Managing Human Resources

Managing Human Resources

FIFTH EDITION

Human Resource Management
in Transition

EDITED BY

Stephen Bach
and
Martin R. Edwards

A John Wiley and Sons, Ltd., Publication

Registered office

John Wiley & Sons Ltd, The Atrium, Southern Gate, Chichester, West Sussex, PO19 8SQ, United Kingdom

For details of our global editorial offices, for customer services and for information about how to apply for permission to reuse the copyright material in this book please see our website at www.wiley.com.

Wiley publishes in a variety of print and electronic formats and by print-on-demand. Some material included with standard print versions of this book may not be included in e-books or in print-on-demand. If this book refers to media such as a CD or DVD that is not included in the version you purchased, you may download this material at http://booksupport.wiley.com. For more information about Wiley products, visit www.wiley.com.

Designations used by companies to distinguish their products are often claimed as trademarks. All brand names and product names used in this book are trade names, service marks, trademarks or registered trademarks of their respective owners. The publisher is not associated with any product or vendor mentioned in this book.

Limit of Liability/Disclaimer of Warranty: While the publisher and author have used their best efforts in preparing this book, they make no representations or warranties with respect to the accuracy or completeness of the contents of this book and specifically disclaim any implied warranties of merchantability or fitness for a particular purpose. It is sold on the understanding that the publisher is not engaged in rendering professional services and neither the publisher nor the author shall be liable for damages arising herefrom. If professional advice or other expert assistance is required, the services of a competent professional should be sought.

Library of Congress Cataloging-in-Publication Data

Managing human resources : human resource management in transition / edited by Stephen Bach and Martin R. Edwards.—5th ed.

p. cm.

Includes bibliographical references and index.

ISBN 978-1-119-99153-3 (pbk.)—ISBN 978-1-118-50997-5 (ebk)

ISBN 978-1-118-50999-9 (ebk)—ISBN 978-1-118-50998-2 (ebk)

1. Personnel management—Great Britain. I. Bach, Stephen, 1963. II. Edwards, Martin R.

HF5549.2.G7M357 2005

658.3—dc23

2012038458

Set in 11/13pt BemboStd by MPS Limited, Chennai, India.

Contents

Notes on Contributors

Stephen Bach, Professor of Employment Relations, Department of Management, King's College London

Corine Boon, Assistant Professor, Amsterdam Business School, University of Amsterdam

Paul Boselie, Professor in Strategic Human Resource Management (SHRM), Utrecht School of Governance, Utrecht University and Associate Professor in SHRM, Department of Human Resource Studies, Tilburg University

Jane Bryson, Associate Professor in Human Resource Management, Victoria Management School, Victoria University of Wellington

Michael Clinton, Lecturer in Work Psychology and HRM, Department of Management, King's College London

Stephen Deery, Professor of Human Resource Management, Department of Management, King's College London

Deanne N. Den Hartog, Professor of Organizational Behaviour, Amsterdam Business School, University of Amsterdam

Virginia Doellgast, Lecturer in Comparative Employment Relations, Department of Management, London School of Economics

Tony Dundon, Senior Lecturer in Employment Relations and HRM, Department of Management, National University of Ireland, Galway

Martin R. Edwards, Senior Lecturer in HRM and Organizational Psychology, Department of Management, King's College London

Tony Edwards, Professor in Comparative HRM, Department of Management, King's College London

Anthony Ferner, Professor of International Human Resource Management, Leicester Business School, De Montfort University

Howard Gospel, Professor of Management and Senior Research Fellow, Department of Management, King's College London

Irena Grugulis, Professor of Employment Studies, Durham Business School, University of Durham

Susan James, Assistant Director of SKOPE and Associate Fellow, Pembroke College and St. Anne's College, Oxford

Ewart Keep, Deputy Director of SKOPE, School of Social Sciences, Cardiff University

Ian Kessler, Professor of Public Sector Management, Department of Management, King's College London

Graeme Lockwood, Senior Lecturer in Law, Department of Management, King's College London

Mick Marchington, Professor of Human Resource Management, Manchester Business School, University of Manchester

Vandana Nath, Teaching Fellow in Human Resource Management, Department of Management, King's College London

Riccardo Peccei, Professor of Organizational Behaviour and Human Resource Management, Department of Management, King's College London

Andrew Pendleton, Professor of Human Resource Management, York Management School, University of York

Stephanie Tailby, Professor of Employment Studies, Bristol Business School, University of the West of England

Marc Van Veldhoven, Professor of Work, Health & Well-Being, Department of Human Resource Studies, Tilburg University

Janet Walsh Professor in Human Resource Management, Department of Management, King's College London

Adrian Wilkinson, Professor and Director of the Centre for Work, Organization and Wellbeing, Griffith University, Australia

Kevin Williams, Reader in law, Sheffield Hallam University

Figures

Tables

Boxes

PART I

Introduction

CHAPTER ONE

Human Resource Management in Transition

Martin R. Edwards and Stephen Bach

The previous version of the book was entitled 'The Management of Human Resources: Personnel Management in Transition', but the idea that personnel management was in transition now seems old hat and this transition seems fully complete. It is now very rare that organisations have a personnel department rather than an HR (Human Resource) department; if a transition is occurring, it is Human Resource Management (HRM) to something else, rather than from Personnel Management (PM) to HRM. The content and breadth of topics included in this book indicate how sophisticated concerns around managing human resources have become. It also highlights that the HR sphere is a fundamentally different and more complex field than the early representations of PM and subsequently HRM were.

Arguments that indicate why the management of human resources and HRM (as a model) is in a state of transition are set out below. Prior to these points, however, it is important to set the scene and reflect upon where HR as a field is now and track its development. An important distinction needs to be made between the general idea of managing human resources, and HRM as a particular people management model. Human resources is fundamentally a term used to describe people in a workplace – managing human resources means the management of people at work. However, the 'human resource' terminology triggers an association with HRM as a particular approach to people management. Loosely defined, HRM can be considered to be a particular model of employment relations that revolves around the management of people, following a particular ideological position; the central principle takes a particular stance on how to get the most out of workers whilst fostering an employment experience that is positive for employees. The Human Resource Management model has certain key assumptions, which include (at its core) what is referred to as a unitarist perspective; that it is possible to sustain an organisation in which all stakeholders share the same set of interests and goals. Indeed this is something which is prevalent in the discourse around HRM. Linked to this assumption is an idea that is central to HRM; work can be organised and employment conditions established that enable employees to achieve the maximum (potential) productive output, whilst ensuring the fulfilment of a range of employee needs. The organisation of work and related working conditions involve a sophisticated coordination of administrative, managerial and strategic activities that require a considerable degree of expertise. People management experts tend to be found in the HR department. Importantly, although these experts are often found within that function, the importance of line management involvement in helping achieve the HRM goals is key (Purcell and Hutchinson 2007). HRM is not just reserved for HR professionals, it is increasingly viewed as a responsibility for all those who manage staff.

Development of HR Theory

The concepts and theories underlying Human Resource Management have developed and matured substantially; the literature discussing HRM as a model is now 30 years old. Frequently cited early US contributions have been associated with the influential Harvard model of HRM (Beer *et al.* 1984; see also Walton 1985). One of the early contributions that defined HRM (based on UK experience) and identified how it was distinct from personnel management, was developed by Guest (1987). In this 1987 paper, Guest attempted to draw some boundaries around what is HRM and how it differs, at least in normative terms, from Personnel Management. As a summary of what Guest set out as a definition of HRM, the model can be distinguished by the following four main aims. Firstly, HRM is a model of employment relations that aims to encourage employee commitment. Secondly, central to its purpose is the achievement of a number of different types of integration (vertical and horizontal). This integration takes two forms: the first being the incorporation of the management of human resources into the strategic planning process to ensure that HR policies and practices *cohere* internally as a system; and the second, externally (i.e. external to the function) with wider business objectives, ensuring that line managers 'buy-in' to HRM initiatives and that employees' interests are aligned with those of the organisation. The third key aim or goal of HRM is to enable the provision of a flexible workforce; enabling functional and employee flexibility. Fourthly, HRM as a model aims to ensure the recruitment and retention of high quality employees who produce quality performance. To achieve these aims, various HR practices and policies need to be put in place. These include setting up clearly defined career development schemes and fostering an internal labour market, organising regular performance appraisal, job design activities that ensure autonomy where possible and voice opportunities, amongst others. From the outset, Guest's definition of HRM was challenged as commentators exposed additional complexity in the people management arena and questioned the assumptions of the model (Legge 1995). An illustration of how analysis evolved was the distinction made between soft and hard HRM (Storey 1989; Legge 1995, see also Chapter 17). The so-called 'hard' version was underpinned by ideological assumptions that employees are resources to be moulded and controlled and that various control strategies are required. The philosophy underpinning the 'soft' version, however, was different; the soft version could be considered to involve a philosophy (and rhetoric) that employees' motivation and participation are important and central concerns of HR. Employee well-being is something that management should strive to enhance, resulting in improved individual and organisational performance.

The soft and hard distinction tends not to be discussed in contemporary literature and this distinction has not been drawn on as a way of framing the HR sphere for some time. The reasons for this may be because contemporary models tend to be more sophisticated and a straightforward division between hard and soft approaches is too simplistic; in addition, many HR models mix hard and soft elements. Further refinements and theoretical development of HRM continued into the 1990s and beyond. Often when theoretical developments and models are discussed, the key debate framing the discussion relates to in which way and why do particular models of HR lead to successful organisational performance. This is not surprising as a central assumption of HRM models is that appropriate HR practices will lead to better performance.

In 1996, Delery and Doty presented a paper that aimed to clarify and define three different theoretical models that set out why and how human resource practices result in successful organisational performance. These three models consisted of the universalistic, contingency and configurational approaches. It is worth summarising these here, as these approaches have been presented as different HR models for a number of years and have only recently begun to be examined with any real scrutiny. The first of these models (*the universalistic perspective*) involves the idea that a particular set of HR practices (so-called 'high performance' or 'strategic' HR practices) will always lead to improved organisational performance. The argument is presented that certain practices will have a universal and positive impact on organisational performance regardless of context. Practices frequently mentioned include: setting up an internal labour market; providing formal training/development opportunities; the use of performance appraisal linked to specific goals; the provision of structured voice mechanisms; and some degree of employment security. The general proposition with this perspective is that the presence of these practices will provide a set of conditions where employees will perform at their best and consequently the organisation will produce higher levels of performance.

In contrast to the universalistic perspective, is an alternative model with different sets of assumptions; this is the *contingency perspective*. The argument is that a key set of conditions exist that determine whether strategic HR practices and policies (as set out with the universalistic perspective) are likely to lead to higher employee and organisational performance. The main contingency is the nature of the firm's strategy, and Delery and Doty (1996) argue that the level of innovation involved in the strategic orientation will be the key factor that determines whether the strategic HRM practices lead to organisational performance; in a high innovation context, strategic HRM practices will show a greater positive relationship with organisational performance than in low innovation contexts. Finally, Delery and Doty outlined a third HRM-performance model, the *configurational perspective* as an alternative. The theoretical assumptions linked to this approach revolve around the idea that *different* HR practices should be put in place (and will be successful), depending upon the nature of the organisation's strategic orientation. This approach is linked to Miles and Snow's (1978) strategic types of 'Prospector', 'Analyser' and 'Defender'. The argument proffered with this approach is that management will need to align and introduce particular employment systems that fit with the firm's strategic configuration. For example, 'Defenders' require long term employment and firm specific knowledge which will require commitment oriented practices; 'Prospectors', however, are constantly changing and, faced with different demands, they rely more on buying in skills and talent from the outside rather than making them. The strategic imperative of the organisation would therefore require different types of employment systems and different ideal sets of strategic HR practices to lead to higher performance. So, unlike the contingency perspective which implies that the strategy will determine whether the universalistic SHRM practices lead to performance, this model suggests that the strategy will require different HR practices to reach full performance potential. These 'models' of HR set the scene of debate around what HRM is and what it should look like for some years, and the arguments presented are still relevant today. This is especially true as the academic and scientific community tries to test a core assumption of HRM: that HR practices, policies and systems can be introduced that foster higher organisational performance. This key assumption explains why most discussion of HRM approaches tends to be linked to debates around HRM and organisational performance. Very rarely, however, are discussions around what HRM should look like, linked to the well-being side of the ideological principles (mentioned above) that form the foundations of HRM (see Peccei 2004 and Chapter 17).

HRM and Performance

In reflecting where the HR field stands at the moment, it is clear that HR researchers have struggled to support the predicted HR-performance relationship to a convincing degree, even though, as Guest argues (2011) 'over the past 20 years there has been a considerable expansion in theory and research about human resource management and performance' (p. 3). The degree to which HR policies and practices have been found to be associated with organisational performance has not necessarily been convincing to critics (or supporters) of the HRM model. A recent theoretical development in the area of HRM and performance is the work by Bowen and Ostroff (2004). These authors explain that organisations are unlikely to have high levels of performance just because HR practices are in place – the degree to which these are enacted and the commitment to ensuring that HR systems are implemented fully across the organisation, will determine whether HR systems lead to enhanced performance. They argue that HR systems need to be 'strong' for increases in performance to be achieved; HR policies need to be visible, distinctive, consistently applied and employees need to have a shared understanding of what they are. Bowen and Ostroff's work is an interesting addition to the theorising in the area of HRM. Central to their argument is the idea that employee perceptions of an HR system will determine whether these systems are likely to have an impact on organisational performance. This adds a considerable degree of complexity to theorising around the expected HRM-performance relationship.

Linked to these debates are broader developments associated with the so-called 'Resource Based View of the Firm' (see Chapter 2). In brief, the core idea is that the key differentiator of successful organisations is the degree to which their human resources are unique and valuable; enabling the organisation to compete successfully. These arguments are used by a number of authors who suggest that the human resources identified as really making a strategic difference should be invested in to a greater extent than other employees. This theory has led to the development of general HR related models, for example Lepak and Snell's 'HR Architecture' model (Lepak and Snell 1999). This trend, a focus on separating employees into groups that receive different treatment, is discussed in more detail below.

All of these approaches and models make their own assumptions as to why, whether and how human resource practices and systems will lead to organisational performance. Despite Guest (2011) arguing that there has been considerable development in the field of HRM, he also concludes that 'after over two decades of extensive research, we are still unable to answer core questions about the relationship between human resource management and performance' (p. 3). This leaves the field in an interesting place at the moment; whilst there is some evidence linking HR practices and positive organisational outcomes (see Chapter 2), the core assumption of traditional models of HRM is yet to be convincingly supported. Examples of existing research examining the relationship between HR and performance are discussed further in Chapter 2 and an important issue in this discussion relates to context. In reflecting on where HR as a field stands at the moment, therefore, we need to consider the wider economic and political context in which it is currently operating.

Current HR Context

There are a number of features of the current global context that cannot be ignored in an introduction to a contemporary edited text that explores employment relationships and human resource management. The main contextual feature is the ongoing global financial crisis (GFC). With its roots in an asset bubble, overheated

Western property markets and 'innovative' investment banking practices, the GFC has cast a long shadow over HR practice. The implications of the GFC for HR practice are wide ranging. The economic crisis is making it more difficult to justify practices traditionally associated with effective HR practice, such as the provision of pensions and other rewards, including, more controversially, bonuses for high performers (see Chapter 12). In many sectors, especially more recently in the public sector, the workforce has been faced with a combination of pay freezes and pay cuts. However, this has frequently not been sufficient to prevent staff reductions in local government, the civil service and the NHS, with profound implications for job security, employee involvement and collective voice (see Chapters 13 and 14). In such a context the function will find it much harder to justify sophisticated or even basic investment in people for central HR activities such as training and development. In such a context it is much harder to motivate and engage staff (Roche *et al.* 2011).

As part of the fallout from the GFC, many, if not most, Western economies have experienced a sustained period of deep recession. As the people usually responsible for managing redundancies, a large portion of HR functions would have been involved in managing this 'downsizing', only to then be required to downsize their own function. At a more macro level, the so-called 'age of austerity' (e.g. as referred to by the UK's Prime Minister, David Cameron) has led to pressure to reduce deficits and to reduce public sector expenditure with knock on effects in terms of staff reductions and service closures. With the 2012 unemployment rate in the UK at its highest since the mid 1990s, the HR employment context is not especially positive.

This period of employment relations that Western economies are experiencing will be familiar to a generation of managers who lived through the last series of recessions, and political rhetoric around spending cuts will also be familiar to students of industrial relations history. Interestingly, what is less apparent in the current crisis is the somewhat muted reaction of UK trade unions, although in many countries such as Greece, Portugal and Spain there has been widespread mobilisation against austerity. This limited mobilisation could be interpreted as an indication of the 'success' of HRM as a model of employment relations. Some commentators have suggested (e.g. Legge 1995) that HRM potentially undermines trade union power for two main reasons. First, it has the potential to individualise the employment relationship and second, the emphasis on employee well-being, if managed effectively, could undermine the role of trade unions that articulate and collectivise employee grievances.

Irrespective of whether HRM has played a role in trade union decline and the difficulties of mobilising trade union members, some theories (e.g. Davies's 1962 J-curve hypothesis) would have predicted a growth in union activity. This is because of a sudden decrease in living standards following the peak of an upturn (where peoples' expectations are high), accompanied by an increase in the experience of actual and relative deprivation as economies suddenly falter. In addition to the recession, 2012 has witnessed a massive amount of uncertainty linked to the sustainability of the European Union's single currency – with Greece and other nations requiring assistance from the International Monetary Fund and the European Central

Bank. As a backdrop therefore to human resource management, all of this points to a considerable degree of uncertainty about the future and this will hinder HR's ability to plan strategically in the long term. Aside from this, it seems that the employment experience for many employees is one of great uncertainty linked to employment insecurity, work intensification and growing income inequality.

Ultimately, the GFC has meant that many organisations have found themselves in a state of distress, and HR is often called upon to help out in this state of distress. This help, however, is (often) in the form of assisting in the shedding of staff. The degree of strategic involvement that HR has in this process will vary (see Roche *et al.* 2011). Some HR functions may be called upon to carry out a fundamental organisation redesign to enable greater efficiency, thus turning a round of job cuts into a more 'positive' adaptive activity for the organisation. Many HR functions will, however, be called upon to purely implement and administer job cuts that are demanded by a financial imperative (from the board or the finance director); HR is often the function that is called upon to wield the axe in such a scenario. Some HR functions help manage this process and make it easier on employees who are made redundant and some now outsource this process to 'out-placement' service providers. Ultimately, as staffing numbers in the HR function are often linked to employee numbers within the organisation, such job cuts can often lead to reductions in the HR function itself.

The contemporary context of HR is one of change and turmoil; in this changing context key questions to ask are, 'Where does HR as a function stand at the moment? What does HR look like now and how has it changed over the last five to ten years?'. The various chapters of this book point to a number of changes which help answer these questions. After reflecting upon recent changes and developments that the authors set out in their chapters, it can be argued that the HR function and the profession look substantively different now from a decade ago.

HRM in Transition?

In this uncertain context, it can be argued that the HR function and the field in general are in a state of transition. Whilst most fields will experience change, there is something distinctive about the range of developments in the HR environment; HRM is therefore in a state of transition. Whilst no single development by itself can be identified as signalling this transition, when the range of developments are considered as a whole, the standard model of HRM (as outlined by Guest 1987) seems untenable. Many of these individual changes have been discussed by various authors in this book; the collection therefore helps build a picture of this transition. In brief, the developments being referred to here can be organised into five main points (discussed below).

First, the HR function is becoming involved in activities that have not traditionally been within the remit of HR, activities which have previously been associated with other disciplines (in particular marketing). This means that questions arise about what HR is and where the boundaries of the function lie.

Second, HR functions are no longer discussing commitment as a goal of their HR systems; the dominant discourse around the aim of the function is linked to employee engagement. This represents a shift away from one of the key aims presented as being central to HRM.

Third, traditional models of HRM suggest that the organisation and its boundaries can be identified, however HR is now operating in an environment where traditional boundaries around the organisation have shifted; the idea of a permanent and stable organisational structure is beginning to look outdated.

Fourth, linked to points two and three, traditional ideas of permanent employment status of the workforce (which is central to HRM because of its focus on organisational commitment) are beginning to seem doubtful. Thus the HRM model needs further refinement or a complete overhaul.

Finally, linked to points one, three and four, traditional models of HRM assume that coherent HR practices and systems can be applied across the workforce in a consistent way; however, such assumptions are under pressure and it is very rare that a single HR system is found within contemporary organisations; this brings into sharp relief the relevance of traditional models of HRM. These developments, amongst others, indicate that the HR arena, the function and its activities are now far more complex than traditional models of HRM are able to assimilate or accommodate.

With regard to the idea that the HR function is now involved in activities that have been traditionally reserved for other functions or disciplines, a key example of this is employer and employee branding (see Chapter 18). Practices that seem to be gaining in dominance in the practitioner field suggest that HR departments are changing fundamentally. Whilst the involvement of HR in branding and marketing functions might reflect an extension of the transition from people management to HRM (which argued for various forms of integration, Guest 1987), the degree to which functions such as marketing are becoming involved in the HR activities seems to be adding another M (Marketing) to HRM. It can be argued that this new model of HRM is quite different, to the extent that the HR in HRM does not fully describe what is happening with the function in these cases. Human Resource Marketing Management is potentially a better description of what is happening, at least in some organisations.

The wholesale use of marketing language across the HR practitioner literature is indicative of key trends. This language includes terms such as 'employee brand management', 'being on brand', having 'brand ambassadors', being a 'walking talking brand agent'; 'employer brand value propositions', 'employer brand equity', 'unique employment brand differentiator', 'employer brand segmentation'; this represents a considerable shift for the HR function. Whilst one might assume that there could be resistance to this development, the fundamental shift in many Western economies to the service sector from manufacturing (see Chapter 6), suggests that in these organisations the pressure to use employees to help become the product differentiators is likely to remain and become a common activity that HR is involved in.

Often, as part of employee attitude (or more accurately engagement) surveys, organisations automatically measure the degree to which employees are taking 'on-board' the corporate brand values.

Another key development across the HR function is the shift from being concerned about fostering commitment to being concerned about fostering employee engagement (see Chapter 16). Although there is still considerable confusion in the practitioner realm about what employee engagement is and how it is measured, the fundamental contemporary concern of HR practitioners is no longer to encourage organisational commitment. This trend represents a shift in one of the central aims of HRM as defined by Guest (1987) and traditional models of HRM will struggle to incorporate this change. The engagement arena is another example of how marketing practices are becoming common across the HR function. Employee surveys are used to measure engagement and the workforce is segmented into 'fully engaged', 'engagement potentials' and 'disengaged' workers, and identifying how best to foster engagement has now become the Holy Grail for the HR function. The companies who run these surveys have market research foundations (e.g. Gallup) and they use market research methodologies applied in the context of employee attitude surveys. These market research agencies have, for decades, developed methodologies to demonstrate the importance of brand awareness, and now apply their methodologies to the employee-customer profit chain. From the point of view of the HR function, one of the main reasons why engagement is so prevalent is that research and arguments presented by many research consultancies claim to show how engaged employees will directly drive bottom-line profits. Also, one of the key reasons why firms like Gallup are so successful is that they provide data analytic tools to automate an element of employee attitude measurement. They also help automate other HR processes such as being able to judge line managers on the basis of how 'engaged' their team members are.

Traditional models of HRM assume some stability and permanency in the organisation's make-up and structure. However, there are various ways in which this assumption is challenged in the contemporary HR field, one of which is the development of various forms of outsourcing. As Doellgast and Gospel (Chapter 15) discuss, the scale and scope of outsourcing have increased considerably. It is not uncommon now for firms (both public and private) to outsource all but their core value maximising activities. Furthermore, many companies are now outsourcing substantial parts of their organisation overseas; 'offshoring' entire functions. This means that large tranches of workers who would previously have been part of a permanent workforce (such as administrative departments, IT support and call-centre operations) are now employed by separate organisations, and of course many of these employers are multi-national corporations with distinctive HR challenges (see Chapter 5). These employees are now only linked to the buyer of an outsourced product through service agreements and contracts between their employer and this buyer; the (people) management of these outsourced employees that the HR function is involved in, or is responsible for, occurs indirectly through the management and negotiation of service contracts. Furthermore, there is also growth in organisations outsourcing central HR related activities such as (for example) the management of pay and benefits, pensions planning and the provision of employment law advice (Gospel and Sako 2010). With more organisations outsourcing large portions of their workforce and elements of the HR function itself, changeable and permeable organisational boundaries place traditional models of HRM (and ideas concerning how the function can and should take a central and strategic role) under considerable pressure. The organisation's ability to implement a coherent HR strategy across the workforce that contributes to the business is reduced, with real challenges occurring in coordination of HR activities across blurred and shifting organisational boundaries (see Chapter 15). The uncertainty around what and who the workforce is, has been further exacerbated over recent years by the considerable strain and state of flux that organisations have been experiencing due to the GFC and global recession. A vast number of organisations have been forced to reduce the number of permanent workers that they employ in an effort to cut costs. The uncertain and changeable nature of organisational boundaries makes it much less likely that HRM aims of commitment and integration (vertical and horizontal, see above) can be achieved easily.

Linked to the point made above, the general HRM model assumes that employees have and want permanent and stable jobs and that they want career development within the organisation. A challenge to this assumption comes from a number of directions. There has been a growing body of literature over recent years arguing that traditional career paths, which HRM as a model would hope to foster, are no longer relevant to today's turbulent business environment. This literature centres on ideas of a boundary-less career (Arthur 2008) which is linked to observations that organisations are unable to offer stability and steady career progression because of the changing context. Whilst there are some problems identified with the theory behind boundary-less careers (Rodrigues and Guest 2010), it is generally recognised that the idea of stable career paths and a linear career development structure, does not take into account the complex nature of contemporary careers; people have changing and sometimes multiple career paths and orientations (Rodrigues and Guest 2010). Another reason why the idea of permanent, stable employment is being challenged is the growth in employment forms that do not fit the full-time permanent template. For example, there has been a steady rise in the proportion of the workforce who have part-time contracts (Chapter 8). Even developments around flexible and remote working bring a degree of challenge in terms of the assumptions associated with HRM and the permanent nature of the relationship between the employee and the organisation. Remote working allows more people to work away from the physical location of their employer; thus bringing further tensions to the idea of permanency and stability of employees' bond with their employer and indeed the idea that people management models assume a strong commitment-based, employee-organisational bond.

One further challenge to traditional models of HRM is the fact that they assume a degree of uniformity or consistency in how and what HR practices should be applied across the organisation. The traditional model of HRM (that has commitment as a core aim along with the aim of ensuring integration) will generally require a consistent set of high commitment HR/management practices applied across the workforce. However, there is little evidence that organisations tend to have the same set of practices applied to all employees (Lawler 2011). Indeed, there is evidence of multiple, identifiable sets of HR practices being in place within organisations (Lepak et al. 2007). As Guest argues 'Many large organisations are likely to have a number of quite highly differentiated internal labour markets, each of which can have a distinctive set of HR policies and practices. In short, one size does not fit all,' (p. 8). This observation in itself accords with many observations made by authors in this book; many of the authors reflect upon variation in HR practices for different reasons, however there is a common thread on this issue throughout the book. For example, Boselie (Chapter 2), discusses strategic HRM and the importance of the resource-based view of the firm as a guiding theoretical model that can signal appropriate organisational variation in HR practices; the suggestion is that different HR practices should be (and are) targeted at different groups of employees (depending upon whether they have strategic 'value' and greater human capital 'worth'). These ideas are now becoming quite commonplace in the HR practitioner field, one of the most obvious examples of this is the growth in various forms of talent management initiatives. Proponents of talent management programmes recommend that the workforce should be segmented into groups of 'talent' versus other/non-talent (see Capelli 2008) and greater developmental (and other) opportunities should be provided to the 'talented' segment. Other examples of talent/potential based segmentation include the Differentiated Workforce model presented by Becker et al. (2009). This involves giving quite different opportunities to 'A players' compared to 'C' and 'B' players, linked to developments in contemporary performance management practices (see Chapter 11). Ultimately, talent management initiatives recommend a form of segmentation and within-organisation HR practice differentiation, which creates a tension for traditional commitment based models of HRM. The idea of segmentation and differentiated HR practices is also discussed elsewhere in this book; for example in relation to remuneration (Chapter 12), employer branding (Chapter 18) and outsourcing (Chapter 15). The very idea of employer branding segmentation challenges the assumption of HRM as a model that has the fostering of commitment across the workforce as a key aim. Ideas behind segmented employment brands indicate that organisations should target varied and tailored HR practices at different groups of employees on the basis of what they want, rather than the necessity of having a uniform and strong set of consistent HR practices designed on the basis of ensuring that the organisation's central business strategy is achieved.

This also raises challenges for the HR function in trying to ensure a degree of consistency in HR practices across countries and organisational boundaries. Whilst there are some models that have been presented which suggest that certain HR practices could be applied differentially to specific groups (Lepak and Snell 2002), at the moment the current HRM models cannot deal with the potential complexity and diversity of HR practices likely to be found across organisations. In summary, what these observations are highlighting is that the current HR environment is much more complex than traditional models and theorising around HRM allows for. In general, the traditional HRM model assumes that commitment fostering policies and practices should be implemented, and opportunities should be provided to all employees (in order to achieve a fully integrated committed workforce).

The Future of HR

This introduction has scoped out what is distinctive about HR as a function and field. It is helpful to extend the discussion and reflect upon what the future of HR might look like. Aside from trends mentioned above as a stimulus for ideas, another possible source of ideas about the future of HR is a recent 2011 special issue of *Organizational Dynamics* which was entitled 'The Future of Human Resource Management'. Many of these predictions reflect the analysis of this collection. An article from this special issue that rings true with some of the arguments of authors in this book is the Galinsky and Matos (2011) paper which focuses on 'work-life fit'. Amongst other things, these authors reflect on developments in technology, which mean that employees are able to connect to their work at any time as well as any place, the changing expectations that the younger generation (the 'Millenials') has from work, and how gender role ideology is more similar within this tranche of the workforce. This generational difference in particular will have a number of implications but a key one is that work-life balance issues and flexible working will become more important with a two working-parent model (who both have equal and strong career ambitions) rather than a one working-parent model (see Chapter 8).

An issue that is also raised by authors from the future of HR special issue is the phenomenon of differentiated HR practices and segmentation of the workforce. This topic is raised by two sets of authors contributing to the 'future of HR' debate. In the articles by Boudreau and Ziskin (2011) and Lawler (2011), clear reference is being made to the idea that HR practices should not be standardised and/or applied equally to all employees as a homogenous workforce. Both authors argue for the need to segment the workforce and target different HR practices according to the needs of each segment. These authors argue that segmentation will be a key activity that any future HR function will need to deal with. Another prediction made by Boudreau and Ziskin (2011) is that future HR departments will need to have permeable boundaries or be boundary spanners, meaning that there will be a need for cross-fertilisation into and from other functions, such as communications, PR and marketing. These predictions accord to a great degree with our analysis about the increasing role that marketing plays in HR activities. Linked to this point and the fact that HR professions will need to increasingly 'look beyond the traditional boundaries of their function' (p. 255), Boudreau and Ziskin (2011) suggest that traditional ideas of what the HR function consists of will need to be fundamentally redefined.

Whilst they do not refer to engagement in their article, Boudreau and Ziskin (2011) suggest that the future of HR will need to pay careful attention to ensuring that their workforce is not exhausted and HR will need to integrate ideas of employee sustainability into what they do. As mentioned above, there is a considerable growth in interest in employee engagement in the practitioner field. Although there are substantial problems with how survey companies measure engagement (see Chapter 16), academic research has (to a degree) considered engagement to be on the other end of the well-being-burnout continuum. Therefore, if practitioners begin to consider engagement from a perspective of energised employees who are full of vigour, this then may be a starting point for Boudreau and Ziskin's (2011) predictions; although there is still some way to go in improving how practitioners measure engagement for this outcome to occur. Engagement aside, there is an increasing place for concentrating on well-being as a special focus of HR activities (see Chapter 17), Clinton and van Veldhoven's contribution clearly indicates that there is an increasing interest in employee well-being within the HRM sphere. In the 'future of HR' special issue, authors discuss the fact that more and more is being expected of employees, potentially to the detriment of their well-being. The arguments resonate with themes raised in the current book. For example, it rings true with points raised about the 'time squeeze' by Walsh in Chapter 8, and more rigorous systems of performance management discussed by Bach in Chapter 11. Edwards (Chapter 18) also discusses the potential for employee branding programmes to represent a potential invasion into the employee sense of self and personal values; this wholesale interference with employees' individual right to privacy and dignity is highlighted in this collection. What these developments potentially lead to (which Boudreau and Ziskin 2011 argue as employees being 'plain exhausted'), is that sustainability linked to employee well-being is something which future HR functions will need to factor in to any HR strategy. The current economic context and many of the developments considered here have the potential to put employees under even greater degrees of strain. The potential effects that this could have on employees in the long term, and the degree to which sustained uncertainty and a ratcheting 'time squeeze' will reduce their ability to function at full potential (over the long term), is something that will need to take centre stage in any future model of HRM.

Conclusion

In summary, traditional models of HRM and the field of HR in general are currently operating within a changing environment and in a state of transition, with the dominant context being the global financial crisis. Although the GFC is the salient contextual event faced by HR in current times, we recognise that there are a number of other significant contextual changes occurring; changes such as a global shift (an increase) in the age of the working population and the challenges that this places HR under; the greater cross-border flow of workers with increases in international

assignments; technological advances meaning that the world of electronic communications is fundamentally different (and instant). Despite these changes, the economic context of the global financial crisis is having such a dominant and profound
effect on organisations (and employees) and HR functions around the world that it
eclipses these (otherwise considerable) contextual developments.

   Our conclusion is that we are in a changing context and a changing (transitioning)
HR field. The change in contributions to this current edited text reflects this
backdrop of change. Whilst the current book includes significant updates of previous
chapters from the earlier edition, there are a number of new contributors who make
this book different and innovative. The new contributions include the following: a
chapter by Boselie (Chapter 2) on HRM and performance; a chapter on employment law and HRM (Chapter 3) by Lockwood and Williams; a chapter reflecting
upon corporate governance, varieties of capitalism and the implications for HRM by
Pendleton and Gospel (Chapter 4) and a new set of contributors (Bryson, James and
Keep) examining recruitment and selection (Chapter 7). Also new is Chapter 9,
which examines skills and training (Grugulis), and Chapter 10 is a completely new
topic for the book with a specific focus on HRM and leadership (Den Hartog and
Boon). Doellgast and Gospel analyse outsourcing and Human Resource Management (Chapter 15) and a new contribution to this edition by Peccei (Chapter 16)
examines employee engagement. There is also a chapter that explores issues around
HRM and well-being, Chapter 17 by Clinton and van Veldhoven. An interesting
development in the current text is the inclusion of a number of Dutch authors; this
reflects the growing role that the Dutch HRM network is having on academic
studies in the field of HR. Whilst the remaining chapters are updated versions, each
of the original contributors has substantially reworked their chapter and added new
content, ensuring that the reader is able to get an up-to-date picture of the contemporary HR context.

REFERENCES

Arthur, M. B. 2008: Examining contemporary careers: A call for interdisciplinary inquiry,
   Human Relations, **61**, 163–186.
Becker, B., Huselid, M. and Beatty, R. 2009: *The differentiated workforce: Transforming talent
   into strategic impact*, Harvard Business Press.
Beer, M., Spector, B., Lawrence, P., Mills, D. Q. and Walton, R. 1984: *Managing Human
   Assets*, New York: Free Press.
Boudreau, J. W. and Ziskin, I. 2011: The future of HR and effective organizations, *Orga-
   nizational Dynamics*, **40**, 255–266.
Bowen, D. and Ostroff, C. 2004: Understanding HRM – firm performance linkages: the role
   of the 'strength' of the HRM system, *Academy of Management Review*, **29**, 203–221.
Capelli, P. 2008: Talent management for the twenty-first century, *Harvard Business Review*,
   March, 74–81.
Davies, J. C. 1962: Toward a theory of revolution, *American Sociological Review*, **27**, 5–19.

Delery, J. and Doty, D. 1996: Modes of theorizing in strategic human resource management: tests of universalistic, contingency and configurational performance predictions, *Academy of Management Journal*, **39**(4), 802–835.

Galinsky, E. and Matos, K. 2011: The future of work-life fit, *Organizational Dynamics*, **40**, 267–280.

Gospel, H. and Sako, M. 2010: The Re-bundling of Corporate Functions: The Evolution of Shared Services and Outsourcing in Human Resource Management, *Industrial & Corporate Change*, March, 1–30.

Guest, D. 1987: Human resource management and industrial relations, *Journal of Management Studies*, **24**, 503–521.

Guest, D. E. 2011: Human Resource Management and performance: still searching for some answers, *Human Resource Management Journal*, **21**, 3–13.

Lawler, E. E. III 2011: Creating a new employment deal: Total rewards and the new workforce, *Organizational Dynamics*, **40**(4): 302–309.

Legge, K. 1995: *Human Resource Management: rhetoric and realities,* Basingstoke: Macmillan.

Lepak, D. and Snell, S. 1999: The human resource architecture: toward a theory of human capital allocation and development, *Academy of Management Review*, **24**, 31–48.

Lepak, D. P. and Snell, S. A. 2002: Examining the human resource architecture: the relationships among human capital, employment, and human resource configurations, *Journal of Management*, **28**, 517–543.

Lepak, D. P., Taylor, S.M., Tekleab, A. G., Marrone, J. M. and Cohen, D. 2007: An examination of the use of high-investment human resource systems for core and support employees, *Human Resource Management*, **46**, 223–246.

Miles, R. E. and Snow, C. C. 1978: *Organizational strategy, structure, and process*, New York: McGraw-Hill.

Peccei, R. 2004: *Human Resource Management and the Search for the Happy Workplace*, Rotterdam: Inaugural Lecture Erasmus University Institute of Management.

Purcell, J. and Hutchinson, S. 2007: Front-line managers as agents in the HRM–performance causal chain: theory, analysis and evidence, *Human Resource Management Journal*, **17**, No 1.

Roche, W. K., Teague, P., Coughlan, A. and Fahy, M. 2011: *Human Resources in the Recession: Managing and Representing People at Work in Ireland*, Dublin: Government Publications.

Rodrigues, R. and Guest, D. E. 2010: Have careers become boundaryless? *Human Relations*, **63**, 1157–1175.

Storey, J. (ed.) 1989: *New Perspectives on Human Resource Management*, London: Routledge.

Walton, R. 1985: From control to commitment in the workplace, *Harvard Business Review*, **63**(2), 77–84.

CHAPTER TWO

Human Resource Management and Performance

Paul Boselie

Introduction

Human resource management (HRM), or the management of people in organisations, can contribute to achieving organisational goals. These goals are strongly related and partly dependent on challenges. Organisations are confronted with major challenges with regard to economic (for example the global financial crisis of 2008–2011), social (for example an aging population in many Western societies) and technological developments (for example the emerging popularity of smartphones).

The search for the potential added value of HRM to performance started in the mid 1990s with empirical studies from, for example Arthur (1994) and Huselid (1995). Their results showed positive effects of human resource practices such as selective recruitment and selection, performance-related pay, extensive training and development, performance appraisal and employee participation on outcome measures such as employee retention (in contrast to employee turnover), labour productivity and firm profits. New theory was developed in the 1990s suggesting the alignment of individual human resource practices into human resource systems or bundles, is even more powerful for increasing performance than applying individual best practices in HRM (Delery 1998; Wall and Wood 2005). The fit or alignment between, for example, selection, socialisation, training, appraisal, rewards and participation is thought to contribute to get the best out of employees. The Swedish company IKEA, for example, has a strong corporate culture supported by a human resource system in which individual human resource practices are aligned to support the strong culture. IKEA employees are recruited and selected not just to fit the job, but to fit the organisation's norms and values. After selection, employees are socialised and trained in a way that strengthens the culture and makes all workers aware of IKEA's business model and way of working.

The concept of human resource management (HRM) basically contains three elements that refer to successful people management. The first element – human – refers to the research object. HRM is (mainly) about people at work. The second element – resource – refers to the assumption that workers can be a powerful source of organisational success. Together with other internal resources such as financial resources and a unique organisational culture, employees can be valuable resources for an organisation. The final element of the concept of HRM – management – refers to the notion that worker attitudes and behaviours can be influenced and affected by managerial interventions. In this chapter human resource management (HRM) is defined as follows: human resource management (HRM) involves all management decisions related to policies and practices that together shape the employment relationship and are aimed at achieving individual, organisational and societal goals. Examples of individual (employee) goals are employee well-being in terms of stress and a good work-life balance. Examples of typical organisational goals are high productivity, high quality levels and innovation and an example of a societal goal is the creation of employment and acknowledging multiple stakeholder interests. This HRM definition explicitly builds on a pluralistic perspective incorporating both multiple stakeholder interests and a multi-dimensional performance construct. This perspective is in line with the Harvard model (Beer *et al.* 1984) and the model presented by Paauwe (2004). In contrast, unitarist perspectives mainly focus on a limited number of stakeholders (shareholders, top management and financiers) and almost exclusively on financial firm performance (Greenwood 2002). The perspective presented in this chapter builds on contextual and institutional notions. It is important to note that the unitarist perspectives on HRM are very popular in Anglo-Saxon contexts such as the USA in both theory and practice. The unitarist perspective pays less attention to situational factors or multiple stakeholders and is mainly focused on financial firm performance and market value as the ultimate business goal (Greenwood 2002). The typical unitarist model for explaining, understanding and predicting HRM and performance is focused on the impact of human resource interventions (HR practices and HR systems) and on human resource outcomes such as employee motivation and commitment that affect productivity and financial performance. In contrast, the pluralist models on HRM and performance are more complex, including multiple variables that potentially mediate and moderate the human resource value chain.

There are three questions that inform the discussion in this chapter:

1. Why can HRM contribute to performance?
2. Does HRM contribute to performance?
3. Institutional context, HRM and performance – under what conditions will HRM contribute to performance?

The chapter starts with a theoretical overview focused on the resource-based view (including the VRIO framework, see Table 2.1) and human capital theory. These theoretical insights help understand why human resource management (HRM) is considered a potential source of organisational success. The next section focuses on how human resource management (HRM) contributes to performance according to scholars and prior empirical research. For a better theoretical understanding of the impact of HRM on performance, the AMO model (ability, motivation, opportunity) or AMO theory will be explained in this section. Together with the RBV (resource-based view), the AMO theory is one of the most popular theories in contemporary HRM (Boselie 2010). The third part of the chapter is focused on under what conditions HRM contributes to performance. Contextual factors are analysed highlighting the relevance of the internal and external organisational context. Applying a simple list of 'best practices' in HRM is not likely to solve the major challenges (economic, social and technological) that contemporary organisations confront. A critical evaluation of the organisation's internal and external context is essential for creating an HR value chain in which HRM adds to performance and contributes to achieving goals set by the organisation.

The theoretical road map for understanding this chapter is as follows. The resource-based view (Barney 1991), the VRIO framework (Barney and Wright 1998) and human capital theory (e.g. Wright *et al.* 2001) are used to explain why, from a theoretical point of view, HRM is assumed to contribute to performance. The main focus is on the 'resource' element of the concept of HRM. Empirical evidence in combination with the AMO theory (e.g. Appelbaum *et al.* 2000) is used to show evidence for the added value of HRM and to provide a framework for understanding how certain HR practices and HR systems contribute to performance. The main focus here is on the 'management' element of HRM. Finally, strategic contingency approaches (e.g. Beer *et al.* 1984) and new institutionalism (e.g. Paauwe and Boselie 2003) are introduced to explain the relevance of context in the HRM and performance area.

Why HRM can Contribute to Performance

When asked what is the most important organisational asset, top managers often reply: our human assets or our employees. This answer might be a socially desirable answer, but it might also be the case that there is a growing awareness that employees can really make the difference between average performance and excellent organisational performance. In the UK study by Guest and King (2004) a majority of top managers saw the potential of the workforce for organisational success. Not all respondents, however, were convinced that human resource management could contribute to achieving success. Perhaps things have changed over the last ten years as a result of new empirical research (e.g. Van de Voorde *et al.* 2010) and HRM in practice.

Before we turn to the impact of HRM on performance we first need to know why human resource management potentially contributes to organisational performance. Just claiming employees are important assets is not sufficient. For a full understanding of the contribution of HRM we need theory: the resource-based view of the firm and human capital theory (Wright *et al.* 2001). These two theoretical frameworks help to structure an understanding of HRM and performance. According to Delery and Shaw (2001), there is general agreement that (1) human capital (for example in terms of employee knowledge and skills) can be a source of competitive advantage, (2) that HR practices such as training and development have the most direct influence on the human capital of a firm, and (3) that the complex nature of HR systems of practice can enhance the inimitability of the system. According to academic literature, human resources belong to a firm's most valuable assets (Boxall and Purcell 2003). Since the late 1990s there is a growing body of literature focused on creating (sustained) competitive advantage for organisations through the development of core competences, tacit knowledge and dynamic capabilities.

One of the dominant theories in the debate on the added value of HRM is the resource-based view of the firm (Boselie *et al.* 2005). The RBV has its roots in the early work of Penrose (1959) and was picked up and applied by Wernerfelt (1984) and Barney (1991) in the 1980s (Boselie and Paauwe 2009). The RBV led to a change in strategic management thinking from an 'outside-in' approach – with an emphasis on external, industry-based competitive issues (Porter 1980) – to an 'inside-out' approach (Baden-Fuller and Stopford 1994), in which internal resources constitute the starting point for organisational success. Barney (1991) argues that the sustained competitive advantage of an organisation is determined by internal resources that are valuable, rare, inimitable, and non-substitutable. Financial resources (equity, debt and retained earnings), physical resources (for example machines, a factory or cranes in a harbour), organisational resources (for example IT systems, organisational design and management information systems) and human resources (in terms of their knowledge, skills, abilities and social network) are potential sources of organisational success when Barney's (1991) four criteria are met.

The concept **'value'** in the RBV represents the economic condition of a resource. For example, a retail firm owns property in terms of the local shops that are owned by the company. The buildings and the building ground can be considered resources of the firm and represent economic value. Sometimes this value can be substantial as a result of the scarcity of building ground in villages and cities where the retail firm operates. The concept **'rare'** in the RBV reflects the scarcity of a resource. When retail shops are built on scarce building ground, for example in a big city, the property (i.e. resource) has economic value and possesses the characteristics of rarity. Banks and financiers will take these issues into account when an organisation wants additional capital (loans, mortgages etc.). The concept **'inimitability'** in the RBV focuses on the degree to which resources are very hard to copy or imitate. Complex oil refineries (for example within BP or Shell) are difficult to imitate for competitors and in particular for potential new entrants. The refinery processes require technology, factories and knowledge of specific business processes which are difficult to imitate by potential new entrants. Toyota, for example, is in the car manufacturing business, but the company cannot simply move to the oil refinery business. It would require specific technology, equipment and the appropriate knowledge. Inimitability can also be embedded in non-tangible resources, for example the culture of an organisation based on specific values, a unique history, the potential role of founding fathers and all other aspects that contribute to a social setting that influences the way an organisation operates. The concept of '**non-substitutability**' in the RBV represents resources that '. . . are very hard to neutralise with other resources which will meet the same ends (Boxall and Purcell 2003: 75).'

Wright *et al.* (2001) have made a valuable contribution to the resource-based debate by linking RBV notions to human capital theory. In their approach a distinction is made between three forms of capital relevant to the HRM and performance debate:

- **Human capital** (for example the knowledge, skills and abilities of workers);
- **Social capital** (for example related to social networks of employees within and outside an organisation);
- **Organisational capital** (for example embedded in the HR practices, HR structure and HR technology in place).

These three capital forms can potentially have the RBV characteristics of value, rarity, inimitability and non-substitutability. In addition, the model by Wright *et al.* (2001) implicitly suggests that unique combinations of human, social and organisational capital are a source of (sustained) competitive advantage. In other words, it is not just the individual employee's abilities in terms of knowledge, skills and abilities that potentially leads to superior performance, but also the workforce's internal and external network (for example with external customers) and the way the employment relationship is shaped through HR practices, HR structures and HR systems (organisational capital).

IKEA, for example, is a company in which a combination of human capital, social capital and organisational capital drives business performance. Employees are selectively recruited and selected, socialised according to IKEA norms, continuously trained and developed, and monitored to evaluate goal achievement. IKEA's organisational capital in terms of the HR infrastructure (in particular related to the training and development infrastructure throughout the company) supports the shaping of HRM. Line managers, for example, spend time working on the shop floor on a yearly basis in order to keep in touch with the workforce on the shop floor and the actual customers. The latter can be considered to increase the social capital, in particular with regard to the relationship between line managers and employees.

The resource-based view and human capital theory provide insights on the value of internal resources such as human resources (employees). There is a related model that is very helpful for understanding the actual impact of RBV and human capital notions on firm performance. Barney and Wright (1998) present the VRIO framework – an abbreviation of Value, Rareness, Inimitability and Organisation. This is a hierarchical framework for determining the potential organisational success through internal resources. The first level in the framework focuses on the question of whether a resource is valuable or not. According to the model, internal resources without value are a source of competitive disadvantage. When resources are valuable, the model suggests the possibility of competitive parity linked to normal performance. Valuable and rare resources can take an organisation to the next level, creating temporary competitive advantage and above normal performance. The highest level is achieved when resources are valuable, rare and difficult to imitate. According to the VRIO framework this is caused by intensive organisational support. The highest level potentially creates above normal performance and sustained (or long term) competitive advantage. Only a few companies are capable of reaching this highest level. IKEA's extensive training and development infrastructure in combination with the company's culture of continuous learning can be labelled 'supported by organisation' in the VRIO framework.

The VRIO framework makes a distinction between different types of performance (see Table 2.1). The lowest level represents resources that do not have any value and are therefore likely to result in below normal performance. This does not automatically mean that these resources will have a dramatic negative impact on firm performance. Some resources need to be installed or in place because of legislation without any potential added value effect, for example health and safety procedures. Linked to the key business processes of an organisation the VRIO framework suggests it is best to avoid the use of resources that have no (economic) value and therefore do not contribute to firm performance. Nowadays these types of resources are often outsourced to other companies in order to reduce costs and focus on the core business activities of the firm. For resources that are valuable without being rare, for example in terms of labour supply or raw materials available for production processes, the framework suggests normal performance outcomes.

The RBV is mainly focused on the next two levels of the VRIO framework: the creation of (temporary) competitive advantage and (sustained) competitive

Table 2.1 The VRIO framework

Is a resource . . . Valuable?	Rare?	Difficult to imitate?	Supported by organisation?	Competitive implications	Performance
No	–	–	↑	Competitive Disadvantage	Below normal
Yes	No	–		Competitive Parity	Normal
Yes	Yes	No		Temporary Competitive Advantage	Above normal
Yes	Yes	Yes	↓	Sustained Competitive Advantage	Above normal

Source: Adapted version of figure in Barney and Wright (1998)

advantage. The framework suggests that above normal performance can be created when resources are valuable, rare and difficult to imitate. Without any structural support by the organisation, the framework suggests these three resource qualities are not likely to result in long term success (sustained competitive advantage). For example, an organisation being first with the introduction of a new product (think of the introduction of the iPad by Apple) might be quite successful, generating above normal performance for a couple of years (temporary competitive advantage). However, soon competitors (e.g. Samsung) will introduce their own products (e.g. smartphones with Android operating systems) in response to the leading firm. The leader will run the risk of losing the initial position and above normal performance outcomes if the unique resources are not 'nurtured' or supported by the organisation. Therefore, sustained competitive advantage is not merely the result of valuable, rare and inimitable resources, but also the result of how these resources are acquired, managed, developed and supported by other organisational systems. The success of Apple since 2006 is not just the result of the iPad and the iPhone, but the shift in Apple's business model from computers and computer software to new forms of digital communication. Illustrative of this is the fact that Apple removed the label 'computer' in its branding, no longer referring to Apple computers. Its new business model is supported by an Apple culture and Apple way of working that goes back to the 1980s and which are difficult to fully understand and imitate by competitors. According to the resource-based view principles, Apple's success is built on unique internal resources.

Inimitability is one of the most important 'qualities of desirable resources' (Boxall and Purcell 2003: 75) in the RBV theory. That is why Barney and Wright (1998) put it on the third level of their VRIO framework. Firm resource can be imperfectly imitable (and difficult to substitute) for one or a combination of three reasons (Dierickx and Cool 1989): the ability of a firm to obtain a resource is dependent on unique historical conditions (**path dependency**); the link between resources possessed by a firm and a firm's sustained competitive advantage is causally ambiguous (**causal ambiguity**); and the resource generating a firm's advantage is socially complex and difficult to understand (**social complexity**). Path dependency captures the idea that valuable resources are developed over time and the fact that their competitive success does not simply come from making choices in the present but has its origin and starting point in a chain of past events, incidents and choices. Barney and Wright's (1998) notion of 'resource support by organisation' is linked to the concept of path dependency. The chain of events and managerial choices over time, in combination with the complexity of social interactions between actors, forms the basis of the second barrier to imitation according to the RBV: social complexity (Dierickx and Cool 1989). Unique networks of internal and external connections are natural barriers for imitation by rivals. The third type of barrier in RBV is causal ambiguity: it is difficult for people who have not been involved in the decision-making process to assess the specific cause-effect relationships in organisations.

In summary, the RBV notions, the VRIO framework and human capital notions provide a theoretical foundation for understanding organisational success through human resources (employees and the social relationships of employees). These insights give us clues about why the people component plays an important role in organisational performance. The 'resource' element in the concept human resource management is theoretically explained and highlighted through the resource-based view of the firm and human capital theory. The next question, of course, is does HRM or the management of people contribute to performance? The next section is therefore focused on the HRM and performance debate.

Does HRM Contribute to Performance?

How do critical HR goals get affected by employees? In other words, what kind of employee attitudes and behaviours have a positive impact on performance? For example, highly committed and motivated employees are potentially more productive (i.e. willing to work harder and smarter) and more flexible (i.e. eager to learn through job rotation) than employees that score very low on employee commitment and motivation. The issues above can be linked to the extensive HRM and performance debate which started some fifteen years ago with publications by Arthur (1994), Huselid (1995) and MacDuffie (1995).

The HRM and performance debate of the last fifteen years is actually threefold. Firstly, the majority of HR research in this area is focused on empirically testing the impact of HRM on performance. These studies were undertaken in different countries, in different branches of industry, with input from different respondents (including HR professionals, line managers, employees and employee representatives), at different levels of analysis (including the individual employee level, the team level, strategic business unit level and company level), in profit and non-profit organisations, using different theories and a diversity of outcome measures. For an extensive overview and critical review of over 104 empirical journal articles in international academic journals on HRM and performance, see Boselie et al. (2005). Secondly, there is a stream of HR research from the year 2000 onwards on the methods used to determine the added value of HRM, for example reflected in the article by Gerhart et al. (2000) on measurement error in previous empirical HR research. Finally, recent overview articles and meta-analyses on HRM and performance were published including the studies by Wall and Wood (2005), Paauwe and Boselie (2005a), Combs et al. (2006), Becker and Huselid (2006), Fleetwood and Hesketh (2006), Paauwe (2009) and Guest (2011). The first stream is focused on empirically testing the impact of HRM on performance. The second stream deals with critically evaluating the methods and research designs applied to empirically test the added value of HRM. The third stream represents overview articles and meta-analysis mainly based on input from the first HRM stream.

The first and the third stream within the HRM and performance debate generated the most output, with empirical evidence that HRM mainly has a modest positive impact on performance and in some cases no impact at all (Purcell 1999).

Becker and Huselid (2000) suggest that the effect of one standard deviation change in an HR system (a statistically technical way to describe the variation in human resource variety and intensity among organisations) is 10 to 20 per cent of a firm's market value. Combs *et al.*'s (2006) meta-analysis on 92 empirical studies found that an increase of one standard deviation in the use of a special type of HRM called high performance work practices, is associated with a 4.6 per cent increase in return on assets (ROA). Therefore, these authors conclude that the relationships between HRM and performance are not just statistically significant, but also managerially relevant (Paauwe 2009).

Overall, there is general agreement among HR scholars that HR practices are at least weakly related to firm performance (Purcell 1999; Wright and Gardner 2003; Wall and Wood 2005; Paauwe and Boselie 2005a), however the results should be treated with caution (Boselie *et al.* 2005; Wall and Wood 2005). The second stream (mainly focused on methods and research design) is much more critical towards the findings because of serious doubts about the research designs (for example surveys sent to organisations to fill in), the quality of the data (for example input from single HR respondents; cross-sectional data), the research methods (for example using simple regression analysis) and the interpretation of the data (for example neglecting contextual factors such as firm size, sectoral differences and country differences caused by institutional differences). Boselie *et al.* (2005) conclude that there is no general agreement and consensus about (1) what constitutes HRM, (2) what is performance, and (3) what is the link between the two, although much progress has been made since Guest (1997) noticed the need for good theory on these three issues.

The first stream has resulted in a large number of empirical studies suggesting the positive impact of HRM on particular outcome variables. Below are some illustrations of findings from empirical studies on the relationship between HRM and performance. *Selective recruitment and selection* of new employees is positively related to labour productivity (Huselid 1995; Koch and McGrath 1996) and negatively related to employee turnover (Huselid 1995). The recruitment and selection of new employees is often the starting point for human resource management. The attraction and retention of highly qualified and motivated workers that fit the job (person–job fit) and fit the organisation (person–organisation fit) is relevant for organisations such as hospitals that are confronted with labour shortages caused by the sector reputation and the aging population.

Excellent *rewards* and *performance-related pay* are positively related to product quality (Kalleberg and Moody 1994), labour productivity (Lazear 1996), customer satisfaction (Banker *et al.* 1996), employee motivation (Dowling and Richardson 1997), organisational commitment and employee trust (Appelbaum *et al.* 2000), and negatively related to employee turnover (Arthur 1994). This empirical evidence stimulated the introduction of performance-related pay in organisations. The empirical research by Cools (2009) on corporate governance and corporate crises, however, suggests that performance-related pay for top management is most likely one of the causes of the 25 largest corporate scandals of the last fifteen years. This puts pay for performance in a different perspective and therefore a critical evaluation of rewards and performance-related pay is necessary before application in practice (see Chapter 12).

Employee autonomy, for example in job planning and decision-making, increases job satisfaction (Wallace 1995). The new way of working in Dutch Telecom as a form of flexible work requires not only the technology for employees working at home, but also line management's trust in employees that they are willing and able to work without direct or close supervision (see introduction of this chapter). This new way of working requires employee autonomy and the direct supervisor's trust in his/her employees. Simply applying employee autonomy as an HR intervention or HR practice is not good enough for making the new way of working successful. It also requires support for, and training of, line managers to implement this alternative way of working.

More recently, Peña and Villasalero (2010) show the positive impact of HR systems on the performance of Spanish banks. Van de Voorde *et al.* (2010) use data from the Netherlands and their findings provide strong empirical evidence that HRM can explain almost 18 per cent of the profitability of business units ($n = 171$) within one large financial institution. These two recent studies highlight the positive effects of HRM on financial performance of financial institutions. And their evidence is quite strong. The findings, however, do not tell us much about how these financial institutions can apply HRM to overcome some of the real challenges financial institutions are confronted with as a result of the global financial crisis. These challenges, for example, relate to regaining customer trust and changing the nature of the performance management systems to new systems that are not exclusively focused on financial performance.

A popular theoretical framework for explaining why certain human resource management practices or systems are contributing is the so-called AMO theory. Boxall and Purcell (2003: 20) argue that according to the AMO model '. . . people perform well when:

They are able to do so (they can do the job because they possess the necessary knowledge and skills);
They have the motivation to do so (they will do the job because they want to and are adequately incentivised);
Their work environment provides the necessary support and avenues for expression (for example, functioning technology and the opportunity to be heard when problems occur).'

Ability practices include selective recruitment and selection (getting the right people) and training and development (development of skills, knowledge and abilities). **Motivation practices** include performance appraisal (evaluation and feedback), performance-related pay, coaching and mentoring, employment security, internal promotion opportunities, fair pay and employee benefits. **Opportunity practices** include autonomy, employee involvement, job rotation, job enlargement, job enrichment, self-directed teamwork, communication and decentralisation of decision-making. A high performance work system can be defined as a bundle of specific HR practices that create employee abilities in terms of knowledge and skills, employee motivation through a sophisticated incentive structure, and employee opportunity to participate in decision-making (Appelbaum *et al.* 2000). The alignment of individual HR practices into a bundle or system of practices is thought to create synergistic effects (Delery 1998). In other words, a fit between individual HR practices will strengthen the impact of HRM on performance outcomes. An internal fit between the individual HR practices combined into a coherent and consistent human resource system is assumed to lead to a higher performance than the sum of the individual HR practices (Kepes and Delery 2007). The underlying theory for the high performance work system and notions of internal fit is known as the AMO theory. The AMO model builds on the notion that HR practices can be bundled to enhance ability, motivation and opportunity to perform (Appelbaum *et al.* 2000; Wall and Wood 2005). The specific HR practices that increase employee abilities (for example extensive skills training), HR practices that contribute to employee motivation (for example career support) and HR practices that stimulate opportunity to participate (for example employee involvement in decision-making) have a positive effect on discretionary effort in task performance (in-role behaviour) and 'the willingness of employees to walk the extra mile' without additional rewards (organisational citizenship behaviour − OCB − or extra-role behaviour) (Boselie 2010). High scores on discretionary effort in task performance and OCB will contribute to organisational performance such as increased labour productivity and service quality according to the AMO model.

The evidence for a relationship between HR practices, HR outcomes and critical HR goals is also visually presented in the model by Paauwe and Richardson (1997). The overview and framework by Paauwe and Richardson (1997) synthesises the results of previous empirical research (See Figure 2.1). HRM practices give rise to HRM outcomes, which influence the performance of the firm. The model does acknowledge potential reversed causality, reflecting the possibility that excellent firm performance or poor firm performance affects HRM and not the other way round. Excellent profits in a given year can have a strong positive effect on HRM in terms of more willingness of the top managers to invest in employees (higher budgets for employee development) and higher compensation for all employees. Poor firm performance, for example as a result of a country's economic crisis, might result in decreasing training budgets and a vacancy freeze. The Paauwe and Richardson (1997) framework also acknowledges the impact of contextual factors on the relationship between HRM and performance. Contextual factors include the type of industry, the firm size, the firm's age and history, the firm's capital intensity, the degree of unionisation, but also the employees' background (gender, level of education, employee age etc.). Some HRM activities or practices influence the performance of the firm directly. Performance-related pay, for example, can have a direct positive effect on labour productivity (Lazear 1996) without any mediating role on HRM outcomes such as employee motivation and commitment.

In summary, the empirical evidence on the added value of human resource management is mounting. The above overview shows HRM does affect performance. We should, however, be modest and critical about simple generalisations based on these findings. Context matters (Boxall and Purcell 2003; Paauwe 2004; Boselie 2010) and HRM effects might differ across organisational contexts depending on factors such as organisational size, branch of industry, country, nature of the workforce and degree of unionisation. The next section will highlight some of these aspects related to the question 'under which conditions does HRM contribute to performance?'

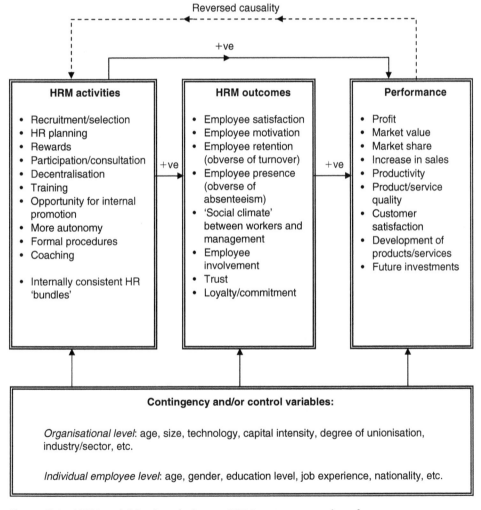

Figure 2.1 HRM activities in relation to HRM outcomes and performance

Source: Paauwe, J. and Richardson, R. (1997). 'Strategic human resource management and performance: an introduction'. *The International Journal of Human Resource Management*, 8/3: 257–262, Routledge (Taylor & Francis Group)

Institutional Context, HRM and Performance – Under What Conditions will HRM Contribute to Performance?

Internal and external contextual factors shape the organisation and the shaping of human resource management in organisations (Paauwe 2004; Boselie 2010). The internal organisational context is also known as configuration. The configuration of an organisation is the organisation's DNA or blueprint reflected in the culture, structure, systems and people's norms and values. The resource-based view ideas, presented earlier, highlight the importance of internal resources and therefore the relevance of the internal organisation context. Causal ambiguity, social complexity and path dependency can contribute to a unique internal organisation. Neglecting the organisation context runs the risk of simply applying 'best practices' in HRM. The overview of Paauwe and Richardson (1997), for example, may suggest simply applying the list of HR practices presented to increase HR outcomes and firm performance. In some cases this (temporarily) works out well, but to gain temporary and sustained competitive advantage according to RBV and human capital standards, a more advanced approach is required. The Apple success is not easily imitated by competitors because of Apple's unique internal organisation. In addition to the difficulty of imitation there is also the possibility that what works well within the Apple context is not applicable in a completely different branch of industry. This is why the conditions of an organisation are relevant for the potential contribution of HRM for improving performance and/or achieving goals. The literature on RBV and human capital theory suggests that HRM can contribute to organisational success when the organisation context and its internal resource are fully taken into account (Wright *et al.* 2001; Boxall and Purcell 2003; Paauwe 2004). However, it's not just the internal organisation context that matters.

The downside of the RBV and the human capital theory in contemporary HR research is the structural neglect of the external organisation context (Boselie and Paauwe 2009). The external organisation context can be characterised by market mechanisms such as new products, markets and technology. Related to this is the concept of competition. Another external organisational context is reflected in the institutional environment of an organisation through, for example, rules, legislation, social partners and the government. New labour legislation, for example, directly affected HR practice. It is therefore important to explicitly take into account both the internal and external organisational contexts to gain a fuller understanding of the conditions under which HRM can contribute to performance. The dominant theories in HRM and performance research (Boselie *et al.* 2005) in particular, structurally neglect the institutional context of an organisation (Boselie and Paauwe 2009). The institutional context of an organisation is represented by legislation, rules, procedures, professional norms, societal norms and values, and the influence of multiple stakeholders. The global and financial crisis has shown the downside of too narrow an agency model that is mainly focused on the interests of agents (top managers) and principals (shareholders/owners), neglecting the interests of other stakeholders such as works councils, trade unions, employees, customers and governments. New agency perspectives explicitly include the involvement of multiple stakeholders in decision-making and include the interests of different stakeholders reflected in new ways of defining organisational performance. The latter refers to the possibility that organisational performance is seen as more than just excellent financial performance. Instead the multi-dimensional performance construct in new agency models includes organisational goals such as social legitimacy and fairness towards individual employees (Paauwe 2004 and 2009). The institutional context and the stakeholder environment cannot be neglected in the HRM and performance debate.

The traditional strategic contingency approaches emphasise the relevance of external factors that shape human resource management and affect performance (Boselie *et al.* 2005). See, for example, the Harvard model by Beer *et al.* (1984) in which both external stakeholders and situational factors are explicitly incorporated as drivers for HR decision-making. These strategic contingency approaches, however, provide little theoretical foundation and explanation for how and why contextual factors matter with regard to the linkage between HRM and performance.

New institutionalism is an alternative theory that can help understand the impact of context in the HRM and performance debate (Paauwe and Boselie 2003). DiMaggio and Powell (1983) present a framework with three institutional mechanisms that affect the shaping of an organisation:

1. **Coercive mechanisms** that stem from legislation and procedures.
2. **Normative mechanisms** that have their origins in the professions (for example the professional education of lawyers and accountants, but also the professional networks that operate to develop and protect certain professions).
3. **Mimetic mechanisms** that are the result of uncertainty or fashion.

Paauwe and Boselie (2003) have translated this theoretical framework to the field of HRM. Coercive mechanisms that affect the HR strategy include national labour legislation, for example on working hours and working conditions, collective bargaining agreements with trade unions and/or works councils, norms and values in a given country or continent, the role of the government or larger entities such as the European Union, and the role of trade unions in the shaping of the employment relationship in an organisation. The coercive mechanisms are manifested in the case of a new labour law, yearly collective bargaining agreements and reorganisation with massive lay-offs.

Normative mechanisms are generally embedded in the employees' professional norms and routines. In other words, these mechanisms determine, to a large extent, how an employee does the job. Medical specialists, for example, are educated and trained in a very specific way. Their routines are not easily changed and influenced by the organisation's new strategy focused on, for example, cost reduction and service quality. The potential tension between the medical specialists and new public management reforms can be found in many hospitals, providing a major challenge for HRM to bridge the two perspectives.

The third institutional mechanism is focused on the general tendency of orga-nisations to copy/imitate others in times of uncertainty or as a result of hype. Mimetic mechanisms can be the result of consultancy interference or the develop-ment of a new fashion in management. The learning organisation, the balanced scorecard, benchmarking, competency frameworks, lean production principles, and the HR scorecard are all potential guru management principles that might lead to mimetic behaviour among organisations in a population. Once several, and often leading, organisations in a population have adopted such a practice, it is likely that other organisations in the population will follow (Paauwe and Boselie 2005b). The imitation of a best practice might be done because of competitive considerations. Then it is not an institutional mechanism but a competitive mechanism that drove the organisation to implement the practice. The imitation of a best practice because others are doing it as well reflects mimetic behaviour potentially caused by legitimacy considerations. In other words, if others are doing it we must do it as well; otherwise we run the risk of reputation damage for not doing it.

In summary, internal and external contextual factors affect the shaping of human resource management and the nature of the human resource value chain. Both strategic contingency approaches (e.g. Beer *et al.* 1984) and new institutionalism (e.g. Paauwe 2004) provide insights into how these contextual or situational factors affect the relationship between HRM and performance, although institutional theory provides a stronger theoretical foundation and explanation. Studying the impact of HRM on performance without taking into account the organisational context runs the risk of oversimplification and stimulating imitation and application of 'best practices' in organisations (Van Hees and Verweel 2006). The real success of HRM interventions for all stakeholders involved (including employees) is often difficult to delineate, to unwrap and to fully understand, partly as a result of causal ambiguity, path dependency and social complexity (Wright *et al.* 2001) and partly as a result of the complex and dynamic nature of organisational concepts such as HRM and performance (Van Hees and Verweel 2006).

Conclusion

This chapter provides an overview of the potential contribution of HRM to per-formance. There are three leading guidelines for the discussion presented here. First, why does HRM potentially contribute to performance? The resource-based view, the VRIO framework and the human capital theory provide frameworks for answering the 'why' question. An important proposition of the RBV and human capital perspectives is that internal resources, in particular human resources, are a potential source of organisational success and performance. In this chapter organi-sational success and performance are defined in terms of achieving certain goals that are directly linked to contemporary organisational challenges related to economics, social issues and technology. These social phenomena form the starting point of the search for the potential added value from employees through human resource management. Social phenomena are often context specific. In other words, organisational challenges can be country, sector and/or company specific. Hospitals are challenged by employee retention issues, while financial institutions are confronted with new ways of working (e.g. new performance management systems) required as a direct consequence of the global financial crisis.

The second guideline or question in this chapter was: does HRM contribute to performance? The empirical evidence shows the added value of people management. Simply applying 'best practice' is not likely to solve major organisational issues. In theory HRM practices affect employee outcomes such as satisfaction and motivation. The latter outcomes affect organisational outcomes such as labour productivity and service quality. Reality, however, is more complex, for example as a result of contingencies at different levels (individual level contingencies and organisation level contingencies) and the possibility of reversed causality.

The third question of the chapter was very much focused on under which conditions HRM contributes to performance. Contextual notions are important for getting a full understanding of HRM and performance. The internal and external organisational context is significant in the shaping of human resource management in the organisation and the potential added value of HRM to performance. It can also be concluded that the institutional context is often neglected while highly relevant. The institutional framework provides structure and understanding of contextual mechanisms (coercive, normative and mimetic) that affect the shaping of HRM and the potential added value of HRM.

There are two issues that could be studied in depth in the near future. First, several scholars (e.g. Greenwood 2002; Paauwe 2004) have argued that mainstream strategic HRM, and HRM and performance in particular, take a unitarist perspective exclusively focused on hard organisational outcomes such as productivity and profits. The Harvard model (Beer *et al.* 1984) and its stakeholder notions in combination with the explicit acknowledgement of organisational outcomes, societal well-being and individual well-being as a multidimensional performance construct, is somewhat lost in the HRM and performance debate. In other words, HRM may contribute to increasing organisational outcomes, but what are the effects on individual well-being and societal well-being? Future research could focus on the societal impact and the individual employee impact of human resource management interventions. The corporate crises and the global financial crisis have shown the limitations of a one-sided view of people management. Performance-related pay for top management to increase financial performance and organisational growth has shown serious negative outcomes for society and individual employees (Cools 2009). There is a growing awareness that all organisations, both public and private, have a public responsibility and public dimension (Rainey 2003). Taking a pluralist perspective in studying HRM and performance is therefore worthwhile for future research and the search for the long term success of organisations.

A second issue that is potentially worthwhile studying in future research is related to the nature of the impact of contextual factors on the HRM and performance relationship. The traditional approaches implicitly build on the notion that institutional mechanisms are hindering factors for organisational interventions including HRM. In other words, institutional mechanisms cause limitations for managerial interventions. There is also a stream of research in strategic management and organisation sociology that builds on notions that institutional mechanisms (for example new legislation) can be a source for creating organisational success. Oliver (1997) and Deephouse (1999), for example, blend new institutionalism and the resource-based view. These approaches are often linked to innovation (Paauwe and Boselie 2005b). Some organisations are better and faster in adaptation of both market and institutional innovations than other organisations. An organisation that is the first to adapt to new institutional arrangements (for example a new law or new procedures) has a potential source of competitive advantage. Deephouse (1999) argues that social legitimacy issues might play a role here related to corporate reputation. Toyota's *Prius*, with its hybrid engine, anticipated institutional developments with regard to environmental pollution. For many years Toyota was, therefore, leading in this segment with a strong reputation towards potential customers. Future research on HRM and performance could focus on the potential added value of HRM to institutional innovations.

REFERENCES

Appelbaum, E., Bailey, T., Berg, P. and Kalleberg, A. 2000: *Manufacturing advantage: why high-performance work systems pay off*, Ithaca: Cornell University Press.

Arthur, J. B. 1994: Effects of human resource systems on manufacturing performance and turnover, *Academy of Management Journal*, **37**(3), 670–687.

Baden-Fuller, C. W. F. and Stopford, J. M. 1994: Creating corporate entrepreneurship, *Strategic Management Journal*, **15**(7), 521–536.

Banker, R. D., Lee, S. Y., Potter, G. and Srinivasan, D. 1996: Contextual analysis of performance impacts of outcome-based incentive compensation, *Academy of Management Journal*, **39**(4), 920–949.

Barney, J. B. 1991: Firm resources and sustainable competitive advantage, *Journal of Management*, **17**, 99–120.

Barney, J. B. and Wright, P. M. 1998: On becoming a strategic partner: the roles of human resources in gaining competitive advantage, *Human Resource Management*, **37**, 31–46.

Becker, B. E. and Huselid, M. A. 2000: Comment on "measurement error in research on human resources and firm performance: How much error is there and how does it influence effect size estimates?" By Gerhart, Wright, McMahan and Snell, *Personnel Psychology*, **53**(4): 835–854.

Becker, B. E. and Huselid, M. A. 2006: Strategic human resource management: Where do we go from here? *Journal of Management*, **32**(6), 898–925.

Beer, M., Spector, B., Lawrence, P., Mills, D. Q. and Walton, R. 1984: *Human Resource Management: a General Manager's Perspective*, New York: Free Press.

Boselie, P. 2010: *Strategic human resource management: A balanced approach*, London: McGraw-Hill.

Boselie, P. and Paauwe, J. 2009: *Human resource management and the resource-based view*. Chapter 25 in: Wilkinson, A., Redman, T., Snell, S. and Bacon, N. 2009: *The SAGE handbook of human resource management*, London: SAGE.

Boselie, P., Dietz, G. and Boon, C. 2005: Commonalities and contradictions in HRM and performance research, *Human Resource Management Journal*, **15**(3), 67–94.

Boxall, P. and Purcell, J. 2003: *Strategy and human resource management*. New York: Palgrave MacMillan.

Combs, J., Liu, Y., Hall, A. and Ketchen, D. 2006: How much do high-performance work practices matter? A meta-analysis of their effects on organizational performance, *Personnel Psychology*, **59**(3), 501–528.

Cools, K. 2009: *Controle is goed, vertrouwen nog beter: Over bestuurders en corporate governance*, Stichting Management Studies, vierde druk, Assen: Koninklijke van Gorcum.

Deephouse, D. L. 1999: To be different, or to be the same? It's a question (and theory) of strategic balance, *Strategic Management Journal*, **20**(2), 147–166.

Delery, J. E. 1998: Issues of fit in strategic human resource management: Implications for research, *Human Resource Management Review*, **8**(3), 289–309.

Delery, J. E. and Shaw, J. D. 2001: *The strategic management of people in work organizations: review, synthesis, and extension*, paper presented at the Academy of Management Meeting 2001 in Washington D.C.

Dierickx, I. and Cool, K. 1989: Asset stock accumulation and sustainability of competitive advantage, *Management Science*, **35**, (12 December).

DiMaggio, P. J. and Powell, W. W. 1983: The iron cage revisited: institutional isomorphism and collective rationality in organizational fields, *American Sociological Review*, **48**(2), 147–160.

Dowling, B. and Richardson, R. 1997: Evaluating performance-related pay for managers in the National Health Service, *The International Journal of Human Resource Management*, **8**(3), 348–366.

Fleetwood, S. and Hesketh, A. 2006: Beyond Measuring the Human Resources Management-Organizational Performance Link: Applying Critical Realist Meta-Theory, *Organization*, **13**(5), 677–699.

Gerhart, B., Wright, P. M. and McMahan, G. 2000: Measurement error in research on the human resource and firm performance relationship: further evidence and analysis, *Personnel Psychology*, **53**(4), 855–872.

Greenwood, M. R. 2002: Ethics and HRM: A Review and Conceptual Analysis, *Journal of Business Ethics*, **36**(3), 261–278.

Guest, D. E. 1997: Human resource management and performance: a review and research agenda, *The International Journal of Human Resource Management*, **8**(3), 263–276.

Guest, D. E. 2011: Human resource management and performance: still searching for some answers, *Human Resource Management Journal*, **21**(1), 3–13.

Guest, D. E. and King, Z. 2004: Power, Innovation and Problem-Solving: The Personnel Managers' Three Steps to Heaven? *Journal of Management Studies*, **41**(3), 401–423.

Huselid, M. A. 1995: The impact of human resource management practices on turnover, productivity, and corporate financial performance, *Academy of Management Journal*, **38**(3), 635–672.

Kalleberg, A. L. and Moody, J. W. 1994: Human resource management and organizational performance, *American Behavioral Scientist*, **37**(7), 948–962.

Kepes, S. and Delery, J. 2007: HRM systems and the problem of internal fit, in Boxall, P., Purcell, J. and Wright, P. M. (eds), 2007: *The Oxford Handbook of Human Resource Management*, Oxford University Press: Oxford, pp. 385–404.

Koch, M. J. and McGrath, R. G. 1996: Improving labor productivity: human resource management policies do matter, *Strategic Management Journal*, **17**, 335–354.

Lazear, E. P. 1996: *Performance pay and productivity*, NBER working paper 5672, Cambridge.

MacDuffie, J. P. 1995: Human resource bundles and manufacturing performance: organizational logic and flexible production systems in the world auto industry, *Industrial and Labor Relations Review*, **48**(2), 197–221.

Oliver, C. 1997: Sustainable competitive advantage: Combining institutional and resource-based views, *Strategic Management Journal*, **18**, 697–713.

Paauwe, J. 2004: *HRM and performance: Achieving long-term viability*, Oxford: Oxford University Press.

Paauwe, J. 2009: HRM and performance: Achievements, methodological issues and prospects, *Journal of Management Studies*, **46**(1), 129–142.

Paauwe, J. and Boselie, P. 2003: Challenging 'strategic HRM' and the relevance of the institutional setting, *Human Resource Management Journal*, **13**(3), 56–70.

Paauwe, J. and Boselie, P. 2005a: HRM and performance: What's next? *Human Resource Management Journal*, **15**(4), 68–83.

Paauwe, J. and Boselie, P. 2005b: 'Best practices . . . in spite of performance': Just a matter of imitation? *International Journal of Human Resource Management*, **16**(6), 987–1003.

Paauwe, J. and Richardson, R. 1997: Introduction special issue on HRM and performance, *The International Journal of Human Resource Management*, **8**(3), 257–262.

Peña, I. and Villasalero, M. 2010: Business strategy, human resource systems, and organizational performance in the Spanish banking industry, *The International Journal of Human Resource Management*, **21**(15), 2864–2888.

Penrose, E. T. 1959: *The theory of the growth of the firm*, Oxford: Blackwell.

Porter, M. E. 1980: *Competitive strategy*, New York: The Free Press/MacMillan.

Purcell, J. 1999: Best practice and best fit: chimera or cul-de-sac? *Human Resource Management Journal*, **9**(3), 26–41.

Rainey, H. 2003: *Understanding and Managing Public Organizations*, 3rd edition, San Francisco, CA: John Wiley & Sons, Inc.

Van de Voorde, K., Paauwe, J. and Van Veldhoven, M. 2010: Predicting business unit performance using employee surveys: monitoring HRM-related changes, *Human Resource Management Journal*, **20**(1), 44–63.

Van Hees, B. and Verweel, P. (eds) 2006: *Deframing organisation concepts*. Advances in Organisation Studies, Copenhagen: Liber and Copenhagen Business School Press.

Veld, M., Paauwe, J. and Boselie, P. 2010: HRM and strategic climates in hospitals: Does the message come across at the ward level? *Human Resource Management Journal*, **20**(4), 339–356.

Wall, T. D. and Wood, S. J. 2005: The romance of human resource management and business performance, and the case for big science, *Human Relations*, **58**(4), 429–462.

Wallace, J. E. 1995: Corporatist control and organizational commitment among professionals: the case of lawyers working in law firms, *Social Forces*, **73**(3), 811–840.

Wernerfelt, B. 1984: A resource-based view of the firm. *Strategic Management Journal*, **5**, 171–180.

Wright, P. M. and Gardner, T. M. 2003: The human resource-firm performance relationship: methodological and theoretical challenges, in Holman, D., Wall, T. D, Clegg, C. W., Sparrow, P. and Howard, A. (eds), *The New Workplace: a Guide to the Human Impact of Modern Working Practices*, Chichester: John Wiley & Sons, Ltd.

Wright, P. M., Dunford, B. D. and Snell, S.A. 2001: Human resources and the resource based view of the firm, *Journal of Management*, **27**(6), 701–721.

CHAPTER THREE

Legal Aspects of the Employment Relationship

Graeme Lockwood and Kevin Williams

Introduction

The British industrial relations system has traditionally been characterised by minimal legal regulation and, as far as possible, the minimum involvement of the state. As such, the system was labelled voluntarist or abstentionist, in contrast to the 'juridification' of other European countries. As Otto Kahn-Freund observed in 1954, 'There is, perhaps, no major country in the world in which the law has played a less significant role in the shaping of industrial relations than in Great Britain and in which today the law and the legal profession have less to do with labour relations'.

However, this description of the role of the law in employment relations is no longer representative of the situation. The law now plays a crucial role in regulating virtually all aspects of the employment relationship from hiring to firing, one result of which is that significant numbers of formal complaints alleging abuse of rights are made every year. The number of claims, however, has been falling, and is now below 200,000 per annum. The legal system operates largely on the basis that it is the responsibility of affected individuals (rather than, say, their trade union) to bring reactive complaints, ordinarily before an employment tribunal. Only rarely are employers or public authorities required to take positive action ahead of time to tackle potential sources of workplace inequity.

Across the last twenty years or so, there has been much debate about how optimal levels of state regulation might be achieved, what that might look like, and the desirability or otherwise of deregulation (Weatherill 2007). In the employment context, the debate has been fuelled by recurring complaints from some quarters that the law, whether emanating from Europe or home-grown, has increasingly imposed unacceptable 'burdens on business', coupled with appeals to government to take steps to combat the alleged (though unproven) growth in frivolous complaints. However, rather than opt for the abolition of substantive rights, by and large the response of successive governments has been to make it more difficult to access them, to simplify procedures or to make tribunals operate more 'efficiently', for example, by giving them extra powers to reject weak cases and to order costs against unreasonable complainants.

In 2011 the Coalition government published an 'Employers' Charter', seemingly designed to reassure anxious employers about some rather basic matters, such as their ability to make staff redundant in the event of a downturn, or to ask employees to take annual leave at a time that suits the business. Whether its present ongoing review of employment law will result in important changes to the law or fewer claims is uncertain. In any event, it seems clear that the rate of claiming is closely connected to fluctuations in the state of the economy and that increases in litigation are usually a side-effect of recession (Department of Trade and Industry 2001). Moreover, the room for radical revision must be limited to the extent that many employment rights (including much of the equality agenda) derive from EU legislation. Even if it were available, there are doubts about the effects of such a strategy. Though the analysis is complex, a study across five countries (UK, USA, France, Germany, and India) concluded that there is very little evidence to support the claim that deregulating labour laws leads to superior economic performance outcomes (Armour, Deakin *et al* 2009).

Nonetheless, at the time of writing in early 2012, the following were under active consideration: increasing the qualifying period for unfair dismissal from one to two years as of 6 April 2012; restricting the consultation rules that operate where a business is transferred or collective redundancies are planned; requiring fees to be paid by all tribunal applicants; empowering tribunal judges to sit alone to dispose of a wide range of cases including unfair dismissal; simplifying the procedure rules in employment tribunals; and compulsory conciliation of all workplace disputes.

This chapter outlines the major 'individual employment protection' rights potentially available to workers and how these affect the practice of human resource management. Given the degree of legal intervention in the employment relationship it is essential for HR students and professionals to be familiar with legal issues that directly impact individual employees and are critical to the organisation.

Individual Employment Protection Rights

Traditionally, the law has differentiated 'employees' from other forms of contracted labour, such as the self-employed, reserving some important rights (including unfair dismissal and redundancy) to the former. Though the vast majority in the workforce are employees, the distinction is sometimes difficult to draw. Moreover, some modern statutes, often influenced by EU law, extend protections (such as those concerning discrimination, working time and the minimum wage) beyond employees to a broader category of persons, often styled 'workers'. For example, s.230(3) of the Employment Rights Act 1996 defines a worker as someone who is an employee or who is individually contracted to perform personally any work or services for another who is not a client or customer of any profession or business carried on by him. It is beyond our scope to examine what precisely distinguishes employees from workers and the self-employed, though it is a significant difference that should be borne in mind. In Autoclenz Ltd v Belcher [2011] IRLR 820, car valeters were held to be employees despite being expressly described in their contracts as self-employed.

The Equality Agenda

Anti-discrimination laws relating to race, sex and pay equality have been in place for over forty years. Others have been added since, such as those providing protection to part-time workers, fixed term employees and agency workers. The law is pervasive throughout the employment relationship, covering recruitment, terms and conditions of employment, promotion, training and termination of employment. Historically the law developed gradually, with separate grounds of discrimination being tackled by separate legislative instruments, such as the Equal Pay Act 1970, Sex Discrimination Act 1975, Race Relations Act 1976, and the Disability Discrimination Act 1995. To comply with European law, legislation outlawing discrimination on the grounds of religion or belief, sexual orientation and age had to be introduced. This incremental development has meant that national legislation has increasingly operated in the context of European law, which has been very influential in driving UK developments (Dickens and Hall 2003).

Whilst the widening scope of legislation to tackle discrimination law was welcomed, critics argued that the law was flawed both in terms of approach and outcome. Its approach was criticised for merely outlawing discrimination, rather than imposing positive duties to promote equality, which arguably undermines its effectiveness. In respect of outcomes, it was observed that relatively few legal actions were taken against employers and that the penalties for failure to comply with the law were weak and ineffective (Dickens 2005:192).

However, the law has since entered a new phase with the introduction of the Equality Act 2010. The Act has brought all of the grounds of discrimination together in one statute, harmonised definitions and concepts, and introduced new requirements. It permits greater scope for positive action, makes express provision for discrimination based on more than one characteristic and strengthens disability protections. Some key aspects of the new law are highlighted below.

The 2010 Act covers both workers and employees. Where there is a reference in the Act to 'employees', this indicates that only employees (within the strict meaning of the word) are affected by the particular provision.

Section 4 of the Act provides that discrimination (less favourable treatment) on the grounds of protected characteristics is prohibited. These include: disability, gender reassignment, marriage and civil partnership, race, religion or belief, sex, sexual orientation, age, pregnancy and maternity.

The Act prohibits several types of conduct in relation to employment. First, direct discrimination; that is, discrimination against a person because they have a protected characteristic. The Act extends direct discrimination by allowing claims for discrimination and harassment to be brought on the basis that the victim is *perceived* to have a protected characteristic (whether or not they do), or because they associate with someone who has a protected characteristic. Second, the Act extends indirect discrimination to cover disability discrimination and gender reassignment. This means that a worker can claim that a particular practice, criterion or provision disproportionately disadvantages persons sharing the same characteristic as the applicant. There is no need to show that the employer knew (or ought to have known) that the person possessed the particular characteristic. Third, discrimination arising from disability occurs where an employer treats a disabled person unfavourably because of something connected with their disability. For example, where an employer dismisses a worker because she has had three months' sick leave, despite the employer being aware that the worker has long term depression and that most of her sick leave is disability-related. Though the employer's decision to dismiss is not because of the worker's disability itself, the worker has been treated less favourably because of something arising in consequence of her disability, namely, the need to take a period of disability-related sick leave. There is no need for a comparator and the employer would have to objectively justify his actions. The 'justification' test asks whether the alleged discriminatory treatment is a proportionate means of achieving a legitimate aim. The employer must produce evidence to support their claim that it is justified and not rely on mere assertion: the action taken by the employer must be 'appropriate and necessary' (Equality Act 2010, Statutory Code of Guidance). This approach requires courts and tribunals to balance the degree of discrimination with the aim to be achieved, taking into account all the circumstances.

The Equality Act 2010 extends third-party harassment to disability, gender reassignment, race, religion or belief, and sexual orientation. Employers are liable for harassment of their employees by a third party (e.g. a customer or client) where: the employer knows the employee has been harassed; harassment occurred at least twice (it is irrelevant whether the third party is the same or a different person on each occasion); and the employer did not take reasonably practicable steps to prevent harassment recurring. In 2011, the government launched a consultation about whether liability for third-party harassment should be abolished.

The Act also included the concept of combined or dual discrimination, which occurs when, because of a combination of two relevant protected characteristics, a person is treated less favourably than others are, or would be treated. For example, suppose a black woman was passed over for promotion to work on reception because her employer thinks black women do not perform well in customer service roles. Because the employer can point to a white woman of equivalent qualifications and experience who has been appointed to the job, as well as to a black man of equivalent qualifications and experience in a similar role, the woman may need to compare her treatment because of race and sex combined to demonstrate that she has been subjected to less favourable treatment because of her employer's prejudice against black women (Government Explanatory Notes 2010, para 68). Section 14 applies only to direct discrimination; there is no equivalent provision for dual discrimination in indirect discrimination (ibid, para 66). However, in March 2011 the Conservative-led Coalition

Government announced that section 14 would not be implemented due to concerns that the provision 'would cost business £3 million per year' (McColgan 2011).

The Act allows (but does not require) an employer to recruit or promote someone because of their protected characteristic in preference to another candidate, if he or she is 'as qualified as the other candidate and the employer reasonably thinks that: people who share the protected characteristic suffer disadvantage connected to the characteristic; participation in an activity by the persons who share a protected characteristic is disproportionately low; and the action is taken in order to overcome or minimise that disadvantage or to promote participation in the activity'.

One provision of the Act that may appease some critics of the enforcement of equality law is that tribunals now have the power to recommend action by the employer which applies to the whole workforce and not just, as previously, to the claimant. This is intended to enable tribunals to help prevent further discrimination by the employer against other employees, and not just the claimant, who may no longer work for the employer.

A significant feature of the Act is that it makes it unlawful for employers to enquire about an applicant's disability or health until after that person has either been offered a job or been included in a pool of successful candidates to be offered a job when a suitable position arises. The restriction is qualified by several exclusions: questions required for national security vetting; making reasonable adjustments to enable the disabled person to participate in the recruitment process; establishing whether a job applicant would be able to undertake a function that is intrinsic to the job, with reasonable adjustments in place as required; monitoring diversity in applications for jobs; supporting positive action in employment for disabled people; if the employer applies a requirement to have a particular disability, establishing whether the applicant has the disability. There is nothing in the Act which prevents employers asking health-related questions of new staff once recruitment decisions have been made.

The restriction on pre-employment health questions is only enforceable by the Equality and Human Rights Commission, though breach constitutes evidence of disability discrimination. For example, an applicant rejected on the basis of the information may sue for direct disability discrimination.

Statistics on discrimination law

Only a small proportion of cases are actually determined by a tribunal hearing and success rates are very low. For example, in respect of sex discrimination claims disposed of during the period April 2010 to March 2011, 49 per cent were withdrawn, 28 per cent were Advisory, Conciliation and Arbitration Service (ACAS) conciliated settlements, 16 per cent were struck out prior to a hearing, 2 per cent were successful, 1 per cent were dismissed at a preliminary hearing and 4 per cent were unsuccessful. The main remedy is a financial one. The median award was £6,078 and the maximum award stood at £289,167. The position relating to the various discrimination jurisdictions is summarised in Tables 3.1 and 3.2 below. The message is that the averages are skewed by a small number of large awards.

Table 3.1 Discrimination claims to employment tribunals 2010–2011

	Sex discrimination	Race discrimination	Disability discrimination	Religious discrimination	Sexual Orientation discrimination	Age discrimination
ACAS conciliated settlement	4300(28%)	1700(36%)	3100(46%)	290(34%)	270(41%)	1300(35%)
Withdrawn	7600(49%)	1400(28%)	2100(31%)	250(29%)	210(31%)	1500(40%)
Cases dismissed by tribunal	590(4%)	800(16%)	640(9%)	120(15%)	62(9%)	320(9%)
Cases successful at tribunal	290(2%)	150(3%)	190(3%)	27(3%)	22(3%)	90(2%)
Dismissed at preliminary hearing	200(1%)	260(5%)	200(3%)	53(6%)	22(3%)	120(3%)
Struck out not at a hearing	2500(16%)	500(10%)	510(7%)	93(11%)	70(11%)	350(10%)

Source: Annual Employment Tribunal statistics 2010–2011
Percentages may not add to 100 due to rounding

Table 3.2 Compensation awards by tribunals by jurisdiction 2010–2011

	Sex discrimination	Race discrimination	Disability discrimination	Religious discrimination	Sexual Orientation discrimination	Age discrimination
Maximum award	£289,167	£62,530	£181,083	£20,221	£47,633	£144,100
Median award	£6,078	£6,277	£6,142	£6,892	£5,500	£12,697
Average award	£13,911	£12,108	£14,137	£8,515	£11,671	£30,289

Unfair Dismissal

Legislation relating to the dismissal of employees was introduced in 1971 and is now to be found in Part X Employment Rights Act 1996 (ERA). In principle, unfair dismissal provides employees (but not mere workers) with an important right to test the fairness of employers' decisions to dismiss. Before then, dismissal was regulated by the contract of employment. The only recourse for a dismissed employee was to claim for *wrongful* dismissal, a common law action alleging the contract had been terminated prematurely or without proper notice, for which the remedy was limited damages.

Meaning of dismissal

ERA 1996 in s.94 (1) provides that an employee has the right not to be unfairly dismissed by his employer, normally after one year's continuous service (increased to two years for those employed on or after 6 April 2012). The employee must first establish that they were dismissed within the meaning of s.95.

Dismissal is defined as the termination of employment by:

- the employer, with or without notice; or
- the expiry of a limited-term contract without its renewal. A limited-term contract is a contract for a specified duration or the performance of a specific task, or one which ends when a specified event does or does not occur; or
- the employee's resignation, with or without notice, because the employer is in breach of the contract of employment (commonly known as constructive dismissal).

For constructive dismissal, the employer's action must be a significant breach of the employment contract, which indicates that they no longer intend to be bound by one or more of its terms. An example might be where the employer arbitrarily demotes an employee to a lower rank or poorer paid position. Western Excavating v Sharp [1978] ICR 221, establishes that there must actually be a breach of contract, not mere unreasonable behaviour. In this case, the fact that an employee was denied an advance of holiday pay was not constructive dismissal. Other examples include: a serious change in the nature of a person's job; failure to provide safety equipment; failure to give proper support to a supervisor; using foul/abusive language.

Reasons for dismissal

Section 98 (4) of ERA 1996 states that the tribunal must decide whether the dismissal was fair or unfair, having regard to the reason shown by the employer, and whether, in all the circumstances (including the size and administrative resources of the employer's undertaking), the employer acted reasonably or unreasonably in treating

Table 3.3 Automatically unfair reasons for dismissal

Dismissal of an employee will be held to be automatically unfair if it is for one of the
following reasons:
  • the employee was, or proposed to become, a member of an independent trade union;
    or had taken part or proposed to take part in the activities of an independent trade
    union at an appropriate time; or was not a member of a trade union, or had refused or
    proposed to refuse to become or remain a member of a trade union.
  • the employee was dismissed or selected for redundancy on maternity related grounds
    or for applying for flexible working;
  • the employee was dismissed or selected for redundancy for having sought to assert
    rights under the Working Time Regulations 1998 or the National Minimum Wage
    Act 1998;
  • the employee was dismissed or selected for redundancy for taking or proposing to take
    certain specified types of action on health and safety grounds; the employee was
    dismissed on the transfer of an undertaking or part of an undertaking, and the transfer
    itself, or a reason connected with it, is the main reason for the dismissal, unless it can be
    established that the dismissal was for an economic, technical or organisational reason
    entailing changes in the workforce;
  • discrimination;
  • dismissal because of a spent conviction;
  • dismissal where the employee has made a protected disclosure;
  • dismissal of employees for pursuing or attempting to enforce their rights under the
    Part-Time Workers Regulations 2000 and the Fixed-Term Employees Regulations
    2002.

that reason as a sufficient reason for dismissing the employee. That question must be
determined in accordance with equity and the substantial merits of the case.

For an employer to dismiss fairly, they must have both a valid reason for dismissing
the employee and have acted reasonably in treating it as a sufficient reason for dismissal. The second of these conditions does not apply where the dismissal is automatically unfair (see Table 3.3). Legislation lists five specific types of reason which can
potentially justify dismissal. They are: conduct, capability and qualifications,
redundancy, a statutory requirement to end employment, and some other substantial
reason. Experience has shown that the latter category is likely to cover almost every
case where dismissal is necessary.

With the exception of transfer of undertakings and spent conviction dismissals,
cases of automatically unfair dismissal do not require a year's continuous service at the
time of the dismissal.

When is dismissal fair or unfair?

If an employer has established a potentially fair reason for dismissal, a tribunal will
then go on to consider the reasonableness of the decision to dismiss. The question

whether the employer acted reasonably not only involves consideration of the way in which the dismissal was carried out, but also whether they acted reasonably in relation to the situation leading up to the decision to dismiss. For example, if the employee was dismissed for misconduct or lack of capability, it is necessary to consider whether they were warned and given a chance to improve or, if redundancy was the reason for dismissal, whether the employee was considered for alternative work within the organisation.

In coming to its decision on fairness, a tribunal is likely to pay particular regard to whether the employer had issued formal policies or rules, for example in a staff handbook or policy document, covering the particular situation (and whether the employee ought to have been aware of them). Thus unfair dismissal has encouraged employers to formalise their approach to disciplinary procedures. The degree to which this has occurred is confirmed by the Workplace Employment Relations Survey 2004, which found that 91 per cent of workplaces in Britain had a formal disciplinary/dismissal procedure, and 88 per cent a formal grievance procedure (Kersley *et al* 2006:215).

When determining the fairness of a dismissal, tribunals apply the 'band of reasonable responses test': only if no reasonable employer would have dismissed will the claimant succeed. The test is generous to employers because only if their response falls outside the band will dismissal be unfair. The test has proved controversial. In *Haddon* v *Van de Bergh Foods* [1999] ICR 1150 the Employment Appeal Tribunal (EAT) disapproved the test believing that its application made it too difficult for a claimant to succeed. However, in *HSBC Bank* v *Madden* [2000] IRLR 827 the Court of Appeal reinstated the test, saying that the EAT in *Haddon* had made an unwarranted departure from binding authority. The case of *Garside and Laycock v Booth* [2011] IRLR 735 provides an illustration of the employer-oriented focus of s. 98(4). The applicant was dismissed for refusing to take a pay cut. The EAT determined that an employer does not need to demonstrate that a pay reduction is the only way to secure the continuation of the business in order to justify such a dismissal. Moreover, the tribunal should focus on the reasonableness of the employer's decision to dismiss rather than the reasonableness of the employee's rejection of the new pay proposal.

The law on unfair dismissal is supplemented by the ACAS Code of Practice on Disciplinary and Grievance Procedures (2009). It sets out detailed guidance and recommendations for employers to follow in relation to discipline and dismissal. While failure to comply with the Code does not 'of itself render a person liable to any proceedings', it is 'admissible in evidence' before a tribunal when deciding whether a dismissal is fair or unfair (Trade Union Labour Relations (Consolidation) Act 1992 (TULRCA) s.207). In addition, where an employer or employee has unreasonably failed to comply with the Code, a tribunal may, if it considers it just and equitable, increase or decrease any award by up to 25 per cent (TULRCA s.207A).

The Employment Relations Act 1999, in s.10 provides a right for all workers (not just employees) to be accompanied at any formal disciplinary or grievance meeting by either a trade union official or a work colleague. The role of the accompanying person is to help represent the worker's case, sum it up, respond on the worker's behalf to any views expressed and confer with the worker during the hearing. The accompanying person may not, however, answer questions asked of the worker directly. If the right to be accompanied is infringed, the employer is liable to pay compensation of up to two weeks' pay following a complaint to a tribunal.

Statistics and impact of unfair dismissal law

Employment tribunals are effectively a barometer of the British economy and it is not surprising to find that, since the summer of 2008, the volume of claims lodged has increased substantially (Senior President of Tribunals, Annual Report 2011). There were 126,300 jurisdictional claims associated with unfair dismissal, breach of contract and redundancy, which is 17 per cent higher than for 2008-09, and 62 per cent higher than in 2007-08. The upward trend reflects the tough economic times the country is experiencing, with the resultant shedding of jobs. The reality is that few cases are actually disposed of by employment tribunals and the success rate is low. During the period April 2010 to March 2011, 8 per cent of unfair dismissal claims were successful after a hearing, 10 per cent were unsuccessful and 3 per cent were dismissed at a preliminary hearing. The majority, 41 per cent, were (ACAS) conciliated settlements. Rather than representing a significant restraint on managerial prerogative, unfair dismissal provides guidelines for employers on how to execute dismissals in a lawful and cost effective manner. Typically, compensation is modest and re-employment rarely awarded. The median award in 2010-2011 was £4,591.

Employers commonly operate from a position of strength when defending unfair dismissal claims. First, they are more likely to be legally represented than the applicant, which is a significant advantage. Second, the fact that employers need not prove actual misconduct or incompetence – it being sufficient to establish a 'reasonable belief' to justify dismissal – means that it is relatively straightforward for an employer to defend claims. Finally, the 'band of reasonable responses' test, used to determine the reasonableness of a dismissal decision, arguably provides employers with too much latitude in making decisions (Collins 1992).

The number of successful cases (8 per cent) seems to illustrate that there is little substance to the claim that the law of unfair dismissal is stacked against employers, though the cost of managing the process and of legal representation is a cause of anxiety to some. The Coalition government is considering proposals for reform. The most far-reaching is scrapping the right to claim unfair dismissal entirely where the employer has fewer than ten staff. These so-called 'micro firms' would instead pay 'no fault' compensation (redundancy pay plus wages in lieu of notice). For employees who started work for their employer on or after 6 April 2012, the qualifying period has been increased from one year to two years, whatever the size of the business. Employers may also be allowed 'protected conversations' with underperforming workers that would not be admissible in tribunal proceedings.

Some practical consequences of unfair dismissal have included the virtual disappearance of 'instant' dismissals, moving the power to sack upwards, closer monitoring of employee absence and disciplinary histories, together with an enhanced role for HR managers in the disciplinary process.

Redundancy Pay

Originally introduced in 1965, the current law concerning redundancy payments is now contained in Part XI of the Employment Rights Act 1996 (ERA). Employees (but not mere workers) with at least 104 weeks' continuous employment whose dismissal is attributable to redundancy are entitled to a tax free lump sum, scale payment based on their years of continuous service (maximum 20), gross weekly earnings (currently capped at £430) and age at dismissal. In 2012, the maximum generated by this statutory formula was £12,900. Additionally, s. 52 of ERA entitles such employees, once under notice of dismissal for redundancy, to a 'reasonable' amount of paid time off (usually considered to be up to two days) to look for other work or to fix up a training opportunity.

While some employers who recognise unions have negotiated agreements supplementing the basic statutory payment, as well as procedures for deciding who is to be selected in the event of unavoidable job losses, they are a minority. Moreover, because length of service — last-in, first-out — continues to be commonly used as a selection criterion, the two-year rule ensures that many who are declared redundant do not qualify for even a minimum statutory payment. The legislation was never intended to prevent job losses, only to compensate the loss of some of them (Fryer 1973) and over the years has become so familiar as largely to escape adverse comment.

Entitlement to a redundancy payment

Section 139 operates a threefold definition of redundancy, which is satisfied where jobs are lost because the business has closed or is expected to close, ceases to operate at the place where the employee in practice worked, or when the demand for employees to carry out work of a particular kind has ceased or diminished (whether permanently or temporarily). In addition, ss. 147 and 148 of ERA provide that lay-off and the introduction of short-time working may constitute redundancy in certain circumstances. Tribunals have no authority to second-guess the business case behind managerial decisions concerning appropriate staffing levels or the need for redundancies (*Moon v Homeworthy Furniture (Northern) Ltd* [1977] ICR 117).

Redundancy is frequently associated with business failure and in the event that an employer is unable to pay, the state will act as a solvent guarantor of last resort (Part XII, ERA). However, redundancy and hard times are not necessarily synonymous: a profitable organisation may decide it needs fewer employees because of techno-logical innovation, for example.

Decisions to change the terms and conditions of employees' contracts so they become less favourable do not amount to redundancy, provided the employer's need for staff to undertake their existing job functions remains the same. Thus, no redundancy payments were due where a police authority, for reasons of efficiency, altered the times when civilian back-room staff were expected to work (*Johnson v Nottinghamshire Combined Police Authority* [1974] ICR 170). That is not to say there is no remedy where an employer insists on varying hours, rates of pay or other promised benefits, only that it does not constitute redundancy. Unilateral changes of that sort will very frequently constitute a serious breach of contract entitling those adversely affected to quit and, where qualified, to claim constructive unfair dismissal, especially where there has been no genuine attempt to consult over the proposed change. Additionally, changes to hours and shift patterns that make, say, child care arrangements harder may well amount to indirect sex discrimination, albeit the employer in question *may* be able to demonstrate justification because the change is a proportionate means of achieving a legitimate aim.

Section 141 disqualifies redundant employees from entitlement to a statutory payment where their employer or an associated employer makes them an offer of 'suitable alternative employment' which they 'unreasonably' refuse. A trial period of up to four calendar weeks is available in which to decide whether or not to accept the new contract. In order to be 'suitable', the employer must prove that the offer entails a job which, judged objectively, is substantially comparable in terms of the demands it makes, the skills it requires, and the benefits and status it provides. The employee, on the other hand, is entitled to have his refusal judged subjectively, though the more suitable the alternative the easier it may be to show unreasonable refusal. Where a firm which had moved some distance offered to keep staff on in their existing jobs at the new location, an employee was held entitled to refuse to go because it was too far to get home at lunchtime to look after his disabled wife.

Redundancy and unfair dismissal

While redundancy is, in principle, a legitimate and potentially fair reason for dis-missal, mismanaging the selection process can give rise to claims of unfair dismissal. Tribunals expect to see that management has made efforts to avoid or minimise the need for compulsory redundancies by considering whether alternative job oppor-tunities might be found, has warned those likely to be affected, consulted them and their representatives, and adopted fair and unbiased selection criteria (*Williams v Compair Maxam Ltd* [1982] IRLR 83). Fair consultation requires employees to be given an explanation about how they have been scored on the criteria and a genuine chance to challenge their score (*Pinewood Repro Ltd (t/a County Print) v Page* [2011] ICR 508. Including length of service in a collectively agreed selection procedure has been held to be lawful despite its potentially indirect age bias, since it serves a legitimate employment policy aim and is proportionate (*Rolls Royce plc v Unite* [2009] IRLR 576).

Where a redundancy situation applies equally to a number of others working in similar positions, s. 105 makes a dismissal automatically unfair where the particular person is picked out for any of the 14 highly various reasons listed as impermissible grounds for selection. Thus, for example, an employer may not select an employee because of family reasons such as maternity leave, having acted in a representative capacity, taken part in official industrial action, or sought to enforce certain statutory rights. Similarly, s. 153 of the Trade Union and Labour Relations (Consolidation) Act 1992 (TULRCA) makes it unfair to base selection on trade union membership (or non-membership) or participation in union activities.

Consultation over redundancy and reorganisation

Special consultation rules were introduced in 1975 in order to implement Directive 75/129/EEC on 'Collective Redundancies'. The provisions are now in Part IV, Chapter II of the TULRCA, as amended. Where a minimum of 20 employees at one establishment are to be made redundant within 90 days, employers must inform and consult any recognised trade union or, in default, specially elected workers' representatives. They must be given written notification of the reasons for the redundancies, the number to be dismissed, the methods of selection and implementation, and how any redundancy payments are to be calculated. The Secretary of State must also be notified on pain of risking prosecution for a fine. Consultation must be in 'good time' and begin at least 90 days before the first dismissal where 100 or more are to go, and at least 30 days beforehand where between 99 and 20 employee job losses are contemplated. In 2011, government proposed that a maximum 30 day consultation period should be introduced. There must be consultation about all of the employees likely to be affected (and not simply those to be made redundant). In the absence of 'special circumstances' which make consultation 'not reasonably practicable', the remedy is a 'protective award' of up to 90 days' pay per dismissed employee. The award is regarded as sanctioning the employer's failure, rather than as compensation to those dismissed, so that a tribunal will focus on the seriousness of the failure (*Susie Radin Ltd v GMB* [2004] IRLR 400). Unusually, a complaint may be lodged by a recognised union on behalf of its members (or the elected representatives on behalf of their constituents), as well as by any individual employee affected.

Quite when the duty to consult in good time is triggered continues to be disputed. A definitive answer from the European Court of Justice is awaited. The Court has been asked to clarify whether consultation must begin when an employer is proposing, but has not yet made, a strategic decision that will foreseeably lead to collective redundancies or whether he need consult only when that decision has actually been made and he is then proposing consequential dismissals (*USA v Nolan* [2011] IRLR 40).

Either way, the legislation in effect creates a breathing space in which the union or employee representatives will hope to be able to negotiate with the employer over matters like selection, timing and, indeed, whether the need for dismissals can be minimised or eliminated by adopting other strategies, such as temporary lay-offs, work-sharing or cutting overtime. Employers must consult about ways of avoiding dismissals, reducing the numbers to be dismissed and mitigating the consequences of any dismissals. This exercise must be undertaken 'with a view to reaching agreement'. Consequently, an employer who consults only after having already decided to dismiss acts unlawfully and cannot plead futility as an excuse (*Middlesbrough BC v TGWU* [2002] IRLR 332).

Section 195 of the 1992 Act defines 'redundancy' for consultation purposes so as to include any dismissal that is 'for a reason not related to the individual'. This is much wider than the definition of redundancy for the purposes of deciding who, when jobs disappear, is entitled to a statutory redundancy payment under the 1996 Act. It will catch various forms of reorganisation. Thus, an employer who imposed new standardised terms and conditions when merging two previously separate workforces should have consulted over the 'technical' dismissals that resulted from this harmonisation exercise, despite having no intention of reducing the size of the workforce overall (*GMB v Man Truck and Bus UK Ltd* [2000] IRLR 636).

The Transfer of Undertakings

When an organisation (or some part of it) changes hands, what happens to the existing workforce? This important question can arise in a variety of contexts – when companies merge, a business is sold, a function is sub-contracted, or some public sector activity is outsourced to the private or voluntary sector. At its simplest, the answer depends on whether the Transfer of Undertakings (Protection of Undertakings) Regulations 2006 (TUPE) apply. If they do not, the employees' contracts ordinarily terminate so that the new owner (the transferee) is free to decide which, if any, of the dismissed staff he wishes to hire and on what terms. Those who are taken on will almost certainly lose any accrued seniority rights, while those who are not hired will have no complaint against the transferee, though their former employer (the transferor) may face claims for redundancy pay and so on.

The TUPE Regulations are designed to implement European legislation, the latest version of which is the Acquired Rights Directive 2001/23/EC. It has two main purposes. First, to safeguard jobs by requiring incoming transferees to continue to employ transferred employees on their existing terms and conditions. Second, by imposing uniform rules governing business restructuring, the Directive aims to ensure that competition between member states is not unduly distorted. By these means, the law attempts to reconcile the protection of social (employment) rights with the promotion of economic (competition) interests.

What is a relevant transfer?

The original 1981 version of TUPE attracted criticism from all sides. One survey suggested that levels of uncertainty over its application were such that some 85 per cent of employers always took legal advice about whether TUPE applied, while over 20 per cent faced employment tribunal litigation (McMullen 2003). The current 2006 version was intended to clarify matters by adopting a broad, two part definition concerning which transfers are covered. First, there is a relevant transfer when an undertaking or part of one is transferred as a going concern or, as Regulation 3 puts it, where there is 'an economic entity which retains its identity', by which is meant 'an organised grouping of resources which has the objective of pursuing an economic activity'. It is irrelevant whether it is central or ancillary and whether or not it is run for profit. There must, however, be a transfer from one party to another. This requirement for a change in the *identity* of the employer is significant because without it TUPE cannot apply. In practice, a significant number of commercial acquisitions in the UK are effected by means of share transfers, which technically involve no change in the *identity* of the employer, only a change in the ownership and control of the company. Consequently, perhaps a majority of corporate take-overs fall outside TUPE, a situation one critic likened to 'Hamlet without the Prince'.

The second category catches any 'service provision change'. The intention here is that TUPE should apply to virtually all outsourcing transactions, whether first or second generation, as well as to cases where services are taken back in-house, so long as the service provided is essentially the same notwithstanding the change of provider (*Nottinghamshire Healthcare NHS Trust v Hamshaw* [2011] EAT 0037/11). Going further than was strictly necessary under the Directive, TUPE now resolves doubts about whether a mere change of service provider can be a relevant transfer. It had previously been arguable that activities such as cleaning, security and maintenance, which are labour-intensive but asset-light, could not constitute a transferable 'economic entity' because there were so few material resources, merely staff providing the service. However, while a 'service provision change' does not require an 'organised grouping of resources', it does require 'an organised grouping of employees ... which has as its principal purpose the carrying out of the activities concerned'. There must be a dedicated team of identifiable employees assigned to meeting the needs of the particular client or service user. Thus, if a courier firm has various staff who collect and deliver to clients on an *ad hoc* basis, TUPE will not apply should a particular client re-allocate the contract to a different provider. The staff will stay with their own employer rather than transfer to the new provider, even though essentially the same type of delivery service is being undertaken.

This provision also has the effect of bringing private sector transfers in to line with those in the public sector, where an earlier combination of ministerial codes and specialist legislation ensured that TUPE-type protections safeguarded public servants whose jobs were outsourced to the private or voluntary sectors or transferred internally to some other part of the public service.

Effects of a TUPE transfer

As we have seen, the major effect is that employees' contracts, rather than terminating, automatically transfer under Regulation 4. Continuity of service is preserved and all the transferor's 'rights, powers, duties and liabilities' are inherited by the transferee. This includes any pre-existing claims an employee may have against the transferor, whether in contract (for unpaid wages, say) or otherwise (such as a claim for damages for personal injury). Criminal liabilities and pension rights do not transfer, however. By virtue of Regulation 11, the transferor must disclose the details of those who are to transfer, their service history across the previous two years and any potential liabilities. Unless not reasonably practical, this information must be given 14 days before the transfer. Failure is actionable before a tribunal, which will normally award a minimum of £500 per employee as compensation to a transferee landed with unexpected or, at least, undeclared obligations.

Dismissals that are 'connected with' (motivated by) a transfer are declared by Regulation 7 to be automatically unfair, provided the employee has the necessary one year qualifying service. This is so, whether dismissal is by the transferor or the transferee, and whether before or after the transfer. So, sacking highly paid staff ahead of a sale in order to make the business more attractive to a potential buyer will be unfair. There can be no automatic finding of unfairness, however, where a dismissal, despite being transfer connected, was done for an 'economic, technical or organisational' reason (ETO). An ETO reason must involve some restructuring – some 'changes in the workforce' – either in terms of staff numbers or roles and functions (*Berriman v Delabole Slate Ltd* [1985] ICR 546). Thus, if a transferee decides the business is overstaffed, he is entitled to declare redundancies without risking a finding of automatically unfair dismissal. Those who lose their jobs thereby will be entitled to have any redundancy payment calculated according to the whole of their service, with both the transferor and the transferee.

In order further to protect employees post-transfer, Regulation 4 (4) declares that attempts to change terms and conditions are 'void' unless, despite being transfer connected, the change was introduced for an ETO reason. Thus, agreeing newly expanded job duties in order to improve output is capable of being defended as fair. Anecdotal evidence suggests that contractual variations are not uncommon in practice. Even so, many employers regard this aspect of TUPE as unduly restrictive, particularly if it frustrates attempts to harmonise terms and conditions. The view of the Labour government and the CBI in 2006 was that employees should be allowed to agree transfer-related contract changes, provided the overall package is no less favourable than previously. Such a move would almost certainly require an amendment to the Directive itself and not merely to TUPE. Post-transfer variation of employee contracts is currently allowed in only one other circumstance, namely as a means of safeguarding jobs and promoting corporate rescues where 'relevant insolvency proceedings' have begun and the changes have been agreed with appropriate workforce representatives (Regulations 8 and 9).

In addition to contracts of employment being transferred, Regulations 5 and 6 provide for the transfer of some industrial relations mechanisms, namely collective bargains and trade union recognition agreements. However, since most collective agreements are not legally binding contracts, it would be open to the transferee to cancel them without incurring any legal penalty, though it would be too late to escape a term once it had become incorporated into the contracts of individual employees (*Robertson v British Gas Corporation* [1983] IRLR 302). Whether this has occurred may be difficult to establish (*Malone v British Airways plc* [2011] IRLR 32).

Consultation and TUPE transfers

Regulations 13-16 require both transferors and transferees to inform and consult either recognised trade unions or elected workforce representatives ahead of time. This must be done 'long enough before' the transfer and provide details of the transfer, information concerning any 'measures' it is envisaged will be taken in connection with it, together with the 'legal, economic and social' implications of the transfer for affected employees. A tribunal may award 'appropriate' compensation having regard to the seriousness of any failure, not exceeding 13 weeks' pay for each employee. As regards failures by the transferor, the transferee is made jointly and severally liable, a system that has been criticised since it may well penalise an employer who is not at fault and had little control over the other party.

Pensions

A pension (or more accurately the right to continuing membership of the transferor's pension scheme) does not transfer alongside the other contract-related benefits. Separate provision is made in the Pensions Act 2004. Broadly speaking, ss. 257-258 provide that where a private sector transferor had an occupational pension scheme pre-transfer and the employee was a member or eligible to join, he has a right to join the transferee's scheme, which need not be comparable. Where no such scheme is in operation, the transferee must match any contributions made by the employee to a stakeholder pension, subject to limits set out in regulations. If the transferor made no pension provision, then neither need the transferee.

As regards employees compulsorily transferred out of the public sector, ministerial guidelines require every transferee to make 'broadly comparable' provision. Since pensions in the public sector are near universal but much less common elsewhere, clearly many who work in the private sector will continue to be worse off than their counterparts in (or transferred from) public sector employment. It has been argued that this system may discourage private and voluntary sector organisations from bidding for public sector contracts.

Minimum Wage Legislation and Working Time

The introduction of a national minimum wage (NMW) in 1999 was a major event which, despite being set at a relatively modest level, immediately benefited some 2 million workers, two thirds of them women. Initially it was controversial, opponents claiming that it would cause damaging wage and price inflation and drive up unemployment. However, subsequent studies showed such fears to be largely groundless. It is now a firmly established plank in the floor of minimum rights. There are three hourly pay rates (for 16-17 year olds, 18-21, and 22 and over) which are revised by government, normally each October, on the recommendation of the Low Pay Commission, which is mindful of what business can afford. Current details can be found on the Department for Business, Innovation and Skills (BIS) website.

The statutory rules are contained in the National Minimum Wage Act 1998 and associated Regulations. Coverage is broad. Virtually all those in the UK workforce, whether employees, or casual, temporary, agency, home or piece workers, are entitled to benefit from the first day of their employment. Apprentices who are under 19 or over 19, but in the first year of their apprenticeship, are also included, though they are paid at a separate (and lower) special rate. Some groups are excluded, such as the genuinely self-employed, volunteers, members of the armed forces and students doing work experience for a year or less as part of their course.

Broadly speaking, whether the minimum hourly rate has been correctly paid is calculated by dividing the wages paid by the hours worked in the relevant 'pay reference period', either a week or a month. Workers are entitled to be paid at the NMW rate for all the time they are expected to be on duty, are on call, or are travelling on the employer's business, whether or not they are actively working throughout the period. They need not be paid during rest breaks, however. All workers must be allowed a twenty minute (unpaid) break after six hours' work by virtue of the Working Time Regulations (below).

Workers are entitled to inspect the records their employer must keep of hours worked and payments made if they believe their pay is below the NMW. So too may compliance officers from HM Revenue & Customs (HMRC), who are responsible for enforcement. Officers may serve a 'notice of underpayment' (against which an employer may appeal to an employment tribunal) requiring payment of arrears (at the current rate) to specified workers within 28 days. The notice must also require the employer to pay a penalty equal to half the arrears due, subject to a minimum of £100 and a maximum of £5,000. Additionally, wilful neglect or refusals to pay and deficient record keeping are crimes triable before magistrates or a Crown Court. From 2011, BIS aims to increase the pressure on employers who persistently flout the legislation by publicly naming them.

As well as underpaid workers lodging claims themselves, somewhat unusually, HMRC compliance officers may bring claims on their behalf, either before an employment tribunal within three months or in a County Court for breach of contract, which has the advantage that the claim may relate to arrears going back six years. Subjecting workers to a detriment (such as refusing to promote) because they claim entitlement under the NMW legislation is also actionable before a tribunal, while the dismissal of an employee is automatically unfair, regardless of their length of service.

Working time and holidays

The common law's view has always been that the number of hours to be worked is primarily a matter for agreement between the parties (whether direct or via collective bargaining). This is subject only to the possibility that insistence on excessive hours might put the health, safety and well-being of an employee at risk and so conflict with their employer's implied duty to provide a reasonably safe system of work (*Johnstone v Bloomsbury Health Authority* [1991] ICR 269). Parliament, on the other hand, beginning in the nineteenth century, enacted a patchwork of miscellaneous provisions intended to protect those thought to be most vulnerable, such as women and young persons in factory employment. Much of this paternalist protection was repealed in the 1980s, however, and it was not until 1998 that what has proved to be a troublingly complicated structure of European-inspired, general regulation of working time was finally introduced in the UK.

The 1993 Working Time Directive 93/104/EEC was designed to promote the health and safety of workers across the Community. The Directive was eventually implemented in the UK in October 1998 by the Working Time Regulations 1998 (WTR), which have been amended several times since. In practice they seem to have had little effect on the long hours' culture (Barnard, Deakin and Hobbs). The main provisions applying to adult workers: limit working time to no more than 48 hours per week on average; impose a six-day working week; provide for a daily rest period of at least 11 hours, and 20-minute rest breaks after six hours' work; restrict night workers (who must be given the opportunity of a free health assessment) to working no more than an average of eight hours in any 24-hour period; and create an entitlement to 28 days' paid holiday a year.

Working time means any period during which a worker 'is working, at his employer's disposal and carrying out his activity or duties.' This includes time on-call provided the worker is required to be present and available at their workplace, when travelling as part of the job (though not simply commuting), or participating in job training. It does not include lunch or rest breaks. Regulation 4 provides that working time, including overtime, must not exceed an average of 48 hours a week. The average is usually calculated over a 17-week 'reference period', though this may be extended to 52 weeks by a 'collective' or 'workforce agreement' with the employer. Controversially, in the view of some, workers can opt out of this otherwise mandatory 48-hour limit, provided they do so in writing. They cannot be subjected to any detriment or lawfully dismissed for refusing to sign or for changing their mind. Protracted attempts to remove the right of workers to opt out (which the UK had consistently opposed) were finally abandoned by the European authorities in April 2009.

Certain groups of workers are exempted from the WTR entirely (notably those in the armed forces and the emergency services) or subjected to specialised, industry-specific regimes, as happens in aviation, fishing, and sea and road transport. Additionally, certain sorts of flexible workers (including managing executives or others with autonomous decision-taking powers) are treated as exempted from the restrictions on maximum hours.

Conclusion

Across the last forty years, legislation has increasingly been used by successive governments to set minimum standards in the workplace; sometimes, as with parts of the equality agenda, to change expectations concerning social and economic fairness. In contrast to the earlier voluntarist tradition of minimal state intervention that held sway for much of the last century, we have witnessed an incremental yet seemingly inexorable growth in legal regulation (so-called juridification) over matters previously thought to be the private preserve of the parties to the employment relationship and, in particular, the preserve of employers. However, once the law began to provide opportunities for workers to challenge basic decisions, such as who should be hired, promoted or fired, it became apparent that the ways in which employers operate would need to become more transparent and ordered if they were to survive external legal scrutiny. This, in turn, created a demand for professionals who understood both the limits of the law and the importance of clear procedures, fairly and consistently applied, which reflect the advice of specialist bodies, such as ACAS. As Anderman (2003) has pointed out, much of the employment protection legislation is designed not merely to protect workers but also to stimulate managers to adopt best practice as set out in codes of practice which 'spell out how managers can best shape organisational rules to comply with the legislation'.

The proper role and effect of the law continue to be contested. Some, particularly smaller employers, regard the system of employment rights and its associated procedures as red tape, while others argue that it hinders economic growth and competitiveness. Whatever the political rhetoric, it seems unlikely, however, that there will be any concerted attempt to cut back the reach of the regulatory regime currently in force, except to the extent indicated earlier. It seems equally unlikely that any major additional new rights will be added to the statute book in the near future. Meanwhile, keeping abreast of the flow of interpretive case law will, no doubt, continue to engage the attention of HR professionals, if only because litigation provides practical illustrations of how workplace relations ought to be managed and how exposure to legal liability can be minimised.

REFERENCES

Anderman, S. 2003: Overview: the law and the employment relationship, in Towers, B. (ed), *The Handbook of Employment Relations, Law and Practice*, 4th edn, London: Kogan Page.

Annual Employment Tribunal Statistics 2010-2011, Employment Tribunal Service, London.

Armour, J., Deakin, S. *et al.* 2009: *Does law really matter to economic development? Top Floor*, issue 16, University of Cambridge: Centre for Business Research.

Barnard, C., Deakin, S. and Hobbs, R. 2003: Opting out of the 48-hour week: Employer necessity or inividual choice, *Industrial Law Journal*, **32** (4) 223–252.

Collins, H. 1992: *Justice in Dismissal: the Law on Termination of Employment*, Oxford: Clarendon.

Dickens, L. 2005: Walking the Talk? Equality and Diversity in Employment, in Bach S. (ed), *Managing Human Resources*, 4th edn, Oxford: Blackwell.

Dickens, L. and Hall, M. 2003: Labour and industrial relations, in Edwards, P. (ed), *Industrial Relations: Theory and Practice*, Oxford: Blackwell.

DTI (Department of Trade and Industry) 2001: *Explaining the growth in the number of applications to Industrial Tribunals* 1972-1997, Employment Relations Research Series, Report no. 10.

Equality and Human Rights Commission, 2011: *Employment Statutory Code of Practice*, London: HMSO.

Fryer, R. H. 1973: Myths of the Redundancy Payments Act, *Industrial Law Journal*, **1**(1), 1-16.

Government explanatory notes to the Equality Act 2010, paragraph 68, http://www.legislation.gov.uk/ukpga/2010/15/notes/division/2/2/2/2, last accessed 22 July 2011.

Kersley, B. *et al.* 2006: *Inside the workplace: findings from the 2004 Workplace Employment Relations Survey*, London: Routledge.

McColgan, A. 2011: *Equality Act 2010*, The Institute of Employment Rights, Liverpool: Russell Press.

McMullen, J. 2003: All in a muddle over TUPE, *The Times*, 25 June 2003.

Senior President of Tribunals 2011: *Annual Report* 2011, Employment Appeal Tribunal, London.

Weatherill, S. 2007: *Better Regulation*, Oxford: Hart Publishing.

PART II

Context

CHAPTER FOUR

Corporate Governance and Human Resource Management

Andrew Pendleton and Howard Gospel

Introduction

This chapter considers the relationship between corporate governance and human resource management (HRM). It is thus concerned with how the ownership and governance of the organisation influences HRM strategies and practices. Since the mid-1990s there has been a growing awareness that corporate governance can have a substantial influence on how organisations are managed and how this may affect HRM. The paradox is that those engaged in corporate governance usually argue that they are not involved in HRM and that corporate governance is not concerned with HRM. This chapter aims to explore this paradox. It does so from a comparative perspective, while focusing mainly on the UK.

We show that the relationship between corporate governance and HRM is mainly indirect, mediated through the business strategies and structures adopted by organisations. This reflects a fundamental tenet of corporate governance in countries such as the UK, that owners and shareholders should not 'micro-manage' how organisations conduct their internal affairs. Nevertheless corporate governance has powerful shaping influences on HRM. Occasionally, it has more direct and immediate effects, such as when ownership changes as a result of mergers and acquisitions (M&A).

In the UK, discussions of corporate governance mainly focus on the relationship between shareholders and top managers of large, stock market-listed companies. But it also refers to the role of owners in private companies and family firms and to the oversight of public sector and voluntary organisations. In the latter, governance has traditionally involved a wide range of actors, including elected and community representatives. In the chapter we will focus mainly on corporate governance of large, listed companies, but will also refer to these other settings where appropriate.

The chapter identifies several key dimensions of corporate governance which can influence HRM. The first dimension concerns the parties involved in governance. Are they primarily owners or shareholders and their immediate managerial representatives, consistent with a so-called 'property rights' conception of governance? Or does governance involve a wider group of actors, such as employees? The norm in most publicly-listed and privately-owned companies in the UK is for owners, shareholders, and senior managers to be the main governance actors, but this is not the case for most public sector bodies and 'third sector' organisations such as charities. In other European countries, such as Germany, it is also common for employees to be involved in governance of large companies via employee representation on the company board.

A second dimension relates to the objectives of those involved in governance and the distribution of returns from organisational activity. How far do the returns from economic activity accrue to shareholders, to managers, to employees, or to other groups? In this respect, there are pronounced differences between countries, and this has consequences for HRM such as the determination of remuneration and relative pay within organisations.

The third issue relates to the nature of involvement of key governance actors. To what extent, and in what ways, are shareholders and stakeholders involved in governance? Many shareholders have traditionally taken a quiescent approach to governance, and this has left power and autonomy with senior managers. But, one of the paradoxes of the UK governance system is that, whilst managers are relatively powerful for most of the time, the market system of governance makes managers and organisations vulnerable to sudden shifts in ownership. This can have profound effects on HRM by imposing intense pressures for reorganisation, downsizing, and divestments of parts of the company.

The identity, objectives, and activities of those involved in governance will affect the management of the organisation. In particular, they influence the business strategies and organisational structures adopted by top management. These, in turn, shape the 'downstream' HR strategies and practices of the organisation (Purcell 1989). Where, for example, governance actors prioritise short-term profits, managers are likely to adopt strategies which generate short-term returns. These strategies may, in turn, discourage HR practices relying on long-term commitments by company and employees within an internal labour market and may instead encourage a reliance on external labour markets for employment and skill formation.

The chapter starts by providing an overview of the dominant perspectives on corporate governance. It then considers broad national and comparative perspectives on business systems to provide a wider context. It proceeds to examine the key dimensions of governance and to provide illustrations and examples of how they may influence HRM.

Perspectives on Corporate Governance

The orthodox and dominant view of corporate governance in the UK and US is that it is a relationship between shareholders and top managers of large companies.

According to this so-called 'shareholder value' view (sometimes termed 'shareholder primacy'), the fundamental purpose of governance is to get managers to do what shareholders want. In Shleifer and Vishny's words, 'corporate governance deals with the ways in which suppliers of finance to corporations assure themselves of obtaining a return on their investment' (1997: 737). This view of governance, widely accepted by many shareholders, managers, and governments, is based on 'property rights' and 'principal agent' theories of the firm. Thus, principals (owners, shareholders) establish governance systems to ensure that agents (managers) run the organisation in the best interests of the former (Jensen and Meckling 1976). A core argument is that owners and shareholders bear risk from investing in the firm, given that shares do not guarantee returns. So, in return for risk-bearing, shareholders have control rights (voting rights attached to shares) and the right to profits, once any prior claimants have been paid ('residual claimants').

However, a fundamental problem is that owners and managers may have different interests: whilst the former seek a return on their investment, the latter may have objectives which conflict with this, such as high salaries for themselves and a 'quiet life' in terms of non-demanding relations with employees. Corporate governance, therefore, is about protecting investors by ensuring that the interests of managers are aligned with those of shareholders. It is aimed at ensuring that managers do not expropriate the gains of economic activity for themselves or distribute too much of the gains to some other party, such as employees. In this view of governance, the key instruments relate to controls and incentives available to owners to ensure that managers do what shareholders want. Some of these are explicitly concerned with HR.

One set of controls arises from regulation of either a 'hard' or 'soft' law. Hard law, in the form of company and securities legislation, regulates the rights and responsibilities of each party, and the UK Company Act 2006 has codified directors' duties to the company and shareholders. Soft law takes the form of codes of conduct and is exemplified by Corporate Governance Codes which have developed over the years since the early 1990s. These codes have dealt with key governance issues, such as the composition, rights, and duties of boards of directors. The key principle in the operation of these codes in the UK is 'comply or explain'. There are no formal sanctions as such for non-compliance, but executives are expected to explain the reasons for non-compliance (Clarke 2004). In recent years this approach to governance has been extended to organisations outside the listed company sector. For instance, since 2006 there has been a corporate governance code of conduct for NHS Foundation Trusts and many of the principles developed in the private sector are incorporated into this, even though the shareholder model is not the underlying mechanism.

These regulatory controls on management have been supplemented by incentives, such as stock options and long-term incentive plans. These are aimed at aligning executives' interests with those of shareholders, though there has been a great deal of criticism that they are, in practice, a means for managerial self-enrichment and have perverse effects on managerial behaviour (Bebchuk and Fried 2004; Froud *et al.*

2006). Indeed, some suggest that one contributing factor in the global financial and economic crisis beginning in 2007 has been the incentives created for executives, which led them to take ever greater risks (Roberts 2010). As we will argue below, incentive systems for managers may also percolate down to lower levels of employees in the organisation and thus affect one very important aspect of HRM.

An alternative view of corporate governance defines it more broadly to cover the relationships between all the parties who have an interest in the organisation, including employees, suppliers and the wider community. This so-called 'stakeholder' model views organisations, including private sector companies, as, in effect, 'public' entities, rather than the 'private' property of owners. According to this view, organisations comprise a number of stakeholders including insiders such as owners, managers, and employees, and outsiders such as lenders, suppliers, customers, and the broader communities within which organisations operate. This model is common in governance of public sector organisations such as schools and hospitals.

The stakeholder model identifies a broader purpose of the organisation than provision of financial returns for shareholders: it is instead about using resources to enhance the well-being of all stakeholders. In a related sense, corporate governance is about checks and balances, so that the interests of all stakeholders are taken into account and balanced against each other. This perspective is also associated with a variety of interest groups, including trade unions and community groups, as well as some influential academic theorists (Donaldson and Preston 1995; Freeman 1984; Kay 1997; Post *et al.* 2002). The essence of this view of governance is that those who are affected by the *de facto* operation of the organisation (i.e. have a stake in it) should *de jure* have some capacity to influence the governance and management of it.

The primary criticism of this stakeholder view is that it is difficult to determine who are stakeholders and who are not. All of us are influenced in some way by the activities of large companies, but this effect can vary greatly. Hence, more sophisticated versions of the stakeholder approach attempt to provide a theoretical basis to identification of key stakeholders. For instance, it has been argued that employees should be seen as stakeholders on a par with owners/investors because, like the latter, they make investments in the firm (their human capital) and the value of this investment is not necessarily transferable to other employment. This exposes employees to the risk that their returns from this investment may not be realised, possibly because of opportunism or short-termism by managers (Blair 1995). In this view, which draws on notions of 'incomplete' and 'implicit' contracts, employees should receive 'control' and 'return' rights to compensate them for bearing uncontracted risk. The corollary then is that employees should have representation in the company, adequate information, and a share of the profits (Blair 1995). This view, however, has been criticised on the grounds that, compared with the nature of risk borne by shareholders, the labour contract is relatively 'complete' or fully specified, and there is little uncontracted risk and hence no justification for employee involvement in control (Hansmann and Kraakman 2000).

There has been an on-going debate as to the relative merits of 'shareholder value' versus 'stakeholder value' approaches to corporate governance and, indeed, the fundamental purpose of companies. In the UK, these issues were paramount in the review of corporate law that took place in the early 2000s (Company Law Review 2001). Critics of prevailing corporate law argued that it had evolved in a way that prioritised owners and shareholders at the expense of other key stakeholders. The review decided in favour of what might be called an 'enlightened shareholder value' view, whereby directors should promote the interests of the company, taking into account relevant interests such as employees, so as to benefit shareholders in the longer run. This view was incorporated in the 2006 Companies Act (Section 172) which requires directors to promote the success of the company in the interests of the shareholders, while also taking into account a wider view of interests, including those of employees (Deakin *et al.* 2006). However, one of the limitations of this is that other aspects of regulation, such as the Corporate Governance Code and the City Takeover Code, still prioritise shareholder interests.

In practice, in the UK, both shareholder primacy and stakeholder value models are present. On the whole, the shareholder primacy model of governance is dominant in most companies which are listed and traded on stock markets – generally larger companies. It also characterises the practice of governance in smaller, privately-owned firms, with the major difference being that many such companies are owner-managed and hence do not have the separation of ownership and management that is found in large listed companies. By contrast, in the public sector, the stakeholder model of governance has tended to be dominant. For example, governing bodies of local authority schools include representatives of the community, parents, and employees. Similarly, as free-standing corporations with a public purpose, universities normally have representatives from private and public sector organisations, local politicians, and staff on their governing bodies. However, some elements of the model developed in the private sector, such as committees to oversee top executive pay, are now also widely found in the public sector. Governance arrangements also incorporate elements of the stakeholder and shareholder models in mutual, 'third' sector and charitable organisations. Building societies, for instance, are 'owned' and governed by their members (customers). Co-operatives are governed by their members, who may be customers (e.g. consumer cooperatives such as the Co-operative) or producers (e.g. agricultural marketing cooperatives, many taxi firms) or employees (workers' cooperatives).

Broad types of business systems, varieties of capitalism and corporate governance

The distinction between shareholder and stakeholder conceptions of corporate governance has been reflected in comparisons of national business systems across different countries. Much of the literature has tried to classify types of governance system within broad national business systems. Some of this has explicitly involved showing links between governance systems and employment, work, and industrial relations. Several distinct types of system have been discerned (Hopt *et al.*1998; Allen and Gale 2000; Amable 2004; McCahery *et al.*2002; Gourevitch and Shinn 2005; O'Sullivan 2000; Gospel and Pendleton 2005).

One body of literature, known as the 'varieties of capitalism' approach (Hall and Soskice 2001), has identified two main types of economic and corporate governance – the 'liberal market' and 'coordinated market' models. In the former, relations between economic actors are achieved predominantly through market mechanisms and corporate governance always has the back-up of the external 'market for corporate control', in other words the threat of M&A. Employees have predominantly market relationships with the firm (i.e. there is a strong reliance on external rather than internal labour markets), so employee interests are assumed to be expressed through market mechanisms. Hence, there is little or no role for employees in governance and, if employees are dissatisfied, they can 'vote with their feet'. As for HRM, reliance on external labour markets tends to inhibit development of firm-specific human capital. There is also an emphasis on general managerial skills and top managers tend to be mobile between companies. For the most part, managers are said to have low commitment to their employing organisation (relative to that found in other governance systems) and this makes corporate governance controls and incentives especially important. A key notion in the 'varieties' literature is complementarity between economic institutions, with each reinforcing the operation and effects of others. Thus, market and competitive models of corporate governance fit with market models of employment and adversarial industrial relations. The US and UK are usually said to exemplify systems of this type.

By contrast, in coordinated market economies, where ownership is typically more concentrated, the firm's operations are substantially coordinated through cooperative relationships between actors. This implies that employees should have a voice in the governance of the firm, and these systems tend to be characterised either by mechanisms of formal representation and works councils or by community norms and understandings, often underpinned by trade unions or works councils. In some instances, employee participation may take the form of involvement of employee representatives on company boards, as in Germany, whilst in others employee voice is achieved via more informal representation in management, as in Japan. In terms of HRM, it is then argued that these arrangements encourage firms to go down the 'high road' route of employee involvement, greater commitment to training, more equality in pay structures, and more high performance orientated work practices (Hall and Soskice 2001). Moreover, it has also been argued that this type of system is conducive to evolutionary product and process innovations, requiring long-term development of firm-specific human capital, whereas liberal market economies tends to favour more risky innovations based on more mobile capital (Hoskisson *et al.* 2004).

Another body of literature has distinguished national systems in terms of 'market-outsider' and 'relational-insider' arrangements (Franks and Mayer 1997; Gospel and Pendleton 2003). Market-outsider systems tend to have large stock markets with a relatively large number of listed firms. They also tend to be dominated by institutional investors with wide portfolios of relatively small shareholdings in a large number of firms. Because ownership is dispersed, governance takes a market or outsider form. Because of the costs of monitoring, it is more efficient for investors to discipline managers by buying and selling shares rather than taking a direct voice in the governance of firms. This means that firms can be at the mercy of the market for corporate control and M&As. The need to maintain stock price to protect the firm or to facilitate takeovers is said to provide strong market-based discipline on managers. Since governance is marketised, it is believed that there is little or no need for employee involvement in governance. Indeed, such systems may set up pressures to minimise labour costs by developing combinations of 'soft' HRM for some (e.g. employees who are strategic and have hard to replace skills) and 'hard' forms for others (e.g. those who are less key). The US and UK are usually said to exemplify systems of economic and corporate governance of this type and to have related HRM systems (Gospel and Pendleton 2003).

By contrast, relational-insider systems are those where firms have relied rather less on markets for raising capital or restructuring transactions and more on relational borrowing from banks and other firms and where ownership is more concentrated in a few large blockholders (families, banks, other companies). In these systems, there are fewer listed firms and stock markets are typically smaller and with lower turnover of shares. This means that the market for corporate control is less developed and hostile takeovers are rare. Governance takes a different form to that found in market-outsider systems. Because owners typically have a large ownership stake, it is worthwhile becoming directly involved in governance as 'insiders'. Their longer-term role in governance protects development in firm-specific human capital and hence tends to encourage high levels of training. It is also more accommodating of employee voice and involvement in the enterprise. As in the 'varieties' typology, Germany and Japan are typically seen as exemplars of this kind of system, with related HRM arrangements, such as longer job tenures, pay and benefits which rise with seniority within the firm, and less dispersion in pay (Gospel and Pendleton 2003).

These bi-polar models of governance have an attractive symmetry, but they have been criticised on several grounds. The most important is that they ignore the diversity of governance and national business systems around the world. They are based primarily on countries such as the US, UK, Germany, and Japan. These typologies ignore countries where the state has played a key role in economic development and coordination such as France or Italy. There is also the question of how emerging and transition economies, such as Brazil, India, Russia and China, are classified. In reaction to this, some analyses have identified a larger number of systems. Thus, Amable (2004) discerns five types: the liberal market, the Continental European, the social democratic, the Mediterranean, and the Asian models (see also Whitley 1999). Another criticism is that the bi-polar typologies portray each category as more homogenous than they are. For instance, the US and UK are usually grouped together, but the US is notable for greater legal regulation of corporate governance, though with even more unregulated labour markets. A further criticism is that there is considerable diversity in governance within countries, as is evidenced by the earlier discussion of governance models within the UK. Moreover, there has also been considerable interest in the last ten years in movements away from the stakeholder model towards elements of the shareholder primacy model in countries such as Germany and Japan (Jackson *et al.* 2005).

Who is involved in governance?

In this section we examine in more detail how corporate governance can shape HRM within the organisation. The relationship between governance and HRM is often indirect, being mediated by management business strategies and structure. Thus, governance has a shaping role on management decisions, setting parameters for decisions. Some of the time it has a stronger, more direct influence on strategic decisions. The 'downstream' nature of HRM makes it difficult to chart relationships between governance and HRM with precision, but the strength of governance factors should not be underestimated. To demonstrate how governance shapes HRM, we discuss key governance dimensions: who is involved, their objectives, and the nature of their involvement.

Corporate governance in UK-listed firms primarily involves large investors and top managers, supported by investor trade associations (e.g. representing pension funds and insurance companies) and a web of business services providers (e.g. company analysts and executive remuneration consultants). As discussed above, and as stressed by 'orthodox' commentators, governance is about getting managers to do what shareholders want.

The standard picture of ownership of large, listed firms in the UK is that it is dominated by institutional investors. Until recently, the bulk of company shares were held by UK pension funds and insurance companies, with a smaller proportion held by unit trusts, investment trusts, and other financial institutions. These institutional investors typically held relatively small proportions of equity in investee companies (often under 1 per cent and usually below the disclosure threshold of 3 per cent) and diversified their investments across a wide range of larger, listed companies. In the last ten years, however, the share of the market accounted for by UK pension funds and insurance companies has fallen from around 50 per cent in the mid-1990s to around 25 per cent in 2010 (Office for National Statistics 2010). Their place has been taken by investors from outside the UK and by other financial institutions, some of which we will discuss below. This has had significant impacts on governance and HRM within firms, involving degrees of involvement and pressures on companies.

Key actors in governance are company chairmen (and very occasionally chair-women) and non-executive directors. Since the Cadbury Reports in 1992 (which resulted in the first Code), a key governance principle has been that the position of Chair of the board should be separate from that of Chief Executive of the company so that the former can reflect and pass on shareholder concerns to the latter and to operational managers without role conflict. This principle is nearly always observed in large companies on a 'comply or explain' basis, though there have been some exceptions. Company boards are also expected to contain a number of non-executive directors, who play key roles in various board committees which companies are expected to have, such as the audit and remuneration committees. A key issue in corporate governance in the UK and elsewhere is the extent to which these board members can be truly independent of executive management in the company. Critics point out that non-executives are usually nominated by company management, especially the Chief Executive, and tend to be drawn from a narrow social circle (see Filatotchev *et al.* 2007 for a review of the literature). This criticism is less applicable to governance in the public sector because many non-executives and governors are chosen by particular constituencies outside the organisation over which the organisation has little or no direct control (for example, teacher and parent governors in schools).

The character of governance in publicly-traded companies has several con-sequences for HRM. First, there is marked under-representation of women and ethnic minorities on company boards. This situation at the top of companies may reinforce 'glass ceilings' further down within company workforces (Pye 2011). Second, non-executive members of company boards are often dependent on the patronage of senior managers and this tends to reinforce the power of the latter in corporate governance. For example, in the case of Royal Bank of Scotland, non-executive directors did not restrain top management from moving away from its traditional banking base towards much riskier involvement in investment banking and large-scale acquisitions. This led ultimately to major redundancies and the state bail-out of the company. Third, it has been argued that the dependence of non-executive directors on company managers has resulted in limited shareholder control of executive pay. Remuneration committees, despite being composed of non-executive directors, have often recommended top executive pay schemes which have been highly favourable to executives, opaque to shareholders, and limited in their performance conditions (Department for Business Innovation and Skills, 2011).

A notable feature of UK private sector corporate governance, compared with many other European countries, is the absence of employees from governance arrangements. Unlike many other European countries, there is no legal underpin-ning of employee representation on company boards or employee rights for works councils. In Germany, the Netherlands, and Norway, for example, employee board representation is widespread (Vitols 2004). This absence appears to limit the extent of consideration of HRM issues in governance discussions between company boards and investors compared with Germany, where more information is supplied and more consideration given to questions such as relative pay (Jackson *et al.* 2005). The situation is rather different, however, in parts of the public sector. Educational organisations such as local authority-run schools and universities usually have pro-vision for staff representation on governing bodies. However, as private sector involvement in the running of key parts of the public sector has increased, and as some parts of the public sector have become more autonomous from state or local authority control, the extent of staff involvement in governance bodies has tended to be reduced.

Objectives and distribution of returns

The dispersed nature of share ownership in UK-listed firms contrasts with the situation in many European countries where ownership is dominated by large block holders whose objectives are said to focus on control and status as well as financial returns. As described above, the nature of institutional shareholding in the UK may be seen as 'low commitment' and characterised by limited engagement by investors in investee companies. It has also been described as 'short-termist' in that investors seek gains and will exit their holdings if company shares under-perform. Further forces leading in this direction include competitive pressures amongst fund management companies to manage pension funds. This has been said to lead to short-termist behaviour by companies, who are impelled to adopt business strategies and investment practices which generate high returns in the short term. In turn, this may lead to low commitment patterns of HRM, with some companies unwilling to make long-term investments in their employees. Hence, for example, there are constraints on training and development and a preference for production systems involving limited skills requirements in many cases (Black *et al.* 2007).

Some investment institutions would take issue with the above. In recent years there has been a growing concentration of ownership in the UK, with the stakes of the largest institutional investors tending to increase. This has locked-in larger investors and encouraged engagement with investee firms. Many institutional investors perceive themselves to be long-term investors and do not actively trade their investments except at the margins. In turn, this has led to growing engagement in governance by major UK institutional investors, as evidenced by rising participation of votes in annual general meetings (AGMs) on executive pay. Also, some investors have adopted 'socially responsible' investment principles, which often include good HRM and high labour standards, to guide their engagement with companies, including their overseas activities.

On the other hand, the nature of listed company ownership has changed in other directions in the last ten years, and there are some renewed pressures towards short-termism running alongside these developments in the direction of engagement. The growth in shareholding by overseas investors has implications for HR. First, overseas investors tend to have a lower commitment to the company, its societal role and its employees. A growing component of overseas ownership is by so-called sovereign wealth funds, from countries like Saudi Arabia, the Gulf States, and China, which generally take an inactive approach to corporate governance so as not to attract unwelcome public attention. Second, the openness of UK firms to overseas share ownership (coupled with the absence of regulatory constraints on overseas takeovers in the UK) exposes them to takeovers by foreign firms. During the 2000s there was a rising trend of acquisitions in the UK by foreign companies, though a dip more recently (Office for National Statistics 2011). Here again, the evidence suggests that overseas companies tend to prioritise the interests of core employees in their home country rather than in the country of their overseas operations, especially when it comes to research and development and high tech investments (see Chapter 5).

There are other new actors amongst owners of UK listed companies, such as private equity and hedge funds. The role of these funds has increased significantly in the UK in the last decade (Gospel *et al.* 2010). We discuss hedge funds here and private equity in the next section.

Hedge funds are pooled investment vehicles open only to large investors, such as institutional investors, banks, and wealthy individuals. They have a variety of investment strategies of which two are especially noteworthy in the context of HR management. First, they can pursue 'activist' strategies, buying shares in companies and then pressuring them to change their strategies, replace top management, pay out cash to shareholders and sell off parts of the company. In this way, they hope to see the price of shares rise and then to sell. Second, many hedge funds engage in 'short-selling'. This involves the borrowing of shares from other owners, such as pension funds, with a view to selling them if the price is expected to decline. The hedge fund then repurchases shares at a lower price and returns the shares to their owner, taking the margin between the sale and repurchase price, minus a fee for borrowing the shares. Institutional investors have supported this activity because the fee generates additional returns. This kind of activity can drive down share prices, especially as much of the trading is computer-generated, leading to a kind of herding behaviour.

There are several potential implications of hedge fund activism and short selling for HRM. Activism can lead to pressure for cost reductions, involving redundancies and tight performance management systems. It can also result in the breaking up of companies, again with job losses and changes in working conditions. Short-selling can lead to reductions in share prices and increases in the vulnerability of companies to takeover. Share price fluctuations, in turn, can lead to instability in strategies, as managers attempt to respond to falls in the valuation of the company. In turn, there can be a diversion of resources to stabilise the share price. A key way of doing this and 'shaking out' hedge funds is for companies to mount share buy-backs (i.e. increasing the share price by increasing demand, thereby threatening the margins made by hedge funds). Share repurchases involve a transfer of resources to shareholders, from other potential claimants such as employees.

The demise of Cadbury, the UK confectioner, and its acquisition by Kraft, the US food group, in 2010 was an example of hedge fund activity. At first, Cadbury was the subject of an activist hedge fund strategy which led to the divestment of the company's beverages division. This, in itself, had major HR implications because it led to the transfer of employees to new employers. It also left a smaller Cadbury open to speculation by hedge funds, involving both short selling and betting on increases in share price. By early 2010, hedge funds owned nearly a third of Cadbury's shares and they were prepared to sell out to Kraft, a larger competitor. Since then, there have been significant redundancies at Cadbury and the transfer of capacity overseas (Gospel *et al.* 2010).

Nature of involvement in corporate governance

Shareholders do not normally expect direct involvement in the management of the firm, but they nevertheless have some influence on the general character of HRM. In the UK, institutional shareholders and managers are united in the view that the latter have responsibility for management and that shareholders should not attempt to 'micro-manage' them. Shareholders argue that they have no expertise in areas like HRM and therefore should not attempt to 'second-guess' management. The logic of this view is that shareholders are unlikely to have a direct involvement in the management of HR within the company, other than the appointment/dismissal of these top managers and the selection of incentive arrangements for such executives.

Institutional investors are often said to take a passive approach to governance because many do not play an active role in governance arrangements such as the annual general meeting (AGM), if indeed they attend at all. Dispersed ownership means that it is not in any shareholder's interests to take a more active role, because they would bear the costs whilst all other shareholders would reap the benefits. However, shareholder quiescence should not be overstated. Major institutional investors do monitor their larger investments, whilst monitoring activity is also undertaken by bodies such as the Association of British Insurers (ABI), the National Association of Pension Funds (NAPF), and Pensions Investment Research Consultants (PIRC). This activity mainly focuses on governance codes and executive pay. For the last decade, it has been a legal requirement that companies' remuneration reports, outlining the rewards made to top executives and the principles upon which they are based, are subject to a vote, albeit non-binding, at the AGM of the company. The propensity to vote by institutional investors is increasing, but a large number of major investors still do not vote. The specific effect this has on HRM is that executive pay has steadily grown at a higher rate than the pay of other employees, despite widespread concerns amongst investors and others that incentive elements of executive reward are often insufficiently challenging (see Bebchuk and Fried (2004) for a broad-ranging US study).

Institutional shareholders can influence the general 'tone' and approach to HRM within investee firms through informal contacts with managers. A key component of corporate governance in the UK is regular meetings between major investors and company managers, at which the latter present their strategies and prospects to investors. Although specific aspects of HRM are rarely discussed, the evidence suggests that investors are interested in whether people management is 'fitting' or 'appropriate'. They may also focus on the level of labour costs. This is backed up by a network of monitoring and information actors such as investment analysts. Although these actors typically have little knowledge of HRM, they nevertheless appear to have views on the general character of HRM within companies and can shape the views of the investor community on this subject (Pendleton and Gospel 2005; Holland 1998; Hendry *et al.* 1997). Thus they may have views on key HRM matters such as total headcount, the need for greater outsourcing, and pension scheme arrangements.

Other aspects of shareholder involvement can pose intense pressures on the management of HR. Given quiescence in governance, the main means for investors to register dissatisfaction with the management of investee companies can be to sell their shares. This facilitates an active market for corporate control, perceived by some as a critically important instrument of governance in countries like the UK (Manne 1965; Fama 1980). The market for corporate control exposes incumbent management to the threat of takeover and the possibility that they may lose their jobs. Arguably, it is this mechanism which forces managers to do what shareholders want. When takeovers occur, this can have very direct and dramatic effects on HRM. Workforce reductions and lay-offs are common after takeovers (Conyon et al. 2002). Takeovers can break 'implicit contracts' between employees and the firm, leading to withdrawal or reductions of employee benefits such as salary progression and pension provision (Shleifer and Summers 1988). At the very least, where merging companies are integrated post-takeover (rather than continuing to operate as autonomous entities), there is often a process of integrating HR systems, with related benefits in terms of efficiencies, and costs in terms of uncertainties.

The threat of takeover, as well as actual takeovers, may have considerable impact on the management of HRM. To prevent takeovers, managers may put shareholders' interests first (or appear to) and may seek to emphasise their contribution to shareholder value. This may affect the distribution of returns between shareholders and employees and encourage a lack of commitment by firms to employee job security. The evidence suggests that employee remuneration tends to be higher when managers are protected against takeovers and where managers have greater control relative to shareholders (Bertrand and Mullainathan 2003; Cronquist et al. 2007).

Although institutional investors are generally seen to be passive in terms of engagement, some owners do take a more activist approach. For example, some major pension funds, such as the BT Pension Fund (Hermes) and the California Public Employees Pension Scheme (CALPERS), are very active in their approach to governance. Both have targeted firms with poor performance and poor corporate governance on the grounds that pressure on management can improve company performance and hence generate returns to its investment (Jacoby 2007). Particular targets of investors such as Hermes and CALPERS tend to be executive pay, with a concern to relate this more tightly to performance targets.

There are other investors who adopt activist strategies. Most significant here has been private equity, which has come to the fore in recent years and may be seen as having profound implications on HRM. Private equity has come to be an important part of the British investment market, with some estimates suggesting that one-eighth of the British private sector workforce is employed in companies owned by such investors. In essence, private equity attempts to reduce the agency problem identified in listed company governance by involving owners (private equity funds) in the strategic direction and management of its investee companies. Private equity funds invite subscriptions from institutional investors, banks and wealthy individuals to make investments in their funds for a fixed period of time (ten to twelve years).

This pooling of capital is used to acquire existing companies or subsidiaries, generally with a view to restructuring and developing their operations prior to a resale or stock-market flotation at some time in the future (generally around five years). Most private equity transactions involve privately-owned firms or subsidiaries of private or publicly-listed firms, but the most dramatic are so-called public-to-private transactions, of which the most notable in the UK is that of Alliance Boots.

In the case of private equity, governance is highly interventionist. The private equity acquirer often installs new management and includes a representative of the fund on the company board of directors. Top management are subject to demanding performance objectives, with their remuneration closely tied to the achievement of these. Extensive 'financial engineering' can intensify the pressure on managers to deliver what investors want (Folkman *et al.* 2009). It is common for much of the purchase price of acquisitions to be financed by debt, much of which is secured against the assets or income stream of the acquired company. Debt puts pressure on managers to do what investors want and to reduce the potential for 'fat' in the company (whilst also minimising tax obligations of the private equity fund and its partners).

There has been extensive debate on the HR outcomes of private equity (Gospel *et al.* 2010). There have been some well-publicised cases of the collapse of firms owned by private equity, such as the bankruptcy of the Southern Cross care-home company in 2011. This company had been forced to sell and leaseback its care homes and was saddled with substantial debts. Critics have argued that the financial and governance pressures imposed on managers of acquired firms force them to cut labour costs by reducing employment, constraining wages and embarking on labour intensification (PSE Group in European Parliament 2007). Against this, it has been argued that evidence of these effects tends to be collected from extreme cases where acquired firms are in serious economic difficulties prior to the takeover, such as was the case with the AA motor services group. Other evidence suggests that private equity firms tend to improve the quality of HRM by enhancing training and by adopting so-called 'high commitment' HR practices so as to improve the performance of the company prior to sale (Bacon *et al.* 2008). Whatever the balance between these two perspectives, it is clear that HR in PE-acquired firms is characterised by an emphasis on performance, as exemplified by enhanced incentives for top managers and often greater use of pay incentives for other employees (Wright *et al* 2009).

Conclusions

In this chapter we have shown that corporate governance and ownership matter for HRM, even though the linkages between the seemingly discrete areas of governance and HRM are highly complex. Corporate governance can have profound effects on HRM, even though those directly involved in governance (major owners, institutional investors, and top managers) emphasise that internal management practices within the firm, other than the appointment and pay of top executives, are the prerogative of managers not shareholders.

However, there are various important ways that governance influences HRM albeit indirectly in most instances. In sum, the corporate governance system influences the nature of business strategies adopted by company managers, and this, in turn, influences HR policies and practices. It is often argued that, in countries such as the UK and US, the pressure for financial returns and shareholder primacy leads companies to adopt business strategies which are relatively short-termist and to undertake investments that have shorter pay-back periods than are observed in countries with more stakeholder-oriented systems of governance such as Germany and Japan. This is said to lead to a reluctance for companies to commit to long-term investments in human capital development, and there is evidence that training is less extensive in countries with certain types of governance systems such as the UK and US (Black et al. 2007). The corporate governance system also shapes management perspectives on the role of management and sets constraints and limits on management action within the firm.

Nevertheless, it remains a striking paradox of the British system that governance arrangements, characterised by apparent passivity of major governance actors and with considerable leeway afforded to managers, can have such profound effects on HR. An important aspect of this is the primacy and liquidity of UK stock markets, the existence of an active market in corporate control, and the looseness of regulatory obstacles to takeovers. The potential for ownership restructuring has a powerful conditioning role on managerial activity. We have seen that restructuring of ownership and governance does indeed affect HRM, often very directly and dramatically.

This is not to portray the governance system as deterministic with managers at the mercy of impersonal capital market forces. A good deal of corporate governance activity occurs 'behind the scenes' and managers have significant autonomy vis-à-vis major investors, because of their superior information and managerial competence and because of shareholders' reluctance to 'micro-manage'. The evidence suggests that shareholders are not necessarily wedded to any particular forms of business strategy or HR practices and that managers can secure the support of shareholders for business strategies and associated HR practices, where there is a long time lag before returns are earned, as in a sector such as pharmaceuticals (Deakin et al. 2006). Moreover, the evidence suggests that listed British firms do tend to operate many 'good' HR practices. The problem is often the fragility of these. Ownership and governance restructuring can lead to dramatic changes in both business strategies and HR practices, as exemplified by the cases of activist hedge funds and private equity.

Currently there are calls for the reform of UK corporate governance in ways that would also impact on HRM. There have also been calls for greater disclosure of the activities of hedge funds and private equity funds. The continuing growth of executive pay and the widening gap between executive remuneration and that of ordinary employees is attracting widespread public and political criticism. Various options for controlling this have been advanced, such as placing employee representatives on company remuneration committees. Further legislation in these areas seems likely. Similarly, there has also been criticism of the openness of the UK system to foreign takeovers and the damaging implications this can have for UK companies and employees. One result of these discussions and initiatives is that the role of governance in shaping HRM is becoming clearer.

REFERENCES

Allen, F. and Gale, D. 2000: *Comparing Financial Systems*, Cambridge, Mass: MIT Press.

Amable, B. 2004: *The Diversity of Modern Capitalism*, Oxford: Oxford University Press.

Bacon, N., Wright, M., Demina, N., Bruining, H. and Boselie, P. 2008: 'HRM, buy-outs, and private equity in the UK and the Netherlands', *Human Relations*, **61**, 1399–1433.

Bebchuk, L. and Fried, J. 2004: *Pay Without Performance: The Unfulfilled Promise of Executive Compensation*, Cambridge, MA: Harvard University Press.

Bertrand, M. and Mullainathan, S. 2003: 'Enjoying the quiet life? Corporate governance and managerial preferences', *Quarterly Journal of Economics*, **111**(5), 1043–1075.

Black, B., Gospel, H. and Pendleton, A. 2007: 'Finance, Governance, and the Employment Relationship'. In Black, B., Gospel, H. and Pendleton, A. (eds), *Industrial Relations*, **46**(3), 643–650.

Blair, M. 1995: *Ownership and Control: Rethinking Corporate Governance for the Twenty First Century*, Washington DC: Brookings Institution.

Brown, C. and Medoff, J. 1988: 'The Impact of Firm Acquisitions on Labor' In Auerbach, A. (ed) *Corporate Takeovers: Causes and Consequences*, Chicago IL: University of Chicago Press.

Clark, G. 2000: *Pension Fund Capitalism*, Oxford: Oxford University Press.

Clark, I. 2009: 'Private Equity in the UK: Job Regulation and Trade Unions', *Journal of Industrial Relations*, **51**(4), 489–500.

Clarke, T. 2004: *Theories of Corporate Governance*, London: Routledge.

Company Law Review, Steering Group 2001: *Modern Company Law: For a Competitive Economy – Final Report*, London: Company Law Review Steering Group.

Conyon, M., Girma, S., Thompson, S. and Wright, P. 2001: 'Do Hostile Mergers Destroy Jobs?' *Journal of Economic Behaviour and Organisation*, **45**(4), 459–473.

Conyon, M., Girma, S., Thompson, S. and Wright, P. 2002: 'The Impact of Mergers and Acquisitions on Company Employment in the United Kingdom', *European Economic Review*, **46**, 31–49.

Cronqvist, H., Heyman, F., Nilsson, M., Svaleryd, H. and Vlachos, J. 2007: 'Do entrenched managers pay their workers more? *Paper presented to American Finance Association, Chicago*, January 2007.

Deakin, S., Hobbs, R., Konzelmann, S. and Wilkinson, F. 2006: 'Anglo-American corporate governance and the employment relationship: a case to answer?', *Socio-Economic Review*, **4**, 155–174.

Department for Business Innovation and Skills 2011: *Executive Remuneration*, London, DBIS.

Donaldson, T. and Preston, L. 1995: 'The Stakeholder Theory of the Corporation: Concepts, Evidence, and Implications', *Academy of Management Review*, **20**, 65–91.

Fama, E. 1980: 'Agency Problems and the Theory of the Firm', *Journal of Political Economy*, **88**, 288–307.

Filatotchev, I., Jackson, G., Gospel, H. and Allcock, D. 2007: *Identifying the Key Drivers of 'Good' Corporate Governance and the Appropriateness of Policy Responses*, DTI Economics Paper, pp. 1–227 URN 07/581/

Folkman, P., Froud, J., Johal, S. and Williams, K. 2009: 'Private equity: levered on capital or labour', *Journal of Industrial Relations*, **51**, 517–529.

Franks, J. and Mayer, C. 1997: 'Corporate Ownership and Control in the U.K., Germany, and the U.S.', in D. Chew (ed.), *Studies in International Corporate Finance and Governance Systems*, New York: Oxford University Press.

Freeman, R. 1984: *Strategic Management: A Stakeholder Approach*, Boston MA: Pitman.

Froud, J., Johal, S., Leaver, A. and Williams, K. 2006: *Financialization and Strategy: Narrative and Numbers*, London: Routledge.

Gospel, H. and Pendleton, A. 2003: Finance, Corporate Governance and the Management of Labour: A Conceptual and Comparative Analysis, *British Journal of Industrial Relations*, **41**(3), 557–582.

Gospel, H. and Pendleton, A. (eds) 2005: *Corporate Governance and Labour Management: An International Comparison*, Oxford: Oxford University Press.

Gospel, H., Pendleton, A., Vitols, S. and Wilke, P. 2010: *The impact of investment funds on restructuring practices and employment levels*, European Foundation for the Improvement of Living and Working Conditions, Dublin, pp. 1–103.

Gourevitch, P. and Shinn, J. 2005: *Political Power and Corporate Control: The New Global Politics of Corporate Governance*, Princeton: Princeton University Press.

Hall, P.A. and Soskice, D. (eds.) 2001: *Varieties of Capitalism: The Institutional Foundations of Comparative Advantage*, Oxford: Oxford University Press.

Hansmann, H. and Kraakman, R. 2000: 'The End of History for Corporate Law', *Georgetown Law Journal*, **89**, 439–468.

Hendry, C., Woodward, S., Harvey-Cooke, J. and Gaved, M. 1997: *Investors' views of people management*, London: Institute of Personnel and Development.

Holland, J. 1998: 'Influence and intervention by financial institutions in their investee companies', *Corporate* Governance, **6**, 249–264.

Hopt, K. J., Kanda, H., Roe, M., Wymeersch, E. and Prigge, S. 1998: *Comparative Corporate Governance*, Oxford: Oxford University Press.

Hoskisson, R., Yiu, D. and Kim, H. 2004: 'Corporate governance systems: effects of capital and labor market congruency on corporate innovation and global competitiveness', *Journal of High Technology Management Research*, **15**, 293–315.

Jackson, G. 2005: 'Towards a Comparative Perspective on Corporate Governance and Labour Management'. In Gospel, H. and Pendleton, A. (eds), *Corporate Governance and Labour Management*, Oxford: Oxford University Press.

Jackson, G., Hopner, M. and Kurdelbusch, A. 2005: 'Corporate Governance and Employees in Germany'. In Gospel, H. and Pendleton, A. (eds), *Corporate Governance and Labour Management*, Oxford: Oxford University Press.

Jacoby, S. 2007: 'Convergence by design: the case of CALPERS in Japan', *American Journal of Comparative Law*, **55**, 239–294.

Jensen, M. and Meckling, W. 1976: 'Theory of the Firm: Managerial Behavior, Agency Costs and Ownership Structure', *Journal of Financial Economics*, **3**, 305–360.

Kay, J. 1997: 'The stakeholder corporation'. In Kelly, G., *et al.* (eds.), *Stakeholder Capitalism*, London: Macmillan.

Manne, H. 1965: 'Mergers and the Market for Corporate Control', *Journal of Political Economy*, **73**, 110–120.

McCahery, J. A., Moerland, P., Raaijmakers, T. and Renneboog, L. 2002: *Corporate Governance Regimes: Convergence and Diversity*, Oxford: Oxford University Press.

O'Sullivan, M. 2000: *Contests for Corporate Control. Corporate Governance and Economic Performance in the United States and Germany*, Oxford: Oxford University Press.

Office for National Statistics 2010: *Share Ownership Survey* 2008, London: Office for National Statistics.

Office for National Statistics 2011: *Mergers and Acquisitions involving UK companies,* London: Office for National Statistics.

Pendleton, A. and Gospel, H. 2005: 'Markets and Relationships: Finance, Governance, and Labour in the UK'. In Gospel, H. and Pendleton, A. (eds), *Corporate Governance and Labour Management*, Oxford: Oxford University Press.

Porter, M. 1992: *Capital Choices. Changing the Way America Invests in Industry*, Boston, MA: Harvard Business School and Council on Competitiveness.

Post, J., Preston, L. and Sachs, S. 2002: *Redefining the Corporation: Stakeholder Management and Organizational Wealth*, Stanford CA: Stanford University Press.

PSE Group in the European Parliament 2007: *Hedge Funds and Private Equity: a Critical Analysis,* Brussels: PSE Group.

Purcell, J. 1989: The Impact of Corporate Strategy and Human Resource Management. In Storey, J. (ed) *New Perspectives on Human Resource Management*, Routledge: London, 67–91.

Pye, A. 2011: *Leading FTSE 100 Companies*, Exeter: Exeter University.

Roberts, J. 2010: Designing Incentives in Organizations, *Journal of Institutional Economics*, **6**, 125–132.

Shleifer, A. and Summers, L. 1988: 'Breaches of trust in hostile takeovers' in Auerbach, A. (ed) *Corporate Takeovers: Causes and Consequences*, Chicago IL; University of Chicago Press.

Shleifer, A. and Vishny, R. 1997: 'A Survey of Corporate Governance', *Journal of Finance*, **52**, 737–783.

Vitols, S. 2004: 'Continuity and Change: Making Sense of the German Model', *Competition and Change*, **8**(4), 331–338.

Whitley, R. 1999: *Divergent Capitalisms. The Social Structuring and Change of Business Systems.* Oxford: Oxford University Press.

Wright, M., Bacon, N. and Ames, K. 2009: 'The impact of private equity on employment, remuneration, and other HRM practices', *Journal of Industrial Relations*, **51**, 501–516.

CHAPTER FIVE

The International Human Resource Function

Tony Edwards and Anthony Ferner

Introduction

Globalisation has become one of the central elements of economic life in the early twenty-first century. While some observers have stressed the historical precedents for some contemporary developments such as migration levels (e.g. Hirst *et al.* 2009), there are unquestionably many novel aspects to how the global economy operates. Multinational companies (MNCs) are at the centre of this process and can be seen as the 'primary drivers of the process of globalization' (Dicken 2011).

Yet some writers have suggested that the MNC is an inadequate focus for understanding globalisation. Delbridge *et al.* (2011: 488), for example, argue that 'the firm as the unit of analysis has become outmoded as corporations have increasingly shifted to networked forms of organisation'. They point, in particular, to the phenomenon of production and service provision processes becoming increasingly coordinated *across* firms in different countries rather than taking place *within* MNCs. This has been referred to as the 'fragmentation' of international economic activity and has been the focus of a large body of literature addressing 'global value chains' (Gereffi *et al.* 2005). While there is undoubtedly a strong element of inter-firm collaboration in the globalisation process, this in our view does not make the multinational an outdated notion; rather, it remains an important and valid unit of analysis. MNCs directly control through ownership more and more resources; their international activities generated 'value-added' of around $16 trillion in 2010, constituting approximately one quarter of global GDP, while the foreign affiliates of MNCs accounted for more than a third of exports in the global economy. Moreover, they remain, to some extent, cohesive entities with strong incentives to manage their operations in an integrated way (Morgan 2011). In terms of how they manage their workforces, there are strong grounds for thinking that MNCs will seek to develop international company-specific policies in such areas as training and development of key staff, communications and managing performance.

Thus, those running MNCs face a number of challenges and opportunities. Much of the academic writing about MNCs has focused on how they respond to 'global competitive pressures' on the one hand, and the pressures to meet 'host country demands' on the other (Doz *et al.* 1981). In the field of international HRM, most work is underpinned by the assumption of a tension between these sets of pressures, variously expressed as the global–local issue, the integration–differentiation dilemma or the centralisation–decentralisation balance (e.g. De Cieri and Dowling 2006; Schuler, Dowling and De Cieri 1993; Stahl and Bjorkman 2006). Thus, MNCs have choices concerning how to organise and manage their international HR function, mirroring the choices they make on 'upstream' issues of business strategy and corporate structure.

Consequently, the international nature of the HR function would appear to be a crucial element of how MNCs achieve their goals. If MNCs are to develop a competitive advantage through the management of the international workforce (Lado and Wilson 1994) then this implies that they need a set of structures capable of performing this role. Specifically, the international human resource (IHR) function has a role in potentially developing rare and hard-to-imitate resources, particularly company-specific skills and competences, and in promoting the organisational learning that is required to exploit them. The IHR function also has a role in global cost control, securing of economies of scale through standardisation of policies, monitoring of outcomes, devising compensation systems that attempt to link reward to outcome, and so on.

The chapter addresses three inter-related questions. First, what does the IHR function look like in MNCs in terms of structure and capabilities? Second, to the extent to which there is variation in these structures and capabilities, how can we explain this variation? Third, why does it matter what the function looks like in terms of HR policy and practice? In tackling these questions we summarise the rather limited existing literature and build on this by reviewing the findings of a large, cross-national project in which both authors have been involved. The project, known as INTREPID, has surveyed MNCs in nine countries over the last few years. Our main focus is on the UK part of this project, with some use being made of data from the three other countries that formed the 'first wave' of the international project, Canada, Ireland and Spain. All four of these first wave countries have an inward stock of foreign direct investment as a percentage of GDP that is higher than the global average, with this reaching over 60 per cent in Ireland (UN 2011). The comprehensive and representative nature of the surveys means that the data constitute a unique opportunity to address these questions in a way that has not been possible hitherto.

Previous Research on the HR Function in MNCs

There are a number of drivers of an international dimension to HR in MNCs. Some of these might be termed 'strategic' in the sense that they are linked to the wider goals of the firm, such as the desire to serve global customers in a standardised manner. Of course, strategies in MNCs are shaped by both the national institutional context in which they originate and the nature of corporate structures within the firm. Thus, if MNCs have choices to make concerning the structure and purpose of the HR function at the international level, then these are likely to be shaped, at least in part, by the nature of the business strategy and corporate structure of the firm and the institutional context in the country of origin. There are a range of strategies and structures which MNCs might tend towards. One of the best known attempts to categorise these is the fourfold typology of Bartlett and Ghoshal (1998) in which we highlight the implications for HR of each category.

The most decentralised of the four types that Bartlett and Ghoshal (1998) identify is the 'multinational'. In such firms there is hardly any role for an international HR function, nor are there global HR policies; instead, local HR functions operate largely autonomously. In stark contrast, in the 'global' firm the central HR function exerts strong control in the search for economies of scale from standardised HR policies. Local HR functions have limited autonomy, mainly serving as implementers of global policies. In the third type, the 'international' firm, there is a central direction that drives broad policy, but the detail of policy is determined by local subsidiaries. Standardisation of HR policies is confined to particular areas, such as management development and organisational learning. The final type, the 'transnational' firm, is the one that Bartlett and Ghoshal advocate as being particularly well placed to meet the various demands of operating internationally, going as far as to term it the 'solution' to managing across borders. It is characterised by an interdependent network in which the IHR function helps provide the 'corporate glue' that holds the network together, which takes the form of the propagation of a strong corporate culture, the development of a cadre of internationally mobile staff and facilitating the flow of organisational learning in all directions.

While Bartlett and Ghoshal's (1998) claim that firms are increasingly moving towards the transnational form may lack empirical backing, it is nevertheless clear that the IHR function is crucial to the achievement of global competitive advantage in all but multi-domestic firms. So, what does the literature tell us about the nature of the IHR function, particularly how internationally integrated is it? Essentially, the literature does not provide a clear answer. It contains many surveys of HR but there are question marks over the generalisability or comprehensiveness of these. The range of weaknesses in existing survey-based studies include: relatively small sample size; a remit that is limited to MNCs in particular sectors or which have grown in particular ways; limited data on employment relations and HR in surveys primarily conducted for other purposes; and, above all, a lack of transparency about the population listings from which samples were generated in many surveys (Edwards *et al.* 2008). Nevertheless, there are a number of studies which throw some light on the nature of the function.

One aspect of the HR function which has been studied is the existence of formal policy-making structures. Most MNCs have at least some mandatory HR policies that operating units across the company have to implement. For example, Wachter *et al.'s* (2006) study of US MNCs identified performance appraisal systems for managers as an issue on which a body, such as an international HR committee, at corporate HQ, designed a mandatory policy that applied across countries. In many cases, however, an internationally coordinated approach to HR emerges in a less overtly top-down way. Farndale and Paauwe (2005: 22) argue that the 'most integrated HR role found in global companies is where HR policy is continually developed by sharing practices amongst the different subsidiaries and head office together, and then implemented jointly across the whole organisation irrespective of where the policy originated'. Tregaskis et al. (2005) make a similar argument concerning the development of HR networks in MNCs (see also Sparrow et al. 2004). This implies that active attempts to bring HR staff together across borders are an element of how the international HR function operates.

The literature also sheds some light on ways in which MNCs concentrate particular HR activities in certain countries. One of the main manifestations of this is the use of HR shared service centres which have an international remit (e.g. Cooke 2006; Farndale and Paauwe, 2007; Sparrow et al. 2004). These bodies tend to have responsibilities for relatively routine aspects of HR, such as handling employee enquiries, and are generally equipped with either multi-lingual staff or staff of a range of nationalities. A further illustration of the concentration of activities in certain countries is the use of HR 'centres of excellence' (Fischer 2003) which have an international remit in generating and spreading HR expertise.

Thus, the literature is suggestive of these international dimensions to the HR function but we cannot say how widespread is each element, nor is it possible to reach a firm assessment of the strength of the international dimension overall. The literature does shed a little more light on why there is variation between MNCs in this respect.

Following the logic above, a central factor in explaining variation is the link with the strategy and structure of the firm. In particular, the extent of the flow of capital, information and people across borders shapes the extent to which the HR function is standardised internationally. In essence, the stronger the flows are, the more likely it is that MNCs will have core business processes in their HR function and have processes of benchmarking and information sharing (e.g. Sparrow et al. 2004). In other words, the degree to which the HR function is internationally organised is contingent on the strategic and structural characteristics of the multinational. What the literature is not so good at, however, is shedding light on the concrete aspects of structure and strategy that matter in this respect. For example, does a high degree of intra-enterprise trade strengthen the international dimension to HR? If so, does this relationship hold for all aspects of how the HR function operates internationally or only some of these aspects?

A second factor which explains why MNCs vary in how they structure the HR function is the nationality of the parent firm. It is well established that there are lasting national differences in the way that firms operate (e.g. Hall and Soskice 2001) and that this influences the HR function. Jacoby's (2004) comparative analysis demonstrated notable differences between Japanese and US firms across a range of dimensions. For instance, in the US the priorities of senior HR executives were geared more towards the share price whilst their Japanese counterparts attached more weight to preserving job security, a difference which he argues is 'emblematic of the distinction between the stakeholder (organisation-oriented) and the shareholder (market-oriented) visions (2004: 154). These national differences not only show up in firms within a country but also across them, in that the character of the IHR function is influenced by the nature of the home country system (Ferner 1997; Fenton-O'Creevy et al. 2008). In the case of Germany, there are grounds for seeing the national context as limiting the potential for senior German HR staff to 'export' their ways of doing things. German HR managers traditionally come from a legal background and spend much of their time on aspects of HR that were shaped by the web of regulations in the German system, such as works councils, and this has meant that their capabilities are German-specific. Consequently, they are not well placed to develop a strong international role (Ferner and Varul 2000). In contrast, senior HR practitioners in the US are much better placed to utilise, at the international level, the expertise that they have acquired at home. Thus, we might anticipate that there is variation in the extent of the international dimension by the country of origin.

A third factor concerns the status of the HR function within the firm. The ability of the HR function to deliver efficient outcomes that are aligned with strategic goals shapes how it is perceived by senior executives (Boselie and Paauwe 2005). One particularly important capability appears to be 'knowledge networking' across borders (Dickmann and Muller-Camen 2006), by which the authors mean the flow of knowledge in multiple directions across the company. However, not all HR functions have the expertise required to develop a role in this respect, or even if they do have this expertise they may not be perceived as being effective in delivering on such issues. Thus, it is the struggle for influence between different functions and groups that shapes the international dimension to HR. The status of the HR function is linked to the sector in which the firm operates. Whilst there is no automatic relationship between the two, it has been argued that firms in sectors in which low cost mass production is the dominant production paradigm, such as textiles or food manufacturing, tend to have smaller HR functions with less strategic influence internationally when compared with those in high-technology production, such as pharmaceuticals (e.g. Brewster et al. 2006).

Turning to the third issue at the heart of this chapter, what do we know about the impact of the organisation of the HR function on various policies and processes? On this issue the main focus of the literature is on how the roles played by HR can shift as the firm internationalises (Piercy and Vernon 2008; Scullion and Starkey 2000; Taylor et al. 1996 for a review). One illustration is the work of Evans et al. (2002) who identify different roles for HR in international firms. One of these is 'change partner'; Evans et al. (2002) see internationalisation as a change management issue and that this is much more straightforward where the broader business strategy is one of either global integration or local responsiveness, but which is more complex where strategy involves elements of both. Another role for HR is that of 'navigator', which is concerned with managing the tensions, dualities and paradoxes inherent in organisational effectiveness, such as between centralisation and decentralisation and between integration and responsiveness. Evans *et al.* (2002: 83) note that the pendulum swings from one priority to the other as strategic priorities fluctuate, and this has led to an emphasis on informal coordination mechanisms, such as lateral networks and socialisation into shared values.

Evans *et al.'s* (2002) analysis goes beyond these roles and identifies areas of HR which are subject to the greatest pressures for centralisation and integration. They argue that issues such as the recruitment of rank and file employees and collective bargaining (where it takes place) should be the responsibility of local subsidiaries. In contrast, those issues such as senior management development and the identification of 'high potentials' should be tightly integrated across borders, with a strong role for the international corporate function. There is also significant scope, Evans *et al.* (2002: 465–466) argue, for HR issues that are not as strategically important as management development and high potentials, to be standardised internationally; the handling of the payroll, employee queries on benefits and some generic training can be handled through outsourcing to global HR suppliers, regional call centres, ICT-based delivery and e-learning, generating cost savings when compared with local provision of these services. A further set of issues may best be handled through balancing integration and differentiation and here the authors identify recruitment for senior or key positions and performance management processes, for which cross-boundary project groups may be well suited.

This strand of the literature tells us something about the link between HR and strategy and how the various areas of HR are differentially affected by this link. In the main, it is based on plausible logic and is sometimes grounded in cases of MNCs. However, in keeping with the other two strands of the literature identified above, it is not supported by large, generalisable survey data. Moreover, it doesn't tell us much about the link between the HR function and such issues as the extent of central control or higher level intervention, organisational learning and the diffusion of practices, and such key practices as those relating to the link between pay and performance and how employees are involved in decision making. In other words, it does not tell us much about why it matters how the HR function is structured. This is a major gap in the literature which we aim to partially fill.

INTREPID Findings

As noted above, there are many challenges in carrying out survey work on HR in MNCs, particularly arising from the difficulties in generating genuinely representative data. Previous surveys have been only partially able to meet these challenges. A further challenge lies in the task of developing questions that result in meaningful measures of policy and practice. One approach to this has been to pose a series of statements concerning the nature of practices that a firm might deploy and ask respondents to indicate the extent to which these statements apply to their subsidiary. This was the approach taken by Pudelko and Harzing (2007), for instance, who sought this information for subsidiaries of German, Japanese and US MNCs across 'all hierarchical levels' of the workforce. They supplemented this with additional data from the HQs concerning whether respondents at this level believed that 'companies of their own country had oriented themselves (in the past) or will orient themselves (in the future) toward HRM practices from the two other countries' (2007: 544–545). Whilst the findings are thought-provoking, there is a high degree of subjectivity in such data and seeking generalisable statements across occupational groups at different levels risks masking considerable variation within subsidiaries.

The approach taken in the INTREPID project is rather different, asking about the existence of specific and concrete structures, policies and practices through a lengthy personal interview. For example, in relation to the organisation of the HR function, respondents were asked whether a range of structures were in place that formed part of an internationally integrated function, such as a policy-making committee, forms of networking within HR across borders, a global philosophy or style on managing staff, and data gathering or monitoring by the corporate HQ of the subsidiaries. Then, in relation to employment policy and practice, questions were asked about four substantive areas, with questions in many cases relating to groups of staff: managers; a 'key' group (defined as a group that is central to the core competence of the firm); and the largest occupational group (or LOG). The project involved a coordinated set of parallel, nationally representative surveys of employment policies and practices in MNCs that would lend themselves to comparative analysis. The UK survey generated a response of 302 firms and it is this which forms the primary data analysed in this chapter, drawing on the summary report (Edwards *et al.* 2007). Teams in Canada ($n = 208$), Ireland ($n = 260$) and Spain ($n = 330$) then carried out the survey and the resulting dataset of 1100 cases in total is also used to set the UK findings in context.

The Nature of the International HR Function and Variation between MNCs

Initially, we deal with the first two questions and split the discussion of them into structures and processes. Building on previous work, there are four aspects of international HR structures that we investigate. The first is an aspect of the international HR function that provides a measure of the degree of control over HR policy across borders, the existence of an international HR policy making body. As indicated in the review of the literature, previous work reveals little about the prevalence of such bodies. Respondents were asked whether there was a 'body within the worldwide company, such as a committee of senior managers, which develops HR policies that apply across countries'. More than half of MNCs in each country reported that there is one, and across the four countries just over six out of ten (61 per cent) are part of a multinational with such a body.

Second, while international policy-making committees are an important indicator of the extent to which the HR function is hierarchically controlled, we can also examine the degree to which it is characterised by a cross-country network. The survey asked about the degree to which the HR function makes a systematic attempt to bring HR managers together across sites in different countries. Around one half of MNCs indicated that this was the case on a global basis and almost a third on a regional basis. Nearly six out of ten (57 per cent) of MNCs across the four surveys did so on either a global or regional basis. The survey then asked about the concrete mechanisms through which contact takes place: international and regular meetings of HR staff were commonly used, as were international HR conferences and virtual groups in HR that have regular contact on at least a quarterly basis. Task forces were also used, though these often were focused on particular issues and met on an *ad hoc* basis. Overall, the findings of the surveys suggest that there are multiple forms of cross-border networking in HR.

As noted in the review of the literature, a further important element of how the international HR function is organised is the prevalence of electronic international 'HR information systems' and 'shared services', which are the third and fourth structures on which we report findings. Respondents were asked whether the worldwide company had an 'HR Information System, such as PeopleSoft or SAP HR, which holds data relating to the firm's international workforce'. Such structures provide a guide as to the ability of corporate management to compare the performance across sites. Just under half of the firms (44 per cent) had such a system. The data on the existence of shared services centres across countries provide a further indicator of the extent to which the conduct of the HR function is integrated across countries. Respondents were asked whether the firm made 'use of "shared services" centres that are part of the company at global or regional level'. These are present in a third (34 per cent) of firms in our surveys. The results for the four issues are presented in Figure 5.1.

Across these four issues, there are two factors that are significant in explaining variation between MNCs. The first is the nationality of the parent firm. In the British data, American MNCs are significantly more likely than those of other nationalities to exhibit these structures on all four issues and French MNCs are significantly more likely to have them on three of the four issues. Indeed, the distinctiveness of US MNCs was a finding in the other national surveys. This confirms the continuing

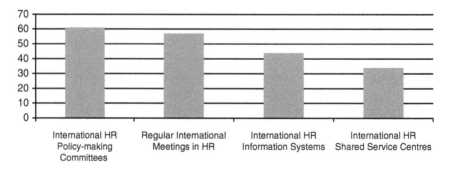

Figure 5.1 The international dimension to the HR function

importance of the influence of the business structures of the country in which the international firm originates in shaping the way that they operate across borders. The other contingent factor is size, with larger firms (by both subsidiary and world-wide employment) being more likely than small ones to have all four structures.

Turning to processes, one aspect of this is the monitoring of practices and outcomes at subsidiary level by higher levels of management. We can think of this as a form of 'output' control, in that it provides information concerning both whether performance is satisfactory and also whether the subsidiary is meeting the MNC's strategic priorities (Ambos *et al.* 2010). Baliga and Jaeger (1984: 26) argue that one advantage of monitoring outcomes in this way is that HQs can use it to influence the ends but allow 'organisational members flexibility in choosing the means'.

Survey respondents were asked whether information on a range of items was collected by management outside the survey country. There were marked differences in the extent of monitoring between the different issues. Those with direct financial implications, such as managerial pay packages, numbers employed and overall labour costs, were monitored by around three-quarters of companies, whereas those issues for which the link to the bottom line is more indirect, such as absenteeism and workforce diversity, were monitored by around one quarter of MNCs (see Figure 5.2).

There were also considerable differences between firms in the overall extent of monitoring. Using the UK data, a count of the number of items for which the UK operations are monitored was constructed, ranging from zero to nine. It is clear that there is considerable variation in the extent to which firms monitored; 29 per cent of firms monitor the UK operations on seven or more of the nine issues, while 18 per cent of firms collect data on two or fewer. How can we explain these differences? One source of difference between firms is their nationality. Japanese firms monitor on the fewest number of items (av = 3.3), significantly less than French (av = 6.2) and American firms (av = 5.1). Japanese firms were particularly less likely to monitor on

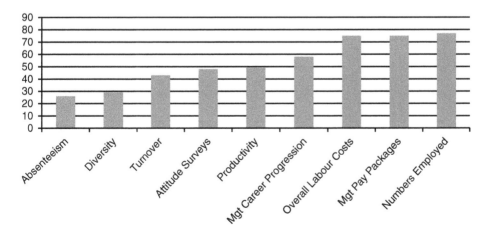

Figure 5.2 The monitoring of HR outcomes

the two managerial items (management pay and managerial career progression), turnover, diversity and employee attitudes. In contrast, American companies were more likely to monitor on absenteeism and on employee attitudes, and French firms more commonly monitored on managerial career progression, headcount, turnover and diversity. Another source of difference is size, with large firms monitoring more widely. This is the case both for UK employment size, with firms of 2,000 or more employees monitoring on more issues than smaller firms, and for worldwide employment size, with firms of 5,000 or more employees monitoring on a wider range of issues (see Edwards *et al.* 2007 for full details).

The surveys across the four countries throw up a marked difference in the extent of monitoring across countries, namely that the subsidiaries of MNCs in Spain are monitored less intensively than those in Canada, Ireland or the UK. In the comparative analysis on this issue (Edwards *et al.* forthcoming) we used seven of the issues and distinguished between those issues for which there was a clear, bottom–line impact, which we termed 'hard' HR issues and which include labour costs, headcount, turnover and productivity. In contrast, a second set of issues, which we termed 'soft', were those for which the bottom–line implications were less direct and which include management careers, diversity and employee attitudes. The figure shows the mean score for each country; for hard issues this could take on a value of between 0 and 4, and for soft issues between 0 and 3. In each case, the Spanish mean was significantly lower than in the other three countries, with the magnitude of the difference being particularly great for hard issues (see Figure 5.3).

One interpretation of this is that it is caused by 'institutional distance' (Kostova *et al.* 2008) in that the Spanish business context is the one of the four that is most distinct; it is a version of a 'coordinated market economy' (Hall and Soskice 2001) in which labour markets are characterised by institutional support for employee voice. In contrast, the main nationalities of MNCs – American, British and to a lesser extent other English-speaking countries – are from 'liberal market economies' with largely deregulated labour markets and weaker support for employee voice. Thus, the

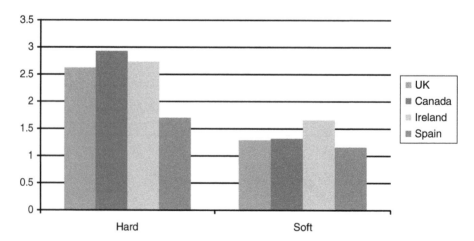

Figure 5.3 The monitoring of HR outcomes across countries

tendency amongst MNCs as a whole to exert less output control over their Spanish subsidiaries, compared with those in the other three countries, could be due to this greater distance in the Spanish case between the home country traditions of MNCs and the host country institutions.

Output control has its limitations as a means of influence since it does not shape the preferences of actors (Paik and Sohn 2004). Thus, mechanisms of 'social control' are rather more subtle and include international management training and the management of career paths, mechanisms that appear to be used increasingly widely, to some extent replacing long-term international assignments (Collings *et al.* 2009). These are ways in which corporate managers seek to instil a 'company way of doing things' (Edstrom and Galbraith 1977) and establish an 'informal network' of managers (Moore 2006).

One aspect of this is the extent to which there is an explicit attempt to establish a uniform management style across borders. Respondents were presented with statements relating to the company's philosophy concerning its management style towards employees and asked the extent to which they agreed or disagreed with it using a 1 to 5 scale. The data show that a worldwide philosophy is widespread: just over six out of ten (61 per cent) of the UK firms agreed or strongly agreed that 'a worldwide philosophy concerning all global operations' existed, almost exactly in line with the average across the four countries. A regional philosophy was also present in a number of firms, though it is rather less common with a little more than four out of ten (43 per cent in both the UK survey and across the four countries) identifying its presence.

The data on this issue were supplemented with an additional question for those respondents that indicated that there was an international philosophy which asked about the extent to which this was influenced by the parent company. For the analysis of the UK data, the same two factors that explained variation in the structures of the HR function are significant once again in explaining variation on this issue. First, American firms are the most likely to say both that a global philosophy is important and that the traditions of the parent company are important in shaping this philosophy. In contrast, French firms, which have been as distinctive as the Americans on many of the issues covered in this chapter, are less likely to see global philosophies as important, raising the possibility that they have a particular pattern of control resting on 'hard' control systems rather than 'soft' philosophies. Japanese firms are also less likely than others to see a global philosophy as important. Second, size was again significant, with larger firms, as measured by UK employment, being those most likely to exhibit a worldwide philosophy. In addition, a third factor was significant, namely that those firms that have been in the UK for the longest were those in which the traditions of the parent company were strongest. This final association sits uneasily with some visions of MNCs evolving over time in such a way that they shed an 'ethnocentric' orientation and suggests instead that this endures, and maybe even strengthens, over time.

A second way of trying to ensure that there is a company way of doing things is through succession planning, which is one of the primary mechanisms firms adopt to identify senior management talent within the organisation. Given that the pool of potential talent spans national borders, we might expect succession planning activity to be global in scope. In the UK data, 65 per cent of multinationals have a succession planning system, the vast majority of which are international in scope. (The findings were similar in the Spanish survey; the issue was not covered in Canada or Ireland.) Interestingly, there are no significant differences between organisations in their adoption of succession planning (global or local) depending on such key strategic factors as the extent of integration across borders or the level of diversification. There is, however, some variation by nationality: in particular, fewer than half of Japanese companies have one. We should see this in the context of Japanese MNCs deploying a high proportion of home-country (i.e. Japanese) nationals in senior positions in their British operations compared with other MNCs; this strong presence of expatriate managers in Japanese MNCs may act as a substitute for formal succession planning systems, and provide Japanese companies with an alternative mechanism for identifying and organising managerial talent internationally. In this respect, the results are consistent with other work that shows that Japanese MNCs are much less likely than European or US MNCs to involve local managerial employees in international development activity (Kopp 1994). Overall, the findings for organisations using succession planning illustrate its central role as a global mechanism for managing managerial talent. However, succession planning is not universally adopted and variation in its use by MNCs from different countries suggests it is an HR tool that, in some instances, remains sensitive to home-country HR traditions and preferences.

A further form of social control concerns the training of 'high potentials'. Organisations were asked if their UK operations had a management development programme specifically aimed at developing its 'high potentials' or senior management potential. The data show that exactly two-thirds of MNCs in the UK had high potential programmes, with a very similar proportion across the three countries in which this was a part of the survey. Of those responding affirmatively, respondents were then asked whether they used a global high potential programme that was adopted elsewhere worldwide, or a local, nationally specific programme. A majority indicated that their programmes were global in scope.

The pattern of variation is explained by quite different factors to those that explain variation in succession planning. In the UK the use of high potential programmes is similar across MNCs irrespective of their national ownership. However, the adoption of global high potential training programmes is related to the extent to which the UK operations are integrated with other parts of the organisation worldwide in operational terms. Specifically, the use of global high potential programmes is much higher among UK operations that have trading relationships with other parts of the worldwide company compared with those that either supply and/or are supplied by other parts of the worldwide company which are more commonly part of global programmes. Thus, the data suggest that high potential training is tied more with the needs of the business than the national training heritage of the parent company.

The final element to our analysis of the extent to which the HR function is internationally integrated concerns whether these various dimensions that we have already considered are inter-related. Starting with the four elements of structure, international HR policy making committees, regular meetings of HR managers across countries, international HR information systems and international shared services centres, are all significantly related to one another. Turning to process, analysis of the data also shows that output and social control are related to one another. For instance, firms with a worldwide philosophy on management style tend to monitor on a larger number of employment issues than do firms without such a philosophy. Moreover, the adoption of succession planning is significantly associated with the collection of data on a range of HR issues (e.g. managerial career progression, managerial pay packages, labour costs, staff turnover and employee attitudes). This suggests that the two forms of control often complement each other. There is also evidence of associations between the structures and the processes. Illustrations of this are that firms with each of the four forms of structure identified above monitor on a wider range of employment issues than firms without these structures. They are significantly more likely to agree or strongly agree that there is a worldwide philosophy concerning the management of staff across borders, and are more likely to have a global approach to succession planning.

To this point we have shed considerable light on the first two questions that the chapter addresses in revealing the extent to which the HR function in MNCs is internationally organised and some factors – particularly nationality of ownership, size and, to a lesser extent, business strategy – that explain variation in this respect. We have shown that in a significant number of MNCs there is a well developed international element to how HR operates, and we can now turn to the third question of what difference this makes and what impact it has.

The Impact of International Integration in HR

In addressing the impact of the HR function we address a number of themes, the first of which is how the organisation of the function affects the control over the formation of HR policies in the subsidiaries. Do the structures and key processes within the function affect the discretion of actors in the subsidiaries? The issue of what predicts subsidiary discretion has been investigated through multivariate analysis of the UK dataset (Ferner *et al.* 2011) on two contrasting HR areas: first, 'performance management', which includes measures of discretion on performance appraisal for managers, performance management for the LOG, variable pay for managers and succession planning; second, 'rank and file' issues, which include discretion over policy on workforce training, employee involvement in work processes, information provision, attitude surveys, union recognition and employee consultation. The results showed that some variables are associated with lower discretion across both sets of issues, namely US ownership and the structure of the multinational (particularly the existence of intermediate structures such as international business divisions between the subsidiary and corporate HQ). The impact of the organisation of the HR function was significant only in relation to performance management, not to rank and file issues. In relation to performance management, it was the bringing together of HR managers from different countries which was the key variable affecting discretion; other HR structures, such as policy-making committees and shared services centres, as well as some processes such as monitoring, were not significant. Ferner *et al.* conclude that the 'relationship of key international HR managers to their subsidiary counterparts is a key aspect of direct personal control' and that 'the "micro-political efficacy" of HR structures lies to a considerable extent in their potential for social control through networking and the resulting acculturation of managers into the cognitive perspectives of higher levels of the MNC' (2011: 503).

A second theme is that of organisational learning and the diffusion of practices across borders. Analysis of the UK data on the issue of organisational learning has been addressed by Tregaskis *et al.* (2010) who examined the incidence of four mechanisms used specifically for international organisational learning: expatriate assignments, international project groups or task forces, international formal committees and international informal networks. These 'transnational social learning structures' were found to be important in shaping the diffusion of best practice and know-how and in the development of a common organisational culture. The multivariate analysis sheds light on the hypothesised relationship between transnational HR structures on the one hand and transnational social learning structures on the other, with the networking of HR professionals across countries being positive and significant in this respect. As Tregaskis *et al.* (2010: 490) put it, 'It might be that the transnational HRM structures evidenced here provide a supportive learning context because they enable international social capital, making it easier for organisations to establish transnational social learning structures'.

The related issue of the diffusion of practices has been investigated by Edwards T. *et al.* (2010a). The focus of this strand of the project was on the extent to which MNCs use their foreign operations as the origin of employment practices that are subsequently transferred across the firm. The main measure of this was derived from a question that asked 'Has the UK company provided any practices in the following areas that have been taken up elsewhere in the worldwide company?', with the areas being pay and performance management, training and development, employee involvement and employee consultation. Regression analysis sought to explain variation between companies on this issue with three broad types of independent variable: nationality of the parent firm, configuration of the firm (essentially capturing some aspects of business strategy and corporate structure), and the 'organisational conduits' through which diffusion can occur. The final category is of particular importance given that it consists of such issues as an HR information system, networking of HR professionals across borders and that professionals were sent from the UK to other parts of the multinational. These factors were significantly associated with diffusion, leading to the assessment that: 'Taken together, these findings provide strong support for the expectation that the extent and nature of international channels in the HR function shapes the likelihood that diffusion from the UK will occur' (Edwards T. *et al.* 2010a: 629).

It is clear from the evidence we have reviewed so far that the organisation of the HR function at the international level affects key processes, including the degree of central involvement in policy-making, organisational learning and diffusion. But what can we say about the nature of practices? Do MNCs with a strong international dimension to the HR function have distinctive practices? We investigate this for two areas of practice: pay and its link with performance, and involvement and communication.

Analysis of the UK data shows some associations between international HR structures and processes and four particular practices in the broad area of pay and performance. The first of these concerns the existence of 'forced distributions' in assessing performance, in which the manager carrying out the assessment must allocate specified proportions of those for whom they are responsible to particular categories. The '10–80–10' distribution is one well-known application of this idea, with 10 per cent of staff classified as outstanding performers, 80 per cent as the solid middle, and 10 per cent as poor performers. MNCs with international HR information systems are almost three times as likely to use forced distributions for the key group as are those without these systems, and are also more likely to have forced distributions for all employee groups. This might be because these systems allow managers at higher organisational levels to monitor how forced distributions are being utilised. The second practice is upward appraisal, in which there is an element of the assessment of performance made by those who work under the individual concerned. This practice is more common where there is an international HR committee, an international HR information system and an international shared HR services centre. Third, variable pay is also more commonly found in MNCs with a strong international structure to HR. Firms in which HR managers are brought together internationally in a systematic way are more likely than others to have variable pay for managers, the key group and the LOG. To varying degrees, the existence of international HR information systems, international shared HR services, and worldwide HR committees are all significantly associated with variable pay. The fourth area is share-based schemes. The collection of data on HR issues in the subsidiaries, HR information systems, international HR policy-making committees and systematic meetings of HR managers across borders are all positively associated with the existence of share schemes. However, an internationally integrated HR function does not affect all practices in this area of HR. For example, the incidence of pay being affected by individual performance is not affected by how the HR function is organised across borders.

Turning to involvement and communication, there are three types of practice that we considered. The first was the extent to which information is provided to staff about the fortunes of the worldwide enterprise. This was significantly more extensive in those MNCs in which there was an international HR policy making committee. As we might expect, the existence of such a body is not associated with the provision of information about the UK subsidiary. The significant association with information provision about the worldwide enterprise, but not the UK subsidiary, suggests that international HR structures do not affect what goes on inside the UK subsidiary in this respect, but it does promote the sharing of information about the wider enterprise with UK employees. Second, we assessed the number of mechanisms that each firm used to communicate with its staff. Those MNCs with an international HR committee were those which used the greatest range of communication mechanisms. Third, we sought to establish an indicator of high employee involvement through a simple index that comprised: the use of problem-solving groups; a large number (seven or more out of a possible nine) of communication mechanisms; and information being provided on several items (four or more out of a possible six). Nearly one-third of MNCs have all three, a further third have two of the three items, a quarter have one item, and the remaining 9 per cent have none. Interestingly, those firms with all three forms of employee involvement also had internationally integrated HR functions.

The analysis of HR practices has been taken further through multivariate analysis of the data across four countries (Edwards P. *et al.* 2010). Their examination of a wide range of practices within the national operations of MNCs in the four countries encompassed those relating to the motivation of the workforce (such as profit sharing and two-way forms of communication), those in the area of opportunities for staff (including international forms of development for managers and problem-solving groups for non-managers) and practices through which management exert control over their workforces (such as appraisal and 'forced distributions'). The authors sought to establish links between clusters of these practices and various aspects of the wider firms of which they were part and concluded that the 'results show that the integration of the firm, the organisational structure and the presence of an international HR committee, as well as size, play an important role on the use of HRMPs'.

These associations raise the issue of what is going on in the relationship between the HR function and HR practices. In particular, why are international HR structures associated with particular substantive policies and practices? One possibility is that HR structures have emerged to cater to a plan to implement certain policies across their operations. Thus, the finding that firms with international HR policy-making bodies more commonly have an international element to management training, for instance, could be interpreted as the former being created to facilitate the latter. This implies a rather ordered world of top-down planning, with both the IHR structures and the HR policies in MNCs reflecting the preferences of senior managers. An alternative, perhaps more plausible, interpretation is that HR structures, once in place, operate in such a way that certain policies, particularly those which are internationally coordinated, are more likely to be put in place. If this is the case then it suggests that the IHR function develops its own logic and influence, which is only partially shaped by higher order issues of business strategy. The summary of the comparative analysis carried out so far is consistent with this second interpretation (Edwards T. *et al.* 2010b).

Conclusion

This chapter has addressed three issues. First, we explored the nature of the international HR function and found that there is a fairly high degree of international integration. The literature had hinted at this and highlighted some of the structures and processes that can constitute an international dimension, but the review of the INTREPID evidence has shed light on the detail and prevalence of a variety of structures in the function.

Second, there is clearly variation in the extent of the international dimension to HR and we have established certain contingent factors that explain this variation. The INTREPID findings confirm the importance of nationality as an important source of variation. US MNCs are evidently distinctive, more commonly employing a range of international HR structures, monitoring their operations more closely and more commonly employing an international philosophy concerning the management of their workforce. French firms were similarly distinctive in some of these respects, notably what we termed the use of 'hard' control systems such as international HR structures and monitoring of outcomes, but were less likely to use the 'soft' forms of international coordination such as global philosophies. At the other end of the spectrum, Japanese MNCs were distinctive in very different ways: they were the least likely to have international HR structures, tended to monitor the fewest HR outcomes, less commonly had a global philosophy, and were the least likely to adopt a common approach to international succession planning. As we argue above, we should not see this as Japanese MNCs having no means of influencing the nature of HR policies in their foreign operations; rather, they appear to have different means, relying on a strong presence of expatriate managers who occupy key positions in their subsidiaries outside Japan. The continuing influence of the national heritage of the firm that shows through from these findings builds on the previous research we reviewed, which indicated that the nature of the business system in the country of origin conditions the potential for HR practitioners to exercise an international influence, illustrated in the contrast between the constrained position of German HR managers and their US counterparts.

A further source of variation is the important, but partial, links between the nature of the IHR function and some key aspects of the strategy and configuration of the firm. One illustration is that MNCs in which there are cross-border intra-firm linkages in production more commonly have an international approach to the training of 'high potential' staff; indeed, the analysis indicated that high potential training is tied more closely with the needs of the business than the national training heritage of the parent company. However, intra-firm linkages in production were not significantly associated with many other elements of an international approach to HR. Our assessment of these patterns is that the HR function operates in a way that is shaped by the wider structure and strategy of the company and, to an extent, therefore, it should be seen as a 'downstream' function which is dependent on 'upstream' levels of strategy and structure. However, this influence is not a determining one: the HR function can develop its own logic, elements of which are arrived at relatively independently of what goes on at higher levels.

The third issue we have addressed concerns why it matters which form the IHR function takes. We have seen that an HR function which is internationally integrated is present in firms in which control over foreign subsidiaries is exercised more tightly and which have a stronger potential to engage in transnational learning and cross-border diffusion. It also makes a difference in terms of the substantive policies that firms deploy. In other words, the nature of the IHR function does indeed matter. One implication concerns an argument that we addressed at the beginning of the chapter, namely the view that the company level is an outdated one if we wish to understand how international activity takes place. Our evidence strongly confirms that this is not at all the case. Indeed, the globalisation of economic activity appears to be strengthening the internal coherence of MNCs, a tendency that can coexist with the process of greater collaboration between firms.

Acknowledgements

There are a number of people who we wish to thank. The other members of the UK research team are Paul Edwards, Paul Marginson and Olga Tregaskis. Duncan Adam has provided invaluable research assistance over many years. We have collaborated closely with teams in Canada (Jacques Belanger, Pierre-Antoine Harvey, Patrice Jalette, Christian Levesque and Gregor Murray), Ireland (David Collings, Paddy Gunnigle, Jonathan Lavelle, Ryan Lamare and Anthony McDonnell) and Spain (Javier Quintanilla, Rocio Sanchez-Mangas and Lourdes Susaeta). We are grateful to all of them for their input to the project and for permission to write this chapter.

REFERENCES

Ambos, T., Andersson, U. and Birkinshaw, J. 2010: What are the Consequences of Initiative taking in Multinational Subsidiaries?, *Journal of International Business Studies*, **41**, 1099–1118.

Baliga, B. R. and Jaeger, A. 1984: Multinational Corporations: Control Systems and Delegation Issues, *Journal of International Business Studies*, **25**, Fall, 25–40.

Bartlett, C. and Ghoshal, S. 1998: *Managing Across Borders: The Transnational Solution*, 2nd edn., London: Hutchinson.

Boselie, P. and Paauwe, J. 2005: Human resource function competencies in European companies, *Personnel Review*, **34**(5), 550–569.

Brewster, C., Wood, G., Brookes, M. and Van Ommeren, J. 2006: What determines the size of the HR function? A cross-national analysis, *Human Resource Management*, **45**(1), 3–21.

Collings, D., Scullion, H. and Dowling, P. 2009: Global Staffing: A Review and Thematic Research Agenda, *International Journal of Human Resource Management*, **20**(6), 1253–1272.

Cooke, F. L. 2006: Modeling an HR shared services center: Experience of an MNC in the United Kingdom, *Human Resource Management*, **45**(2), 211–227.

De Cieri, H. and Dowling, P. 2006: Strategic IHRM in Multinational Enterprises: Developments and Directions, in G. Stahl and I. Bjorkman (eds.), *Handbook of Research in International Human Resource Management*, 15–35. Cheltenham: Edward Elgar.

Delbridge, R., Hauptmeier, M. and Sengupta, S. 2011: Beyond the Enterprise: Broadening the Horizons of International HRM, *Human Relations*, **64**(4), 483–505.

Dicken, P. 2011: *Global Shift*. London: Sage.

Dickmann, M. and Muller-Camen, M. 2006: A typology of international human resource management strategies and processes, *International Journal of Human Resource Management*, **17**(4), 580–601.

Doz, Y., Bartlett, C. and Prahalad, C.K. 1981: Global Competitive Pressures and Host Country Demands: Managing Tensions in MNCs, *California Management Review*, **23**(3), 63–74.

Edstrom, A. and Galbraith, J. 1977: Transfer of Managers as a Co-ordination and Control Strategy in Multinational Organizations, *Administrative Science Quarterly*, 22 June, 248–263.

Edwards, P., Edwards, T., Ferner, A., Marginson, P. and Tregaskis, O. 2007: *Employment Practices of MNCs in Organisational Context: A Large-Scale Survey*, Report of the Main Survey, available at: http://www2.warwick.ac.uk/fac/soc/wbs/projects/mncemployment/conference_papers/full_report_july.pdf

Edwards, T., Edwards, P., Ferner, A., Marginson, P. and Tregaskis, O. 2010a: Multinational Companies and the Diffusion of Employment Practices: Explaining Variation Across Firms, *Management International Review*, **50**(5), 613–634.

Edwards, P., Lévesque, C., McDonnell, A., Quintanilla, J., Sanchez, R. and Tregaskis, O. 2010: *Human Resource Practices in the Multinational Company: A Test of System, Societal and Dominance Effects*, Paper presented at Cornell University, 12 September.

Edwards, T., Marginson, P. and Ferner, A. 2010b: *Multinational Companies in Comparative Context*, paper presented at Cornell University, 12 September.

Edwards, T., Tregaskis, O., Collings, D., Jalette, P. and Susaeta, L. forthcoming: Explaining Similarities and Variation in Control over Employment Practices in Multinationals: Subsidiary Functions, Corporate Structures and National Systems, *Industrial and Labour Relations Review*.

Edwards,T., Tregaskis, O., Edwards, P., Ferner, A. and Marginson, P. with Arrowsmith, J., Adam, D., Meyer, M. and Budjanovcanin, A. 2008: *Charting the Contours of Multinationals in Britain: Methodological Issues Arising in Survey Research*, Warwick Papers in Industrial Relations, No 86, Coventry: IRRU/Leicester Business School Occasional Paper, Leicester: De Montfort University.

Evans, P., Pucik, V. and Barsoux, J.-L. 2002: *The Global Challenge: Frameworks for International Human Resource Management*, Boston: McGraw-Hill/Irwin.

Farndale, E. and Paauwe, J. 2005: *The Role of Corporate HR Functions In Multinational Corporations: The Interplay Between Corporate, Regional/National And Plant Level*, Cornell, Centre for Advanced Human Resource Studies, no. 05 - 1. Ithaca.

Farndale, E. and Paauwe, J. 2007: Restructuring the HR function: HR shared service centres in the Netherlands in G. Martin, M. Reddington and H. Alexander (eds.), *Technology, Outsourcing and HR Transformation*, UK: Butterworth Heinemann.

Fenton-O'Creevy, M., Gooderham, P. and Nordhaug, O. 2008: HRM in US Subsidiaries in Europe and Australia: Centralization or autonomy?, *Journal of International Business Studies*, **39**, 151–166.

Ferner, A. 1997: Country of Origin Effects and HRM in Multinational Companies, *Human Resource Management Journal*, **7**(1), 19–37.

Ferner, A. and Varul, M. Z. 2000: Internationalisation and the personnel function in German multinationals, *Human Resource Management Journal*, **10**(3), 79–96.

Ferner, A., Edwards, P., Edwards, T., Marginson, P. and Tregaskis, O. 2011: HRM Structures and Subsidiary "Discretion" in Multinationals, *International Journal of Human Resource Management*, **22**(3), 483–509.

Fischer, K. 2003: Transforming HR globally: The center of excellence approach, *Human Resource Planning*, **26**(2), 9.

Gereffi, G., Humphrey, J. and Sturgeon, T. 2005: The Governance of Global Value Chains, *Review of International Political Economy*, **12**(1), 78–104.

Hall, P. and Soskice, D. 2001: *Varieties of Capitalism: The Institutional Foundations of Comparative Advantage*, Oxford: Oxford University Press.

Hirst, P., Thompson, G. and Bromley, S. 2009: *Globalisation in Question*, 3rd edn., London: Polity.

Jacoby, S. 2004: *The Embedded Corporation: Corporate Governance and Employment Relations in Japan and the United States*, New York: Princeton University Press.

Kopp, R. 1994: International human resource policies and practices in Japanese, European and United States multinationals', *Human Resource Management*, **33**(4), 581–599.

Kostova, T., Kendall, R. and Dacin, T. 2008: Institutional Theory in the Study of MNCs: A Critique and New Directions, *Academy of Management Review*, **33**(4), 994–1007.

Lado, A. and Wilson C. 1994: Human Resource Systems and Sustained Competitive Advantage: A Competency-based Perspective, *Academy of Management Review*, **19**(4), 699–727.

Moore, F. 2006: Strategy, Power and Negotiation: Social Control and Expatriate Managers in a German Multinational Corporation, *International Journal of Human Resource Management*, **17**(3), 399–413.

Morgan, G. 2011: Reflections on the Macro-politics of Micro-Politics in C. Dorrenbacher, and M. Geppert (eds.), *Politics and Power in the Multinational Corporation: The Role of Institutions, Interests and Identities*, Cambridge: Cambridge University Press.

Paik, Y. and Sohn, J. 2004: Expatriate Managers and MNCs' Ability to Control International Subsidiaries: the Case of Japanese MNCs, *Journal of World Business*, **39**(1), 61–71.

Piercy, K. and Vernon, P. 2008: Globalisation of the HR function: The next step in HR's transformation?, *Global Business and Organisational Excellence*, **27**(2), 42–51.

Pudelko, M. and Harzing, A.-W. 2007: Country of Origin, Localization or Dominance Effect? An Empirical Investigation of HRM Practices in Foreign Subsidiaries, *Human Resource Management*, **46**(4), 535–559.

Schuler, R., Dowling, P. and De Cieri, H. 1993: An Integrative Framework of Strategic International Human Resource Management, *Journal of Management*, **19**(2), 419–459.

Scullion, H. and Starkey, K. 2000: The Changing Role of the Corporate Human Resource Function in the International Firm, *International Journal of Human Resource Management*, **11**(6), 1061–1081.

Sparrow, P., Brewster, C. and Harris, H. 2004: *Globalizing Human Resource Management*, Routledge: London.

Stahl, G. and Bjorkman, I. (eds.) 2006: *Handbook of Research in International Human Resource Management*, Cheltenham: Edward Elgar.

Taylor, S., Beechler, S. and Napier, N. 1996: 'Toward an integrative model of strategic international human resource management', *Academy of Management Review*, **21**(4), 959–985.

Tregaskis, O., Glover, L. and Ferner, A. 2005: International HR Networks in Multinational Companies, *CIPD Research Report*, London: CIPD.

Tregaskis, O., Edwards, P., Edwards, T., Ferner, A. and Marginson, P. 2010: Determinants of Transnational Learning Capability in Multinational Firms: the Effects of Organisational

Structure, Corporate Governance and Country of Origin, *Human Relations*, **63**(4), 471–499.

United Nations 2011: *World Investment Report: Non-Equity Modes of International Production and Development*, New York: UN.

Wachter, H., Peters, R., Ferner, A., Gunnigle, P. and Quintanilla, J. 2006: The Role of the International Personnel Function in P. Almond and A. Ferner (eds.), *American Multinationals in Europe: Managing Employment Relations Across National Borders*, Oxford: Oxford University Press.

CHAPTER SIX

Customer Service Work, Employee Well-being and Performance

Stephen Deery and Vandana Nath

A majority of workers in industrialised nations are employed in the service sector. Employees engaged in service work are often recognised as important resources that contribute to an organisation's performance. Many service jobs require employees to interact directly with customers. Whether they are lawyers, nurses, hairdressers or call centre staff, their work involves a high degree of personal contact with the public and the enactment of 'emotional labour' (Hochschild 1979). They must present their emotions and manage their behaviour in such a way that both complies with the service standards of the organisation and help create a desired 'state of mind' in the service recipient. Organisations can also demand that employees regulate their appearance and modulate their speech during service interactions to appeal to customer senses. This market of 'looking good' and 'sounding right' is known as 'aesthetic labour' (Witz *et al.* 2003). Often, these emotional, visual and vocal service standards are embodied in the employment contract and are used to judge worker performance (Morris and Feldman 1997; Warhurst *et al.* 2000).

Service work involving employee-customer interaction exhibits certain features that are quite different from jobs performed in the manufacturing sector. The principal difference relates to the participation of the customer in the process of service work. The customer plays a role in determining the way in which the work is performed. It is the customer whose requirements must be satisfied and whose orders must be met. In some cases, service recipients may act as co-producers while in others, they may be enlisted jointly by the organisation to supervise workers and help manage the labour process (Fuller and Smith 1996). This triangular relationship between the customer, the employee and management distinguishes interactive service work from industrial production where customers are normally external to the labour process and where the dynamics of management control are more firmly located within the boundaries of the worker-management dyad. As the quality of the interaction between the employee and the customer is frequently part of the service delivered, MacDonald and Sirianni (1996: 15) argue that in service jobs 'the producer in some sense equals the product'. Consequently, 'workers' looks, words, person-alities, feelings, thoughts and attitudes may all be treated by employers as legitimate targets of intervention' (Leidner 1996: 30).

This chapter begins by examining the nature of customer service work. This is followed by a consideration of the ways in which emotional and aesthetic labour is managed by organisations. Employee responses to these managerial demands and to customer interactions are explored. It is observed that jobs involving close customer contact can often result in emotional exhaustion, stress and work alienation. The final part of the chapter analyses the relationship between the service work labour process and employee well-being and organisational performance.

The Nature of Customer Service Work

Customer service work is performed in a diverse range of industries from hospitality and recreation to banking, retailing and professional services. The work has a number of common characteristics (Korczynski 2002). Firstly, it is intangible. In contrast to a manufactured product, services such as advice provided over the telephone cannot be held or touched. Secondly, service work is perishable. It is transitory and cannot be stored and made use of later. Thirdly, it is characterised by inseparability as services are produced and consumed simultaneously. Unlike manufacturing firms, customer service organisations cannot place a quality control buffer between the production of a service and its consumption. Fourthly, due to real-time human interactions, service work is variable. Customer demands are often idiosyncratic and service providers possess different skills, temperaments and varying levels of commitment to the customer (Peccei and Rosenthal 2001). As customers generally participate in the production of the service, they can not only be a source of great satisfaction for the service provider but also a cause of intense anxiety and stress (Korczynski and Macdonald 2009).

These characteristics have important implications for the way in which customer service work is managed. Perhaps the most significant of these features relates to the scope for variability in service provision and the absence of a buffer between pro-duction and consumption. Controlling service quality is seen to be difficult because of the day-to-day variability in employee attitudes and behaviour and because ser-vices cannot be inspected after they are produced and before they are consumed. In response to this problem, service organisations have often sought to prescribe tight rules of interaction to narrow the scope for provider-customer variability and to restrict opportunities for employee discretion in service delivery. Many organisations thus attempt to control worker behaviour through designing jobs based on an 'efficiency approach' of task simplification, specialisation and standardisation. Task simplification and specialisation create a division of labour and reduce the amount of skills and training required to carry out a service, while task standardisation allows consistency and control over service conditions. Therefore, employee autonomy is reduced considerably and management can closely supervise work activities. Ritzer (2004) contends that such 'McDonaldized' processes represent work dimensions of efficiency, calculability, predictability and control (see Table 6.1).

The importance of the front-line worker to the success of interactions has given rise to different approaches to oversee the service provider's encounters with customers. In some cases, it has led to particularly invasive forms of workplace control. In telephone call centres, for example, computer technology is a critical component of workplace management (Batt and Moynihan 2004). It is used to monitor the speed of work and assess the quality of the interaction between the service provider and the customer. Furthermore, employees are invariably required to follow a tightly scripted dialogue with customers. Deery *et al.* (2002) provide an example of a call centre where all service representatives were directed to follow a sequence of five specified tasks: greet and build rapport with the customer; fact-find; provide solutions; close conversation; and follow (or wrap) up. These tasks had to be completed with each customer within a short and fixed period. The close monitoring of words and the often limited variation that employees are allowed in service interactions has meant that call centre workers lose a large measure of control over their self-presentation.

Not all service workers, however, are so constrained in their interactions with customers. Where service work requires subjective interpretation, and where employees must exercise judgement to meet customer needs, it is more probable that they will be granted greater discretion and control over their conduct. In these

Table 6.1   Ritzer's (2004) dimensions of McDonaldized service production

Dimension	Definition	Corresponding work systems
Efficiency	The optimum method of completing a task	Emphasis on adhering to a pre-arranged set of procedures and stages during service delivery which is monitored by management
Calculability	The estimation of quantitative performance	Quantitative measurement of work outcomes such as the rapidity of customer turnover
Predictability	The guarantee of uniformity and standardisation of outcomes	Forms of work routinisation such as the use of a conversational script during customer interaction
Control	The attempted elimination of risk	Minimisation of decision-making. This may entail task simplification and standardisation, heavily laden organisational rules and the use of technology to control work pace and monitor employee performance

Source: Ritzer (2004)

circumstances, employees are more likely to be armed with information rather than instructions (Macdonald and Sirianni 1996). Work systems that are built upon recognised professional qualifications and skills provide workers with greater autonomy. Such work tends to be complex, non-routine and cannot be easily monitored or controlled. Occupations that might lie within this category include lawyers, doctors and university lecturers (Herzenberg *et al.* 1998).

It is widely recognised that tight control over the labour process can deliver efficient task completion, but is unlikely to elicit high-quality performance from employees. Control workers too completely, as Fuller and Smith (1996: 76) observe, and management will 'extinguish exactly those sparks of worker self-direction and spontaneity' that are so critical for service quality. Customers care how services are delivered and therefore the way in which employees display their feelings towards them can have an important effect on the perceived quality of the interaction (Ashforth and Humphrey 1993). Many front-line employees nevertheless are presented with the twin demands of being both efficient and appealing to the customer's sense of sovereignty. Employees have to balance task proficiency with relationship-orientated behaviour. Such service work organisation is seen as a form of 'customer oriented bureaucracy' (Korczynski 2002).

Encounters or relationships

Gutek (1995) has highlighted the role of the customer in helping to shape the way that service work is organised and managed. She argues that organisations can choose to structure interactions with customers as 'encounters' or 'relationships'. They can either seek to limit the contact between the service provider and the customer to an impersonal encounter where transactions are completed in the shortest duration possible, or they can seek to develop a relationship between the service provider and recipient where personalised knowledge of the customer is emphasised and future interactions are expected. Where the service is dispensed as an encounter, the organisation's objective will be to maximise operational efficiency and the number of transactions handled. Where the service is structured as a relationship, the organisation's objective will be to maximise the repeat business of the customer by delivering a service tailored to the recipient's special needs. As Batt and Moynihan (2004:30) note, 'The longer a client stays with one provider, the more difficult it is to shift to another provider not only because of personal relations of trust, but because of the wide variety and complexity of services that are provided'.

These different forms of interaction tend to be associated with differing work regimes. Encounters call for little employee discretion and draw heavily on standardised and codified procedures, while relationships emphasise interpersonal skills and worker expertise in dealing with idiosyncratic information and situation-specific needs. With organisations increasingly seeking to cut the costs of customer services, there have been strong pressures to make interactions less time-consuming and more standardised. However, Gutek (1995) believes that encounters have a number of major weaknesses as a means of servicing customers. Firstly, individual service providers do not have an incentive to deliver a high quality service as they are unlikely to have contact with the same customer in the future. Secondly, encounters do not encourage the customer to be polite or civil and service providers may experience rude and abusive behaviour. Thirdly, in encounters, problems and mistakes can be more difficult for the customer to report and have rectified. Consequently, Gutek (1995: 68) reports that many organisations have encouraged their front-line service staff to 'make each encounter as relationship-like as possible' and to manufacture intimacy as a way of personalising the service. She has called this form of interaction a 'pseudo-relationship'. At Asda, one of Britain's largest supermarket chains, employees are asked to provide 'real' smiles to customers, 'Asda has mystery shoppers measuring . . . [store] warmth. They check on the friendliness of the staff, eye contact, use of the customer's name at checkout, even smiles ...What Asda is trying to achieve in its company culture requires employees' emotional investment' (*The Observer* 11 July 2004).

Emotional labour

Service work is characterised by interactional uncertainties. The use of emotional labour to service customers is emphasised in the recruitment, training and performance monitoring in organisations and is achieved by the company stipulating certain policies or self-monitoring 'rules' that employees need to follow during interactions. These rules have been designed to ensure that workers act and behave in ways that are consistent with the organisation's customer service objectives. Irrespective of how the worker may feel towards the customer, he or she is expected to follow the company's instructions for the performance of emotional labour. According to Wharton (1996:92), the critical task for these workers 'is to display publicly an emotion that they may not feel privately'. This can take the form of an employee refraining from responding to abusive customers in a call centre or to a flight attendant maintaining a constant smile while serving passengers (Hochschild 1983). When organisations require employees to display emotions publicly that they may not feel privately, it can lead to what has been called 'emotive dissonance' (Hochschild 1983: 90).

In order to adhere to the organisation's display rules during customer interaction, service employees may voluntarily, or at management's suggestion, engage in two types of coping behaviours: surface acting or deep acting (Hochschild 1983). Surface acting involves the modification of outward expressions without transforming inner feelings. For example, when faced with an irate customer the service employee may 'fake' sympathy while secretly feeling annoyed and resentful. Deep acting involves employee attempts to transform their inner state of mind such that they adhere to the emotional display rules set by the organisation. For instance, the service employee may try to empathise with the customer and see the predicament 'through the customer's eyes'. Surface acting has been found to be more emotionally exhausting than deep acting, creating greater emotive dissonance (Chau *et al.* 2009), generating negative moods and lowering job satisfaction (Judge *et al.* 2009).

Some services may entail repeated interactions between the service recipient and provider. The frequent contact between staff and the customer provides an opportunity for the development of a relationship. In healthcare, Theodosius (2008) provides examples of how nurses come to internalise the emotional feeling rules of the profession and deep act by empathising with the suffering and vulnerability of their patients. As explained by Korczynski (2009), 'caring work' that emphasises relationship building and greater customer dependency might lower employee feelings of job alienation. In her research on hairdressers, Cohen (2010), however, reveals that deep acting can also be emotionally problematic and reach a 'breaking point' if the emotional 'favours' that employees give to customers are not reciprocated or go unacknowledged.

Aesthetic labour

The commodification of an employee's projected demeanour can extend to how they 'look' and 'sound' in the presence of customers. Obtaining the 'right' appearance from employees involves careful recruitment and selection. Companies can stipulate, encourage and indeed train front-line workers to reflect an appropriate image to customers through their make-up, clothes, hairstyle and physique. These aesthetic standards also form part of the performance appraisals in many organisations (Hall and van den Broek 2011). An example of such 'lookism' is described in Box 6.1. Aesthetic rules allow a firm to stamp its employees with an image that is consistent with its corporate brand. As Warhurst *et al.* (2000) point out, the hospitality and retail sector is particularly disposed towards capitalising on workers' looks. In the UK retail sector, Nickson *et al.* (2011) suggest that a large proportion of employers seek recruits with the 'right appearance', often seen as a pivotal factor in determining employment. Wijesinghe and Wills (2010: 156–157) report the experience of a trainee hotel receptionist:

> Part of our induction into the job at the Goldmark [hotel] involved learning its style in personal grooming in order to ensure our image met the requirements of the corporate hospitality image of feminised attractive receptionist . . . we wore pink uniforms, which made us look very feminine and docile. We were expected to look attractive at all times; we were often sent back to the locker rooms to put on make-up if we came plain-faced or if we wore a lipstick colour that our manager thought was too bold or too pale; we were reprimanded if we wore flat shoes or didn't wear stockings.

Additionally, in certain organisational settings, aesthetic labour can manifest itself in 'sexualised labour'. Warhurst and Nickson (2009: 386) suggest that, 'in prescribing the looks of employees, some organisations then further refine their desired corporate image to include the mobilisation, development and commodification of employee sex appeal'. The marketing strategies of airlines such as Virgin Blue and Air Asia are also understood to sexually appeal to customer senses through their

---

Box 6.1 A look at Abercrombie & Fitch

Abercrombie & Fitch (A&F) describes itself as an all-American lifestyle clothing company and is well known for its 'look policy'. Although A&F's London store frontage does not display any company insignia, shoppers manage to locate the club-like outlet by the unmistakable branding of its employees (Pettinger 2004). The 'attractive' staff recruited under the job description of 'models' greet customers at the entrance and offer shoppers the opportunity of being photographed alongside them. The interiors provide other compelling facets of a distinctive shopping experience. Dark walls, dim lights and an infusion of heady perfumes contribute to a nightclub atmosphere, with staff strategically placed on the balconies, dancing to the latest music.

Front-line employees at A&F have to meet exacting grooming standards. According to the BBC (26 June 2009), the typical 'look' for female employees includes being 'attractive', sporting long hair, having a slender figure, and wearing close-fitting denims. The production of such a service design is maintained through careful recruitment practices for both sexes, in addition to a policy of 'style policing' by the organisation. These aesthetic labour guidelines have, however, come into the firing line. A&F's appearance policy has been subject to a number of controversies and lawsuits, including allegations of racial and disability discrimination and unfair dismissal.

---

advertising slogans with subtle (and sometimes not so subtle) innuendos involving the aesthetic appeal of their in-flight employees (Spiess and Waring 2005).

Other features of a person's identity such as their linguistic mannerisms are also amenable to aestheticisation. To cater for customers in the West, offshored call centre employees in India are provided with accent training to encourage them to 'neutralise' their native speech patterns or to adopt a British or American accent (Taylor and Bain 2005). Such aestheticisation of one's identity can be reinforced though an employee's 'cultural cache' – their ability to engage with the customer on a cultural level (Baum 2007: 1393). Significantly, employees can find aesthetic performances stressful. The tight monitoring of 'vocal aesthetics' in offshored Indian call centres, for instance, can intensify language insecurities and self-consciousness and limit the ability of employees to 'be themselves' during interactions (Nath 2011). In many instances, however, an organisation's subjective evaluation of what signifies 'aesthetic' labour could mean that a number of potential workers are denied employment opportunities based on their gender, age, race and social class (Williams and Connell 2010).

Forms of Management Control and HR Practice

There will be limitations on the ability of firms to standardise the behaviour of the customer and completely routinise the work of the service provider. Rigid control of the labour process can result in job dissatisfaction and employee withdrawal. The way employees are treated will affect the quality of the service that is provided. Positive displays of emotion by employees can create favourable impressions in customers' minds while negative behaviours can create unfavourable impressions. This has been called 'emotional contagion' (Ashkanasy and Daus 2002). A major problem for management therefore is 'how to direct, control and monitor customer service interactions without disrupting them' (Macdonald and Sirianni 1996: 6). Work regimes that are too tightly specified or are too intrusive run the risk of jeopardising the quality of the service.

Therefore, combinations of control and commitment strategies are most likely to be used in service work. Quite invasive methods of overseeing and controlling customer service interactions can be mixed with teamwork for peer support and problem solving. In call centres, for example, Kinnie *et al.* (2000: 967) observed that high-commitment management practices as well as team competitions and games were often used 'to offset some of the worst features of call centre working'. They referred to this combination as 'fun and surveillance'. In their research on call centres, Fleming and Sturdy (2011), however, contended that management's discourse and encouragement of 'fun' can be seen as a method of 'distracting' workers from the more coercive forms of employee surveillance and job monotony. They found that employees were given opportunities for self-expression mainly '*around* the work' (p. 190) rather than *in* their work tasks, and therefore such diversions failed to truly empower staff.

Most companies have also sought to instil values of good customer service in their staff through normative control strategies. This may be seen as an attempt to change workers' personalities and their underlying feelings and values with the purpose of developing an internalised commitment to quality service. Thompson *et al.* (2001) point to the importance of recruitment in this process of control, with firms focusing on personality traits and service-orientated attitudes. In their research on interactive service work in the banking industry, they found that recruitment was strongly orientated towards the selection of people with certain desired social skills and attitudes rather than a particularly strong knowledge of banking. Confidence, con-centration, communication skills, energy and enthusiasm were judged as highly important competencies. Leidner (1996: 46), however, believes that it is difficult to make a distinction between skills and attitudes in interactive service work because 'the willingness and capacity of workers to manipulate and project their attitudes in the organisation's interests are central to their competence on the job'.

Thompson *et al.* (2001: 936) have also observed that companies not only seek to 'recruit attitude' but also 'shape it'. 'Trainees are encouraged to make the necessary changes to their 'state of mind', and told that sufficient concentration will improve sincerity and that by consciously working on levels of enthusiasm they can 'change themselves''. Korczynski *et al.* (2000: 676) have also noted that induction and training are used to promote self-control through an identification with customers – an active 'self-as-customer orientation'. Furthermore, they show how this form of normative control can be used as a means of obtaining acceptance of management's performance measurement and monitoring procedures.

Different forms of management control can be used simultaneously. 'Customer control' or 'management by customers' has been identified as an important means through which worker behaviour can be directed (Fuller and Smith 1996). Most service firms solicit customer feedback through telephone or internet surveys, comment cards or through the use of 'mystery shoppers' – individuals employed by management to act anonymously as clients, guests or passengers. While pretending to be customers, these 'shoppers' monitor and report on front-line staff as well as on service quality.

The information that is collected from customers on their perceptions of service providers can have quite a significant effect on the employment prospects of those workers. For example, Fuller and Smith (1996: 80) reported one manager as saying that 'the customer survey is important for monitoring workers because, 'It's like a report card on individual employees''. Data gathered on employees from customers' observations can be used in performance reviews as well as disciplinary action and placed in individuals' personnel files. Fuller and Smith (1996: 84–5) claim that the implications of these customer feedback techniques are that interactive service workers gain an 'additional boss': 'feedback from customers strengthens employers' hold over the workplace by providing them with an additional source of data they can use for control, evaluation and discipline'. In interactive service work, therefore, a range of control methods ranging from simple control by managers through to normative techniques and customer feedback can be used to direct the labour process and effect service delivery.

Service Work and Employee Well-being

The performance of emotional labour can have negative consequences for workers. Where front-line staff are expected to smile regularly and be friendly and enthusiastic in all their service interactions, it can affect their psychological well-being. Some employees find it difficult to contain their true feelings or emotions when serving customers. Tensions between the employees' inner feelings and the requirements of outward display can cause stress and burnout. Aesthetic labour also demands effort. The pressure of keeping up appearances can take a mental toll and the requirement to sustain aesthetic displays can produce personal insecurities and stress reactions that need to be concealed and managed during service encounters. In such instances, the demands of aesthetic labour can manifest in the experience of emotional labour during service interactions as employees cope with the negative emotions generated from the anxiety of 'keeping up appearances' (Nath 2011). Moreover, employees can find it difficult to achieve the visual and vocal standards set by their organisation, possibly posing a risk to their job performance and continued employability.

However, not all front-line service workers suffer negative effects from emotional and aesthetic labour. Service work can also provide pleasure and stimulation and a high degree of job satisfaction (Frenkel *et al.* 1998; Korczynski 2002). This may be due to the personality and disposition of the employee, the nature of the job or because of the HRM practices in the workplace.

HR policies and worker well-being

There is a considerable body of research to indicate that certain types of work practices and HRM policies can affect the psychological consequences of emotional labour. One of the most important would appear to be the degree of autonomy and control that interactive service workers have over their job. This is particularly salient in relation to the opportunities that employees have for self-direction in conducting their interactions with customers. In her study of banking and healthcare workers in the USA, Wharton (1993) found that workers who experienced greater job autonomy and opportunities for self-monitoring were significantly less likely to suffer from emotional exhaustion and job burnout. Johnson and Spector (2007) similarly found that greater job autonomy helped minimise the negative effects of deep and surface acting in jobs with high emotional labour requirements.

This issue also lies at the heart of the problems encountered by call centre workers where employees are invariably limited in their opportunities for self-direction and their ability to exercise control over their interactions with customers. Deery *et al.* (2002) observed that call centre workers who did not like following a conversational script were more likely to feel emotionally exhausted. There was clear evidence to indicate that the adoption of HRM policies that would have allowed employees to depart from the script and interact more naturally with their customers would have reduced anxieties associated with the work. This is consistent with other research findings. Jenkins *et al.* (2010) found that call centre staff who were allowed to exercise discretion in interacting with customers displayed a greater sense of positive self-identity and higher job satisfaction.

In his study of worker well-being in three call centres in the UK, Holman (2004) also identified that workers who exercised greater control over how they talked to customers were found to be less likely to suffer from anxiety at work. Furthermore, where customer service representatives were engaged in a wider variety of tasks, they enjoyed their jobs more. He additionally suggested that monitoring could indeed lower work performance as 'higher levels of anxiety brought about by excessive monitoring may cause people to devote their cognitive resources to dealing with this anxiety rather than focus on providing a quality customer service' (p. 238).

Surveillance technology imposed by management to monitor employees in the 'care' sector can also be in conflict with the service philosophy of the profession. In local government services for home care in the UK, Brown and Korczynski (2010) found that the introduction of real-time work scheduling, monitoring and tracking technology for care workers was experienced as highly intrusive. Carers felt that the IT systems de-personalised their relationships with clients and compromised the time they devoted to delivering 'meaningful care' (p. 425).

High workloads also affect worker well-being. Burnout is more likely to occur in jobs with sustained customer contact and where staff have fewer opportunities to vary the nature of their displayed feelings. Higher levels of interpersonal contact have consistently been linked to emotional exhaustion (Cordes and Dougherty 1993; Lee and Ashforth 1996). This has been identified as a common phenomenon in the caring professions and in customer service occupations where the strain of frequent and often intense contact with people can result in anxiety and frustration and feelings of being emotionally drained (Cordes and Dougherty 1993). In their call centre research, Deery et al. (2002) identified high workload as the most important determinant of emotional exhaustion. It was noteworthy that they also found that those employees who spent longer with customers on each call experienced significantly lower levels of emotional exhaustion. In these circumstances, service providers had greater opportunities to build a rapport with customers, thereby making the interaction more rewarding.

It has been suggested that certain personality types are also more likely to fit the requirements of customer service work and therefore personnel selection policies can play a role in the job satisfaction of interactive service workers. Service sector employers are found to be particularly sensitive of the need to select staff for high-contact service roles who have strong interpersonal and 'people' skills (Wharton 1996: 103). Outgoing or extrovert individuals are said to be better suited to this form of work because of their more sociable personalities (Rafaeli and Sutton 1987). Field research into call centres indicates that managers do seek to employ more outgoing or sociable employees who enjoy interacting with others (Kinnie et al. 2000).

Customers and worker well-being

Invariably, front-line staff are discouraged from arguing with customers and are expected to maintain a polite and calm demeanour in all circumstances. However, customers can be abusive and their demands may be unreasonable. For some employees, customer complaints are a regular part of their work experience, while verbal abuse is cited as the most common form of customer hostility (Yagil 2008). This has become even more apparent over recent years with rising customer expectations about service quality, often being primed by the organisations themselves. Bolton and Houlihan (2005) argue that as customers themselves can often fall into the 'victim' category through services promised but not delivered, it is likely that they will therefore vent their anger and frustration at front-line staff. It has also been suggested that customers are able to discern the difference between genuine and 'feigned quality service' (Taylor 1998: 87). Customer dissatisfaction with the service provision can increase if they perceive employees as displaying inauthentic emotions (Grandey *et al.* 2005). 'Manufactured' aesthetics can also exasperate service recipients. Customer ire can then be directed towards front-line staff, thereby exacerbating the demands of emotional labour on employees (Nath 2011).

In order to protect themselves from abuse and mistreatment, employees are often encouraged to emotionally detach themselves from hostile or difficult customers (Frenkel *et al.* 1998). However, this can be a difficult process for individual staff in the absence of institutionally sanctioned policies such as 'time out' to recover from customer abuse. Ill treatment from customers can result in depersonalised relationships, diminished self-esteem and higher turnover. Employees may also experience sustained mistreatment or bullying from regular customers, which can translate into anxiety and depression (Bishop and Hoel 2008). Worker performance can be adversely affected by episodes of customer incivility (Sliter *et al.* 2012), thereby threatening their continued employability. Studies in the UK National Health Service reveal that verbal abuse and harassment by patients and their relatives is a major cause of absenteeism amongst front-line nursing staff (Oakley *et al.* 2003). Deery *et al.* (2011) also found that nurses who faced harassment from patients and their relatives reported greater job burnout and higher quit intentions.

Macdonald and Sirianni (1996) have argued that there is an asymmetry in the exchange of respect between customers or patients and front-line service workers. They assert that, 'the idiom of servant and master is alive and well in many kinds of service workplaces'. They cite the case of clerical workers at Harvard University who were counselled to be passive and servile in the face of aggressive student behaviour, 'think of yourself as a trash can. Take everyone's little bits of anger all day, put it inside you, and at the end of the day, just pour it in the dumpster on your way out the door' (p.17). Korczynski and Bishop (2008) reveal how management may even systematically blame employees' lack of skills for inciting abusive and violent customer behaviour. Organisations might additionally attempt to 'bury' customer incivility through denial and customers may therefore never be held accountable for their words or actions (Yagil 2008).

Job satisfaction

The discussion of emotional labour and worker well-being so far has tended to concentrate on the negative aspects of interactive service work. It has also been suggested that aesthetic labour can have harmful effects on a worker's self-image. However, as stated earlier, service employees can receive great pleasure from their work. It can also be argued that the rewards of emotional labour have been understated relative to other types of work (Korczynski 2002). Holman's (2004) research indicated that call centre workers obtained greater job satisfaction than shop floor manufacturing workers. Moreover, they reported less anxiety and depression. He asserted:

> The findings from this study go some way to challenging the stereotyped image of all call centres as 'electronic sweatshops' or 'human battery farms'. Call centre work compares favourably to shop floor manufacturing work and clerical work with regard to well-being. Indeed, at two call centres, the level of well-being was equivalent to, and in many cases better than, these forms of work (Holman 2004: 239–40).

Cross-national studies of interactive service workers conducted by Frenkel *et al.* (1999) also suggest quite high levels of overall job satisfaction. Wharton (1996) believes that this may be because the work can provide important rewards that are not available in other types of jobs. There is evidence to indicate that service workers derive their greatest pleasure from 'helping people' and 'assisting others' (Frenkel *et al.*1999). Employees might find personal use-value in giving their emotions philanthropically to customers as 'gifts' (Bolton and Boyd 2003). In his study of US nursing homes, Lopez (2006) found that staff who were allowed emotional discretion in dealing with residents voluntarily engaged in compassionate care-giving and assistance.

In some caring occupations such as nursing, job satisfaction is closely associated with the attachment felt towards patients (Lewis 2005). Korczynski (2002: 99) reports the case of one nurse who stated, 'I just love the close contact with the patient. I love the chance to . . . be involved in their lives'. Research suggests that if front-line service workers are encouraged by management to use their full array of skills and abilities to meet customer needs they will obtain greater job satisfaction (Deery *et al.* 2004). In her study of retail work, Godwyn (2006) found that when an organisation permitted staff to develop and implement creative sales ideas, it resulted in employees' experiencing a sense of pride and greater job satisfaction.

Workers can similarly derive pleasure from jobs that require aesthetic labour. In the high-end retail sector, for instance, it is suggested that employees can feel privileged by being associated with a particular corporate image. Staff who identify with a company's brand may view themselves as ambassadors of a particular lifestyle or simply welcome being employed by a 'cool' organisation (Williams and Connell 2010: 359). Additionally, some workers might perceive themselves as personally benefitting from the 'grooming' they receive as a route to upward social mobility.

Employee Resistance to Management Control

Organisational efforts to manage the emotions and identity of employees can often spark opposition and resistance. The use of control strategies to restrict and regulate role behaviour can clash with the desire of employees to preserve their sense of self-worth and the need to defend the dignity of their work (Hodson 2001). Employees can engage in a range of activities to challenge management decision-making and resist unfair treatment and unacceptable customer behaviour. Such contests, however, are often more implicit than explicit (Macdonald and Sirianni 1996). Although collective action in the form of strikes is not uncommon among interactive service workers, resistance is more likely to be covert, individual and temporary (Sturdy and Fineman 2001).

This can take a number of different forms. Rosenthal (2004), for example, shows how workers can use management's forms of normative control – the language of customer service and direct control – the performance monitoring and measurement systems to turn the tables on management and defend their rights and protect their interests. She argues that the espoused values of customer service invariably emphasise respect for employees, as well as for customers, and that the language of such programmes can supply workers with an effective means of enforcing standards of fair treatment. She also notes how normative control can be used as a collective worker resource by providing the example of a strike in British Telecom, where the workers resisted pressures to increase customer throughput by invoking the managerial language of service quality.

Service workers may confront management in other ways as well. Mulholland (2002), for example, has reported that call centre agents often challenge management's discourse about care, quality and teamwork by subjecting it to derision. She argues that 'making fun of a management style is a form of resistance' (p. 299). Front-line employees can also turn to internet blogs to vent their frustrations about management policies and practices (Richards 2008). Sturdy and Fineman (2001) believe that employees can shield themselves from the psychological costs of interactive work by limiting their full engagement with their role. This can be done by finding weaknesses in the organisation's control systems and creating free space for themselves, by ridiculing or questioning the social order or by using cynicism to create a distance between themselves and their work role.

Some forms of resistance may be less covert and less benign. An organisation's scripted conversational rules, for example, may be openly disregarded. Service staff may withhold communication, feign ignorance in dealing with customer requests or misinform customers (Fisk and Neville 2011). Call centre representatives may deliberately redirect calls to other service operators in an effort to boost their own productivity, 'mouth words' to fictional callers to confuse supervisors or just hang up on offensive customers (Knights and McCabe 1998; Mulholland 2004). They may find loopholes in the surveillance systems and engage in opportunistic 'tricks' such as bumping customers to the end of caller queues (Townsend 2005).

Employee opposition can also be organised and take a collective form. Union representation has long been an embedded feature of healthcare, banking and retailing. Moreover, the growth of call centres has been accompanied by an expansion of unionism and the use of industrial action to address issues such as the intensification of work and the abuse of monitoring systems (Bain and Taylor 2002; van den Broek 2004).

Resistance is not only directed towards management. Front-line service workers may also feel the need to establish a more balanced relationship with their customers and exercise a greater degree of control over their service interactions. Employees may conceal customer complaints from the organisation if they perceive the customer to be rude or offensive (Harris and Ogbonna 2010). They may also invoke interactional scripts and cite company 'rules' to their own advantage, adopting the organisational policies 'strictly' in order to control conversations and to avoid emotional entanglements with customers. Service employees can target customers for ridicule, which can be seen as a form of opposition to the unstated relational superiority of the customer (Darr 2011: 249).

Customer Service Work and Performance

A considerable body of HRM research suggests that certain types of work systems and employment practices are associated with better organisational performance. Work systems that provide employees with greater discretion, more information, enhanced skills and extended opportunities for teamwork, for example, have been found to enhance organisational performance (Arthur 1994; Becker and Huselid 1998; Huselid 1995). This is particularly the case when those practices are combined or bundled together into what has been called a high-involvement or high-performance work system. It has been suggested that a coherent set of HR practices is needed; firstly, to create a motivated workforce that is willing to expend discretionary effort; secondly, to provide the necessary skills to make that effort meaningful; and thirdly, to supply the workforce with the opportunity to participate in substantive workplace decisions (Appelbaum et al. 2000).

Much of the empirical evidence on the association between high-involvement work systems and organisational performance has been based on research in the manufacturing sector and on blue-collar workers. There are those, however, who have argued that the HR-performance link may be stronger in customer service settings than in manufacturing. The attitude and motivation of workers is likely to be more important in interactive service jobs because satisfaction or dissatisfaction with work can more easily spill over into customer interactions, thereby directly affecting the quality of the service and the volume of sales (Batt and Moynihan 2004; Brown and Lam 2008). Where the behaviour of the employee is said to play such a pivotal role in shaping customer perceptions, it has been argued that the empowerment of front-line workers will generate pro-social customer-oriented behaviour that can inspire customer satisfaction and loyalty (Liao and Chuang 2004).

Batt (2002) believes that high-involvement practices are important for performance because they help employees develop a detailed knowledge of the firm's products, customs and work processes that assist them to interact more effectively with customers. A more elaborate conception of the relationship between HR practices and organisational performance in interactive services has been presented in what has been termed the 'service profit chain' (Heskett et al. 1997). According to this concept of service management, HR practices that enhance the satisfaction and competence of service workers will result in greater customer satisfaction and retention and ultimately in better performance and higher profits. Indeed, research indicates that certain types of organisational and HR practices correlate strongly with customer perceptions of high quality service. These pertain, firstly, to the selection procedures of the organisation, secondly, to the management practices that are used to motivate employees, and thirdly, to the development of a 'service-orientated' climate.

HR practices and service performance

Customer perceptions of service quality can be affected by an organisation's selection procedures. There is some evidence to indicate that certain types of employees may be predisposed towards providing customers with more positive service encounters, and that by selecting applicants with those characteristics an organisation may be able to deliver better quality service. Liao and Chuang (2004) provide some support for this argument. They found that employees in a US restaurant chain who were more conscientious and more extravert reported higher service performance levels. They were found to be more friendly and helpful to customers and more responsive to their needs. It is also suggested that employees who are extravert find surface-acting strategies less stressful and are able to employ such an emotion management style more effectively when performing emotional labour (Chi *et al.* 2011).

A second factor that has been associated with customer satisfaction and service performance relates to the personnel policies and practices of the organisation. Job autonomy and high-involvement work systems, including employee participation and skills training, contribute significantly to both customer-orientated employee behaviour and organisational performance. On the basis of their findings in front-line service work in restaurants, Liao and Chuang (2004) claimed, 'Empowered employees can meet a wide range of customer demands and are able to share the information they collect about customer behaviours, thereby serving customers better and helping to improve service quality' (p. 45). In the banking sector, Aryee *et al.* (2011) demonstrated that the use of high performance work systems including self-managed teams and employee participation promoted a climate of empowerment, which was associated with both higher levels of individual service performance and branch-level market performance. Peccei and Rosenthal (2001) have also observed that job autonomy and the systematic provision of training in both service values and skills were positively associated with stronger customer-orientated behaviour among front-line retail workers. HRM policies that promote organisational justice can affect both employee behaviour and customer satisfaction. Where organisations treat their staff fairly, it can be argued that it will generate positive attitudes and behaviour, which, in turn, will affect customers' reactions (Masterson 2001). Furthermore, HRM policies that affect worker well-being can influence performance. Singh (2000), for example, found that worker burnout was associated with the provision of lower service quality. He observed that the principal way of reducing burnout was to introduce practices that gave workers greater task control or job autonomy.

The development of a 'service-oriented' climate in an organisation is the third factor that has been associated with enhanced service quality and higher customer satisfaction and retention (Salanova *et al.* 2005; Towler *et al.* 2011). Research indicates that if organisations are able to create an overall climate that values and rewards high quality service, employees will be more likely to deliver a good service and customers will be more likely to provide higher service ratings (Schneider *et al.* 1998; 2005). In their analysis of almost 600 stores of a large US retail company, Borucki and Burke (1999) found that service climate predicted employee service performance, which, in turn, predicted store financial performance. Chuang and Liao (2010) also demonstrated the link between high performance work systems and market performance in 133 stores in Taiwan. They found that HR practices such as investment in training, workplace participation and performance feedback promoted a service climate that emphasised both a concern for customers and for employees. Such an environment resulted in staff providing superior customer services and also engaging in supportive behaviour towards their co-workers, which subsequently resulted in greater sales growth and profitability. Other research has also highlighted the importance of supervisory and co-worker support in fostering a positive service climate and providing employees with an enhanced capacity to deliver a quality service to customers (Sergeant and Frenkel 2000; Suskind *et al.* 2003).

Summary and Conclusion

A large proportion of the workforce in industrialised nations is now employed in customer service jobs (Eurostat 2008; US Bureau of Labor Statistics 2011). Many front-line service workers are involved in quite routine and standardised activities where both their emotions and their image are dictated by commercial decision-making. Others are more fortunate. Their guidelines for emotional and aesthetic labour are collegially determined and are largely self-supervised. These types of professional employees – doctors, lawyers, academics – are, however, in a minority. The majority of interactive workers are closely supervised and monitored by managers or customers. Because of the absence of any buffer between the production of the service and its consumption, most organisations have explicit interactional guidelines, attempting to limit any possible variation in the quality of service delivered to the customer.

This has often resulted in quite invasive forms of management control. Perhaps the most obvious of these have been documented in telephone call centres (Taylor and Bain 1999). In some cases, management control has been extended to nearly all areas of a worker's demeanour, self-expression and appearance (Thompson *et al.* 2001). This, of course, can stifle creativity, spontaneity and subjective judgement, which are qualities that are often needed if service providers are to satisfy the varying needs of customers. Standardised work practices can also result in boredom, job dissatisfaction, emotional exhaustion and a lack of personal accomplishment (Holman 2004). Such feelings can be transmitted to customers who may be 'infected' by the negative emotions of the service provider (Ashkanasy and Daus 2002).

Dissatisfaction can also manifest itself in high employee turnover and absenteeism. This, in turn, can impair service quality and organisational performance.

A number of writers have observed that there is always a strong temptation for service organisations to pursue cost minimisation strategies, while at the same time declaring a desire to customise services and provide employees with specialist skills and independent discretion (Kinnie *et al.* 2000). In this context, Korczynski (2002) has argued that interactive service work is often infused by two contradictory and competing logics: a need to be cost efficient and a desire to be customer-orientated. Batt and Moynihan (2004) have called this a 'mass customisation' model of service delivery where firms adopt some form of standardisation and rationalisation along with some level of attention to service quality.

Organisational efforts to direct and control the work activities of front-line service providers can often provoke resistance. Managerial language of service quality may be used to resist organisational pressures to increase customer throughput at the expense of quality (Rosenthal 2004). In other cases, workers may openly challenge or question the espoused values of the organisation and subject them to ridicule in order to create a distance between themselves and their work role. Underlying this resistance is the continuous struggle by workers to establish an appropriate level of recognition and respect from both their organisation and the customer.

Issues of recognition and respect underpin worker dignity and well-being and according to some writers provide the key to understanding why employees may be purposeful and productive or resistant and uncooperative (Hodson 2001). Research into customer service work has found that organisational practices that emphasise skill formation and employee participation in decision-making enhance motivation, effort and performance. This is most apparent when those practices are combined with high relative pay and job security as well as policies that emphasise fairness and organisational justice (Batt 2002; Masterson 2001). The creation of an internal climate of service excellence buttressed by supportive co-workers and immediate supervisors also encourages customer-orientated behaviour and is associated with higher service quality. Although services can be distinguished from manufacturing work because of the interposition of the customer in the labour process, the types of HR policies that promote both job satisfaction and organisational performance are remarkably similar in both work settings.

REFERENCES

Appelbaum, E., Bailey, T., Berg, P. and Kalleberg, A. 2000: *Manufacturing Advantage*, Ithaca NY: Cornell University Press.

Arthur, J. 1994: Effects of human resource systems on manufacturing performance and turnover, *Academy of Management Journal*, **37**(3), 670–687.

Aryee, S., Walumbwa, F. O., Seidu, E. Y. M. and Otaye, L. E. 2011: Impact of high-performance work systems on individual- and branch-level performance: Test of a multilevel model of intermediate linkages, *Journal of Applied Psychology*, published online before print.

Ashforth, B. and Humphrey, R. 1993: Emotional labor in service roles: The influence of identity, *Academy of Management Journal*, **18**(1), 88–115.

Ashkanasy, N. and Daus, C. 2002: Emotion in the workplace: The new challenge for managers, *The Academy of Management Executive*, **16**(1), 76–86.

Bain, P. and Taylor, P. 2002: Ringing the changes? Union recognition and organization in call centres in the UK finance sector, *Industrial Relations Journal*, **33**(3), 246–261.

Batt, R. 2002: Managing customer services: Human resource practices, quit rates and sales growth, *Academy of Management Journal*, **45**(3), 587–597.

Batt, R. and Moynihan, L. 2004: The viability of alternative call centre production models, in S. Deery and N. Kinnie (eds.), *Call Centres and Human Resource Management: A Cross-National Perspective*, 25–53. Houndmills: Palgrave Macmillan.

Baum, T. 2007: Human resources in tourism: Still waiting for change, *Tourism Management*, **28**(6), 1383–1399.

BBC News magazine 2009: What is the Abercrombie look?, 26 June.

Becker, B. and Huselid, M. 1998: High performance work systems and firm performance: A synthesis of research and managerial implications, *Research in Personnel and Human Resource Management*, **16**(3), 53–101.

Bishop, V. and Hoel, H. 2008: The customer is always right? Exploring the concept of customer bullying in the British Employment Service, *Journal of Consumer Culture*, **8**(3), 341–367.

Bolton, S. C. and Boyd, C. 2003: Trolley dolly or skilled emotion manager? Moving on from Hochschild's Managed Heart, *Work, Employment and Society*, **17**(2), 289–308.

Bolton, S. C. and Houlihan, M. 2005: The (mis)representation of customer service, *Work, Employment and Society*, **19**(4), 685–703.

Borucki, C. C. and Burke, M. J. 1999: An examination of service-related antecedents to retail store performance, *Journal of Organizational Behavior*, **20**(6), 943–962.

Brown, K. and Korczynski, M. 2010: When caring and surveillance technology meet, *Work and Occupation*, **37**(3), 404–432.

Brown, S. P. and Lam, S. K. 2008: A meta-analysis of relationships linking employee satisfaction to customer responses, *Journal of Retailing*, **84**(3), 243–255.

Chau, S. L., Dahling, J. J., Levy, P.E. and Diefendorff, J. M. 2009: A predictive study of emotional labor and turnover, *Journal of Organizational Behavior*, **30**(8), 1151–1163.

Chi, N.-W., Grandey, A. A., Diamond, J. A. and Krimmel, K. R. 2011: Want a tip? Service performance as a function of emotion regulation and extraversion, *Journal of Applied Psychology*, **96**(6), 1337–1346.

Chuang, C.-H. and Liao, H. 2010: Strategic human resource management in service context: Taking care of business by taking care of employees and customers, *Personnel Psychology*, **63**(1), 153–196.

Cohen, R. L. 2010: When it pays to be friendly: Employment relationships and emotional labour in hairstyling, *The Sociological Review*, **58**(2), 197–218.

Cordes, C. L. and Dougherty, T. W. 1993: A review and integration of research on job burnout, *Academy of Management Review*, **18**(4), 621–656.

Darr, A. 2011: Humour in retail work: Jokes salespeople tell about their clients, in I. Grugulis and O. Bozkurt (eds.), *Retail Work*, 235–252. Hampshire: Palgrave-Macmillan.

Deery, S., Iverson, R. and Walsh, J. 2002: Work relationships in telephone call centres: Understanding emotional exhaustion and employee withdrawal, *Journal of Management Studies*, **39**(4), 471–496.

Deery, S., Iverson, R. and Walsh, J. 2004: The effect of customer service encounters on job satisfaction and emotional exhaustion, in S. Deery and N. Kinnie (eds.), *Call Centres and Human Resource Management: A Cross-National Perspective*, 153–173. Houndmills: Palgrave-Macmillan.

Deery, S., Walsh, J. and Guest, D. 2011: Workplace aggression: The effects of harassment on job burnout and turnover intentions, *Work, Employment and Society*, **25**(4), 742–759.

Eurostat 2008: Industry trade and services: Main features of the EU-27 services sector, Report: European Commission.

Fisk, G. M. and Neville, L. B. 2011: Effects of customer entitlement on service workers' physical and psychological well-being: A study of waitstaff employees, *Journal of Occupational Health Psychology*, **16**(4), 391–405.

Fleming, P. and Sturdy, A. 2011: 'Being yourself' in the electronic sweatshop: New forms of normative control, *Human Relations*, **64**(2), 177–200.

Frenkel, S., Korczynski, M., Shire, K. and Tam, M. 1998: Beyond bureaucracy? Work organization in call centres, *International Journal of Human Resource Management*, **9**(6), 957–979.

Frenkel, S., Korczynski, M., Shire, K. and Tam, M. 1999: *On the Front-line Organization of Work in the Information Economy*, Ithaca, New York: ILR Press.

Fuller, L. and Smith, V. 1996: Consumers' reports: Management by customers in a changing economy, in C. L. Macdonald and C. Sirianni (eds.), *Working in the Service Society*, 74–90. Philadelphia: Temple University Press.

Godwyn, M. 2006: Using emotional labor to create and maintain relationships in service interactions, *Symbolic Interaction*, **29**(4), 487–506.

Grandey, A. A., Fisk, G. M., Mattila, A. S., Jansen, K. J. and Sideman, L. A. 2005: Is "service with a smile" enough? Authenticity of positive displays during service encounters, *Organizational Behavior and Human Decision Processes*, **96**(1), 38–55.

Gutek, B. 1995: *The Dynamics of Service: Reflections on the Changing Nature of the Customer/Provider Interface*, San Francisco: Jossey-Bass Publishers.

Hall, R. and van den Broek, D. 2011: Aestheticising retail workers: Orientations of aesthetic labour in Australian fashion retail, *Economic and Industrial Democracy*, published online before print.

Harris, L. C. and Ogbonna, E. 2010: Hiding customer complaints: Studying the motivations and forms of service employees' complaint concealment behaviours, *British Journal of Management*, **21**(2), 262–279.

Herzenberg, S., Alic, J. and Wial, H. 1998: *New Rules for a New Economy*, Ithaca, New York: Cornell University Press.

Heskett, J., Sasser, W. E. and Schlesinger, L. 1997: *The Service Profit Chain: How Leading Companies Link Profit and Growth to Loyalty, Satisfaction and Value*, New York: Free Press.

Hochschild, A. 1979: Emotion work, feeling rules, and social structure, *American Journal of Sociology*, **85**(3), 551–575.

Hochschild, A. 1983: *The Managed Heart: Commercialization of Human Feeling*. Berkeley: University of California Press.

Hodson, R. 2001: *Dignity at Work*, Cambridge: Cambridge University Press.

Holman, D. 2004: Employee well-being in call centres, in S. Deery and N. Kinnie (eds.), *Call Centres and Human Resource Management: A Cross-national Perspective*, 223–244. Houndmills: Palgrave-Macmillan.

Huselid, M. 1995: The impact of Human Resource Management practices on turnover, productivity and corporate financial performance, *Academy of Management Journal*, **38**(3), 635–672.

Jenkins, S., Delbridge, R. and Roberts, A. 2010: Emotional management in a mass customised call centre: Examining skill and knowledgeability in interactive service work, *Work, Employment and Society*, **24**(3), 546–564.

Johnson, H.-A. M. and Spector, P. E. 2007: Service with a smile: Do emotional intelligence, gender and autonomy moderate the emotional labor process?, *Journal of Occupational Health Psychology*, **12**(4), 319–333.

Judge, T. A., Woolf, E. F. and Hurst, C. 2009: Is emotional labor more difficult for some than for others? A multilevel, experience sampling study, *Personnel Psychology*, **62**(1), 57–88.

Kinnie, N.J., Purcell, J. and Hutchinson, S. 2000: 'Fun and surveillance': The paradox of high commitment management in call centres, *International Journal of Human Resource Management*, **11**(5), 967–985.

Knights, D. and McCabe, D. 1998: What happens when the phones go wild? Staff, stress and spaces for escape in a BPR telephone banking work regime, *Journal of Management Studies*, **35**(2), 163–194.

Korczynski, M. 2002: *Human Resource Management in Service Work*, Basingstoke: Palgrave

Korczynski, M. 2009: The mystery customer: Continuing absences in the sociology of service work, *Sociology*, **43**(5), 952–967.

Korczynski, M. and Bishop, V. 2008: 'The Job Center: Abuse, violence and fear on the front-line: Implications of the rise of the enchanting myth of customer sovereignty, in S. Fineman (ed), *Emotions in Organisations: Critical Voices*, 74–87. Oxford: Blackwell.

Korczynski, M. and Macdonald, C. L. 2009: Critical perspectives on service work: An introduction, in M. Korczynski and C.L. MacDonald (eds.), *Service work: critical perspectives*,1–10. New York: Routledge.

Korczynski, M., Shire, K., Frenkel, S. and Tam, M. 2000: Service work in customer capitalism: customers, control and contradictions, *Work, Employment and Society*, **14**(4), 669–688.

Lee, R. T. and Ashforth, B. E. 1996: A meta-analytic examination of the correlates of the three dimensions of job burnout, *Journal of Applied Psychology*, **81**(2), 123–133.

Leidner, R. 1996: Rethinking questions of control: Lessons from McDonald's, in C.L. MacDonald and C. Sirianni (eds.), *Working in the Service Society*, 29–49. Philadelphia: Temple University Press.

Lewis, P. 2005: Suppression or expression: an exploration of emotion management in a special care baby unit, *Work, Employment and Society*, **19**(3), 565–581.

Liao, H. and Chuang, A. 2004: A multilevel investigation of factors influencing employee service performance and customer outcomes, *Academy of Management Journal*, **47**(1), 41–58.

Lopez, S. H. 2006: Emotional labor and organized emotional care: Conceptualizing nursing home care work, *Work and Occupations*, **33**(2), 133–160.

MacDonald, C.L. and Sirianni, C. (eds.) 1996: *Working in the Service Society*, Philadelphia: Temple University Press.

Masterson, S. S. 2001: A trickle-down model of organizational justice: Relating employees' and customers' perceptions of and reactions to fairness, *Journal of Applied Psychology*, **86**(4), 594–604.

Morris, J. and Feldman, D. 1997: Managing emotions in the workplace, *Journal of Managerial Issues*, **9**(3), 257–274.

Mulholland, K. 2002: Gender, emotional labour and teamworking in a call centre, *Personnel Review*, **31**(3), 283–303.

Mulholland, K. 2004: Workplace resistance in an Irish call centre: Slammin', scammin', smokin' an' leavin', *Work, Employment and Society*, **18**(4), 709–724.

Nath, V. 2011: Aesthetic and emotional labour through stigma: National identity management and racial abuse in offshored Indian call centres, *Work, Employment and Society*, **25**(4), 709–725.

Nickson, D., Warhurst, C., Commander, J., Hurrell, S. A. and Cullen, A-M. 2011: Soft skills and employability: Evidence from UK retail, *Economic and Industrial Democracy*, Published ahead of print.

Oakley, P., Guest, D. and Deery, S. 2003: Developing core practice standards to retain staff in three London Trusts, King's College London, mimeo.

Observer. 2004: Where it Asda be a real smile, 11 July.

Peccei, R. and Rosenthal, P. 2001: Delivering customer-oriented behaviour through empowerment: An empirical test of HRM assumptions, *Journal of Management Studies*, **38**(6), 831–857.

Pettinger, L. 2004: Brand culture and branded workers: service work and aesthetic labour in fashion retail, *Consumption Markets and Culture*, **7**(2), 165–184.

Rafaeli, A. and Sutton, R. 1987: Expression of emotion as part of the work role, *Academy of Management Review*, **12**(1), 23–37.

Richards, J. 2008: 'Because I need somewhere to vent': The expression of conflict through work blogs, *New Technology, Work and Employment*, **23**(1–2), 95–110.

Ritzer, G. 2004: *The McDonaldization of Society*, London: Sage.

Rosenthal, P. 2004: Management control as an employee resource: The case of front-line service workers, *Journal of Management Studies*, **41**(4), 601–622.

Salanova, M., Agut, S. and José María, P. 2005: Linking organizational resources and work engagement to employee performance and customer loyalty: The mediation of service climate, *Journal of Applied Psychology*, **90**(6), 1217–1227.

Schneider, B., White, S. and Paul, M. 1998: Linking service climate and customer perceptions of service quality: Test of a causal model, *Journal of Applied Psychology*, **83**(2), 150–163.

Schneider, B., Ehrhart, M. G., Mayer, D. M., Saltz, J. L. and Niles-Jolly, K. 2005: Understanding organization-customer links in service settings, *The Academy of Management Journal*, **48**(6), 1017–1032.

Sergeant, A. and Frenkel, S. 2000: When do customer contact employees satisfy customers?, *Journal of Service Research*, **3**(1), 18–34.

Singh, J. 2000: Performance, productivity and quality of frontline employees in service organizations, *Journal of Marketing*, **64**(2), 15–34.

Sliter, M., Sliter, K. and Jex, S. 2012: The employee as a punching bag: the effect of multiple sources of incivility on employee withdrawal behavior and sales performance, *Journal of Organizational Behavior*, **33**(1), 121–139.

Spiess, L. and Waring, P. 2005: Aesthetic labour, cost minimisation and the labour process in the Asia Pacific airline industry, *Employee Relations*, **27**(2), 193–207.

Sturdy, A. and Fineman, S. 2001: Struggles for the control of affect – resistance as politics and emotion, in A. Sturdy, I. Grugulis, and H. Willmott (eds.), *Customer Service*, Basingstoke: Palgrave.

Suskind, A. M., Kacmar, K. M. and Borchgrevink, C. P. 2003: Customer service providers' attitudes relating to customer service and customer satisfaction in the customer-server exchange, *Journal of Applied Psychology*, **88**(1), 179–187.

Taylor, P. and Bain, P. 1999: An 'assembly line in the head': The call centre labour process, *Industrial Relations Journal*, **30**(2), 101–117.

Taylor, P. and Bain, P. 2005: India calling to the far away towns: the call centre labour process and globalization, *Work, Employment and Society*, **19**(2), 261–282.

Taylor, S. 1998: Emotional labour and the new workplace, in P. Thompson and C. Warhurst (eds.), *Workplaces of the Future*, London: Macmillan.

Theodosius, C. 2008: *Emotional Labour in Health Care*, Oxon: Routledge.

Thompson, P., Warhurst, C. and Callaghan, G. 2001: Ignorant theory and knowledgeable workers: interrogating the connection between knowledge, skills and services, *Journal of Management Studies*, **38**(7), 923–942.

Towler, A., Lezotte, D. V. and Burke, M. 2011: The service climate-firm performance chain: The role of customer retention, *Human Resource Management*, **50**(3), 391–406.

Townsend, K. 2005: Electronic surveillance and cohesive teams: Room for resistance in an Australian call centre?, *New Technology, Work and Employment*, **20**(1), 47–59.

US Bureau of Labor Statistics 2011: Occupational Employment Statistics, Report: United States Department of Labor.

van den Broek, D. 2004: Call to arms? Collective and individual responses to call centre labour management, in S. Deery and N. Kinnie (eds.), *Call Centres and Human Resource Management: A Cross-national Perspective*, 267–284. Houndmills: Palgrave Macmillan.

Warhurst, C. and Nickson, D. 2009: 'Who's got the look?' Emotional, aesthetic and sexualized labour in interactive services, *Gender, Work and Organization*, **16**(3), 385–404.

Warhurst, C., Nickson, D., Witz, A. and Marie Cullen, A. 2000: Aesthetic labour in interactive service work: Some case study evidence from the 'New' Glasgow, *The Service Industries Journal*, **20**(3), 1–18.

Wharton, A. 1993: The affective consequences of service work, *Work and Occupations*, **20**(2), 205–232.

Wharton, A. 1996: Service with a smile: Understanding the consequences of emotional labor, in C. L. Macdonald and C. Sirianni (eds.), *Working in the Service Society*, 91–112. Philadelphia: Temple University Press.

Wijesinghe, G. and Wills, P. 2010: Receiving and shaping the tourist appraising gaze: The lived experience of reception work in the tourism and hospitality industry, in P.M. Burns, C. Palmer and J.-A. Lester (eds.), *Tourism and Visual Culture: Volume 1 Theories and Concepts*, 150–164. Cambridge: CAB International.

Williams, C. L. and Connell, C. 2010: "Looking good and sounding right": Aesthetic labor and social inequality in the retail industry, *Work and Occupations*, **37**(3), 349–377.

Witz, A., Warhurst, C. and Nickson, D. 2003: The labour of aesthetics and the aesthetics of organization, *Organization*, **10**(1), 33–54.

Yagil, D. 2008: When the customer is wrong: A review of research on aggression and sexual harassment in service encounters, *Aggression and Violent Behavior*, **13**(2), 141–152.

PART III

Resourcing and Development

CHAPTER SEVEN

Recruitment and Selection

Jane Bryson, Susan James and Ewart Keep

Introduction

Recruitment and selection (R&S) often appears as one of the 'Cinderella' aspects of Human Resource Management (HRM) policy and practice, valuable as a hygiene factor, but not up there with the really important or trendy issues like 'talent management', mentoring/coaching, performance management, reward system design or aligning HR with the organisation's strategic goals and capabilities. Much of the practitioner-oriented literature reinforces this view, with an often highly technocratic, how-to-do-it approach at its core.

This chapter suggests this perception may be partly misplaced. R&S is, we argue, a key focal point where HR prescriptions clash with reality, and where traditional best practice models meet with challenges from a range of sources. These tensions have major implications for HR practitioners and the organisations employing them. Moreover, a range of power relationships are mediated through R&S, consequently some of the most important points of contention arise between what organisations want and tend to do, and what public policy would like them to do. For example, issues such as employment discrimination and disadvantage, social mobility and social justice often revolve to a considerable extent around R&S practices and the outcomes they do and do not generate.

Drawing on three main bodies of research – HRM, labour economics and work psychology – this chapter outlines what we know about recruitment and selection, specifically in the UK, but with some reference to other Anglo-Saxon countries. It identifies areas of R&S policy and practice about which research can currently tell us relatively little. In exploring these topics through disciplinary perspectives and bodies of theory and research that go beyond the mainstream literature, we conclude with a discussion on the wider implications for R&S and HRM strategy and practice.

The Textbook Model and Disciplinary Perspectives

There is an extensive literature on R&S, predominantly in work psychology and human resource management (HRM). Within this, R&S are terms that refer to two different sets of activity. Recruitment is the process of defining a role to be filled and the type of person to fill it, developing an attraction strategy which will yield good numbers of applicants appropriately qualified for the role, and the initial screening of applicants to proceed to the selection process (Cascio 2006; Searle 2003). Some would claim recruitment also encompasses the selection process and induction of the new employee (Wood and Payne 1998).

Selection is then the process of assessing applicant suitability for the job or the organisation through the use of various selection methods (Guion 1998; Wood and Payne 1998). Selection research has become almost solely the preserve of work psychology and HRM.

The textbook model

The textbook model is heavily normative, is focused on the micro practices of 'how' to conduct R&S and aimed at what proponents term, the 'scientist practitioner' (Latham 2007). The underlying assumptions are of rationality, objectivity, measurability, validity and meritocracy, underpinned by procedural rigour. The implication is that R&S is, or least can be, a scientific and objective process in which there is a single, readily identifiable best outcome. The standard HRM textbook model of R&S (in times past, often linked to 'manpower planning' or human resource planning – see Hendry 1995), is based upon a sequence of stages or processes that revolve around:

1. Defining the job or role to be filled;
2. Attracting applicants;
3. Managing the application, sifting and selection process; and
4. Making an appointment.

This cycle illustrates one of the key theoretical underpinnings of the standard R&S model, which is the concept of person–environment fit (Anderson *et al.* 2004; van Vianen 2005). Traditionally the predictivist or objective psychometric approach to selection has assumed relative stability of the job role. In this scenario, seeking and achieving person–job fit lends itself to measurement and validation. As will be explored below, this notion of the 'best' person for the job is a major source of tension and difficulty.

Textbook approaches to the first stage of the cycle, job analysis and definition, offer an extensive range of well-debated techniques from task analysis through to competency modelling. These produce job descriptions and person specifications leading to selection criteria. From the textbook perspective, not accurately knowing the nature of the job seriously undermines the ability to select appropriately for it; therefore, this stage is important, but as we will see, in practice it is often ignored or subverted.

In the second stage the textbook approach promotes a neutral, unbiased attraction phase. In practice, however, this phase has always featured the use of potentially biased social networks, whether by low-tech 'who you know' connections or high-tech social media. Moreover, attracting applicants has changed significantly in the last decade with the entrance to HRM of both marketing and communication technology, particularly online technology. For instance: corporate websites to inform and capture potential employees; social media such as Facebook and LinkedIn to create and maintain linkages; job boards to target a global or a specialist labour market (CIPD 2011; Parry and Wilson 2009). Use of external recruitment agencies is also popular, particularly in the private sector (CIPD 2011).

The third stage of managing applications, sifting and selecting has also been impacted by technology. Online application systems automatically manage acknowledgement of submission and communication with candidates. Increasingly, they also perform initial sifting of applicants through entry progression/elimination questions, psychometric testing or work simulations (Anders 2011). Applicants are then screened against key selection criteria in order to reduce numbers and to decide who proceeds to the next step. This process may involve screening CVs or brief telephone interviews. A smaller number of applicants then progress to further selection methods such as interviews, tests, assessment centres, etc. (see Table 7.2 later in this chapter for a list of methods currently in use). The textbook representation of selection is dominated by assumptions of various methods predicting job performance or person-organisation fit. It is this selection phase that receives the greatest attention in textbook approaches.

In contrast, the fourth stage, making an appointment, is presented as a natural outcome of the rigorous selection process and thus is not always well discussed. The textbook approach presents all four stages as a logical flow of job definition to establish selection criteria, a perfectly targeted attraction strategy, and a set of formal selection methods to measure and predict the best person for the job.

Policies and practices that do not conform to this model are seen as more likely to lead to discrimination (Jewson and Mason 1986; Fevre 1989) and to produce a poorer fit between candidate and job, and are often labelled 'informal'. As will be explored below, despite this belief, it is not always clear that informal methods are *a priori* inherently liable to lead to any less effective outcomes and decisions, at least from the firm's point of view. Furthermore, this approach is, in part, founded upon and at the same time a promoter of an industry whose products include the design and management of assessment centres; the design, administration and interpretation of psychometric tests; and headhunting and recruitment agency services. The technocratic vision that this industry has spawned is best exemplified by Farr and Tippins (2010) blockbuster *Handbook of Employee Selection*, which runs to 1,032 pages.

Disciplinary Perspectives

Having outlined the textbook model, we now briefly explore how the various academic disciplines with an interest in R&S approach the subject, and what theoretical perspectives they bring with them. Their starting points are varied and each discipline has specialised in certain aspects of the R&S process. Table 7.1 shows a summary of the questions that the three main disciplines pose.

In the work psychology and HRM literature there are two broad approaches to R&S. One is characterised as more scientific, sometimes referred to as the objective psychometric or predictivist approach (Searle 2003; Newell 2005). It focuses on measurement in order to predict the candidate who will perform best in the role, and is concerned with identifying the factors that underpin success in the job and the organisation, establishing selection criteria that reflect these and devising ways of measuring candidates against these criteria.

Central to this approach is proving the validity and reliability of the selection process. In particular, criterion-related validity demonstrates that the chosen selection methods result in the choice of candidates who then go on to perform successfully in the organisation (Cook 2000; Guion 1998). The appeal of this objective psychometric approach is that HRM departments regard it as providing a defence against legal challenges to R&S decisions, mainly because it lends itself to standardised practice. Added to which, a large recruitment consulting and psychometric testing industry is keen for employers to utilise its services and products.

Table 7.1   R&S focus of the three main disciplines

Discipline focus	Types of questions this discipline asks in R&S
HRM *Focus: organisational processes*	How does it impact organisation performance? Is it legal? Does it manage risk for the organisation? Can we implement a standard policy for managers to follow? How quickly and cost effectively can we recruit? Does this align with other strategies in the organisation?
Work psychology *Focus: individual behaviour*	How can we measure and predict job performance? What is the most valid and reliable way to select? What is the impact of other variables on applicant performance?
Labour economics *Focus: the labour market*	How do agents/individuals overcome information asymmetry in the labour market? What impacts the labour market supply and demand? How can government policies influence the labour market?

The second approach focuses on how and why a more pragmatic and socially oriented process is conducted. Greater attention is directed at the role of intuition and 'gut feel' about a candidate in selection decision making. Selection methods may consist solely of an interview. Research suggests that the employer appeal of the social approach is its simplicity, flexibility and cost efficiency (see below). In addition, it takes account of applicant views of the selection process and their need for information in order to make decisions about the job.

Labour economics studies the demand for, and supply of, people to meet the productive needs of organisations. A prominent theoretical approach is *signalling theory* in which Spence (1973) suggests that signals from job applicants (for example their qualifications) allow the employer to evaluate their potential. The majority of the economics research on job market signalling tends to examine the relationship between education levels and occupational attainment or pay, thus inferring whether education acts as a signal or not – Bills (2003) provides a comprehensive and useful overview of the arguments. However, research investigating recruiter or employer reaction to signals at the time of recruitment is sparse.

Summary

On the one hand, these disciplines have a point in common: using the best prediction method for successful performance or fit in the job or organisation. On the other hand, although the prescriptive literature acknowledges educational credentials as a prerequisite for some jobs, research demonstrates that there are many instances where this is not the case and recruiters prefer to rely on other signals and indicators, such as work experience, personal recommendation, cognitive ability, personality or to defer to an extended job trial – essentially the 'try before you buy' strategy (see below).

Moreover, these bodies of literature pose a problem in that there is often very little knowledge of, and therefore crossover between, research in the different disciplines. To give just one example, as noted above, HRM specialists often view informal methods that are outside the traditional model as being inherently less rigorous, less objective and therefore less effective. Some economists (see Pellizzari 2004) argue the opposite – that informal methods, for example nominations and recommendations of candidates from existing workers, friends and family, may provide more accurate information than the textbook R&S techniques and are therefore associated with higher pay and better quality work. Neither school of thought seems aware of the other's reasoning or conclusions.

The Reality of Recruitment and Selection Practice

The formalised R&S model – job definition, recruitment, application form and CV, sifting and short-listing, psychometric tests, assessment centre, interview – was arguably created from observed 'best practice' for appointments to graduate train-eeship and managerial or professional posts in large, bureaucratic organisations during the 1970s and 1980s such as BP, Shell, the BBC, IBM, and other Association of Graduate Recruiters (AGR) members. All of these organisations could support an HR function and indeed specialist recruitment staff with high levels of expertise for delivery. In other words, the ideal type is expensive. Those wishing to adopt this model must make similar investments, either in-house or via outside consultancies and agencies (Lockyer and Scholarios 2007).

This formal model arguably faces two linked challenges. First, as many observers have pointed out over the years (Oliver and Turton 1982; Hedges 1983; Windolf and Wood 1988; Fevre 1989; Lockyer and Scholarios 2007), in some sectors, occupations and organisations, the costs may outweigh their benefits to organisations and, as a result, different models of R&S may pertain across much of the economy. Second, even in organisations where the formal model is in use, it faces constant challenge, by either being ignored or subverted by line managers acting in the face of incentives that push them away from the model. Thus, a central issue is, to what extent is the textbook depiction of R&S an accurate picture of what actually happens?

To answer this we need to review what we know about how R&S is currently conducted, in terms of who is being recruited, what (skills, competences, attributes, etc.) are being recruited, how they are being recruited (what methods are being deployed), and by whom this R&S activity is being conducted. Once we have a clear picture of what is known on these fronts, we will turn to discuss the implications for policy and practice.

Unfortunately, our knowledge of R&S practice and of the policies that underlie it is patchy. There are good case studies of individual firms and of particular sectors (see Nickson et al. 2008 for the voluntary sector; and Lockyer and Scholarios 2004 and 2007 for hotel staff and the construction industry respectively) and of particular techniques such as psychometric testing (Kersley et al. 2006: 75–78; Jenkins 2001; Jenkins and Wolf 2002) and interviews (Rynes et al. 2000), and a rich research literature that examines R&S for signs of bias against different groups (see below).

What is lacking is a robust time series or even a comprehensive, contemporary overview of how the broad mass of organisations is undertaking R&S activity for various groups of workers. There is some survey evidence, but much of it comes from surveys whose chief focus is not R&S (for example, the UK Commission for Employment and Skills' National Employer Skills Survey – see Shury et al. 2010; and the Workplace Employment Relations Survey – see Kersley et al. 2006). Although it is now somewhat dated, Spilsbury and Lane's survey of R&S in central London (2000) provides a useful snapshot of the rich variety of policy and practice to be found, and for a more recent examination of the practices of 200 large employers, see Learning and Skills Council (2008). Unfortunately, there is no counterpart of equal quality to cover the R&S practices of small firms. A key problem with many existing R&S-focused surveys, particularly those run by the Chartered Institute of Personnel and Development (CIPD), is that they are directed at HR professionals and therefore responses tend to reflect organisational policies and what ought to be happening rather than what line managers may actually end up doing. With these caveats about the information available borne in mind, what do we know?

Who is being Recruited?

Impact of labour markets

Within the HRM literature, R&S is conceived of primarily as a micro-level activity, involving firms, individual candidates and particular jobs, but as economic theory reminds us, it takes place against, and is influenced by, the external macro-level backdrop of national, regional, local and occupational labour markets and their regulation structures. For example, in tight labour markets (which in some occupations can exist even during a recession as the jobs are simply so unattractive or the skills required so scarce), employers may have to take what is on offer, so that, 'the problem becomes one of recruitment rather than selection' (Lockyer and Scholarios 2007: 531).

In slack labour markets, such as we are generally currently experiencing, in conditions where skills are in over-supply, and where access to migrant labour is relatively easy, the balance of power often rests with the employer, allowing them to raise the criteria for who they are willing to recruit (and dictate on what terms and conditions people are employed). In some cases this power may lead to credentialism and inflated entry requirements (usually specified in terms of qualifications) in sought-after jobs. For employers, the main downside of a buyer's market is that they may be deluged with applications for attractive jobs, which need to be processed. For example, in 2010 UK's Price Waterhouse Coopers received 18,000 applicants for 1,200 graduate places (Grimston and Gourlay 2010), and for some apprenticeship places in blue-chip engineering firms, 100 applicants per training place are not uncommon.

Given this, one of the most striking paradoxes within current R&S debates is the existence of a discourse of scarcity – a 'war for talent' (CIPD 2010a). Thus, if the respondents to the CIPD's 2010a 'Resourcing and talent planning' survey are to be believed, the perception of 41 per cent of HR practitioners (up from 20 per cent in 2009) is that, 'competition for talent is greater as the pool of available talent to hire has fallen sharply' (CIPD 2010a: 3). Furthermore, this perception exists in a labour market where there are significant indications of rising levels of over-qualification (Felstead *et al.* 2007; UKCES 2009 and 2010).

How can this paradox be explained? As Brown and Hesketh (2004) and Brown *et al.* (2010) argue, by choosing to define talent in a very narrow way, and by using passage through a tiny, global group of elite educational institutions as a key proxy for it, it has proved possible for consultants (see Chambers *et al.*1998) and HR practitioners to create a discourse of scarcity in the midst of a world of apparent plenty.

Thus, there may be more graduates than ever before, but only a small minority are deemed to have 'talent', and the route via which they were educated serves as a proxy for this 'talent' (see Keep and James 2010a).

Labour market regulation

Another example of external influences on R&S is that of labour market regulation. The less regulated the labour market is, the greater the freedom employers have both to specify the characteristics and skills they want to recruit and to choose who to employ. UK employers have relatively considerable latitude on the former point (see Cox *et al.* 2009 and Devins *et al.* 2009 for an overview). Unlike many other OECD countries, including other Anglo-Saxon nations (e.g. individual states in the USA, Australia and Canada), there is relatively little licence to practise regulation (legal requirements about minimum levels of skill or qualification needed to perform a particular job) outside of the professions (law, medicine, accountancy, teaching), and a few occupations where health and safety issues loom large, such as security contractors (Pratten 2007), aircraft technicians (Haas 2008), carers (Gospel and Lewis 2010) and fitness instructors (Lloyd 2005). Nor, unlike in some European countries, do trade unions, via co-determination, participation in company management or collective agreements, normally have much influence over R&S criteria and practices.

Labour market legislation

In terms of legislative intervention in R&S choices, in recent times UK law has sought to change or influence employers' behaviour in terms of both R&S processes and the outcomes they generate. Chapter 3 addresses labour law but for the purposes of this chapter it is important to note that legislation has sought to outlaw bias against candidates on the grounds of race, sex preference, gender, age, disability or religious belief, although discrimination on the grounds of social class remains perfectly legal. Thus, public policy has a major stake in trying to ensure that the HR textbook approach to R&S does meet its claims to promote meritocracy, deliver an objectively measured 'fit' and, most importantly, eliminate, or at least minimise, bias or discrimination. The response from HR functions has been to adopt a 'compliance officer' model and seek to ensure that managers follow bias-free R&S procedures (CIPD 2010a).

One result of this public policy focus on discrimination has been much research, often conducted from outside the HRM discipline, that has sought to probe this issue: Fuller *et al.* (2005) on gender and career choice; Brown and Hesketh (2004), Sutton Trust (2005 and 2006), and Panel on Fair Access to the Professions (2009) on social stratification in the employment market; and Goldthorpe and Jackson (2007) on class and how employers define desirable candidate attributes in ways that privilege individuals with certain class backgrounds. Overall, the research suggests that although the HR function expends much time and energy trying to enforce a bias-free, textbook model, there remain major problems that reflect structurally embedded forms of bias in R&S patterns – both within large, sophisticated organisations that are liable to try to follow the textbook model and in organisations and sectors where this is much less likely to be the case (Jewson and Mason 1986; Fevre 1989; Jackson 2006; Ashley 2010).

What is being Recruited?

External conceptions of jobs and occupations

The skills, attributes and forms of potential employers are seeking relate to how they and wider society conceive of the nature of jobs and occupations. There is now considerable research evidence suggesting that the UK has a radically different conceptualisation of the nature of, and skills needed to perform, many non-professional forms of work compared to expectations in much of the rest of Europe. Put simply, UK employers often have a far narrower and shallower view of what skills are needed to be a bricklayer or lorry driver, and do not think in terms of the job's place within a wider occupation within which the worker may progress (see Brockmann *et al.* 2011). In other words, UK firms often recruit to fill a specific job opening, rather than with an eye for any future progression. In turn, how we define and specify the type, level, breadth and depth of the vocational skills needed has influenced the design of our vocational qualifications (Green 1998; Wolf 2011). For many non-professional forms of work, our conception of what is required to function successfully is set at a much lower level than would be the norm in Europe.

One structural issue requires some elaboration: the scale and nature of contemporary internal labour markets (ILMs). This is a complex topic, and one that cannot be debated at length here, but it is important to stress that, despite all the talk of an end to careers and to 'jobs for life', in many large organisations there still remain opportunities to progress upwards within the firm, albeit often more limited and fragmented than those that existed in earlier eras (Beynon *et al.* 2002). The key issue is the degree to which candidates are being selected to fill entry-level positions, with little or no regard to their ability to be developed and to subsequently progress. If the assumption is that individuals are there to fill a particular current job opening, then the R&S criteria applied (the person description in terms of skills, knowledge, capabilities, attributes, etc.), will often be somewhat different than if R&S is predicated on the assumption that the capacity to progress to more complex and demanding work is important.

Moreover, while attention has focused on R&S for initial entry, selection for progression within internal labour markets (ILMs) is comparatively under-researched (Keep and James 2010a). Our knowledge about who progresses, why and how, within altered and fragmented ILMs is very poor. Given the importance of promotion, certainly in managerial and professional work, this is a surprising gap.

Internal conceptions of jobs and occupations

R&S needs (in terms of numbers, skills, the relative importance of formalised qualifications, and other attributes or experience) vary enormously, and different employers, depending on size, sector, occupation and skill level, may deploy very different approaches to R&S activity, within and between one another. For instance, the Learning and Skills Council's very detailed survey of R&S policies and practices among 200 large national companies (LSC 2008) demonstrates variations between firms and sectors, and also within organisations when recruiting for different levels of their job hierarchy.

Within this wider context, a key issue is the nature of what employers are seeking to recruit. In academic analyses this is often depicted as being a contest between the importance of human and social capital; or between hard/technical skills and knowledge, and 'soft', interpersonal skills, attitudes and personality traits.

Vast amounts of UK public policy relating to education and training have assumed that human capital, represented by formal certification, is key to who gets appointed in a modern economy. Unfortunately, the evidence suggests that in many instances this is at best partly true and in some cases probably more or less entirely mistaken (for a fuller discussion, see Keep and James 2010a, b). For many vacancies, holding the required certification may get the candidate onto the short list, but will not be the deciding factor thereafter in securing them the job. In other occupations soft skills, attitudes and appearance will be key.

The importance of soft or generic skills is not a new phenomenon (see Oliver and Turton 1982), but their importance is deemed to have grown with the rise in employment in the service sector (Grugulis et al. 2004; Payne 1999). Aesthetic skills (appearance, accent, voice, dress sense, deportment) are also not new, but their importance as selection criteria in many types of inter-active service work (and even high-end graduate jobs – see Ashley 2010) has only been explicitly recognised and researched over the last two decades (Warhurst and Nickson 2001, 2007). For a fuller discussion of their importance relative to qualifications in the R&S process, see Keep (2009) and Keep and James (2010a). There is also a burgeoning literature on the concept of employability and how education and training institutions can inculcate the skills and attributes needed to make their students employable (for an overview of this topic see Gleeson and Keep 2004; and UKCES, 2011).

Increasingly, therefore, some organisations are seeking more flexible employees to fit rapidly changing roles, project-based work etc. Consequently, the concept of candidates' fit has expanded to include broader notions of person-organisation fit (Anderson et al. 2004; Kristof-Brown et al. 2005) and has reshaped and changed the emphasis of many selection processes. In particular, traditional task-focused job analysis methods have often been superseded by competency frameworks which permit a focus on broader, often less well-defined motivations, skills and attitudes (Shippmann *et al.* 2000; Wood and Payne 1998). This, in turn, has led to selection methods aimed at measuring these competencies, such as behavioural and situational interviews (for example, Barclay 2001). Behavioural interviews assume that past behaviour is a good indicator of future behaviour, thus they ask candidates to discuss examples from their work experience of how they have demonstrated a particular characteristic (e.g., 'tell us about a time when you have successfully dealt with conflict'). Situational interviews are forward-looking; they present the candidate with scenarios of things that might happen on the job and ask for explanation of how they would deal with the situation.

The desire for 'fit' would lead many to believe that the strategic intent that underlies organisations' R&S policies and practices would be research worthy; however, there is a dearth of attempts to explore this area in detail. As noted earlier, much of the HR literature stresses the processes and technologies of R&S practice in a search for perfect matching and securing the 'best person' for the job. Unfortunately, the question of how this ties back to the organisation's wider competitive strategy, product market strategy, product or service specification or even other elements of its HRM strategy, is often simply implied or sketched in with scant detail. There are a few exceptions, perhaps the most important is Brown and Hesketh's (2004) detailed study of graduate recruitment in blue-chip UK companies, but overall research on, and understanding of, this aspect of R&S and its relationship with HR and corporate strategy is weak.

How is R&S Activity Occurring?

Overview

Over the last two decades there has been a profound shift in who is undertaking R&S activity. In many organisations, part or all of the R&S processes have been out-sourced to a burgeoning industry of contractors and recruitment agencies (see Chapter 15). Furthermore, although the textbook norms for R&S are heavily marketed and have appeal, actual practice often still favours the informal approach.

The survey data presented in Table 7.2 shows those selection methods which are often classified as informal (i.e., unstructured interview, CV, references, trial periods) were the most frequently used. Formalised methods (i.e. psychometric tests, assessment centres, work samples) were more rare across the range of jobs, but more frequently deployed in graduate selection.

Thus, choice of selection method may vary according to type of job, industry sector and size of organisation (see below). However, the most common methods remain the traditional triad (Cook 2000) of application form, interview and references. International studies comparing selection methods across different country

Table 7.2 Recent research on selection methods used by UK employers

Selection method	Branine (2008) 350 UK large & small organisations Graduate selection % using method	Zibarras and Woods (2010) 579 UK large & small organisations Range of jobs % using method
Interview		
Unspecified type	100	
Structured		69.4
Unstructured		41.8
CV/letter	73	84.8
References		
Unspecified timing	90	71.5
After selection	34	
Application form		
Unspecified type		59.6
Employer form	76	
Standard form	63	
Ability/aptitude test	72	39
Work placement/trial period	60	58.2
Assessment centre	50	17.3
Literacy/numeracy test		28.2
Biodata		27.3
Criminal check		26.6
Personality test		25.6
Work sample		19.3
Drug/medical test		15.9
Other	21	

samples, find that those most popular with applicants are: interviews, work sample tests and CVs (Anderson and Witvliet 2008). It may be that this is why employers more frequently use these methods. Branine (2008) also shows that employers favour methods which are easy to use, cost effective and which **they** perceive as accurate and fair. Interviews, in particular, are popular with employers because they allow a two-way exchange of information, and 'they enabled judgements based on instinct to be made, to find out more about the applicants' personalities, to gather crucial information quickly and simply to see applicants' (2008: 508). This employer desire to rely on gut instinct to judge applicants is exactly what textbook models aim to constrain through formal, standardised methods. This is a key selection tension between a social versus a scientific process.

With this overview in mind, we now turn to a more detailed examination of some of the issues raised by this tension between social and science, and textbook and practice.

Macro-level issues

The ways in which R&S processes are designed and delivered varies significantly across the hierarchy within organisations, and also by sector and sub-sector (see Nickson *et al.* 2011). A case in point would be retailing. In large chain retailers, appointments to graduate traineeships and to relatively senior positions in the management team probably conform to the textbook model, but for the bulk of the shop floor workforce, the model is either diluted or ditched in favour of more 'informal' methods (see Lockyer and Scholarios 2004; and Nickson *et al.* 2011). As Cook (2000) demonstrates, even in very large, sophisticated employers (in this case one of the UK's biggest and most successful multiple retailers), the standard, officially prescribed R&S process for shop floor staff – a behavioural questionnaire, an interview conducted by two managers and a 20-minute work trial – can be attenuated or discarded when time pressure on managers builds. R&S, as with so many other HR procedures, is often very dependent upon the time, energy and compliance of line managers whose priorities may diverge from those of the HR department.

As noted above, there is a significant tension between the restricted list of R&S techniques prescribed by the textbook model and the enthusiasm that many employers demonstrate for other approaches. There are many reasons why employers resort to 'informal' methods.

One is that the formal textbook model often assumes a slowly changing or static workplace where current job specifications and definitions are liable to hold good for a reasonable time; however, this is often no longer the case. This issue often crystalises around the preparation of job descriptions and person specifications. Some organisations overlook this stage and question the usefulness of detailed approaches to job definition in a rapidly changing work environment (Voskuijl 2005). Alternatively, in the haste to advertise and fill vacancies, organisations simply recycle job descriptions without much further analysis.

Another reason for abandoning the formal approach is cost. As already suggested, the textbook model requires a considerable amount of expertise, formalised processes and recourse to techniques (e.g. assessment centres and psychometric tests) that are expensive, in terms of both time and money, to administer. For jobs at the lower end of the occupational spectrum, quicker and cheaper approaches that stress a rapid assessment of personal traits, such as reliability, motivation and attitude are quite often deemed sufficient (Atkinson and Williams 2003). For low-paid and/or low-skilled work in the UK, employers are far more likely to either mix a range of 'informal' R&S methods with elements of the textbook model, or simply rely wholly on informal techniques (Bunt *et al.* 2005). As Gatta (2011) discusses, in the US retail labour market, small retailers are often making hiring decisions largely based on 'blink of the eye' assessments that predominantly reflect the candidate's appearance and voice (aesthetic labour) and the class connotations that are thereby inferred.

One example of low-cost informality would be the use of recommendations from existing employees or the use of employees and family to advertise job openings rather than use press adverts and/or the web. However, it would be dangerous to assume that this technique, and possibly other forms of non-standard approach, are the mark of small firms or low-end jobs. Indeed the LSC's (2008) survey of large employers (201 firms with 5,000 or more staff) shows that 30 per cent used word-of-mouth advertising of posts, and nearly 20 per cent recommendations from existing employees. For example, in the UK the Siemens subsidiary that deals with railway train maintenance (with 650 employees) uses a 'refer a friend' scheme called Talentspot to help provide candidates to fill highly skilled technical and engineering posts (Modern Railways 2011).

Another example of an informal or non-standard approach that has rapidly been gaining favour in the UK over the past decade is work trials and internships. For example, the latest report on graduate recruitment to 'blue-chip' companies in the UK (High Fliers Research 2011: 5) notes that overall, 'a third of this year's entry-level positions are expected to be filled by graduates who have already worked for their organisations – through industrial placements, vacation work or sponsorship – and therefore are not open to other students from the "Class of 2011". Moreover, 'at least half of the entry-level vacancies advertised this year by City investment banks and the leading law firms are likely to be filled by graduates who have already completed work experience with the employer' (2011: 6).

Another way that work trials have been made possible is via the use of agency labour. In a number of sectors, such as cleaning, food processing, call centres and hotels (Lloyd *et al.* 2008), agency work is now an important means of entry into the mainstream workforce, with firms' managements using agency employment as a screening device whereby they can pick the best of agency temps and offer them a job inside the organisation (James and Lloyd 2008). For some types of work with some employers, agency work now provides the sole port of entry into the organisation's lower tier job openings (Beynon *et al.* 2002).

There appear to be a number of reasons for this emphasis on using observation of applicants or potential applicants at work as a key R&S sifting technique. The first is again cost. Internships are a useful source of cheap or 'free' labour (where the intern is a worker in all but name, but is not paid, or is only very poorly paid) (CIPD 2010b), not least because there is no legal limit in the UK on how long an internship can last. In small firms in areas such as fashion, interns can outnumber workers (see Elliott 2010). The owner-manager of one internet website for interns (Interns Anonymous) has argued that, 'Posts that were previously offered to new graduates are now being staffed by unpaid interns, so entry level jobs are disappearing. Why would a company fork out £15,000 to £20,000 a year for an entry-level fashion designer, when they have an endless supply of people willing to do it for free?' (Elliott 2010: 2). In some cases, the internships are now being auctioned off to the highest bidder (sometimes in aid of charities or other forms of fund-raising), or arranged for a fee by a company that specialises in such activity.

The second reason is the strength and reliability of the data obtained. Internships and work trials allow managers to observe a candidate's performance in their own workplaces and work routines (Lockyer and Scholarios 2007). This is a very rich and reliable source of performance data that cannot easily be derived from traditional CVs and psychometric testing; from simulated work environments and situations, such as assessment centres; or from what candidates say in an interview. Although adherents of the HR textbook model of R&S might see internships as informal, the validity of the information they can generate may be equal, if not superior, to that derived from a battery of textbook techniques.

Interestingly, government policy now supports internships as an R&S method, and the UK Commission for Employment and Skills (2011:33) has commented:

> Internships and work-experience programmes for graduates and non-graduates alike represent a low-risk way for employers to take young people on. Work experience placements provide reliable information for prospective employers on key attributes which are rarely accounted for within formal qualifications. They give the employer a chance to recruit someone with relatively little risk for a sufficient period to thoroughly assess them...the average cost of filling a vacancy is over £6,000, so the benefit of a more reliable recruitment process is also of economic interest to employers.

In the CBI/EBD (2010) survey of business priorities for education and skills, 72 per cent of respondents saw offering work experience as having benefits for future recruitment, making this the most popular reason for employer involvement in work experience. It is worth noting that in countries such as Germany, Austria and Switzerland, which have mass apprenticeship systems that entail employers taking on more trainees than they expect to keep, apprenticeships have long been seen as a form of 'extended interview'.

Overall, an argument can be made that organisations are often adopting informal or non-textbook standard methods and approaches to R&S, not out of ignorance or apathy, but rather because there is what Lockyer and Scholarios (2007) dub, a 'logic of informality'. Non-standard approaches may make sense in that they provide richer or more reliable forms of information. They may also be quicker and cheaper to deploy in organisations where resources and time (not least managerial time) are in short supply, or where labour turnover is high (see below) (Lockyer and Scholarios, 2004). Their chief drawback may not be their cost to the organisation, but to candidates who may suffer disadvantage as a result of the possibly potentially greater likelihood of discrimination that they may foster, though as Brown and Hesketh (2004) suggest, even the most formalised R&S process can be subverted by the humans who administer it. The counter argument would be that discrimination means that organisations risk not getting the best people, but in many instances managers may be willing to make this trade-off.

Micro-level issues

At every stage of the recruitment and selection process, decision makers are drawing inferences about how an applicant will perform and 'fit' in the organisation or job. Hence, recruiters and selectors are constantly looking for reasons to accept and to reject applicants (sometimes with good reason, sometimes not). For example, Cole *et al.* (2003) examined the conclusions that recruiters drew from reading CVs of job applicants. In particular they found that they used information provided on education, work experience and special skills to make assumptions about mental ability and personal traits. Proenca and de Oliveira (2009) highlighted the paradoxical behaviour of HR managers who described rational selection processes, but in practice used emotional and intuitive resources to sift CVs.

From the limited research that examines recruiter or employer screening behaviour, it would appear that this is likely to be the least rigorous stage of the recruitment and selection process (Brown and Hesketh 2004). It is, after all, the point with the maximum number of applicants to assess and very little information. Recent research has indicated a growth in the use of internet-based recruitment methods, which have the benefit of attracting more applicants and allowing speedy screening (Anderson 2003; Parry and Wilson 2009). However, some estimates of the scale of internet-based R&S (see Gallagher and O'Leary 2007 for an upbeat assessment) need to be treated with caution (see Parry and Tyson 2008).

Overall there is far less research and validation of this initial screening phase, i.e. response to signals, than any other part of the recruitment and selection process (see Orlitzky 2007). This is worrying given that large numbers of job applicants never proceed further than the job application, and often that initial screening decision is made for the employer by a recruitment agency (see Hoque *et al.* 2008 and Kirkpatrick *et al.* 2009 for examples within the healthcare sector).

One could argue that the focus on the micro practices of R&S by HRM, and more particularly work psychology research, is aimed at reducing or managing hiring uncertainty. For instance, trying to develop recruitment strategies that are more likely to attract appropriately qualified applicants and using selection techniques which lead to the appointment of someone who will be productive for the organisation. But is this what most employers do?

The job market signalling theory (Spence 1973) rests on the core assumption that the signal is meaningful to the employer. Hence, if there is a proliferation of educational credentials from a plethora of education providers, it is questionable whether signalling equilibrium is attainable (Coughlan 2008). This is arguably the case in the United Kingdom. For example, employers discover or believe that not all credentials are the same, thus some only recruit from certain universities or colleges with which they are familiar (Brown and Hesketh 2004; Chillas 2010). In this case the signal is not the educational credential but the reputation of the education provider who has granted the credential, and also the rigour of the education provider's own selection system (Keep and James 2010a). Moreover, traditional approaches to sifting CVs have centred on using qualification levels as bars, but as qualification achievement and alleged 'grade inflation' has taken hold, this has become a less and less effective strategy. For example, the use of a 2:1 degree or above as a filter has dwindled in effectiveness; more and more UK graduates reach this threshold. Price Waterhouse Coopers (the large accountancy and consultancy firm) argue that, 'there's been an incredible boom in the number of 2:1s, which means that as a differentiator it is not significant. We have seen grade drift' (quoted in Grimston and Gourlay 2010). As a result, PWC are introducing an on-line aptitude test for all candidates. Other firms (Accenture and BT) are raising their graduate recruitment bar by including 'A' level scores in their degree-level entry requirements (Grimston and Gourlay 2010).

Recruitment versus Retention

Much of the R&S literature notes that there is a relationship within organisations between job tenure and labour turnover, and the levels of recruitment that this necessitates. The HR literature often depicts high levels of labour turnover as a 'bad thing', stresses the costs of hiring replacements (e.g. see Gallagher and O'Leary 2007) and argues that better HR practices, and hence improved retention rates, would save money. However, caution is needed here. The recruitment costs frequently cited (£2,930 for employees who were not senior managers or directors – CIPD 2010a: 10) are somewhat misleading. They are an average, derived from a sample of 262 respondents, and are produced from a dispersion ranging from a maximum cost of £40,000 per employee to just £50 per worker at the other end. Interestingly, only 14 per cent of employers in the CIPD's survey bothered to calculate turnover costs.

This may not be all that surprising. In some sectors and occupations, rapid labour turnover is culturally ingrained. One recruitment industry representative posed the challenge: 'Too often recruitment has been dismissed by employers as an administrative chore, a burdensome process designed to fill an empty slot. Imagine if we were so casual in choosing our life partners?' (Future of Employment Working Group 2010: 1). Unfortunately, the analogy is, in some instances, a poor one. In many industries, 'divorce rates' are high because employers expect (and may actually wish) to part company with labour on a regular basis. Life partners are precisely not what are being recruited, and may not be what is wanted. This is because employers may believe that it would cost them more to reduce turnover by improving terms and conditions, or re-designing work to make it more interesting and less stressful, than it is to live with employee burnout and turnover and the R&S costs they impose (Keep and James 2010a). In other words, organisations have designed work in ways that minimise the skill content of individual jobs, and thereby created a 'disposable workforce', whose replacement costs are limited.

There is some evidence (Beynon et al. 2002) that employers may be making an entirely rational calculation on this point. In a country where the vast bulk of initial education and training is provided in further and higher education and paid for from general taxation and/or by the student, the issue of training costs for new workers may not always apply, particularly for less highly skilled work. Moreover, the wider context – a slack labour market, often relatively easy access to migrant labour, an over-supply of qualified labour in many areas, lack of labour market regulations that impose Licence to Practice requirements, and relatively hollow and thin conceptions of the skills needed for many lower end jobs – all help support such an approach.

Wider Implications and Conclusions

One key finding from research across many Anglo-Saxon countries is that there is a large and growing mis-match between the qualification levels of the workforce and the skill levels that actually appear to be needed to perform the jobs by workers. There is now a substantial body of evidence that points to skills at aggregate level being in over-supply, with workers holding higher qualifications than needed to either do their current job or to obtain it (for the UK, see Felstead *et al.* 2007; for the Canadian story, see Livingstone 2010). This suggests that insofar as the textbook model of R&S is meant to be a matching process, the matching is not being undertaken very well. In essence, the massive expansion of post-compulsory education that has taken place over the last few decades has not been met by a corresponding expansion in real demand for skills across the whole economy, with the result that supply has outstripped demand. Employers have often responded to this situation by gradually 'raising the bar' in terms of qualification requirements for even quite mundane jobs (Livingstone 2010).

There are numerous implications arising from this situation. For the purposes of this chapter, two are mentioned here. The first is that employers may find that job satisfaction will be limited in cases where an individual's skills and education are not tapped into and not rewarded – indeed the over-qualified often appear to suffer a long-term scarring effect on their wage levels (Green and Zhu 2010). The second, much broader, issue, is the wider cost to society of skills developed through initial education and training, often created at public expense, not being used to maximum productive effect. This issue has become a major public policy feature in Scotland (Scottish Government 2007), with attempts being made to assist organisations to make better use of the skills that the publicly-funded education and training system has provided them with. Awareness of the problem has spread to England (DBIS 2010) and is currently the subject of work by the OECD (2011). As Livingstone (2010: 225) argues:

> The extent of underemployment has now become such a widespread problem that it seriously inhibits 'normal' adjustments of labour markets in advanced economies. Underemployment is likely to become an increasingly serious social problem – unless there is a significant change in the way workers' abilities are utilised in their jobs.

These issues highlight that R&S is a process through which various types of positional competition get played out – a fact that makes its conduct and outcomes potentially highly contentious. At one level, there is intense competition to secure employment. Jobs are scarce and valuable in an era of high unemployment, and good jobs are very scarce and valuable in terms of the social and economic prizes they afford those who obtain them (Brown and Hesketh 2004; Keep and James 2010a). At another level, there is also competition between sectors and occupations for what is often seen as a finite supply of better-educated and more motivated young people. In both forms of competition, not everyone can come out a winner. For employers in less fashionable sectors the likely outcome is that they will be losers (for a more detailed discussion of this issue and its consequences, see Keep and James 2010a: 23–27). One response is to seek to use employer branding as a means of building and promoting the attractiveness of what individual organisations have to offer (Chapter 18).

At a wider level, R&S's role in determining who gains access to which type of job makes it controversial. As the supply of those nominally qualified to undertake many jobs far exceeds the opportunities on offer, how and to whom the prized employment openings in our economy are offered is liable to be subject to intense public scrutiny. From a societal perspective, rather than being a technocratic process, R&S can be viewed as the point at which a number of forces and interests are bargained over and power relationships established. Rather than the traditional economics or HRM view of R&S as a procedure for bargaining or matching needs between employer and potential employee, it is in fact a procedure through which a complex range of forces and interests are mediated (Keep and James 2010a).

This, in turn, has major implications for the HR function, and particularly those elements of it that focus on R&S. As argued above, to date much of the contemporary HR approach to recruitment and selection in the UK has centred on forms of compliance management, with the aim of avoiding legal claims of unfair or discriminatory practices. However, the issues may now go considerably wider than that. Intense positional competition for a finite supply of good jobs, particularly in the context of high unemployment (especially youth unemployment) and suspicions that the upper and upper-middle classes are seeking forms of labour market closure in order to ration competition, have the potential to provoke outside interest in HR policies and practices in ways that have relatively few parallels (perhaps the exception would be pay and bonuses for senior staff).

It can be argued that, on the whole, recruitment and selection activity serves as a somewhat depressing illustration of the fading of the original HRM 'dream' (Bach and Sisson 2000: 36), whereby HRM would propel old-style personnel management out of the slough of welfare work and routine administration and power it into the world of corporate decision making, thereby securing the HR director a seat at the boardroom table, if not one at the right hand of the CEO.

Sadly, the reality is that some HR activity is being outsourced, not least R&S (to recruitment agencies and head-hunters), and much of the HR activity around R&S, at least in large organisations, is focused around a process-driven compliance model. Insofar as the practitioner-oriented R&S literature reflects higher level organisational strategy, this often appears to be linked (Brown and Hesketh 2004; Brown et al. 2010) to the 'war for talent' – a concept that, as indicated above, is probably of dubious value.

However, an opportunity may be opening up for HR thinkers and practitioners to link up a number of issues, including R&S, to address an emerging agenda around concerns that have been highlighted in this chapter. As noted above, the UK has a distinctively narrow and shallow conception of the vocational skills needed to do many lower level jobs, and lacks well-developed notions of occupational identity in many areas. There is also quite high-profile public disquiet about who gains access to the better paid jobs and professions, a growing over-supply of qualified labour at aggregate level, and the start of public policy interventions to try to improve skill usage within the workplace. Read in one way, this represents another threat to HR managers. However, approached as an opportunity it could allow the HR function to take a strategic lead in addressing public policy concerns and threats to organisational reputation/brand by making a business case for initiatives that address these issues holistically, and at the same time boost organisational performance. If R&S and workforce training could be linked to wider efforts to re-engineer productive processes and re-design organisations and jobs to optimise the deployment of skills and knowledge in the shop floor workforce, there could be an opportunity for some real progress.

REFERENCES

Anders, G. 2011: The games they make you play, *The Guardian*, (work supplement), 29 October, 1–2.

Anderson, N. 2003: Applicant and recruiter reactions to new technology in selection: a critical review and agenda for future research, *International Journal of Selection and Assessment*, **11**(2/3), 121–136.

Anderson, N. and Witvliet, C. 2008: Fairness Reactions to Personnel Selection Methods: An International Comparison between the Netherlands, the United States, France, Spain, Portugal, and Singapore, *International Journal of Selection and Assessment*, **16**(1), 1–13.

Anderson, N., Lievens, F., van Dam, K. and Ryan, A. M. 2004: Future perspectives on employee selection: key directions for future research and practice, *Applied Psychology: An International Review*, **53**(4), 487–501.

Ashley, L. 2010: Making a difference? The use (and abuse) of diversity management at the UK's elite law firms, *Work, Employment and Society*, **24**(4), 711–727.

Atkinson, J. and Williams, M. 2003: Employer perspectives on the recruitment, retention and advancement of low-pay, low-status employees, *Strategy Unit Occasional Paper Series* No. 2, London: Cabinet Office.

Bach, S. and Sisson, K. 2000: Personnel management in perspective, in S. Bach and K. Sisson, (eds.), *Personnel Management*, 3rd edn, 3–42. Oxford: Blackwell.

Barclay, J. 2001: Improving selection interviews with structure: organisations' use of "behavioural" interviews, *Personnel Review*, **30**(1), 81–101.

Beynon, H., Grimshaw, D., Rubery, J. and Ward, K. 2002: *Managing Employment Change – The New Realities of Work*, Oxford: Oxford University Press.

Bills, D. 2003: Credentials, Signals, and Screens: Explaining the Relationship between Schooling and Job Assignment, *Review of Educational Research*, **73**(4), 441–469.

Branine, M. 2008: Graduate Recruitment and Selection in the UK: A Study of the Recent Changes in Methods and Expectations, *Career Development International*, **13**(6), 497–513.

Brockmann, M., Clarke, L. and Winch, C. 2011: *Knowledge, Skills and Competence in the European Labour Market*, London: Routledge.

Brown, P. and Hesketh, A. 2004: *The Mismanagement of Talent: Employability and Jobs in the Knowledge Economy*, New York: Oxford University Press.

Brown, P., Lauder, H. and Ashton, D. 2010: *The Global Auction*, Oxford: Oxford University Press.

Bunt, K., McAndrew, F. and Kuechel, A. 2005: *Jobcentre Plus Employer (Market View) Survey 2004*, London: Department for Work and Pensions.

Cascio, W. 2006: *Managing human resources: productivity, quality of work life, profits*, 7th edn, New York: McGraw Hill Irwin.

CBI/EBD, 2010: Ready to Grow: business priorities for education and skills, *Education and Skills Survey 2010*, London; CBI.

Chambers, E., Foulon, M., Handfield-Jones, H., Hankin, S. and Michaels III, E. 1998: The war for talent, *The McKinsey Quarterly*, No. 3.

Chartered Institute of Personnel and Development 2010a: Recruitment: an overview, *CIPD Factsheet*, www.cipd.co.uk/hr-resources/factsheets/recruitment-over... (accessed 26 July 2011).

Chartered Institute of Personnel and Development 2010b: Internships: To pay or not to pay?, *Policy analysis and recommendations June 2010*, http://www.cipd.co.uk/NR/rdon lyres/5A28F718–CC39–4B95–97BC-B0C93123BF8D/0/5258_Internships_report1.pdf (accessed 7 September 2011).

Chartered Institute of Personnel and Development 2011: Resourcing and Talent Planning, Annual Survey Report 2011. http://www.cipd.co.uk/hr-resources/survey-reports/ resourcing-talent-planning-2011.aspx (accessed 17 October 2011)

Chillas, S. 2010: Degrees of fit: matching in the graduate labour market, *Employee Relations*, **32**(2), 156–170.

Cole, M., Field, H. and Giles, W. 2003: What can we uncover about applicants based on their resumes? A field study, *Applied HRM Research*, **8**(2), 51–62.

Cook, M. 2000: *Personnel Selection*, Chichester: John Wiley & Sons Ltd.

Coughlan, S. 2008: *Degree Grades Arbitrary: Watchdog* http://news.bbc.co.uk/2/hi/uk_news/ education/7469396.stm (accessed 24 June 2008).

Cox, A., Sumption, F., Hillage, J. and Sloan, J. 2009: Review of employer collective measures: policy review, *UKCES Evidence Report 8*, London: UK Commission for Employment and Skills.

DBIS, 2010: *Skills for Sustainable Growth: Strategy Document*, London: DBIS.

Devins, D., Nunn, A., Stewart, J. and Stansfield, C. 2009: Review of employer collective measures: policy prioritisation, *UKCES Evidence Report 9*, London: UK Commission for Employment and Skills.

Elliot, J. 2010: Fashion industry internships: exploitation or experience?, *The Guardian*, 24 July 2010, http://www.guardian.co.uk/money/2010/jul/24/fashion-industry-interns (accessed 8 September 2011).

Farr, J. and Tippins, N. 2010: *Handbook of Employee Selection*, London: Routledge.

Felstead, A., Gallie, D., Green, F. and Zhou, Y. 2007: *Skills at work 1986–2006*, Oxford: Oxford University, SKOPE.

Fevre, R. 1989: Informal practices, flexible firms and private labour markets, *Sociology*, **23**(1), 90–109.

Fuller, A., Beck, V. and Unwin, L. 2005: Employers, young people and gender segregation (England), Occupational Segregation, *Working Paper Series* No. 208, Manchester: Equal Opportunities Commission.

Future of Employment Working Group. 2010: *Gateway to Success – Recruitment 2020*, London: Recruitment and Employment Confederation.

Gallagher, N. and O'Leary, D. 2007: *Recruitment 2010 – How Recruitment is Changing and Why it Matters*, London: Demos.

Gatta, M. 2011: In the blink of an eye - American high-end small retail businesses and the public workforce system, in I. Grugulis and O. Bozkurt, *Retail Work*, Basingstoke: Palgrave Macmillan.

Gleeson, D. and Keep, E. 2004: Voice without accountability: the changing relationship between employers, the State and education in England, *Oxford Review of Education*, **30**(1), 37–63.

Goldthorpe, J. and Jackson, M. 2007: Intergenerational class mobility in contemporary Britain: political concerns and empirical findings, *The British Journal of Sociology*, **58**(4), 525–546.

Gospel, H. and Lewis, P. 2010: Who cares about skills? The impact and limits of statutory regulation on qualifications and skills in social care, *SKOPE Research Paper* No. 89, Cardiff: Cardiff University, SKOPE.

Green, A. 1998: Core skills, key skills and general culture: in search of a common foundation for vocational education, *Evaluation and Research in Education*, **12**(1), 23–43.

Green, F. and Zhu, Y. 2010: Overqualification, job dissatisfaction, and increasing dispersion in the returns to graduate education, *Oxford Economic Papers*, **62**(4), 740–763.

Grimston, J. and Gourlay, C. 2010: Employers sideline 'devalued' degrees', *Sunday Times*, 10 October, 18.

Grugulis, I., Warhurst, C. and Keep, E. 2004: What's Happening to 'Skill', in C. Warhurst, I. Grugulis and E. Keep (eds.), *The Skills That Matter*, 1–18. Basingstoke: Palgrave Macmillan.

Guion, R. 1998: *Assessment, Measurement, and Prediction for Personnel Decisions*, New Jersey: Lawrence Erlbaum.

Haas, J. 2008: Occupational Licensing Versus Company-Led Training: The Controversy over the Competence Assurance System for European Aircraft Technicians, *European Societies*, **10**(4), 597–617.

Hedges, B. 1983: *Survey of Employers' Recruitment Practices* (1982), London: Social and Community Planning Research.

Hendry, C. 1995: *Human Resource Management – a strategic approach to employment*, Oxford: Butterworth Heinemann.

High Fliers Research 2011: *The Graduate Market in 2011 – Annual review of graduate vacancies & starting salaries at Britain's leading employers*, London: High Fliers Research.

Hoque, K., Kirkpatrick, I., De Ruyter, A. and Lonsdale, C. 2008: New Contractual relationships in the Agency Worker Market: The Case of the UK's National Health Service, *British Journal of Industrial Relations*, **46**(3), 389–412.

Jackson, M. 2006: Personality traits and occupational attainment, *European Sociological Review*, **22**(2), 187–199.

James, S. and Lloyd, C. 2008: Supply Chain Pressures and Migrant Workers: Deteriorating Job Quality in the United Kingdom, in C. Lloyd, G. Mason and K. Mayhew (eds.), *Low Wage Work in the United Kingdom*, 211–246. New York: RSF.

Jenkins, A. 2001: *Companies' Use of Psychometric Testing and the Changing Demand for Skills: A Review of the Literature*, London: London School of Economics, Centre for the Economics of Education.

Jenkins, A. and Wolf, A. 2002: *Why Do Employers Use Selection Tests? Evidence from British Workplaces*, London: London School of Economics, Centre for the Economics of Education.

Jewson, N. and Mason, D. 1986: Modes of Discrimination in the Recruitment Process: Formalisation, Fairness and Efficiency, *Sociology*, **20**(1), 43–63.

Keep, E. 2009: Internal and External Incentives to Engage in Education and Training – A Framework for Analysing the Forces Acting on Individuals?, *SKOPE Monograph* No. 12, Cardiff: Cardiff University, SKOPE.

Keep, E. and James, S. 2010a: Recruitment and selection – the great neglected topic, *SKOPE Research Paper* No. 88, Cardiff: Cardiff University, SKOPE.

Keep, E. and James, S. 2010b: What incentives to learn at the bottom end of the labour market? *SKOPE Research Paper* No. 94, Cardiff: Cardiff University, SKOPE.

Kersley, B., Alpin, B., Forth, J., Bryson, A., Bewley, H., Dix, G. and Oxenbridge, S. 2006: *Inside the Workplace: Findings from the 2004 Workplace Employment Relations Survey*, London: Routledge.

Kirkpatrick, I., Hoque, K., Lonsdale, C. and De Ruyter, A. 2009: Outsourcing the procurement of agency workers: the impact of vendor managed services in English social care, *Nottingham University Business School Working Paper*, Nottingham: Nottingham University.

Kristof-Brown, A., Zimmerman, R. and Johnson, E. 2005: Consequences of individuals' fit at work: a meta-analysis of person-job, person-organization, person-group, and person-supervisor fit, *Personnel Psychology*, **58**, 281–342.

Latham, G.P. 2007: A Speculative Perspective on the Transfer of Behavioral Science Findings to the Workplace: 'The times they are a-changin', *Academy of Management Journal*, **50**, 1027–1032.

Learning and Skills Council 2008: *Recruitment and Training Among Large Employers – Final Report*, Coventry: LSC.

Livingstone, D. 2010: Job requirements and workers' learning: formal gaps, informal closure, systemic limits, *Journal of Education and Work*, **23**(3), 207–231.

Lloyd, C. 2005: Training standards as a policy option? The regulation of the fitness industry, *Industrial Relations Journal*, **36**(5), 367–385.

Lloyd, C., Mason, G. and Mayhew, K. 2008: *Low Wage Work in the United Kingdom*, New York: The Russell Sage Foundation.

Lockyer, C. and Scholarios, D. 2004: Selecting hotel staff: why best practice does not always work, *International Journal of Contemporary Hospitality Management*, **16**(2), 121–135.

Lockyer, C. and Scholarios, D. 2007: The "rain dance" of selection in construction: rationality as ritual and the logic of informality', *Personnel Review*, **36**(4), 528–548.

Modern Railways 2011: 'The right people', Evolution in motion – *Siemens and UK Rail* (A special Modern Railways supplement in association with Siemens), March, 7.

Newell, S. 2005: Recruitment and Selection. In S. Bach (ed.), *Managing Human Resources* 4th edn, Oxford: Blackwell.

Nickson, D., Hurrell, S., Warhurst, C. and Commander, J. 2011: Labour supply and skills demands in fashion retailing. In I. Grugulis and O. Bozkur (eds.) *Retail Work. Critical Perspectives on Work and Employment.*, 68–87. Basingstoke: Palgrave.

Nickson, D., Warhurst, C., Dutton, E. and Hurrell, S. 2008: A job to believe in: recruitment in the Scottish voluntary sector, *Human Resource Management Journal*, **18**(1), 20–35.

Oliver, J. and Turton, J. 1982: Is There a Shortage of Skilled Labour?, *British Journal of Industrial Relations*, **20**(2), 195–217.

Organisation for Economic Cooperation and Development 2011. *Towards an OECD Skills Strategy*, Paris: OECD.

Orlitzky, M. 2007: Recruitment strategy. In P. Boxall, J. Purcell and P. Wright (eds.), *The Oxford Handbook of Human Resource Management*, Oxford: Oxford University Press.

Panel on Fair Access to the Professions 2009: Unleashing Aspiration: The Final Report of the Panel on Fair access to the Professions, London: Cabinet Office.

Parry, E. and Tyson, S. 2008: An analysis of the use and success of online recruitment methods in the UK, *Human Resource Management Journal*, **18**(3), 257–274.

Parry, E. and Wilson, H. 2009: Factors influencing the adoption of online recruitment, *Personnel Review*, **38**(6), 655–673.

Payne, J. 1999: All Things to All People: Changing Perceptions of 'Skill' Among Britain's Policy Makers Since the 1950s and Their Implications, *SKOPE Research Paper* No. 1, Coventry: University of Warwick, SKOPE.

Pellizzari, M. 2004: Do Friends and Relatives Really Help in Getting a Good Job?, *CEP Discussion Paper* No. 623, March, London: London School of Economics, Centre for Economic Performance.

Pratten, J. 2007: Securing the Doors: Bouncers and the British Licensed Trade, *International Journal of Contemporary Hospitality Management*, **19**(1), 85–91.

Proenca, M. and de Oliveira, E. 2009: From Normative to Tacit Knowledge: CV Analysis in Personnel Selection, *Employee Relations*, **31**(4), 427–447.

Rynes, S., Barber, A. and Varma, G. 2000: Research on the Employment Interview, in C. Cooper and E. Locke (eds.) *Industrial & Organizational Psychology: Linking Theory and Practice*, Oxford: Blackwell.

Scottish Government 2007: *Skills for Scotland: A Lifelong Skills Strategy*, Edinburgh: The Scottish Government.

Searle, R. 2003: *Recruitment & Selection: A Critical Text*, Milton Keynes: The Open University and Palgrave Macmillan.

Shippmann, J., Ash, R., Battista, M., Carr, L., Eyde, L., Hesketh, B., Kehoe, J., Pearlman, K., Prien, E. and Sanchez, J. 2000: 'The Practice of Competency Modelling', *Personnel Psychology*, **53**, 703–740.

Shury, J., Winterbotham, M., Davies, B., Oldfield, K., Spilsbury, M. and Constable, S. 2010: *National Employer Skills Survey for England 2009: Main report*, Wath-upon-Dearne: UK Commission for Employment and Skills.

Spence, M. 1973: Job market signalling, *The Quarterly Journal of Economics*, **87**(3), 355–374.

Spilsbury, M. and Lane, K. 2000: *Skill Needs and Recruitment Practices in Central London*, London: FOCUS Central London.

Sutton Trust 2005: *Sutton Trust Briefing Note: The Educational Backgrounds of the UK's Top Solicitors, Barristers and Judges*, London: Sutton Trust.

Sutton Trust 2006: *The Educational Background of Leading Journalists*, London: Sutton Trust.

UK Commission for Employment and Skills 2009: *Ambition 2020 – world class skills and jobs for the UK*, London: UKCES.

UK Commission for Employment and Skills 2010: *Skills for jobs: Today and tomorrow the national strategic skills audit for England 2010, Volume 1: key findings*, London: UKCES.

UK Commission for Employment and Skills 2011: *The Youth Inquiry: Employers' perspectives on tackling youth unemployment*, London: UK Commission for Employment and Skills.

van Vianen, A. 2005: A review of person-environment fit research: prospects for personnel selection, in A. Evers, N. Anderson and O. Voskuijl (eds.), *The Blackwell Handbook of Personnel Selection*, Malden, MA: Blackwell.

Voskuijl, O. 2005: Job Analysis: Current and Future Perspectives, in A. Evers, N. Anderson and O. Voskuijl (eds.), *The Blackwell Handbook of Personnel Selection*, Malden, MA: Blackwell.

Warhurst, C. and Nickson, D. 2001: *Looking Good, Sounding Right* London: Industrial Society.

Warhurst, C. and Nickson, D. 2007: Employee experience of aesthetic labour in retail and hospitality, *Work, Employment and Society*, **21**(1), 103–120.

Windolf, P. and Wood, S. 1988: *Recruitment and Selection in the Labour Market*, Aldershot: Avebury.

Wolf, A. 2011: *Review of vocational education – The Wolf Report*, London: Department for Education.

Wood, R. and Payne, T. 1998: *Competency Based Recruitment and Selection: A practical guide*, Chichester: John Wiley & Sons Ltd.

Zibarras, L. and Woods, S. 2010: A Survey of UK Selection Practices Across Different Organization Sizes and Industry Sectors, *Journal of Occupational and Organizational Psychology*, **83**, 499–511.

CHAPTER EIGHT

Work–Life Balance: The End of the 'Overwork' Culture?

Janet Walsh

Work-life balance is an issue that continues to have a high public profile. In the UK and the United States, as well as in other advanced economies, there has been intense debate about the time demands and pressures of work and their impact on employees' ability to juggle their work and personal or family commitments. Such concerns have surfaced in the argument that employees are experiencing a 'time squeeze' (Hochschild 1997), with some commentators pronouncing that people are indeed 'fighting for time' (Epstein and Kalleberg 2004). An important consequence of this debate is that governments and employers have become increasingly more involved in formulating and implementing policies designed to enhance the ability of employees to manage their work and family/personal life demands. In the UK context in particular, a wide variety of policy initiatives promoting work-life balance employment practices have been enacted over the past decade and a half. Some of these initiatives have sought to impose statutory obligations on employers, for instance enhanced maternity and paternity leave, and the 'right to request' flexible work practices, while others have been designed to encourage diffusion of work-life policies through persuading employers of their positive consequences (Hooker *et al.* 2007). Overall, however, such policies have sought to enhance employees' work-life balance and their ability to manage their work and non-work demands.

Against this backdrop this chapter examines developments in working time and work-life balance, investigating, in particular, human resource policy making in this area. In the first section we outline key labour market trends, particularly changes in the gender pattern of employment and developments in working hours. The next section explores the concept of work-life conflict and examines the causes and effects of work-life conflict on organisations and employees. Following this, evidence on work-life policy making is considered, including the way in which work-life initiatives can assist employees in coordinating their work and family/life activities. Particular attention is paid to the extent of adoption of work-life policies in the UK and the effect of such policies on employees and organisations. Finally, the implementation of work-life policies is addressed and a number of issues for human resource managers are highlighted.

The Struggle for Work-Life Balance: Context of the Debate

Working time: towards a time squeeze?

It is often claimed that the time demands and pressures of paid employment have escalated, with serious negative consequences for employees' family and social lives (Bunting 2004). A number of factors have prompted contemporary concerns about the issues of overwork and work-life balance. Perceptions of an intensification of work activity have occurred, in part, because of the employment reductions that have accompanied successive waves of corporate restructuring. For those employees who retain their jobs, greater job insecurity and higher workloads have often been the consequence (Cappelli 1995). New information technologies have also placed increasing demands on employees due to the fact that employers can more intensively monitor the time employees spend at work. Computer-mediated communication technologies, such as e-mail and mobile phones, mean that employees are able to stay connected to work even when not formally in the office or at work, thereby leading to the phenomenon of '24/7' access (Boswell and Olson-Buchanan 2010; Spector *et al.* 2004).

In this context, much attention has been paid to the phenomenon of the 'long hours work culture'. There are, however, important international variations in the extent to which employees work long hours. Employees in the United States, the United Kingdom, Australia and Japan have been more likely to work longer hours (48 hours plus) than employees in continental Europe and Scandinavia (Kodz *et al.* 2003: 87). Moreover, in the United States, the UK, Australia and Japan, long hours working has not only been evident among professional and managerial employees, but also workers in lower level jobs. According to Kodz *et al.* (2003: 15) two factors contribute to inter-country variations in working hours. Firstly, (paid) long hours, especially among manual workers, are more prevalent in countries that have higher levels of income inequality, mainly because overtime work is used to supplement relatively low hourly wage rates. Secondly, countries that have not sought to regulate working time, through either legislation or collective agreements, have significantly higher proportions of employees working long hours.

Furthermore, the inclination of employees in some countries, such as the USA, to work long hours may not simply be due to shorter holiday entitlements and a minimally regulated labour market, but also reflect a distinctive cultural orientation to work. Wharton and Blair-Loy's (2002: 56) cross-national study of finance professionals found that American employees were the least inclined to consider working part-time. Such reluctance to cut back on their hours they argue, reflects 'greater individualism and a stronger equation of work with individual achievement and identity in the United States than in England and Hong Kong'.

Trends in UK working hours

In contrast to the US, the UK's own working hours are determined partly by European regulations. In 1998 the Labour government introduced the Working Time Regulations which sought to implement the EU Working Time Directive. This stipulated a 48-hour maximum on employees' weekly working hours, including overtime, albeit averaged over 17 weeks. It is important to note that employers can agree individual opt-outs from the legislation. Moreover, certain categories of employees do not fall within the rubric of the 48-hour weekly limit, such as senior management and individuals who determine their own working time (Barnard *et al.* 2003: 225).

Despite these exemptions, however, there has been a relatively steady decline in the proportion of all employees working more than 45 hours a week since the enactment of the legislation. Such a trend reflects the fall in the working hours of male employees. As Figure 8.1 demonstrates, the percentage of males working more than 45 hours a week fell from 39 per cent in 1998 to 27 per cent by 2011, which suggests that the legislation has had some tangible effects in this respect. In addition, the Third Work-Life Balance Employee Survey found a significant fall in the incidence of both paid and unpaid overtime (from 67 per cent of employees in 2003 to 52 per cent in 2006)

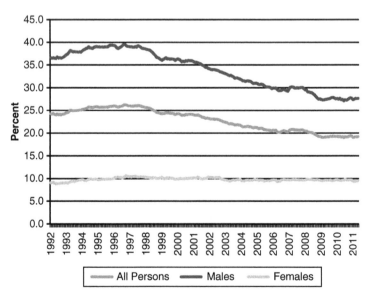

Figure 8.1   Percentage of employed people working more than 45 hours per week, 1992–2011

Source: Labour Force Survey

(Hooker *et al.* 2007: 32). People's perceptions of how hard they are working also seem to have stabilised, with evidence of little change in indicators of work effort between 1997 and 2006 (Green and Whitfield 2009). Consequently, Green (2011: 124) argues that the main period of work intensification in Britain occurred during the 1990s, before the Labour government came to power, and has thus levelled off since 1997.

Nevertheless, despite such positive trends, a significant proportion of British employees still work more than 45 hours a week, especially male employees, and long hours working remains widespread among managers. Indeed, despite the enactment of working time regulations, recent data on working hours suggest that full-time employees in the UK still work, on average, longer hours per week than in most other EU countries, and well above the EU average (see Figure 8.2) (ONS 2011). The British 2004 Workplace Employment Relations Survey (WERS 2004) also revealed that managers were more likely to work long hours than non-managerial employees and they were less likely to be able to work flexitime or reduce their hours (Kersley *et al.* 2006: 251, 267). Similarly, the Third Work-Life Balance Employee Survey found that long hours working was most marked for managers and professionals and was more pronounced in industries such as construction, transport and communications and in private sector establishments (Hooker *et al.* 2007: 22). Moreover, the Survey indicates that there is a persistent gender division in long hours working, with 22 per cent of men working an average in excess of 48 hours a week compared with 8 per cent of women.

In certain occupations, such as hospital medicine, it appears difficult to eradicate the long hours work culture despite implementation of the European Working Time Directive (Walsh 2012). In 2009 one half of all junior doctors surveyed by the British Medical Association were still working more than 56 hours a week, while one in

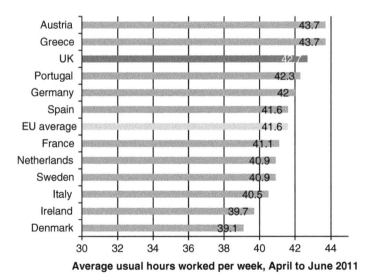

Figure 8.2   Full-time employment – selected European countries, 2011
Source: Labour Force Survey – Office for National Statistics (2011) Eurostat

three were working in excess of 65 hours (BMA 2010). It has been observed that 'doctors frequently work longer hours than those on official returns', mainly to deliver continuity of patient care and to access training (Bax *et al.* 2009: 21). Thus, even when working time is regulated, as is the case in the UK and in other European countries, long working hours remain a characteristic of many types of managerial and professional work.

Female employment and family structures

Perceptions of a 'time squeeze' are also fuelled by changes in the nature of people's domestic obligations. The erosion of the 'male-breadwinner' family and the shift to dual-income and lone parent households, rather than simply the length of weekly working hours, are critical to understanding why employees may be experiencing heightened time pressures. One of the most important developments in the UK labour market in recent years has been the dramatic increase in female employment. By 2010 around 70 per cent of women were active in the labour market compared with less than half in 1963 (OECD 2011: 241). At the same time there has been an increase in the employment rate of women with dependent children from 57 per cent in 1990 to 71 per cent in 2010 (ONS 2011). Dependent children thus appear to be 'a declining barrier to work' (Desai *et al.* 1999).

The increase in female employment rates has been particularly pronounced among those women with working partners and those that are better educated. This has spearheaded major changes in family structures. As noted above, recent decades have seen a rapid decline in the male breadwinner model of employment as the numbers of dual earner and single adult households have grown (Harkness 2003: 151). This reflects the increase in families with a male full-time earner and a female full- or part-time worker. High rates of female employment have important implications for men, since men are increasingly in relationships with women who are likely to be in the labour force.

Despite growth in the numbers of dual earner couples and some evidence that working fathers are participating more actively in parenting and housework, the gender balance in unpaid work remains unequal, with women continuing to play a much greater role than men (Kan *et al.* 2011). Evidence from sixteen countries suggests that women still undertake the bulk of child care and routine housework, while men have greater involvement in more masculine-oriented, less routine types of tasks such as DIY and shopping (Kan *et al.* 2011). Obstacles to gender equality in the allocation of domestic work still persist therefore.

The growth of dual earner households and lone parent families is crucial in understanding why workers across the socioeconomic spectrum may perceive a 'time squeeze'. Jacobs and Gerson (2001, 2004) observe that while average working time in the US has remained relatively stable, this masks a large increase in the combined working time of married couples – from 52.5 hours a week in 1970 to 63.1 a week in

2000. In the British context it is argued that 'full-time working mothers in dual-career couples and single parents are particularly burdened by long hours of paid and unpaid work, and this is true even before account is taken of time spent on childcare.' (Harkness 2003: 168). The work-life dilemmas of employees are also more extensive than simply caring for dependent children. Increasingly employees are experiencing pressures to manage care for both young children and elderly relatives, commonly referred to as the phenomenon of the 'sandwiched employee' (Lobel and Kossek, 1996: 230). From this perspective, therefore, it is the growth of dual-earner households that underpins people's perceptions of a 'time squeeze', with women's employment activity providing the main increase in couples' working time.

Working Hours and Work-Life Conflict

Although people's perceptions of a 'time squeeze' may be underpinned by a complex range of factors, including women's growing labour market participation, the number of hours people work and the times at which they work have an important bearing on how individuals manage their work and family/personal life commitments. As we have seen, although there are international variations in working hours, there is a distinct tendency for certain kinds of workers, most notably managerial and professional employees, to work long hours in most modern economies (Kodz et al. 2003: 14). Why might employees have a propensity to work long hours? Many organisations operate on the basis of a social norm that presumes that an employee's presence at work, sometimes referred to as 'face time', is indicative of their commitment to the job and their productivity (Perlow 1998). Such a norm is especially prevalent in managerial and professional work. Indeed, it has been shown that promotions at managerial level are associated with working long hours (Judge et al. 1995). Hence, in many organisations a process of 'competitive presenteeism' can occur whereby individuals seek to compete over who works the longest hours (Simpson 1998).

There are a number of factors that create and sustain an 'overwork culture'. Firstly, as noted above, managers play an active role in encouraging employees to work long hours. In her study of software engineers Perlow (1998: 328) observed that managers did this by *establishing work demands*, for instance arranging meetings and setting deadlines; *monitoring employees*, including inspecting their work and observing them perform tasks; and acting as *role models* by displaying the work patterns they expect their subordinates to imitate. Secondly, long working hours may reflect the contemporary dynamics of technical, professional and managerial work. In these types of knowledge-based jobs the productivity or commitment of employees is not easily ascertained and therefore managers tend to rely on work hours as a convenient indicator of an employee's job performance.

The behaviour of co-workers may also be an important contributory factor. An analysis of law firms (Landers et al. 1996) suggests that junior lawyers were inclined to work longer hours if they perceived their co-workers had increased their hours. Such 'positional competition' compels individuals to work progressively longer hours, thereby leading to an outcome that is less optimal than one in which all worked fewer hours. This vicious cycle of escalating work hours has been aptly characterised as a prisoner's dilemma (Eastman 1998).

In respect of people's reasons for working overtime, it appears that work overload ('too much work to finish in normal hours') is a critical factor. Such a rationale was cited by 44 per cent of employees in the Third Work-Life Balance Employee Survey, followed by financial reasons (19 per cent) (Hooker *et al.* 2007: Table 2.4). Gender role expectations and childcare responsibilities can also shape people's hours of work. As we have seen, (full-time) male employees are significantly more likely to work longer hours than their female counterparts, as are men with dependent children (Kodz *et al.* 2003: 42; Hooker *et al.* 2007: 22). The persistence of long working hours for fathers employed in full-time jobs is considered to highlight 'the salience of father as breadwinner' in the British context (Biggart and O'Brien 2009: 2).

Individuals may not necessarily perceive long hours as 'overwork', however, particularly if they are strongly committed to their work activity. Brett and Stroh (2003) found that male managers who worked very long hours (61 hours plus) not only benefited financially, but also experienced a heightened sense of self-esteem and accomplishment. Nevertheless, although long work hours may not be perceived as uniformly burdensome, there is evidence that such work patterns can impair people's health and well-being. An analysis of 21 studies concluded that people who worked longer hours experienced poorer physical and psychological health (Sparks *et al.* 1997). It is against this backdrop that public concern about employees' work-life balance has grown. In particular, there has been intense debate regarding the causes and effects of work-life conflict and the appropriate policy responses.

Work-family/life conflict

Much of the debate about employees' growing work-life imbalances presumes that time spent participating in work activities inhibits the fulfilment of obligations and responsibilities in the family or personal life domains. The involvement of individuals in work and family activities may not necessarily be a source of conflict, however. Indeed, multiple roles may have a positive impact on employees' well-being, commonly referred to as work-family/life enrichment, particularly when the roles are fulfilling and rewarding (Greenhaus and Powell 2006: 73). For instance, women managers who are involved in multiple roles, such as parent, spouse and employee, appear to be satisfied with their lives in general and have a positive sense of their self-esteem and self-worth (Ruderman *et al.* 2002). Nevertheless, although participation in work and family roles can be positive for an individual's well-being, it is generally argued that there is a point beyond which such commitments can become 'burdensome' and 'stressful' (Ruderman *et al.* 2002: 73).

Certainly time-based pressures, such as long work hours, variable and inflexible work schedules, weekend and shift work can be important catalysts for work-family/life conflict, commonly defined as a 'form of inter-role conflict in which the role pressures from the work and family domains are mutually incompatible in some respect' (Greenhaus and Beutell 1985: 77). Long work hours not only lead to family conflict, but are also indirectly associated with increased depression and other stress-related health problems (Major *et al.* 2002). Excessive work-family/life conflict, however, does not necessarily mean that employees prefer to spend less time at work. Although around a quarter wanted to work fewer hours in the Third Work-Life Balance Survey (Hooker *et al.* 2007: 34) two thirds of these respondents also stated that 'they would not be interested if it meant earning less money as a result'. Employees may only be inclined, therefore, to seek shorter work schedules when they are well off financially (Reynolds 2003).

The nature of people's jobs and work regimes also has an influence on people's perceptions of work-life conflict. Employees who face excessive work demands, as well as those who have limited job autonomy and discretion, are more likely to report work-family/life conflict (Eby *et al.* 2005). Those employees who have low job autonomy appear less able to control the timing of work and thus may have difficulties in managing their work and personal life activities. The use of computer-mediated communication technologies (mobile phones, e-mail) after hours has also been found to be associated with employee perceptions of work-life conflict. Boswell and Olson-Buchanan (2010) attribute the negative impact on employees' personal lives to the 'connectivity' and 'flexibility' afforded by such technologies when used after hours.

Furthermore, particular types of employees, such as dual-earner couples and individuals with caring responsibilities, are prone to higher levels of work-family/life conflict (Eby *et al.* 2005; Roehling *et al.*, 2003). Disparities in work and family/life role pressures can also lead to gender differences in perceptions of work-family/life conflict. Some evidence suggests, for instance, that women experience greater work-family/life conflict, particularly when working longer hours (Gutek *et al.* 1991; Batt and Valcour 2003). People's experiences of their organisations can be important too. When individuals perceive that their managers are unsupportive over their efforts to balance work and family personal life responsibilities, they perceive greater work-family/life conflict (Anderson *et al.* 2002).

A particular focus of the debate on work-life balance has been the implications of excessive work-family/life conflict for people's health and well-being. Overall, studies suggest that greater levels of work-family/life conflict are directly related to stress at work and greater job burnout (Allen *et al.* 2000). Work to family/life conflict also appears to promote lower levels of life satisfaction, as well as physical and mental health complaints, such as fatigue, nervous tension, heavy alcohol use and depression (Thomas and Ganster 1995; Frone *et al.* 1997). Furthermore, work-family/life conflict can have negative consequences for organisations. People with high levels of work-family/life conflict tend to be less satisfied with their careers (Martins *et al.* 2002) and jobs in general (Allen *et al.* 2000). There is also evidence that individuals experiencing higher work-family/life conflict display less organisational commitment and higher turnover (Allen *et al.* 2000). Employees with more work-family/life conflict also have higher levels of self-reported absenteeism and lower levels of job performance (Kelly *et al.* 2008: 329–330).

In light of the negative outcomes associated with work–family/life conflict, it is not surprising that programmes and policies have been developed with the aim of alleviating such pressures. The focus of human resource policy making has thus shifted in recent years to measures that are designed to ease employees' work–life imbalances. It is the nature of these organisational work–life policies that will be explored in the next section.

Work-Life Policies

Work-life policies have been defined as 'any organisational programmes or officially sanctioned practices designed to assist employees with the integration of paid work with other important life roles such as family, education or leisure' (Ryan and Kossek 2008: 295). There are three types of work-life initiative that organisations might introduce to enhance employees' work-life balance:

- policies that respond to employees' desire for reduced working hours in order to fulfil their caring responsibilities or educational and leisure pursuits, such as part-time, term-time working;
- policies that enable workers to have greater flexibility or control over the scheduling of work hours and the location of work, such as flexitime arrangements, compressed work weeks, job sharing and teleworking;
- policies and practices that provide financial, informational and organisational support for employees including assistance with childcare or eldercare and sick child support.

Although these initiatives may not fully eradicate employees' work-life pressures, they are nonetheless an essential basic requirement of any employer strategy to reduce work-life tensions and difficulties among employees and thus to facilitate a more satisfactory reconciliation of work and personal life.

Employee preferences

Employers often introduce work-life policies in order to improve the recruitment and retention of staff (DTI/HM Treasury 2003). Exactly what employees expect or desire from such programmes is more difficult to ascertain, however. Individuals may have very different family and life needs and their requirements may change over the work-life cycle. Hence, policies designed for one segment of employees may not satisfy the work-life requirements of another group, or even those of the same employees at a different point in the work-life cycle (Glass and Estes 1997). The

Third Work-Life Balance Employee Survey sheds some light on demand for work-life initiatives among those employees who either did not have an arrangement available to them or did have it available but had not taken it up (Hooker *et al.*, 2007: 49–50). The arrangement which employees expressed greatest interest in was flexitime, with 42 per cent of employees not currently working flexitime saying that they would like to do so. One third of employees (32 per cent) would have liked a compressed work week, and just over a quarter reduced hours for a limited period or annualised hours. In addition, almost one in four respondents would have liked the opportunity to work from home on a regular basis. There was less demand, however, for permanent reduced hours working (e.g. part-time, term-time, job-share), possibly due to the negative financial effects of such arrangements.

Legislative context

The availability of work-life policies depends on the degree to which governments seek to regulate employees' entitlements to work-life benefits. In the United States, for example, despite the unpaid parental leave provisions of the 1993 Family and Medical Leave Act, the state has played a comparatively weak role in the regulation of work-life benefits. Minimal state entitlements and low levels of trade union membership have meant that employers have had a greater role in the development of family responsive policies in the United States than elsewhere (Glass and Fujimoto 1995). By contrast, in northern Europe, especially the Nordic countries, there have been strong state policies on family welfare and benefits. Moreover, over the past two decades, the European Union has encouraged member states to introduce legislation and develop policies that seek to reconcile work and family life. Governments in Europe have thus had to be responsive to European Commission Directives and the requirement for the provision of certain minimum standards and entitlements across Europe (Hooker *et al.* 2007: 9–10).

Against this backdrop the Labour government in Britain introduced a series of measures over the period 1997 to 2010 designed to improve the work–life balance of employees. The government implemented EU legislation on working time (1998), parental leave (1999), paid paternity leave (1993), equality in the treatment of part-time workers (2000), and employees' rights to time off work for family reasons (1999). In addition, for the first time in Britain, the government put in place a comprehensive approach to family policy, enshrined in the National Child Care Strategy (1998) and the National Carers Strategy (1998), as well as a range of work-life balance initiatives for working parents (Dex and Forth 2009). In respect of the latter, measures were taken to enhance and extend maternity leave, maternity rights and pay, and to introduce the 'right to request' flexible working for parents with a child under six in 2003 and then for all carers of adults in 2006. The right to request a flexible working pattern was further extended in 2009 to people with parental responsibility for children aged 16 years and under, with the intention to offer such arrangements to all employees by the end of the decade.

Under the 'right to request' legislation employers have a statutory requirement to consider applications for flexible working seriously, although there is scope to reject them on business grounds. Specifically, eligible employees can request:

- a change to the hours they work;
- a change to the times when they are required to work;
- to work from home.

As indicated in Table 8.1, flexible working can encompass a broad spectrum of arrangements.

The Labour government's approach to work-life policy, therefore, had three crucial elements:

- the strengthening of existing leave entitlements (holiday, maternity leave) and the introduction of new forms of leave (parental leave, paid paternity leave);
- expanded support for childcare (childcare subsidies, out of school care);
- the introduction of a statutory 'right to request' flexible work arrangements accompanied by a work-life balance campaign (and funding) to encourage employers to adopt best practice and to innovate in respect of their work-life policies.

Recent assessments have been largely positive. For instance, Lewis and Campbell (2007: 5) argue that 'measured in terms of the increase in annual government spending... the initiatives are hugely significant, especially in respect of childcare,

Table 8.1 Flexible work arrangements

Annualised hours	Working time is organised on the basis of the number of hours to be worked over a year rather than a week: it is usually used to fit in with peaks and troughs of work.
Compressed hours	Individuals work their total number of agreed hours over a shorter period. For example, employees might work their full weekly hours over four rather than five days.
Flexitime	Employees can choose their actual working hours, usually outside certain agreed core times.
Homeworking	This does not have to be on a full-time basis and employees can divide their time between home and office.
Job-sharing	Typically involves two people employed on a part-time basis, but working together to cover a full-time post.
Shift working	Gives employers the scope to have their business open for longer periods than an eight-hour day.
Staggered hours	Employees start and finish their day at different times.
Term-time working	Employees can take unpaid leave of absence during the school holidays.

Source: Adapted from DTI (2003: 10)

and have also imposed costs on employers', while Waldfogel (2011: 144) contends that there has been a 'veritable "sea change" in the support available for working parents...'. Similarly, Green (2011: 118–9) argues that the government's legislation has helped to 'embed attitudinal changes, and enabled some doors to be opened.' Importantly, moreover, the Coalition government (2010–) has not sought to reverse many of Labour's work-life initiatives but appears to be committed to their extension, as indicated by their 'consultation on modern workplaces' launched in May 2011 (HM Government 2011: 11). In particular, the government is consulting on proposals to implement a system of flexible shared parental leave, as well as extending the right to request flexible working to all employees.

Work-life policy provision

Not surprisingly, there has been an improvement in work-life policy provision in Britain over the past decade. The percentage of workplaces with flexible work policies, such as flexitime, part-time work, compressed hours (nine-day fortnights, four-and-a-half-day week), job sharing and working from home all increased between 1998 and 2004 (see Figure 8.3). In addition, there have been substantial increases in the availability of paid paternity leave, parental leave and emergency paid leave. The 2004 Workplace Employment Relations Survey indicates that the ability to reduce working hours (70 per cent of workplaces) and to increase working hours (57 per cent of workplaces) were the most common flexible working arrangements,

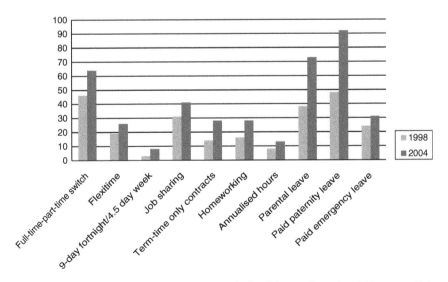

Figure 8.3 Percentage of establishments with flexible work and paid leave policies, 1998–2004

Source: WERS, 1998 and 2004, Kersley *et al.*, 2005, Table 9; Kersley *et al.*, 2006: 254

while flexitime was available in just over a third of workplaces (35 per cent) (Kersley *et al.* 2006: 250). There also appear to have been changes in employer attitudes towards work-life policy provision, with fewer managers stating that they considered work-life balance to be solely the individual's responsibility (Kersley *et al.* 2006: 273).

Of course, managers may make overly generous estimates of their provision in order to create the impression that they are 'good employers'. Employees' perceptions of provision in their workplaces are therefore a useful corrective. Figure 8.4 indicates that, compared with managers' reports, employees were less likely to perceive the availability of many kinds of flexible work arrangements. Moreover, while employees perceived an overall increase in the availability of flexible work arrangements, they believed certain types of provision to be far less widespread than others. In general, job sharing, working from home and term-time only working were considered by employees to be much less widely available than flexitime and reduced hours working. A striking finding is also the extent of uncertainty among employees about the availability of work-life policies. Between 16 and 37 per cent of employees were unaware whether such benefits were available to them, arguably reflecting poor communication by organisations (Kersley *et al.* 2006: 252).

Finally, it is important to examine whether employees in Britain are actually using (as opposed to reporting the availability of) work-life policies. The Third Work-Life Balance Employee Survey (Hooker *et al.* 2007: 57) indicates that 17 per cent of employees had made use of their legal right to request flexible working in 2006, with 78 per cent of these requests either fully or partially granted by their employers. The incidence of flexible working is much higher than the number of formal requests

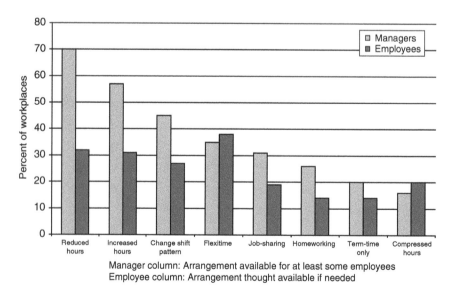

Figure 8.4 Perceived availability of flexible working arrangements (manager and employee reports)

Source: Kersley *et al.*, 2006 (p. 250 and p. 252)

made, however. Over half of employees (56 per cent) worked flexibly in 2006 which suggests that there is a high level of informal and short-term flexible working in British workplaces (Hooker *et al.* 2007: 62). Overall then, evidence from Britain indicates that legislation on work-life policies has stimulated increases in the provision of work-life policies, including paid leave and a variety of flexible work arrangements. Not only are most formal requests to work flexibly granted by employers, but there is also evidence of flexible working occurring informally in British workplaces. Nevertheless, uncertainty regarding availability of work-life programmes may be exerting a negative effect on employee uptake of such policies.

Determinants of work-life policy provision

Although certain types of work-life policies have become more prevalent in British workplaces, they are not necessarily available uniformly in all organisations. Research demonstrates that the adoption of work-life policies is strongly affected by workplace and organisational size. In general, larger organisations in both the US and Britain appear more likely to provide work-life policies (Goodstein 1994; Glass and Fujimoto 1995; Wood *et al.* 2003). Such benefits are also more common in organisations with large specialised human resource departments and those with equal opportunities or diversity management provisions (Osterman 1995; Wood *et al.* 2003). Institutional and societal pressures have also been proven to be important influences on organisations. For instance, Goodstein (1994) found that the more widely diffused work-life practices were within an industry, the more likely that individual firms would adopt those practices. Organisations with a high proportion of female employees, as well as those that are reliant on professional and technical employees, are also more likely to offer work-life policies (Osterman 1995).

In Britain in the late 1990s there appeared to be a higher incidence of 'family friendly flexible management' practices (e.g. part-time work, job sharing, working from home, parental leave) in public sector workplaces, the health industry and the financial services industry (Wood *et al.* 2003), although by 2004 there was no longer a significant disparity between public and private sector provision (Whitehouse *et al.* 2007). Nonetheless, work-life policies were still more prevalent in large workplaces, in the financial services industry and in workplaces with a high proportion of female and technical employees (Whitehouse *et al.* 2007).

Interestingly, senior human resource managers can also affect the diffusion of work-life policies. Drawing on US evidence, Milliken *et al.* (1998) found that work-life benefits were more likely to be adopted by organisations where senior human resource staff viewed work and family concerns as important, and perceived that such matters would negatively affect employee productivity if they were not acted upon. Organisations that collected data on demographic and work-family matters, including employee surveys and exit interviews, were also more responsive to work-family issues.

Unions, too, may affect the adoption of work-life practices. According to Budd and Mumford (2004) unions may 'voice' employee demands for certain types of benefits and also provide information about policies and assist workers in using them. Their analysis of WERS 98 showed that union presence reduced the availability of some work-life balance practices, for example working from home and flexible hours arrangements, but was positively associated with others, such as job sharing and parental leave (Budd and Mumford 2004). Unions appear, therefore, to have an ambiguous influence on work-life policy provision. Finally, there is some evidence from the US that high performance/high commitment work practices (viz. quality circles, employee participation and discretion) may enhance both the availability of work-life benefits and people's perceptions of their work-life balance (Berg *et al.* 2003; Osterman 1995), although studies conducted in Britain have failed to confirm such findings (White *et al.* 2003).

Work-Life Policies: The Business Case

The business case benefits of work-life policies are widely cited rationales for their introduction in both small and larger organisations (see Dex and Scheibl 2001). There has been speculation, for example, that the introduction of work-life policies is likely to enhance an organisation's corporate reputation. Firms should therefore be able to attract a larger, and potentially superior, pool of potential recruits who are likely to improve productivity and profits. At the same time, work-life programmes should enable firms to improve the retention of their employees. It is argued that work-life policies are likely to engender greater commitment and stability among employees, thereby lowering a firm's costs and enhancing its profitability (Arthur and Cooke 2004).

Certainly, work-life policies can have beneficial effects on individuals and their organisations. Employees whose organisations provide more work-life benefits appear to hold more positive work attitudes, including greater organisational commitment and less intention to leave their organisations (Thompson *et al.* 1999). Indeed, people appear to be more attached to organisations that offer work-life policies whether or not they have actually used those policies. According to Grover and Crooker (1995: 274) work-life policies have this effect because they symbolise a 'wider corporate concern' for employees. Furthermore, work-life policies may engender among employees a 'generalised sense of obligation to the workplace', with people more likely to engage in organisational citizenship behaviour, such as helping co-workers and supervisors with their job duties and suggesting improvements, the more useful they perceive the work-life benefits available to them (Lambert 2000: 811).

However, some commentators are rather sceptical of the wider business case for work-life policies. For instance, Sutton and Noe (2005) have argued that work-life policies do not necessarily enhance organisational effectiveness, with limited tangible effects on employee recruitment, retention, well-being or productivity. Similarly, Kelly *et al.* (2008: 307) observe that the 'empirical evidence that work-family initiatives have strong economic pay-offs for organisations is fairly weak and yet many organisations have put these policies and programmes in place.'

In respect of the evidence, Perry-Smith and Blum (2000) found that organisations with more extensive 'bundles' of work-life policies, including childcare provision and assistance, flexible scheduling, parental leave, elder care support, experienced higher perceived organisational performance. Konrad and Mangel (2000) also demonstrate that work-life programmes have a positive influence on the (actual) productivity of firms, especially when the workforce is composed of large numbers of women and professionals. There is very little research on the impact of work-life policies on financial performance, however, although some studies suggest that work-life programmes improve shareholder return. An investigation of Fortune 500 companies found that announcements of work-family initiatives prompted increases in share prices, which suggests that investors consider such measures to be beneficial for firms (cf. Arthur and Cook 2004: 610). According to Arthur (2003: 504) 'the average dollar value of the change in share price associated with a work-family initiative is approximately 60 million dollars per firm'.

Overall, however, there is only limited evidence on the link between work-life policy provision and business performance. Moreover, very little research provides rigorous analysis of the costs and benefits of these initiatives (Kelly *et al.* 2008). On the other hand, there is evidence that certain kinds of work-life policies, particularly forms of flexible working, can have positive consequences for employees and their organisations. Hence, research has sought to disaggregate work-life initiatives and to analyse the implications of individual policies, such as flexible working and telecommuting.

Flexible working

Flexible work arrangements typically describe a variety of initiatives such as flexi-time, reduced hours, compressed workweeks, job sharing, and term-time working. In a review of over thirty studies, it was found that employees on flexible work schedules experienced greater satisfaction with their jobs and work schedules, were less likely to be absent and were more productive (Baltes *et al.* 1999). In addition, flexible schedules have been associated with higher organisational commitment (Grover and Crooker 1995) and lower turnover intentions (Batt and Valcour 2003). Importantly, workers that are employed in organisations offering flexible work hours tend to have higher organisational commitment regardless of whether or not the employee makes use of such arrangements (Scandura and Lankau 1997). In this case flexible work hours appear to signal to employees that their organisation is sensitive to work-life balance issues and prepared to respond to employees' needs.

A rather more controversial issue is the extent to which flexible scheduling and reduced hours enable individuals to integrate more effectively their work and non-work obligations. Research suggests that flexible schedules can enhance people's perceptions of control over the work-life interface. Such improved control, more-over, appears to lower people's perceptions of work-family conflict, enhances their physical and mental health and increases their job satisfaction (Thomas and Ganster 1995). Nevertheless, although reduced hours work can result in less work to family/ life conflict and greater life satisfaction for women in both higher and lower level jobs, such individuals may experience disadvantages, such as higher workloads and reduced promotional opportunities (Higgins *et al.* 2000: 17). Walsh (2007) also found that part-time female service workers were not immune from work-life tensions, mainly because they were expected to work overtime at short notice, attend training sessions outside of work hours and had work scheduled during school holidays and after the school day. Furthermore, flexible workers may experience pressures to work more intensively (Kelliher and Anderson 2010), although it is uncertain whether employees engaged in reduced hours work or telework are likely to experience greater work intensification than non-flexible workers.

Teleworking

Teleworking or telecommuting has become more widespread in recent years. Employees perform tasks in the home or elsewhere that are usually done in an office or workplace, often using communication technologies to maintain contact with their managers and colleagues (Gajendran and Harrison 2007). It is commonly presumed that teleworking is favourable for an individual's work-life balance, mainly because it can improve employees' flexibility and autonomy and reduce time spent commuting. On the other hand, there can be negative consequences of teleworking for employees, including greater professional isolation, reduced promotional opportunities and lack of social integration (Cooper and Kurland 2002; Hill *et al.* 1998).

In a review of 46 studies, Gajendran and Harrison (2007) found that tele-commuting had small but mainly favourable effects on employee autonomy and work-family conflict, as well as other outcomes including employees' job satisfaction, turnover intentions and role stress. Telecommuting in general did not impair significantly employees' perceptions of their career prospects. Neither did it damage the overall quality of workplace relationships, particularly with supervisors. Interestingly, home-centred or high-intensity telecommuting (e.g. more than two-and-a-half days a week) had a particularly beneficial impact on employees' perceptions of work-family conflict, although it did lead to the deterioration of co-worker relationships. The authors conclude that 'the more extreme loss of "face time" that comes with being a high-intensity telecommuter undermined the depth of ties with peers in the workplace' (Gajendran and Harrison 2007: 1536). Hence, the effects of telecommuting may vary depending on its frequency and intensity.

Managing Work-Life Policies

Although organisations might have formal work-life policies in place, employees may not take advantage of such benefits. Many employees are reluctant to utilise work-life programmes, such as reduced hours work, working from home, and extended leave, because of the fear that it will damage their career prospects. Moreover, such perceptions may be most pronounced in organisations which value 'face time' as an indicator of an employee's productivity or commitment. The Second Employee Work-Life Balance Survey indicated that around one half of employees believed that working reduced hours would negatively affect their career advancement. In addition, around 43 per cent reported that it would harm their job security. Two fifths (42 per cent) of employees also thought that not working beyond their contracted hours would damage their career prospects (Stevens *et al.* 2004: 108).

Managers and supervisors play a critical role in deciding which employees are able to access such policies. Hence, work–life programmes may be under-utilised because managers and supervisors are reluctant to allow their employees to participate or apply the policies inconsistently. Nord *et al.'s* (2002) investigation of work-life programmes showed that employees believed that the support of first-line supervisors was even more vital than that of senior management, particularly in the day-to-day implementation of policies. Indeed, employees whose supervisors are supportive of their efforts to integrate their work and family/life demands are much less likely to experience work-life conflict (Batt and Valcour 2003; Thomas and Ganster 1995).

The social context of the workplace appears, therefore, to affect whether or not employees use work-life programmes. According to Grover and Crooker (1995: 285) 'even the most family friendly workplace policies are at best useless, or worse, counter-productive, if the work climate does not support them.' Not surprisingly, supportive work-family cultures, defined as 'the extent to which an organisation supports and values the integration of employees' work and family lives' are associated with greater utilisation rates of work-life policies (Thompson *et al.* 1999). Furthermore, employees who perceive a supportive work-life culture are less likely to experience work to family/life conflict and display greater commitment to their organisations (Thompson *et al.* 1999: 409).

Work-life policies: inequity or inclusivity?

Work-life policies have focused predominantly on employees with children (e.g. mothers) or other caring responsibilities. Employees without family or caring responsibilities can therefore perceive that they are 'excluded' from the scope of such policies and therefore treated inequitably compared with parents or carers. There may also be inequities in the implementation of work-life policies. Such problems may occur as a consequence of the informal actions of managers, particularly in the allocation of tasks and workloads. Nord *et al.* (2002) observed, for instance, that 'employees with children were able to choose their flexible schedules first, forcing single/non-parent employees to work around those schedules.' As a consequence, employees without children were scheduled to work later shifts, regardless of their own non-work commitments. Users of work-life policies may, therefore, encounter a significant 'backlash' from their co-workers due to the perceptions that they are receiving, in some way, unfair advantages at the expense of their peers. Poor communication, especially about the effectiveness of work-life programmes, can also lead to the stigmatisation of policy users, reflected in cynical or critical comments about those who use flexitime and telecommuting (cf. Nord *et al.* 2002: 229).

It is not necessarily easy to quantify the significance of 'family friendly' backlash. The Third British Work-Life Balance Employee Survey asked employees whose co-workers had worked one or more flexible arrangements if there had been any negative consequences to them of their co-workers' arrangements (Hooker *et al.* 2007: 82, 192). Around one third of respondents reported negative consequences, with 15 per cent citing work-related outcomes, such as 'having to cover colleagues' workload', 'increased workload', 'staff shortages' etc. Communication problems, such as 'colleagues not being available for meetings' and 'lack of interaction', were perceived to be the most negative effect of colleagues' working from home. Other research suggests that male employees and parents of older children are most likely to view work-family/life policies unfavourably, primarily because such programmes are less relevant to their needs (Parker and Allen 2001). However, it is important to note that, in the Third Work-Life Balance Survey, over two fifths of employees (45 per cent) perceived there were *no* negative consequences of colleagues' flexible working arrangements (Hooker *et al.* 2007).

Organisational responses to the 'backlash' phenomenon vary. Some organisations have sought to broaden the scope of work-life policies to embrace a variety of non-work commitments, including employees' leisure interests and voluntary work activities. Organisations may also consider integrating their work-life programmes into their more general diversity initiatives in order to meet the needs of employees with different work and personal life profiles (Lobel and Kossek 1996: 241). Inevitably such a focus involves organisations assessing the needs and preferences of their employees and designing programmes that take into consideration their individual requirements. For instance, employees at an international consulting firm wanted new programmes, including paid sabbatical leave and improved technical support for telecommuters, in addition to existing work-life initiatives (Nord *et al.* 2002: 230). According to Ryan and Kossek (2008: 303–304) 'the most inclusive approach to implementing a work-life policy would be one where the organisation obtains a direct assessment of needs and preferences rather than assumes these.' Involving employees in the planning and implementation of work-life initiatives may therefore widen the scope and relevance of programmes and improve their effectiveness (Sutton and Noe 2005).

Work-family programmes may therefore need to be reconfigured as work-life programmes in order to reduce the possibility of employee 'backlash'. In this context, Ryan and Kossek (2008: 296) identify four 'implementation' factors that affect the extent to which work-life policies are compatible with the inclusive treatment of employees, specifically a culture that '. . . values differences within its workforce and uses the full potential of all employees'. These factors are:

- the extent of supervisor support for users of work-life policies;
- whether policies are universally available to all employees, regardless of job level and position;

- the degree to which individuals need to negotiate with supervisors before they can use such policies and the perceived 'fairness' of decision making over policy use;
- the quality of organisational communication regarding such policies.

If supervisors display strong support for work-life policies, and in so doing recognise and value the diversity of individual needs and preferences, an inclusive workplace culture is more likely to result. Similarly, if work-life policies are perceived as available for use by all employees, regardless of their level or job, barriers to inclusiveness within the organisation are reduced. The extent to which work-life policies need to be negotiated with organisational actors, such as human resource managers and supervisors, may have a more ambiguous effect on 'inclusivity', however. According to Ryan and Kossek (2008), inclusive implementation of policies does not simply mean meeting all employee requests but ensuring that such negotiations are approached consistently across all employees. Finally, backlash is less likely to occur if implementation of policies is communicated effectively. Formal policies that are poorly publicised and communicated will limit employee perceptions of availability and the likelihood of takeup. In such circumstances supervisors may not be aware of such programmes and thus do little to recommend them to employees. The effective communication of policies is thus an indicator of an organisation's overall support for such initiatives.

Of course, in order to reduce potential inequities, human resource managers may need to take an active role in reshaping the organisation's human resource practices (Nord *et al.* 2002: 236). Firstly, formal procedures governing the allocation of work assignments may be required to ensure that all employees are treated equitably and in particular, to inhibit employees without children being overloaded. Secondly, alternative work arrangements, such as flexitime and telecommuting, are likely to require changes in training, performance evaluation and compensation systems so that employees are both developed and recognised for their organisational inputs. According to Nord *et al.* (2002: 236), it is important that organisations 'overcome tendencies to underutilise telecommuters or devalue the contributions or commitment of flexitime employees.' Thirdly, career and promotion systems may need to be restructured so that they are compatible with work-life policies, especially if employees are able to take leave for personal development or family care, and are deployed on work assignments that are less demanding in terms of travel and client contact.

There may also need to be a more radical reframing of organisational norms, including those relating to time, autonomy, commitment and equity, so that organisations genuinely accommodate employees' diverse work-life requirements (cf. Bailyn 1993: 79–96, 105–120). This change in norms would require organisations to:

- shift the measurement of productivity/successful performance away from hours of input (time) to output or client load (results of work);
- enhance employees' discretion over the conditions of work;

- define commitment as the exercise of mutual respect and trust, and not simply the prioritisation of work above all other activities;
- view equity in terms of justice and fairness in accordance with employees' diverse needs rather than the uniform requirements of a homogeneous workforce.

Organisations may therefore need to move beyond a piecemeal response to work-life matters based on separate, discrete initiatives, such as flexitime and job sharing, and embrace instead comprehensive 'culture change' programmes that seek to re-fashion organisational norms and practices (Bailyn 1993: 70). Such a radical trans-formation of organisational practices requires changes in the orientation of senior managers and human resource practitioners. In particular, higher-level managers need to be actively committed and involved in both policy formulation and implementation. As noted above, operational changes in human resource processes and practices, such as staffing, training provision, performance management and job design, may also need to occur in order to facilitate broader shifts in the norms and values of organisations. Human resource managers may play a vital role in this context, notably by managing communication flows between the users of work-life initiatives and senior management and providing information about the experiences of employees on such programmes (Nord *et al.* 2002: 236–237).

Summary and Conclusion

The issue of work-life balance has attracted considerable attention from both aca-demics and policy makers in recent years. Intense concern over the time demands and pressures of paid employment has been prompted by organisational restructuring and the development of new communication technologies. The growing use of e-mail and mobile phones enhances the 'connectivity' between employees and employers (and clients), thus facilitating '24/7' access and the erosion of the boundaries of the conventional workday. The 'time squeeze' may be more evident in some countries than others, however. In the United States, the UK, Japan and Australia, long hours working has been evident not only among professional and managerial employees, but also among employees lower down the occupational ladder. Nevertheless, long work hours may not necessarily be the only (or most important) factor underpinning employees' work-life imbalances. The erosion of the male breadwinner family and the shift to dual earner and lone parent households underpin people's perceptions of a 'time squeeze', with women's employment activity providing the main increase in households' working time.

Concern about employees' work-life imbalances has necessitated interventions from policy-makers, including the development of work-life policy initiatives. The broad aim of work-life policies is to assist employees with the integration of paid employment with their family and personal life activities. The role played by employers in the provision of such initiatives, however, is very much dependent on the degree of governmental regulation of employees' work-family/life entitlements. In the UK a wide variety of policies promoting work-life balance employment practices were enacted by the Labour government over the period 1997 to 2010, including regulations on working time, parental leave, paid paternity leave and employees' rights to time off work for family reasons. Measures were also taken to enhance and extend maternity leave, maternity rights and pay and to introduce a 'right to request' flexible working for an increasingly large number of employees. Moreover, despite a change in government in 2010, such employment policies have not been overturned. Indeed the current Coalition government is seeking to extend the right to request flexible working to all employees, regardless of parental status, and to introduce flexible parental leave (HM Government 2011).

The Labour government's legislative measures and associated work-life policy initiatives appear to have had positive effects. Indeed, Waldfogel (2011: 149, 151) contends that 'the change in support for working parents over the past decade is nothing short of remarkable' with the consequence that Britain is no longer a 'laggard in the childcare arena'. Such improvements are important because childcare provision is a critical support for parental employment, particularly for mothers and lone parents. On the other hand, policies on childcare and early learning have entailed large governmental expenditure, which, in an age of austerity and cutbacks in public spending, may not be so easily sustained.

In respect of flexible working, the evidence suggests that the 'right to request' legislation has been implemented successfully, with the vast majority of employee requests being granted by employers. Overall, an increase in the availability and take-up of flexible working, as well as the incidence and duration of parental leave, indicates that employers have grown more responsive to employees' attempts to reconcile their work and family/personal lives. In addition, employees perceive an overall increase in their access to flexible work arrangements, with flexitime, part-time work and working from home most commonly utilised if available. Along-side a decline in the proportion of employees who work long hours, there is a view that employees have experienced improvements to their work-life balance and that the pressures of balancing work and personal/family life have been eased (Green 2011).

Nevertheless, certain problems remain. For instance, the working hours of full-time employees in the UK are still longer, on average, than in many other EU countries. The continuity of long working hours for fathers employed in full-time jobs has also been highlighted as an issue in the UK context (Biggart and O'Brien 2009). Moreover, the tendency for managers and professional employees to work long, and in some cases very long, hours persists, as does their more limited access to flexible work arrangements. A significant proportion of employees also appear uncertain whether such arrangements are available to them, which may reflect the poor communication of work-life policies by organisations (Kersley et al. 2006:252).

Furthermore, an emerging issue for policy-makers, including human resource managers, is the use of communication technologies at work. Although such technologies may facilitate modes of flexible working, such as teleworking, their use after hours appears to heighten employees' work–life conflict. It is argued that organisations may need to formally or informally constrain employees in their use of communication technologies, such as prohibiting e-mail correspondence on weekends and dissuading managers from e-mailing employees after hours (cf. Boswell and Olson-Buchanan 2010: 605). In addition, organisations may need to publicise more strenuously the availability of work–life policies for those most affected by communication technology use, particularly the provision of flexible working and personal leave policies.

Despite the potential benefits of work–life policies for both individuals and organisations, such initiatives are not necessarily straightforward to implement. In order to increase the utilisation of work–life policies, organisations need to foster a supportive work climate, such that managers and supervisors are responsive to employees' non-work activities and commitments. Moreover, employees, particularly those in managerial and professional occupations, will need to be assured that usage of such policies will not lead to career penalties or diminished promotional opportunities. There has also been concern regarding the potential inequities of work–life policy implementation, particularly when such initiatives are orientated towards the needs of parents (mothers) with young children. Employees without children or caring responsibilities may feel 'excluded' and inequitably treated, thereby giving rise to co-worker resentment, commonly known as 'family friendly backlash'. The focus of work–life policy making is therefore shifting to cater for the needs and requirements of a wider range of employees, rather than simply employees with children. Such developments are a response to the growing diversity of employees' personal lifestyles, as well as a pragmatic attempt to deal with the threat of 'backlash' from employees that have been considered ineligible for traditional work–family/life programmes.

In order to overcome 'backlash' problems and to foster 'inclusivity', organisations may need to consider making work–life policies universally available to all employees (Ryan and Kossek 2008). Such universality will require the involvement of employees in the planning and implementation of work–life policies in order to reflect the potential diversity of employees' work–life requirements. The inclusive implementation of work–life policies is also likely to require consistent, decision making, particularly in the handling of employee requests, as well as effective communication of the scope and nature of such policies. In this context, supervisor and line manager support for organisational work–life policies is an essential precondition for successful policy implementation. Finally, human resource practitioners have an important role to play in the effective delivery of work–life policies, particularly in ensuring that training, appraisal, promotion and reward systems are compatible with policy goals, and that users and non-users experience fair treatment at work. In this context, work–life policies will need to be integrated into organisational diversity and broader 'culture change' programmes, particularly if organisational norms of 'face time' and presenteeism are to be challenged.

REFERENCES

Allen, T.D., Herst, D.E.L., Bruck, C.S. and Sutton, M. 2000: Consequences Associated With Work-to-Family Conflict: A Review and Agenda for Future Research, *Journal of Occupational Health Psychology*, **5**(2), 278–308.

Anderson, S.E., Coffey, B.S. and Byerly, R.T. 2002: Formal Organizational Initiatives and Informal Workplace Practices: Links to Work-Family Conflict and Job-Related Outcomes, *Journal of Management*, **28**(6), 787–810.

Arthur, M.M. 2003: Share Price Reactions to Work-Family Initiatives: An Institutional Perspective, *Academy of Management Journal*, **46**(4), 497–505.

Arthur, M.M. and Cook, A. 2004: Taking Stock of Work-Family Initiatives: How Announcements of "Family-Friendly" Human Resource Decisions Affect Shareholder Value, *Industrial and Labor Relations Review*, **57**(4), 599–613.

Bailyn, L. 1993. *Breaking The Mold: Women, Men, and Time in the New Corporate World*, New York: Free Press.

Baltes, B.B., Briggs, T.E., Huff, J.W., Wright, J.A. and Neuman, G.A. 1999: Flexible and Compressed Workweek Schedules: A Meta-Analysis of Their Effects on Work-Related Criteria, *Journal of Applied Psychology*, **84**(4), 496–513.

Barnard, C., Deakin, S. and Hobbs, R. 2003: Opting Out of the 48–Hour Week: Employer Necessity or Individual Choice? An Empirical Study of the Operation of Article 18(1) (b) of the Working Time Directive in the UK, *Industrial Law Journal*, **32**(4), 223–252.

Batt, R. and Valcour, M.P. 2003: Human Resources Practices as Predictors of Work-Family Outcomes and Employee Turnover, *Industrial Relations*, **42**(3), 189–220.

Bax, N.D.S., Farrell, K. and Thwaites, B.D. 2009: *Survey on 49 hour week. Working Time Directive Readiness*: Final Report prepared for the Department of Health, Sheffield: University of Sheffield.

Berg, P., Kalleberg, A.L. and Appelbaum, E. 2003: Balancing Work and Family: The Role of High Commitment Environments, *Industrial Relations*, **42**(3), 168–188.

Biggart, L. and O'Brien, M. 2009: Fathers' Working Hours: Parental analysis from the Third Work-Life Balance Employee Survey and Maternity and Paternity Rights and Benefits Survey of Parents, *Employment Relations Occasional Paper*, London: Department for Business Innovation & Skills.

Boswell, W.R. and Olson-Buchanan, J.B. 2010: The Use of Communication Technologies After Hours: The Role of Work Attitudes and Work-Life Conflict, *Journal of Management*, **33**(4), 592–610.

Brett, J.M. and Stroh, L.K. 2003: Working 61 Plus Hours a Week: Why Do Managers Do It? *Journal of Applied Psychology*, **88**(1), 67–78.

British Medical Association 2010: BMA Survey of Junior Doctors' Working Arrangements 2010, *BMA Junior Doctors Committee: Health Policy & Economic Research Unit*, London: British Medical Association.

Budd, J.W. and Mumford, K.A. 2004: Trade Unions and Family-Friendly Policies in Britain, *Industrial and Labor Relations Review*, **57**(2), 204–220.

Bunting, M. 2004: *Willing Slaves: How the Overwork Culture is Ruling Our Lives*, London: HarperCollins.

Cappelli, P. 1995: Rethinking Employment, *British Journal of Industrial Relations*, **33**(4), 563–602.

Cooper, C.D. and Kurland, N.B. 2002: Telecommuting, Professional Isolation, and Employee Development in Public and Private Organizations, *Journal of Organizational Behavior*, **23**, 511–532.

Department of Trade and Industry/Her Majesty's Treasury 2003: *Balancing Work and Family Life: Enhancing Choice and Support for Parents*, January, London: DTI/HM Treasury.

Desai, T., Gregg, P., Steer, J. and Wadsworth, J. 1999: Gender and the Labour Market, in P. Gregg and J. Wadsworth (eds.), *The State of Working Britain*, 168–184. Manchester: Manchester University Press.

Dex, S. and Forth, J. 2009: Equality and Diversity at Work, in W. Brown, A. Bryson, J. Forth and K. Whitfield (eds.), *The Evolution of the Modern Workplace*, 230–254. Cambridge: Cambridge University Press.

Dex, S. and Scheibl, F. 2001: Flexible and Family-friendly Working Arrangements in UK-Based SMEs: Business cases, *British Journal of Industrial Relations*, **39**(3), 411–432.

Eastman, W. 1998: Working for position: women, men, and managerial work hours, *Industrial Relations*, **37**(1), 51–66.

Eby, L.T., Casper, W.J., Lockwood, A., Bordeaux, C. and Brinley, A. 2005: Work and Family Research in IO/OB: Content Analysis and Review of the Literature (1980–2002), *Journal of Vocational Behavior*, **66**(1), 124–197.

Epstein, C.F. and Kalleberg, A.L. 2004: Time and Work: Changes and Challenges, in C.F. Epstein and A.L. Kalleberg (eds.) *Fighting for Time*, 1–21. New York: Russell Sage Foundation.

Frone, M.R., Russell, M. and Cooper, M.L. 1997: Relation of work–family conflict to health outcomes: A four-year longitudinal study of employed parents, *Journal of Occupational and Organizational Psychology*, **70**(4), 325–335.

Gajendran, R.S. and Harrison, D.A. 2007: The Good, the Bad, and the Unknown about Tele-Commuting: Meta-analysis of Psychological Mediators and Individual Consequences, *Journal of Applied Psychology*, **92**(6), 1524–1541.

Glass, J.L. and Estes, S.B. 1997: The Family Responsive Workplace, *Annual Review of Sociology*, **23**, 289–313.

Glass, J.L. and Fujimoto, T. 1995: Employer Characteristics and the Provision of Family Responsive Policies, *Work and Occupations*, **22**(4), 380–411.

Goodstein, J.D. 1994: Institutional Pressures and Strategic Responsiveness: Employer Involvement in Work-Family Issues, *Academy of Management Journal*, **37**(2), 350–382.

Green, F. 2011: Job quality in Britain under the Labour Government, in P. Gregg and J. Wadsworth (eds.), *The Labour Market in Winter*, 111–127. Oxford: Oxford University Press.

Green, F. and Whitfield, K. 2009: Employees' Experience of Work, in W. Brown, A. Bryson, J. Forth and K. Whitfield (eds.), *The Evolution of the Modern Workplace*, Cambridge: Cambridge University Press.

Greenhaus, J.H. and Beutell, N.J. 1985: Sources of Conflict between Work and Family Roles, *Academy of Management Journal*, **10**(1), 76–88.

Greenhaus, J.H. and Powell, G.N. 2006: When Work and Family Are Allies: A Theory of Work-Family Enrichment, *Academy of Management Review*, **31**(1), 72–92.

Grover, S.L. and Crooker, K.J. 1995: Who Appreciates Family-Responsive Human Resource Policies: the Impact of Family-Friendly Policies on the Organizational Attachment of Parents and Non-Parents, *Personnel Psychology*, **48**(2), 271–288.

Gutek, B.A., Searle, S. and Klepa, L. 1991: Rational versus Gender Role Explanations for Work-Family Conflict, *Journal of Applied Psychology*, **76**(4), 560–568.

Harkness, S. 2003: The Household Division of Labour: Changes in Families' Allocation of Paid and Unpaid Work, 1992–2002, in R. Dickens, P. Gregg and J. Wadsworth (eds.), *The Labour Market Under New Labour*, 150–169. Basingstoke: Palgrave Macmillan.

Higgins, C.A., Duxbury, L. and Johnson, K.L. 2000: Part-Time Work for Women: Does It Really Help Balance Work and Family? *Human Resource Management*, **39**, 17–32.

Hill, E.J., Miller, B.C., Weiner, S.P. and Colihan, J. 1998: Influences of the Virtual Office on Aspects of Work and Work/Life Balance, *Personnel Psychology*, **51**, 667–683.

HM Government 2011: Consultation on Modern Workplaces, May 2011, London: HM Government.

Hochschild, A.R. 1997: *The Time Bind*, New York: Henry Holt & Company.

Hooker, H., Neathey, F., Casebourne, J. and Munro, M. 2007: *The Third Work-Life Balance Employee Survey*, DTI Employment Relations Research Series No. 58, London: DTI.

Jacobs, J.A. and Gerson, K. 2001: Overworked Individuals or Overworked Families? *Work and Occupations*, **28**(1), 40–63.

Jacobs, J.A. and Gerson, K. 2004: Understanding Changes in American Working Time: A Synthesis, in C.F. Epstein and A.L. Kalleberg (eds.) *Fighting for Time*, 25–45. New York: Russell Sage Foundation.

Judge, T.A., Cable, D.M., Boudreau, J.W. and Bretz, R.D. Jr. 1995: An Empirical Investigation of the Predictors of Executive Career Success, *Personnel Psychology*, **48**, 485–519.

Kan, M.Y., Sullivan, O. and Gershuny, J. 2011: Gender Convergence in Domestic Work: Discerning the Effects of Interactional and Institutional Barriers from Large-Scale Data, *Sociology*, **45**(2), 234–251.

Kelliher, C. and Anderson, D. 2010: Doing More With Less? Flexible Working Practices and the Intensification of Work, *Human Relations*, **63**(1), 83–106.

Kelly, E.L., Kossek, E.E., Hammer, L.B., Durham, M., Bray, J., Chermack, K., Murphy, L. A. and Kaskubar, D. 2008: Getting There From Here: Research on the Effects of Work-Family Initiatives on Work-Family Conflict and Business Outcomes, Chapter 7, *The Academy of Management Annals*, **2**(1), 305–349.

Kersley, B., Alpin, C., Forth, J., Bryson, A., Bewley, H., Dix, G. and Oxenbridge, S. 2005: *Inside the Workplace: First Findings from the 2004 Workplace Employment Relations Survey* (WERS 2004), London: DTI.

Kersley, B., Alpin, C., Forth, J., Bryson, A., Bewley, H., Dix, G. and Oxenbridge, S. 2006: *Inside the Workplace: Findings from the 2004 Workplace Employment Relations Survey*, London: Routledge.

Kodz, J., Davis, S., Lain, D., Strebler, M., Rick, J., Bates, P., Cummings, J., Meager, N., Trinczek, R. and Palmer, S. 2003: *Working Long Hours: A Review of the Evidence. Volume 1 – Main Report*, Employment Relations Research Series No. 16, London: Department of Trade and Industry.

Konrad, A.M. and Mangel, R. 2000: The Impact of Work-Life Programs on Firm Productivity, *Strategic Management Journal*, **21**(12), 1225–1237.

Lambert, S.J. 2000: Added Benefits: The Link Between Work-Life Benefits and Organizational Citizenship Behavior, *Academy of Management Journal*, **43**(5), 801–815.

Landers, R.M., Rebitzer, R.B. and Taylor, L.J. 1996: Human Resources Practices and the Demographic Transformation of Professional Labor Markets, in P. Osterman (ed.), *Broken Ladders: Managerial Careers in the New Economy*, 215–246. New York: Oxford University Press.

Lewis, J. and Campbell, M. 2007: UK Work/Family Balance Policies and Gender Equality, 1997–2005, *Social Politics*, **14**(1), 4–30.

Lobel, S. and Kossek, E.E. 1996: Human Resource Strategies to Support Diversity in Work and Personal Lifestyles: Beyond the "Family Friendly" Organization, in E.E. Kossek and S. A. Lobel (eds.), *Managing Diversity*, 221–244. Oxford: Blackwell.

Major, V.S., Klein, K.J. and Ehrhart, M.G. 2002: Work Time, Work Interference with Family, and Psychological Distress, *Journal of Applied Psychology*, **87**(3), 427–436.

Martins, L.L., Eddleston, K.A. and Veiga, J.F. 2002: Moderators of the Relationship between Work-Family Conflict and Career Satisfaction, *Academy of Management Journal*, **45**(2), 399–409.

Milliken, F.J., Martins, L.L. and Morgan, H. 1998: Explaining Organizational Responsiveness to Work-Family Issues: The Role of Human Resource Executives as Issue Interpreters, *Academy of Management Journal*, **41**, 580–592.

Nord, W.R., Fox, S., Phoenix, A. and Viano, K. 2002: Real-World Reactions to Work-Life Balance Programs: Lessons for Effective Implementation, *Organizational Dynamics*, **30**(3), 223–238.

Office for National Statistics (ONS) 2011: Hours Worked in the Labour Market – 2011, 8 December 2011.

Organisation for Economic Co-operation and Development (OECD) 2011: *Employment Outlook*, Paris: OECD.

Osterman, P. 1995: Work/family Programs and the Employment Relationship, *Administrative Science Quarterly*, **40**(4), 681–700.

Parker, L. and Allen, T.D. 2001: Work/Family Benefits: Variables Related to Employees' Fairness Perceptions, *Journal of Vocational Behavior*, **58**(3), 453–468.

Perlow, L.A. 1998: Boundary Control: The Social Ordering of Work and Family Time in a High-tech Corporation, *Administrative Science Quarterly*, **43**(2), 328–357.

Perry-Smith, J.E. and Blum, T.C. 2000: Work-Family Human Resource Bundles and Perceived Organizational Performance, *Academy of Management Journal*, **43**(6),1107–1117.

Reynolds, J. 2003: You Can't Always Get the Hours You Want: Mismatches between Actual and Preferred Work Hours in the U.S, *Social Forces*, **81**(4), 1171–1199.

Roehling, P.V., Moen, P. and Batt, R. 2003: Spillover, in P. Moen (ed.), *It's About Time: Couples and Careers*, 101–121. ILR/Cornell University Press.

Ruderman, M.N., Ohlott, P.J., Panzer, K. and King, S.N. 2002: Benefits of Multiple Roles for Managerial Women, *Academy of Management Journal*, **45**(2), 315–330.

Ryan, A.M. and Kossek, E.E. 2008: Work-life policy implementation: breaking down or creating barriers to inclusiveness? *Human Resource Management*, **47**(2), 295–310.

Scandura, T.A. and Lankau, M.J. 1997: Relationships of Gender, Family Responsibility and Flexible Work Hours to Organizational Commitment and Job Satisfaction, *Journal of Organizational Behavior*, **18**(4), 377–391.

Simpson, R. 1998: Presenteeism, Power and Organisational Change: Long Hours as a Career Barrier and the Impact on the Working Lives of Women Managers, *British Journal of Management*, **9**(s1), 37–50.

Sparks, K., Cooper, C., Fried, Y. and Shirom, A. 1997: The Effects of Hours of Work on Health: A Meta-Analytic Review, *Journal of Occupational and Organizational Psychology*, **70**, 391–408.

Spector, P., Cooper, C.L., Poelmans, S., Allen, T.D., O'Driscoll, M., Sanchez, J.I., Siu Ling, O., Dewe, P., Hart, P. and Lu, L. 2004: A Cross-National Comparative study of Work-Family Stressors, Working Hours, and Well-being: China and Latin America Versus The Anglo World, *Personnel Psychology*, **57**(1), 119–142.

Stevens, J., Brown, J. and Lee, C. 2004: The Second Work-Life Balance Study: Results from the Employees' Survey, *DTI Employment Relations Research Series* No. 27.

Sutton, K.L. and Noe, R.A. 2005: Family Friendly Programs and Work-Life Integration: More Myth than Magic? In E.E. Kossek and S.J. Lambert (eds.), *Work and Life Integration: Organizational, Cultural and Individual Perspectives*, 151–170. Mahwah, NJ: Erbaum.

Thomas, L.T. and Ganster, D.C. 1995: Impact of Family-Supportive Work Variables on Work-Family Conflict and Strain: A Control Perspective, *Journal of Applied Psychology*, **80**(1), 6–15.

Thompson, C.A., Beauvais, L.L. and Lyness, K.S. 1999: When Work-Family Benefits Are Not Enough: The Influence of Work-Family Culture on Benefit Utilization, Organizational Attachment, and Work-Family Conflict, *Journal of Vocational Behavior*, **54**(3), 392–415.

Waldfogel, J. 2011: Family-Friendly Policies, in P. Gregg and J. Wadsworth (eds.), *The Labour Market in Winter*, Oxford: Oxford University Press, 144–154.

Walsh, J. 2007: Experiencing Part-time Work: Temporal Tensions, Social Relations and the Work-Family Interface, *British Journal of Industrial Relations*, **45**(1), 155–177.

Walsh, J. 2012: Gender, the Work-Life Interface and Wellbeing: A Study of Hospital Doctors. *Gender, Work and Organization*, early online: doi10.1011/j.1468–0432.2012.00593.x

Wharton. A.S. and Blair-Loy, M. 2002: The "Overtime Culture" in a Global Corporation, *Work and Occupations*, **29**(1), 32–63.

White, M., Hill, S., McGovern, P., Mills, C. and Smeaton, D. 2003: 'High-Performance' Management Practices, Working Hours and Work-Life Balance, *British Journal of Industrial Relations*, **41**(2), 175–195.

Whitehouse, G., Haynes, M., MacDonald, F. and Arts, D. 2007: *Reassessing the 'Family-Friendly Workplace': Trends and Influences in Britain, 1998–2004*, DTI Employment Relations Research Series, No. 76, London: Department of Trade and Industry.

Wood, S.J., De Menezes, L.M. and Lasaosa, A. 2003: Family-Friendly Management in Great Britain: Testing Various Perspectives, *Industrial Relations*, **42**(3), 221–250.

CHAPTER NINE

Skills and Training

Irena Grugulis

Everyone is in favour of training. For national governments it has the potential to increase productivity and facilitate knowledge-based competition; it enhances the bargaining power of collective bodies such as professional associations and trade unions and it helps individuals to progress in the labour market. Yet any and all of these outcomes are the result, not of training in isolation, but of training in combination with supportive national institutions, education systems, organisational strategies, supply chains, customer bases, job design and market demand (among others). As Keep and Mayhew (1999) point out, skills are a third order issue. They do not drive practice themselves but follow on from decisions about corporate strategy, market competition and national policies.

Such interdependency is rarely included in accounts praising training, or suggesting it as a solution to a myriad ills, instead the hopes are that 'publicly funded skills supply will, of itself, stimulate moves to higher value-added products and services, high performance work organisation and greater innovation in products and services – what the government terms a 'supply-push' effect' (Keep and Mayhew 2010: 569). This failure to mention wider issues is understandable since the practicalities of changing supply chain relationships, of redesigning jobs or of changing organisational strategies are far more fraught than those involved in putting on another course (see also Cutler 1992). However, without these adjustments training is little more than a placebo. This is intervention-free intervention (Keep and Mayhew 2010: 567).

It may be, of course, that it is this very prospect of resolving problems without fundamental change that makes training so popular. But this chapter is concerned not with training as a political device, a type of neutered mechanism for countering criticism without providing solutions, but rather a focus on what is happening in practice and the impact that this has. Accordingly, this chapter will consider both training and skills, since micro-level practices within firms are embedded in wider sets of institutions. The chapter begins by setting out the nature of skill, the different approaches nations take to skill formation and, at micro-level, the way people learn at work. It explains the nature of skill before reviewing current developments in both skills and training. These are confusing, since despite widespread rhetorical support, training levels are actively falling, particularly for the highly educated knowledge workers most governments see as their key resource. Set against this, skills are rising against a range of indicators, individuals are more highly qualified and work is more demanding, although discretion is falling. The nature of skills is also changing, with soft skills such as communication and customer service now dominating employers' lists of the elements they are most keen to recruit.

The Nature of Skill

Since this chapter will consider skills as well as training, it would be helpful to begin by reviewing what skills are. Cockburn (1983), in her detailed study of the very gendered nature of technological change in the printing industry, defined skill in three ways: skill in the person, skill in the job and skill in the social setting. Skill in the person is the accumulation of education, experience and expertise that each individual worker brings to their task; the competences, qualities and attributes that most employers mean when they use the term. Skill in the job is the way work is designed: the discretion it allows and the challenges it presents. So, for example, Darr's (2004) computer sales staff regularly spent weeks tailoring systems to clients' needs, a process which required learning on both sides, while Finegold's (1999) work on Silicon Valley reveals the way professionals working on cutting-edge tasks would draw on individual networks to solve problems and devise new applications. In both cases levels of formal training were low but the nature of the work meant that professionals were constantly developing their personal skills. At the other extreme, work can be so codified and scripted that there is no room for individual discretion, as in McDonald's where work systems, buzzers, lights, machinery, pre-prepared foods and scripts are all designed to ensure homogeneity of products and service and a 600-page work 'bible' sets out routines and responses to ensure homogeneity in every outlet (Royle 2000).

Finally, skill in the social setting acknowledges that the way skills are judged also depends on a jobholder's social status, from Penn's (1984) account of 'big piecers' and 'little piecers' in the nineteenth-century cotton industry, who did exactly the same work but got paid very different rates, to the general assumption that managerial work is more skilled than that conducted by non-managers, to divisions of labour that are gendered and racialised (Reskin and Roos 1990). These were recently illustrated by the film *Made in Dagenham*, a fictional version of the 1968 strike by women workers at Ford. At the time Ford's pay scales differentiated between skilled workers, semi-skilled workers, unskilled workers and women, with women paid at 85 per cent of the wage of an unskilled man. The strike resulted in a wage rise to 92 per cent of the unskilled male workers' rate but, more importantly, also helped to stimulate legislation stipulating equal pay for work of equal value. The undervaluing of women's skills continues to the present day (see Grugulis 2007). As Green and Ashton (1992: 296) point out 'the labels used to describe job vacancies as 'skilled' often tell us less about the actual technical content of the job than about the sex of the persons likely to get the jobs'. Skills are social constructs and people who are already disadvantaged in the labour market by their gender, race or class are likely to be viewed as less skilled than high status workers regardless of what their job involves or how well they do it.

This broader definition of skill in the person, skill in the job and skill in the social setting is valuable since it locates skill firmly in the work process and the social system, which serves both to make skills a meaningful analytic device through which work can be assessed and ensure that skills-based interventions are more likely to have an impact on practice.

Skill Formation Systems

When reviewing skills it is also useful to consider the very different national systems of provision that exist. Clearly, different nations vary greatly in the extent to which they support skills, the way they support skills and the skills that are supported; in particular, the extent to which the state will intervene to regulate or provide skills, as in Germany, Taiwan and Denmark, or to which skill provision is left to the market, as in the UK and USA. Germany is a good example of highly regulated provision and has an excellent system of apprenticeships. They are designed by a consortia of educationalists, employers and trade unions and young people undertake specially designed work projects, placements and college courses over a period of several years. This ensures that nearly two-thirds of the workforce are qualified to intermediate level (roughly the equivalent of academic 'A' levels, the qualification taken at age 18 in the UK) in the area they are employed in, although provision beyond this level is much less certain (Lane 1989). At the other end of the spectrum, the USA is primarily market-oriented and world-leading universities provide graduates for the financial services, aero engineering, enter-tainment, biotechnology and software industries. There is also, however, a chronic shortage of low- and intermediate-level provision, which raises particular problems of social inclusion in a nation where health benefits are often dependent on employment (Rubery and Grimshaw 2003).

In Taiwan and Denmark, both of which are dominated by small and medium sized enterprises (which are far less likely to train and develop workers than their larger competitors), the state has intervened to ensure that vocational education and training take place and that activities are of high quality, but these interventions take very different forms. In Taiwan extensive technical and vocational skills were introduced into the education system. Despite the fact that most of the demand was for (high status) academic courses, and that these would have been cheaper to provide, the Taiwanese government invested extensively in the education of scientists and engineers. Access to academic courses was officially restricted, more than half of school children were channelled into technical training and, at university level, more courses were made available for scientists and engineers and new Institutes of Technology launched. Student numbers, textbooks and curricula were state controlled, and this meant that Taiwan succeeded in both increasing the numbers of low-cost industrial products for export and also managed the transition from this to higher value-added production across many, if not all, sectors without significant reported skills shortages (Green *et al.* 1999). In Denmark, a long legacy of strong and collaborative trade unions meant that workplace learning programmes could be set centrally (by both employers and unions) to ensure high standards and consistency, while state subsidy provided for a high uptake by firms and apprentices (Ashton 2004).

These differences in national policy and practice have a significant impact on the way firms choose to compete, as Mason *et al's* (1996) comparative study of biscuit manufacturing reveals. In Germany, where the majority of workers were trained apprentices, one skilled worker could run two or three lines and workers were involved in implementing and improving the way new machinery worked. Regular maintenance ensured that machines were in full working order and products were of high quality, with most effort going into those aspects of production which would earn the firm additional revenue in store, such as adding fillings, variegated coatings, decoration and packaging. In the UK the biscuits produced were simple and mass manufactured. Unskilled workers were taught only part of the production process and worked repetitively, so that several were required on each line, while 24–hour working left no time for regular maintenance, so machinery was constantly breaking down. At the UK plant additional labour was employed clearing up after such breakdowns and sweeping broken biscuits away (see Clarke and Wall 1996; Prais 1995 for similar assessments of other industries).

Each is a legitimate way to compete (and Mason and his colleagues were careful to note that in each country the demand was for their own, national type of biscuit). Moreover, the firm-level strategic choices about product markets and skill utilisation are heavily influenced by factors such as labour markets and competition policies. Interestingly, many of these differences seem to be fairly stable (Whitley 1999; 2003).

Learning at Work

Given this broader focus on the individual, the nature of work and the social setting, this chapter goes on to consider what is happening to training and also what is happening to learning in the workplace. It is a truism that in times of recession, training is one of the first casualties (though, see Felstead and Green 1994 for an account of the resilience of training in the 1980s-1990s recession). The Chartered Institute of Personnel and Development's (CIPD) *Learning and Talent Development* survey of 2011 (CIPD 2011) certainly shows some signs of retrenchment (see below for further concerns) with external practitioners, workshops and conferences still common for leaders, but much else moved in-house. When asked which practices they found most effective, some 54 per cent of organisations named e-learning, 47 per cent coaching by line managers, 45 per cent in-house development programmes and 37 per cent internal knowledge sharing events. Most organisations had reported a decline in both provision and the funds available for training over the recession, and although many had seen improvements over the last year, the decline in public sector training was particularly marked. This is a matter for concern since the public sector has traditionally been one of the strongest sites for skills development.

Unsurprisingly the survey found little evidence of the sort of structured training needs analysis, delivery and evaluation that so many textbooks advocate. However, just over half of organisations planned training, at least to the extent of discussing it with trainees, and 84 per cent evaluated it (although in most cases this was limited to 'happy sheets' following courses).

Encouragingly, there is considerable evidence of good practice with developmental opportunities that benefit people at every level of the workforce. Two initiatives in particular are worth mentioning here, 'unionlearn', which encourages and funds a whole range of skills-based activities through trade unions, and the NHS Skills Escalator, which stimulates skills and progression within the NHS. The Union Learning Fund was established in 1998 to provide resources for unions to support learning at work. By 2010, 230 learning centres had been established and 514 learning agreements signed with employers, with training from these initiatives addressing basic skills gaps, work related and non-work related learning covering an estimated 250,000 learners each year, with 91 per cent of projects open to all employees, regardless of union membership. Practice covered the full range of learning from Bombardier and the CSEU's provision of IT, mentoring and support at their East Midlands base, to Mersey Travel's success in getting 98 per cent of its workforce qualified at NVQ levels 2 and 3 and reducing sickness absence (Stuart *et al.* 2010). One union branch secretary, working with the NHS on a successful 'unionlearn' project maintained that, 'If people are given a basic right of education and are helped and supported, it produces a better workforce ... There's less sickness, less discontent, less people moving on' (Warhurst *et al.* 2007: 10). The initiative may also encourage collaborative relations between unions and employers (Findlay and Warhurst 2011).

In the NHS, the Skills Escalator was set up in 2002 to increase participation in learning, meet skills shortages, expand opportunities for career development and increase productivity; it has proved extremely effective at linking training opportunities to job redesign and, through this, to career progression. For most of the low-skilled workers on the Skills Escalator, training takes the form of NVQs. These are low-level, problematic qualifications which rarely benefit the people who gain them (Grugulis 2003; Wolf 1995). However, because the NHS specifically links training to pay and progression by, for example, creating new roles such as that of Ward Housekeeper for cleaners or Junior Doctor's Assistant for Health Care Assistants,

---

Box 9.1 Migrant workers' project, London, UNITE

The project promotes learning with migrant and other vulnerable workers in the contract-cleaning sector in London, building on the Justice for Cleaners campaign, and covers workers from over 25 countries. With an estimated 25,000 migrant workers involved in cleaning services in the capital, the project has sought to organise these workers to promote labour rights, using education as a means of giving them access to trade union representation. It started with 15 learners at a Saturday English class, but demand soon grew. Over 1,000 vulnerable workers have received learning and 1,479 have received information, advice and guidance. Currently there are 240 worker learners that attend sessions on Saturdays and Sundays at premises provided by Syracuse University; employers provide no facilities. Twenty-seven new ULRs [Union Learning Representatives] have also been trained, the majority of which are migrant workers.

"This project has opened people's eyes to migrant workers and its multicultural aspect has had an impact on the union, as well as making the union more attractive for migrant workers. It would not have happened as quickly without the project but it will continue because it is member-led".

(National Union Learning Organiser) Taken from Stuart *et al.* (2010: 18)

NVQs are connected to developmental work and so become opportunities for development themselves. The initiative is not without its problems. There is far more demand for career opportunities than there is a supply of posts to meet them and the generation of progression routes has created turnover problems for facilities departments (Cox *et al.* 2008). The new roles are not all examples of up-skilling and there are wider problems with the NHS reforms (Bach *et al.* 2007; Cooke 2006; Bach *et al.* 2008).

These are both substantial initiatives, with many millions of pounds and extensive resources invested in making them successful, but it is also possible to observe excellent developmental practice in small firms with formal and informal opportunities to learn.

Indeed, much of the exchange of knowledge and expertise depends, at its most basic, on occupational groups. Orr's (1996) ethnography of photocopier repair technicians reveals the way groups used to meet at the same cafe for lunch and talk about problems, exchange histories of well-known machines or simply tell 'war stories'. While Lave and Wenger (1991) draw on studies of workers from butchers

---

Box 9.2 The hairdressing salon

This small, single owner hairdressing salon in a market town in the East Midlands has eight staff and an annual turnover of £200,000, of which ten to fifteen per cent is net profit reinvested into the business every year. The owner belongs to an elite club of hair designers, of which there are about 500 members in the UK. Annual membership of the club (which has just celebrated its 25 year anniversary) costs several thousand pounds per year. As a result of adopting the club's sales techniques, the salon's annual turnover of products has increased by 500 per cent. The motivation to learn in the salon is stimulated by the desire to earn money and to ensure that the salon achieves maximum capacity. If stylists can continually reach their targets, they will be promoted every three months and could end up as a profit-sharing partner in the business. This competitive approach did not appear to undermine team-based approaches to learning. Staff described how they learn informally, from each other in the salon, through observation and through discussing the best techniques in relation to each other's clients. They also coach each other to improve their skills and learn by reading trade magazines.

Taken from Unwin, Felstead and Fuller (2007: 6-7)

---

and recovering alcoholics to midwives to describe a process they term 'situated learning'. In this, novices are legitimate peripheral participants; their group membership is justified by the fact that they perform routine tasks, fetching and carrying for their more expert colleagues, and this membership allows them to watch, learn and progress in their chosen occupation.

Fuller and Unwin (2004), in an attempt to theorise the differences between organisations where staff have opportunities to develop and those where they do not, coined the terms 'expansive' and 'restrictive' workplaces. This is very useful since it allows analytical attention to extend beyond formal training (at best an imperfect proxy for skills). So, in expansive workplaces, a breadth of work, experience and contacts facilitate learning. Workers are likely to be given discretion, to have a wide range of contacts both inside and outside the firm and to be engaged with a range of tasks. By contrast, in restrictive workplaces, tasks and responsibilities are narrowly defined; expertise is automated, scripted away or physically relocated so novices have less access to expert and experienced workers. Work is simplified and codified so that extensive skills development is considered less necessary (see Grugulis and Vincent 2005 for a discussion of the effect of fragmenting organisations on skills). Learning can and does occur naturally at work, but, for this to happen, work, workplaces and workers need to be structured appropriately, for although the process is natural, it is not inevitable.

What is Happening to Skills and Training?

Given this, and having established what skills are, looked at some of the different national systems that they can be located in and the detail of skills development in the workplace, this chapter goes on to review the current trajectories in both skills and training in practice.

Training

Despite the positive rhetoric that surrounds training (see, for example, Leitch 2006), actual provision is often dependent on state intervention either directly, through legislation over particular areas such as health and safety and the provision of colleges and courses, or indirectly through industry regulation. In France, levies fund much vocational training, while German licences to practice ensure that people are appropriately qualified. However, as observed above, not all countries accept regulation so readily and in the market-based Anglo-American economies, it is generally both fragmented and less effective. In the US, some sectors do regulate training practice, but this is becoming increasingly rare, with amendments generally limiting regulation rather than extending it. This liberation rarely increases provision – levels of training fell in the construction industry following deregulation (Bosch 2005).

In the UK, training levels rose through the 1980s and 1990s before declining from 2002 and by 2009 they had fallen back to 14 per cent, equivalent to 1993 levels (Mason and Bishop 2010). This is of particular concern since part of the earlier increase involved provision being spread more thinly. Courses became shorter but more workers benefitted from them and as part of this change, there was a greater emphasis on informational workshops rather than skills development (Keep 1989). Since the current fall in training levels is not coupled with any evidence that courses are lengthening again, it seems that provision is now both shorter and less widely available. This fall in provision has hit the best qualified the most. Vocational training has always raised issues of social inclusion, since it has effectively served the function of a hospital for the healthy, with most (and often most well-funded) provision available for those who were already the best qualified. In this latest decline, this gap has narrowed slightly, since training levels for those with the fewest qualifications have remained fairly steady, while those for the best qualified have declined. However, as Mason and Bishop (2010) point out in their assessment, it is difficult to celebrate such a narrowing of differentials as more socially inclusive, when it represents a levelling down, rather than a levelling up. Declining training levels for the highly skilled do not fit well with official attempts to foster a national knowledge economy with more knowledge-based jobs and competition fuelled by innovation.

Yet, at the same time, official support for training has increased. Although the UK has never regulated employment issues heavily, vocational training has received both practical and rhetorical support from governments of every persuasion and subsidies are extensive, with 45 per cent of adult education and training funded by government in 2007–2008 (IFLL 2009). A considerable proportion of this goes directly to firms and McDonald's received £37 million in 2009 (James and Keep 2010). UK vocational training and apprenticeship programmes, unlike their German equivalents, vary greatly in quality. Some are excellent and those run by British Gas are regularly over-subscribed. Others are far less rigorous (Grugulis 2003) and even officially approved qualifications often fail to have the depth and breadth observed elsewhere (Wolf 2011). Subsidy, it seems, is no guarantee of quality. In this instance, given how tightly controlled McDonald's catering is, and how unlikely it is that any skills learned would be transferable outside their restaurants, it is difficult to justify such extensive funding. As Keep (2011) argues, it appears that some employers have learned to play the system, because employer withdrawal will always be countered by additional state funding.

Skills

While training levels are in decline, the findings on skills are more positive, in that employee skills are rising across the developed world. In Britain 30 per cent of jobs required level four qualifications (degree level or its vocational equivalent) on entry in 2006, compared to 20 per cent in 1986. At the other end of the spectrum, the proportion of jobs which require no skills has declined from 38 per cent to 28 per cent, findings that are reinforced by the time employees report they need to learn to do a job well. They show the proportion needing more than two years' experience to do well rising from 22 per cent to 30 per cent and those needing less than one month falling from 27 per cent to 19 per cent (Felstead *et al.* 2007:53–54). In both the US and Germany qualifications have risen and the proportion of jobs which demand at least college-level education has dramatically increased (Green 2006).

So far so good. However, while qualifications are rising there are also instances of deskilling and it may be that the labour market is polarising around an hour-glass shape, with most jobs either low- or high-skilled (Nolan and Slater 2003; Holmes 2011). In the retail banking industry, where traditionally male employees were encouraged to progress through a hierarchy of job roles to management, the disaggregation of products into specialist processing 'warehouses', dedicated central lending departments and computerised credit scoring have all resulted in the dramatic deskilling of branch staff. Strong internal labour markets and lifetime careers for men have been replaced by routinised jobs (Crompton and Jones 1984; Hasluck 1999). Elsewhere in the economy the number of knowledge intensive jobs is rising, but so too is demand for low-level service work, for cleaners, carers and security guards (Goos and Manning 2003; Nolan and Slater 2003).

This has two implications. Firstly it raises issues of progression. The clearly demarcated and well understood career ladders of bureaucratic firms rely on intermediate-skilled jobs as stepping stones. A polarised labour market, shaping and shaped by the fragmentation of organisational structures observed above, offers few such links. This is a concern since traditionally people have been able to find a way into 'good' jobs (better paid, more secure, more prospects of career progression) through work and particularly by gaining skills. When these links are shattered, progression is harder and much of the 'churn' at the bottom end of the labour market is between 'bad' jobs with low pay and little access to career ladders and unemployment, rather than bad jobs and better jobs (Kenway 2011).

Secondly, when the differences in trajectory between individuals and jobs are considered, it becomes apparent that there is a mismatch between the skills individuals possess and those that their jobs require. In the UK there is an oversupply of skilled workers at every level of qualification, and the demand for unskilled workers far outstrips supply. This has largely been caused by individual successes in gaining qualifications. Between 1986 and 2006 the number of people with no qualifications fell by 5.5 million; the number of jobs which require no qualifications at entry fell by only 1.2 million (Felstead *et al.* 2007: 59). More broadly, it seems that employers are taking advantage of this increase in credentials to hire better qualified people, whether or not their skills are needed on the job. Some 40 per cent of workers now protest that they are more highly skilled than their work demands and only 14 per cent of employees, most of whom are older workers, are under-qualified for the tasks that they perform (p. 63).

There is also an additional area of concern. While skill levels in general have risen, discretion has actively declined and this can be seen most dramatically among professional workers. In 1986, 72 per cent of professionals reported that they had 'a great deal' of choice over the way that they worked. By 2001 this figure had fallen to 38 per cent (Felstead *et al.* 2002: 71).

A review of many traditionally high discretion occupations demonstrates this decline in practice. Barrett's (2005) study of computer programmers reveals workers largely engaged in repetitive tasks, cutting and pasting code and checking detailed sections over and over again, while Hales (2000) reveals the restrictions on managerial work (see also Grugulis, Bozkurt and Clegg 2011). Many attempts to control highly skilled workers have proved counterproductive (see, for example, Whalen and Vinkhuyzen 2000), but others have proved enduring. In the UK in particular, public sector reforms, target setting and the introduction of the national curriculum have had dramatic effects on the work of those affected (Bach *et al.* 2007). In the private sector, technology makes a high degree of control possible and it is now common, for example, for lawyers and accountants to monitor their billable time in six minute sections.

This also has implications for where work is done. Until relatively recently the traditional global model of off-shoring was that predictable, generally physical production was undertaken in developing, low-wage countries while research and development, product innovation and high-tech tasks were confined to the developed world, effectively justifying higher wage costs. However, the exceptionally highly-educated workforce in China has enabled it to effectively leapfrog this development curve and set up enclaves of highly-educated production with high-skill but low-wage workers. High-skill production is not immune from the reverse auction pushing down wage costs and nor is it free from detailed control, as increasingly restrictive routines are applied to high-tech and high-skill jobs, a process Brown *et al.* (2011) describe as digital Taylorism.

This has worrying implications for the extent to which high wage competition is ever possible, since low-wage, high-skill production seems to overturn the normal expectations of economic competition. The decline of discretion is also a conundrum. Discretion is a pre-requisite for many high-skill jobs and it is often the space that discretion provides which enables workers to develop their skills. When workers judge the quality of their own work, make decisions, problem solve and take responsibility for actions they are able to use and acquire higher levels of skill. This is not to argue, as some theorists have, that discretion is skill and skill is discretion: an anaesthetist is tightly monitored by sophisticated machinery and follows set procedures during an operation but few would argue that their work is less highly skilled than that of a gardener who is free to decide when, where and how they work (Noon and Blyton 2007). However, in general, reductions in discretion are closely linked to reductions in skill (Braverman 1974). It is difficult to resolve the paradox of a labour market with ever higher levels of skill and declining levels of discretion.

Soft skills

Traditionally, references to skill have assumed physical, technical and generally male activities, with full-time work ensuring a 'family' wage and unions safeguarding skill recognition. Today, just as the typical worker has changed, so too have shared understandings of skill, with soft and social skills most in demand by employers (Payne 2000; Keep 2001). With the majority of the workforce in the developed world located in the service sector, it is not surprising that customer service and communication skills dominate organisational requirements.

Soft and social skills are vital to almost every form of work. Technical and engineering factories require teamwork and problem-solving skills to ensure smooth running and to resolve issues. Shibata's (1999, 2001) study of a Japanese firm and its US subsidiary reveals that workers were trained in quality circles and Kaizen (continuous improvement) circles as well as mathematics and production, so that they could solve maintenance problems and this work involved predicting breakdowns, analysing problems and solving them. In Thompson *et al.*'s (1995: 735) research into bus and truck manufacture, a frame assembly production manager said that what he was looking for in a worker was:

> The skill I am looking for is the ability of a person to completely motivate himself, use his initiative, have an understanding of what he needs to do and be able to complete it

and overcome any of the minor problems which may crop up and have the *nous* to alert somebody if he still has a problem.

In the service sector, particularly in customer and client-facing roles where the process of being served is as much a part of the transaction as any product exchanged, these soft skills are even more vital (Noon and Blyton 2007). The extent of this is shown in one survey where respondents said that if they were unable to obtain help from a colleague who was both pleasant to work with and capable of answering their technical query (a 'star'), they would far rather seek advice from 'lovable fools', who were nice to deal with but would be unable to answer questions accurately, than 'competent jerks' who could deal with technical issues but had few social skills (Casciaro and Lobo 2005). This, however, also presents us with a dilemma. At one level, soft skills are a necessary and integral part of any workplace activity, without which, activities such as team-working, communication and problem solving would be impossible. At another, they are defined in ways that are so elusive that they are meaningless and effectively act as legitimation for gendered, racialised and class-based stereotypes, with skills ascribed rather than observed.

In practice, different employers emphasise different social attributes so the soft skills desired are many and varied, with lists including everything from presentation skills and self esteem to problem solving, team-working and loyalty. There is nothing new about employers focusing on their employees' character, indeed this is a familiar feature of most accounts of work; however, calling these qualities skills is both a new development and inaccurate. These are personal qualities, psychological attributes, virtues and competencies, they are not skills. This is of more than semantic interest since the re-labelling effectively individualises responsibility for each characteristic. If loyalty is part of a work relationship, then reciprocity is expected through good treatment, reasonable workloads, appropriate tasks or terms and conditions; if loyalty is a *skill*, then individuals are assumed to possess and demonstrate it regardless of treatment (Lafer 2004).

One US study reported marked differences in the employment experiences of the staff of two warehouses in Los Angeles (Moss and Tilly 1996, 2001). Both businesses recruited from the same population of ex-gang members, but while one condemned turnover rates of 25 per cent, criticised workers' lack of commitment, their preference for gang-colours and their poor personal hygiene, the owner of the second warehouse reported excellent staff who followed the firm's dress code, turnover rates of 2 per cent and high levels of loyalty. Tellingly, the second warehouse paid between 50 cents and $2.50 per hour more than the first.

Classifying such attributes as skills also legitimises judgements based on stereotypes. Again there is little that is novel about this in the workplace. Collinson *et al*'s (1990) detailed study of recruitment reveals women and men had a preference for jobs 'appropriate' for their gender and were discriminated against when they had to apply for less 'suitable' posts. This gendered division of labour is not something the labour market has outgrown. Even recent studies of reorganisations demonstrate gendered restructuring, generally with women concentrated in low-paid, customer facing roles with limited prospects (Skuratowicz and Hunter 2004; Grugulis *et al.* 2003). But such segregation can now be justified on the basis that women have more customer service skills than their male colleagues, just as promotions can be denied for lack of aggression or gravitas.

In practice, too, the impact that soft skills have also seems very different for those who are highly skilled than for the low-skilled, low-wage workers at the bottom of the labour market. Early accounts of soft skills argued that women's skills were undervalued because they could not be labelled and that, once suitable labels had been devised, women's wages would be boosted. Unfortunately, this greater recognition of, and additional labels for, women's skills has not resulted in additional payments and may have actually led to more women being allocated gender-based work. It seems that at the bottom end of the labour market, soft skills are a passport to low-level, poorly paid jobs which often have high levels of turnover. Training courses, designed to get the unemployed into work in Britain, the US and Canada involve little substantive content (see, for example, Lafer 2004; Cohen 2003), equipping workers only for low-level work. Small wonder then that, as Bolton (2004) notes, 'soft skill' shortages, in marked contrast to those of technical skills, are rarely resolved by wage premia.

It may be that soft skills disadvantage all workers, since they exist largely in the eye of the beholder. Traditional skills are readily visible to all, so a well-engineered bridge, a finely soldered join or a solidly built wall will be appreciated by all those with expertise in the area, effectively conferring status on the craftsperson. By contrast soft skills are subjective and intangible. Frequently demanded traits such as loyalty, customer focus and helpfulness are only valuable if they are demonstrated in ways and places acceptable to management, and then only if also observed and appropriately labelled by management. In place of independent artisans leaving tangible records of their accomplishments we have courtiers pleasing the current monarch (Grugulis and Vincent 2009). However, in practice, rather than disadvantaging all, soft skills seem to polarise the workforce, effectively advantaging those who are already highly skilled. In Grugulis and Vincent's (2009) study of housing benefit caseworkers and IT consultants, while both groups were expected to demonstrate soft skills, benefit caseworkers were deskilled as a result, since the job was seen as only requiring soft skills. Training times were reduced, less well-qualified applicants recruited, managers with no experience of housing benefit appointed and the technical aspect of the job devalued. By contrast the IT consultants' technical skills were highly valued and a great deal of effort was put into developing them, for this group soft skills were important, but in addition to their existing skills, not instead of them. As Dickerson and Green (2002) observe, skills need to be put into practice to be of organisational value, so an IT specialist would need to communicate their skills, fit systems to organisational requirements and problem solve when errors arose, but they also need to be valued by management.

Discussion

There are a number of contradictory changes here. Training levels and discretion have declined, in some cases dramatically, but skills, gauged against a number of indicators, have risen. This fits neither of the principal theories of skill trajectories particularly comfortably. The first focuses on observations of deskilling. In *Labour and Monopoly Capital*, Harry Braverman (1974) attempted to reconcile the very modern dilemma of rising educational qualifications and ever more tightly controlled jobs. At the other extreme, advocates and gurus predicting the knowledge economy, argue that the evolution of work has demanded increasingly intelligent workers. These professionals, who are hired for their brainpower, rather than the strength in their hands and bodies, represent the future of work when automation and out-sourcing will strip the developed world of routine jobs and firms will compete on the basis of knowledge and innovation (see, for example, Leadbeater 2000).

Both positions are oversimplified. Braverman successfully incorporates detailed observations of real work into his analysis, together with references to pay and status. But he romanticises the freedoms historically available to craft workers (his implicit and explicit comparators) and, as Rose *et al.* (1994) point out, skill levels are actually rising rather than falling. Writers on the knowledge economy generally have less empirical evidence on their side. Their evidence is more often anecdotal, with examples taken from a narrow range of jobs, so that it is difficult to see how their conclusions could be extended beyond a small group of privileged professionals (for an excellent critique, see Thompson 2004). Some accounts do indeed claim high numbers of knowledge workers in the economy, but these tend to reclassify all service sector workers as knowledge workers, and while it is true that the service sector includes consultants, teachers, academics and medics it also, and in far greater numbers, covers waiters, carers and caterers. Even Robert Reich (1991), who coined the term 'symbolic analyst' to describe the knowledge working professionals who manipulate symbols rather than physical objects, argued that such workers would always be in a minority.

It seems doubtful whether any skills trajectory, deskilling or upskilling is inevi-table. National policies, sectoral institutions, inter-firm competition, supply-chain networks and technological innovations all serve to drive skills down as well as up. The workplace of the future is as likely to be a technically sophisticated but low-skill call centre, a shop where innovations have allowed head office to take ever more control over the activities of customer-facing staff, or a consultancy firm where technologies are shaped and re-shaped by highly skilled consultants. All are likely to exist, in some form or other, and organisations can and will make very different choices on the skills that staff can exercise.

Within firms, particularly given this book's focus on HRM, it is also worthwhile considering HRM's influence on skills and training. Theoretically this is significant.

Skills and training are key features of 'soft' HRM (Legge 1995) and, as Keep and Mayhew (1996) argue, they are the pivotal aspect of HR practice. When firms focus on skills development, employees can contribute more to work and it makes sense to involve them in workplace decisions or vary their pay by the strength of that contribution. When firms fail to invest in skills and see labour as a cost to be limited rather than a resource to be developed, then other HR practices, such as employee involvement or performance related pay, make little sense either. Small wonder, then, that training is one of the consistent elements in the many varied lists of 'best practice' HRM, High Performance Work Practices or High Commitment Management. On this basis, a broader definition of skill should enhance Strategic HRM (see, for example, Arthur 1999).

However, as the evidence above indicates, while some firms, institutions and nations are encouraged by this theoretical logic to offer excellent developmental opportunities which fit seamlessly into wider organisational strategies (Boxall and Purcell 2003), not all practice is quite so neat and while the advantages of implementing groups of cumulative HR practices can readily be seen, this does not necessarily translate into practice.

Conclusions

What implications do all these have, both for skills and for workers and workplaces? Firstly it is clear that changes will be very different for varying groups of workers. The polarisation of pay observed elsewhere is also apparent in skills, for while it is difficult to claim that a knowledge economy exists anywhere in the world, there are certainly knowledge intensive jobs which are extremely highly rewarded. Far from spreading to the labour market more generally, such work may be considered distinctive, the preserve of an elite, exceptional few (Michaels *et al.* 2001) despite recent increases in educational attainment (Brown and Hesketh 2004).

This is worrying since many of the traditional structures for developing skills have collapsed and the new ones are often uneasy. The division between the highly-paid elite and low-paid routine workers seems to take place in the education system, with access to the best jobs confined to graduates from a small number of universities (Brown and Hesketh 2004). In other words, changes to the graduate labour market and increasing numbers of people gaining degrees have not been taken as an opportunity to redesign work so that it can exercise more of workers' talents; rather recruiters aim to find new methods to identify the top fraction. Ironically, the one economy where more highly-qualified labour market entrants have influence on work and vocational training is Germany. There, although graduate numbers are deliberately kept low, at around 17 per cent, an influx of well-educated school-leavers has been used as a stimulus to make apprenticeships and jobs more demanding (Bosch 2010).

Elsewhere, while knowledge economy jobs do exist, they are easily outnumbered by no- and low-skill *McJobs* which are poorly paid, often insecure and frequently fail to link to traditional career ladders, making it harder for workers to progress out of them to other types of work. The shift in emphasis to focus on soft skills seems to feed into this polarisation, with soft skills under- and un-valued at the *McJobs* end of the labour market, but attracting respect and pay premia in high-skilled work.

HR departments have a choice in the way they respond to these challenges. Some, no doubt, will follow the example of the NHS with its Skills Escalator and actively look for ways that workers can progress out of dull, restrictive and low-paid jobs through training, secondments and work-redesign. For others, the developmental focus will be restricted to highly skilled knowledge workers and higher level managers, with 'soft' HR practices a perk for high status workers, while those highly qualified workers who have not gained high-status jobs become a source of discontent and alienation. Clearly, the demand and supply sides of the labour market are out of kilter, with demand failing to keep pace with individual improvements to qualification levels. It is possible that in the absence of formal job redesign, such a change to the supply side could result in a type of grass-roots revolution in which individuals 'grew' their own jobs, taking on more tasks and more responsibilities because they were more capable. Such is the optimistic potential. It is also possible, particularly given the decline in discretion, that this increase in qualified workers at entry level will simply result in higher levels of frustration and alienation since talented, qualified people will be trapped in tightly controlled jobs that they cannot change. Realistically, both types of jobs are likely to exist in the future. It would be nice to believe that jobs with capacity for growth will outnumber the alienated and alienating ones, but the evidence on discretion provides few grounds for optimism.

REFERENCES

Arthur, J.B. 1999: Explaining variation in human resource practices in US steel mini-mills, in P. Cappelli (ed.), *Employment Practices and Business Strategy*, 11–42. Oxford and New York: Oxford University Press.

Ashton, D. 2004: The political economy of workplace learning, in H. Rainbird, A. Fuller and A. Munro (eds.), *Workplace Learning in Context*, London and New York: Routledge.

Bach, S., Kessler, I. and Heron, P. 2007: The consequences of assistant roles in the public services: degradation or empowerment? *Human Relations*, **60**(9), 1267–1292.

Bach, S., Kessler, I. and Heron, P. 2008: Role redesign in a modernised NHS: the case of health care assistants, *Human Resource Management Journal*, **18**(2), 171–187.

Barrett, R. 2005: Managing the software development labour process: direct control, time and technical autonomy, in R. Barrett (ed.), *Management, Labour Process and Software Development: Reality Bytes*, Abingdon: Routledge.

Bolton, S.C. 2004: Conceptual confusions: emotion work as skilled work, in C.W. Warhurst, I. Grugulis and E. Keep (eds.), *The Skills that Matter*, 19–37. Basingstoke: Palgrave Macmillan.

Bosch, G. 2005: Employability, Innovation and Lifelong Learning. Presented at *Second International Conference on Training, Employability and Employment*, 21–23 September, Monash University Centre, Prato.

Bosch, G. 2010: The Revitalization of the Dual System of Vocational Training in Germany, in G. Bosch and J. Charest (eds.), *Vocational Training: International Perspectives*, pp. 136–161. New York and Abingdon: Routledge.

Boxall, P. and Purcell, J. 2003: *Strategy and Human Resource Management*, London: Palgrave.

Braverman, H. 1974: *Labour and Monopoly Capital*, New York: Monthly Review Press.

Brown, P. and Hesketh, A. 2004: *The Mismanagement of Talent: employability and jobs in the knowledge economy*, Oxford: Oxford University Press.

Brown, P., Lauder, H. and Ashton, D. 2011: *The Global Auction*, Oxford University Press.

Casciaro, T. and Lobo, M.S. 2005: Competent jerks, lovable fools and the formation of social networks, *Harvard Business Review*, **83**(6), 92–99.

CIPD 2011: *Learning and Talent Development, Annual Report 2011*, London: Chartered Institute of Personnel and Development.

Clarke, L. and Wall, C. 1996: *Skills and the Construction Process: a comparative study of vocational training and quality in social housebuilding*, Bristol: Policy Press.

Cockburn, C. 1983: *Brothers: male dominance and technological change*, London: Pluto Press.

Cohen, M.G. 2003: *Training the excluded for work*, Vancouver and Toronto: UBC Press.

Collinson, D., Knights, D. and Collinson, M. 1990: *Managing to Discriminate*, London and New York: Routledge.

Cooke, H. 2006: Seagull management and the control of nursing work, *Work, Employment and Society*, **20**(2), 223–243.

Cox, A., Grimshaw, D., Carroll, M. and McBride, A. 2008: Reshaping internal labour markets in the National Health Service: new prospects for pay and training for lower skilled service workers?, *Human Resource Management Journal*, **18**(4), 347–365.

Crompton, R. and Jones, G. 1984: *White Collar Proletariat: Deskilling and Gender in the Clerical Labour Process*, London: Macmillan.

Cutler, T. 1992: Vocational training and British economic performance: a further instalment of the 'British Labour Problem?, *Work, Employment and Society*, **6**(2), 161–183.

Darr, A. 2004: The interdependence of social and technical skills in the sale of emergent technology, in C. Warhurst, I. Grugulis and E. Keep (eds.), *The Skills that Matter*, Basingstoke: Palgrave Macmillan.

Dickerson, A. and Green, F. 2002: The growth and valuation of generic skills in *SKOPE Research Paper*, Oxford and Warwick: Universities of Oxford and Warwick.

Felstead, A. and Green, F. 1994: Training during the recession, *Work, Employment and Society*, **8**(2), 199–219.

Felstead, A., Gaillie, G. and Green, F. 2002: *Work Skills in Britain 1986–2002*, Nottingham: DfES Publications.

Felstead, A., Gallie, G., Green, F. and Zhou, Y. 2007: *Skills at Work 1986–2006*, Oxford: SKOPE and ESRC.

Findlay, P. and Warhurst, C. 2011: Union Learning Funds and Trade Union Revitalization: A New Tool in the Toolkit?, *British Journal of Industrial Relations*, **49**(s1), s115–s134.

Finegold, D. 1999: Creating self-sustaining, high-skill ecosystems, *Oxford Review of Economic Policy*, **15**(1), 60–81.

Fuller, A. and Unwin, L. 2004: Expansive learning environments: integrating organisational and personal development. In Rainbird, H., Fuller, A.F. and Munro, A. (eds) *Workplace Learning in Context*, London and New York: Routledge.

Goos, M. and Manning, A. 2003: McJobs and MacJobs: the growing polarisation of jobs in the UK, pp. 70–85. In Dickens, R., Gregg, P. and Wadsworth, J. (eds) *The Labour Market under New Labour*, Houndsmills: Palgrave Macmillan.

Green, F. 2006: *Demanding Work: the paradox of job quality in the affluent economy*, Princeton and Oxford: Princeton University Press.

Green, F. and Ashton, D. 1992: Skill shortages and skill deficiency: a critique, *Work, Employment and Society*, **6**(2), 287–301.

Green, F., Ashton, D., James, D. and Sung, J. 1999: The role of the state in skill formation: evidence from the republic of Korea, Singapore and Taiwan, *Oxford Review of Economic Policy*, **15**(1), 82–96.

Grugulis, I. 2003: The contribution of NVQs to the growth of skills in the UK, *British Journal of Industrial Relations*, **41**(3), 457–475.

Grugulis, I. 2007: *Skills, training and human resource development: a critical text*, Basingstoke: Palgrave Macmillan.

Grugulis, I. and Vincent, S. 2005: Changing boundaries, shaping skills: the fragmented organisational form and employee skills, in M. Marchington, D. Grimshaw, J. Rubery and H. Willmott (eds.), *Fragmenting Work: blurring organisational boundaries and disordering hierarchies*, Oxford: Oxford University Press.

Grugulis, I. and Vincent, S. 2009: Whose skill is it anyway? 'Soft' skills and polarisation, *Work, Employment and Society*.

Grugulis, I., Bozkurt, O. and Clegg, J. 2011: No place to hide? The realities of leadership in UK supermarkets, in I. Grugulis and O. Bozkurt (eds.), *Retail Work*, 193–212. Houndsmills: Palgrave Macmillan.

Grugulis, I., Vincent, S. and Hebson, G. 2003: The rise of the 'network organisation' and the decline of discretion, *Human Resource Management Journal*, **13**(2), 45–59.

Hales, C. 2000: Management and Empowerment Programmes, *Work, Employment and Society*, **14**(3), 501–519.

Hasluck, C. 1999: Employment Prospects and Skill Needs in the Banking, Finance and Insurance Sector, *Skills Task Force Research Paper*, Sudbury, Suffolk: DfEE Publications.

Holmes, C. 2011: Implications of polarisation for UK policymakers in *SKOPE Issues Papers*, Oxford and Cardiff: SKOPE, Universities of Oxford and Cardiff.

IFLL 2009: Inquiry into the future of Lifelong Learning in *Learning Through Life*, Leicester: National Institute of Adult Continuing Education.

James, S. and Keep, E. 2010: Are bad jobs inevitable? Incentives to learn at the bottom end of the labour market in *International Labour Process Conference*, Rutgers, NJ.

Keep, E. 1989: Corporate training strategies: the vital component? In J. Storey (ed.), *New Perspectives on Human Resource Management*, 109–125. London: Routledge.

Keep, E. 2001: If it moves, it's a skill. Presented at *ESRC seminar on The Changing Nature of Skills and Knowledge*, 3–4 September, Manchester.

Keep, E. 2011: Education and Industry - taking two steps back and reflecting, *Education and Employers Taskforce Seminar*, London.

Keep, E. and Mayhew, K. 1996: Evaluating the assumptions that underlie training policy, in A. Booth and D.J. Snower (eds.), *Acquiring Skills*, 303–334. Cambridge: Cambridge University Press.

Keep, E. and Mayhew, K. 1999: The assessment: knowledge, skills and competitiveness, *Oxford Review of Economic Policy*, **15**(1), 1–15.

Keep, E. and Mayhew, K. 2010: Moving beyond skills as a social and economic panacea, *Work, Employment and Society*, **24**(3), 565–577.

Kenway, P. 2011: What does 'exiting' a bad job mean and whose business is it?, *SKOPE Making Bad Jobs Better Seminar*, Cardiff.

Lafer, G. 2004: What is skill? In C. Warhurst, I. Grugulis and E. Keep (eds.), *The Skills that Matter*, 109–127. Basingstoke: Palgrave Macmillan.

Lane, C. 1989: *Management and Labour in Europe*, Aldershot: Edward Elgar.

Lave, J. and Wenger, E. 1991: *Situated Learning: legitimate peripheral participation*, Cambridge: Cambridge University Press.

Leadbeater, C. 2000: *Living on Thin Air*, London: Viking.

Legge, K. 1995: *Human Resource Management, Rhetorics and Realities*, London: Macmillan.

Leitch, S. 2006: *Prosperity for all in the global economy – world class skills*, Leitch Review of Skills, final report, London: The Stationery Office.

Mason, G. and Bishop, K. 2010: Adult Training, Skills Updating and Recession in the UK: the implications for competitiveness and social inclusion in *LLAKES Research Paper*, London: Institute of Education.

Mason, G., Van Ark, B. and Wagner, K. 1996: Workforce skills, product quality and economic performance, in A. Booth and D.J. Snower (eds.), *Acquiring Skills*, 175–198. Cambridge University Press.

Michaels, E., Handfield-Jones, H. and Axelrod, B. 2001: *The War for Talent*, Harvard Business School Press.

Moss, P. and Tilly, C. 1996: Soft skills and race: an investigation into black men's employment problems, *Work and Occupations*, **23**(3), 252–276.

Moss, P. and Tilly, C. 2001: *Stories employers tell: race, skill and hiring in America*, New York: Russell Sage Foundation.

Nolan, P. and Slater, G. 2003: The labour market: history, structure and prospects, in P. Edwards (ed.), *Industrial Relations: Theory and Practice*, Oxford: Blackwell.

Noon, M. and Blyton, P. 2007: *The Realities of Work*, Houndsmills: Palgrave.

Orr, J. 1996: *Talking about Machines*, Ithaca and London: ILR Press/Cornell University Press.

Payne, J. 2000: The unbearable lightness of skill: the changing meaning of skill in UK policy discourses and some implications for education and training, *Journal of Education Policy*, **15**(3), 353–369.

Penn, R. 1984: *Skilled Workers in the Class Structure*, Cambridge: Cambridge University Press.

Prais, S. 1995: *Productivity, Education and Training: an international perspective*, Cambridge: Cambridge University Press.

Reich, R. 1991: *The Work of Nations: Preparing Ourselves for 21st Century Capitalism*, New York: Vintage Books.

Reskin, B.F. and Roos, P.A. 1990: *Job queues, gender queues: explaining women's inroads into male occupations*, Philadelphia: Temple University Press.

Rose, M., Penn, R. and Rubery, J. 1994: Introduction, the SCELI skill findings, in R. Penn, M. Rose and J. Rubery (eds.), *Skill and Occupational Change*, Oxford: Oxford University Press.

Royle, T. 2000: *Working for McDonald's in Europe: the unequal struggle*, London: Routledge.

Rubery, J. and Grimshaw, D. 2003: *The Organization of Employment*, Basingstoke: Palgrave Macmillan.

Shibata, H. 1999: A comparison of American and Japanese work practices: skill formation, communications and conflict resolution, *Industrial Relations*, **38**(2), 192–214.

Shibata, H. 2001: Productivity and skill at a Japanese transplant and its parent company, *Work and Occupations*, **28**(2), 234–260.

Skuratowicz, E. and Hunter, L.W. 2004: Where do women's jobs come from? Job resegregation in an American bank, *Work and Occupations*, **31**(1), 73–110.

Stuart, M., Cook, H., Cutter, J.C. and Winterton, J. 2010: Assessing the impact of union learning and the Union Learning Fund: union and employer perspectives, *CERIC Policy Reports*, Leeds: Centre for Employment Relations, Innovation and Change, Leeds University Business School.

Thompson, P. 2004: Skating on thin ice: the knowledge economy myth, Glasgow: University of Strathclyde/Big Thinking.

Thompson, P., Wallace, T., Flecker, J. and Ahlstrand, R. 1995: It ain't what you do, it's the way that you do it: production organisation and skill utilisation in commercial vehicles, *Work, Employment and Society*, **9**(4), 719–742.

Unwin, L., Felstead, A. and Fuller, A. 2007: Learning at Work: towards more 'expansive' opportunities, *NIACE Commission of Inquiry into 'The Future for Lifelong Learning'*, Leicester: National Institute for Adult and Continuing Education.

Warhurst, C., Findlay, P. and Thompson, P. 2007: Organising to learn and learning to organise in *Research Paper*, unionlearn.

Whalen, J. and Vinkhuyzen, E. 2000: Expert systems in (inter)action: diagnosing document machine problems over the telephone, in C. Heath, J. Hindmarsh and P. Luff (eds.), *Workplace Studies: Recovering Work Practice and Information Systems Design*, Cambridge: Cambridge University Press.

Whitley, R. 1999: *Divergent Capitalisms: the social structuring and change of business systems*, Oxford: Oxford University Press.

Whitley, R. 2003: The Institutional Structuring of Organizational Capabilities: The Role of Authority Sharing and Organizational Careers, *Organization Studies (after Jan 1, 2003)* **24**(5), 667–695.

Wolf, A. 1995: *Competence-Based Assessment*, Buckingham and Philadelphia: Open University Press.

Wolf, A. 2011: *Review of Vocational Education – the Wolf Report*, London: Department for Education.

CHAPTER TEN

HRM and Leadership

Deanne N. Den Hartog and Corine Boon

Human Resource Management (HRM) and leadership are both relatively large areas of research that have developed largely independently of each other. Research shows that both HRM practices and leaders can affect employee attitudes and performance, yet little work has focused on integrating or linking elements of these fields. This is somewhat surprising for two reasons. First, management tends to form a core group of employees for whom often specific HR tools, especially in terms of development, are in place. However, there is only limited attention relating to leaders as a specific and important group of 'receivers' of HR. Secondly, and perhaps even more pressing, is the lack of attention to formal leaders as the ones who tend to implement HR practices (e.g. Den Hartog *et al.* 2004). This important role of leaders, especially line managers, in delivering HRM to employees and communicating and giving a face to the policies and practices developed by the HR department, forms the focus of this chapter.

An HR department can create elaborate HR policies and develop (or even buy in) sophisticated HR tools. However, whether these policies and practices achieve the positive effects often heralded in the HR literature depends on the appropriate enactment, implementation, or delivery of HR tools by line managers (e.g. Gratton and Truss 2003). The line managers' consistency, fairness and skill in using HR tools and implementing HR policies will, to a large degree, determine whether such tools indeed generate positive effects on employee commitment, motivation and performance. HR practices such as a specific type of performance appraisal process or career development plan can be equitable on paper but if these practices are not implemented fairly by individual line managers, employees will question the procedural fairness of the HR policies of the organisation. How specific managers implement HRM will affect employees' perceptions of the content and fairness of the firm's HR policies and practices. This chapter therefore focuses on the role of leaders in implementing HR practices, and by linking the HR and leadership literature it tries to bring further insight in this role.

We start by going back to some of the earlier work on HRM as compared to personnel management. This work highlights that one of the key differences between classical personnel management and HRM is that the responsibility for many HR tasks shifts from central personnel departments to individual line managers. This shift implies a central role for line managers as leaders in the HR process. However, research that examines the role of line managers and their leader behaviour in implementing HRM is scarce. We identify differences that exist between line and HR managers and between managers and employees in their views on HR tasks and the importance of HR. We note that such differences can form a barrier to the effectiveness of HR. We then discuss the research on the role of managers as leaders and how their leadership styles affect employees. As HRM and leadership form completely separate fields of research that have typically not been connected, we offer some suggestions for a more integrated view on leadership and HR implementation. Finally we conclude that this changing role of line managers also has an impact on HR practices aimed at these managers. The organisation's HR tasks also include ensuring that line managers have the skills and motivation to be able to carry out the needed HR tasks effectively.

HRM and Line Managers

Since the emergence of HRM as a field of research, the focus of the management of human resources has changed from classical personnel management to HRM. While the classical personnel management approach can be characterised by a high emphasis on standardised rules and procedures with an operational focus, human resource management regards people as (strategic) assets of the company and focuses on the integration of HRM with strategic goals (Storey 1992). Researchers stress that an important consequence of managing human resources in a strategic way is that HRM should be carried out by all managers in the organisation, not only by the personnel department (Storey 1992; Thornhill and Saunders 1998). Even by 1992, Storey emphasised the key role of line managers in implementing HRM. Storey went further, suggesting that due to the more strategic focus of HR, business and line managers are the key managers involved in HRM, and that the management style that fits best with HRM is so-called transformational leadership. We will go into more detail about this style of leadership later.

Similarly, Sisson (1994) also mentions the important role of managers at different levels of the organisation in implementing HR practices. He also stresses the importance of transformational leadership at the top management level, and a focus on inspiring and developing employees and encouraging middle and lower level managers to implement HRM effectively. Thus, the change from personnel management to HRM implies a change in the roles taken on both by HR managers and (line) managers, and the responsibility for many HR tasks shifts from the HR department to line managers (McConville and Holden 1999; Sisson 1994; Storey

1992; Ulrich 1997a, 1997b; Ulrich and Brockbank 2005). As Purcell and Hutchinson (2007: 3) put it, 'The HR practices perceived or experienced by employees will, to a growing extent, be those delivered or enacted by line managers, especially front-line managers with direct supervisory responsibility'. These line managers will take on the 'employee champion' role proposed by Ulrich (1997a), having direct contact with employees and fulfilling their needs, for example by motivating them and supporting their development.

One example of a core HR task in which this key role of line managers is very clear is performance management (see Chapter 11). Performance management refers to the integrated set of HR activities engaged in by an organisation to enhance the performance of a target person or group, with the ultimate purpose of improving organisational effectiveness (Den Hartog et al. 2004). Among other things, performance management tasks include setting individual performance targets that are linked to the goals of the organisation, ensuring sufficient skills and motivation of employees to meet these targets, evaluating progress towards targets and rewarding high performance. The role of line managers who are the direct supervisors or leaders of employees is crucial in such performance management systems. The line managers' consistency, fairness and skill in using tools such as conducting appraisal interviews, working with personal development plans and holding consultation meetings will, to a large degree, determine whether the often sophisticated performance management tools HR departments develop actually generate the desired effects in terms of employee commitment, effort and performance. An HR department can thus develop (or buy in) sophisticated performance management tools; however, whether these really achieve the desired effects depends on the appropriate *enactment* of these tools by line managers. Performance management thus clearly and directly involves managers in the process (e.g. Den Hartog et al. 2004; Gratton and Truss 2003).

It is the line manager or direct supervisor in setting challenging, yet attainable, objectives who monitors, evaluates and appraises performance and also who gives performance feedback to employees. They see where subordinates' development and training are needed, can help enrich the tasks of employees and stimulate a climate in which high performance is emphasised. These line managers are the ones who can offer participation in decision–making or stimulate teamwork. They also often play a role in selecting new employees. Thus, line managers' skill and fairness in performing such crucial HR tasks, as well as their leadership styles and relationships with their different subordinates, will play a key role in the success of HR systems. HR tools aimed at developing line managers should ensure that such managers have the right skills to be able to perform these tasks, which is an issue to which we return later.

Clearly, the role of line managers as leaders in enacting or implementing HRM is crucial for HRM to have a positive impact. However, studies that examine the changing role of managers and the consequences of this change for the effectiveness of HRM have been limited to date. Only recently have HRM researchers called attention to the role of (line) managers in implementing HR practices (e.g. Caldwell 2003; Nishii and Wright 2008; Purcell and Hutchinson 2007). In this regard a somewhat worrying outcome of some studies that have looked at HR managers', line managers' and employees' views of HRM is that these are often only moderately correlated. An example of the disconnect between managers and employees is seen in the work of Liao *et al.* 2009, who find only a moderate correlation (.39) between aggregated perceptions of managers and employees of the HR practices in the same units. The existence of this type of disagreement is problematic if the impact of HR practices on outcomes is argued to (at least in part) come about via the effect of practices on individual employees.

In addition, Wright *et al.* (2001) found little agreement between HR and line managers' evaluations of both the relative and the absolute effectiveness of the HR function in terms of service delivery, roles and contributions to the firm; HR managers gave significantly higher ratings than did line managers. In this study, Wright *et al.* (2001) did, however, find that HR and line managers tend to agree on the *importance* of HRM. Interestingly, they found that line managers rated HRM as slightly more important than HR executives did, but overall there was a high correlation (.77) between HR and line manager scores on the importance of HRM. Combined, these studies suggest that although HRM tasks are seen as important, a lack of agreement on the delivery and effectiveness of HRM exists between HR managers, line managers and employees. But why might there be such a disconnect? Here we focus on the implementation role of line managers and how that might influence employee perceptions.

Intended HR policies versus implemented and perceived HR practices

A few models have been proposed that help understand why there might be a lack of agreement between HR managers, line managers and employees on how they perceive HRM. Purcell and Hutchinson (2007), for example, argue that given that line managers are involved in enacting HR practices and engage in leadership behaviours, they should be included in models that link HRM to performance. They propose the 'people management–performance causal chain', which is shown in Figure 10.1.

The proposed HRM causal chain distinguishes between intended practices, actual practices and employee perceptions of HR practices. Intended practices are HR practices as designed by the organisation, or to what extent HR practices

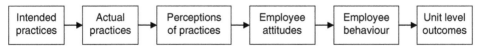

Figure 10.1 People management–performance causal chain

Source: Adapted from Purcell & Hutchinson (2007) in *Human Resource Management Journal* **17** (1), 3–20, Oxford: Wiley Blackwell

are present 'on paper'; actual practices are the HR practices that are actually implemented in the organisation by the line managers responsible. HR departments may, for example, have tools available to help managers determine training and development needs in their unit, but not all managers will find development of their employees equally important at a given moment, and thus whether such tools are used can differ over time and between units. The actual implementation of HR practices could be assessed, for example, by asking line managers to report on the extent to which a number of HR practices are implemented in their department.

Thus, actual HR practices may differ between units or departments. Each individual employee, in turn, forms perceptions of HR practices based on the actual practices and the way they are implemented in the organisation. 'Employee responses to HR practices are at the heart of all HRM-performance models' (Purcell and Hutchinson 2007: 6; see also Purcell and Kinnie 2006). These responses are mainly a result of their perceptions of the degree to which they feel HR practices are offered to them and not so much a result of intended or actual practices (Guest 1999). In other words, if employees do not perceive a practice, it is not likely to affect their motivation. Therefore, perceptions of HR practices are related to employee attitudes, employee behaviours and, in turn, to unit level outcomes.

For example, an organisation might have a policy in place calling for regular performance appraisals including a meeting between each employee and his/her supervisor, to discuss their assessment of the employee's strengths and weaknesses relative to required competencies and behaviours for his/her specific job, and to formulate a development plan for the employee. All line managers in the organisation are asked to follow this procedure – this forms the 'intended' HR practice. Some line managers may follow the exact procedure, some may do it their own way, some may not undertake performance appraisals at all, and some managers may be better at appraisal than others. All of this can lead to variation in the 'actual' HR practice. In turn, each employee is likely to experience the performance appraisal differently, as individual differences in employees will play a role here. Their expectations and traits may differ, what they value may differ, and the process they go through may differ. One individual employee might have had a performance appraisal in which they felt the line manager was very helpful and supportive, yet another might have had a bad experience in their meeting – expectations were not met. Thus, employee perceptions of implemented practices will vary.

Nishii and Wright (2008) present a model (the 'Process Model of HRM'; see Figure 10.2) linking intended, actual, and perceived HR practices to employee reactions and organisational performance. Nishii and Wright (2008) focus mainly on the variability that may emerge when HR practices are implemented in an organisation. While most studies seem to assume that all employees receive and perceive the same practices, variability in HR practices may exist between units or departments as a result of differences in implementation, and between individuals as a result of differences in perceptions of HR practices.

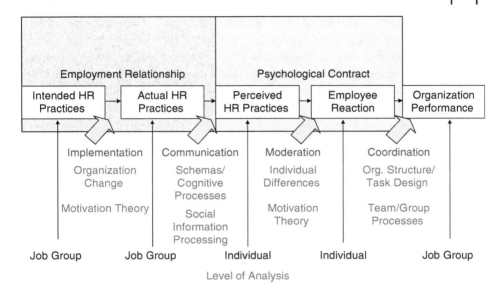

Figure 10.2 The Process Model of HRM

Source: adapted from Nishii & Wright (2008) in *The People Make the Place*, Psychology Press, New York: Taylor & Francis Group

Line managers act as agents of the organisation in managing employees (Rhoades Shanock and Eisenberger 2006), and tend to have the ultimate responsibility for executing HRM (Ulrich and Brockbank 2005). Based on social exchange theory and organisational support theory, the central assumption is that 'HRM practices are viewed by employees as a "personalised" commitment to them' (Hannah and Iverson 2004: 339), which is delivered by the organisation through line managers. Therefore, as we also noted above, employees are likely to be influenced by both HR practices themselves and the quality of their implementation by managers (Purcell and Hutchinson 2007).

Authors such as Nishii and Wright (2008) and Purcell and Hutchinson (2007) argue that (line) managers influence the HRM implementation process in two ways. First, the relationship between *intended* and *actual* practices is influenced by managers because of differences in implementation. While organisations may have centralised HR practices, line managers are likely to differ in how they implement these practices. Line managers usually have some freedom in the way they implement practices, and the way in which HR practices are implemented largely depends on their leadership style (Purcell and Hutchinson 2007). As a result, employees might receive different HR practices. For example, in selecting new employees, some managers might find educational background more important, whereas others find it more important that the person fits well in the team. Or, looking at coaching of employees, line managers vary in the importance they attach to coaching and also have different coaching styles. This leads to differences in the implementation of HR practices.

Second, besides differences in the actual HR practices that employees receive, employee *perceptions* of HR practices and their *reactions* to these practices are likely to be directly influenced by line managers, both as a result of their aforementioned role as implementers of HR practices and also as a result of their leadership style (Nishii and Wright 2008; Purcell and Hutchinson 2007). For example, managers can make specific choices in the interactions with specific subordinates, which could lead to differences in HRM perceptions between individuals (Nishii and Wright 2008; Zohar 2000). One employee may have performed better than another, leading their line manager to treat them differently.

Thus, line managers may influence the actual delivery of practices and the perceptions of these practices. For example, in a company in which employee development is seen as important, it is not only relevant to know whether individual line managers do indeed offer development opportunities to their subordinates, but in addition, the way in which these opportunities are offered can make a difference. If managers inspire and coach employees, this might influence employee perceptions and attitudes and the effectiveness of the development practices of the firm.

Only a few studies have simultaneously examined (perceptions of) HR practices and of leader behaviour. Purcell and Hutchinson (2007), for example, examined the extent to which employee perceptions of, and satisfaction with, both HR practices and leader behaviour relate to job attitudes such as commitment, autonomy and job challenge. They found that both HRM perceptions and leadership behaviour strongly affect employee attitudes, which shows that not only the HR practices themselves, but also the way they are implemented, affects employee attitudes. Searle *et al.* (2011) argue that unless HRM systems such as high involvement work practices are implemented consistently and fairly by managers, their positive effect on a number of outcomes at the individual level is not likely to occur. This again suggests that the (perceived) content of HRM practices and the fair and consistent implementation by managers are both relevant and complement each other. In sum, line managers have an important role in influencing perceptions, attitudes and behaviours of employees, and both line managers' role in HRM implementation and their leadership styles are discussed in more detail below.

Line Managers as Implementers

The limited empirical evidence indicates an important role for line managers in the HRM process (e.g. Purcell and Hutchinson 2007). Who then should take the lead in HRM issues – HR or the line manager? Dany *et al.* (2008) highlighted the importance of whomever takes the lead in the design and implementation of HR practicing, influencing effectiveness, assuming that a well-integrated HR system is a necessary, but not a sufficient, condition for HRM effectiveness. More specifically, they examined whether the relationship between the integration of business strategy and HRM and organisational performance (product/service quality, level of productivity, profitability, rate of innovation and stock market performance) depends on the distribution of influence between HRM specialists and line managers. These results show that when HRM decisions are mainly taken by either HRM specialists or line managers, the relationship between HRM integration and performance is not significant. If, however, responsibilities are shared between HRM specialists and line managers, there is a significant relationship between HRM integration and performance. This study clearly suggests that the most effective option is one of cooperation between HRM specialists and line managers, with HRM specialists having a prominent role.

It also seems logical that HR departments and line managers are not equally involved in every specific HR task, thus some researchers have looked at how HRM responsibilities are typically shared between HR managers and line managers. Rhoades *et al.* (2006: 689), for example, state that managers tend to play a larger role in the more individualised treatments such as informal feedback concerning job performance or evaluating individual employees performance, whereas the HR department plays a larger role in practices that are 'provided indiscriminately to groups of employees'. Hall and Torrington (1998) found that HRM managers played the biggest role in systems of rewards and benefits, whereas line managers were responsible for appraisals, communications, and quality initiatives. In general, HRM managers are more involved in tasks that require specialist expertise, whereas line managers tend to be more involved in issues related to day-to-day management (Whittaker and Marchington 2003).

As a result of the changing role of HRM in organisations, line managers are thus involved in delivering a whole range of HR practices such as selection, individual training, development and coaching, performance appraisal, and rewards, and in doing this they can influence employees' attitudes and behaviours to a large extent. However, discrepancies between intended and implemented HR practices can occur when line managers are not able or willing to perform these tasks. So, the question is whether this increasing involvement of line managers in HRM tasks is always straightforward and desirable? On the one hand, research shows line managers are generally positive about taking on HR work, adopt a professional attitude, and take into account employee needs and wishes (Renwick 2003; Whittaker and March-ington 2003). In addition, they have closer contact with employees than the HR department, which may make them better able to select new employees as they know better what the department needs, and they are also likely to have more insight on how their subordinates perform, which might make them better able to do performance appraisal and determine appropriate rewards and promotions as well as training needs.

On the other hand, line managers have many other more pressing priorities on their hands and at times face conflicting demands on their time and it is thus not unlikely that HRM issues will be taken less seriously or seen as less urgent than meeting production or service goals. Line managers are usually not experts in HRM; they will thus not always possess the skills and competencies necessary to perform HRM tasks effectively without support from personnel practitioners, and they sometimes lack commitment. Even when line managers have responsibility for HRM tasks, they often feel they have little autonomy in what they can offer, which leads to tensions between line managers and HR about line managers' HR duties (Renwick 2003; Whittaker and

Marchington 2003). As a result, line managers may be reluctant to take on HR responsibilities (Bos-Nehles 2010; Whittaker and Marchington 2003).

Thus, consistent implementation of HR practices and aligning employee perceptions, attitudes and behaviours throughout the organisation is likely to be a major challenge, influenced greatly by the abilities, motivation, and leadership styles of line managers. As line managers are increasingly involved in implementing HR practices, more attention needs to be directed at consistent implementation of HRM. How can organisations make sure HRM is implemented consistently by line managers? Developing an effective implementation and communication process, coordinating this process, and training and motivating line managers in performing HR tasks seems a crucial, but challenging, task. Given that line managers are crucial to implementation, organisations need to ensure that line managers understand that HR tasks are part of their core duties. Organisations also need to ensure that attention is given to training, supporting and motivating line managers in order to increase the quality of HRM implementation. This development and support of managers in their HR role could form a key area in which HR specialists could add value to the organisation.

While some research attention has been paid to barriers to effective implementation of HR practices by line managers, less research has focused on the role of leadership styles in influencing employee perceptions of HRM, as suggested by Purcell and Hutchinson. Below we will explore how leadership styles may influence HRM implementation.

Line Managers' Leadership Styles

In addition to line managers' explicit attention to HR tasks, the relationship between leaders and followers is also very important for the successful implementation of HR practices. The leadership styles and behaviours of line managers also influence employees' perceptions of HRM (e.g. Den Hartog *et al.* 2004; Nishii and Wright 2008; Purcell and Hutchinson 2007). Uhl-Bien *et al.* (2000) already indicated over a decade ago that the role of interpersonal relationships between managers and employees has been largely disregarded in strategic HRM research and this, perhaps with a few exceptions, still holds. Yet, clearly, social interaction between managers and employees helps shape employees' perceptions of HR practices. Through their leadership behaviours, line managers can, for example, influence employees' job experience, desired behaviours, and employees' sensemaking by communicating their perception of the HR practices (Nishii and Wright 2008).

Several main trends can be distinguished in the development of the study of what makes leaders in organisations effective. A categorisation of approaches to leadership often distinguishes early trait research, style or behavioural approaches, contingency approaches, and the transformational/charismatic approach (see e.g. Bass and Bass 2008; Day and Antonakis 2011; Den Hartog and Koopman 2001; Yukl 2010 for overviews). Here we focus on leadership styles, in other words, the behaviours leaders show. The style approach treated leadership as a behavioural pattern, which can be learned. The HR implication is that once the most effective leadership style has been identified, people can be trained to exhibit that specific style of behaviour and become better leaders (Bass 1990; Bryman 1992). However, subsequent work showed that, often, the context in which leadership took place also played a role and therefore it is hard to pinpoint one single style that is always most effective. Below, we briefly discuss three dominant leadership style models, namely consideration versus initiating structure or task versus relationship oriented styles, the transactional versus transformational leadership model, and the recent research on ethical leadership. This is not meant as an exhaustive review of leadership styles, but as indicative of the current debates.

Styles of leadership

Some of the most influential older studies on leadership styles were the questionnaire-based Ohio State studies. The Ohio State researchers concluded that leadership style could best be described as varying along two dimensions, i.e. 'consideration' and 'initiating structure' (e.g. Fleishman and Harris 1962). Consideration includes leader behaviour indicating mutual trust, respect and a certain warmth and rapport between leader and subordinate. Initiating structure describes task related behaviour in which the leader organises and defines group activities and his/her relation to the group. This distinction between 'task' oriented and 'relationship' oriented leader behaviour is still widely known and used.

Since the early eighties several new leadership theories have been proposed, using terms such as transformational, charismatic or value-based (Bass 1985; 1997; Bryman 1992; House, 1977; 1996). As noted above, this style of leadership is considered important for line managers in HR implementation (Storey 1992). Transformational leaders articulate an attractive vision for the organisation and behave in ways that reinforce the values inherent in that vision. They inspire followers to transcend their own self-interests for the sake of the collective. Followers become highly committed to the goal of the collective and perform beyond expectations (Bass 1985; Burns, 1978).

Transformational leadership is usually contrasted with transactional leadership. Transactional leadership theories are founded on the idea that leader-follower relations are based on a series of exchanges or implicit bargains between leaders and followers (Burns 1978; Bass 1985). The leader clarifies performance criteria, in other words what he expects from subordinates, and what they receive in return. In return for such promised rewards, subordinates deliver the agreed results. Transformational leadership goes beyond the cost-benefit exchange of transactional leadership by motivating and inspiring followers.

Bass (1985; 1997) defines both transactional and transformational leadership as comprised of several dimensions. Transactional leadership consists first of contingent rewards. The leader rewards followers for attaining the specified performance levels. The other form of transactional leadership is active management-by-exception (or performance monitoring). When practising active management-by-exception, a leader actively monitors followers' task behaviour, checks for mistakes, seeks deviations from standard procedures, and takes action when irregularities occur. Leaders avoid giving directions if the old ways work and allow followers to continue doing their jobs as always, as long as performance goals are met (Hater and Bass 1988).

Bass's (1985; 1997) model of transformational leadership has four dimensions. The first is labelled charisma or idealised influence. The charismatic leader provides vision and a sense of mission, instils pride, gains respect and trust, and increases optimism. Such leaders excite, arouse and inspire subordinates. The second dimension, inspirational motivation, describes a leader's capacity to act as a model for subordinates and their inspiring communication of a vision to focus efforts. The third dimension is individual consideration, which includes coaching and mentoring. It provides for continuous feedback and links the individual's current needs to the organisation's mission. Some commentators suggest that individualised consideration is similar to the Ohio State notion of consideration (Bryman 1992). Bass and Avolio (1993), however, state that the two are related, but that individualised consideration builds on two aspects of behaviour – that is individualisation *and* development of followers– whereas earlier consideration scales were primarily concerned with whether a leader was seen as a 'good guy or gal' (p. 63). The fourth dimension is intellectual stimulation. An intellectually stimulating leader provides subordinates with a flow of challenging new ideas to stimulate rethinking of old ways of doing things (Bass 1985; 1997). Other authors have suggested more dimensions of transformational leadership, for instance, vision, role-modelling, demonstrating trust in subordinates, and expressing high performance expectations (House 1996).

Many empirical studies and a number of meta-analyses have found positive relationships between transformational leadership and a range of outcome measures including subordinates' satisfaction, organisational commitment, and perceptions of leader effectiveness (see the meta-analysis by Lowe *et al.* 1996). Other outcomes that were found to be positively related to transformational leadership include well-being related outcomes such as lower levels of burnout (De Hoogh and Den Hartog 2009) as well as task and contextual performance outcomes both at the individual level, such as organisational citizenship behaviour (Den Hartog *et al.* 2007; Podsakoff *et al.* 1996) and group or organisational level, such as business–unit performance (Howell and Avolio 1993) and organisational profitability (De Hoogh *et al.* 2004). These positive effects on performance and employee related outcomes tend to be far less strong or even non–existent for transactional leadership.

Ethical leadership

The pressure on firms and their leaders at all levels of the hierarchy to behave ethically has increased due to media attention and government regulation following recent business scandals. Showing ethical behaviour is currently critical to leaders' credibility and their potential to have meaningful influence on followers at all levels in the organisation (Piccolo *et al.* 2010). Therefore, line managers' ethical behaviour may be important in implementing HR practices. In addition, ethical leadership stresses fairness and fairness and consistency are crucial to HR implementation. We return to the linkages of this leadership style with HR practices below. Ethical leadership can be defined as 'the demonstration of normatively appropriate conduct through personal actions and interpersonal relationships, and the promotion of such conduct to followers through two-way communication, reinforcement, and decision-making' (Brown *et al.* 2005: 120). Over the last decade, the effects of ethical leadership on follower attitudes and behaviours have been the subject of multiple studies. Combined, the results suggest that, like transformational leadership, ethical leadership also relates positively to employee outcomes (Brown *et al.* 2005; Kalshoven *et al.* 2011; Mayer *et al.* 2009; Piccolo *et al.* 2010).

This attention to morality and ethics as elements of leadership is not new and was already evident in the work on transformational leadership. Bass (1985) originally argued that transformational leaders can take ethical as well as unethical forms. In later work, Bass and Steidlmeier (1999) distinguished between authentic and pseudo-transformational leaders based on the moral character of the leaders and their concerns for self and others; the ethical values embedded in the leaders' vision and behaviour and the morality of the processes of social ethical choices and action leaders pursue. However, this distinction is not without problems. For example, as Dasborough and Ashkanasy (2002) note, it is hard for followers to see the difference between authentic and pseudo transformational leadership as, while the intentions of such leaders differ, they display similar behaviours.

More recently, researchers have started to focus on ethical leadership as a behavioural style in itself rather than on ethical aspects of other leadership styles. Ethical leader behaviours include acting fairly and justly, promoting and rewarding ethical conduct among followers, allowing follower voice and sharing information and power, showing concern for followers, demonstrating consistency and integrity, and taking responsibility for one's actions (Brown *et al.* 2005; Brown and Trevino 2006; Kalshoven *et al.* 2011). As indicated, research suggests ethical leadership has positive effects. For example, ethical leaders help to make the work of followers more meaningful and motivating (Piccolo *et al.* 2010). Ethical leaders also positively affect follower attitudes and behaviours. For example, studies show that ethical leadership relates positively to commitment (Brown *et al.* 2005), negatively to employee cynicism (Kalshoven *et al.* 2011) positively to perceived leader and top management team effectiveness (De Hoogh and Den Hartog 2008) and to follower citizenship behaviours such as helpfulness (Mayer *et al.* 2009; Piccolo *et al.* 2010).

Linking HR practices and leadership styles

The above overview of different leadership styles indicates that HR tasks are not often explicitly mentioned in these styles, but there are some links between certain styles and specific HR practices. One way to integrate HR tasks and leadership styles might be to focus on how different leadership styles relate to different

HR tasks. For example, the core of transactional leadership focuses on performance monitoring and contingent rewards. Thus, the line managers' HR tasks of evaluation, monitoring and rewarding of good performance in that sense form part of a transactional leadership style. Transformational leadership is focused on the development of followers through the component of individualised consideration; the coaching and development of employees is a key concern. Emphasis is placed on the shared responsibility and shared goals that these leaders convey as well as empowering elements. Transformational leadership, therefore, relates to the participative practices that tend to be seen as central to effectiveness in the high involvement work systems literature (Batt 2002). Earlier studies (Storey 1992; Sisson 1994) noted that transformational leadership is especially important in the HRM process.

Although the leadership styles literature mostly focuses on the type of direct influencing behaviour used by leaders and typically does not explicitly talk about the role of line managers in HR tasks, one can look at the relationship between HR practices and different leader behaviours and styles. Bamberger and Meshoulam (2000) distinguish three human resource 'subsystems' or bundles that combine a wide range of HR practices in one broad typology: people flow, appraisal and reward, and employment relations. Each of these suggests several important tasks for leaders. The *employment relations bundle* has a broader perspective on the nature of jobs, stimulating employees to identify with the organisation, and balancing employee expectations; it includes practices such as job design, flexible job arrangements, and participation (Bamberger and Meshoulam 2000; Sun *et al.* 2007; Zhang and Jia 2010). This bundle is perhaps most directly linked to leadership styles. For example, transformational leadership especially has been shown to enhance identification and commitment (Bycio *et al.* 1995). Also, both transformational and ethical leadership have been shown to affect how employees evaluate the characteristics of their jobs, which, in turn, affects outcomes. For example, both these leadership styles relate to employees evaluating their job as more meaningful, which, in turn, motivates them to show increased effort at work (Piccolo and Colquitt 2006; Piccolo *et al.* 2010). In addition, these styles both have an empowering element relating to participation because such leaders enhance perceived autonomy, encourage subordinates to speak up and allow them influence in decision making (Den Hartog and De Hoogh 2009). Thus, both ethical and transformational styles clearly fit the employment relations bundle.

The *appraisal and reward bundle* focuses on motivating employees to contribute to and stay with the organisation and covers performance appraisal and rewards practice. Leaders have a crucial role in monitoring and evaluating performance and in ensuring that rewards and praise are linked to performance. As noted, this links to transactional leadership, which is focused on motivating through rewards. In addition, fairness (a core element of ethical leadership) is also very important when it comes to performance and rewards related issues.

The *people flow bundle* focuses on employee development and on getting the required skills and competencies in place and covers staffing, training, development, mobility, and job security. As noted, leaders can differ in the extent to which they focus on people's development through individualised consideration and coaching and mentoring. In addition, leaders have several tasks related to this bundle that are not specifically covered in leadership styles, such as planning, selecting employees, and assessment of training needs. This illustrates that leadership behaviours and HRM tasks can overlap but are not the same.

In sum, some leadership styles fit better with certain types of HR practices or HR bundles than others. If HR practices are implemented by managers who adopt a leadership style that supports the practices and the HR strategy or philosophy behind the practices, implementation is likely to be more effective. In contrast, implementation of HR practices using a leadership style that does not match with the practices, or even goes against them, is likely to hinder the potentially positive impact of the practice on employees, and consequently on organisational performance. For example, transformational leaders are typically well able to vary their behaviour and adapt it to what is needed. They tend to use both transformational and transactional behaviours to influence subordinates (Bass 1985). Thus, transformational leadership seems to fit very well with a broad range of HR practices as well as many practices that are typically included in high performance work systems.

Yet, if HR systems are not focused on extensive sets of integrated high performance or high involvement work systems and instead are focused more on cutting costs and efficiency, such leadership might fit less well. In addition, certain leadership styles can go against core HR practices. For example, more autocratic and authoritarian styles typically centralise decision-making and limit participation of employees in decisions, thereby going against the aforementioned participation element of high involvement work systems. Also, *laissez-faire* leaders are passive in their approach, and their unwillingness to take responsibility can hinder fair and consistent HR implementation.

Functional leadership

A somewhat different approach to leadership that more explicitly takes HR related tasks into account is the functional approach to leadership which is found in the team leadership literature. As Morgeson *et al.* (2010) outline, functional leadership theory suggests that the core of the leadership role is 'to do, or get done, whatever is not being adequately handled for group needs' (McGrath 1962: 5). The functional view shifts the focus from the leader of a team to the leadership processes within teams and acknowledges the diverse sources of leadership that are possible within a team, including the informal ones. Morgeson and colleagues (2010) developed a research based taxonomy of team leadership functions. In this taxonomy they differentiate between two team phases. The transition phase is the period when teams focus on activities related to structuring the team, planning the team's work, and evaluating the team's performance such that the team will ultimately be able to achieve its goal or objective. The action phase is the period where the team is focused on activities that directly contribute to accomplishing its goals (Marks *et al.* 2001; Morgeson *et al.* 2010).

In the transition phase, the focus of leadership is not so much on driving forward the task at hand, but rather on establishing the structures and processes that can enable future performance of the team. Team leadership functions in this phase include selecting the team members to ensure the right composition; defining the team's overall mission, goals, and the appropriate standards of performance; structuring and clarifying roles and responsibilities; developing team members and ensuring that they are capable of performing effectively; and facilitating feedback processes in the team. Enacting these leadership functions over time helps the team to develop the basis to perform future team actions that contribute directly to goal accomplishment. During the action phase, important team leadership functions include monitoring team performance, acquiring resources for the team, managing the boundaries between the team and the organisational environment, performing the team's tasks, solving problems, challenging the team to keep performing and improving, encouraging the team to act autonomously and self-manage, and developing and supporting a positive social climate in the team (see Morgeson *et al.* 2010 for a detailed discussion of these functions). This functional view of leadership more clearly incorporates HR tasks in the leadership role. Although to date this approach in the literature focuses explicitly on team leadership, additional empirical work may help to develop a functional leadership approach in other contexts. This will help further our understanding of the linkages between leadership and HR.

Conclusions and Implications

In this chapter we have linked leadership and HRM by focusing on the HR tasks of line managers. They have a key position in HR implementation and, as we have outlined, their fair and consistent implementation of HR practices as well as their overall leadership styles will affect the extent to which employees perceive and appreciate the HR practices that are offered to them. As noted, research shows presently that the views of line managers and employees tend to only correlate moderately, which suggests improvements in communication about HR practices within organisations might help their effectiveness.

As many HR practices work through their impact on employee motivation, the perceptions of employees are crucial. If employees do not perceive that they are offered a practice or negatively evaluate it, the practice is not likely to have a motivating effect on employees. Thus, line managers' skills in leading and inspiring others and in performing motivation related HR tasks such as performance evaluation need to be developed in organisations to gain optimal success through HRM. In other cases, HR practices will work through enhancing skills and abilities of the workforce, for example selection. In addition to line managers' skills in, for example, selecting highly competent employees, their behaviour can also affect overall workforce capabilities and the intellectual capital of the firm (Youndt and Snell 2004). In sum, managers play a key role both in building intellectual capital and in leading and motivating employees to use their abilities effectively.

Through these motivational and capital building leadership roles, line managers play a crucial role in the success of using HR instruments. Leadership and HRM currently are separate research areas, although the central role of line managers in HR implementation implies that more integration is needed here. Devolving HR tasks to line managers can have both advantages and disadvantages. On the one hand, line managers have closer contact with employees and tend to have a better view on what the department or team needs and how employees are performing. On the other hand, line managers might lack the time, skills and motivation to perform HR tasks, and involvement of many different line managers increases possible inconsistencies of HR implementation throughout the organisation. Therefore, aligning and supporting line managers in this area is an increasingly important task for organisations.

This central role of line managers suggests that line managers themselves need to be carefully selected and developed, with an eye on being able and motivated to perform such HR tasks and provide leadership in ways that are both competent and that fit the organisation's values. Thus, line managers should also be considered as a special group of 'receivers' of HR practices. As noted, research currently suggests that not all managers are at present willing or able to perform HR tasks (Whittaker and Marchington 2003). Also, a clear process needs to be in place that guides line managers in implementing HR practices as consistently as possible. Developing such a framework for implementation fits well with the 'new' division of tasks between the HR department and line managers that is increasingly found in organisations; the HR department could take a leading role in developing HR practices, tools, and guidelines for implementation, and support line managers who are the ones performing many of the actual HR tasks and roles.

In many large firms the responsibility for the development of line managers is placed outside the HR department and rests with specific management development staff. Although this may ensure that special attention goes to this group, this runs the risk of a division between what HR sees as key for employees and what managers find important. As noted earlier, research suggests that HR and line managers' views on what is implemented also typically differ from each other (Wright et al. 2001). Research has suggested that partnership between HRM and line management is important in effectively implementing HRM (Dany et al. 2008). This implies that when HR managers and line managers cooperate to establish and implement HR tasks, it could increase agreement about HRM practice and what is successful HRM. Also, developing and communicating an integrated vision for the organisation in terms of HR for both managers and employees is important.

Finally, both HR and line managers could improve the effectiveness of HR implementation by learning more about HR research and practising what is often called evidence based management. Rynes et al. (2002) reported large discrepancies between research findings on HRM and HR practitioners' beliefs about HR practices and their effectiveness. Rynes and colleagues surveyed 959 HR managers, directors and vice-presidents. The survey contained 39 true/false questions about various facets of HRM, all based on research findings. Results showed that there was a lack of agreement between managers' beliefs and research evidence. Five of the largest discrepancies involved selection-related issues. For example, research has shown that companies that screen job applicants for intelligence have higher performance than those that screen for values, whereas only 16 percent of the (HR) managers thought this was indeed true. Also, only 42 percent gave the correct answer on the statement 'There is very little difference among personality inventories in terms of how well they predict an applicant's likely job performance', which is false, according to research. Thus, although HRM tasks are seen as important by both line and HR managers, we see a lack of agreement on the delivery and effectiveness of HRM and, in addition, managers' research based knowledge on the effects of HR practices is limited. Both the within firm lack of agreement on HRM and the lack of evidence based management in HRM are clearly in need of attention in organisations. Reducing these knowledge gaps could help line managers to more successfully implement HRM.

REFERENCES

Bamberger, P. and Meshoulam, I. 2000: *Human resource strategy*, Newbury Park, CA: Sage.

Bass, B.M. 1985: *Leadership and Performance Beyond Expectations*, New York: Free Press.

Bass, B.M. 1990: *Bass and Stogdill's Handbook of Leadership: Theory, Research and Managerial Applications* 3rd edn, New York: Free Press.

Bass, B.M. 1997: Does the transactional – transformational paradigm transcend organizational and national boundaries?, *American Psychologist*, **52**, 130–139.

Bass, B.M. and Avolio, B.J. 1993: Transformational leadership a response to critiques. In: M.M. Chemers and R. Ayman (eds.), *Leadership theory and research*, San Diego: Academic Press.

Bass, B.M. and Bass, R. 2008: *The Bass Handbook of Leadership: Theory, Research and Managerial Applications,* New York: Free Press.

Bass, B.M. and Steidlmeier, P. 1999: Ethics, character and authentic transformational leadership behavior, *Leadership Quarterly*, **10**, 181–217.

Batt, R. 2002: Managing customer services: human resource practices, quit rates, and sales growth, *Academy of Management Journal*, **45**(3), 587–597.

Bos-Nehles, A.C. 2010: *The line makes the difference: line managers as effective HRM partners*, Doctoral thesis, the Netherlands: Universiteit Twente.

Brown, M.E. and Treviño, L.K. 2006: Ethical leadership: A review and future directions, *The Leadership Quarterly*, **17**, 595–616.

Brown, M.E., Treviño, L. K. and Harrison, D. A. 2005: Ethical leadership: A social learning perspective for construct development and testing, *Organizational Behavior and Human Decision Processes*, **97**, 117–134.

Bryman, A. 1992: *Charisma and Leadership in Organizations*, London: Sage.

Burns, J.M. 1978: *Leadership*, New York: Harper and Row.

Bycio, P., Hackett, R.D. and Allen, J.S. 1995: Further assessments of Bass's (1985) conceptualization of transactional and transformational leadership, *Journal of Applied Psychology*, **80**, 468–478.

Caldwell, R. 2003: The changing roles of personnel managers: old ambiguities, new uncertainties, *Journal of Management Studies*, **40**(4), 984–1004.

Dany, F., Guedri, Z. and Hatt, F. 2008: New insights into the link between HRM integration and organizational performance: the moderating role of influence distribution between HRM specialists and line managers, *The International Journal of Human Resource Management*, **19**(11), 2095–2112.

Dasborough, M.T. and Ashkanasy, N.M. 2002: Emotion and attribution of intentionality in leader-member relationships, *The Leadership Quarterly*, **13**, 615–634.

Day, D. and Antonakis, J. (eds). 2011: *The Nature of Leadership,* 2nd edn, Thousand Oaks, CA: Sage.

De Hoogh, A.H.B. and Den Hartog, D.N. 2008: Ethical and despotic leadership, relationships with leader's social responsibility, top management team effectiveness and subordinates' optimism: A multi-method study, *The Leadership Quarterly*, **19**, 297–311.

De Hoogh, A.H.B. and Den Hartog, D.N. 2009: Neuroticism and locus of control as moderators of the relationships of charismatic and autocratic leadership with burnout, *Journal of Applied Psychology*, **94**, 1058–1067.

De Hoogh, A.H.B., Den Hartog, D.N., Koopman, P.L., Thierry, H., Van den Berg, P.T., Van der Weide, J.G. and Wilderom, C.P.M. 2004: Charismatic Leadership, Environmental Dynamism and Performance, *European Journal of Work and Organizational Psychology*, **13**(4), 447–471.

Den Hartog, D.N. and De Hoogh, A.H.B. 2009: Empowerment and leader fairness and integrity: Studying ethical leader behaviour from a levels-of-analysis perspective. *European Journal of Work and Organizational Psychology,* **18**, 199–230.

Den Hartog, D.N. and Koopman, P. L. 2001: Leadership in organizations, in N. Anderson, D. S. Ones, H. Kepir-Sinangil and C. Viswesvaran (eds.), *International handbook of industrial, work and organizational psychology* (Vol. 2), London: Sage.

Den Hartog, D.N., Boselie, P., and Paauwe, J. 2004: Performance management: A model and research agenda, *Applied Psychology: An International Review*, **53**, 556–569.

Den Hartog, D.N., De Hoogh, A.H.B. and Keegan, A.E. 2007: Belongingness as a moderator of the charisma – OCB relationship, *Journal of Applied Psychology*, **92**(4), 1131–1139.

Fleishman, E.A. and Harris, E.F. 1962: Patterns of leadership behavior related to employee grievances and turnover, *Personnel Psychology*, **15**, 43–56.

Gratton, L. and Truss, C. 2003: The three-dimensional people strategy: Putting human resources policies into action. *Academy of Management Executive*, **17**(3), 74–86.

Guest, D.E. 1999: Human resource management – the worker's verdict, *Human Resource Management Journal*, **9**(3), 5–25.

Hall, L. and Torrington, D. 1998: Letting go or holding on: The devolution of operational personnel activities, *Human Resource Management Journal*, **8**(1), 41–55.

Hannah, D. and Iverson, R. 2004: Employment relationships in context: implications for policy and practice, in J. A.-M. Coyle-Shapiro, L.M. Shore, S. Taylor and L. Tetrick, (eds.), *The employment relationship: Examining psychological and contextual perspectives*, 332–350. Oxford: Oxford University Press.

Hater, J.J. and Bass, B.M. 1988: Superiors' evaluations and subordinates' perceptions of transformational and transactional leadership, *Journal of Applied Psychology*, **73**, 695–702.

House, R.J. 1977: A 1976 theory of charismatic leadership, in J.G. Hunt and L.L. Larson (eds.), *Leadership: the Cutting Edge*, 189–204. Carbondale, IL: Southern Illinois University Press.

House, R.J. 1996: Path-Goal theory of leadership: Lessons, legacy and a reformulated theory, *Leadership Quarterly*, **7**, 323–352.

Howell, J.M. and Avolio, B.J. 1993: Transformational leadership, transactional leadership, locus of control and support for innovation, *Journal of Applied Psychology*, **78**, 891–902.

Kalshoven, K., Den Hartog, D.N. and De Hoogh, A.H.B. 2011: Ethical leadership at work questionnaire (ELW): Development and validation of a multidimensional measure, *The Leadership Quarterly*, **22**, 51–69.

Liao, H., Toya, K., Lepak, D.P. and Hong, Y. 2009: Do they see eye to eye? Management and employee perspectives of high-performance work systems and influence processes on service quality, *Journal of Applied Psychology*, **94**(2), 371–391.

Lowe, K.B., Kroeck, G. K. and Sivasubramaniam, N. 1996: Effectiveness correlates of transformational and transactional leadership: a meta-analytic review, *Leadership Quarterly*, **7**, 385–425.

Marks, M.A., Mathieu, J.E. and Zaccaro, S.J. 2001: A temporally based framework and taxonomy of team processes, *Academy of Management Review*, **26**, 356–376.

Mayer, D.M., Kuenzi, M., Greenbaum, R., Bardes, M. and Salvador, R. 2009: How low does ethical leadership flow? The relative effects of top management and supervisors on employee ethical behaviors and job attitudes, *Organizational Behavior and Human Decision Processes*, **108**, 1–13.

McConville, T. and Holden, L. 1999: The filling in the sandwich: HRM and middle managers in the health sector, *Personnel Review*, **28**(5/6), 406–424.

McGrath, J.E. 1962: *Leadership behavior: Some requirements for leadership training*, Washington DC: U.S. Civil Service Commission, Office of Career Development.

Morgeson, F.P., DeRue, D.S. and Karam, E.P. 2010: Leadership in teams: A functional approach to understanding leadership structures and processes, *Journal of Management*, **36**, 5–39.

Nishii, L.H. and Wright, P.M. 2008: Variability within organizations: Implications for strategic human resource management, in D. Brent Smith (ed.), *The People Make the Place: Dynamic Linkages Between Individuals and Organizations*, New York: Taylor and Francis Group.

Piccolo, R.F. and Colquitt, J.A. 2006: Transformational leadership and job behaviors: The mediating role of core job characteristics, *Academy of Management Journal*, **49**, 327–340.

Piccolo, R.F., Greenbaum, R., Den Hartog, D.N. and Folger, R. 2010: Task Significance and Job Autonomy as Motivational Mechanisms in the Ethical Leadership Process, *Journal of Organizational Behavior*, **31**, 259–278.

Podsakoff, P.M., MacKenzie, S.B. and Bommer, W.H. 1996: Transformational leader behaviors and substitutes for leadership as determinants of employee satisfaction, commitment, trust and organizational citizenship behaviours, *Journal of Management*, **22**, 259–298.

Purcell, J. and Hutchinson, S. 2007: Front-line managers as agents in the HRM-performance causal chain: theory, analysis and evidence, *Human Resource Management Journal*, **17**(1), 3–20.

Purcell, J. and Kinnie, N. 2006: HRM and business performance, in P. Boxall, J. Purcell and P. Wright (eds.), *The Oxford Handbook of Human Resource Management*, Oxford: Oxford University Press.

Renwick, D. 2003: Line manager involvement in HRM: an inside view, *Employee Relations*, **25**(3), 262–280.

Rhoades Shanock, L. and Eisenberger, R. 2006: When supervisors feel supported: Relationships with subordinates' perceived supervisor support, perceived organizational support, and performance, *Journal of Applied Psychology*, **91**(3), 689–695.

Rynes, S. L., Colbert, A. E. and Brown, K. G. 2002: HR professionals' beliefs about effective human resource practices: Correspondence between research and practice, *Human Resource Management*, **41**(2), 149–174.

Searle, R., Den Hartog, D.N., Weibel, A., Gillespie, N., Six, F., Hatzakis, T., and Skinner, D. 2011: Trust in the employer: The role of high-involvement work practices and procedural justice in European organizations. *The International Journal of Human Resource Management*, **22**(5), 1069–1092.

Sisson, K. 1994: Personnel management: paradigms, practice and prospects, in K. Sisson (ed.), *Personnel Management: A Comprehensive Guide to Theory and Practice in Britain* 2nd edn, 3–52. Oxford: Blackwell Publishers.

Storey, J. 1992: *Developments in the management of human resources*, Oxford: Blackwell Publishers.

Sun, L.-Y., Aryee, S. and Law, K.S. 2007: High-performance human resource practices, citizenship behavior, and organizational performance: A relational perspective, *Academy of Management Journal*, **50**(3), 558–577.

Thornhill, A. and Saunders, M.N.K. 1998: What if line managers don't realize they're responsible for HR?, *Personnel Review*, **27**(6), 460–476.

Uhl-Bien, M., Graen, G. and Scandura, L. 2000: Indicators of leader–member exchange (LMX) for strategic human resource management systems, *Research in Personnel and Human Resources Management*, **18**, 137–185.

Ulrich, D. 1997a: *Human resource champions*, Boston, MA: Harvard Business School Press.

Ulrich, D. 1997b: Measuring Human Resources: An Overview of Practice and a Prescription for Results, *Human Resource Management*, **36**(3), 303–320.

Ulrich, D. and Brockbank, W. 2005: *The HR value proposition*, Boston, MA: Harvard Business Press.

Whittaker, S. and Marchington, M. 2003: Devolving HR responsibility to the line, *Employee Relations*, **25**(3), 245–261.

Wright, P. M., McMahan, G. C., Snell, S. A. and Gerhart, B. 2001: Comparing line and HR executives' perceptions of HR effectiveness: Services, roles, and contributions, *Human Resource Management*, **40**(2), 111–123.

Youndt, M.A. and Snell, S.A. 2004: Human Resource Configurations, Intellectual Capital, and Organizational Performance, *Journal of Managerial Issues*, **3**, 337–360.

Yukl, G. 2010: *Leadership in Organizations,* 7th edn, Englewood Cliffs, NJ: Prentice Hall.

Zhang, Z. and Jia, M. 2010: Using social exchange theory to predict the effects of high-performance human resource practices on corporate entrepreneurship: Evidence from China, *Human Resource Management*, **49**(4), 743–765.

Zohar, D. 2000: A group-level model of safety climate: testing the effect of group climate on micro-accidents in manufacturing jobs, *Journal of Applied Psychology*, **85**(4), 587–596.

PART IV

Performance and Rewards

CHAPTER ELEVEN

Performance Management

Stephen Bach

Employers and employees are living through a period of heightened economic uncertainty in which the economic crisis has cast a long shadow over public and private sector organisations. HR professionals have emphasised the necessity of enhanced individual and organisational performance in response to more volatile economic and political circumstances whilst seeking to maintain employee engagement in tough times. Performance management has become a key tool in these attempts to reconcile the increased demands placed on employees whilst signalling that employee development and engagement remain important concerns for employers. Reconciling these complex and frequently contradictory organisational requirements, however, has placed severe strains on performance management practice and uncertainties about its effectiveness remain a prominent topic of debate (Brown 2010).

The evolution of performance management reflects wider trends in human resource management. Performance management has its origins in systems of performance appraisal, traditionally associated with a relatively straightforward process in which line managers met annually to review the performance of their subordinates, assigned a rating based on the previous year's performance, and filled in the requisite form, with little happening until the process was repeated the following year. Performance appraisal has evolved, becoming far more than an annual ritual and an important lever to enhance organisational performance. West *et al.* (2002), in their study of hospitals, suggested that effective performance appraisals by providing role clarity, identifying training needs, and making staff feel valued led to improved patient care and contributed to reductions in patient mortality. Over time, performance appraisal became one dimension of more integrated systems of performance management and the terms were often used interchangeably.

In the last decade the label 'performance appraisal' has been used less and has frequently been replaced by the term 'performance management'. It remains important, however, to differentiate between the two concepts rather than to assume that performance appraisal has been replaced by performance management. Performance appraisal is concerned mainly with the individual review of performance and setting individual objectives, whilst performance management encompasses the whole orga-nisation and extends beyond setting individual objectives to include broader organisa-tional priorities such as talent management. In this chapter, performance appraisal is viewed as one component of these broader approaches to performance management.

This accords with HR professionals' own understanding of the variety of practices associated with performance management. In a Chartered Institute of Personnel and Development (CIPD 2009) survey, in response to a question about what activities they understood to be included under the banner of performance management, over 90 per cent of respondents included 'regular review meetings', 85 per cent 'objective or target setting', 83 per cent 'performance appraisal' and 75 per cent 'assessment of development needs'. In terms of what actually happens under the heading of per-formance management, performance appraisal remains the most prevalent charac-teristic of performance management systems, identified by over four-fifths of respondents (CIPD 2009).

The higher profile of performance management has, however, been accompanied by a recognition that the process has often fallen short of managerial expectations. This has led to ongoing adjustments to performance management processes, with a tighter link between individual targets and corporate objectives, ensuring 'there is a clear line of sight' between organisational and individual requirements. Employees have been assigned an increased role in steering the performance management process and this has often been accompanied by the growth of more varied forms of 'upward' feedback. Employers are also using performance management to identify future talent and to highlight the behaviours expected of staff (IDS 2011).

This chapter starts by charting the evolution from performance appraisal to per-formance management. It proceeds to examine the forms and extent of performance appraisal and to discuss the problems associated with it. It argues that a great deal of the literature concentrates on implementation problems which are viewed as remedial through proper training and communication. Radical critiques of perfor-mance management, influenced by labour process and Foucauldian traditions, raise more fundamental questions about the purpose of performance management, but are too one-dimensional in their assessment. The final part of the chapter examines attempts to overcome many of the problems of performance management, exam-ining the growth of employee involvement and multi-source feedback. It also considers other recent trends, highlighting the impact of technology and cultural diversity on the evolution of performance management.

The Evolution of Performance Management

The evolution of performance management reflects the broader emphasis within HRM on establishing coherent and integrated bundles of HR practice. In the 1990s there was a move away from stand-alone, ratings-driven systems of performance appraisal towards more integrated systems of performance management, with line managers becoming more pivotal to their implementation. This trajectory continued into the noughties with more ambitious attempts to integrate performance management into organisational HR architecture by the use of competency frameworks and systematic links to talent management and employee engagement processes. The risk, however, is that performance management systems become overloaded as organisations seek to address a wide variety of HR challenges via their performance management system (Brown and Hirsh 2011).

These shifts in emphasis stem from the more competitive environment in which firms operate. This has placed a premium on firms' abilities to measure and improve the performance of their staff. This pressure has not been confined to the private sector. Within public services, the international adoption of systems of new public management has been characterised by an emphasis on tighter management of performance and raised expectations of staff. This shift has been especially pronounced in Britain, with public service employers required to meet a range of central government targets, placing direct pressure on the workforce to meet demanding service standards (Bach and Kessler 2012).

Advocates of performance management claim that its value resides in the cycle of integrated activities, which ensure that a systematic link is established between the contribution of each employee and the overall performance of the organisation. This strategic approach contrasts with the free-standing nature of performance appraisal, in which the outcomes of each individual appraisal are rarely linked to overall corporate objectives. Line managers, rather than HR specialists, have the dominant role in the design and management of the performance management process and a premium is placed on ensuring effective communication and feedback. Armstrong and Baron (2005: 17) suggest the main value of performance management is to:

- communicate a shared vision of the purpose and values of the organisation;
- define expectations of what must be delivered and how it should be delivered;
- ensure that people are aware of what constitutes high performance and how they need to achieve it;
- enhance motivation, engagement and commitment by providing a means of recognising endeavour and achievement through feedback;
- enable people to monitor their own performance and encourage dialogue about what needs to be done to improve performance.

The extent to which these objectives have been achieved can be gauged from surveys of performance management practice.

Trends

The most detailed UK surveys of performance management arrangements have been undertaken for the CIPD in 1998, 2004 and 2009 with respectively 562 (1998), 506 (2004) and 507 (2009) HR respondents (Armstrong and Baron 1998; 2005; CIPD 2009).

The 2009 survey was web-based and fewer data are provided on the characteristics of the respondents. Between 1998 and 2004 the number of organisations with a formal process of performance management increased from 69 per cent to 87 per cent, although comparison between the surveys needs to be treated with caution as the profile of respondents differed (Armstrong and Baron 1998; 2005).

During the 1990s there was a shift from an emphasis on reward-driven systems, based on individual performance-related pay and quantifiable objectives, towards more rounded systems of performance management with a stronger developmental focus; over two-thirds of organisations included personal development plans in their performance management systems, a trend that continued throughout the noughties. Consequently, performance-related pay was a feature of only 31 per cent of performance management systems in 2004, compared to 43 per cent in 1998 (Armstrong and Baron 2005: 68). By 2009, less than a third of respondents identified performance-related pay as a feature of their performance management approach (CIPD 2009: 8).

The 2009 survey draws attention to two main issues. First, the main components of performance management had not altered markedly since the previous survey in 2005, with individual performance appraisal, objective setting and drawing-up personal development plans remaining the main characteristics of performance management. This does not necessarily indicate stability in performance management processes, as linked practitioner interviews suggested that a very high proportion of organisations had recalibrated performance management arrangements to improve effectiveness, for example, revamping competency frameworks or other changes 'to drive a performance culture' (CIPD 2009: 14). Second, the trend to integrate performance management more tightly to other HR processes continued, with respondents advocating further integration between performance management activities and programmes to coach staff and manage well-being.

Despite these changes, however, the CIPD survey revealed limited consensus about the benefits of performance management and considerable scepticism that performance management was delivering the anticipated benefits. These issues are not new. Previous surveys highlighted similar concerns, with Armstrong and Baron reporting that 37 per cent of their respondents viewed performance management as 'ineffective' or only 'slighty effective' in improving organisational performance, a figure that had not altered by 2004 (Armstrong and Baron 1998: 109; 2005: 66). One reason is the increased use of competency-based assessment, which is often difficult to use effectively. Behaviours such as 'leadership' are hard to define and this has led to considerable scepticism amongst managers about the value of competencies in judging performance, although they are more suited to identifying development needs (Strebler et al. 2001).

Despite these shortcomings, performance management systems are designed with the assumption that managers within organisations can establish clear, unambiguous goals which can be broken down into individual components, are accepted by the individuals concerned and can be easily measured. The extent to which these assumptions are valid highlights the dilemmas associated with performance appraisal, which forms the core component of all systems of performance management.

| Performance Appraisal: Policy and Practice |

A variety of studies have tracked the incidence of performance appraisal arrangements over time, focusing on the increased uptake of appraisal schemes which have been applied to larger proportions of the workforce. In the first large-scale survey commissioned by the Institute of Personnel Management (IPM) (Gill *et al.* 1973), 74 per cent of respondents had an appraisal scheme in place for some of their workforce, a figure which rose to over 80 per cent by 1977 and remained at that level in 1986 (Long 1986). The 1998 Workplace Employee Relations Survey (WERS) noted that formal performance appraisals were conducted in 73 per cent of workplaces with more than ten employees, with appraisal being more common in the public sector (79 per cent) than the private sector (72 per cent). By 2004, the overall figure had increased by five per cent to 78 per cent and there had been a very sharp increase in the public sector (91 per cent) and a smaller increase in the private sector (75 per cent). Performance appraisal was not, however, always conducted on a systematic basis, nor did it include all employees (Kersley *et al.* 2006: 87).

As significant as the widespread use of appraisal schemes has been the increased importance of performance review. A striking finding of Gallie's work is that between 1986 and 1992 the role of appraisal in determining how hard employees worked had increased substantially and had become more important than pay incentives in controlling work behaviour, the reverse of the position in 1986 (Gallie *et al.* 1998: 68-9). Updating this data set provides further support for such findings with appraisals 'influencing employees' feeling of working under high demands' (McGovern *et al.* 2007: 184).

The purpose of performance appraisal

It is often assumed that the growth of performance appraisal stemmed from the extension of performance-related pay in the 1980s and 1990s and the need to support these PRP systems. This assumption does not provide the full picture, not least because the biggest increase in the uptake of performance appraisal occurred during the 1970s. Long (1986: 15) reported that assessment of salary increases was not viewed as one of the main purposes of performance review and there had been little change since 1977. It is more plausible to argue that during the expansion of performance-related pay in the early 1990s, this growth shaped the type of scheme adopted rather than being a key influence on the increasing use of performance appraisal (Storey 1992: 107).

An important influence on the increased use of performance appraisal has been the commitment of successive governments to modernise public service HR practice as part of attempts to enhance managerial authority and increase efficiency (Bach and Kessler 2012). The establishment of appraisal within the public sector in the 1980s and 1990s initially proved contentious because employees and trade unions viewed it as a means to reinforce managerial control and ensure conformity with government priorities (Healy 1997). It has become a more accepted feature of performance management practice, but professionals, such as medical staff, often view it as a laborious tick-box exercise rather than as a tool to enhance performance (McGivern and Ferlie 2007). An additional reason to introduce or revamp performance management arrangements arises from employer interest in gaining external acreditation such as Investors in People and ISO 9000. The use of a formalised appraisal scheme with a prominent personal development component can be used as evidence to demonstrate investment in staff. For example, the BIG Lottery Fund overhauled its performance management process in response to feedback from Investors in People (IDS 2011: 15).

For HR specialists, performance appraisal and other components of performance management systems ensure the systematic collection of information about employees, which provides the bedrock of all HR practice. Training and development needs analysis, career planning and talent management processes can be implemented and monitored as part of an integrated approach to performance management. HR intranets are increasingly used to move performance management processes online, and in many organisations employees can access their performance and relevant guidance and training materials from their desktop. For HR and line managers, this enables them to keep track of the completion of performance appraisals and generate a series of reports about the performance and potential of their team or particular individuals within it. Overall, appraisal data is a valuable source of information about the effectiveness of HR policies and process including recruitment and selection and diversity policies.

Managers are often asked to identify the main objectives of their schemes. In an e-rewards (2005) survey of 181 organisations, almost two-thirds cited either 'aligning individual and organisational objectives' or 'improving organisational performance' as their top priority, with more than a third identifying personal development as the key goal of performance management; only a quarter of respondents emphasised its role in informing performance pay decisions. The responses indicate that employers have multiple objectives for their performance management systems and it is these potentially conflicting objectives which account for many implementation difficulties (Strebler et al. 2001).

Traditional performance appraisal tended to be divided between what was termed development-driven versus rewards-driven systems. The emphasis has shifted increasingly to embrace both objectives, with an emphasis on short-term performance coupled with a more developmental orientation in which line managers are increasingly cast in the role of coaches and mentors (IDS 2011). Identifying and dealing with poor performance has always been one objective of appraisal systems. Grey (1994), in his study of trainee accountants, notes that, although performance appraisal was presented as an aid for career management, in practice it was used to discipline employees and weed out poor performers in the annual 'cull'. Increased awareness of the prevalence of forms of bullying at work has been accompanied by a recognition that performance assessments which assign staff 'unsatisfactory' ratings, often without any prior warning, may constitute a form of bullying behaviour (Lee 2002). The absence of a third person during appraisal interviews, in marked contrast to most selection interviews, provides greater scope for bullying behaviour than in other organisational settings.

Despite these concerns, a more common worry amongst HR managers is that line managers are reticent in addressing poor performance, reflected in ambivalent attitudes towards performance management. Three quarters of HR managers suggested that line managers are reluctant to conduct performance reviews and are not committed to performance management (e-reward 2005). Addressing poor performance has become a higher priority for organisations and performance management systems have been reformed to address this issue. Luton Borough Council, for example, shifted from an appraisal system focused on development towards an approach that focuses more on achieving individual objectives that are linked to the council's business strategy, making under-performance more visible (IDS 2011: 33).

Who is appraised?

In 2004, WERS data reported that in almost three-quarters (73 per cent) of workplaces employing managers, their performance was formally appraised. Besides managers, professional workers (82 per cent), personal service staff (79 per cent) and associate professionals and technical staff (77 per cent) were the categories of staff most commonly subject to formal appraisal (Kersley *et al.* 2006: 88). Overall the trend has been towards inclusivity, with the proportion of workplaces where *only* managers were appraised declining to 3 per cent by 2004 (8 per cent in 1998). In the public sector, this trend towards inclusivity has been accelerated by harmonisation of the conditions of employment of manual and non-manual workers, as exemplified by the 1997 single status agreement in local government. Townley (1989) put a different gloss on these developments, suggesting that, in essence, appraisal is being used as a more subtle form of managerial control, with tighter monitoring of workers' performance (Townley 1989). By 2004, the proportion of workplaces conducting appraisal for non-managerial staff had reached 86 per cent in the public sector and 68 per cent in the private sector (Kersley *et al.* 2006: 88).

A long-standing exception to these patterns have been board level directors. Long (1986: 9) reported that the coverage of appraisal arrangements for directors was almost half the figure for other managers and there was little alteration during the 1990s (Industrial Society 1997). This started to change, however, because of the increased interest in corporate governance and the important role assigned to non-executive directors in the wake of US corporate scandals such as Enron. Performance reviews of board level directors are now a requirement of the UK Corporate Governance Code and senior independent chairmen and non-executive directors are required to meet at least annually to appraise the chairman's performance. Boards are also required to undertake performance reviews (see Chapter 4). This represents a far-reaching reform of the manner in which British boards have traditionally operated.

What is appraised?

At the core of the appraisal process is the type of performance criteria used for rating individuals. In traditional appraisal schemes, the personality traits of individuals have been rated based on the 'commonsense' assumption that traits such as leadership skills and loyalty are important for effective performance. The use of personality traits has been subject to extensive criticism as a result of subjective characteristics and because of the difficulty of isolating the particular facet of personality responsible for effective job performance. The use of trait-based methods waned over the course of the 1970s and 1980s, although this did not preclude appraisers making judgements on the basis of personality traits, even if this was justified in terms of more acceptable performance criteria (Barlow 1989). Since the 1990s there has been a revival of interest in assessing personality, but it has been imbued with greater authority than in the past by establishing scales to measure emotional intelligence, enabling the ambiguous to be made tangible by a process of measurement and quantification (Fineman 2004: 721).

The dominant approach, particularly for managerial staff, continues to be the assessment against an individual's objectives, with reference to the previous appraisal round and organisational priorities. It is usually suggested that this process is most effective when individual objectives are aligned to organisational goals enabling individuals to understand how their role fits into overall divisional objectives and when the number of objectives is limited to ensure that individuals can focus on a smaller number of challenging objectives (CIPD 2009). Employers increasingly expect individuals to set their objectives in reference to corporate priorities. For example, at the BIG Lottery Fund individuals are required to record which corporate priority each of their objectives is linked to, a process facilitated by the online system which requires a selection to be made by the appraisee (IDS 2011).

A number of challenges remain for managers in establishing agreed performance criteria. In service industries in the past, it has been difficult to establish tangible and quantifiable performance objectives, but these problems are being surmounted by electronic surveillance (see Chapter 6) and the use of technology to assist in the appraisal process (Miller 2003). Challenges remain, especially in politically sensitive sectors such as health and education in which the key performance criteria for staff may be contested. A related concern is that individuals' tenacious pursuit of their own performance targets may lead them to neglect other aspects of their job or to focus on achieving their objectives to the detriment of teamwork or other important aspects of organisational performance. There is a heightened danger of this occurring in a context in which managers complain that they are being pressurised to achieve harder performance targets. These concerns have led many organisations to modify their performance criteria so that staff are assessed on the manner in which they achieve their results as well as the targets themselves (IDS 2011).

This development signals an increasing emphasis on a shift from job-related to person-related performance criteria. As job roles evolve constantly, the person rather than the job becomes the key focus of performance management systems.

Employers are therefore placing more emphasis on measuring behaviours associated with emotional intelligence because of the assumption that managers who exhibit characteristics such as enthusiasm, honesty, empathy and self-assurance are more effective (Fineman 2004). Moreover, it is argued that assessing competencies is effective because results may not relate to individual performance, but arise from fortuitous circumstances; assessing behaviour therefore provides a better guide to high performance (Pulakos 2009).

This change in emphasis is reflected in the widespread adoption of competencies and behaviours to underpin performance management. Performance criteria are being extended beyond a sole focus on what has been achieved, to encourage staff to consider how they achieve results and to encourage them to follow corporate values. Various dimensions of performance are linked to a series of behavioural statements and employees are assessed according to the extent to which they demonstrate these behaviours. Typically, competence frameworks refer to communications, teamwork, relationship management, decision making and customer focus, with organisations sometimes differentiating competencies by level or job family (IDS 2011).

There has also been a trend to simplify competency frameworks because they have proved to be too complicated and time consuming to operate. Reinsurance company MunichRe shifted from 18 competencies to four core competency areas relating to customers, innovation, co-operation and being solution-focused (IDS 2011: 40). The role of competency frameworks in assessing performance varies between organisations. It is not unusual to be assessed separately against results and behaviours and for these ratings to be combined to generate an overall rating. This occurs at DHL, the international logistics company, with individual achievement based on a combined assessment of achieving personal targets (individual key objectives – IKOs) and competences, ranked from 'far exceeds – role model' to 'does not meet' indicating that expected behaviours are not demonstrated (Armstrong 2009: 340).

Employers have also developed more wide-ranging frameworks to assess organisational performance. Kaplan and Norton (1996, 2001), in their 'balanced scorecard' framework, suggested that organisations needed a more rounded assessment of performance than solely short-term financial returns. They suggest that balanced, but objective, measures of performance can be derived from four perspectives:

- *The financial perspective:* How do we appear to our shareholders?
- *The customer perspective:* How do we appear to our customers?
- *The internal/business perspective:* What business process must we excel at?
- *The innovation and learning perspective:* How do we continue to sustain our ability to learn and grow?

According to this model organisations develop a small number of key indicators in each quadrant that reflects key performance drivers and which enables employees' individual objectives to be aligned to corporate objectives. Many large organisations, including the retailer Tesco and the oil company Shell, use versions of the balanced scorecard. Whilst the 'Innovation and Learning perspective' has a strong people management component, the balanced scorecard has been criticised for paying insufficient attention to a company's human resources and may underplay the external environment (Maltz et al. 2003). Companies such as Tesco that have adapted the balanced scorecard (termed the Tesco steering wheel) to bring in aspects of corporate responsibility such as environmental issues and other variants of the balanced scorecard, including the 'performance prism', are designed to take more account of other stakeholder interests (Bourne and Bourne 2011).

The Limitations of Performance Appraisal

Concerns about performance appraisal are long-standing, stretching from McGregor's (1957) 'uneasy look' at appraisal, to Deming's (1982) suggestion that appraisal was 'a deadly disease' which blamed individuals for problems systemic to organisations. Despite repeated gloomy predictions, the use of performance appraisal has continued to evolve, but there is recognition within the HR profession of the difficulties of ensuring its effective use, indicated by the rather mixed evaluations of performance management systems (Armstrong 2009; Brown 2010). These criticisms arise from within a conventional management framework, in the sense that they do not challenge the underlying, managerially-defined purpose of performance review, but rather they seek to remedy the imperfections in the design and implementation of existing approaches.

A widely acknowledged problem is that the appraisal process is used for a variety of conflicting purposes. An Institute of Employment Studies survey of 926 managers in 17 public and private sector organisations reported that performance review had become 'a bottleneck of stark contradictions' (Strebler et al. 2001: 54). It can be used to motivate staff to improve performance by establishing clear objectives for the future and letting them know what is expected of them. This contrasts with a review process which is primarily concerned with distributing rewards based on an assessment of past performance. Finally, the appraisal process can be more geared to development, with training needs identified either to assist in remedying deficiencies or to assist in talent management. The difficulty is that these different elements are often blended together in an ill-defined manner. The reviewer is forced to adopt conflicting roles, cast as both a monitor and judge of performance, but also as an understanding counsellor and mentor. It is pointed out that employees are unlikely to confide their limitations and anxieties about job performance to their appraiser, not least because it may impact on their remuneration or career progression (Newton and Findlay 1996).

A major preoccupation of the performance appraisal literature has been to view appraisal as a measurement problem, focusing on ways to increase the validity and reliability of the process and to understand the cognitive biases of raters

(Spence and Keeping 2011). Given the problems of biased assessment raised in Chapter 7 in relation to the selection interview, it is not surprising that similar problems occur in appraisal interviews. There is less systematic evidence available, however, on the outcomes of appraisal interviews compared to the numerous studies that have examined selection interviews (Fletcher 2001). The first problem is the 'halo effect' distortion. This arises when one attribute of the individual is used as the basis to rate the overall performance of the person, largely irrespective of the stated criterion. A second problem relates to the reluctance of managers to be too judgemental, which can result in an error of central tendency in which everybody is rated as average. This reluctance to differentiate between appraisees undermines the value of the review process. A third problem is called 'recency bias'. Because managers rarely keep detailed notes about their appraisees, and are not very precise about rating all the behaviours they are required to judge, there is a tendency to base reviews on the recent past, regardless of how representative it is of performance over the year. This shortcoming may be tempered by the shift within some organisations from appraisal as an annual process to a more continuous process of performance review (IDS 2011).

More recently there has been a recognition that bias may arise not only from unintended actions of appraisors but also consciously, in that managers may distort ratings to pursue their own interests (Spence and Keeping 2011). These insights stem from long-standing awareness that managers are reluctant to judge individuals. In McGregor's (1957) terms, managers are uncomfortable 'playing God' and are reluctant to transmit negative feedback to employees. Consequently, managers may deliberately distort ratings and their own motives in the performance appraisal process need to be considered in addition to the focus on the appraisee. Longnecker et al 's (1987) study of sixty senior managers found that a variety of factors, other than the appraisees' actual performance, influenced the ratings managers allocated. They were more concerned to enhance and protect their own interests than to provide accurate ratings. Managers' motives were varied, including a recognition that their own lack of support and guidance may have contributed to poor performance and a more straightforward concern to avoid conflict (Longnecker et al. 1987).

Compounding the managerial problems of rater bias is the existence of the inflation of performance feedback. In other words, even when poor ratings are allocated to employees, there is a tendency for supervisors to explain away lower ratings, diluting the impact of poor ratings (Waung and Highhouse 1997). Some commentators suggest that these problems may be exacerbated by the physical removal of HR support arising from outsourcing and the moves towards shared services, leaving line managers unsupported in the performance management process (Brown 2010). Employers seek to ensure consistency by encouraging benchmarking forums before ratings are finalised. At Sony Europe calibration sessions are held between managerial peers to discuss and benchmark performance expected at different grades (IDS 2011: 13).

The appraisal interview is also influenced by the gender and ethnic origins of the appraisee and appraiser (Geddes and Konrad 2003). Chen and DiTomaso (1996), surveying mainly US studies, suggest that women in similar jobs to men and performing to the same level gain similar ratings. However, they contend that gender impacts on ratings in two main ways. First, women gained better ratings when they were evaluated in 'women's jobs' and second, cultural assumptions or implicit theories of performance criteria, i.e. the choice of performance standards actually used, may be unconsciously biased towards the values of white men. Many employees, especially women, complain of a competitive masculine culture at the workplace in which long hours are equated with loyalty and commitment to the organisation, with detrimental implications for appraisal ratings of those workers not prepared, or able, to demonstrate this level of 'commitment' (Lewis and Taylor 1996; Simpson 1998).

Employers have adopted a variety of measures to improve the consistency and credibility of their appraisal systems, with most approaches underpinned by five levels of performance category. To avoid problems of central tendency, some organisations use forced-distribution systems, which means that raters have to conform to a set proportion of ratings at different levels. Most famously associated with Jack Welsh's 20:70:10 rank and yank system at GE, the bottom-ranked 10 per cent of managers were removed annually and a similar system was employed by Enron before the company collapsed. Hewlett Packard used to use such an approach, but abandoned it because the perception amongst staff was that their rankings depended on the negotiation skills of their manager rather than their own performance. Instead, managers are provided with guidelines about the proportion of staff which would be expected to be in the top and bottom portions of the distribution (IDS 1997). In addition to being unpopular with managers and encouraging perverse behaviour, there is little evidence that forced distribution systems are an effective approach (Armstrong 2009).

The most common response to these challenges is to redouble training efforts to ensure that line managers are trained in conducting appraisals, to recognise good and bad performance, and to be aware of sources of potential bias. With the growth of HR metrics there is also much more effort to try and evaluate and demonstrate the benefits of performance management (CIPD 2009). Despite these efforts, managers remain uncertain about the effectiveness of their performance review systems. Within the HR literature there is a strong awareness of the limitations of performance review and numerous suggestions on how to remedy these problems. The underlying philosophy that unites these accounts is essentially unitarist. It is assumed that employees and employers both derive equal benefits from appraisal, and this is especially likely to be the case when the appraisal process is as open and objective as possible. In short, it is the implementation of performance appraisal that is at fault rather than more fundamental problems associated with the assumptions that lie behind it.

The radical critique

A different set of assumptions about the purpose of performance appraisal is influenced by Foucault (1981), with appraisal interpreted as part of a more sinister management regime to control all aspects of employee behaviour and ensure that employees adhere to management objectives (Barlow 1989; Grey 1994; Healy 1997; Newton and Findlay 1996; Townley 1993). These accounts reject most of the assumptions that underpin the practitioner-orientated analysis of performance appraisal. Instead of a concern to prescribe how appraisal can operate effectively, the focus is on understanding the actual practice of appraisal within the workplace, with greater emphasis on its specific context. Unitary assumptions about the benevolent purposes of appraisal are replaced by a more radical ideology concerned to examine managerial objectives, especially tighter control over behaviour and performance, the potential to individualise the employment relationship, and the scope for managers to use appraisal as a veneer to legitimise informal management practice.

A dominant thread running through these accounts is the emphasis placed on the manner in which appraisal is used to bolster managerial power and control. Barlow's (1989) study of a petrochemicals firm highlights many of the shortcomings of appraisal as perceived by line managers. But he departs from the prescriptive literature in suggesting that these 'problems' do not undermine the utility of the appraisal system to managers. Indeed, quite the reverse is true, because it allows managers discretion to promote favoured individuals but, if challenged, to legitimise them by referring to the formal appraisal process. The spread of performance appraisal to manual workers and public service professionals has similarly been interpreted as a means to increase managerial control over diverse occupational groups formerly immune from these processes (Townley 1989, 1999; Healy 1997).

Within many of these critical accounts, there are strong leanings towards Foucault's (1981) conception of power, with appraisal used by managers as a form of disciplinary gaze (Townley 1993; Grey 1994) which complements other forms of electronic and personal surveillance found in call centres and the like. The starting point for this literature is Foucault's discussion of Bentham's 'Panoptican', the model prison in which prisoners can always be observed by the prison guards, but they cannot be seen by the prisoners. Because prisoners would never know whether they were being observed, the Panoptican combines surveillance and discipline. For Townley (1993), the relevance to appraisal within the university sector is clear, 'Appraisal operates as a form of panoptican with its anonymous and continuous surveillance as seen in the articulation of a monitoring role' (Townley 1993: 232). Grey (1994) pursues similar themes, suggesting that, for trainee accountants, the appraisal process is used as a form of disciplinary technology, with those rated as 'satisfactory' running the risk of being summarily dismissed in the annual 'cull'.

There is a tendency, however, to assume that managerial intentions are necessarily translated into managerial actions, ignoring the issue of human agency (Newton and Findlay 1996). Both Barlow (1989) and Townley (1989) view the achievement of managerial objectives as straightforward, ignoring scope for employee resistance. This is curious when, as noted earlier, the management literature is replete with evidence about the ambivalent feelings of line managers towards appraisal and commentators express exasperation at the leniency shown by managers in rating employees.

Despite their limitations, these critical accounts have challenged many of the traditional assumptions about performance appraisal and helped to advance understanding of why the anticipated benefits of appraisal do not always emerge in practice. Critical perspectives highlight that it is not sufficient to assume that clearer objectives and training of appraisers will yield satisfactory results. The contested nature of appraisal, the specific managerial objectives sought, and the nature of the context in which it is applied all have an important bearing on the impact of the appraisal process. These insights have informed many of the current developments in performance appraisal.

Collaborative Performance Review

The changing shape of organisations, with more reliance on a variety of external partners, often associated with network forms of organisation and more diverse workforces, has encouraged shifts in performance management practice. This emphasis has several distinct dimensions, with increased interest in how performance needs to be managed across organisational boundaries to satisfy the requirements of end users (Busi and Bititci 2006). A second dimension focuses on greater collaboration between employees and their managers in the performance management process, with the involvement of a wider range of stakeholders that may extend beyond the firm.

One important element is placing more responsibility on employees to manage the performance review process. This stems, in part, from a recognition that performance review is shaped by the behaviour of two parties and is more effective when appraisees are active participants rather than passive recipients of line management evaluations. This includes influencing the objectives that are established in the annual performance appraisal cycle. Employees are often expected to undertake a self-appraisal prior to discussion with their line manager, which may include gathering evidence to highlight achievements against objectives. Employees are also being assigned an enhanced role in following up on development needs after the annual review.

The emphasis on engaging a wider range of stakeholders in performance review, indicating that the process is no longer solely the preserve of managers appraising their employees, is intended to ensure a more rounded view of overall performance. Multi-source feedback, particularly upward feedback from direct reports, has attracted much attention (Ghorpade 2000; Silverman et al. 2005). It is the combination of information from self-appraisal, subordinate appraisal, peer appraisal and feedback from other internal and external customers which has been termed '360-degree' feedback. The term can be misleading because the most widely adopted part of the process, and the aspect which has attracted most attention, has been the appraisal by staff of their managers, i.e. 'upward' appraisal. Other sources of feedback from internal/external peers and from customers are also utilised in some organisations, but predominantly for developmental purposes.

The overall rationale for 360-degree appraisal is that it can enhance self awareness by providing feedback on performance from a variety of perspectives, enabling managers to learn about their strengths and weaknesses and alter their behaviour. Moreover, changes in organisational structures with more fluid working arrangements, such as project teams, and multiple reporting lines make it inappropriate to rely solely on the judgement of one individual who may not be sufficiently close to gauge performance accurately. The emphasis on teamwork and collaboration assigns greater responsibility to employees and 360-degree appraisal enlists employees' active participation in improving performance, especially amongst managers.

It is also suggested that 360-degree appraisal overcomes many of the limitations of traditional appraisal systems. Advocates maintain that upward appraisal may provide a more accurate view of performance because direct reports are in closer contact with their manager and are more directly affected by the manager's style than the manager's superior (Ward 1997). Upward appraisal therefore provides a direct source of information about whether managers are able to achieve results through their people and to what extent they are effective in dealing with a variety of customer requirements (Kettley 1997). Take the case of the Department of Health, which introduced this form of upward coaching in 2005 on a voluntary basis; pairing a senior civil servant with a more junior manager who provides face-to-face feedback on performance. Eighty-six senior civil servants have opted to work with a buddy to assist senior management development. The scheme has encouraged a culture in which staff provide feedback, increasing their confidence, and making junior staff more aware of the challenges faced by senior staff (Arkin 2011).

Awareness of multi-source feedback and its usage has increased, with some surveys pointing to 360-degree feedback being used for some staff by 30 per cent of organisations, predominantly for developmental purposes (e-rewards 2005). These developments have been influenced by its widespread usage in the USA and its advocacy by management consultants. Many commentors suggest that when organisations shift their use of 360-degree feedback to appraise, rather than develop, managers, problems arise as the 360-degree process becomes entangled and confused with appraisal, undermining its usefulness as a developmental tool (De Nisi and Kluger 2000; Ghorpade 2000). By contrast Bracken *et al.* (2001) disagree, because they argue that it is only if the process is used to inform decisions that ratees and raters will engage with and benefit fully from the process.

A questioning tone towards the utility of multi-source feedback is widespread (Armstrong 2009; Bracken *et al.* 2001; Ghorpade 2000; Luthans and Peterson 2003). Meta-analysis of the effectivness of feedback on performance indicated that in more than one-third of cases feedback lowered subsequent performance because negative feedback, perhaps not surprisingly, discouraged rather than motivated people to improve (Kluger and DeNisi 1996). Research on the validity of multi-source ratings by using externally validated criteria demonstrated non-significant correlations

(Van Hooft *et al.* 2006). There is also a recognition that 360-degree appraisal can generate an overwhelming amount of feedback, which is difficult to evaluate. This has encouraged the use of facilitators to provide feedback and coaching (Luthans and Peterson 2003). In many organisations, however, the emphasis is on managers taking personal responsibility for addressing shortfalls in their competencies, which may prove to be a recipe for inaction. Silverman *et al.* (2005) concur, suggesting that many organisations concentrate on initial implementation, but do not consider adequately how they will use the feedback to assist their managers to benefit from the process.

A prominent issue in any discussion of 360-degree appraisal is the degree to which the process is anonymous and confidential. The majority of organisations provide feedback on an anonymous basis and it is often confidential to the manager that has been rated, being used to aid that individual's self-development. Anonymity is primarily to reassure participants that there will be no repercussions as a result of their feedback and is designed to encourage honest feedback. As Ghorpade (2000) points out, however, honest ratings are not necessarily accurate or valid, because of the degree to which participants' views may be distorted by organisational politics or personality differences. These type of distortions may often arise because many individuals are not provided with any clear guidance about what is expected of ratee roles. Forty-five per cent of employers using 360-degree appraisal suggested that direct reports who provide feedback felt threatened and unable to be honest and 36 per cent of employers suggested that the process is threatening to participants (Handy *et al.* 1996).

Several key issues are rarely considered adequately. It is not self-evident that multi-source feedback challenges the basic assumptions underpinning all appraisal systems as is often claimed. The method of 360-degree appraisal shares with more traditional appraisal the assumption that performance improvements arise from measuring and rewarding the performance of individuals, but uses a different process (i.e. subordinate feedback) to measure it. Nonetheless, the focus remains on variations between *individuals* rather than examining the context in which those individuals work, which may have a greater impact on performance. The use of 360-degree appraisal is trumpeted as 'empowering', but it does not necessarily challenge existing power relationships and behaviour within organisations. Employers decide whether to use such a system and take all the key decisions about its design and operation.

There is a high level of consensus that this type of feedback is likely to prove most effective within relatively high-trust organisations, in which managers are prepared to accept criticism and be open enough to alter their behaviour as a result of the feedback provided. As Kanouse (1998) warns, multi-rater feedback can easily fail; for example, if a company is about to restructure and shed jobs, then feedback mechanisms can be viewed as a means to select employees for redundancy. Despite continuing uncertainties about multi-source feedback, web-based, rather than paper-based, systems enable the process to be administered more easily, which may encourage increased take up (Fletcher 2001).

Discussion

This chapter has highlighted the paradox that, although performance appraisal is being used more extensively than ever before, there is a much greater awareness of its limitations. Some writers have gone further and proposed that employee appraisals are abolished (Culbert 2010). These criticisms have encouraged considerable change in practice and an emphasis on performance appraisal giving way to more rounded forms of performance management. This shift in emphasis has been influenced by criticism in the prescriptive literature but also from more radical critiques of performance appraisal. The latter have revealed some of the questionable assumptions embodied in traditional appraisal practice and hastened the search for alternatives. They have also illustrated the importance of the context in which performance appraisal is implemented. This has allowed much greater clarity in designing and implementing performance appraisal, with an explicit consideration of the primary purpose of appraisal.

Over recent years a number of issues have become more prominent, reflecting broader changes in the business context. The first relates to the changing composition of the workforce and the second concerns cultural diversity. Increased attention is being paid to the different components of the workforce and the implications for performance management in terms of the differing expectations of distinct employee groups. For example, an important issue relates to the performance management of volunteers who make a vital contribution to the delivery of many services within non-profit and public service organisations. The CIPD is heavily reliant on volunteers to maintain its branch and national network and developed a series of competencies required by its national directors who are regularly reviewed against these competencies via a 'conversations with a purpose' process. This appraisal process assists in setting clear expectations about the director role (cited in Pointon 2010).

Another component of the workforce that is attracting increased attention relates to the ageing of the workforce. Studies have noted that many employers have stereotypical attitudes towards older workers that include assumptions about performance declining with age and concerns such as increasing ill-health absence (Loretto and White 2006). Analysis of 117 studies of age stereotypes in workplace settings, however, indicates the erroneous nature of most of these assumptions, for example, that performance declines as workers age. Detailed workplace studies such as those of judges' decision-making has indicated that there are quantitative and qualitative dimensions of performance and that they are affected in opposite ways by the ageing process (Backes-Gellner *et al.* 2011). For employers, as Pointon (2010) points out, two issues are dominant: how to capitalise on the knowledge of older workers prior to their retirement and second, how to maintain high levels of performance.

A second relates to performance management within a global business context, and especially to what extent performance appraisal systems need to be adapted to the specific institutional context in which appraisal occurs. Much attention has focused on how far multinationals should adopt standardised systems or if they should be adapted to local circumstances, and to what extent performance management should take account of different cultural assumptions about good performance (Claus and Briscoe 2009). This literature draws heavily on the work of Hofstede (1980) and his dimensions of national culture. In countries with high-power distance, in which superiors and subordinates do not view themselves as equals, it is predicted that there will be a reluctance to use upward feedback or allow subordinates much input into their appraisal. Milliman *et al.* (2002) argue that these propositions are broadly borne out by the existing, albeit limited, research evidence of performance appraisal in countries outside of the US and UK, with little support for subordinate input in countries such as Korea. The experience of performance appraisal in China has received considerable attention, and within Chinese firms it has been noted that more emphasis is placed on personal attributes such as loyalty and punctuality, but this is not incompatible with individualistic results-orientated systems (Taormina and Gao 2009). Although the work of Hofstede has been subject to extensive criticism, as Fletcher (2001: 481) highlights, it does draw attention to the fact that generalising from US studies in other institutional contexts may be unwise.

If our knowledge and understanding of the impact of performance appraisal processes in different national contexts remains uneven, in general we have gained a much better appreciation of why performance appraisal appears to be more accepted in some organisations than others. Employer practices which genuinely sustain trust by promoting transparency and procedural fairness, alongside respect for the individual, are more likely to lead to appraisal systems which are accepted and valued by the workforce.

It is the sustained criticism of the imprecision and lack of objectivity of performance appraisal, and a recognition that too much weight has been attached to the annual appraisal interview, which has generated a search for more rounded forms of assessment and ones less reliant on a manager's rating of their employees. The shift towards an element of self-appraisal, the more diverse criteria used within performance management systems and the interest in multi-source feedback all testify to the emergence of a broader approach to performance appraisal. It appears that organisations are trying to make a virtue out of the different perspectives on performance which different stakeholders bring to the appraisal process. Another dimension of this broadening of approach is that more emphasis is being placed on using performance appraisal not only to consider current performance, but as a means to manage talent and bolster employee engagement.

These developments also suggest that, while performance appraisal will remain at the heart of human resource management practice, it is likely to be increasingly facilitated by software that makes it more straightforward to draw on a wider network of performance measures from both inside and outside the organisation. Some of these indicators arise from the scope to monitor performance more easily by deploying information technology. Other forms of performance information will be generated from surveillance by fellow employees, customers or mystery shoppers.

These developments, while often viewed negatively within Foucauldian accounts, potentially provide opportunities for a more nuanced approach, which moves away from the rightly and increasingly much-criticised one-dimensional view of individual performance.

REFERENCES

Arkin, A. 2011: The Odd Couple, *People Management*, October, 44-46.

Armstrong, M. 2009: *Armstrong's Handbook of Performance Management* 4th edn, London: Kogan Page.

Armstrong, M. and Baron, A. 1998: *Performance Management: The New Realities*, London: Chartered Institute of Personnel and Development.

Armstrong, M. and Baron, A. 2005: *Managing Performance: Performance management in action*, London: Chartered Institute of Personnel and Development.

Bach, S. and Kessler, I. 2012: *The Modernisation of Public Services and Employee Relations: Targeted Change*, Basingstoke: Palgrave Macmillan.

Backes-Gellner, U., Schneider, M. and Veen, S. 2011: Effect of workforce age on quantitative and qualitative organizational performance: conceptual framework and case study evidence, *Organization Studies*, **32**(8), 1103-1121.

Barlow, G. 1989: Deficiencies and the Perpetuation of Power: Latent Functions in Management Appraisal, *Journal of Management Studies*, **26**(5), 499-517.

Bourne, M. and Bourne, P. 2011: *Handbook of Performance Management*. Chichester: John Wiley & Sons Ltd.

Bracken, D., Timmereck, C., Fleenor, J. and Summers, L. 2001: 360 Feedback from Another Angle, *Human Resource Management*, **40**(1), 3-20.

Brown, D. 2010: *Performance Management: Can the Practice Deliver the Policy?*, Brighton: Institute of Employment Studies.

Brown, D. and Hirsh, W. 2011: Performance Management: Fine intentions, *People Management*, September, 34-37.

Busi, M. and Bititci, U. 2006: Collaborative performance management: present gaps and future research, *International Journal of Productivity and Performance Management*, **55**, 7-25.

Chen, C. and DiTomaso, N. 1996: Performance Appraisal and Demographic Diversity, in E. Kossek and S. Label (eds.), *Managing Diversity*, Oxford: Blackwell.

CIPD (Chartered Institute of Personnel and Development) 2009: *Performance Management in Action: Current Trends and Practice*, London: Chartered Institute of Personnel and Development.

Claus, L. and Briscoe, D. 2009: Employee performance management across borders: A review of relevant academic literature, *International Journal of Management Reviews*, **11**(2), 175-196.

Culbert, S. 2010: *Get Rid of the Performance Review!*, New York: Hachette Book Group.

Deming, W.E. 1982: *Out of the Crisis* Cambridge, MA: MIT.

De Nisi, A. and Kluger, A. 2000: Feedback effectiveness: Can 360 degree appraisals be improved?, *Academy of Management Executive*, **14**(1): 129-139.

e-reward 2005: *What is Happening in Performance Management Today: Part 1 – Survey Findings*, available at: www.e-reward.co.uk

Fineman, S. 2004: Getting the measure of emotion – and the cautionary tale of emotional intelligence, *Human Relations*, **57**(6), 719-740.

Fletcher, C. 2001: Performance appraisal and management: The developing research agenda, *Journal of Occupational and Organizational Psychology*, **74**(4), 473-487.

Foucault, M. 1981: *Power/Knowledge: Selected Interviews and other Writings*, Brighton: Harvester Press.

Gallie, D., White, M., Cheng, Y. and Tomlinson, M. 1998: *Restructuring the Employment Relationship*, Oxford: Oxford University Press.

Geddes, D. and Konrad, A. 2003: Demographic differences and reactions to performance feedback, *Human Relations*, **56**(12), 1485-1513.

Ghorpade, J. 2000: Managing five paradoxes of 360-degree feedback, *Academy of Management Executive*, **14**(1), 140-150.

Gill, D., Ungerson, B. and Thakur, M. 1973: *Performance Appraisal in Perspective: a Survey of Current Practice*, London: Institute of Personnel Management.

Grey, C. 1994: Career as a Project of the Self and Labour Process Discipline, *Sociology*, **28**(2), 479-497.

Handy, L., Devine, M. and Health, L. 1996: *360 Degree Feedback: Unguided Missile or Powerful Weapon?*, Ashridge: Berkhampstead.

Healy, G. 1997: The industrial relations of appraisal: The case of teachers., *Industrial Relations Journal*, **28**(3), 206-220.

Hofstede, G. 1980: *Culture's Consequences*, California: Sage Publications.

IDS (Incomes Data Services) 1997: *Performance Management*, London: Incomes Data Service.

IDS (Incomes Data Services) 2011: *Performance Management*, London: Incomes Data Service.

Industrial Society 1997: *Appraisal*, No. 37, London: Industrial Society.

Kanouse, D. 1998: Why Multi-rater Feedback Systems Fail, *HRFocus*, 3 January.

Kaplan, R. and Norton, D. 1996: *The Balanced Scorecard: Translating Strategy into Action* Boston, MA: Harvard Business School Publishing.

Kaplan, R. and Norton, D. 2001: Transforming the balanced scorecard from performance management to strategic measurement: Part 1, *Accounting Horizons*, **15**(1), 87-104.

Kersley, B., Alpin, C., Forth, J., Bryson, A., Bewley, H., Dix, G. and Oxenbridge, S. 2006: *Inside the Workplace: Findings from the 2004 Employment Relations Survey*, London: Routledge.

Kettley, P. 1997: *Personal Feedback: Cases in Point*, Sussex: Institute for Employment Studies, IES Report 326.

Kluger, A and DeNisi, A. 1996: 'The effects of feedback interventions on performance', *Psychological Bulletin*, **119**, 254-284.

Lee, D. 2002: Gendered workplace bullying in the restructured UK civil service, *Personnel Review*, **31**(2), 205-227.

Lewis, S. and Taylor, K. 1996: Evaluating the Impact of Family-Friendly Employer Policies: A Case Study, in S. Lewis and J. Lewis (eds.), *The Work-Family Challenge*, London: Sage.

Long, P. 1986: *Performance Appraisal Revisited*, London: Institute of Personnel Management.

Longnecker, C., Sims, H. and Gioia, D. 1987: Behind the Mask: The Politics of Employee Appraisal, *Academy of Management Review*, **1**(3), 183-193.

Loretto, W. and White, P. 2006: Employers' attitudes, practices and policies towards older workers, *Human Resource Management Journal*, **16**(3), 313-330.

Luthans, F. and Peterson, S. 2003: 360-degree feedback with systematic coaching: Empirical analysis suggests a winning combination'. *Human Resource Management*, **42**(3), 243-256.

Maltz, A., Shenhar, A. and Reilly, R. 2003: Beyond the Balanced Scorecard: Refining the Search for Organizational Success Measures, *Long Range Planning*, **36**(2), 187-204.

McGivern, G. and Ferlie, E. 2007: 'Playing tick-box games: Interrelating defences in professional appraisal', *Human Relations*, **60**(9), 1361-1385.

McGovern, P., Gratton, L., Hope-Hailey, V., Stiles. P. and Truss, C. 1997: Human Resource Management on the Line, *Human Resource Management Journal*, **7**(4), 12-29.

McGovern, P., Hill, S., Mills, C. and White, M. 2007: *Market, Class and Employment*, Oxford: Oxford University Press.

McGregor, D. 1957: An Uneasy Look at Performance Appraisals, *Harvard Business Review*, **35**(3), 89-95.

Miller, J. 2003: High Tech and High Performance: Managing Appraisal in the Information Age, *Journal of Labor Research*, **24**(3), 409-424.

Milliman, J., Nason, S., Zhu, C. and De Cieri, H. 2002: An Exploratory Assessment of the Purposes of Performance Appraisals in North and Central America and the Pacific Rim, *Human Resource Management*, **41**(1), 87-102.

Newton, T. and Findlay, P. 1996: Playing God? The Performance of Appraisal, *Human Resource Management Journal*. **6**(3), 42-58.

Pointon, J. 2010: Performance Management in J. Beardwell and T. Claydon (eds.), *Human Resource Management: A Contemporary Approach,* 6th edn. Harlow: Pearson.

Pulakos, E. 2009: *Performance Management: A New Approach for Driving Business Results,* Chichester: Wiley-Blackwell.

Silverman, M., Kerrin, M. and Carter, A. 2005: *360-Degree Feedback: Beyond the Spin*, Sussex: Institute for Employment Studies.

Simpson, R. 1998: Presenteeism, power and organizational change: long hours as a career barrier and the impact on the working lives of women managers, *British Journal of Management*, **9** (Special Issue), 37-50.

Spence, J. and Keeping, L. 2011: Conscious rating distortion in performance appraisal: A review, commentary, and proposed framework for research, *Human Resource Management Review*, **21**, 85-95.

Storey, J. 1992: *Developments in the Management of Human Resources*, Oxford: Blackwell.

Storey, J., Edwards, P. and Sisson, K. 1997: *Managers in the Making: Careers, Development and Control in Corporate Britain and Japan*, London: Sage.

Strebler, M., Robinson, D. and Bevan, S. 2001: *Performance Review: Balancing Objectives and Content*, IES Report 370. Brighton: Institute for Employment Studies.

Taormina, R. and Gao, J. 2009: Identifying acceptable performance appraisal criteria: an international comparison, *Asia Pacific Journal of Human Resources*, **47**(1), 102-125.

Townley, B. 1989: Selection and Appraisal – Reconstituting Social Relations? In J. Storey (ed.), *New Perspectives on HRM*, London: Routledge.

Townley, B. 1993: Performance Appraisal and the Emergence of Management. *Journal of Management Studies*, **30**(2), 221-238.

Townley, B. 1999: Practical Reason and Performance Appraisal, *Journal of Management Studies*, **36**(3), 287-306.

Van Hooft, E., van Flier, H. and Minne, M. 2006: Construct Validity of Multi-Source Performance Ratings: An Examination of the Relationship of Self-, Supervisor-, and Peer-Ratings with Cognitive and Personality Measures, *International Journal of Selection and Assessment*, **14**, 25-81.

Ward, P. 1997: *360-Degree Feedback*, London: Chartered Institute of Personnel and Development.

Waung, M. and Highhouse, S. 1997: Fear of Conflict and Empathic Buffering: Two Explanations for the Inflation of Performance Feedback, *Organizational Behavior and Human Decision Processes*, **71**(1), 37-54.

West, M., Borrill, C., Dawson, J., Scully, J., Carter, M., Anelay, S., Patterson, M. and Waring J. 2002: The Link between the Management of Employees and Patient Mortality in Acute Hospitals, *International Journal of Human Resource Management*, **13**(8), 1299-1310.

CHAPTER TWELVE

Remuneration Systems

Ian Kessler

In general, remuneration refers to the way in which organisations reward their employees for work performed. Remuneration can take various forms, reflected in Bloom and Milkovich's (1992: 22) definition of it as a 'bundle of returns offered in exchange for a cluster of employee contributions'. These returns can be extrinsic, assuming a concrete monetary or non-monetary form as a wage or a fringe benefit, usually provided by the employer. They can also be intrinsic, self generating outcomes such as personal esteem and fulfilment derived from, say, undertaking 'interesting' work or developing enriching relationships with colleagues.

As a central pillar of the employment relationship, often conceptualised as the effort-reward bargain, remuneration has attracted considerable attention. The seemingly endless search for 'new and better' ways to reward employees has focused on the perennial theme of how to balance the link between reward and three contingencies: job, person and performance (Mahoney 1989). For researchers and other interested actors, this search has generated a number of more refined, but equally enduring, questions: What approaches have organisations adopted in connecting reward to these contingencies? How have particular approaches operated in practice? How have these approaches impacted upon various outcomes and stakeholders?

Broadly, these questions have been addressed in two closely-related ways. The first approach has been based on established analytical and theoretical frameworks, regularly tested and modified, but rooted in long-running debates and embedded in disciplinary assumptions and premises. Behavioural psychologists have explored remuneration as a means of stimulating and reinforcing particular individual and work group actions, while cognitive psychologists have concentrated more on how employee perceptions of reward systems have mediated attitudinal and behavioural outcomes (Arnold *et al.* 2010: 306–360). Economists have been concerned with how employers and employees have used pay in the rational pursuit of their objectives, typically on the assumption of utility maximisation, in a labour market context (Gerhart and Rynes 2003). Sociologists have placed more emphasis on non-rational social norms and values in shaping the design and implementation of reward systems at the workplace level and beyond. These norms and values have been seen as diverse and power-driven, encouraging a sociological interest in pay processes and outcomes as contested, and as a site for employer-worker conflict (Wajcman and Edwards 2005: 87–114).

The other approach to these questions has recognised remuneration's sensitivity to the prevailing and changing socio-economic and political context. This is not to deny the value and use of different disciplinary models in exploring contemporary remuneration issues. It is, however, to suggest that the emphasis given to the various questions, and their more precise formulation, have been influenced by developments in the political economy. Most obviously, the trend towards the de-industrialisation of developed countries over the last 50 years or so (Webster 2010) has had a profound effect on the nature of work and the occupational composition of the workforce, affecting, in turn, the viability and incidence of different reward systems (Drucker and White 2009: 3–6). More recently, the financial crisis in 2008 has framed and influenced debates on and practice as it relates to employee reward, unleashing changes likely to have long-term consequences for organisational approaches to remuneration.

This chapter mainly focuses on extrinsic rewards and, in particular, on pay. It uses the contingencies outlined above – job, performance and person – as a framework for evaluating recent developments in organisational approaches to pay. Initially it draws upon these contingencies to identify and define such approaches. It moves on to review how the emphasis given to the link between pay and these various contingencies has been influenced by recent pressures on the political economy in Britain and in other developed economies. The chapter explores two broadly conceived, and partly overlapping, sets of pressure on remuneration: competitive and regulatory. It is argued that while changes in organisational approaches to rewards induced by recent developments in the political economy should not be overstated, there has been a marked shift in the framing of reward issues founded upon new uncertainties, exercising some influence over policy and practice.

Types of Reward

Pay and the job

The link between pay and a job, defined as a stable configuration of tasks and responsibilities, has traditionally been the building block of grading structures. Individual jobs within an organisation will be of differential worth to the employer, prompting the need for them to be grouped into a grading hierarchy as the basis for determining their pay. As Figure 12.1 indicates, in establishing job worth, a distinction can be drawn between approaches which rely upon external comparisons and ones driven by internal organisational comparisons; in other words, job worth may be underpinned by notions of external equity or internal equity.

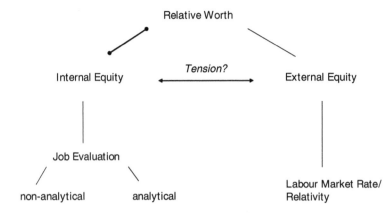

Figure 12.1 Pay and the job

External job worth will depend on the state of the outside labour market for a job. Is there a national or local market for the job? How 'tight' is labour supply in these different markets? How strong is the employer's need or demand for the job? What is the going rate for similar jobs given these labour market conditions? Organisations will often seek information from a range of sources to establish a job's external labour market worth, including pay surveys undertaken by consultants. However, the data from these sources are not always unproblematic. Organisations may well design jobs in distinctive ways, making it difficult to find comparable outside posts for benchmarking purposes.

The principle mechanism used to establish *internal* occupational worth is job evaluation. It seeks to determine the relative size of jobs within an organisation, independent of the performance of the post holder. While a structured and systematic approach, involving the consistent application of a given set of rules (ACAS 2009), job evaluation inevitably involves a degree of subjectivity. This subjectivity might, however, still vary according to the type of job evaluation technique used, in particular whether it assumes a non-analytical or an analytical form.

An extensive prescriptive and descriptive literature surrounds the use of both approaches (for more detail see, for example, Armstrong and Cummins 2008), but in general terms, non-analytical schemes, such as job ranking and paired comparisons, are founded on whole job comparisons. Comparing full job descriptions directly with one another, a non-analytical approach can be a quick, low-cost solution to establishing internal job worth, and viable in small organisations employing a limited range of easily distinguishable job roles. However, it typically involves the exercise of high levels of personal judgement, and, partly as a consequence, fails to provide organisational protection against equal-value pay claims.

Analytical schemes involve unpacking jobs according to key factors: their attitudinal, behavioural and technical attributes. For instance, the Hay scheme, widely used to evaluate senior management grades, is based on three main factors – know-how, problem solving and accountability (e-reward 2007: 25). Under a factor points JE

Table 12.1 Job evaluation weighting scheme, National Health Service Agenda for Change

Factor	1	2	3	4	5	6	7	8
Communication	5	12	21	32	45	60		
Knowledge, training and experience	16	36	60	88	120	156	196	240
Analytical skills	6	15	27	42	60			
Planning/organisation skills	6	15	27	42	60			
Physical skills	6	15	27	42	60			
Responsibility-patient care	4	9	15	22	30	39	49	60
Responsibility-policy/service	5	12	21	32	45	60		
Responsibility-finance/physical	5	12	21	32	45	60		
Responsibility-staff	5	12	21	32	45	60		
Responsibility-information	4	9	16	24	34	46	60	
Responsibility-research & development	5	12	21	32	45	60		
Freedom to act	5	12	21	32	45	60		
Physical effort	3	7	12	18	25			
Mental effort	3	7	12	18	25			
Emotional effort	5	11	18	25				
Working conditions	3	7	12	18	25			

Source: NHS Staff Council 2010

scheme, jobs are scored according to these factors, so establishing their relative size. This facilitates comparisons between diverse jobs, allowing them to be bundled into grades, and is more likely to provide a defence against equal pay claims. Table 12.1 sets out the key features of the job evaluation scheme underpinning the pay structure in the British National Health Service, applied to over a million workers in a diverse range of groups ranging from porters and cleaners, through nurses to consultants. Table 12.1 sets out the factor plan and weightings for the JE scheme. It can be seen that there are 16 factors, with 'knowledge, training and experience' heavily weighted, although some quite unusual factors such as 'emotional effort' are also included. One thousand points are available under this plan and each job will be assessed using it, with Table 12.2 indicating how scores then relate to pay bands. Indicative of the allocation of occupational roles to pay bands under this scheme, healthcare assistants are found in Bands 2 and 3 with nurses pitched at Bands 5 and 6.

External or internal comparisons are not necessarily mutually exclusive organisational approaches to determining job worth and the 'appropriate' rate of pay. On completion of a job evaluation exercise, an organisation will still need to position pay rates for its evaluated jobs in relation to the external labour market. Will the organisation be a 'high' payer within the labour market or set rates more in line with the median? The use of shared consultant-designed job evaluation schemes facilitates pay-rate comparisons between companies for similarly sized jobs. At the same time, there may well be tensions between internal and external worth: jobs rated as

Table 12.2 NHS pay: Pay and job weight

Pay Band	Job Weight
1	0–160
2	161–215
3	216–270
4	271–325
5	326–395
6	396–465
7	466–539
8a	540–584
8b	585–629
8c	630–674
8d	675–720
9	721–765

Source: NHS Staff Council 2012

equivalent in an internal job evaluation might be subject to contrasting external labour market conditions suggesting different pay rates. Although there is no easy pay response to such tensions, organisations often use (temporary) market supplements to deal with them (e-reward 2007: 35).

Pay, Person and Performance

The relationship between pay and the other two contingencies, *person and performance*, takes the discussion into the realm of pay systems. If 'job' is the basis for establishing the grading structure, a pay system is the mechanism driving pay movements once the post has been allocated to a grade. Pay systems have been underpinned by two basic criteria, time and performance (Brown 1989), with person overlapping in various ways with both.

Time-based pay systems reward the employee for the period of attendance at the workplace, with managerial advantages, such as the low cost of administration, and with employee benefits including predictability and transparency. However, time-based pay has no incentive effect, requiring other techniques to manage staff performance. Time-based pay systems are often intimately related to the job, with a particular job attracting a given rate of pay in the form of a daily or hourly rate, a weekly or monthly wage or an annual salary. This job rate may be pitched at an external market level, while recognised unions engaging in collective bargaining might seek a regular up-rating of such a rate to sustain living standards for the post holders.

A pay system driven by time can also interface with person and performance, particularly where the grading structure operates on the basis of service. Traditional grading structures have allowed progression along fixed incremental points to a scale maximum, according to the time served or the seniority of the person in post. The rationale for this form of progression is an assumed link between pay and the person's development in the role.

In seeking to characterise the more direct link between pay and performance, three basic questions need to be addressed: Whose performance is being assessed? How is performance being measured? How is it being rewarded? The first question relates to the unit of performance, with scope to link pay to individual, group or company performance. The second question focuses on the nature and evaluation of performance. Performance might refer to outputs, for example, the achievement of individual or group targets or objectives. Performance might also relate to inputs. These input measures of performance are likely to overlap with the person, pay being driven by the skills, knowledge and behaviours individual post holders bring to the role.

The third question encourages an interest in the performance-pay link: how a given level of performance translates into a particular payout. This link can be founded on a relatively fixed relationship, where a given performance level produces an automatic payout, or on a less mechanistic connection, founded on an assessment of performance. Payment systems might also be distinguished according to how the performance-related award connects to base pay: whether the payment is earned on a recurring basis or, once awarded, ratchets up pay to a new and sustained level. The former approach assumes the form of a non-consolidated pay increase, often seen as a variable element in pay; the latter is typically consolidated into base pay and given on a recurring basis.

The various dimensions and distinctions associated with performance combine to produce various types of pay system (CIPD 2011). These are presented in Figure 12. 2 below, and suggest a number of generic pay systems. The first relates pay to an individual employee's appraised or assessed performance. Founded upon inputs, these systems are often referred to as merit, skills or competency schemes, rewarding individuals for the capabilities they bring to or display on the job. These might be 'hard' competencies related to work standards or 'softer' behavioural competencies such as the capacity to communicate or co-operate with work colleagues and customers (Neathey and Reilly 2003).

Linked to outputs these appraised or assessed pay systems are labelled 'individual performance related pay' (IPRP). These schemes are founded upon the setting of individual employee objectives, assessed at the end of a given period, and then linked through an overall box marking to pay progression. A hybrid approach, 'contribution pay' (Armstrong and Brown 1999), has also emerged as a means of addressing some of the perceived weaknesses in individual input and output schemes. Output schemes have sometimes been seen to narrow the employees' focus on the achievement of a limited number of tightly defined personal objectives, in so doing, driving out the behaviours needed to maintain ongoing customer and co-worker relations. In linking pay to both individual employee inputs and outputs, contribution pay is seen as ensuring a 'sensible' balance between the two. Schemes based on an assessment of the individual employee's performance tend to generate a

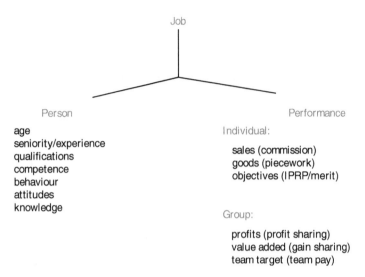

Figure 12.2 Types of payment system

consolidated payment, integrated into base salary either in the form of a percentage increase or additional increments on a pay scale.

The second type of system relates pay in a mechanistic way to individual production, sales or other tangible outputs, and is often viewed as an individual bonus. The payment takes the form of an unconsolidated lump sum and includes traditional piecework and commission on sales schemes.

The third type of system is a collective bonus linking pay to group work in terms of team, department, establishment or company performance. Again producing largely unconsolidated payments, it includes profit sharing and employee ownership plans, which in many developed countries are sponsored and encouraged by governments (Kessler 2010). In Britain there are various approved schemes (HM Revenue and Customs 2011): share incentive plans and save as you earn schemes, which must be open to all eligible employees; and enterprise management and company share-option plans, discretionary schemes which companies can choose to apply to discrete groups of workers. (For more details see http://www.hmrc.gov.uk/shareschemes/welcome.htm)

Organisations often use the three pay contingencies – job, performance and person – in complementary ways. A typical pay system provides for steady movement up a scale on the basis of a person's service to a point which equates with a 'competitive market rate' for the job. This rate would regularly be revised to reflect any changes in external market conditions, with any scope for the individual to move beyond this point dependent on performance. Moreover, a given contingency might be used in different ways, with pay related to both individual and collective performance. It is this search for what organisations and other stakeholders regard as the 'right balance' between pay and the three contingencies which provides the dynamic for pay developments. It is towards these developments that attention now turns.

Competitive Pressures

Models of strategic pay

An interest in the strategic use of human resources as a means of addressing the intensification of product market competition over recent decades has endured and deepened (Guest 2011). However, it has been given a new 'twist' by the acute competitive challenges created by the recent economic and financial crisis. In this context, pay has continued to be presented as a strategic lever in the pursuit of 'competitive advantage' (Armstrong and Brown 2009), although the form taken by pay in supporting such an objective, and its capacity to do so, have been subject to continued debate.

Strategic pay emerged in harness with a broader emphasis on strategic human resource management (SHRM), reflected in the notion of the 'New Pay' (Schuster and Zingheim 1992). This was articulated as 'a pay design process that starts with business strategy and organisational change' (Lawler 1995: 14). Implicitly, previous organisational approaches to pay had been opportunistic and *ad hoc*, although it still remained open to debate as to how pay might effectively be related to business strategy. The answer to this question lay in different models of strategic human resource management, with pay being drawn into broader debates and controversies associated with the use of HR practices to enhance corporate performance in the context of increasingly intense product-market competition.

As a key lever in the management of employee performance, pay has figured prominently in the three main strategic human resource management models based on universal, matching and resource-based 'recipes', hypothesising the relationship between HR practices and corporate performance in different ways. The 'universalistic' or 'best practice' model has invariably included payment systems, usually based on individual or collective performance, in its bundle of 'high commitment' HR practices (Pfeffer 1998). There has, however, been inconsistency in the type of payment systems included in this bundle, reflecting different views on the efficacy of such systems in promoting 'desired' employee attitudes and behaviours. There has, for example, been debate about whether individual performance pay generates effective employee commitment or rather is a coercive technique, spawning defensive and instrumental worker responses (Kohn 1993).

Pay systems have also been integral to matching or 'best fit' models of SHRM, usually predicated on notions of vertical and horizontal 'fit'. Vertical fit suggests that corporate performance is dependent on the close alignment between an organisation's pay system and its business objectives. This was most prominently theorised by Schuler and Jackson (1987) who suggested that different strategic orientations, based on quality, costs or innovation, would best be served by the adoption of payment (and other HR) systems able to generate the in-work employee attitudes and behaviours needed to support them. Attempts to provide an evidence base for this model have, however, proved elusive, not least as a consequence of difficulties faced in classifying organisations by strategy, let alone by the pay systems appropriate to support the corporate strategy.

Horizontal fit points to the organisational value of ensuring congruence between payment systems and other personnel practices: pay and other HR systems need to be bundled together in mutually supportive ways (Kroumova and Lazarova 2009). Most obviously the importance of such a fit might be seen in the relationship between work design and payment systems. For example, the adoption of team working, with its assumed emphasis on joint and co-operative behaviours, would appear to sit uneasily with individual performance pay, which often places weight upon the achievement of personal goals. Unilever revised the payment system for staff at its Leeds deodorant site, moving from a reliance on individual performance pay to 'rate for the job', so ensuring alignment with a model of production based on semi-autonomous work teams (IDS 2009a). Indeed research suggests that the use of team pay to support job design may have positive outcomes in terms of individual and organisational performance (Pearsall *et al.* 2010).

Interest in horizontal fit overlaps with the final SRHM model, informed by the resource-based view (RBV) of the firm. The RBV suggests 'sustained competitive advantage' is largely based on the development of an inimitable organisational approach to the management of resources. In this context, an idiosyncratic relationship between pay and other HR practices becomes a potential source of such inimitability (Gerhart *et al.* 1996). As Cox and Purcell (1998: 65) note, 'The real benefit in reward strategies lies in complex linkages with other human resource management policies and practices'. It also encourages consideration of a pay system as making a contribution to competiveness, 'adding value' through its distinctive design or impact on employee attitudes and behaviours. The longevity or path dependence of Lincoln Electric's piecework scheme, in place for almost a century and often cited as contributing to high employee productivity, might be seen as an example of a pay system making such a contribution (Kessler 2001).

Rhetoric and practice

While the value of these strategic models of human resource management in explaining the take-up and consequences of pay systems and structures remains uncertain and contested, the notion of strategic reward continues to exert a hold over commentators, policy makers and practitioners (Armstrong and Brown 2009: 2). The prescriptive rhetoric surrounding strategic reward has drawn upon all three models of SHRM in various ways. It is, however, the matching model which has tended to dominate this rhetoric. Thus, Armstrong and Brown define strategic reward as 'a forward-looking approach to reward management that is characterised by an emphasis on integrating reward strategies with the business and HR strategies, and aligning reward management processes with other key HR activities' (ibid: 8–9).

More specifically, the influence of the matching model can be seen in the narratives used by companies to justify the development of pay systems and structures.

As an example of vertical fit – the link between business goals and pay practices –corporate mergers have often prompted an overhaul of pay systems and structures as the organisation seeks to harmonise practices and prompt behaviours which support a new and integrated organisational culture. For example, the formation of Virgin Media from a merger between Telewest and ntl in 2006, and the acquisition of Virgin Mobile in 2007, led to the development of job families 'that would be relevant and fit the newly merged organisation' as the basis for a new pay system (e-reward 2011a: 6). Similarly the merger of the UK and German operations of management consultant KPMG in 2007–8, resulted in a harmonised approach to pay as a means of 'driving the behaviours needed to facilitate the cross-border approach to working with clients' (e-reward 2011b: 5).

As an instance of horizontal fit – the connection between pay and other HR practices – companies have sought to review and tighten the link between performance management systems and rewards. For instance, Ladbrokes, a leading sports betting company, redesigned its performance management and appraisal scheme so that it had standard criteria and objectives for all grades, in turn linking this new scheme to its refreshed bonus scheme (e-reward 2009).

Constraint and control

Whilst strategic reward rhetoric has continued to frame corporate developments some 20 or so years after the emergence of the New Pay, the plausibility of such an approach has been subject to an ongoing critique. This critique has assumed different forms. In part, it has referred to the limited adoption of corporate practices indicative of a strategic approach to pay. For example, a CIPD survey (2010: 7) revealed that barely a third of organisations (35 per cent) had a reward strategy, a figure that has remained the same over the last five years.

There has also been long-standing research literature questioning the operational capacity of pay systems and structures to deliver on managerial objectives. Much of this literature has focused on pay determination as susceptible to influence or control from various workplace actors, in the process subverting its original purpose. This partly reflects the importance of line managers in implementing pay practices. Purcell and Hutchinson (2007) have highlighted how the pursuit of corporate aims through pay has often been undermined by uneven line management interpretations of pay practices, or by the lack of organisational support for these managers in implementing such practices. Individual performance-related pay, in particular, has been seen as 'plagued' with these difficulties (Kessler and Purcell 1992). Founded upon a considerable degree of managerial discretion, IPRP has generated: inconsistencies in the setting of performance objectives, subjectivity in the assessment of performance, and distortions in the link between such an assessment and pay progression (Marsden and Richardson 1994). More generally, these managerial difficulties might be seen as related to attempts made by shop floor groups to capture or colonise pay systems in pursuit of their own, sectional interests. Classic workplace studies have highlighted the 'battle' between supervisors and workers over the functioning of traditional, factory piecework schemes, each group seeking to optimise the balance between effort and reward in accordance with their own needs and circumstances (Lupton 1963; Brown 1973).

A closer examination of organisational decision-making casts further doubt on the strategic intent underlying approaches to reward. The prerequisites of a strategy are choice and means-ends rationality (Trevor 2009). However, patterns in the take-up of different payment systems suggest that choice is constrained by various contingencies. For example, industry technologies affect the viability of a payment system, the continued application of piecework schemes in footwear, for example, being related to a production process which allows pay to be linked to unambiguous units of individual worker output. In addition, organisation size is related to the incidence of payment system. The CIPD's (2011: 22) reward survey in 2011 found that that while just over half (56 per cent) of organisations had pay incentives for some of their workers, this was the case in the overwhelming proportion of organisations (80 per cent) with more than 10,000 employees. This pay-firm size link provides some support for agency theory, which suggests that incentives are more likely to be used where worker performance is less easily monitored.

Moreover, there are some striking differences between approaches to pay in the public and the private sector, which suggests the constraining influence of sector. Thus, a recent CIPD survey (2009: 7) revealed that while the public sector places considerable weight on internal worth in pay determination, the private sector is more interested in external worth. This is particularly reflected in the differential use of job evaluation: in the public sector most employers (80 per cent) had pay structures underpinned by JE, with under half of private sector employers (49 per cent) covered by JE (e-reward, 2007: 6). More striking is the fact that pay systems in the private sector are much more likely to be driven by performance, with those in the public sector still attaching greater weight to person. In over three-quarters of private sector organisations, salary progression is based on individual performance, well under 10 per cent using length of service. In the public sector, under a third of organisations (31 per cent) use individual performance to determine base pay, and over a half rely on length of service (CIPD 2011: 16).

The lower incidence of performance pay in the public sector should not detract from attempts by the British government over the years to pursue this form of pay. Conservative governments in the eighties and early nineties retained a strong commitment to individual performance pay, modifying civil service pay progression accordingly; while the New Labour government initially displayed a strong interest in team-based pay (Makinson 2001). However, the relatively low take-up of such pay reinforces the views that structural features of a sector might well constrain approaches to pay. The public sector workforce comprises a significant proportion of professional workers (Audit Commission 2002), with some doubts cast on the viability of setting them individual performance targets and their receptiveness to them (Prentice et al. 2007; Courty and Marschke 2004). Indeed the weight placed on internal worth and job evaluation in the public sector might similarly be related to the gendered nature of its workforce: with two thirds of this workforce made up of women, the sector needed to address statutory equal pay for work of equal value issues, through equality-proofed job evaluation.

Finally, national institutions might also be seen to influence or constrain the adoption of pay systems. In accounting for the much higher take-up of all forms of incentive pay in France than in Britain, Marsden and Belfield (2010) highlight national differences in the institutional support for such pay schemes: state sponsorship of profit sharing is much stronger in France, while its relatively well developed employer networks encourage the transfer of support for and experience and knowledge of individual performance pay.

French employer networks additionally draw attention to non-rational forms of decision making, which belie the notion of a means-end strategic intent in the take-up of a pay system. The close engagement between employers in these networks might well have generated normative pressure (Oliver 1997) to adopt incentive pay, so driving out economic rationality, in this instance, a proven link between pay and corporate or individual performance. The adoption of a pay system might relate to less instrumental, more affective and values-based forms of rationality. Attention has been drawn to the mimetic isomorphism which encourages conformance in the pursuit of fashions and fads in the selection of pay systems; for example, Fernandez-Alles et al.'s (2006) case study of a Spanish bank that implemented performance pay in a search for legitimacy within the wider business community, rather than because the scheme directly improved organisational performance.

The economic crisis

A final set of challenges to strategic reward has emerged in the context of the competitive pressures created by the economic and financial crisis breaking in 2008: thus, with downward pressure on reward and pay bill costs, elaborate, planned approaches to reward have become highly problematic. This downward pressure on reward has had a marked impact on pensions, the most significant non-pay element of remuneration in terms of cost and value. Pension arrangements in most developed countries have been confronted with deep-seated pressures from secular demographic trends: an aging population placing an increasing onus on a smaller working population to support increasing numbers of retired workers (World Aging Population 2009). The resultant long-run pressures on pensions have, however, been intensified by more immediate economic uncertainties: the volatility of stock market performance raising doubts about the sufficiency of pension fund payouts; faltering corporate performance leading to questions about the affordability of schemes; and government deficit reduction measures prompting a renewed public policy interest in pensions.

These uncertainties and difficulties have led many private sector companies to close their defined benefits pensions, including final salary schemes. A survey of over 300 pension schemes conducted by the Association of Consulting Actuaries

(ACA 2007) reported that 81 per cent of defined benefit schemes were closed to new recruits. There have been such closures in a host of major companies. Between 2010 and 2011, these included Aviva, Unilever, Alliance Boots, Barclays, Morrisons, Vodafone and IBM, who all shut their schemes (BBC 2011). Indeed, early in 2012 Shell became the last FTSE 100 company to close its final salary pension scheme for new employees (*Financial Times* 2012).

The design of pension schemes has also been subject to revision, most strikingly illustrated in the case of pensions for public service workers in Britain. Again the long-standing sustainability of schemes given demographic shifts has become entangled with government attempts to re-order the funding of public service pensions as a means of addressing the public expenditure deficit run up to deal with the economic crisis. A government commissioned report by John Hutton (2011) suggested: a pension for public service workers based on career average salary rather than final salary; tying the retirement age to the state retirement age; and the introduction of a new tiered level of employee contribution according to earnings. The government's decision to take forward and build upon the main Hutton recommendations, not least requiring increased employment contributions, has generated considerable industrial conflict in the public services.

The economic crisis has also called into question forward-looking approaches to pay. This is most obviously reflected in a retreat from long-term pay deals, particularly in the private sector (IDS 2009b). At the same time, it might be argued that the very intensity of these pressures has forced companies to depart the 'comfort zone' of strategic reward rhetoric, and more meaningfully engage with their workforces in the search for tangible pay solutions to shared economic difficulties. The value of this more nuanced view to pay in times of crisis is reflected in the use of pay freezes. Most commonly cited and trailed as an organisational response to the crisis, in practice, total pay freezes have been experienced by a limited proportion of workers (IDS 2009c). In the main, freezes have related to the annual, across-the-board pay settlement, the normal progression mechanisms driving a pay system continuing to function (IDS 2010a). Moreover, bonus schemes have often continued, explicitly to counter the freeze in base pay. For example, insurance company AXA allowed bonus payments in the context of a pay freeze in 2009 of around 5 per cent for front-line staff (IDS 2010b). Indeed, generally in the manufacturing sector, the incidence of lump sum payments in lieu of base pay has increased: motor industry firms, for instance, have sometimes rewarded staff with a loyalty bonus as a *quid pro quo* for agreeing cost-saving measures during the downturn (IDS 2010c).

The crisis has also encouraged a shift toward more contingent forms of pay. For instance, workers at Jaguar Land Rover sought to secure the future of their plant by agreeing to move from a pay system based on general increases to one driven more by individual performance (IDS 2010d). Moreover, there has been some re-balancing between monetary and non-monetary rewards: for example, life insurance company AEGON UK and Kwik Fit improved holiday entitlements to compensate for the pay squeeze (IDS 2009d).

Regulatory Pressures

In 2001, Tony Blair, British Prime Minister at the time, stated that 'Justice for me is concentrated on lifting incomes of those that don't have a decent income. It's not my burning ambition to make sure that David Beckham earns less money' (quoted in Geogiadis and Manning 2008). Implicitly such a statement dismisses the significance of pay inequality as long as those less well placed in the labour market are safeguarded with the guarantee of a 'decent' basic wage. However, in the succeeding decade or so, the issue of pay inequality has become one of the most contentious public policy issues. Across most developed countries, there has been heated debate and concern about the socio-economic and political consequences of such inequality, leading, in turn, to a search for the more efficient and effective regulation of pay. This final section covers three themes: it assesses developments in pay inequality over recent years, then moves on to consider these debates and concerns as they relate to low and then high-paid workers.

Pay inequality

In many developed economies, pay inequality has been rising since the late 1970s (Antonczyk *et al.* 2010: 1). This picture is confirmed on a slightly wider canvas by the ILO (2008: 23–30). Comparing the wages below which the bottom 10 per cent of workers and the top 10 per cent of workers were paid between two periods, 1995–97 and 2004–06, the ILO found that more than two-thirds of their sample countries had experienced an increase in wage inequality. The exceptions were mainly Latin American countries, with most European and other developed countries following the majority trend.

This long-run, global trend should not detract from ongoing national variation in pay dispersion or from differences in the pattern of this dispersion, possibly related to its causes. Thus, the ILO distinguishes between three forms of pay inequality. 'Flying top' pay inequality is where high-wage earners are moving faster than low earners. It is a development which might most plausibly be linked to skill-biased techno-logical change (Autro *et al.* 2003). This suggests that the supply of workers capable of undertaking new and more complex technical tasks is falling short of demand, therefore increasing the price of labour at the top end. 'Collapsing bottom' inequality is the result of a deterioration in the lowest wages, possibly reflecting a weakening of collective wage-setting arrangements, particularly apparent in the decline of unionisation and the shrinking coverage of collective bargaining. 'Polarisation' is where low and high earners move away from each other, and points to the inter-action between these different influences. The ILO finds that, in the main, developed countries such as the US have experienced a 'flying top', with developing countries – Argentina, Chile and Thailand – subject to a 'collapsing bottom' (ILO 2008: 26).

This ILO analysis categorises Britain as a 'flying top' country, although detailed analysis reveals a more nuanced picture. In the 1980s there was a sharp polarisation between high- and low-paid workers, which continued in the 1990s albeit in a more muted form. The noughties saw a change in the pattern of pay inequality and an uncanny realisation of Blair's aspirations: the development of a flying top, as wage inequality at the upper end continued to rise, but at the bottom end stagnated (Machin 2011).

The rise in wage inequality in Britain and beyond has prompted considerable public policy debate, particularly related to the 'so what?' question: whether and in what sense pay inequality matters. In general, there has been a strong backlash against 'trickle down' philosophies, which suggest a win–win situation as those lower down the pay hierarchy benefit from the expenditure of increasingly high earners. More recently, attention has been drawn not only to the dangers of pay inequality for social cohesion, but for individual physical and psychological well-being. Indeed, Wilkinson and Pickett (2010), exploring the consequences of (in) equality for a range of outcomes, turn the 'trickle down' approach on its head, claiming that a 'win–win' solution lies in equality rather than inequality.

Wage inequality has also prompted a wider debate on 'fair pay' (Toynbee and Walker 2008). This debate has encouraged a renewed interest in worker voice and process, on the assumption that fairness equates with worker engagement and understanding of pay determination. Brown (2011), for example, makes this link, pointing to a study of 50 organisations which revealed that around half believed reward communication 'not to be effective'. More profoundly, it is a debate which has re-opened more fundamental concerns about the value society places upon different sorts of work or jobs (Wootton 1955: 9). Such valuations have often been highly gendered, with matters of fairness often overlapping with those of pay equity (Brown 2009: 3), especially a concern with equal pay for work of equal value. Others have given greater attention to person and performance. Will Hutton, for example, (2011: 13–26) in his report on senior management pay in the public sector, suggests that pay fairness resides in 'just desserts', tempered by an acknowledgement that work and pay chances are tempered, to some degree, by personal 'luck'. Indeed, over recent years it is an apparent disconnect between pay and 'just desserts', particularly amongst higher earners, and especially in the context of the financial and economic crisis, which has generated disquiet amongst a range of interested stakeholders. Before turning to this issue, however, consideration is given to the management of low pay.

Low pay

Over the years, the regulation of low pay has played an important part in moderating pay inequality. Indeed, differences in the form assumed by regulation have been seen to account for significant variation in the incidence of low pay within and between developed countries. More specifically, low pay emerges as deeply embedded in the political economy, influenced by the distinctive configuration of

Table 12.3   Proportion of low paid workers by country 2003-05

	Denmark 2005	France 2005	Germany 2005	Netherlands 2005	United Kingdom 2005	United States 2003-05
Percentage of employees below low pay threshold	8.5	11.1	22.7	17.6	21.7	25.0

Source: Mason and Salverda, in Gautie J and Schmitt, J (eds) *Low Wage Work in the Wealth World*, New York: Russell Sage

national institutions associated with pay determination, welfare and labour activation. These configurations have often been differentiated in terms of 'low' and 'high road' approaches. The former is based on limited workforce capacity, leading to low productivity and therefore poor pay, while the latter is founded on more elevated levels of skill, productivity and reward. Appelbaum *et al's* (2003) study of low wage work in the United States suggests that weak product and labour market regulation helped account for the fact that many of the country's employers adopted a 'low road' approach. In contrast, the much stronger regulation in continental Europe, not least reflected in more robust welfare states and collectively bargained terms and conditions of employment, reduced the incidence of low-wage work and enhanced the job quality for low-wage workers (Bosch 2009).

This view finds some confirmation in Table 12.3, below which sets out the proportion of employees below the low-pay threshold, defined as two-thirds of the national median of gross hourly earnings, in the US and five European states. The contrast between the United States, with the highest proportion of low-paid employees at a quarter, and the European countries would be even sharper if the social wage were taken into account: in European countries non-pay benefits associated, holidays and healthcare are provided on a statutory basis while in the United States they remain discretionary. Certainly, these country differences should not obscure the fact that the probability of being low paid is greater in all six countries for women, the young, the low skilled and migrants (Mason and Salverda 2010). However, as Bosch (2009: 341) notes, 'There are remarkable inter-country differences in the quantitative importance of these effects.'

Whilst a configuration of regulatory institutions impacts on the incidence and effects of low pay, collective bargaining and a national minimum wage are typically associated with less wage inequality (Freeman 2007). It is beyond the scope of this chapter to explore national differences in the structure of collective bargaining and their impacts on low pay. It is, however, worth stressing that low pay is most likely to be ameliorated where minimum pay rates are collectively agreed and supported by statutory mechanisms. In France and the Netherlands, for instance, collective agreements set minimum rates at industry level, usually extended by the government to uncovered workers. In Germany, minimum rates are similarly enshrined in sector agreements, while in Denmark a relatively high national minimum wage is agreed by the social partners at national level. In the United States and Britain a national minimum wage is only set by statutory means (Bosch 2009). This should not detract from the contribution made by NMW to addressing low pay, particularly in Britain, but a sole reliance on a statutory NMW has been the source of some contention.

More specifically, in Britain, there have been long-standing attempts to regulate low pay through wages councils, setting minimum rates in selective industries, and a Fair Wage Resolution, encouraging government contractors to pay 'decent' rates. These mechanisms were withdrawn by Conservative governments, the latter being rescinded in 1983 and the former essentially abolished in 1993, but the New Labour government introduced a national minimum wage (NMW) in April 1999. The Low Pay Commission survived the Conservative-led Coalition's 'bonfire of the Quangos' and currently sets four minimum hourly pay rates: an adult rate for those at 21 years old and above standing at £6.08 from October 2011; a development rate for those between 18–20 years old, at £4.98; a 16–17 age rate, at £3.68; and an apprentice rate, at £2.60.

While directly covering only some 10 per cent of employees, Britain's NMW has nonetheless contributed to a stagnation of pay inequality at the bottom end (Machin 2011: 162). Indeed, over its first ten years (1999–2010), the minimum wage has risen by nearly 65 per cent, a much higher increase than price inflation or average earnings growth (Low Pay Commission 2011). Moreover, these improvements in living standards for the low paid have not been at the expense of adverse economic consequences originally predicted by certain employer groups (Low Pay Commission 2011: 7–53). The NMW has prompted some important changes in terms and conditions: some employers have adjusted non-wages cost and changed pay structures. However, the Low Pay Commission (2011) stresses, 'the evidence available to date suggests that minimum wages do not appear to have cut employment to any significant degree.'

In part these outcomes have been carefully crafted, being closely related to the level set for the NMW. This has, however, raised considerable debate about the appropriate rate for a minimum wage, in particular, whether it constitutes a living wage. Calculations of a living wage typically put it much higher than the current NMW. The 'basic living cost' approach, developed by the Family Budget Unit, estimates the living wage by reference to 'a low-cost but acceptable budget'. The 'income distribution' approach takes the low-pay threshold figure of 60 per cent of median income. In 2011, the Greater London Authority averaged these figures to come up with a living wage rate of £8.30 per hour (GLA Economics 2011). Using a living wage calculation challenges the assumption that low pay only exists at the fringes of the economy, a study by Resolution finding that a quarter of the workforce fell below it (Savage 2011). Indeed, the living wage has mobilised considerable campaigning support, particularly in London, where it has been taken forward by the East London Communities Organisation. It is a cause which has achieved some success, not least reflected in the Greater London Authority's will-ingness to adopt a contract compliance approach, requiring its contractors to pay a living wage.

High/top pay

The controversies associated with wage inequality have been fuelled by pay arrangements for certain high-paid groups, especially in the wake of the financial crisis and the subsequent economic downturn. Two sets of issues, often overlapping and entangled, can be distinguished: the first, long running and related to executive compensation; the second, more recent, focusing on pay practices in financial ser-vices, and even more particularly in investment banking. In broad terms, both sets of issues have touched on similar concerns. These have related to:

- the relatively high level of remuneration;
- the lack of transparency in determining reward;
- the emphasis on incentives and particularly the 'dysfunctional' worker beha-viours these have prompted; and
- the opaque relationship between reward and corporate performance.

The overlapping interest in executive and financial sector pay was apparent in the case of Fred Goodwin, Chief Executive of the Royal Bank of Scotland. In 2007, the year before the bank collapsed, Goodwin earned over £4 million and then walked away with an annual pension of over £700,000. However, this overlapping interest in executive and financial sector pay should not detract from a separate consideration of the respective sets of issues, revealing a difference in the emphasis given to, and the development of, these different concerns.

Executive pay

The debate associated with executive pay has an extended history, which, in Britain, can be traced back to the late seventies and earlier eighties with the 'fat cats' who benefited from the share option schemes and salary hikes accompanying the priva-tisation of various public utilities. This debate has, however, intensified over the years. As Richard Lambert (2010), former head of the CBI, noted, 'It is difficult to persuade the public that profits are no more than the necessary lifeblood of a suc-cessful business if they see a small cohort at the top reaping such large rewards.'

This debate has been driven by a number of factors. First, executive pay has risen exponentially over the last decade or more, linked in part to the increasing value of bonus payments. The High Pay Commission (2011: 26) revealed that, for the same on-target performance, lead executives in the FTSE 100 companies doubled their bonuses from 48 per cent of salary at the median in 2002, to 90 per cent in 2010. This was not at the expense of base salary pay, which increased by almost two-thirds (64 per cent) over the same period. These increases placed CEOs of private sector companies amongst the highest earners: in 2009 a third (34 per cent) of the top 47,000 adults who made up the top 1 per cent of the income distribution were company executives.

Second, the link between these increases and corporate performance has increasingly been called into question. As Vince Cable (2011), Secretary of State for Business, Innovation and Skills has stressed, 'Ridiculous levels of remuneration are going unchallenged as the norm, when there is no clear evidence of a correlation with performance'. The High Pay Commission (2011: 39) has, for example, noted that between 1998 and 2009 the remuneration of chief executives of FTSE 100 companies rose by 6.7 per cent a year to an average of £3–4 million, while earnings per share fell by 1 per cent per year over the same period.

Third, this debate has been driven by disquiet about process, in particular the apparent lack of transparency and accountability in the governance procedures underpinning executive remuneration. In Britain, public policy attempts to regulate executive compensation have mainly focused on these process issues, reflected particularly in the development of corporate remuneration committees. The Cadbury report in 1992 recommended the appointment of such committees to determine senior management pay, bolstered by the Greenbury report a few years later in 1995 requiring the appointment of independent members to such committees (see Chapter 4).

More recently, one of the few attempts to develop a mechanism with implications for substantive pay outcomes took the form of calls for a restriction on pay-multiples. This call emerged in the public sector, the Cameron government asking Will Hutton's (2011) public sector fair pay commission to consider the viability of a fixed limit on pay dispersion, with the pay of a senior manager in the sector not exceeding more than twenty times the pay of the lowest paid employee. The suggestion was ruled out by Hutton as unfair in hitting some public sector organisations more than others and likely to create perverse incentives.

The most prominent of these moves to regulate the process of wage setting has been in a strengthening of remuneration committee accountability to shareholders. This approach was put on a statutory basis by the New Labour government under its Director's Remuneration Report regulations, 2002, requiring companies to produce a remuneration report, approved by an ordinary resolution at the Annual General Meeting. This has prompted instances of shareholder resistance to executive pay: for example, two thirds of investors at construction product company SIG voted down the remuneration report following its call for a 14.5 per cent rise for its CEO (*The Telegraph* 2010); while at BT's 2011 AGM, a quarter of proxy shareholder votes failed to back the renewal of the executive share incentive scheme (*Financial Times* 2011). Views on the impact of these developments have differed. It has been suggested, for example, that remuneration committees are taking greater care over their report, reflected not least in their increasing length. At the same time, the result of the ordinary resolution to AGMs is purely advisory, with the remuneration report being seen solely as compliance documents (Allen 2010).

Pay in the finance sector

Many of these concerns have been played out in the finance sector, with some viewing pay systems in the sector as contributing to the financial crisis. In his review of the regulatory response to this crisis, Adair Turner, at the time head of the Financial Services Agency (2009: 80) noted that, 'There is a strong *prima facie* case that inappropriate incentive structures played a role in encouraging behaviour which contributed to the financial crisis.' The House of Commons Treasury Committee, in particular, drew attention to the pernicious effect of variable pay in investment banking. It found that 'bonus driven remuneration structures encouraged reckless and excessive risk-taking and that the design of bonus schemes was not aligned with the interest of shareholders and the long-term sustainability of banks'. (House of Commons Treasury Committee 2009: 3). These concerns about pay were not confined to Britain. In the US the 'Wall Street bonus culture' was similarly seen as the root cause of the financial crisis, while across Europe, there was 'outrage' at banker incentives (Conyon *et al.* 2011: 71–85).

In their defence, the banks claimed that such incentives were the norm in international investment banking, needed to generate income levels high enough to attract staff in a global labour market for 'talent'. Such claims largely failed to impress policy makers across the world, with the crisis stimulating domestic attempts to tighten regulation of compensation. There was, however, some acknowledgement of the need for regulation to cut across borders, not least as a means of protecting national competitiveness in the financial service sector. In Britain, this tighter reg-ulation was mainly driven by the Turner review, which stressed the need for remuneration policies to be much more sensitive to risk and opportunism (FSA 2009). The FSA Code of Practice, effective from 1 January 2010, called on bonuses to be based primarily on profit, with the profit pool fully adjusted to reflect risk, and on any assessment of performance to be extended beyond a year.

The development of cross national forms of regulation emerged as guidelines on financial sector pay published by the European Commission in April 2009, calling *inter alia* for member states to set a maximum on the variable component of com-pensation. They were also evident in pronouncements at G20 meetings following the crisis. The leaders' statement following the London G20 meeting in early 2009 committed 'to endorsing and implementing tough new principles on pay and compensation' (e-reward 2009).

The efficacy of national and international moves to regulate remuneration in the finance sector still remains open to debate, with mixed evidence on the contribution of pay practices to the financial crisis. Fahlenbach and Stulz (2010) found no evidence that US banks with CEOs whose incentives were poorly aligned with the interests of shareholders performed relatively weakly during the crisis. Similarly, a study of executive compensation in Britain found that while pay was relatively high in financial services, the cash-plus-bonus pay performance sensitivity of firms was not significantly higher than in other sectors, leading the authors to conclude that 'it is unlikely that the incentive structure could be held responsible for inducing bank executives to focus on short-terms profits' (Gregg *et al.* 2011). In contrast, Erkens *et al.* (2009), examining 306 financial companies across 31 countries, reveal that CEOs holding compensation contracts with a heavier emphasis on bonus rather than equity performed worse and took more risks during the crisis.

Given the ambiguity of these findings, the political sensitivity associated with compensation in the finance sector is unlikely to abate. There has been a considerable ratcheting-up of concern as the payment of high bonuses returns (IDS 2010e), following government bail-outs of the banks with taxpayers' money. In the US this concern reached its height with the revelation that Merrill Lynch had paid bonuses of $1 million to each of 700 employees just prior to its acquisition by Bank of America in early 2009. In Britain, the four major banks – Barclays, HSBC, Lloyds and RBS – noted, under the Project Merlin agreement, setting out how they would support the economic recovery, their willingness to 'show more responsibility on pay', although the undertakings provided went little further than those already set out in the FSA Code.

Summary and Conclusions

Founded in part on traditional debates from across the range of academic disciplines with an interest in remuneration, this chapter sought to highlight the sensitivity of contemporary reward issues to recent developments in the political economy. In so doing, it has become clear that organisations, nations and indeed regional and international communities face new challenges as to how they approach the management of reward. Secular, competitive, workforce and regulatory pressures have intensified, forcing a re-evaluation of the relationship between rewards, job, person and performance. In part, this has been reflected in an increased mutuality between management and workers, forced to adopt more co-operative approaches to reward in the shared pursuit of economic survival. More striking, however, has been a growing conflict between actors with a stake in remuneration, not least related to new uncertainties about what and who society values, and, as a consequence, how rewards should be distributed.

More intense competitive pressures in the wake of economic recession have not shaken the organisational rhetoric associated with strategic pay. It was suggested, however, that strategic pay continue to be constrained by structural features associated with the organisation, the sector and the economy. Moreover, at workplace level the 'best laid pay plans' could easily be subverted by shortcomings and conflict during the implementation phase. Economic crises have also rendered forward-planning on pay problematic, the downward cost pressure on reward particularly illustrated by changes to pension arrangements in the public and private sectors. There are, however, signs that such pressures have forced organisations beyond the 'comfort zone' of their rhetoric to a new reality, which often involves a more direct and constructive engagement with their workforce to devise imaginative approaches to reward. There are instances of unions and employees long opposed to performance pay and the trade-off between variable and guaranteed pay increases accepting such changes, not least as a means of preserving jobs in difficult times.

A deepening of pay inequalities over recent years has been seen to generate the most striking social and political unrest. A long-run trend towards increasing pay inequality was given a twist by the financial crisis and economic recession. The regulation of low pay through a range of institutions related to pay determination, not least designed to provide minimum pay rates, has placed some check on such inequality. However, the rapid growth of top pay has stimulated growing public policy concern and debate. This has been fuelled not only by the high absolute levels of pay, but the apparent disconnect between pay and individual as well as corporate performance. Indeed, it has been suggested that in investment banking, incentive pay systems encouraged attitudes and behaviours contributing to the financial crisis. National and international attempts to regulate top pay appear to have been ineffective in addressing the deepening social divide prompted by pay inequality. Punitive measures taken by governments to deal with the crisis have only exacerbated this divide, being widely perceived to have fallen disproportionately on those least involved in causing it. At the time of writing, pay inequality, linked to the notion of 'corporate greed', has been a rallying call for the 'Occupy Wall Street' movement, encouraging demonstrations in financial capitals across the world. How these concerns about pay inequality play out remains uncertain, but they might yet have further, more fundamental social, economic and political consequences.

REFERENCES

ACAS 2009: *Job Evaluation: Considerations and Risks*, London: ACAS.

Allen, A. 2010: Hanging in the balance, *Personnel Management*, December 2010, 14–16.

Antonczyk, D., DeLeire, T. and Fitzenberger, B. 2010: *Polarization and Rising Wage Inequality: Comparing the US and Germany*, Bonn: Institute for the Study of Labour.

Applebaum, E., Berg, P., Frost, A. and Preuss, G. 2003: *Low Wage America: How Employers are Re-Shaping Opportunity in the Workplace*. New York: Russell Sage Foundation.

Armstrong, M. and Brown, D. 1999: *Paying for Contribution: Real Performance-related Pay Strategies for the Next Millenium*, London: Kogan Page.

Armstrong, M. and Brown, D. 2009: *Strategic Reward*, London: Kogan Page.

Armstrong, M. and Cummins, A. 2008: *Valuing Roles: How to Establish Relative Worth*, London: Kogan Page.

Arnold, J., Randall, R., Patterson, F. and Silvester, J. 2010: *Understanding Human Behaviour in the Workplace*, 5th edn, Harlow: Pearson Education.

Association of Consulting Actuaries, UK 2007: *Pension Trends Survey Report*, London: ACA.

Audit Commission 2002: *Recruitment and Retention: A Public Service Workforce for the 21st Century*, London: Audit Commission.

Autro, D., Levy, F. and Murnane, R. 2003: The skill content of recent technological change: an empirical investigation, *Quarterly Journal of Economics*, **118**, 1279–1333.

BBC 2011: Public sector pensions report explained, BBC News [online] 10 March, available at http://www.bbc.co.uk/news/business-11466273.

Bloom, M. and Milkovich, G. 1992: Issues in Managerial Compensation Research, in C. Cooper and D. Rousseau (eds.), *Trends in Organizational Behavior*, Chichester: John Wiley & Sons Ltd.

Bosch, G. 2009: Low-wage work in five European countries and the United States, *International Labour Review*, **148** (4), 337–355.

Brown, D. 2009: *Fairness: The Ultimate Reward Goal*, IES Opinion, Sussex: IES.

Brown, D. 2011: *Reward communication: why does it never seem to get any better?, What's Happening to Reward?* Stockport: e-reward.co.uk.

Brown, W. 1973: *Piecework Bargaining*, London: Heinemann.

Brown, W. 1989: Managing Remuneration, in K. Sisson (ed.), *Personnel Management in Britain*, Oxford: Blackwell.

Cable, V. 2011: Speech at Association of British Insurers Conference, 22 June.

CIPD 2009: *Reward Management Annual Survey Report*, London: Chartered Institute of Personnel and Development.

CIPD 2010: *Reward Management Annual Survey Report*, London: Chartered Institute of Personnel and Development.

CIPD 2011: *Reward Management Annual Survey Report*, London: Chartered Institute of Personnel and Development.

Conyon, M., Fernandes, N., Ferreira, M., Matos, P. and Murphy, K. 2011: *The Executive Controversy*, Fondazione: Rodolfo de Benedetti.

Courty, P. and Marschke, G. 2004: An empirical investigation of gaming responses to explicit performance incentives, *Journal of Labour Economics*, **22**(1), 23–56.

Cox, A. and Purcell, J. 1998: Searching for leverages, in S. Perkins and S. Sandringam (eds.), *Trust Motivation and Commitment*, Farringdon: Strategic Remuneration Centre.

Drucker, J. and White, G. 2009: Introduction in J. Drucker and J. White (eds.) *Reward Management: A Critical Text*, Abingdon: Routledge.

e-reward 2007: *The e-reward Job Evaluation Survey*, Stockport: e-reward.co.uk.

e-reward 2009: *The Regulation of Remuneration Polices in the Financial Services Sector*, Stockport: e-reward.co.uk.

e-reward 2011a: *Case Study: Virgin Media*, Stockport: e-reward.co.uk.

e-reward 2011b: *Case Study: KPMG*, Stockport: e-reward.co.uk.

Erkens, D., Hung, M. and Matos. P. 2009: *Corporate Governance in the 2007–2008 Financial Crisis: Evidence from Financial Institutions Worldwide*, University of Southern California Working Paper.

Fahlenbach, R. and Stulz, R. 2010: Bank CEO Incentives and the Credit Crisis, *Journal of Financial Economics*, **99**, 11–26.

Fernandez-Alles, M., Cuevas-Rodriguez, G. and Valle-Cabrera, R. 2006: How symbolic remuneration contributes to the legitimacy of the company, *Human Relations*, **59**(7), 961–992.

Financial Services Agency 2009: *The Turner Review: A Regulatory Response to the Global Banking Crisis*, London: Financial Services Authority.

Financial Times 2011: BT executive pay scheme challenged, 13 July.

Financial Times 2012: Shell ends an era with pensions retreat, 6 January.

Freeman, R. 2007: *Labor Market Institutions Around the World*, Cambridge, Massachusetts: National Bureau of Economic Research Working Paper No. 13242.

Geogiadis, A. and Manning, A. 2008: Spend it like Beckham, *Centrepiece*, Autumn, London: LSE.

Gerhart, B. and Rynes, S. 2003: *Compensation: Theory, Evidence and Strategic Implications*, London: Sage.

Gerhart, B., Trevor, C. and Graham, M. 1996: New Directions in Compensation Research: Synergies, Risk, and Survival, *Research in Personnel and Human Resource Management*, **14**, 143–203.

GLA Economics, Living Wage Unit 2011: *A Fairer London: The Living Wage in London*, London: GLA.

Gregg, P., Jewell, S. and Tonks, I. 2011: *Executive Pay and Performance: Did Bankers' Bonuses Cause the Crisis?* Bath: University of Bath.

Guest, D. 2011: HRM and performance: Still searching for some answers, *Human Resource Management Journal*, **21**(1), 3–13.

High Pay Commission 2011: *More for Less*, London, High Pay Commission.

HM Revenue and Customs 2011: *Employee Share Schemes: Statistics for 2009–10*. London: HMRC.

House of Commons Treasury Committee 2009: *The Banking Crisis: Reforming corporate governance and pay in the city*, 9th report of sessions 2008–9, London: HMSO.

Hutton, J. 2011: *Independent Public Services Pension Commission: Final Report*, London: Pensions Commission.

Hutton, W. 2011: *Fair Pay in the Public Sector*, London: Treasury.

IDS 2009a: *Unilever New Pay System*, Pay Report 1032, 12–13 September.

IDS 2009b: *Economic uncertainty leads to fewer long term deals*, Pay Report 1034, 2–3 October.

IDS 2009c: *How progression can make for zero awards*, Pay Report 1037, 6–7 November.

IDS 2009d: *Dealing with the downturn*, Pay Report 1024, 23–24 May.

IDS 2010a: *Progression gains importance as firms go for growth*, Pay Report 1062, 11–12 December.

IDS 2010b: *Bonus Pay*, Pay Report 1055, 2–5 August.

IDS 2010c: *Pay in the motor industry*, Pay Report 1053, 7–11 July.

IDS 2010d: *Jaguar employee vote on landmark deal*, Pay Report 1061, 11–12 November.

IDS 2010e: *Pay in the financial sector*, Pay Report 1055, 7–10 August.

ILO 2008: *Global Wage Report, 2008/9*, Geneva: ILO.

Kessler, I. 2001: Reward System Choices in J. Storey (ed.) *Human Resource Management: A Critical Text*, London: Thompson.

Kessler, I. 2010: Financial Participation, in A. Wilkinson, P. Gollan, M. Marchington and D. Lewin (eds.), *The Oxford Handbook of Participation in Organizations*, Oxford: OUP.

Kessler, I. and Purcell, J. 1992: Performance related pay: Objectives and application, *Human Resource Management Journal*, **23**(3), 34–59.

Kohn, A. 1993: Why Incentive Plans Cannot Work, *Harvard Business Review*, September-October, 54–63.

Kroumova, M. and Lazarova, M. 2009: Broad based incentive plans, HR practices and company performance, *Human Resource Management Journal*, **19**(4), 356–374.

Lambert, R. 2010: Speech to RSA, 30 March.

Lawler, E. 1995: The New Pay: A Strategic Approach, *Compensation and Benefits Review*, July, 14–20.

Low Pay Commission 2011: *National Minimum Wage Report*, 2011, London: HMSO.

Lupton, T. 1963: *On the Shop Floor*, Oxford: Pergamon Press.

Machin, S. 2011: Changes in UK Wage Inequality over the Last Forty Years, in P. Gregg and J. Wadsworth (eds.) *The Labour Market in Winter*, Oxford: OUP.

Mahoney, T. 1989: Multiple Pay Contingencies: Strategic Design of Compensation, *Human Resource Management*, **28**(3), 337–347.

Makinson Report 2001: *Incentives for Change*, London: HMSO.

Marsden, D. and Belfield, R. 2010: Institutions and the Management of Human Resources: Incentive Pay Systems in France and Great Britain, *British Journal of Industrial Relations*, **48** (2), 235–283.

Marsden, D. and Richardson, R. 1994: Performing for pay? The effects of merit pay on motivation in a public service, *British Journal of Industrial Relations*, **32**(2), 243–261.

Mason, G. and Salverda, W. 2010: Low pay: Living standards and employment, in J. Gautie and J. Schmitt (eds.), *Low Wage Work in the Wealthy World*, New York: Russell Sage.

Neathey, F. and Reilly, P. 2003: *Competency Based Pay*, Brighton: IES.

NHS Staff Council 2010 *NHS Job Evaluation Handbook*, London: Staff Council.

NHS Staff Council 2012 *NHS Terms and Conditions Handbook*, London: Staff Council.

Oliver, C. 1997: 'Sustaining Competitive Advantage: Combining Institutional and Resource Based Views', *Strategic Management Journal*, **18**(9) 697–713.

Pearsall, M., Christian, M. and Ellis, A. 2010: Motivating Independent Teams: Individual Rewards, Shared Rewards or Something Inbetween, *Journal of Applied Psychology*, **95**(1), 183–191.

Pfeffer, J. 1998: *The Human Equation*. Boston: HBS Press.

Prentice, G., Burgess, S. and Propper, C. 2007: *Performance Pay in the Public Sector: A Review of the Issues and Evidence*, Bristol: University of Bristol.

Purcell, J. and Hutchinson, S. 2007: *Rewarding Work: The Vital Role of Line Managers*, London: Chartered Institute of Personnel and Development.

Savage, L., 2011: *Low Pay in Britain*, London: Resolution.

Schuler, R. and Jackson, S. 1987: Linking Competitive Strategies with Human Resource Management Practices, *Academy of Management Review*, **1**(3), 202–219.

Schuster, J. and Zingheim, P, 1992: *The New Pay*, New York: Lexington Books.

The Telegraph 2010: Executive Pay Report 2010: How the recession has reshaped pay. May 16.

Toynbee, P. and Walker, D. 2008: *Unjust Reward: Exposing Greed and Inequality in Britain Today*, London: Granta.

Trevor, J. 2009: Can pay be strategic? In S. Corby, S. Palmer and E. Lindop (eds.) *Rethinking Reward*, Basingstoke: Palgrave.

Wajcman, J. and Edwards, P. 2005: *The Politics of the Workplace*, Oxford: Oxford University Press.

Webster, D. 2010: *Impacts of de-industrialisation of the labour market and beyond*, PhD thesis, University of Glasgow.

Wilkinson, R. and Pickett, K. 2010: *Spirit Level: Why equality is better for everyone*, London: Penguin.

Wootton, B. 1955: *The Social Foundation of Wages Policy*, London: Allen and Unwin.

World Aging Population 2009. New York: United Nations.

CHAPTER THIRTEEN

Employee Involvement and Voice

Adrian Wilkinson, Tony Dundon and Mick Marchington

Introduction

In its various guises, the topic of employee involvement and voice has been a recurring theme in British employment relations. Different periods have embraced new forms of participation which have sometimes replaced, and at other times existed alongside, those which already existed. The wider political and economic environment has had a key influence in facilitating particular forms. In the 1970s, for example, developments centred around notions of power-sharing through industrial democracy and representative participation through trade unions. The decline in union membership and influence and changes in public policy both conspired to move industrial democracy off the domestic agenda during the 1980s and 1990s. However, the regulatory mandate for employee voice arising from European Directives has led to renewed debate (Gomez *et al.* 2010; Gollan 2002; Gospel and Willman 2003).

Notwithstanding regulatory impact, the last twenty years have witnessed growing managerial interest in the area of employee involvement and voice. Recent initiatives have been management-sponsored and, not surprisingly, have reflected a management agenda concerned primarily with employee motivation and commitment to organisational objectives. The new approach has focused on direct involvement by and with small groups and individual employees sharing information at work-group level. As such, direct involvement and voice is fundamentally different from industrial democracy and representative participation schemes (Wilkinson 2002). In this chapter, we analyse employee involvement (EI) and voice.

One of the major factors shaping EI and voice within organisations is competition, restructuring and product market change, owing to global financial pressures in the private sector. The public sector has also been subjected to such forces, arising from deregulation and commercialisation and linked to notions of customer choice. Secondly, government policy has set the scene for wider changes in management approaches, and in particular the free market stance advocated by successive governments has lifted restrictions on employers in order to encourage 'enterprise'.

This fits well with political changes in North America, although it has remained at odds with European developments that seek a more uniform social framework. Thirdly, in addition to shifts in the structure of employment in Britain away from manufacturing to services (see Chapter 6) which have impacted on EI and voice, there have also been changes in patterns of employment and the increased use of outsourcing and sub-contracting (see Chapter 15). In these situations, where the employer is 'elusive' and there is no simple relationship between a single employer and its employees, it is difficult to devise appropriate systems of participation which apply to workers on different contracts of employment (e.g. agency workers) (see Marchington *et al.* 2005).

Whilst each of these factors is important in shaping the environment within which direct involvement and voice operates, we also need to examine how these macro-level changes interact with developments at organisational level, where business decisions are made, with implications for the management of employment. An important influence here is management choice for voice; for example, the *way* in which employers adapt to commercial pressures or decide strategic priorities can be as important as *what* sorts of EI schemes are implemented as sources of improved performance and innovation (Marchington *et al.* 2001; Poole *et al.* 2000: 497). Compliance, hierarchy and following rules are seen as supposedly less appropriate for employees who are expected to work beyond contract and exercise their own initiative. Best practice HRM or high-commitment management (Huselid 1995; Huselid and Becker 2009; Wood 2010) emphasise the importance of employee involvement by drawing on an array of sophisticated statistical evidence (Edwards and Wright 2001; Lewin 2010; Ramsay *et al.* 2000). Of course, there is a danger that such perspectives are viewed solely in a positive and upbeat manner, so ignoring the more contested and mundane nature of participation. For example, rather than leading to autonomy and self-management, empowerment or teamworking may merely produce greater work intensification, increased stress levels and redundancies.

This introduction sets the scene for the remainder of the chapter. First, we review briefly the dynamics and patterns of involvement and voice, focusing in particular on cycles and waves as competing explanations of how and why participation has varied in extensiveness and importance over time. Second, we unpick the term as an all-embracing concept and analyse different types of involvement and voice, considering, in each case, some of the major characteristics, problems and different interpretations of EI and voice. We then look at the role of line managers and trade unions in direct EI, leading on to a critique of the often-claimed link between voice and performance. Finally, we evaluate the role of direct EIP involvement and voice by assessing a number of key themes and emergent issues such as the role of informal voice and the embeddedness of voice over time.

Patterns of employee involvement and voice

A central issue is that employee involvement and voice are very broad terms with considerable width in the range of definitions given by authors (see, for example,

Dietz *et al. 2009*; Poole 1986; Budd *et al.* 2010). This width is particularly evident across different disciplinary traditions – from human resource management, political science, psychology, law and industrial relations – that have distinct perspectives on voice (Wilkinson *et al.* 2010). It appears that scholars from diverse traditions often know relatively little of the research that has been done in other areas. Equally, terms carry different connotations or have ideological baggage. Perhaps the best exposition of the term 'voice' goes back to Hirschman's (1970) classic work, although the notion of employee voice could be dated to the ideas of the human relations school. Hirschman, however, conceptualised 'voice' in a very specific way and in the context of how organisations respond to decline, 'any attempt at all to change rather than to escape from an objectionable state of affairs' (1970: 30). If exit is reduced, this may force the discontented to take action within the organisation, hence making voice more powerful (Wilkinson and Fay 2011).

We can try to make sense of the elasticity of the terms by seeing employee voice as an opportunity to have 'a say' and indeed this is central to most definitions (Marchington 2004; Freeman *et al.* 2007). But as Strauss (2006) points out, voice is a weaker term than some of the others – such as participation – as it does not denote influence and may be no more than spitting in the wind. Voice is a necessary precursor for participation, but does not, in itself, lead to participation. So voice has multiple 'meanings' and can be interpreted in different ways, such as being seen as a countervailing source of power on management action, or perhaps part of a mutual gains process (Dundon *et al.* 2004).

It is, therefore, helpful to deconstruct voice as a broad term. One framework in which to do so is to assess the 'degree, form, level and range' of issues subject to EI. Taking the first of these, *degree* indicates the extent to which employees are able to influence decisions about various aspects of management – whether they are simply informed of changes, consulted or actually make decisions. The escalator of participation (see Figure 13.1) illustrates this; it implies a progression upwards rather than simply a move from zero participation to workers' control. Secondly, there is the *level* at which participation takes place; task, departmental, establishment, or corporate. The *range* of subject matter is the third dimension, ranging from the relatively

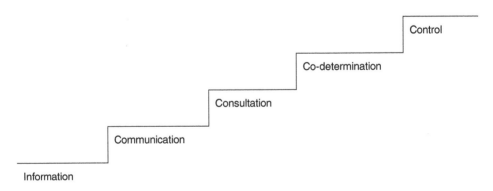

Figure 13.1 The escalator of participation

trivial – such as canteen food – to more strategic concerns relating, for example, to investment strategies. Fourthly, there is the *form* that participation takes. Indirect participation is where employees are involved through their representatives, usually elected from the wider group. Financial participation relates to schemes such as profit-sharing or gain-sharing whereby employees participate directly in the commercial success or failure of the organisation, usually linking a proportion of financial reward to corporate or establishment performance. Direct involvement and voice, the subject of this chapter, is concerned with face-to-face or written communications between managers and subordinates that involve individuals rather than representatives. This is referred to as 'on-line' (Appelbaum and Batt 1995), where workers make decisions as part of their daily job responsibilities, as distinct from 'off-line', where workers make suggestions through a formal scheme. In our view, empowerment relates to all aspects of direct participation, given that it covers a very broad range of initiatives (Wilkinson 2002; Psoinos and Smithson 2002; Wall *et al.* 2004).

There have been various attempts to trace the dynamics of participation, of which the cycles of control thesis (Ramsay 1977) is one of the best known. This argued that we have seen four broad cycles of interest in participation over the last 100 years, starting with profit sharing in the late nineteenth century. The second and third related to consultative arrangements between management and workers and included the Whitley Committees during and just after the First World War and the Joint Production and Advisory Committees (JPACs) of the 1940s. In the 1960s and 1970s, attention changed to new forms of participation in the shape of productivity bargaining and worker directors. The reason for this waxing and waning of interest is simple according to Ramsay. Employers are attracted to the notion of participation only if their authority is under threat from below and, by appearing to share some elements of control, they are able to regain it. Once the threat from labour has abated, management loses interest in participation and allows schemes to fade into more trivial forms or to vanish altogether. Ramsay (1983) later updated and refined the cycles thesis in the context of early 1980s Thatcherite industrial relations, arguing that the potential for industrial democracy had been 'swept under the carpet' through the new managerial offensive. He concluded (1983: 219) that the cycles analysis had been more dramatically vindicated than could readily have been imagined in the mid-1970s.

The 'cycles' theory appeared plausible as an explanation for some developments in participation, but it has been criticised as a general, all-encompassing explanatory theory (Ackers *et al.* 1992). Firstly it is essentially rooted in manufacturing and public sector workplaces and has less relevance where trade unions are weaker or among the majority of unorganised firms. Secondly, looking principally at extensiveness and interest, it fails to take into account how schemes are actually used at the workplace and assumes that participation has a single, universal meaning. Thirdly, it assumes labour relations are of paramount importance to employers and that control over the labour process is one of their principal objectives. Fourthly, it fails to explain more recent developments in direct participation where we have witnessed a huge array of initiatives in a climate where, according to Ramsay, one would expect decline (Marchington 2004; Wilkinson *et al.* 2004).

An alternative thesis has been advanced by Marchington *et al.* (1993), termed the 'waves' analysis. The argument here is that a single, all-embracing explanation of change is inappropriate, and that EI can be driven by a variety of motives. For example, developments in profit sharing in the 1980s were facilitated by politically-driven legal changes which were seen to improve recruitment and retention. Similarly, some employers introduce participation for moral, religious or philosophical reasons, and the early profit sharing schemes were implemented by the likes of Quaker owners who held religious-paternalist views. Once the analysis is broadened to allow for pressures other than from organised labour, we can look more closely at the role managers play. A central component of the waves analysis is that internal managerial relations help to explain the ebb and flow of schemes, and the shape of EI in organisations varies significantly over time and can be characterised in terms of wave patterns. These are subject to a range of forces, one of the most important being the career aspirations and mobility of managers, and conflicts between different functions and levels in the organisational hierarchy. The impetus behind many voice schemes is the career aspirations of managers in various functions, and the dynamics of EI are related to internal political rivalries within management. In other words, patterns of EI in particular workplaces owe as much to relations *within* management as they do to relations between managers and workers (Marchington *et al.* 1993).

The detailed and longitudinal case studies on which the waves thesis was based demonstrated clearly that, irrespective of broader developments, the dynamics of involvement and voice at workplace level were highly uneven and contested (Dundon *et al.* 2004). Significantly, subsequent case study research by the same team confirmed the unevenness of developments, and that newer schemes – such as partnership or engagement – may have been operating for years, although under different labels (Marchington *et al.* 2001; Ackers *et al.* 2004). A key point to emerge from the waves concept is that much more attention needs to be focused on the meanings and micro-political motives for voice at workplace level, as well as the contextual circumstances surrounding the dynamics of EIP (Marchington and Kynighou 2012).

Definitional Issues and Debates

The terminology employed in analyses of employee voice and involvement is often vague and imprecise, making it difficult to draw meaningful comparisons between findings. On some occasions, the same term is used for quite different practices; for example, a daily team-briefing just before a shift commences may be quite different from one which is held on a quarterly basis. The latter could be seen as a bolted-on, off-line activity which involves little in terms of time and has minimal impact on daily work, whilst the former is far more significant in relation to everyday work activities. Moreover, the *way* in which direct involvement is introduced can be as significant as the form it takes. Analysis based on survey data which is abstracted from organisational context can gloss over the real meaning and interpretation of these processes (Marchington *et al.* 1994), so it is important to ensure that direct participation is analysed in the context of organisational policies (see also Foster and Hoggett 1999).

Survey questions about extensiveness (or absence and presence) tell us nothing about the degree to which schemes are embedded within a workplace or an organisation. A particular technique may have been in operation for many years but be marginal to everything that occurs at the workplace; for example, a briefing group may only tell workers information they already know or are not interested in. Moreover, if more than one scheme is in operation, it is not possible to work out which has the greater influence or importance in the organisation, nor can we assess how different stakeholders feel about participation at work.

There is a clear polarisation in much of the writing in this area. On the one hand, prescriptive writers see it as something of a panacea (working smarter) which offers benefits to all (Byham 1991; Foy 1994), part of the re-enchantment of work and the gradual democratisation of the workplace. On the other hand, EI can be regarded as wholly exploitative (working harder), with benefits accruing only to employers (Sewell and Wilkinson 1992). Thus, rather than employees being allocated greater power to do things, being entrusted with authority and achieving higher levels of control over their work, it is argued that any increase in authority is heavily circumscribed within the confines of managerial control systems. Under such schemes, performance is often analysed by breaking down the work process into constituent parts, with performance that deviates from set targets being rendered transparent and subject to discipline. Actions which appear to empower employees may actually be disempowering, as workers collaborate in their own exploitation (Wilkinson and Willmott 1994). Rather than gaining greater power, workers assume higher levels of accountability and responsibility, and can be more easily blamed when things go wrong. Table 13.1 summarises these contrasting meanings of EI.

Table 13.1 Contrasting meanings of participation

Bouquets	Brickbats
Education	Indoctrination
Empowerment	Emasculation
Liberating	Controlling
De-layering	Intensification
Teamwork	Peer group pressure
Responsibility	Surveillance
Post-Fordism	Neo-Fordism
Blame-free culture	Identification of errors
Commitment	Compliance

Source: Wilkinson *et al.* 1997

Voice and Management Choice: Practice and Public Policy Developments

Over the last 20 years employee involvement and voice has been a major growth area in employment relations, coinciding with (and perhaps related to) reductions in collective bargaining (Kersley *et al.* 2006). Despite the decline in union membership, the overall incidence of employee voice has remained consistent over time, which can be attributed to greater emphasis on direct voice and non-union representative channels (Dundon *et al.* 2005). Similar tendencies are evident across much of the rest of Europe, America and Australia (Lewin 2010; Gomez *et al.* 2010). Regardless of growth, there are major problems with the terminology and consequently it is difficult to make precise comparisons about the extent of change over time. Furthermore, there are dangers that generalisations are made when, in fact, different practices are being compared. For this reason, it is necessary to outline briefly the range of practices which are included under the title of employee involvement and voice. Drawing upon previous categorisations by the authors (Marchington *et al.* 1992; Wilkinson and Dundon 2010) we employ a four-fold schema: *downward communications; upward problem-solving; task participation;* and *teamworking and self-management.* This schema is discussed below.

Downward communications represent the most dilute form of direct involvement, to some extent because of the direction of the communication, but also due to the fact that it is typically 'bolted-on' to the work process rather than forming part of everyday life. It takes a number of forms in practice – ranging from formalised written documents to all employees through to face-to-face interactions between line managers and their staff – although it has a common purpose to inform and 'educate' employees about managerial actions and intentions. This can be viewed as nothing more than a mechanism to convey information about a particular issue (e.g. a new order, a change to car parking arrangements or a reminder about work standards), although alternatively it could be interpreted as an instrument to reinforce management prerogatives and shape employee expectations. More extensive and open communications are often seen as an important precursor to 'fuller' employee involvement. In the sense that information is rarely neutral, however, messages may have a more insidious intent and/or consequences (Tebbutt and Marchington 1997).

The principles behind face-to-face communication systems are simple. They rely on bringing small 'natural' groups of staff together at predetermined times (say, once a month) to hear about new developments direct from their line manager, who is responsible for conveying relevant information, as well as using the briefing session to help build teams. Information is cascaded down the organisational hierarchy, with the original core message being adapted to suit specific audiences. Although briefings themselves are intended as one-way, downward communications, there is often provision for feedback up the line management chain in order to clarify issues and ensure that senior managers are aware of workers' feelings. Although there is widespread support for team briefings in principle, in practice they can run into a number of problems – such as line managers not being able to communicate effectively, the information lacking relevance or not being timely, and trade unions seeing briefing as a device to undermine or marginalise their role.

Upward problem-solving incorporates a range of techniques designed to tap into employee knowledge and ideas, typically through individual suggestions or through *ad hoc* or semi-permanent groups brought together for the specific purpose of resolving problems or generating ideas. As with downward communications, these schemes tend to be 'bolted-on' rather than integral to the work process. These types of schemes have also grown considerably in extensiveness and importance over the last two decades (Kersley *et al.* 2006). These practices are designed to increase the stock of ideas available to management and increase cooperation at work, encouraging the acceptance of change. Although clearly offering a greater degree of voice than downward communications, they are also seen by critics as problematic precisely because they encourage employees to collaborate with management in helping to resolve work-related problems.

Task-based participation represents the third category, differing from the first two in being integral to the job and forming a part of everyday working life. As with certain aspects of upward problem-solving, the practices included under this heading have a much longer history, especially under the guise of Quality of Work Life Programs in the USA and Sweden in the 1960s and 1970s (Heller *et al.* 1998). De-layering, devolution and the removal of demarcations have increased pressure on employees to take responsibility for a greater range of tasks than under previous organisational structures, potentially encouraging empowerment. However, as with employee involvement generally, task-based participation illustrates elements of both 'soft' and 'hard' human resource management, regarding employees not only as resourceful humans but also as a cost that has to be minimised.

Task-based participation can occur both horizontally and vertically. The former is where workers undertake a variety of tasks at the same skill level, something which has now become a common feature in many workplaces. The range of tasks may be relatively small and require little additional training or skills acquisition, especially on assembly lines where each individual task can be learned without much difficulty. Whilst offering a way in which to alleviate boredom, in terms of employee involvement, the improvements may be minimal; as Herzberg (1972: 118) famously wrote, when 'adding another meaningless task to the existing one, the arithmetic is adding zero to zero'. Vertical task-based participation comprises two different forms. Employees may be trained to undertake tasks at a higher skill level or they may be given some managerial and supervisory responsibilities, such as taking over the planning and design of work as well as its execution. At one level, this is a genuine attempt to give non-managerial employees greater discretion over how their own work is organised. On the other hand, devolving responsibility may increase stress levels and have a detrimental effect on workers' home and family lives as well as their health (Hochschild 1997).

The final category is *teamworking and self-management*, both of which have been central to recent discussions about employee voice. As with many 'new' initiatives, one of the problems in attempting to analyse teamworking is the breadth and inconsistency in definition. Drawing on a range of definitions (Banker *et al.* 1996; Cordery 2003), teamworking and self-management are seen to incorporate the following sorts of elements: responsibility for a complete task; working without direct supervision; discretion over work methods and time; encouragement for team members to organise and multi-skill; influence over recruitment to the team. Clearly, teamworking is more far reaching than other forms of direct involvement due to its centrality to work processes, and the level and scope of subject matter which can be under the influence or control of employees. In theory, increasing team autonomy may improve collective motivation (Cordery 2003: 109) but it may also enable learning and knowledge-based action in furtherance of improved task performance (Parker *et al.* 2001).

Because of this, some analysts regard self-managing teams as the ultimate in direct participation, but others see this as merely increasing the pressure on workers to perform, exposing them to the vagaries of their team-mates and to interpersonal tensions. Barker (1993: 408) suggests that self-managing teams produce 'a form of control more powerful, less apparent and more difficult to resist than that of the former bureaucracy'. Under a teamworking regime, pressure for performance comes from peers rather than from managers, and whilst some would see this as liberating and genuinely positive, others would view it as management control at its most subversive and effective because workers take over responsibility for peer surveillance.

Informal voice

Each of the above four classifications – *downward communications, upward problem-solving, task participation,* and *teamworking and self-management* – can function in various ways. Indeed, one of the more neglected aspects of how these schemes function in practice is the important dimension of 'informal' dialogue across and within different mechanisms (Boxall *et al.* 2007; Mohr and Zoghi 2008; Townsend *et al.* 2011). Whilst formal EI relates to codified, prearranged structures that are typically captured in most studies and surveys, informal voice refers to *ad hoc* or non-programmed interactions between managers and their staff which provide opportunities for information-passing, consultation and the seeking of ideas. Most definitions refer to methods, mechanisms and structures rather than processes and face-to-face dialogue (Dundon and Rollinson 2004; Wilkinson *et al.* 2010; Wilkinson and Fay 2011). Strauss (1998: 15) specifically defines informal involvement as 'the day-to-day relations between supervisors and subordinates in which the latter are allowed substantial input into decisions . . . a process which allows workers to exert some influence over their work and the conditions under which they work.' Perhaps 'substantial' input accords too great a degree of influence to informal voice, although at least this directs us away from focusing solely on formal practices. The importance of informal dialogue is similarly noted by Purcell and Georgiadis (2007: 197), 'employers who want to gain the maximum value from voice systems would do well to note that all the evidence points to the need for direct face-to-face exchange with employees at their work stations and in groups.'

Informal involvement is attractive to line managers because it provides them with opportunities to explain issues directly to workers, while also exercising some choice about whether or not to incorporate employee ideas (Marchington *et al.* 2001). It also allows them to develop closer relationships with some employees more than with others (Liden *et al.* 2004). This view is supported by recent research. In the study of RestaurantCo by Marchington and Suter (2013), all the branch managers believed that informal EI was critical to effective operations in restaurants where close teamworking and interaction with customers were pivotal. The notion of devolved decision-making came up regularly, especially where it had implications for how staff worked together and it could improve operations; for example, seeking ideas on how to design seating plans in the restaurant, or taking over responsibility for how tips were distributed and tables handed over to the next shift. One manager reported that informal chats accounted for the vast majority of what he learned about the restaurant. In short, managers regarded informal voice as crucial to the generation of worker commitment to the goals of the firm, as well as helping to make it a more pleasant environment in which to work.

Workers also like informal voice. For example, Gollan (2006) notes that e-mail and word-of-mouth were cited as particularly valuable, whereas Kessler *et al.* (2004: 528–529) found from their study of different EU countries that one-to-one meetings and informal discussions proved much more useful than arms-length forms of communication. Townsend *et al.'s* (2012) study at a hotel showed very similar results. Research into leader–member exchange (LMX) theory suggests that positive outcomes flow from informal EI because line managers empower employees in exchange for high levels of performance or organisational citizenship behaviours (Wayne *et al.* 1997). In these situations, both parties report higher levels of job satisfaction and work performance (Gerstner and Day 1997), and employees have enhanced organisational commitment due to stronger exchange relationships with line managers (Farndale *et al.* 2011; Marchington and Suter 2013).

Links obviously occur between formal and informal voice practices. Firstly, they can operate in parallel, with each being used for different issues and/or for different degrees of involvement. Formal systems may be more useful if senior managers wish to cascade information down the hierarchy and ensure it reaches the maximum number of staff possible. Second, formal systems act as a safety net for informal dialogue by ensuring that a cross-section of workers receive information. Whilst informal EI might be preferred, it can be overlooked if managers are too busy or preoccupied with operational issues (Marchington and Suter 2013). Finally, and perhaps most importantly, formal and informal voice can interact and coexist sequentially to lubricate the wheels of involvement. Managers tend to use informal voice to ask what employees think about new ideas or changes that are being planned before these are raised via the formal machinery. In this way the informal system offers the chance to reflect on issues before they are formally discussed. Managerial preference for informality is clear, but it is tempered by a realisation that formal practices offer additional support that helps to sustain and embed involvement.

Impact and Performance

Evaluating the impact of direct participation on performance is tricky for a number of reasons. Firstly, there is a range of measures which can be used to evaluate success – such as increases in productivity, improved employee attitudes, or changes in the balance of power – that depend on the standpoint of the observer. In most estimates of EI, however, workers' needs are typically subordinate to production or service goals. Secondly, given that direct voice is only one factor amongst many which can affect performance, it is difficult to disentangle the impact of EI from that of other variables – such as a change in technology, shifts in the external labour market or even exchange rate fluctuations. Thirdly, even when authors do find a significant association between voice and performance, it is very difficult to determine the direction of causality. It could be argued that superior organisational performance contributes to positive employee attitudes rather than the conventional view that direct EI causes employees to be more satisfied or to work harder and more effectively. In short, the view that employee voice is connected with high levels of commitment and organisational performance is predicated upon a series of assumptions, none of which can be taken for granted. As Boxall and Purcell (2003: 17) note:

> The problems of evaluation are threefold. First, given the very wide range of schemes, it is impossible to take a unified approach boiled down to one question. Second, while one can measure the existence of a structure, mechanism or arrangement, one cannot impute that these lead to certain behaviours. We know that the crucial variable is how, and to what extent, line managers support and activate employee involvement as a process ... Third, the idea of a bundle of HR practices is that it is a combination of mutually supportive practices which appear to have performance outcomes where these are appropriate to firm strategy ... Thus it becomes hard to sort out individual policies.

The impact of direct involvement on employee attitudes and commitment appears to be influenced by a number of factors, not least the type of scheme which is introduced. In general terms, the more comprehensive and participative the scheme, the greater the impact in terms of its effects on employee behaviour; depending on one's standpoint, this could be seen as good or bad for workers. Studies by the authors (Marchington et al. 2001; Wilkinson et al. 2004; Dundon et al. 2005) have suggested that three sets of factors are important irrespective of the specific schemes which are implemented. These are workers' prior experiences of voice and work in general; management's approaches to employment relations; and recent and projected performance of the organisation. Inevitably, these can be interrelated. Prior experience of voice schemes means that there may be occasions when similar types of scheme are perceived in quite different ways by workers. For example, members of staff with relatively little experience of EI are more likely to welcome any initiative which gives them some opportunity to become involved, no matter how limited. On the other hand, employees who work for organisations with a long history of EI may well react negatively to schemes which offer them less than they are accustomed to. Experience of participation may also generate a desire for more – the so-called 'taste for power' hypothesis (Drago and Wooden 1991). However, prior experience is only one factor, and much depends on how workers interpret management's approach to employment relations in general. For example, at each of the organisations studied by Marchington *et al.* (1994: 888), 'employees were less positive about EI where they saw a tightening-up of management styles on the factory floor or in the office'. Of course, it is relatively easy for management to maintain an inclusive style in an environment where competitive prospects are rosy in comparison to recession or downsizing. Not surprisingly, workers are likely to be sceptical if schemes do not offer long-term employment security, even having a voice makes work more interesting and enjoyable.

Empowerment is a central issue in considerations of employee involvement and voice, although much depends on what one means by the term. There is overwhelming evidence that empowerment has not been associated with a significant shift in the locus of power (Harley 1999) and it has even been referred to as 'mythical' (Sewell 2001). There is no doubt that participation schemes are located within a strict management agenda which is largely confined to operational issues and does not extend to significant power sharing or involvement in higher-level decision-making (Edwards *et al.* 1998; Wilkinson *et al.* 2004). However, since those implementing schemes do not intend them to produce radical changes, nor do those whose working lives it affects expect this, it is hardly surprising to find the balance of power does not shift or that direct involvement fails to resolve contradictions within the employment relationship. It is perhaps too easy to compare some naive vision of empowerment with the mundane reality, and then dismiss initiatives as either a conspiratorial management trap, or too inconsequential to be worthy of further analysis.

If 'full participation' (Pateman 1970) is not on offer, does that mean we should dismiss other employee voice initiatives as small beer? Evidently, workers may favour the removal of what are sometimes referred to as 'sand in shoe' irritations (Morton 1994) – for example, 'over-the-shoulder supervision' – and welcome the opportunity to allocate work amongst themselves and also to address work-related problems. This may not be earth shattering or full-blown participation in management decision-making, but in a working environment where there is little opportunity to exercise discretion, it may improve working lives. Even where workers are well aware of the underlying managerial motivations for introducing different employee voice schemes, they may still be well disposed to the initiative. It is also clear that opportunities to feel engaged relate to the knowledge requirements of the work itself; if these are low, there is little scope for knowledge development and fewer opportunities for empowerment (Wall *et al.* 2004).

The Role of Line Managers and Trade Unions

The prescriptive literature suggests an optimistic scenario in which line managers who develop employee involvement move from being holders of expert power to facilitators (or from 'cops to coaches') and hence take on new skills and responsibilities. However, this picture contrasts with research investigating the reactions of line managers and supervisors about employee voice (Denham *et al*.1997; Wilkinson *et al*. 2004).

First, it is suggested that line managers do not believe in the principles underlying direct involvement or participation. Attempts to involve and engage workers are often regarded as 'soft management' or pandering to the workers, as opposed to a more traditional view that 'a branding iron is a more suitable instrument to work with than any concept of employee involvement' (Wilkinson *et al.* 1993). This illustrates succinctly the gap between the values of senior management and those of line managers and supervisors. Secondly, while some line managers may see the value of employee voice and engagement in principle, they have concerns as to its actual operation in the context of current organisational pressures. This is due to conflict between giving employees a voice and external commercial market pressures and meeting production targets. In this context, employee relations considerations are typically regarded as secondary to production or service goals. The failure to reward line managers for meeting EI goals, and in some cases their lack of skill in implementing EI methods due to lack of training, in itself provides telling insights about the relative importance senior managers attach to employee involvement (Fenton-O'Creevy 2001). Thirdly, line managers are anxious about their own futures, whether or not they will continue to have jobs and, if so, the extent to which these will differ dramatically from current activities. A paradox of change operates here. Jobs at the interface between managers and managed are likely to alter most, but equally supervisors are required to play a critical change-agent role in relation to engaging employees. Given a mix of disbelief and agnosticism in their views, and a lack of skills and confidence in their ability, in addition to uncertainty as to the value that senior management attaches to direct involvement, it is hardly surprising that problems occur. Evidently, senior managers have often been less than enthusiastic about EI and have tended to blame line managers (Edwards and Wright, 1998).

The relationship between direct employee involvement and trade unions is also complex. A variety of outcomes is possible, ranging from compatibility or even synergy through to tension between management and union representatives as competitive sources of power. Equally, the relationship may be relatively unaffected and direct employee involvement can complement collective forms of trade union representation co-existing in quite separate zones (Dundon *et al.* 2004). It has been common to suggest that there are *a priori* reasons why direct employee involvement schemes represent a challenge to trade unions, or that a non-union voice serves to marginalise collective participation. Employee involvement and voice can offer an alternative source of information that is managerial-led to that provided by union channels of information. There are examples where managers have introduced a barrage of direct communications aimed at employees, with the objective of marginalising trade unions. This also makes it more difficult for union representatives to challenge management's interpretation of issues (Beale 2003: 86).

There are also situations where direct employee involvement and collective union representation coexist, in either competitive or complementary forms. In recent years attention has been directed towards 'dual' union and non-union voice channels (Boxall and Macky 2009; Budd *et al.* 2010). One area of growing importance here is what has been labelled double-breasting voice: a practice in which companies simultaneously operate on both a union and non-union basis. Three interrelated features are thought to underpin this voice system. First, double-breasting is seen as an intentional choice by an employer in order to shape and mould the patterns of voice and involvement. Second is that such an approach can be motivated by a desire to avoid or at least marginalise union voice within a union-recognised workplace. Finally, the union and non-union voice arrangements compete with one another for aspects of employee loyalty, commitment and social identity (Donaghey *et al.* 2012). Of course, dual involvement and voice does not exist in a vacuum, nor is it determined solely by management action. Trade unions themselves can limit the development of direct involvement, especially in situations where employees are suspicious of management intentions or in workplaces characterised by low-trust relations.

Embedding Involvement and Voice at Work

Many studies of EI and voice use measures of absence and presence alone, rather than examining how these practices are implemented and perceived at workplace level. This is a very narrow way to evaluate its significance, for a number of reasons. First, relying on questions about absence or presence takes no account of *how* these schemes work in practice; for example, one employer might hold problem-solving groups every six months whilst at another it happens every morning as a prelude to work, or every week to allow for staff training. Second, asking questions about absence or presence, without any follow-up about the proportion of workers involved, overlooks the possibility that only a minority of those employed are able to take advantage of the scheme. Finally, questions about extensiveness tell us nothing about the importance of particular voice practices or the interplay between union and non-union channels of involvement within an organisation. Indeed, a particular technique may have been in operation for many years but remains marginal to everything that occurs in the workplace, especially informal dialogue which may be more important than a formal policy. By using the concept of embeddedness (Granovetter 1985), it is possible to assess how individual practices and the voice system as a whole are configured within organisations. Cox *et al.* (2006, 2009) developed this idea to analyse the *breadth* and *depth* of involvement, and these have subsequently been adopted by several other authors (Butler 2009; Danford *et al.* 2009).

Breadth can be measured by the number of EI practices operating at the workplace. Single voice practices are likely, other things being equal, to have less effect than a number of practices operating together because they lack reinforcement. They can be more easily dismissed as 'bolted-on' or out of line with other HR practices, and not taken seriously by workers. Combinations of voice mechanisms provide the potential for employees to be involved in different ways. For example, employees can receive information from and ask questions of their line managers through team briefings, give their views on aspects of work via surveys, resolve issues about quality through problem-solving groups and interact with their representatives who can exercise collective influence at establishment level through meetings with senior managers, which may or may not be based on informal dialogue. Information received in one forum can be used in others, and influence on decision making at a more senior level can help to shape employment relations at workplace level. If managers show they value employee views and share information, this helps to build trust.

Depth can be assessed, amongst other things, by the frequency with which meetings take place, the opportunity for employees (or their representatives) to raise issues and the relevance and importance of subjects considered at meetings. The more frequently meetings take place, and the more that employees are directly involved in the process – for example via their contribution to team briefings or to problem solving groups – then the more embedded the practice, and potentially the stronger and more positive its association with employee perceptions. Without regular meetings to discuss views, issues may be forgotten, and without opportunities for upward communication, employees may assume their views are not sincerely valued. Survival of the mechanisms in an organisation over time may indicate commitment to making them worthwhile and useful. Greater depth reduces the possibility that techniques will be regarded as superficial.

Cox *et al.* (2006, 2009) used the Workplace Employment Relations Survey (WERS) data to examine associations between voice embeddedness and employee outcomes. These show that the *breadth* of EI had consistently positive and significant associations with organisational commitment and job satisfaction. Indeed, combinations of involvement and voice had a substantially stronger association with employee perceptions than single practices alone. The *depth* of voice also showed significant positive associations with organisational commitment and job satisfaction. In short, the more embedded EI is at the workplace, the more positive are levels of organisational commitment and job satisfaction. Additive combinations of *direct* voice that were embedded in the workplace had positive and statistically significant associations with both organisational commitment and job satisfaction. This suggests that worker attitudes are more positive if voice practices have a close and immediate impact on them. Of course, we might not be convinced by such data because it focuses solely on psychological involvement and does not examine concrete practices themselves, or the interplay between related mechanisms, although it does go some way towards measuring impact in different ways and on various levels.

Conclusion

A major theme running through this chapter has been that it can be too simplistic either to celebrate involvement and voice as a panacea for organisational ills, or equally to dismiss it because it has failed to transform the employment relationship. To celebrate involvement as empowerment or engagement is to ignore the major operational and human obstacles to its implementation. Likewise, to dismiss involvement and voice because it does not fundamentally challenge existing relations between capital and labour is to overstate its potential contribution. Indeed, as we have argued elsewhere (Wilkinson *et al.* 1997), management initiatives are probably more limited than the enthusiasts claim, but more constructive than the critics admit. So much depends on the context in which schemes are introduced – the competitive situation, management style, employee expectations, and other human resource practices – as well as on the types of schemes themselves. A fundamental paradox of management is that whilst they require employee commitment and high trust, at the same time, they can erode any basis for such relations to develop and be sustained. This takes us back to the critical issues of context, power and authority: individuals involved in decision-making may also feel continually under the watchful eye of 'Big Brother'.

In our chapter in the previous edition we suggested that most British employers have implemented direct involvement in a half-hearted and partial way, adopting techniques in an *ad hoc* and piecemeal manner, thus falling short of the holistic, integrated approach which research suggests is required to make EI work effectively. Faddism and fashion in management approaches have been noted by a number of writers (e.g. Collins 2000; Micklethwait and Woolridge 1996), and we ourselves have written about this in the area of employee involvement and participation (Marchington *et al.* 1993; Wilkinson *et al.* 2004). We noticed that many of the techniques examined in the early 1990s have been replaced or recast, and sometimes fused into a more all-embracing voice mechanism combining union and non-union channels (Ackers *et al.* 2004; Dundon *et al.* 2005). There appears to be less informality and fragmentation and more evidence that schemes are now better integrated with each other, in particular with other forms of upward problem-solving and several non-union forms of voice appear as robust as collective representation. In addition, senior managers now appear to see greater value in working with trade unions and sharing information with union representatives at earlier stages in the process. We know that involvement and voice waxes and wanes over time, taking on different forms with several schemes operating alongside each other. However, we now know that involvement and voice remains a constant, yet also contested, facet of employee-management relations (Gomez *et al.* 2010). It is important to note in this regard that management's repeated return to the idea of involvement and voice as part of their search for more effective ways to run organisations is likely to continue. This suggests that enabling and empowering employees to have a say does have some value, even if it does not remove problems at work. As Boxall and Purcell (2003: 182) argue:

> Few voice systems and positive union–management relations will exist, or exist for long, unless they are valued in their own right as legitimate and morally necessary activities irrespective of the performance outcomes. They have to have social legitimacy.

Given the recent obsession with finding how HRM can lead to improved performance, this is a timely and useful reminder that involvement and voice are complex and multi-faceted phenomena that illustrate the contractions of the employment relationship.

REFERENCES

Ackers, P., Marchington, M., Wilkinson, A. and Dundon, T. 2004: Partnership and Voice, With or Without Trade Unions: Changing UK Management Approaches to Organisational Participation, in M. Stuart and M. Martinez-Lucio (eds.), *Partnership and Modernisation in Employment Relations*, London: Routledge.

Ackers, P., Marchington, M., Wilkinson, A. and Goodman, J. 1992: The use of cycles? Explaining employee involvement in the 1990s, *Industrial Relations Journal*, **23**(4), 268–283.

Appelbaum, E. and Batt, R. 1995: Worker Participation in Diverse Settings: Does the Form Affect the Outcome, and if so, Who Benefits?, *British Journal of Industrial Relations*, **33**(3), 353–378.

Banker, R., Field, J., Schroeder, R. and Sinha, K. 1996: Impact of Work Teams on Manufacturing Performance: A Longitudinal Field Study, *Academy of Management Journal*, **39**(4), 867–890.

Barker, J. 1993: Tightening the Iron Cage: Concertive Control in Self-Managing Teams, *Administrative Science Quarterly*, **30**, 408–437.

Beale, D. 2003: Engaged in Battle: Exploring the Sources of Workplace Union Militancy at Royal Mail, *Industrial Relations Journal*, **34**(1), 82–95.

Boxall, P. and Macky, K. 2009: Research and Theory on High-performance Work Systems: Progressing the High-involvement Stream, *Human Resource Management Journal*, **19** (January), 3–23.

Boxall, P. and Purcell, J. 2003: *Strategy and Human Resource Management*. London: Palgrave.

Boxall, P., Haynes, P. and Freeman, R. 2007: Conclusion: What Workers Say in an Anglo-American World, in R. Freeman, P. Boxall and P. Haynes (eds.), *What Workers Say in an Anglo-American World*, New York: ILR Press/Cornell University Press.

Budd, J., Gollan, P. and Wilkinson, A. 2010: New Approaches to Employee Voice and Participation in Organizations, *Human Relations*, **63**(3), 303–310.

Butler, P. 2009: "Riding Along on the Crest of a Wave": Tracking the Shifting Rationale for Non-union Consultation at FinanceCo, *Human Resource Management Journal*, **19**(2), 176–193.

Byham, W. 1991: *Zapp! The Lightning of Empowerment*. London: Century Business.

Collins, D. 2000: *Management Fads and Buzzwords: Critical-Practical Perspectives*. London: Routledge.

Cordery, J. 2003: Team Work in D. Holman, T.D. Wall, C.W. Clegg, P. Sparrow and A. Howard, (eds.), *The New Workplace: A Guide to the Human Impact of Modern Working Practices*, Chichester: John Wiley & Sons Ltd.

Cox, A., Marchington, M. and Suter, J. 2009: Employee Involvement and Participation: Developing the Concept of Institutional Embeddedness, *International Journal of Human Resource Management*, **20**(10), 2150–2168.

Cox, A., Zagelmeyer, S. and Marchington, M. 2006: Embedding Employee Involvement and Participation at Work, *Human Resource Management Journal*, **16**(3), 250–267.

Danford, A., Durbin, S., Richardson, M., Tailby, S. and Stewart, P. 2009: "Everybody's Talking at Me": The Dynamics of Information Disclosure and Consultation in High-skill Workplaces in the UK, *Human Resource Management Journal*, **19**(4), 337–354.

Denham, N., Ackers, P. and Travers, C. 1997: Doing Yourself Out of a Job? How Middle Managers Cope With Empowerment, *Employee Relations*, **19**(2), 147–159.

Dietz, G., Wilkinson, A. and Redman, T. 2009: Employee voice and participation in A. Wilkinson, N. Bacon, T. Redman and S. Snell (eds.), *The Sage Handbook of Human Resource Management*, London: Sage.

Donaghey, J., Cullinane, N., Dundon, T. and Dobbins, T. 2011: Non-union employee representation, union avoidance and the managerial agenda, *Economic and Industrial Democracy*, **33**(2), 163–183.

Drago, R. and Wooden, M. 1991: The Determinants of Participatory Management, *British Journal of Industrial Relations*, **29**(2), 177–204.

Dundon, T. and Rollinson, D. 2004: *Employment Relations in Non-union Firms*, London: Routledge.

Dundon, T., Wilkinson, A., Marchington, M. and Ackers, P. 2004: The Meanings and Purpose of Employee Voice, *International Journal of Human Resource Management*, **15** (September), 1150–1171.

Dundon, T., Wilkinson, A., Marchington, M. and Ackers, P. 2005: The Management of Voice in Non-Union Organizations: Managers' Perspectives, *Employee Relations*, **27** (June), 307–319.

Edwards, P. and Wright, M. 1998: HRM and Commitment: A Case Study of Teamworking in P. Sparrow and M. Marchington (eds.), *HRM: The New Agenda*, London: Pitman.

Edwards, P. and Wright, M. 2001: High-involvement Work Systems and Performance Outcomes, *International Journal of Human Resource Management*, **12**(4), 568–585.

Edwards, P., Collinson, M. and Rees, C. 1998: The Determinants of Employee Responses to Total Quality Management, *Organization Studies*, **19**(3), 449–475.

Farndale, E., Van Ruiten, J., Kelliher, C. and Hope-Hailey, V. 2011: The Influence of Perceived Employee Voice on Organisational Commitment: An Exchange Perspective, *Human Resource Management*, **50**(1), 113–129.

Fenton-O'Creevy, M. 2001: Employee Involvement and the Middle Manager: Saboteur or Scapegoat?, *Human Resource Management Journal*, **11**(1), 24–40.

Foster, D. and Hoggett, P. 1999: Change in the Benefits Agency: Empowering the Exhausted Worker?, *Work, Employment and Society*, **13**(1), 19–39.

Foy, N. 1994: *Empowering People at Work*. London: Gower.

Freeman, R, Boxall, P. and Haynes, P. (eds.) 2007: *What Workers Say: Employee Voice in the Anglo-American Workplace*. New York: Cornell University Press.

Gerstner, C.V. and Day, D.V. 1997: A Meta-analytic Review of Leader-Member Exchange Literature: Correlates and Construct Issues, *Journal of Applied Psychology*, **82**(6), 827–844.

Gollan, P. 2002: So What's the News? Management Strategies Towards Non-union Employee Representation at News International, *Industrial Relations Journal*, **33**(4), 316–331.

Gollan, P. 2006: Editorial: Consultation and Non-union Employee Representation, *Industrial Relations Journal*, **37**(5), 428–437.

Gomez, R., Bryson, A. and Willman, P. 2010: Voice in the Wilderness? The Shift from Union to Non-Union Voice in Britain in A. Wilkinson, P. Gollan, M. Marchington and D. Lewin, (eds.), *The Oxford Handbook of Participation in Organizations*, Oxford: Oxford University Press.

Gospel, H. and Willman, P. 2003: *High Performance Workplaces: the Role of Employee Involvement in a Modern Economy Evidence of the EU Directive Establishing a General Framework for Informing and Consulting Employees*. London: Centre for Economic Performance.

Granovetter, M. 1985: Economic Action and Social Structure: The Problem of "Embeddedness", *American Journal of Sociology*, **91**(3), 481–510.

Harley, B. 1999: The Myth of Empowerment: Work Organisations, Hierarchy, and Employee Autonomy, *Work, Employment and Society*, **13**(1), 41–66.

Heller, F., Pusić, E., Strauss, G. and Wilpert, B. 1998: *Organisational Participation, Myth and Reality*, Oxford: Oxford University Press.

Herzberg, F. 1972: One More Time: How Do You Motivate Employees? In L. Davis and J. Taylor (eds.), *Design of Jobs*, London: Penguin.

Hirschman, A. 1970: *Exit, Voice and Loyalty: Responses to Decline in Firms, Organizations and States*. Cambridge: Harvard University Press.

Hochschild, A. 1997: *The Time Bind: When Work Becomes Home and Home Becomes Work*, New York: Metropolitan Books.

Huselid, M. 1995: The Impact of Human Resource Management Practices on Turnover, Production and Corporate Financial Performance, *Academy of Management Journal*, **38**(3), 635–672.

Huselid, M. and Becker, B. 2009: Strategic Human Resource Management: Where Do We Go from Here? In A. Wilkinson, N. Bacon, T. Redman and S. Snell (eds.), *Sage Handbook of Human Resource Management*, London: Sage.

Kersley, B., Alpin, C., Forth, J., Bryson, A., Bewley, H., Dix, G. and Oxenbridge, S. 2006: *Inside the Workplace: Findings from the 2004 Workplace Employment Relations Survey*, London: Routledge.

Kessler, I., Undy, R. and Heron, P. 2004: Employee Perspectives on Communication and Consultation: Findings from a Cross-national Survey, *International Journal of Human Resource Management*, **15**(3), 512–532.

Lewin, D. 2010: Employee Voice and Mutual Gain, in A. Wilkinson, P. Gollan, M. Marchington and D. Lewin (eds.), *The Oxford Handbook of Participation in Organizations*, Oxford: Oxford University Press.

Liden, R., Bauer, T. and Erdogan, B. 2004: The Role of Leader-Member Exchange in the Dynamic Relationship Between Employer and Employee: Implications for Employee Socialization, Leaders, and Organizations, in L. Shore, S. Taylor, J. Coyle-Shapiro and L Tetrick (eds.), *The Employment Relationship: Examining Psychological and Contextual Perspectives*, Oxford: Oxford University Press.

Marchington, M. 2004: Employee Involvement: Patterns and Explanations, in B. Harley, J. Hyman and P. Thompson (eds.), *Essays in Honour of Harvie Ramsay, Participation and Democracy at Work*, London: Palgrave.

Marchington, M. and Kynighou, A. 2012: The Dynamics of Employee Involvement and Participation During Turbulent Times, *International Journal of Human Resource Management*, **23**(16), 3336–3354.

Marchington, M. and Suter, J. 2013: Where informality really matters: patterns of employee involvement and participation in a non-union firm, *Industrial Relations*, **52**(1), (forthcoming).

Marchington, M., Goodman, J., Wilkinson, A. and Ackers, P. 1992: *New Developments in Employee Involvement*, Research Paper No. 2, London: Employment Department.

Marchington, M., Grimshaw, D., Rubery, J. and Willmott, H. (eds.) 2005: *Fragmenting Work: Blurring Organisational Boundaries and Disordering Hierarchies*, Oxford: Oxford University Press.

Marchington, M., Wilkinson, A., Ackers, P. and Dundon, T. 2001: *Management Choice and Employee Voice*, London: Chartered Institute of Personnel and Development.

Marchington, M., Wilkinson, A., Ackers, P. and Goodman, J. 1993: The Influence of Managerial Relations on Waves of Employee Involvement, *British Journal of Industrial Relations*, **31**(4), 553–576.

Marchington, M., Wilkinson, A., Ackers, P. and Goodman, J. 1994: Understanding the Meaning of Participation: Views from the Workplace, *Human Relations*, **47**(8), 867–894.

Micklethwait, J. and Woolridge, A. 1996: *The Witch Doctors: What the Management Gurus are Saying, Why it Matters and How to Make Sense of It*, London: Heinemann.

Mohr, R. and Zoghi, C. 2008: High Involvement Work Design and Job Satisfaction, *Industrial and Labour Relations Review*, **61**(3), 275–296.

Morton, C. 1994: *Becoming World Class*, London: MacMillan.

Parker, S. K., Wall, T. D. and Cordery, J. 2001: Future Work Design Research and Practice: Towards an Elaborated Model of Work Design, *Journal of Occupational and Organisational Psychology*, **74**, 413–440.

Pateman, C. 1970: *Participation and Democratic Theory*, Cambridge: Cambridge University Press.

Poole, M. 1986: *Towards a New Industrial Democracy: Workers' Participation in Industry*, London: Routledge and Kegan Paul.

Poole, M., Lansbury, R. and Wailes, N. 2000: A Comparative Analysis of Developments in Industrial Democracy, *Industrial Relations*, **40**(3), 490–525.

Psoinos, A. and Smithson, S. 2002: Employee Empowerment in Manufacturing: A Study of Organisations in the UK, *New Technology, Work and Employment*, **17**(2), 132–148.

Purcell, J. and Georgiadis, N. 2007: Why Should Employers Bother with Employee Voice? In R. Freeman, P. Boxall and P. Haynes (eds.), *What Workers Say: Employee Voice in the Anglo-American Workplace*, New York: Cornell University Press.

Ramsay, H. 1977: Cycles of Control. Worker Participation in Sociological and Historical Perspective, *Sociology*, **11**(3), 481–506.

Ramsay, H. 1983: Evolution or Cycle? Worker Participation in the 1970s and 1980s, in C. Crouch and F. Heller (eds.), *Organisational Democracy and Political Processes*, Chichester: John Wiley & Sons Ltd.

Ramsay, H., Scholarios, D. and Harley, B. 2000: Employees and High-performance Work Systems: Treating Inside the Black Box, *British Journal of Industrial Relations*, **38**(4), 501–531.

Sewell, G. 2001: What Goes Around, Comes Around: Inventing a Mythology of Teamwork and Empowerment, *The Journal of Applied Behavioural Science*, **37**(1), 70–89.

Sewell, G. and Wilkinson, B. 1992: Empowerment or Emasculation? Shopfloor Surveillance in a Total Quality Organisation, in P. Blyton and P. Turnbull (eds.), *Reassessing Human Resource Management*, London: Sage.

Strauss, G. 1998: Participation Works – If Conditions are Appropriate, in F. Heller, E. Pusic, G. Strauss and B. Wilpert (eds.), *Organisational Participation: Myth and Reality*, Oxford: Oxford University Press.

Strauss, G. 2006: Worker participation – some under-considered issues, *Industrial Relations*, **45**(4), 778–803.

Tebbutt, M. and Marchington, M. 1997: Look Before You Speak: Gossip and the Insecure Workplace, *Work Employment and Society*, **11**(4), 713–735.

Townsend, K., Wilkinson, A. and Burgess, J. 2012: *Economic and Industrial Democracy* (forthcoming).

Wall, T.D., Wood, S.J. and Leach, D. 2004: Empowerment and Performance, in C. Cooper and I. Robertson (eds.), *International Review of Industrial and Organisational Psychology*, New York: John Wiley & Sons Inc.

Wayne, S.J., Shore, L.M. and Liden, R.C. 1997: Perceived Organisational Support and Leader-Member Exchange: A Social Exchange Perspective, *Academy of Management Journal*, **40**(1), 82–111.

Wilkinson, A. 2002: Empowerment, in M. Poole and M. Warner (eds.), *International Encyclopaedia of Business and Management Handbook of Human Resource Management*, London: ITB Press.

Wilkinson, A. and Dundon, T. 2010: Direct Employee Participation, in A. Wilkinson, P. Gollan, M. Marchington and D. Lewin (eds.), *The Oxford Handbook of Participation in Organizations*, Oxford: Oxford University Press.

Wilkinson, A. and Fay, C. 2011: New times for employee voice? *Human Resource Management*, **50**(1), 65–74.

Wilkinson, A. and Willmott, H. 1994: Total Quality: Asking Critical Questions, *Academy of Management Review*, **20**(4), 789–791.

Wilkinson, A., Godfrey, G. and Marchington, M. 1997: Bouquets, Brickbats and Blinkers: Total Quality Management and Employee Involvement in Practice, *Organization Studies*, **18**(5), 799–820.

Wilkinson, A., Dundon, T., Marchington, M. and Ackers, P. 2004: Changing Patterns of Employee Voice, *Journal of Industrial Relations*, **46**(3), 298–322.

Wilkinson, A., Gollan, P., Marchington, M. and Lewin, D. 2010: Conceptualising Employee Participation in Organisations, in A. Wilkinson, P. Gollan, M. Marchington and D. Lewin (eds.), *The Oxford Handbook of Participation in Organizations*, Oxford: Oxford University Press.

Wilkinson, A., Marchington, M., Ackers, P. and Goodman, J. 1993: Refashioning the employment relationship? The experience of a chemical company over the last decade, *Personnel Review*, **22**(3), 22–38.

Wood, S. 2010: High Involvement Management and Performance, in A. Wilkinson, P. Gollan, M. Marchington and D. Lewin (eds.), *The Oxford Handbook of Participation in Organizations*, Oxford: Oxford University Press.

CHAPTER FOURTEEN

Employee Representation

Stephanie Tailby

Introduction

Trade unions have been the principal institutions for worker representation in the UK where industrial relations were 'voluntarist' until the late twentieth century (Dickens and Hall 2010). Their principal method of representing their members' interests to employers has been collective bargaining (sometimes denoted as 'joint regulation' of the employment relationship, the contrast being unrestrained management prerogative). At the level of government they have lobbied in respect of economic policy and employment law (Quinn 2010). However, the past three decades have presented political and labour law challenges in the context of economic restructuring and assessed on the range of conventional measures, trade union vitality has shown a marked decline. There were 6.5 million union members in 2010, which is a sizeable 27 per cent of employees, but half the total achieved when trade union membership peaked in 1979. Sixty per cent of union members currently are in the public sector, which is exposed to the Conservative-Liberal Democrat coalition government's deficit reduction priorities. In the private sector, which employs the majority of the workforce, 70 per cent of workplaces had no union presence on the weakest of measures (no union members) according to Labour Force Survey estimates, although there was variation by workplace size and industry sector (Achur 2011). Collective bargaining on pay covered 71 per cent of the workforce in 1979 (Ewing 2003: 145). In 2010 the employee coverage overall was 30 per cent and 17 per cent in the private sector.

Union decline has not been unique to the UK. That said, the UK experience has been protracted and relatively dramatic (Simms and Charlwood 2010: 131). Attention has centred on the 'representation gap' at the level of the workplace (Towers 1997) and the potential for union revitalisation as the means of redress. Nonetheless academic interest in non-union employee representation has been stimulated by European Union legislation; the 1994 European Works Council and 2002 Information and Consultation of Employees Directives. In addition, increased complexity of employee representation has been identified in analyses of Workplace Employment Relations Survey (WERS) data (Charlwood and Terry 2007). A central issue is whether non-union employee representation complements trade unions and can support their rebuilding, or threatens to substitute for them (Heery *et al.* 2004: 21–32). The picture is complicated by diversity. Non-union representation embraces employer-sponsored systems of indirect representation through joint consultation structures, the statutory provision and civil society organisations. The last are organisations beyond the workplace – charities, voluntary associations, social movement and other non-governmental organisations – that promote the interests of sections of the workforce 'often as part of a broader remit that embraces other social domains', provide advocacy and other labour market services to workers and campaign for changes in employment law (Heery 2010: 544; Williams *et al.* 2011). Non-union employee representation has gained salience and yet there is limited evidence of an absolute increase in the incidence of collective consultation. In fact the 2004 WERS suggested the reverse (Kersley *et al.* 2006: 126).

In evaluating employee representation institutions, the most obvious criterion is effectiveness in representing employee interests (Hyman 1997, Heery 2010). That point may seem obvious and provocative: how are employee interests to be discerned; which are to be prioritised? It deserves emphasis nonetheless. There is a large, prescriptive management literature that discusses direct employee participation (the types of arrangements examined in the preceding chapter) and indirect representation (where mentioned at all) as techniques that find their utility in corporate objectives. That is to say, the provision (at management's discretion) of opportunity for employees to participate in aspects of organisational decision-making at the level of their job or task is recommended for the purpose of enlisting their knowledge, skill and effort to the organisation's goals for productivity, efficiency and financial performance improvement. The discourse is in sharp contrast with the emphasis in academic industrial relations (Terry 2010: 275–6), as in pluralist academic HRM (Boxall and Purcell 2011: 162) on workers' right to be represented by strong independent organisations as a counter to the power asymmetry in the employment relationship and means of presenting interests that may diverge from those of other organisational stakeholders.

An approach in the academic analyses of institutions of worker representation has been to survey workers for their preferences in respect of representation and make recommendations on this basis (Freeman *et al.* 2007). Yet it is problematic, for reasons discussed by Heery (2010). Reported preferences may reflect immediate experience; the majority of non-union members have never experienced union membership, often because they have been in workplaces where there is no union to join (Bryson and Forth 2010). They may be shaped by dominant ideologies and norms. An alternative is to conceptualise from theory and evidence of the situation of the workforce (or its non-managerial population) where worker interests may lie. In this way Heery constructs a checklist for evaluating the *societal* impact of union and non-union institutions for worker representation that he offers as a 'device for comparing these institutions in an explicitly normative sense' (2010: 546–7).

His claim is that worker interests embrace redistribution (of income and economic risk), work quality, the representation of diversity, multi-level representation (at the workplace and above), conflict as well as cooperation (the capacity to challenge) and in relation to this the accumulation of power resources. He adds that it is desirable that representation institutions balance the interests of working people against other stakeholders with equally legitimate interests.

With that checklist in mind, this chapter sketches the contexts of union decline in the UK before turning to indirect employee representation at the workplace in its union, non-union and hybrid forms. The third, substantive section is concerned with the legislative framework for employee representation and, in particular, the influence of EU law. Most western European countries have long had national systems for company-level employee representation – works councils or similar – that are institutionalised by collective agreement or, more typically, by statute, alongside trade unions and collective bargaining at industry or sector level (see Hyman 2010; Rogers and Streeck 1995). In Germany, which is often regarded as the most developed model, works councils elected by the workforce have extensive statutory participation rights – to information, consultation and on some issues co-determination – although also 'peace obligations' (and industrial action is proscribed). There was anticipation that the EU Information and Consultation Directive would stimulate works council-like arrangements in the UK but its limited provisions were diluted in the transposition to UK legislation as the 2004 Information and Consultation of Employees (ICE) Regulations. The German industrial relations model itself has not been immune to the pressures of economic restructuring.

Labour governments in the UK from 1997 to 2010 kept in place much of the legislation enacted by Conservative governments in the period 1979–97 that was restrictive of trade unions. They conceded few new union rights, although it is relevant to consider the statutory union recognition procedure that came into effect from 2000. New or enhanced individual employment rights enforceable at an Employment Tribunal or via a state agency were enacted in support of 'fairness at work' (and are currently being eroded). Aside from EU law, there was pressure from the trade unions and the Trades Union Congress (TUC). It is ironic, therefore, that individual rights are sometimes seen as union-substituting (Metcalf 2005). However, there is the issue of how unorganised workers become informed of their rights and achieve redress for problems at work (Colling 2010). Some evidence is considered. The fourth section turns to trade union revitalisation. Unions have pursued a wide range of initiatives but debate in the past decade centred on the relative merits of *partnership* and *organising*. Summarised crudely, these aspire to accumulate the power resources of employer legitimacy and internal union strength respectively. Partnership was proposed by the TUC as a new accommodation in capital-labour relations that, at the level of the enterprise, would be embodied in formal, joint agreements committing the parties to a joint problem-solving approach in the interests of mutual gain. It achieved limited political support or employers' take-up, which is a measure, perhaps, of the cold climate in which unions in the UK have operated (Kelly 2005).

The Contexts of Union Decline

Union decline has not been unique to the UK but neither has it been an international phenomenon: there has been substantial demand for representation at work and in pay determination among the production workforce in rapidly industrialising countries including China (Grammaticas 2010). In the European Union, union density (members as a proportion of employees) declined in all 27 member states in the period 2000 to 2008. Bryson *et al.* caution (2011: 98–99) that while it is tempting to look for general causes either in the unions' external environment (forces of globalisation, changes in labour markets, management practices and politics) or in their internal organisation and policies, or both, there is sufficient inter-country difference to suggest the approach is inadequate. On the dimension of union density alone (just one among the proxy measures of union strength), the range in 2010 was from 70 per cent in the Nordic countries (Sweden, Denmark, Finland) to 8 per cent in France, where, until recently there has been state support for industry-level collective agreements and the unions have shown capacity to mobilise workers in mass demonstrations notwithstanding their low membership (Fulton 2011). It is necessary to consider the specific economic, social, political and legal contexts in which unions operate in interaction with challenges that are common: the local in interaction with the global.

Forces of globalisation

For example, much attention has focused on the impact of intensified product market competition, stimulated by trade liberalisation, the increased flow of foreign direct investment that now integrates into production for market exchange the vast 'labour reserves' of formerly non-capitalist countries, the resultant expansion of trade (much of which is within multinational companies) and the *financialisation* of corporate ownership. Among the impacts identified is employers' resistance to collective bargaining of a 'distributive' kind and willingness to include unions only on the terms of a 'productivity coalition'. Brown (2010) identifies these pressures bearing on UK industrial relations from the third quarter of the twentieth century. Yet he notes that 'voluntarist' collective agreements were relatively easy for inward investors to side-step, encouraging other employers to withdraw from multi-employer bargaining at industry level in order to develop organisation-specific employment relations regimes and tighter systems of performance management (see also Purcell 1991). In addition, there was government policy from 1979 and the legal restriction of union activity including the capacity to engage in lawful industrial action in support of bargaining claims.

Local history

UK industrial relations were largely decentralised, in the unionised sector of private industry at least. In manufacturing from the Second World War, if not before, workplace-based trade unionism had re-grown to engage in collective bargaining at this level with supervisors and local management. Shop stewards, or lay union representatives elected by and accountable to the work groups from which they were drawn, were central within this (see Terry 2003; 2010). Participative trade unionism was the large strength. However, workplace trade unionism was highly uneven in its development, even within manufacturing. The model spread to the public services, but in many of the private services that were also expanding by 'mobilising' a female labour supply, union presence at the workplace was at best patchy. Hence, one critique of the unions' commitment to 'free collective bargaining' was that it favoured work groups with 'positional power' in the production chain or had the advantage of occupational solidarity but was inadequate for others (Rubery 1995).

At national level the unions had been drawn into the process of government as government itself had become more interventionist in the economy. However, this was a weak version of 'corporatism' by comparison with arrangements in some western European countries. In the 1974–79 'social contract' between the unions and Labour government, the 'political exchange' was wage restraint for legislation more favourable for unions. In the context of high inflation and public expenditure cuts (under pressure from the International Monetary Fund), the arrangement was unstable and broke down in the 1978–9 *winter of discontent*. The 'new right' Conservative government from 1979 opted for industrial relations reform of a different kind. In the context of an economic downturn (abroad as in the UK), it determined to break with the Keynesian 'full employment' commitments to which governments from 1945 (abroad and in the UK) had broadly adhered, elevate low inflation as the key goal of macro-economic policy, and use the resources of the state to liberate 'markets' – in particular the labour market – from social and legal regulation (see Nolan 2011).

Comparative institutional permissiveness

The UK economy has become progressively integrated with the economies of other EU member states in the process of European economic integration and EU enlargement. Yet it has remained distinctive from other western European economies. Its peculiarities are often presented within the *Varieties of Capitalism* framework (Hall and Soskice 2001); it is (or has become increasingly) a 'liberal market economy' that relies on markets and contracts to coordinate economic actors rather than legal and social regulation, as in 'coordinated market economies' of which Germany is taken as the exemplar. The framework can appear rather static; there are certainly dangers in under-estimating the extent of de-regulation across EU member states that gathered pace from the 1990s. The point, nonetheless, is that 'comparative institutional permissiveness' in industrial relations (Marginson and Meardi 2010: 207–8) in the UK has offered inward-investing corporations (and employers more generally) more than average scope to assert their 'employee voice regime' preferences. And while the rootlessness of multinational capital can be greatly exaggerated, the permissiveness of UK corporate law, as well as employment law, has meant that companies can exit with above average ease (or make credible threats to do so). Comparative wage costs have meant that, for inward investors, the UK has often been favoured as a site for routinised operations (e.g. assembly in manufacturing). Investment in knowledge-intensive processes goes to higher wage countries, notably Germany (Marginson and Meardi 2010: 213) whose economy has been powered by its large manufacturing sector that employed 7.2 million in 2010. Accelerated de-industrialisation in the UK in the 1980s and 1990s had reduced manufacturing employment to 2.5 million in 2010 (Froud et al. 2011).

Over that period there has been a renaissance in the small firms sector resulting, in not insignificant part, from large firms' (and public sector organisations') use of sub-contracting relationships (Ram and Edwards 2010). Small firms (0–49 employees) were 99.3 per cent of the 4.8 million private sector enterprises recorded in 2009, which, with the 0.3 per cent of medium-sized enterprises (50–249 employees), accounted for 59.8 per cent of private sector employment (BIS 2010a). The small firms sector is enormously diverse and its employment regimes are varied. Overall, however, small firms are significantly less likely than medium-sized or large enterprises to have a union presence (Kersley et al. 2006). Small firms have 'figured prominently in policy-oriented discourses on the 'burden of regulations'' (Ram and Edwards 2010: 231).

In the context of some substantial union membership loss, the TUC and many of its affiliated unions or their leaderships had become pro-EU by the late 1980s, in aspiration that the 'European social model' would diffuse to UK legislation. New Labour from 1997 reversed the UK's opt-out from the EU social chapter but pledged to make the case for labour market flexibility within Europe. Its approach in macro-economic policy was broadly consistent with that of the 1979–97 Conservative governments. In respect of industrial relations, the difference was that New Labour sought to 'domesticate, rather than exclude, workers' voices' (Smith and Morton 2006: 405). 'Partnership' became the central theme and voluntary initiatives were supported by public funds, but the government accorded the unions no special status in the relationship; it advocated labour-management cooperation, with or without trade unions.

New Labour presided over what Mervyn King, Governor of the Bank of England, described as a 'nice' decade of non-inflationary continuous economic expansion. That assessment was made in 2007, just before the banks began to topple in the capitals of global finance, London and New York. The UK's success was celebrated by many as the product of 'globalisation' (delivering cheap manufactured imports), its 'flexible labour market' and the government's de-politicisation of interest-rate policy through its delegation to the Monetary Policy Committee of the Bank of England (Ward 2007). Those conditions were not benign for the trade unions; low inflation in its own right removed an incentive to union joining (Charlwood 2004) and they collapsed, to make obvious the unbalanced economic growth of the preceding decade, internationally and (over some longer period of time) in the UK (Froud *et al.* 2011; Nolan 2011).

Representation at the Workplace

The WERS series from 1980 has recorded for Britain (*cf.* the UK) the erosion of the traditional system of employee representation, sometimes summarised as 'single channel' union representation. A 'hard' measure (and what Millward *et al.* 2000: 1000 describe as the 'most telling indicator of employee voice') is management's recognition of one or more trade unions for the purposes of collective bargaining over pay. There was continual decline from the mid-1980s to a rate of 27 per cent in 2004 among workplaces with 10 or more employees, although there was variation by industry and public/private sector and the positive association between recognition and workplace size meant 48 per cent of employees were covered (or at least in workplaces with pay bargaining for some groups). De-recognition contributed in the 1980s and 1990s, although most analyses highlight changes in the composition of the economy and unions' difficulties in obtaining negotiation rights in newer workplaces. The rate of decline in union recognition tempered from 1998, at least among private sector workplaces with 25 or more employees (ibid. 121). The contribution of the statutory union recognition procedure from 2000 is considered in the next section of this chapter, which also provides details of the content of the EU-derived Information and Consultation of Employees (ICE) Regulations that came into effect, initially for undertakings with 150 or more employees, from April 2005. This section is concerned with the increased diversity in employee representation systems detected in the WERS findings to 2004 and that drew attention as indicative perhaps of ways in which employers would respond to the ICE Regulations. The focus allows some comparison of union and non-union employee representation in the workplace.

Diversity within decline

The large change recorded by the WERS series was the growth in workplaces without any on-site indirect employee representation; 83 per cent of private sector workplaces with five or more employees and 21 per cent in the public sector in Charlwood and Terry's (2007: 324) analysis of the 2004 data. In short, direct employer communication with employees was now dominant in many parts of the economy (DTI 2007:21). As regards indirect employee representation, aside from its diminished incidence, there was change in the composition of the population of workplace employee representatives. Shop steward numbers fell, most sharply in the 1980s as managements asserted their 'right to manage' (Terry 2003).

Non-union employee representatives increased in number and in 2004 nearly equalled the total of workplace union representatives: 200,000 inclusive of health and safety and union learning representatives (discussed later in relation to social partnership). The total of 350,000 workplace employee representatives was concentrated in 14.5 per cent of workplaces with five or more employees, albeit larger workplaces so that around 50 per cent of employees were in workplaces with representatives (Charlwood and Terry: 323; DTI 2007). Most employee representation was union or non-union, the former predominating but the latter was the structure at a not insubstantial 6 per cent of private sector workplaces covering 13 per cent of private sector employees. Hybrid or dual channel representation – the inclusion of employee representatives in a consultation forum, alongside union recognition – attracted interest as a possible employer's response to the ICE Regulations. Yet its incidence was less obvious; less than 2 per cent of workplaces (Charlwood and Terry 2007). Moreover, the proportion of workplaces with joint consultative committees at this level fell after 1998; among workplaces with 10 or more employees, from 20 per cent to 14 per cent in 2004. Small workplaces and those without union recognition accounted for most of the change (Kersley et al. 2006: 126–7). Nonetheless, the effectiveness of non-union and hybrid employee representation compared to union representation merited attention. The evidence is sifted first by considering the processes (consultation and negotiation) and structures (union and non-union representation) involved.

Process and structure

Joint consultation in the UK has been an employer-led arrangement and, as already hinted, there is not much evidence to date to suggest the situation has been altered by the ICE Regulations. While in practice it can be varied, it is generally understood in relation to collective bargaining as a weaker form of 'collective engagement', situated further towards the management prerogative end of the 'continuum of employee participation' (Blyton and Turnbull 2004: 255; Boxall and Purcell 2011: 162–3). The reasons are elaborated by Terry (2010: 280–281). Collective bargaining is a process of negotiation in which the parties may deploy (or threaten) 'economic sanctions (strikes, lockouts) as well as arguments in order to obtain their objectives'. The 'outputs' are joint or collective agreements. Joint consultation is a process in which management invites or listens to employee views through their representatives but retains the right to take the final decision. In the absence of legislation providing for co-determination, it is 'ultimately a process of unilateral regulation'. Second, the process is one of dialogue; the use of sanctions is considered inappropriate. Third, the issues may be more wide-ranging but different from those of collective bargaining; production-focused, relating to customer service and so on. For these reasons it is understood as a process that is 'integrative' in objective, as distinct from 'distributive' collective bargaining on pay and conditions (see also Kim 2009).

In the decades after the Second World War, the ability of workplace trade unionism to extend the scope of collective bargaining beyond pay to include issues of labour use (and other dimensions of the quality of working life in Heery's evaluation framework), appeared to obviate the need for works councils, as in Continental Europe (Clegg 1976), or to render joint consultation unstable (liable to 'capture' within collective bargaining – McCarthy in Clegg 1979: 155). Non-union employee representation was relatively rare (and in fact there is less evidence of its recent growth than of decline in union representation). It was often concentrated in industries with the structural characteristics associated with unionisation and attracted limited academic interest, the presumption being that the employer's objective was union avoidance (Terry 1999). Research subsequently has highlighted the respects in which it can be limited as a means of amplifying employees' voice (ibid.; Blyton and Turnbull 2004). The process is joint consultation and the employee representation body lacks the power resources of a union beyond the workplace (advice, research, expertise brought in) or within it (a mobilising ideology). By the same token, however, non-union representation instituted simply to counter employees' interest in unionisation could be thought potentially unstable, if it lacks legitimacy or is unable to deliver the interests employees have in representation (Terry 1999). Dundon and Gollan (2007) are inclined to locate it as a low-cost approach to union avoidance, in comparison to 'soft HRM'. Tailby *et al.'s* (2007) study of *FinanceCo* records management's initiatives to make the existing 'partners council' system more salient to employees at the time the statutory union recognition procedure was brought into law.

In the 1980s there was speculation that employers would take advantage of weakened unions to substitute joint consultation for collective bargaining. By the 1990s the larger danger appeared to be atrophy in the scope of collective bargaining, its 'hollowing out' to constitute little more than joint consultation (Brown 2010). Yet developments were uneven, as between workplaces. And Kersley *et al.'s* (2006: 181) analysis of the 2004 WERS data cautioned against dismissing joint regulation over pay and conditions, for many employees the 'bread and butter' issues (Hyman 1997), 'as things of the past'. On this score, unions certainly out-performed 'pure' non-union employee representation since negotiation over any terms and conditions of employment was almost exclusively within workplaces with recognised unions. The 'union wage mark-up', the differential between the unionised and non-union workforce, had declined but persisted (at 5 per cent and rather higher for women according to Bryson and Forth's 2010 analysis for the late 2000s). Collective agreements cover union and non-union employees in a bargaining unit.

Effects and effectiveness

Lay union representatives have a multifaceted role as representatives of the union and of union members in the workplace. Central responsibilities are recruitment and the representation of members individually (e.g. in grievance and disciplinary hearings) and collectively (negotiation). The 2004 WERS allowed comparison with non-union workplace representatives on a range of dimensions. Union representatives were more likely to have been elected to their position by an employee constituency (in this case union members). Charlwood and Terry (2007) detect a spill-over effect in that non-union representatives in hybrid systems were more likely to have been elected than those within 'pure' non-union employee representation systems. The apparent paradox was that non-union representatives, on average less accountable to an employee constituency, were more likely than the union to report being consulted regularly by management, in particular in hybrid systems (p. 327). Most representatives spent time in discussion with employers and employees on issues relating to terms and conditions, welfare (e.g. health and safety), staff selection and development. Yet union representatives were much more likely than non-union to spend time on personal cases such as disputes about individual grievances or disciplinary matters (cited by DTI 2007: 21). Union representatives on average spent significantly more time on their range of representation duties than non-union representatives.

Union representatives have had a statutory right to reasonable paid time-off to fulfil a defined set of union duties since 1975. Legislation in the past decade extended entitlement to paid time-off to union learning representatives (from 2002) and time-off for workers formally appointed as information and consultation representatives under the ICE Regulations. Employers are not obliged to better the statutory requirements but there are often negotiated agreements. In the 2004 WERS, 89 per cent of union representatives reported employer-paid time for representation work, as did 83 per cent of non-union representatives in joint consultation committees (Kersley *et al.* 2006). Most union representatives receive training in their functions; only a fifth of non-union representatives had training for their role. TUC accredited training delivered within further education has benefited from public support. The 'value for money' was reckoned within the Department for Trade and Industry's (now BIS) cost-benefit review of the facilities and time available to workplace representatives (union and non-union) for the Labour government in 2006–7; an exercise towards the government's *Success at Work* agenda for improvement in workplace performance and employment relations. This utilitarian calculation of the effects of representation in pursuit of employee welfare and fairness at work interests estimated the societal benefit, employer and public purse savings worth between £476 million and £1,133 million (the reduction in employment tribunal cases, working days lost due to workplace injury and work-related illness). The TUC and CBI in May 2009 issued a joint statement on the positive role of workplace union representatives (TUC 2010). However, that did not restrain sections of the press and the Taxpayers' Alliance from effort to vilify employers', or more specifically public sector employers', facilities time expenditure (e.g. Copping and Malnick 2010).

Charlwood and Terry (2007) used the 2004 WERS data to assess the effectiveness of union, non-union and hybrid employee representation systems in respect of employee interests in equity and employers' interest in efficiency. Their principle was to follow the tradition of industrial relations theory that has debated representation in terms of how best to balance these respective interest claims. Equity impacts are considered in terms of the narrowing of wage dispersion and reduction of dismissal rates (a function of procedural fairness or the restraint of arbitrary management); the efficiency measure is productivity and the data source the manager survey. There is no attempt to assess redistribution from profits to wages. It could be said, however, that Kersley *et al.'s* (2006) analysis of WERS in respect of the incidence of pay negotiation (reported above) resolved that non-union representation on its own could not have a redistributive impact. Charlwood and Terry conclude from their statistical investigation that a union presence is a pre-requisite for positive employee and employer outcomes. Hybrid representation delivered on both, while 'pure' non-union representation was associated with no tangible employee or employer gain (unless, of course, the objective was purely union avoidance).

Legislation and Employee Representation

'Voluntarism' in UK industrial relations was amended from the 1960s. The radical break was from 1979 (Dickens and Hall 2010). Conservative governments employed the law to shift the 'balance of power' in industry and de-regulate the labour market. Labour governments from 1997 made 'partnership' the theme for employment relations 'modernisation' and enacted new individual employment rights for which a business efficiency case could be made over and beyond considerations of social justice. At the same time they retained a good deal of the Conservatives' industrial relations legislation, in particular that restricting industrial action. Colling (2010) identifies the shift to *legal enactment* as one mirrored in other liberal market economies where collective bargaining has contracted substantially, notably the USA. In the case of the UK, a principal source of new employee rights has been the EU.

The long history of statutory employee rights in most western European countries, as Taylor *et al.* (2009: 28) summarise, was 'integrated and made a key plank in the formation of the Single European Market in 1992'. The Social Chapter of the Maastricht Treaty covered areas including employment security, health and safety, working time and rights to information and consultation. The rationale was that 'firstly, a single market in labour should be based on harmonisation of employment conditions and secondly, that competition within Europe should be tempered by a concern with the employment and social conditions of Europe's citizens' (ibid.). The harmonisation of 'labour standards', industrial relations structures and processes was challenging even among countries with similar legal systems and traditions (Hyman 2010). The UK did not have a past of positive employment rights and from 1979 its governments were neo-liberal in orientation. New Labour in 1997 reversed the Social Chapter 'opt out' that Margaret Thatcher's Conservative government had negotiated for the UK. Yet its pledge was to take labour market flexibility (and 'light touch' regulation, UK style) to the European agenda. The UK government opposed or sought dilution of a number of employment directives. The commitment to partnership notwithstanding, these included the Information and Consultation Directive that (amended) was adopted in 2002.

This section looks very briefly at the statutory union recognition procedure enacted by the Labour government, one of the few new collective employment rights conceded, before turning to the EU Information and Consultation Directive, its transposition into UK employment law and the evidence available to date of its impact. The section also considers the 1994 European Works Council Directive ('recast' in 2009) that aimed to coordinate national provisions in order to create a European legal framework for transnational information and consultation procedures within 'community-scale' enterprises. It concludes with some attention to the issue of the adequacy of statutory employment rights without representation in the workplace, and the current UK coalition government's proposed reforms of the Employment Tribunal system.

The union recognition legislation

The 1999 Employment Relations Act provided for a statutory procedure through which a union could seek an enforceable award from the Central Arbitration Committee that an employer recognised it for collective bargaining. The legislation was important but fell short of what the unions had pressed for and, in the form in which it came into law from 2000 (with limited revision in 2003), incorporated most of the amendments that the CBI (that opposed the legislation) had lobbied for (Dickens and Hall 2010). Small firms (with fewer than 21 employees) are excluded. The CAC may award recognition without a ballot if 50 per cent of the workers in a 'bargaining unit' are union members, although it has to make consideration of 'good industrial relations'. Otherwise, in a secret ballot, there must be a majority vote in favour among those voting and among at least 40 per cent of workers in the bargaining unit. There was significant growth in union recognition agreements in anticipation of the law and after its enactment, although that tailed off as recognition campaigns faced the more challenging workplace sites. The majority were voluntary agreements, concluded in 'the shadow of the law'. The number of applications received by the CAC has fallen sharply: from 106 in 2003–4 to 28 in 2010–11 (Wright 2011). The Labour government enacted a worker the right to be accompanied by a trade union official or fellow worker at workplace disciplinary hearings. This was a significant measure, given that union accompaniment was irrespective of whether the union had recognition at the workplace or not, although did not amount to a full-fledged 'right to representation' (Dickens and Hall 2010: 310).

The ICE age?

Most western European countries have long established national systems of company level employee representation (works councils or similar). They include the six founding member states of the EU (or European Economic Community as it was known). Efforts to generalise the arrangements by EU legislation proved contentious for reasons elaborated by Hyman (2010: 69–72) and that include the UK's lack of comparable provision and the diversity between national systems that increased with EU enlargement. The first steps towards 'common rules' for the 'establishment of a representation structure at the workplace for the purpose of informing and consulting' employees were achieved in the 1970s (Picard 2010:16). The 1975 Collective Redundancies and 1977 Acquired Rights Directives each required the establishment of information and consultation procedures in relation to their specific issues. The provisions were transposed to the UK to apply only to organisations with recognised trade unions. The accommodation conserved the UK's traditional 'voluntarist' policy in respect of employee representation and the 'single channel' of trade union representation but became more contentious as the incidence of trade union recognition declined over the 1980s and 1990s. An important ruling of the European Court of Justice in 1994 affirmed that the obligation of employers to consult with employee representatives on the issues prescribed applied generally; in organisations without, as well as those with, union recognition. Subsequently the UK Labour government introduced EU information and consultation regulations relating to aspects of health and safety, working time agreements and parental leave. The piecemeal developments, and in particular the 2002 Information and Consultation Directive, challenged the traditional framework for employee representation.

The Directive created, in principle, an employer obligation 'to inform and consult employee representatives on recent and foreseeable developments in the firm's financial situation, employment and work organisation, with opportunities for representatives to respond and seek agreement before the implementation of change' (Hyman 2010: 71). It did not embrace co-determination and the procedures prescribed were dilute rights of employee representation in comparison with those of most western European countries. The UK government, under pressure from the CBI, had opposed the draft Directive issued in 1998. When the 'blocking minority' disintegrated, the government sought amendment and dilution of the provisions. There was further dilution in the transposition to UK law as the 2004 ICE Regulations, phased in from April 2005 and applying to undertakings with 50 or more employees from April 2008.

The Regulations provide employers substantial flexibility. The trigger mechanism means they need not act at all unless 10 per cent of employees request negotiation of an information and consultation agreement. They encourage arrangements tailored to organisations' specific circumstances. They allow for information and consultation bodies to be constituted as voluntary 'pre-existing agreements' (PEAs) that may effectively pre-empt the use of the Regulations' procedures; negotiated agreements reached via the Regulations' procedures; or, where no agreement is reached, 'standard' or default arrangements. It is also possible for employers to determine arrangements unilaterally outside the scope of the Regulations (Hall and Purcell 2011). Only in the event that the Regulations' procedures are triggered but no agreement is reached are (minimally prescriptive) 'standard' or default information and consultation provisions enforceable, via complaints to the CAC and from there to the Employment Appeals Tribunal. Trade unions acquire no statutory rights; the ICE Regulations confer employee rights to information and consultation with employers.

There were contrasting prognoses of the impact on UK employment relations. The TUC was optimistic for employee representation and for trade union opportunity within the information and consultation bodies formed. However, there was division of opinion among trade unions and in academic analyses; for example, suspicion that rather than filling the 'representation gap' in UK workplaces, the statutory support for a second channel of communication would enable employers to undermine union representation where that was established and substitute consultation for collective bargaining (Smith and Morton 2006). A comprehensive, economy-wide assessment of the institutional adjustments made (or otherwise) at the workplace will be provided by the sixth WERS (its findings had not been published at the time of writing). The 2004 WERS, as noted, recorded an overall fall in the incidence of joint consultative committees, although these remained common in large workplaces. The small-scale survey and case study evidence since 2004 suggests the ICE Regulations have given some impetus to the trend towards hybrid arrangements (Hall and Purcell 2011). Obviously the stability of such arrangements remains to be seen.

Hall and Purcell (2011) draw on their longitudinal research (with others) among 25 private and voluntary sector organisations, small and large, to assess the arrangements adopted against the standard provisions of the ICE Regulations. Under these, information on the undertaking's activities and economic situation must be provided and consultation should take place on probable developments in employment. Where a decision is likely to lead to substantial change in work organisation, consultation should be 'with a view to reaching agreement'. The majority of the information and consultation bodies in the companies studied were either elected by all employee constituencies or hybrid in type (eleven of the fourteen organisations with recognised trade unions). The majority of the arrangements were subject to voluntary agreements. Of the organisations that participated throughout the research, eight were 'active consultors' who put strategic issues on the agenda and could take on board employee views. Twelve used the information and consultation bodies primarily to communicate to the workforce and expected employee representatives to assist in this process. Of the eight active consultors, three met the criterion of consulting with a view to reaching agreement. Overall management was the dominant partner in consultation, a situation that Hall and Purcell ascribe to insufficiently effective employee representation bodies and, among union representatives, insufficient trust in management objectives.

Marginson *et al.* (2010) surveyed employment practice in the UK operations of 302 multinational companies (MNCs) in 2006. The findings present a contrast with those of the 2004 WERS. The ICE Regulations were apparently prompting 'representative arrangements which are not union-based' and 'significant activity in establishing new indirect consultative structures where these did not previously exist'. On this evidence, MNCs represent 'a leading force in the changing contours of representation and voice practice in Britain' (p. 174). Continuity and change are suggested by Taylor *et al.'s* (2009) case study research in six companies (each MNC owned and unionised at least in part) in four industry sectors (financial services, motor vehicle manufacture, electronics, and aerospace/engineering). The firms had accommodated the ICE Regulations in varying ways. Consultative arrangements had provided opportunity to by-pass the union in three cases. The ICE Regulations had not deterred 'shock redundancies' announced in the press, with the information provided to employee representatives at the last minute.

European Works Councils

The 1994 EWC Directive provided for the establishment of a representation structure at European level in community-scale undertakings (those with at least 1,000 employees within the EU and operations employing at least 150 in at least two member states) for the purposes of information and consultation on matters of a transnational nature affecting employee interests. The rationale for the Directive was that 'nationally-based rights of employee participation were being outflanked by the transnationalisation of corporate structures' given impetus by the Single European Market project (Hyman 2010: 69; Picard 2010; 16). Hyman notes a concern among EU policy-makers that such restructuring should have 'social acceptability' and also that there had been trade union pressure and the precedent set by the voluntary establishment of 'prototype' EWCs in some companies. An example is Volkswagen, which, in 1992, recognised formally the European employee representatives' body that German works councillors had initiated (Greer and Hauptmeier 2008). More broadly, while international union cooperation was not novel, there was registered some urgency for *labour transnationalism* in response to the internationalisation of markets and firms that threatened the national industrial relations systems that had developed over the twentieth century, or their capacity to accommodate enterprise and worker well-being claims. The incentive for firms to regulate their (domestic) 'market relations' through multi-employer bargaining was eroded while transnational enterprise (dependent on form) had capacity to by-pass local labour organisation and engage in 'coercive comparison' of the performance of subsidiary operations spread internationally (ibid.). The potential for EWCs to develop 'actor qualities' (Hertwig *et al.* 2011), however, was not obvious for some observers (and not desired by others).

The European Commission campaigned over two decades for the adoption of a measure on transnational information and consultation. The acceptance of the EWC Directive in 1994 was facilitated by a number of factors: the extension of qualified majority voting in the Council of Ministers for a range of social policy issues including employee participation and the Commission's shift away from 'hard law' and towards 'soft regulation' that provided scope to negotiate the terms and operation of EWCs (Waddington 2011). Also relevant was the UK's opt out from the Social Chapter of the Maastricht Treaty, although that did not exempt UK based MNCs with the requisite employment figures in EU member states other than the UK. With the Labour government's reversal of the opt-out, the Directive was extended to the UK with effect from 2000. Its coverage was extended further with EU enlargement in 2004 and 2007. However, the highest rate of EWC creation remains the 1994–6 period when voluntary agreements were permitted that did not have to conform to the Directive's minimum standards (for example, for an annual information and consultation meeting with central management). While around 2,400 MNCs potentially are covered by the EWC Directive, the European Trade Union Institute's (ETUI) database (www.ewcdb.eu) recorded only 944 as having active EWCs in 2012. However, the rate was higher among larger MNCs and varied by industry sector. It was above the European Economic Area (EEA) average (36 per cent) among UK-owned MNCs (42 per cent) in the late 2000s (BIS 2010:10).

Waddington's (2011) survey of 941 EWC employee representatives over 2005–8 suggests that for these participants the quality of information and consultation on average is poor. Waddington concludes that 'At best, the majority of EWCs are institutions at which managers disclose information' (p. 347). However, he understands EWCs as an 'institution in process'. Managers with experience of EWCs in surveys are generally positive, seeing the merit as a channel for two-way communication for providing information and eliciting employee views that have a capacity to develop cooperation and involve employees more fully in the business (cited in Marginson and Meardi 2010: 225). The surveys also find that in most instances managers reckon the EWC impact on transnational business decisions is marginal.

The European Trade Union Confederation (ETUC) campaigned for years for the revision of the 1994 Directive. Its criticisms included the lack of any definition of information and the imprecise definition of consultation; the omission of any reference to trade unions; and the exclusion of co-determination on any issue. The recast Directive (that came fully into force in 2011) makes some amendment as regards the first two points. Academic analysis and debate, as Waddington (2011) summarises, has made the central issue the capacity of union organisation. That is to say that while there is broad agreement that the Directive in content is deficient and other factors (the different languages and industrial relations backgrounds of EWC representatives) complicate, evaluation divides on unions' capacity to meet the challenges. These are within EWCs, to achieve information exchange and consultation of the quality to enable EWC representatives to influence developments within MNCs, and beyond EWCs, to establish an infrastructure of support and integration (to prohibit EWC representatives' isolation from other, within-company institutions of labour representation) (Ibid.). Variability in EWC functioning and effectiveness has been identified, and for the European auto industry analysed with reference to 'actor strategies' (Greer and Hauptmeier 2008) in interaction with structures (company type, 'home country' industrial relations systems) and economic conditions (Hertwig et al. 2011).

Rights without representation

In the UK, Labour governments from 1997 enacted an extensive programme of individual employment rights, many EU-derived. For reasons outlined by Colling (2010), however, a larger volume of law is not a sufficient condition for justice at work. The difficulties include the UK's common-law based system, piecemeal legislation and enforcement agencies that remain fragmented in spite of some recent measure of joining-up. Successive governments have argued that the Employment Tribunal system is overloaded by 'frivolous' or 'litigious' claims. That overload is explained more adequately in terms of legal enactment in place of the social regulation of the workplace via collective bargaining. The majority of employers never face a claim (ibid.: 338). Employees are rarely well placed to pursue their rights through that process, and where they are, their chances of success at an Employment Tribunal are not large. In the absence of clear and well enforced law, employees – acutely those without representation at work – are dependent on management's assiduity in complying with the law. Citing Casebourne *et al.'s* (2006) employee survey research, Colling (p. 339) writes that management is 'now the principal actor in disputes resolution' in the UK, given that a minority of workers have access to a union representative for advice, and that managers are 'the most common source of advice and principal actors in addressing workplace issues irrespective of whether advice is sought'. There are 'public interest, legal organisations' (Williams *et al.* 2011) that provide employment law advice – the Citizens' Advice Bureaux and Law Centres – yet their funding has always been stretched. It has come partly from local authorities that are currently obliged to retrench, while Legal Aid is a further casualty of 'rapid deficit reduction'. The current coalition government has resolved to push disputes resolution back into the workplace. Access to the ET system is to be further restricted, and that system's caseload cut by the erosion of unfair dismissal rights (Carley 2011).

Partnership in Employment Relations

The concept of union revitalisation embraces all policy innovation to redress the challenges unions have faced (Frega and Kelly 2003), and in the UK trade unions have pursued a diversity of initiatives to counter falling membership and to take unionism to a 'new workforce'. These include reform of their own governance structures to be inclusive of hitherto under-represented sections of the workforce: women, black and ethnic minority workers, young workers. However, academic debate in the past decade has centred on the relative merits, tensions between or potential symbiosis of *organising* and *partnership* approaches. The former can mean different things in practice (see Simms and Charlwood 2010). However, the focus is on understanding worker interests, collectivising around common grievances, building activism and internal strength and participation in collective action.

Partnership when applied to employment relations can mean many things. As an approach to union revitalisation, however, it is predicated on the understanding that there are issues of common or complementary employee and employer interest that can be developed to the mutual benefit of all parties through a joint problem-solving approach at company level and in the workplace. It is sometimes summarised as a reciprocal exchange: of greater security of employment for employees' co-operation with flexibility and more extensive employee participation (direct and indirect) in exchange for worker commitment. The TUC championed social partnership from the 1990s. The attention to business efficiency and competitiveness made the strategy controversial within the union movement. The TUC hoped to find support among employers' organisations and, in turn, a lobby for supportive measures from government. The realisation of campaigns for labour standards (a re-regulation of the labour market) required some audience at the level of public policy formulation.

The provenance of partnership

The TUC's principal reference point was the 'European social model' and more specifically the 'German model' of industrial relations. That has embraced 'dual channel' worker representation: works councils at the level of the enterprise that have statutory participation rights and at industry or sector level, collective bargaining between trade unions and employers' associations on pay, working hours and other issues. There is substantial inter-dependence between works councils and unions. Further, the unions under most coalition governments in Germany have been included alongside employers' representation bodies as 'social partners' in economic and policy forums at the level of government (Hyman 2010). In the UK the infrastructures beyond the enterprise are largely missing. And Germany's co-ordinated industrial relations institutions were weakened somewhat from the 1990s by changes in capital markets that increased the 'shareholder value' orientation of firms, union membership decline, the 'flight' of large employers from peak-level associations and the vertical disintegration of large firms (Doellgast and Greer 2007).

A second point of reference has been the American partnership literature and theory of the *mutual gains enterprise* (Kochan and Osterman 1994). The terrain for labour-management cooperation is located in the work design principles and HRM practices of 'high commitment management' (HCM). A company-level collective consultation forum is advocated on the principle that the 'high road' requires champions, and employees and their representatives are the most likely among the organisation's stakeholders to be concerned about job quality and employee voice, and are more likely to engage in workplace change where they feel their interests are represented. The improvement of working life actually gained through HCM practices, of course, remains a matter of debate (see Godard 2004).

The TUC emphasised joint regulation as the means of achieving the transition to the 'high road' to competition in a global-market age. Its principles of partnership, or pre-conditions for a new accord in labour-management relations, emphasised formal, negotiated joint agreements that committed the parties (management, unions, employees) to a joint commitment to enterprise success, employment security, recognition of differences of interest, information sharing, broadening the scope of the issues tackled jointly, and the objective of mutual gain (TUC 1999). New Labour championed partnership at work but interpreted the relationship as 'little more than an antonym for conflict and an assertion of commitment to co-operative relations and increased productivity', its 'primary axis the individual and employer' (McIlroy 2008: 289). The unions' inclusion was left a matter for employers to concede voluntarily or, of course, for unions to achieve through organising and successful activation of the statutory union recognition procedure, in which case the emergent workforce preference might be for traditional collective bargaining.

Debate and numbers

The labour gains or risks of union-employer partnerships dominated academic industrial relations debate for the best part of a decade, until the mid-2000s. From the outset there were optimistic and pessimistic prognoses of partnership as a strategy for union re-building; that it would yield a more secure institutional presence once unions turned the 'rhetoric of employee involvement' around (Ackers and Payne 1998); risked union incorporation in management and loss of legitimacy among members and potential members (Taylor and Ramsay 1998); or risked membership 'demobilisation' (Kelly 2005) and union marginalisation within a company consultation structure (Danford *et al.* 2005). A substantial body of case study research evidence was accumulated but different evaluation criteria were applied, making comparison of findings problematic. Kelly (2005) was the most insistent critic. He highlighted the conditions that made liberal market economies an especially inhospitable environment for partnership agreements. 'Stock market capitalism' was oriented to short-term profits maximisation, subject to limited legal or institutional pressure to invest in workforce training and functional flexibility and, in the absence of encompassing industry-level collective agreements, had substantial freedom to achieve profitability by exerting downward pressure on wage rates. Trade unions had access to few power resources other than those they could build themselves. In the absence of labour, organising the partnerships that emerged would be employer-dominant rather than labour-parity.

Opinion on the possible worker gains continued to differ. By the mid-2000s, however, there was substantial convergence on the view that the UK was not a hospitable environment for the partnership approach in enterprise employment relations. The number of formal partnership agreements concluded that conformed (on paper) to TUC principles was modest; around 80. They were concentrated in industries undergoing substantial restructuring (manufacturing, the privatised utilities) and among companies that had experienced a labour-management crisis of some kind, quite a few of these in the financial services (Kelly 2005). Bacon and Samuel (2009) identified a larger number of formal agreements; 248 concluded in the period between 1990 and 2007, the great majority in New Labour's period in government. However, most were thin in content, 'substantively hollow and procedurally biased' (Samuel and Bacon 2010: 443). And three-quarters of the agreements signed in the period 2001–7 (over half of the total number) were in the public sector, where the government was pursuing structural 'modernisation'. Many of these public sector partnership agreements appeared to be industry or sectoral framework agreements.

Social partnership

The TUC had aspired for inclusion alongside employers' organisations as a 'social partner' at the level of government. In the Labour government period union leaders achieved increased contact with ministers, at least in comparison with their near total exclusion under 1979–97 Conservative administrations. Yet New Labour was inclined to provide them the status of one among a range of interest groups. Business leaders had the premier position (Quinn 2010). It is true that the TUC and major unions were integrated within the infrastructure of training and skills policy formulation. Yet they pressed for, and did not achieve, legislation that would oblige employers to engage in collective bargaining on workforce training (McIlroy 2008). They did gain the Union Learning Fund from 1998 to support projects, and the new role of Union Learning Representatives in the workplace – assisted access to training for worker groups formerly marginalised in employers' provision. The contribution to workplace organising continues to divide views, however (ibid., Stuart and Rainbird 2011).

Conclusion

The UK's traditional system of employee representation, based on trade unions and collective bargaining, has been subject to substantial erosion over a period of three decades. Analyses have weighed unions' external environment (ideological, political, legal, economic and social) and the adequacy of their organisation and policies, although to contribute differing prognoses of their prospects (e.g. Simms and Charlwood 2010, Bryson and Forth 2010). Union decline in the UK, as in other liberal market economies, has been coterminous with increased inequality; a widening gap between high and low incomes (Schulten 2010).

Non-union employee representation has come under scrutiny. To substitute for trade union representation it has, in principle, to be as effective at the task of worker interest representation. The 2002 EU Information and Consultation Directive has been criticised as limited; it omits co-determination rights. The UK ICE Regulations were framed to be permissive for employers. Studies of the employer-initiated arrangements put in place to date tend to the view that the ICE Regulations have 'provided an additional channel for management but have failed to provide new opportunities for employee consultation' (Hyman 2010: 72). Hall and Purcell (2011) identify a problem of insufficiently effective employee representation and urge trade unions to become more engaged. An issue is how unions are to insert themselves in information and consultation bodies in workplaces where they currently do not have a presence. Where they have a presence, the issue is how they build membership – rather than losing it, for example because members see no reason to pay union subs for representation in an all-employee information and consultation forum. An approach of servicing-in expertise from the external union (research and assistance in preparing a response to the company's business plans) is not necessarily incompatible with one of organising to build participative unionism locally, and yet there are tensions.

The financial crisis from 2008 injected uncertainty on a broad range of fronts; indeed at the beginning of 2012 the future of the EU was in doubt. The UK public deficit was inflated by revenues lost in the 2008/9 recession, expenditures made on unemployment benefits and the large expenses incurred in the rescue of financial institutions and markets. There was opportunity for a shift of approach in the management of the economy; the state was obliged to nationalise leading banks but potentially gained leverage to redirect their activity towards industry and employment reconstruction (Froud *et al.* 2010). However, such a shift required champions. The Conservative-Liberal Democrat coalition government from May 2010 opted to write-down the deficit with speed and through 'savage cuts' in public expenditure, in particular welfare expenditure. Unemployment continued to rise, notably for youth, as economic growth flat-lined. To the total is being added the estimated 0.75 million jobs that are to be axed in the public services, which, in aggregate, have a predominantly female workforce and have been relatively highly unionised. Prime Minister Cameron's case for national unity ('we are all in this together') casts opposition as the pursuit of sectional interests. Nonetheless a shared sense of injustice has galvanised protests by students (facing a hike in university tuition fees), public sector workers (against job and service cuts, privatisation and pensions' reform), community groups (losing local services), disability activists, and civil society organisations (on behalf of the elderly, or against child poverty). New grassroots campaigning and direct action groups have formed. The challenge for the unions (as ever) is to forge and conserve unity among existing and potential constituencies, in order to make effective representation of labour's interests.

REFERENCES

Achur, J. 2011: *Trade Union Membership 2010.* Office for National Statistics. Department for Business, Skills and Innovation.

Ackers, P. and Payne, J. 1998: British Trade Unions and Social Partnership: Rhetoric, Reality and Strategy, *The International Journal of Human Resource Management,* **9**(3), 529–550.

Bacon, N. and Samuel, P. 2009: Partnership Agreement Adoption and Survival in the British Private and Public Sectors, *Work, Employment and Society,* **24**(3), 231–248.

BIS (Department for Business, Innovation & Skills) 2010a: Statistical Release, October 13, http://stats.bis.gov.uk/ed/sme

BIS (Department for Business, Innovation and Skills) 2010b: Impact Assessment. Implementation of the Recast European Works Council Directive. April, URN 10/889.

Blyton, P. and Turnbull, P. 2004: *The Dynamics of Employee Relations* 2nd edn, Houndsmill: Palgrave Macmillan.

Boxall, P. and Purcell, J. 2011: *Strategy and Human Resource Management* 3rd edn, Houndsmill: Palgrave Macmillan.

Brown, W. 2010: Negotiation and Collective Bargaining in T. Colling and M. Terry (eds.), *Industrial Relations: Theory and Practice*, Chichester: John Wiley & Sons Ltd.

Bryson, A. and Forth, J. 2010: *Trade Union Membership and Influence 1999–2009*. Centre for Economic Performance, CEP Discussion Paper No. 1003, September.

Bryson, A., Ebbinghaus, B. and Visser, J. 2011: Introduction: Causes, consequences and cures for union decline, *European Journal of Industrial Relations*, **17**(2), 97–105.

Carley, M. 2011: Government launches consultation on workplace disputes resolution. Eironline, March 15. http://www.eurofound.europa.eu/eiro/2011/02/articles/uk1102019i.htm

Casebourne, H., Regan, J., Neathey, F. and Tuohy, S. 2006: 'Employment Rights at Work – Survey of Employees', *Employment Relations Research Series*, No. 51, Department of Trade and Industry.

Charlwood, A. 2004: The new generation of trade union leaders and prospects for union revitalization. *Work, Employment & Society* **42**(2), 379–398.

Charlwood, A. and Terry, M. 2007: 21st-century models of employee representation: structures, processes and outcomes. *Industrial Relations Journal*, **38**(4), 320–337.

Clegg, H. A. 1976: *Trade Unionism Under Collective Bargaining: A Theory Based on Comparisons of Six Countries*, Oxford: Blackwell.

Clegg, H. 1979: *The Changing System of Industrial Relations in Great Britain*, Oxford: Blackwell.

Colling, T. 2010: Legal Institutions and the Regulation of Workplaces in T. Colling and M. Terry (eds.), *Industrial Relations: Theory and Practice*, Chichester: John Wiley & Sons Ltd.

Copping, J. and Malnick, E. 2010: Taxpayers spend millions paying for trade union activities. *The Telegraph*, September 4.

Danford, A., Richardson, M., Stewart, P., Tailby, S. and Upchurch, M. 2005: *Partnership and the High Performance Workplace. Work and Employment Relations in the Aerospace Industry*, Houndmills: Palgrave Macmillan.

Department for Trade and Industry (DTI) 2007: Consultation Document. *Workplace representatives: a review of their facilities and facility time.*

Dickens, L. and Hall. M. 2010: The Changing Legal Framework of Employment Relations in T. Colling and M. Terry (eds.), *Industrial Relations: Theory and Practice*, Chichester: John Wiley & Sons Ltd.

Doellgast, V. and Greer, I. 2007: Vertical Disintegration and the Disorganization of German Industrial Relations, *British Journal of Industrial Relations*, **45**(1), 55–76.

Dundon, T. and Gollan, P.J. 2007: Re-conceptualizing voice in the non-union workplace, *The International Journal of Human Resource Management*, **18**(7), 1182–1198.

Ewing, K. 2003: Labour Law and Industrial Relations, in P. Ackers and A. Wilkinson (eds.), *Understanding Work & Employment*, 138–160. Oxford: Oxford University Press.

Freeman, R.B., Boxall, P. and Haynes, P. 2007: *What Workers Say: Employee Voice in the Anglo-American Workplace*, Ithaca and London: ILR Press.

Frega, C. and Kelly, J. 2003: Union Revitalization Strategies in Comparative Perspective, *European Journal of Industrial Relations*, **9**(1), 17–24.

Froud, J., Moran, M., Nilsson, A. and Williams, K. 2010: Wasting a crisis? Democracy and markets in Britain after 2007. *The Political Quarterly*, **81**(1) 25–38.

Froud, J., Johal, S., Law, J., Leaver, A. and Williams, K. 2011: *Rebalancing the Economy (Or Buyer's Remorse)*, Centre for Research on Socio-Cultural Change (CRESC) Working Papers Series, Working Paper No.87, January.

Fulton, L. 2011: Trade Unions. Worker representation in Europe, Labour Research Department and ETUI (online publication) http://worker-participation.eu/layout/set/print/National-Industrial-Relations/Acr

Godard, J. 2004: A Critical Assessment of the High-Performance Paradigm, *British Journal of Industrial Relations*, **42**(2), 349–378.

Grammaticas, D. 2010: China's factories hit by waves of strikes. BBC News Asia Pacific, 28 June. http://www.bbc.co.uk/news/10434079.

Greer, I. and Hauptmeier, M. 2008: Political Entrepreneurs and Co-Managers: Labour Transnationalism at Four Multinational Auto Companies, *British Journal of Industrial Relations*, **46**(1), March, 76–97.

Hall, M. and Purcell, J. 2011: *Employee consultation – a mixed picture*, IRRU Briefing Number 20, Warwick Business School, Spring.

Hall, P. and Soskice, D. (eds.) 2001: *Varieties of Capitalism, The Institutional Foundations of Comparative Advantage,* Oxford: Oxford University Press.

Heery, E. 2010: Worker Representation in a Multiform System: A Framework for Evaluation. *Journal of Industrial Relations*, **52**(5), 543–559.

Heery, E., Healy, G. and Taylor, P. 2004: Representation at Work: Themes and Issues, in G. Healy, E. Heery, P. Taylor and W. Brown (eds.), *The Future of Worker Representation*. Houndmills: Palgrave Macmillan.

Hertwig, M., Pries, L. and Rampeltshammer, L. 2011: Stabilizing effects of European Works Councils: Examples from the automotive industry, *European Journal of Industrial Relations*, **17**(3), 209–226.

Hyman, R. 1997: The Future of Employee Representation, *British Journal of Industrial Relations*, **35**(3), 309–336.

Hyman, R. 2010: British Industrial Relations: The European Dimension, in T. Colling and M. Terry (eds.), *Industrial Relations: Theory and Practice*, Chichester: John Wiley & Sons Ltd.

Kelly, J. 2005: Social partnership agreements in Britain, in M. Stuart and L. Martínez (eds.), *Partnership and Modernisation in Employment Relations*, Abingdon: Routledge.

Kersley, B., Alpin, C., Forth, J., Bryson, A., Bewley, H., Dix, G. and Oxenbridge, S. 2006: *Inside the Workplace: Findings from the 2004 Employment Relations Survey*, London: Routledge.

Kim, Dong-One 2009: Employees' Perspective on Non-Union Representation: A Comparison with Unions, *Economic and Industrial Democracy*, **30**(1), 120–151.

Kochan, T.A. and Osterman, P. 1994: *The Mutual Gains Enterprise: Forging a Winning Partnership Among Labor, Management and Government*, Boston: Harvard University Press.

Marginson, P. and Meardi, G. 2010: Multinational Companies: Transforming National Industrial Relations? In T. Colling and M. Terry (eds.), *Industrial Relations: Theory and Practice*. Chichester: John Wiley & Sons Ltd.

Marginson, P., Edwards, P., Edwards, T., Ferner, A. and Tregaskis, O. 2010: Employee Representation and Consultative Voice in Multinational Companies Operating in Britain, *British Journal of Industrial Relations*, **48**(1), 151–180.

McIlroy, J. 2008: Ten Years of New Labour: Workplace Learning, Social Partnership and Union Revitalization in Britain, *British Journal of Industrial Relations*, **46**(2), June, 283–313.

Metcalf, D. 2005. Trade unions: resurgence or perdition? An economic analysis, in S. Fernie and D. Metcalf (eds.), *Trade Unions: Resurgence or Demise?* London: Routledge .

Millward, N., Bryson, A. and Forth, J. 2000: *All Change at Work?* British employment relations 1980–1998, as portrayed by the Workplace Industrial Relations Survey series, London and New York: Routledge.

Nolan, P. 2011: Money, markets, meltdown: the 21st-century crisis of labour, *Industrial Relations Journal*, **42**(1), 2–17.

Picard, S. 2010: *European Works Councils: a trade union guide to Directive 2009/38/EC*. Brussels: ETUI aisbl.

Purcell, J. 1991: The Rediscovery of the Management Prerogative: The Management of Labour Relations in the 1980s, *Oxford Review of Economic Policy*, **7**(1), 33–43.

Purcell, J. and Hall, M. 2011: UK: EIRO CAR on "The effect of the Information and Consultation Directive on Industrial Relations in the EU Member States five years after its transposition" http://www.eurofound.europa.eu/eiro/studies/tn1009029s/uk1009029q.htm

Quinn, T. 2010: New Labour and the Trade Unions in Britain, *Journal of Elections, Public Opinion and Parties*, **20**(3), 357–380.

Ram, M. and Edwards, P. 2010: Industrial Relations in Small Firms, in T. Colling and M. Terry (eds.), *Industrial Relations: Theory and Practice*. Chichester: John Wiley & Sons Ltd.

Rogers, J. and Streeck, W. (eds) 1995: *Works Councils. Consultation, Representation, and Cooperation in Industrial Relations*, Chicago: University of Chicago Press.

Rubery, J. 1995: The Low-paid and the Unorganised, in P. Edwards (ed.) *Industrial Relations, Theory & Practice in Britain*, Oxford: Blackwell.

Samuel, P. and Bacon, N. 2010: The contents of partnership agreements in Britain 1990-2007. *Work Employment & Society*, **24**(3) 430–448.

Schulten, T. 2010: 'Minimum wages under the conditions of the global economic crisis', in J. Heyes and L. Rychly (eds.), *Labour Administration and the Economic Crisis. Challenges, Responses and Opportunities*, Geneva: International Labour Organisation.

Simms, M. and Charlwood, A. 2010: Trade Unions: Power and Influence in a Changed Context, in T. Colling and M. Terry (eds.), *Industrial Relations: Theory and Practice*, Chichester: John Wiley & Sons Ltd.

Smith, P. and Morton, G. 2006: Nine Years of New Labour: Neoliberalism and Workers' Rights, *British Journal of Industrial Relations*, **44**(3), 401–420.

Stuart, M. and Rainbird, H. 2011: The state and the union learning agenda in Britain, *Work, Employment & Society*, **25**(2), 202–217.

Tailby, S., Richardson, M., Upchurch, M., Danford, A. and Stewart, P. 2007: Partnership with and without trade unions in the UK financial services: filling or fuelling the representation gap? *Industrial Relations Journal*, **38**(3), 210–228.

Taylor, P. and Ramsay, H. 1998: Unions, Partnership and HRM: Sleeping with the Enemy? *International Journal of Employment Studies*, **6**(2), 115–143.

Taylor, P., Baldry, C., Danford, A. and Stewart, P. 2009: ' "An umbrella full of holes?": Corporate Restructuring, Redundancy and the Effectiveness of ICE Regulations', *Relations Industrielles/Industrial Relations*, **64**(1), 27–49.

Terry, M. 1999: Systems of collective employee representation in non union firms in the UK, *Industrial Relations Journal*, **30**(1), 16–30.

Terry, M. 2003: Employee Representation: Shop Stewards and the New Legal Framework, in Edwards, P. *Industrial Relations, Theory and Practice*, Oxford: Blackwell.

Terry, M. 2010: Employee Representation, in T. Colling and M. Terry (eds.), *Industrial Relations: Theory and Practice*, Chichester: John Wiley & Sons Ltd.

Towers, B. 1997: *The Representation Gap: Change and Reform in the British and American Workplace*, Oxford: Oxford University Press.

Trades Union Congress 1999: *Partners for Progress: New Unionism at the Workplace*, London: TUC.

Trades Union Congress 2010: *The Facts About Facility Time for Union Reps*, London: Congress House, September.

Waddington, J. 2011: European works councils: the challenge for labour, *Industrial Relations Journal*, **42**(6), 508–529.

Ward, K. 2007: How the 'nice' decade has turned nasty, *The Independent,* 10 December.

Williams, S., Abbot, B. and Heery, E. 2011: Non-union worker representation through civil society organisations: evidence from the United Kingdom, *Industrial Relations Journal*, **42**(1), 69–85.

Wright, C. 2011: *What role for trade unions in future workplace relations?* Acas Future of Workplace Relations discussion paper series.

PART V

Process and Outcomes

CHAPTER FIFTEEN

Outsourcing and Human Resource Management

Virginia Doellgast and Howard Gospel

Introduction

Historically, outsourcing has always existed, as firms put out work to suppliers, contractors, and intermediaries to organise the production of goods and services (Doellgast and Gospel 2011).* In recent years, however, outsourcing has increased in both scale (the volume of outsourcing) and scope (the number of activities outsourced). This has several related causes. First, the advent of new transportation systems, such as the growth of maritime, rail, and road logistics and the advent of new information and communications technologies (ICTs) have facilitated ordering, monitoring, and delivery of products and services. Second, as markets have extended and become more competitive, firms increasingly seek to save costs through focusing on their core value-maximising activities, handing other activities over to suppliers. Third, the relaxation of trade barriers, emergence of new markets, and expansion of a more highly skilled labour force in Asia have increased the ease and cost savings of outsourcing to these regions. Fourth, in the public sector, organisations have been prompted by politicians to look to outsourcing as a way of cutting costs and introducing greater flexibilities. Finally, management fashion has played an important role in popularising production and service models, as firms watch and imitate their competitors (IMF 2007; OECD 2007ab).

These trends have a number of implications for the management of human resources across firms' increasingly diverse (and often international) procurement and supply chains. Managers face choices concerning how to help employees adjust during worker transfer or downsizing following the decision to outsource work. Networked relationships across core firms and their subcontractors introduce new

*This chapter draws on and updates Doellgast, V. and Gospel, H. 2011: 'Outsourcing and International HRM' in T. Edwards and C. Rees *International Human Resource Management*, Harlow: Pearson. We would like to thank the previous two editors and Pearson.

demands, in terms of resources and monitoring, as firms seek to coordinate practices and incentives across organisations. In addition, the human resource management (HRM) function itself is increasingly being outsourced to specialist organisations, often involving substantial restructuring and rationalisation.

We first provide background on outsourcing trends and then discuss the HRM issues and choices associated with outsourcing. Throughout, we examine the ways in which national institutions affect the costs and benefits of different strategic choices by firms, as well as the particular challenges multinationals face as they seek to manage outsourcing contracts across national borders. We show that outsourcing is both driven by and used to facilitate globalisation. However, outsourcing strategies and their impact on different stakeholder groups continue to be embedded in distinct national settings.

Understanding Outsourcing and Related Activities

There are several dimensions to the outsourcing of activities by an organisation. Here we consider the process, what may be outsourced, and to whom and where the out-sourcing may take place. First, there is a decision as to whether or not to outsource. We deal with this below, but here we state that this involves a calculation of relative benefits and costs. Benefits may involve the ability to secure inputs more cheaply, to access new technologies, and to concentrate on core activities. It may also provide the opportunity to get around certain labour problems e.g. involving difficult trade union situations. Costs involve searching for a supplier, negotiating a deal, and then monitoring and enforcing that deal. It may be difficult and risky coordinating such activities and may potentially lead to a loss of control and 'hold up' by the supplier or provider. In these latter circumstances, it has also sometimes happened that firms which have outsourced decide later to bring activities back in-house again – or insource.

Second, outsourcing involves the decision *to carry out certain activities inside or outside the boundaries of the firm*. Economists have described this as the use of the 'visible hand' of management or the 'invisible hand' of the market, representing a choice between internal or external methods of coordination. They have also seen it in terms of 'make' or 'buy' decisions, or the decision either to make or do something oneself or to buy it in from others (Coase 1937; Williamson 1975). More recently, scholars have begun to refer to the 'vanishing hand', as once highly integrated businesses and organisations are reducing coordination via internal mechanisms and are increasing coordination via market mechanisms (Langlois 2003). In practice, firms typically use a combination of internal and external arrangements, shifting the balance between in-house and outsourced production over time. In addition, some activities may lie in an area between the firm and the market – for example, where a company contracts with a supplier or subcontractor that it partly owns, or with an association of which it is a member. This first aspect of outsourcing can be seen in terms of a simple horizontal spectrum from *internal* to *external*, or *insourcing* to *outsourcing*.

Third, firms face decisions concerning *what to outsource*. Here a distinction may be made between *people* and *activities*. The firm can outsource workers who have previously been employed within the firm, transferring them to another firm on a permanent basis. The firm can also outsource activities, which can be further categorised as *'primary'* and *'support'* activities (Porter 1985). Primary activities are those that are integral to the firm's value chain, such as components in a manufacturing company or accounts processing in a service organisation. Support activities are those processes that facilitate the firm's value chain, such as IT, advertising, accounting and HRM.

Fourth, firms must decide on *the location of outsourced operations*, or to which regions, countries, or continents outsourcing will occur. Historically, outsourcing was largely domestic, to other firms or organisations in the near vicinity of the outsourcing firm. The geographical scope of outsourcing then extended to the national level as communications improved, transportation developed, and markets expanded. More recently, with further improvements in ICT, outsourcing has come to cross national boundaries and continents, with increased outsourcing by firms in developed countries to developing countries. The term *offshoring* is used to describe transactions that take place across international boundaries. We can distinguish further between *nearshoring*, in which work is moved to a neighbouring country (such as when a German firm shifts production to Poland) and *farshoring*, in which work is moved over a greater geographical distance (such as when a UK firm shifts production or service delivery to India).

Figure 15.1 shows the main distinctions made so far diagrammatically. The two entries on the right-hand side cover outsourcing. The bottom two entries cover offshoring. In this chapter, we are primarily concerned with the two entries to the right, or outsourcing that occurs domestically and internationally. Here, though, it should also be taken into account that what is outsourced at one point in time may be taken back into the firm later, as circumstances, incentives, and fashion change.

In the rest of this chapter, we examine the particular implications of outsourcing for the management of human resources. We focus on three themes: employment restructuring associated with outsourcing, especially where this involves transfers and/ or redundancy of workers; the challenges of coordinating HRM across organisational boundaries after outsourcing has occurred; and the particular case of the outsourcing of the HRM function itself.

		Internal v. External	
		Internal	*External*
Geographical location	*Domestic*	in-house production	domestic outsourcing
	Overseas	in-house offshoring	offshore outsourcing

Figure 15.1 Outsourcing and offshoring

Outsourcing and the Restructuring of Employment

One set of HRM challenges associated with outsourcing concerns the transfer or dismissal of current employees, following the decision to move the activities that they perform out of the core organisation. Companies typically choose among several organisational forms for a new outsourced operation. These include the following: the establishment of a *subsidiary* which remains under their direct control; the shifting of work to a *third-party subcontractor*; and the establishment of a *joint venture* with a third-party subcontractor. Subsequent to this, managers then face the decision either to dismiss the workforce performing the outsourced functions or to transfer a portion or all workers to the new organisation.

The decision to adopt a particular organisational and staffing strategy has important HRM implications. The retention of staff during outsourcing may be useful in transferring firm-specific knowledge, particularly for more complex business processes such as IT, research and development, or HRM. It also avoids costs associated with layoffs and new recruitment. However, the transfer of existing workers may also conflict with plans to implement new working practices or reduce direct labour costs and is impractical when outsourcing is undertaken with the intention of shifting work to another region or country.

Viewed from an employee's perspective, the opportunity to transfer to a new employer is generally preferable to layoffs. There may be additional positive aspects of moving to a more specialist organisation, such as new opportunities for career development (Kessler *et al.* 1999). However, employees also often experience disruption associated with broken career ladders and changes in management practices and style, which may negatively affect motivation and commitment. For example, one study found that outsourced workers who were more satisfied in their jobs had more difficulty adjusting to a new employer compared to those with lower job satisfaction (Logan *et al.* 2004). The decision to adopt a more intermediate organisational form such as a wholly-owned subsidiary or joint venture can create more continuity in management and reduce disruption to employees, while allowing the core firm to retain additional control during the outsourcing process.

While employers face similar challenges in managing employee transfer or downsizing regardless of location, national contexts will influence the costs and benefits of different strategic choices. Two institutions at the national level are particularly important in this respect: legal regulation and industrial relations systems.

Legal regulations

Laws concerning employee rights during the so-called 'transfer of undertakings' affect the ease with which management can downsize the workforce or alter employment contracts when outsourcing work. In the European Union (EU), the *Acquired Rights Directive* seeks to safeguard employees' rights in the transfer of ownership of a business or part of a business, defined to include the transfer of employees between organisations. The directive specifies that the terms and conditions in a collective agreement must be observed until the agreement expires, the transfer of ownership does not constitute justifiable reason for dismissals and the status of existing employee representatives should be preserved (i.e. the new employer must continue to recognise and negotiate with existing unions or works councils). In addition, these representatives are entitled to be consulted as to the 'likely or planned economic and social implications of the transfer' 'in good time' before the transfer (Eurofound 2007). The European Court of Justice has broadly interpreted this to apply to the transfer of work associated with outsourcing, even when a contract is shifted from one outsourced firm to another and involves no transfer of 'tangible or intangible assets' (Justice 2002). Thus, the directive covers cases where services are outsourced, insourced, or assigned to a new contractor.

The implication of these rules is that staff transfers or downsizing associated with outsourcing are more strongly regulated in Europe compared to North America or Asia. For example, in the US, employment contracts are 'at will' unless otherwise agreed through individual contracts or collective bargaining agreements, meaning the employer can terminate the contract at any time without giving cause. There is thus no legal protection of contracts following the transfer of work through outsourcing, either to a third party or a subsidiary. In Japan the *Labour Contract Succession Law* was passed in 2000, giving the parent company the right to transfer its existing workforce employed in a line of business to a separate company (Sako 2006). Existing employment contracts and collective agreements are automatically transferred to a spin-off. However, this does not apply to transfer of undertakings associated with outsourcing to a third party (Araki 2005).

Despite overall stronger employment protection in Europe, there is also significant variation between EU member states in the terms of national regulations. In the UK, the *Transfer of Undertakings Protection of Employment* (TUPE) legislation safeguards, to a degree, the terms and conditions of employees affected by outsourcing . For instance, the 'transferee' (the firm taking in the outsourced staff) takes on the liability for the key aspects of the contract of employment, while the 'transferor' (the firm sending the outsourced staff) is obliged to undertake a 'full and meaningful' consultation process as early as is practical. However, some aspects of terms and conditions, such as pensions, are not fully protected in the transfer and the consultation process does not oblige management to negotiate.

In continental Europe, consultation requirements are substantially stronger. For example, in the Netherlands, management must inform works councils and union representatives of the decision to transfer part of the business, provide information on the likely impact and justification of its decision, and show that it has taken account of workers' interests. If works councils challenge the proposals, they must be postponed for a month, and the works council can subsequently go to a labour court to formally contest the decision. In addition, once the process of outsourcing has begun, the employer must consult with the works council on any contract changes with the subcontractor (Caprile and Llorens 2000). France, Italy and Spain also have additional regulations that make it difficult for employers to use subcontracting arrangements that do not involve the transfer of staff to terminate employment contracts or change working conditions, and that establish joint responsibility by the client and subcontractor for observing employment rights (Caprile and Llorens 2000). These different regulations affect the extent to which workers are able to have a say in the restructuring process, as well as the cost advantages of different organisational forms to employers.

Industrial relations

A second set of national-level institutions which can influence outsourcing decisions is the national industrial relations system. This can take a number of different forms, depending again, in part, on the law, but also on the arrangements established by employers and trade unions.

First, negotiation and consultation rights affect employees' ability to participate substantively in restructuring decisions – and thus may shape both the form that outsourcing takes and outcomes for employees. These rights can be important for the implementation of transfer of undertakings rules. In many continental European counties, employees have additional representation rights on corporate boards which allow them to have prior knowledge and to be consulted on restructuring decisions.

Second, the bargaining power of trade unions can influence their ability to negotiate job security provisions, which makes it difficult or costly to lay off workers, or to oppose outsourcing through strikes or other forms of industrial action. In countries where unions are weak, with lower bargaining coverage, membership density, and participation rights, such as the US and UK, workers are less likely to have these forms of leverage. For example, under the UK's TUPE regulations, an employer can dismiss workers if it can be demonstrated that it was undertaken for economic, technical, or organisational reasons; and employment contracts can be changed with the approval of individual employees. These conditions can be easy to meet, in the absence of strong unions or works councils to inform workers of their legal rights or to contest decisions. A study by Cooke et al. (2004), based on a series of UK case studies, showed that employers had broad discretion in reducing staff numbers and altering working practices following the transfer of workers, for example through dismissing employees for economic reasons and then re-hiring them under less favourable contracts.

Third, variation in bargaining coverage, or the number of workplaces covered by central collective agreements, may influence employers' ability to use outsourcing to reduce labour costs through varying employment terms and conditions. Companies may seek to use new organisational forms to escape or renegotiate strong collective agreements. This means that the ease of renegotiating agreements can influence employers' cost-benefit calculus. For example, in France, the government typically extends agreements negotiated between the major employers' association and trade unions in a sector to all firms, while in Germany employers must agree to such an extension (which rarely occurs). France has sectoral collective agreements that cover all firms and subsidiaries in major industries like telecommunications and banking, as well as for the contractors that service these industries (Doellgast *et al.* 2009). In Germany, many subcontractors do not have agreements, and firms often form subsidiaries to move work out of stronger sectoral or company agreements (Doellgast and Greer 2007). For example, German banks have set up 'direct banks' for their call centres in order to transfer work to new companies not covered by the sectoral banking agreement. This has largely been uncontested following one unsuccessful strike by workers at Citibank facing redundancy (Holtgrewe 2001). Inclusive sectoral or national bargaining also exists in Austria, Denmark and Spain, among other countries, which may affect firms' ability to vary working conditions across their 'production chain' (Shire *et al.* 2009; Sørensen and Weinkopf 2009).

Finally, differences in union strategies may also affect outsourcing decisions. Worker representatives have distinct interests in keeping work in-house or maintaining a coherent framework of collective bargaining. Sako (2006: 4) argues that unions themselves choose to extend or contract their boundaries, and these decisions can then affect management's choice of a corporate structure. As representation rights regarding outsourcing are often weak, unions may draw on distinct forms of bargaining power in other areas to try to influence employment restructuring decisions. For example, in a comparison of call centre outsourcing strategies, Doellgast (2008) finds that US unions adopted strategic campaigns and strike tactics to extend agreements to new organisations and protect the working conditions of members, while German unions relied more on the co-determination rights of works councillors.

In some cases, unions have tried to organise subcontractors and extend legal regulations to these workplaces in countries or sectors where they are more poorly regulated – which may, in turn, affect the cost and/or skill differential between the in-house and subcontracted workforce. For example, in India a union was recently formed in India's call centre and business process outsourcing sector (Taylor *et al.* 2009). However, these efforts are often limited by the mobility of much subcontracted work and employer resistance in those sectors or activities where there is a perceived need to keep labour costs low as a source of competitive advantage.

International outsourcing within the EU – or nearshoring between EU countries – has created particular challenges for labour unions in recent years. Increasingly, transnational subcontractors in project-based industries employ 'posted workers' on a short-term basis, many of whom are migrants from eastern European countries with weaker labour market regulations. Following the terms of the European Union Posted Workers Directive, posted workers are entitled to the statutory minimum conditions of their host state or sending state, whichever is better from the worker's perspective. However, a series of legal decisions by the European Court of Justice has clarified that governments and unions cannot enforce standards that are not laid out explicitly in the directive and covered by national law. This means that where minimum pay and working conditions are typically set by collective agreement in a host country, these standards cannot legally be enforced. Lillie (2010; 2011ab) has argued that the result is a trend toward increasingly segmented labour markets in industries like construction and shipbuilding, where there is heavy use of posted workers: growing numbers of posted workers are competing with domestic workers who are paid higher wages and have more tightly regulated employment terms and conditions. This suggests that opportunities to 'escape' national regulations and industrial relations institutions through subcontracting can also be shaped by supra-national forms of regulation.

Institutions and strategic choice

The above discussion raises the question of to what extent these national differences in institutions influence the strategic choices of firms. We focus here on staff transfers and layoffs associated with outsourcing, as well as the organisational form adopted.

The results of a survey by Kakabadse and Kakabadse (2002) suggest that the cross-national differences in outsourcing strategies between the more 'liberal' US and more 'social' Europe may not be as large as we might expect. They found that staff were transferred to a supplier following outsourcing in 38 per cent of US and 39 per cent of European companies surveyed; post-transfer redundancies occurred in 28 per cent of US and 24 per cent of European companies; while managers adopted new terms of employment for redeployed workers in 13 per cent of US and 10 per cent of European cases. Although the extent of employment change associated with out-sourcing appears to be somewhat higher in the US, with more firms pursuing redundancies or changing HRM practices, these differences are relatively small.

Other studies find more substantial differences in outsourcing decisions within Europe. Barthelemy and Geyer (2001) conducted a survey of firms undertaking IT outsourcing and found that 69 per cent of these decisions involved personnel transfers and layoffs in France compared to 42 per cent in Germany. They argue this is explained by the greater power of German trade unions, which allows employees to oppose measures disruptive to employees. Grimshaw and Miozzo (2006) con-ducted a similar study of IT outsourcing in Germany and the UK, based on in-depth case studies of 13 outsourcing contracts. They show that all of these contracts involved some staff transfer through direct outsourcing, joint venture, or a captive market subsidiary. However, national differences in consultation rights and the period of protection against dismissal affected how the transfer was managed in each country. In Germany, management typically conducted six months of commu-nications and negotiations with works councils, and demonstrated a stronger determination to win the 'hearts and minds' of IT workers through designing a restructuring process that allowed staff to adjust to changes. In the UK, they found minimal consultation, little labour influence over the transfer, and, subsequently, substantial resistance – in one case resulting in a strike. These procedural differences also resulted in different organisational strategies: the German firms initially adopted joint ventures between client and supplier to transition workers to the subcontractor, because this was viewed as better for employees; while the UK firms all relied on direct outsourcing, with an immediate shift from in-house to externalised provision.

Thus, institutional factors which vary across countries, including legal systems and industrial relations arrangements, can influence employment restructuring decisions associated with outsourcing. Stronger laws protecting employee rights during the transfer of assets or people and more inclusive bargaining systems create constraints on strategic choice, encouraging consultation and discouraging the renegotiation of employment contracts at a lower level. While these constraints may represent short-term costs for firms, they also can have long-term advantages, in terms of higher levels of employee commitment and cooperation with restructuring plans. The Grimshaw and Miozzo (2006) study cited above found that German client firms were more satisfied with the HR practices and service quality of new supplier firms than those in the UK, which they attribute to the more extensive process of consultation in Germany.

Coordination of HRM Across Organisational Boundaries

A further set of HRM challenges associated with outsourcing concerns the co-ordination of management decisions and processes between the relevant organisations. Here we refer to the firm that outsources work as the *client* and the firm that performs the outsourced work as the *subcontractor*. The following areas of HRM tend to be the focus of coordination efforts.

- *Employee selection and skill development*: Clients may seek to establish a common set of standards for employee qualifications and training across their subcontractors. This may be particularly important for higher-skilled jobs or services in which the subcontractors' workers are interacting with the clients' customers.
- *Performance management*: Clients may seek to harmonise incentives to promote shared goals, such as meeting sales or performance targets. Monitoring practices that track individual and group performance are often important for ensuring that standards are met.
- *Work design*: Clients may seek to encourage shared principles of work design, such as use of teams, participation or suggestion initiatives, and the use of shared procedures. This may be most important where employees work with each other across organisations, or in cases where a firm is strongly committed to particular principles of work organisation (such as lean production historically in Japan).
- *Scheduling and staffing*: Clients often demand a certain level of flexibility from subcontractors in adjusting the volume of goods or service production at short notice. This can have a direct effect on scheduling practices, with higher requirements for employees to be flexible with their own schedules, more use of part-time or temporary contracts, and lower job security.

Below we consider the conditions under which client firms are more likely to seek to influence or jointly manage subcontractors' HRM practices. We then discuss the challenges of coordinating HRM across organisational boundaries. Again, we show that national context can have an important influence on management strategy and outcomes, affecting the costs and benefits associated with coordination. In addition, the international character of many outsourcing contracts – and the internationalisation of subcontractors themselves – create distinct coordination challenges.

The decision to coordinate or differentiate HRM practices

It is not obvious that a client should seek to intervene in the HRM decisions of subcontractors or to coordinate these decisions in some way. Companies often outsource certain functions to reduce costs, concentrate on their core competencies, or rely on a specialist organisation's expertise – with the option of terminating the contract or switching providers if quality does not meet expectations. In other words, one of the attractions of outsourcing might be to differentiate HRM between occupational groups. However, there are certain conditions under which a client may have more of an interest in its subcontractors' HRM practices, depending on the nature of the contracted product or service, the extent of joint production carried out across organisations, and the national (or international) context of the contracting relationship.

First, where the product or service is more intangible or complex, contracting firms may take more interest in management practices used at the point of production. In settings such as business services or call centres, services are simultaneously produced and consumed, and thus the client is typically unable to rely on quality control mechanisms used in manufacturing at the point of delivery to prevent 'defective' products from getting to the customer. The reasons for outsourcing this work may also play a role: clients pursuing a business strategy focused on quality rather than cost reduction may be particularly concerned with ensuring that successful practices used in-house are extended to subcontractors, or that workers in the subcontracted firm develop a shared organisational identity with the client firm.

Second, where the outsourcing contract involves substantial collaboration or joint production with in-house staff, the client may encourage the coordination of practices to facilitate cooperation and harmonise incentives. Under so-called 'relational contracting', managers seek to encourage the development of social capital or collective goals across organisations (Dyer and Singh 1998). However, even in more transactional or mixed settings, there can be incentives for developing shared procedures and skills. For example, Rubery et al. (2003) show, in a case study of 'multi-agency' subcontracting relationships in the airline industry, that a high level of interdependence between staff from different organisations meant that employees were subject to 'multiple sources of control and evaluation' as organisations attempted to 'control staff employed by other organisations and through actions designed to encourage these staff members to increase identity with, and thus commitment to, the goals of the client ... organisation' (285).

Third, as stated above, national context can influence strategy concerning HRM coordination. Geographical or cultural distance between the client and subcontractor(s) may have contradictory influences on the extent and goals of coordination. On the one hand, a client may be more likely to allow its sub-contractors to adopt HRM practices that are consistent with the local conditions and business environment. Companies may also be more likely to offshore the pro-duction of products or services that are relatively standardised or easily codified, allowing them to engage in more arms-length contracting. On the other hand, cultural distance may increase uncertainty, leading firms to seek tighter control over HRM. In addition, firms with subcontractors in developing countries are increas-ingly concerned about the negative effects on their image associated with labour standard violations, and thus may establish codes of conduct with monitoring mechanisms to ensure that suppliers meet minimum terms and conditions.

Other national institutions of corporate governance, industrial relations, or tra-ditions of corporate organisation may also influence the extent and nature of HRM coordination. For example, Japanese firms traditionally developed close, trust-based relational contracting with suppliers, based on the *Keiretsu* form of business organi-sation. Core firms sought to influence the promotion, training and work design practices of their subcontractors, even moving employees across firms to adjust to changing demand in different areas of the business. In Germany, strong industry-based unions have coordinated HRM to some extent across core firms and suppliers through sectoral agreements, while strong business associations serve to diffuse best practices and establish shared rules and acceptable behaviour of members. In contrast, US and UK firms have pursued more arms-length contracting relationships, explained in part by weaker organisation of employers, distinct traditions of law, and more decentralised or disorganised industrial relations institutions (Helper 1991; Lane and Bachmann 1997).

Challenges of HRM coordination

Where firms do seek to coordinate HRM across organisational boundaries, a further set of issues concerns the particular challenges clients, subcontractors and employee representatives face in managing coordination and how these may be overcome.

A first set of challenges for client firms concerns the potentially high costs of enforcement or monitoring when seeking to promote a shared set of standards or practices across subcontractors, where they do not now have direct control over management. They thus often develop complex systems for ensuring compliance with contract terms; for example, through assigning special account managers to meet regularly with subcontractors or requiring detailed information on success in meeting training goals or quality targets. Third-party certification through con-sultants also plays an increasingly important role, with the growing popularity of both general certifications such as ISO 9000 and more targeted certification for particular industries or types of work.

A second set of challenges is faced by the subcontractors themselves, as they seek to adapt internal HRM practices to the demands of multiple clients. Contracts with different customers or clients may have widely varying terms concerning quality specifications and flexibility in adjusting the volume of goods or service production at short notice. This, in turn, affects the subcontractor's ability to invest in training or to offer its employees predictable schedules and long-term contracts. In addition, clients may provide different variable incentives or offer contract terms that allow vendors to pay certain employees at a higher level. These difficulties are particularly pronounced in service settings, such as call centres or technical support, in which different groups of employees are 'dedicated' to a particular client. Under these conditions, managers face the potential problem of managing widely varying HRM practices within the firm (and often in one location), as well as dealing with possible negative effects on employee motivation of this internal variation. Grimshaw and Miozzo (2009) found that the global IT services firms EDS and IBM faced the challenge of managing multiple 'employment subsystems', as clients transferred groups of dedicated workers across subcontractors, while seeking to retain partial control over staff skill and expertise.

A third set of challenges exists for worker representatives, such as unions and works councils, which confront the question as to whether and how to coordinate collective bargaining across organisational boundaries. In many countries, HRM practices are regulated by collective agreements at the industry, firm, or establishment level. However, these structures are typically organised around traditional industry or firm boundaries, which may not fit the 'networked firm' model characteristic of outsourcing relationships. Different unions may be responsible for in-house and outsourced firms whose workers carry out similar functions, or, as discussed above, were formerly employed in the same organisation. Improving bargaining coordination between these unions and works councils at different organisations can be quite difficult due to conflicting interests and increased variation in pay and working conditions across in-house and outsourced firms (Doellgast and Greer 2007; Holtgrewe and Doellgast 2012).

These coordination issues usually have an important international dimension. Multinationals face distinctive challenges in coordinating HRM across international borders (see Chapter 5). This can be exacerbated by the fragmented ownership structures associated with subcontracting. Performance management and monitoring practices may be particularly important in helping to facilitate coordination, and thus there may be more focus on standardisation in a multinational setting. For example, Indian call centres have received a lot of attention in the media in recent years for their intensive monitoring practices, with workers' calls often listened to by both internal managers and a series of additional quality control managers from client firms seeking to harmonise standards across subcontractors (Taylor and Bain 2004). A study by Batt *et al.* (2006) showed that subcontracted call centres in the US were more heavily monitored than in-house centres, but that monitoring was even more intensive in offshore settings such as India. In addition, subcontractors themselves are often multinationals, possibly serving other multinational clients. This poses multiple coordination issues as firms seek to provide a standardised service across national boundaries.

This additional focus on coordination and harmonisation can help to ensure a standardised product, but may also have costs, as local managers are constrained from adapting to local conditions. Case study research has shown that outsourced staff often experience reduced skill and discretion as their new employers intensify monitoring (Grugulis and Vincent 2005). The study by Batt *et al.* (2006) cited above found that higher monitoring rates were associated with high employee turnover, indicating possible negative implications in terms of employees' satisfaction and commitment of attempts to control performance management too closely. Yu and Levy (2010) found that radiology professionals working in the Indian offshore sector experienced a deskilling of their work, with negative effects on worker motivation. Another recent UK study found that increased internationalisation of the value chain for IT services contributed to a falling domestic demand for technical IT skills, with negative effects on career development and professionalisation in the sector (Donnelly *et al.* 2011).

The success of companies in responding to these challenges depends on a combination of management strategy and supportive institutions. Donnelly *et al.* (2011) show that collective social actors in the UK largely failed in their attempt to professionalise the workforce in the IT services sector through joint investment in training, due to weak coordination among the actors and marginal support from firms. In contrast, Kuruvilla and Ranganathan (2010) found that in the Indian business process outsourcing industry, high turnover rates among an increasingly mobile, middle-class workforce led companies to experiment with new HRM strategies aimed at improving recruitment, retention and training. These initiatives were complemented by those of actors outside of the firm: industry associations and the state and national governments in India adopted a range of policies aimed at overcoming persistent problems of skill shortages (Kuruvilla and Ranganathan 2008).

The Outsourcing of the HR Function

The outsourcing of HR activities and even of a large part of the HR department is one specific form of outsourcing and offshoring that has very direct effects on HRM. Here we refer to the firm that performs the outsourced work as a *service provider*, consistent with the terminology used in this industry. As we noted in the introduction, firms have long outsourced support services, including HR activities such as recruitment or executive salary and benefit comparisons. In some countries, such as Germany and the Scandinavian countries, firms have also handed over aspects of their dealings with trade unions to employers' organisations, which is, in a way, a form of outsourcing. Here, however, we are primarily concerned with the relatively recent phenomenon of the outsourcing of a significant part of HR departments and HR activities.

Several factors have combined to facilitate the growth of HR outsourcing. These include the development of ICT platforms, pressures to reduce support costs, and the growth of provider companies. Adler (2003) describes several recent trends that have been particularly important: HR departments have been the target of 'belt-tightening' as firms seek to focus on core activities; the HR legal environment has become increasingly complex, requiring subject matter experts (particularly for international firms); M&As create new challenges in managing the cross-border movement of employees; and improvements in HR information systems have made it easier to outsource information in areas such as payroll.

Responding to these trends, several segments of HR service providers have developed. First, specialised consultants supply a particular service, such as recruitment support, pensions planning, or wage and benefit surveys and systems. Second, technology providers supply specialist technological support services such as customised HR software. Third, a growing number of very large providers (such as IBM, Accenture, Exult and HP) provide a wide range of HR services and operate on a global scale. These often involve multi-billion pound deals lasting up to 10 years. Overall, it has been estimated that the global market for HR outsourcing is growing rapidly, and may rise from $30 billion in 2005 to $50 billion by 2010 (Sako and Tierney 2005; Gospel and Sako 2010).

The recent increase in the demand for such services started with a small number of large firms in the private sector in the US and UK. However, in more recent years demand has grown among smaller companies and public sector organisations across countries. National context again appears to have some effect on strategies: firms in countries such as Germany or Japan have preferred to keep more of their HR in-house, perhaps reflecting greater risk aversion and a willingness to continue to accept support services as a fixed cost. However, even in these countries, firms have recently shown a greater willingness to outsource support services. Despite some reversions to insourcing, it is likely that the outsourcing of many aspects of HR will continue (Adler 2003; Gospel and Sako 2010).

Firms face a number of considerations in managing the outsourcing of HR processes. Here we consider initial cost and benefit calculations and then more down-stream decisions about how and what to outsource. First, managers must evaluate the pros and cons of moving these activities to a provider. Advantages are similar to those of other forms of outsourcing, including lower costs through the reduction of overall headcount, the payment of lower salaries, the greater division of labour, and access to better ICT systems, higher quality work with fewer mistakes, especially in routine areas, and the freeing up of internal staff to concentrate on more important strategic or operational matters. Estimates suggest the average annual HR cost per supported employee is between $1,500 and $2,000 when carried out by an outsourced HR service provider, compared to $5,000 in-house (Sako and Tierney 2005). However, there are also disadvantages and risks, such as reduction in morale both among transferred and retained staff, the risk of losing core competencies and control over activities, and the costs of administering what are often very lengthy contracts. Because of the sensitive nature of these contracts and because they often run for up to 10 years, there has been little research to date evaluating these costs and benefits.

Second, managers must decide which HR functions to outsource. For the most part, strategic and high value-added activities will be kept in-house. These usually include the management of senior managers, the development of HR strategy, and the development of HR policy. Sensitive issues such as dealings with works councils and trade unions will also typically be kept in-house. More transactional services are more often outsourced, including the running of HR information systems (including call centres), the administration of recruitment and exits, payroll processing, compensation and benefits, pensions administration, training administration, and expatriate and travel arrangements. Outsourcing the 'transactional' and retaining the 'strategic' activities has been a way in which HR professionals working in different functions have sought to improve their profile within their organisations.

In practice, there are a number of borderline or 'grey' areas where the advantages of outsourcing are more ambiguous. For example, an employee at a manufacturing plant might have a complaint about his or her level of pay. This may seem to be a simple individual issue, for which the facts are easily ascertained and where, if necessary, corrective action can be taken by the service provider. However, several employees may start to make similar complaints, contributing to a collective grievance and possible trade union involvement in an industrial dispute. If payroll is outsourced, it may be unclear who should spot this escalating problem and who should intervene at what stage. Such contingencies are usually set out in the service contract, with procedures for resolving disputes between the user and the provider about 'who does what'. For the most part, however, the parties prefer to deal with these issues through personal contact and trust rather than on a purely contractual basis – and this may become more difficult when one or more service providers are involved. Overall, in deciding what to keep in-house and what to outsource, firms have to think through what aspects of HR add value, based on their core competencies or strategies. (Adler 2003; Gospel and Sako 2010).

Third, managers face the choice among different routes to outsourcing. One decision concerns whether to integrate and transform HR arrangements before handing them over to a provider or to first hand them over and let the provider transform systems (Sako and Tierney 2005). Large multinational companies typically have different HR arrangements that cover distinct product or service areas and geographical areas, which may be the legacy of mergers and acquisitions or a decentralised organisational structure. The decision to transform and integrate these HR systems before outsourcing may allow the firm to form a better opinion about what to outsource and what to keep in-house and to retain knowledge and capability in core areas. The firm will also pay a lower price for the service contract since much of the hard work of integrating and standardising HR will have already been done.

From the 1990s onwards, an increasingly popular strategy for transforming HR systems has been to create a Shared Services Centre (SSC) that brings together business processes shared across units within a company. A recent survey of MNCs in the UK revealed that around one-third of the companies operated an international SSC in the HR function (Edwards *et al.* 2007). A large multinational may establish a limited number of these centres in different parts of the world covering all its global activities. A related decision is then whether to outsource HR for a particular country or region or to do this worldwide. This latter decision will depend on factors that have been discussed elsewhere in this volume, such as how centralised the company already is and whether it has gone down the SSC route (Gospel and Sako 2010).

A final consideration relates to the effects of outsourcing on HR professionals. Here, two main groups should be considered *viz.* those who are transferred or hired by the service provider and those who stay within the firm. The first group are the HR managers who are transferred to or hired by the service provider. On the one hand, some of these employees will have to concentrate on rather narrow areas, losing their ability to perform generalist roles. On the other hand, they are able to move into an organisation specialising in their area, rather than working in a department that is an adjunct to the primary activity of the firm. They may, therefore, feel that their careers have been enhanced. One important consideration for the client is that, at first at least, sufficient ex-employees remain with the provider so as to be able to deliver a satisfactory level of service.

The second group of HR managers are those who stay within the firm. On the one hand, these employees can be freed up from more routine matters and allowed to become so-called 'business partners', where they may work as part of more value-adding line management teams. On the other hand, there may be a continuing need for some 'experts' who will have a more detailed knowledge of one particular area, such as the design of executive compensation plans. There will also be a need for a new class of managers whose job is to administer the contract with the service provider and deal with 'seam' issues when they arise. These include issues that are in grey areas, which have not been sufficiently thought through when the contract was negotiated, or that are new to the contract; for example, when an acquisition is made and new employee groups have to be integrated in the contract (Gospel and Sako 2010; Ulrich 1997).

Conclusions

The management of outsourcing is increasingly important to the HRM strategies of both national and international firms. This chapter has presented a number of issues that managers face in deciding to outsource various aspects of production or service provision and in managing contracts with subcontractors. On the basis of this discussion, we can draw several broad conclusions concerning the role of national context and firm strategies in outsourcing decisions.

First, while management faces an increasing range of choices concerning the structure of outsourcing and activities outsourced, these choices are often influenced by distinctive institutional constraints. Transfer of undertakings rules, industrial relations institutions, and the strategies of trade unions and other worker representatives can affect the cost of outsourcing and its impact on employees. Continental Europe stands out as having stronger protections than those in most other parts of the world, including organised consultation mechanisms to ensure that employee interests are considered in outsourcing decisions.

Second, however, firms may increasingly be able to by-pass or circumvent these constraints. Outsourcing may weaken collective bargaining institutions; for example, by moving work outside of establishments covered by collective agreements or disrupting coordinated bargaining across a firm's production network. The threat of outsourcing or offshoring may allow firms to gain concessions from worker representatives. The HR function itself within large multinationals is increasingly shifted to SSCs, and then often transferred to outsourced providers. This drives standardisation and benchmarking of practices across countries, creating pressure to adopt a common HRM strategy across organisations or regions.

All of this suggests that outsourcing will remain a contentious (and contested) area of firm strategy. Consideration of this phenomenon has shed further light on the extent to which firms are embedded in distinct contexts, demonstrating that they have increasing scope to globalise their operations. We have also seen that as they do so, they face competing incentives to differentiate the way that different occupational groups are managed but also to achieve a degree of integration across them. Managing the process of outsourcing and its long-term effects on employees will be an increasingly important area for international HRM practitioners.

REFERENCES

Adler, P. S. 2003: 'Making the HR Outsourcing Decision', *MIT Sloan Management Review*, **45**(1), 53–60.

Araki, T. 2005: Corporate Governance, Labour, and Employment Relations in Japan: The Future of the Stakeholder Model, in H. Gospel and A. Pendleton (eds.), *Corporate Governance and Labour Management*, 254–283. Oxford: Oxford University Press.

Barthelemy, J. and Geyer, D. 2001: IT Outsourcing: Evidence from France and Germany', *European Management Journal*, **19**(2), 195–202.

Batt, R., Doellgast, V. and Kwon, H. 2006: Service Management and Employment Systems in U.S. and Indian Call Centers, in S.M. Collins and L. Brainard (eds.), *Offshoring White-Collar Work*, Washington, D.C.: Brookings Institution Press.

Caprile, M. and Llorens, C. 2000: *Outsourcing and industrial relations in motor manufacturing 2000* [cited February 2005. Available from http://www.eiro.eurofound.eu.int/2000/08/study/tn0008201s.html.

Coase, R. H. 1937: The Nature of the Firm. *Economica*, **4**, 386–405.

Cooke, F., Earnshaw, L., Marchington, M. and Rubery, J. 2004: For better and for worse: transfer of undertakings and the reshaping of employment relations, *International Journal of Human Resource Management*, **15**(2), 276–294.

Doellgast, V. 2008: National industrial relations and local bargaining power in the US and German telecommunications industries, *European Journal of Industrial Relations*, **14**(3), 265–287.

Doellgast, V. and Gospel, H. 2011: 'Outsourcing and International HRM' in T. Edwards and C. Rees *International Human Resource Management*, Harlow: Pearson.

Doellgast, V. and Greer, I. 2007: Vertical Disintegration and the Disorganization of German Industrial Relations, *British Journal of Industrial Relations*, **45**(1), 55–76.

Doellgast, V., Nohara, H. and Tchobanian, R. 2009: Institutional Change and the Restructuring of Service Work in the French and German Telecommunications Industries, *European Journal of Industrial, Relations*, **15**(4), 373–394.

Donnelly, R., Grimshaw, D. and, Miozzo, M. 2011: Does the UK have a 'comparative institutional advantage' that is supportive of the IT services sector?, *New Technology, Work and Employment*, **26**(2), 98–112.

Dyer, J. H. and Singh, H. 1998: The Relational View: Cooperative Strategy and Sources of Interorganizational Competitive Advantage, *The Academy of Management Review*, **23**(4), 660–679.

Edwards, P., Edwards, T., Ferner, A., Marginson, P. and Tregaskis, O. 2007: 'Employment Practices of MNCs in Organisational Context: A Large Scale Survey', Survey Report, http://www2.warwick.ac.uk/fac/soc/wbs/projects/mncemployment/

Eurofound 2007: Acquired Rights Directive. Review of Reviewed Item. *European Foundation for the Improvement of Living and Working Conditions, European Industrial Relations Dictionary*, http://www.eurofound.europa.eu/areas/industrialrelations/dictionary/definitions/acquiredrightsdirective.htm.

Gospel, H. and Sako, M. 2010: The Re-bundling of Corporate Functions: The Evolution of Shared Services and Outsourcing in Human Resource Management, *Industrial & Corporate Change*, **19**(5), 1367–1396.

Grimshaw, D. and Miozzo, M. 2006: Institutional Effects on the IT Outsourcing Market: Analysing Clients, Suppliers and Staff Transfer in Germany and the UK, *Organisation Studies*, **27**(9), 1229–1259.

Grimshaw, D. and Miozzo, M. 2009: New human resource management practices in knowledge-intensive business services firms: The case of outsourcing with staff transfer, *Human Relations*, **62**, 1521–1550.

Grugulis, I. and Vincent, S. 2005: Changing boundaries, shaping skills: The fragmented organisational form and employee skills, in M. Marchington, D. Grimshaw, J. Rubery and H. Willmott (eds.), *Fragmenting work: Blurring organizational boundaries and disordering hierarchies*, 199–216. Oxford: Oxford University Press.

Helper, S. 1991: How much has really changed between U.S. automakers and their suppliers, *Sloan Management Review*, 15–28.

Holtgrewe, U. 2001: Recognition, Intersubjectivity and Service Work: Labour Conflicts in Call Centres, *Industrielle Beziehungen*, **8**(1), 37–54.

Holtgrewe, U. and Doellgast, V. 2012: A service union's innovation dilemma: Limitations on creative action in German industrial relations, *Work, Employment and Society*, **26**(2), 314–330.

IMF 2007: *World Economic Outlook*, International Monetary Fund, Washington.

Justice, E. C. O. 2002: Temco Service Industries SA, Judgement of the Court (Sixth Chamber), Directive 77/187/EEC – Safeguarding of employees' rights in the event of transfers of undertakings, 24 January 2002. Review of Reviewed Item, http://curia.europa.eu/jurisp/cgi-bin/gettext.pl?lang=en&num=79979875C19000051&doc=T&ouvert=T&seance=ARRET&where=().

Kakabadse, A. and Kakabadse, N. 2002: Trends in Outsourcing: Contrasting USA and Europe, *European Management Journal*, **20**(2), 189–198.

Kessler, I., Coyle-Shapiro, J. and Purcell, J. 1999: Outsourcing and the employee perspective, *Human Resource Management Journal*, **9**(2), 5–19.

Kuruvilla, S. and Ranganathan, A. 2010: Globalisation and outsourcing: confronting new human resource challenges in India's business process outsourcing industry, *Industrial Relations Journal*, **41**(2), 136–153.

Kuruvilla, S. and Ranganathan, A. 2008: Economic Development Strategies and Macro and Micro Level Human Resource Policies: The Case of India's Outsourcing Industry, *Industrial and Labor Relations Review*, **62**(1), 39–72.

Lane, C. and Bachmann, R. 1997: Co-operation in Inter-firm Relations in Britain and Germany: The Role of Social Institutions, *British Journal of Sociology*, **48**(2), 226–254.

Langlois, R. N. 2003: The Vanishing Hand: The Changing Dynamics of Industrial Capitalism, *Industrial and Corporate Change*, **12**(2), 351–385.

Lillie, N. 2010: Bringing the Offshore Ashore: Transnational Production, Industrial Relations and the Reconfiguration of Sovereignty, *International Studies Quarterly*, **54**(3), 683–704.

Lillie, N. 2011a: National Unions and Transnational Workers: The Case of Olkiluoto 3, Finland, *Work Employment & Society*, **25**(2), 292–308.

Lillie, N. 2011b: Subcontracting, Posted Migrants and Labour Market Segmentation in Finland, *British Journal of Industrial Relations*, early view 17 May 2011.

Logan, M., Faught, K. and Ganster, D. 2004: Outsourcing a satisfied and committed workforce: A trucking industry case study, *International Journal of HRM*, **15**, 147–162.

Miozzo, M. and Grimshaw, D. 2011: Capabilities of large services outsourcing firms: the "outsourcing plus staff transfer model" in EDS and IBM, *Industrial and Corporate Change*, **20**(3), 909–940.

OECD 2007a: *Economic Outlook*, Organisation for Economic Cooperation and Development, Paris.

OECD 2007b: *Offshoring and Employment: Trends and Impacts*, Organisation for Economic Cooperation and Development, Paris.

Porter, M.E. 1985: *Competitive Advantage: Creating and Sustaining Superior Performance*. New York: The Free Press.

Rubery, J., Cooke, F.-L., Earnshaw, J. and Marchington, M. 2003: Inter-organisational Relations and Employment in a Multi-employer Environment, *British Journal of Industrial Relations*, **41**(2), 265–289.

Sako, M. 2006: *Shifting Boundaries of the Firm: Japanese Company – Japanese Labour*. Oxford: Oxford University Press.

Sako, M. and Jackson, G. 2006: Strategy Meets Institutions: The Transformation of Labor Relations at Deutsche Telekom and NTT, *Industrial and Labor Relations Review*, **59**(3), 347–366.

Sako, M. and Tierney, A. 2005: Sustainability of Business Service Outsourcing: The Case of Human Resource Outsourcing, *AIM Research Working Paper*, 19 June 2005.

Shire, K., Schönauer, A., Valverde, M. and Mottweiler, H. 2009: Collective Bargaining and Temporary Contracts in Call Centre Employment in Austria, Germany and Spain, *European Journal of Industrial Relations*, **15**(4), 437–456.

Sørensen, O. and Weinkopf, C. 2009: Pay and Working Conditions in Finance and Utility Call Centres in Denmark and Germany, *European Journal of Industrial Relations*, **15**(4), 395–416.

Taylor, P. and Bain, P. 2004; 'India Calling to the Far Away Towns': The Call Centre Labour Process and Globalisation, *Work, Employment and Society*, **19**(2), 261–282.

Taylor, P., D'Cruz, P., Noronha, E. and Scholarios, D. 2009: Indian Call Centres and Business Process Outsourcing: A Study in Union Formation, *New Technology, Work and Employment*, **24**(1), 19–42.

Ulrich, D. 1997: *Human Resource Champions*. Boston, MA: Harvard Business School Press.

Williamson, O. E. 1975: *Markets and Hierarchies: Analysis and Antitrust Implications*, New York: Free Press.

Yu, K.-H. and Levy, F. 2010: Offshoring Professional Services: Institutions and Professional Control, *British Journal of Industrial Relations*, **48**(4), 758–783.

CHAPTER SIXTEEN

Employee Engagement: An Evidence-based Review

Riccardo Peccei

Introduction

Employee work engagement is a relatively new construct that was first introduced in the academic literature in the early 1990s (Kahn 1990, 1992). However, because of its presumed positive effect on a range of important employee and organisational outcomes, such as job satisfaction, organisational commitment and various aspects of job and organisational performance (Halbesleben 2010), the notion of engagement has attracted increasing interest amongst organisational scholars and practitioners alike over the past decade (Schaufeli and Bakker 2010). On the academic side, this growing interest is reflected in the publication, in the past few years, of two major edited books (Albrecht 2010a; Bakker and Leiter 2010a) and three journal special issues on engagement (*European Journal of Work and Organizational Psychology*, 1, 2011: *Industrial and Organizational Psychology*, 1, 2008; *Work and Stress*, 3, 2008), as well as several large-scale meta-analyses of the relationship between engagement and its main correlates, antecedents and outcomes (Christian *et al.* 2011; Cole, *et al.* 2011; Crawford *et al.* 2010; Halbesleben 2010; Newman *et al.* 2010). The interest on the practitioner side has been even greater. This is reflected in the growing emphasis placed by organisations, management consultancies and policy-makers on employee engagement in the last few years (Vance 2006), including the recent publication of an official government sponsored report on the topic in the UK (MacLeod and Clarke 2009). Employee engagement, in fact, is routinely claimed by many human resource consultancy firms to be central to organisational success and is increasingly regarded by management in both the private and public sectors as a key business priority (MacLeod and Clarke 2009).

Despite this growing interest, however, there is still no clear agreement about the meaning of work engagement and how it should be measured. There are also important unanswered questions about the antecedents and consequences of engagement for both employees and organisations. For example, claims about the benefits of employee engagement and, in particular, about the importance of engagement for business success, are especially common in the practitioner literature (Vance 2006). As noted by Schaufeli and Bakker (2010), however, these claims are not necessarily based on systematic research or scientific evidence. They therefore require closer and more critical scrutiny. The aim of the present chapter is to address these issues by providing an up-to-date evidence-based review of the engagement area, focusing specifically on the nature, antecedents and consequences of employee engagement at work. To this end, I first critically examine the main ways in which work engagement (WE) has been conceptualised and measured in the extant literature, followed by a review of the key antecedents and outcomes of engagement at work. The chapter concludes by highlighting important directions for future research.

The general framework underpinning the review and its overall coverage are summarised in Figure 16.1. In this context it is important to emphasise that, as important as the antecedents and consequences of engagement are, the first priority of the present review is to explore the problems and issues surrounding the meaning and measurement of the notion of engagement itself. The reason for this is that unless basic problems of conceptualisation and operationalisation are addressed and resolved, there is little hope of making substantive, systematic progress in the study of engagement. This position is reflected in the balance of the present review. Thus, even though both the antecedents and consequences of work engagement are examined, relatively more space is devoted in the review to a consideration of the meaning of engagement, including a discussion of current debates about the theoretical and empirical distinctiveness of the WE construct.

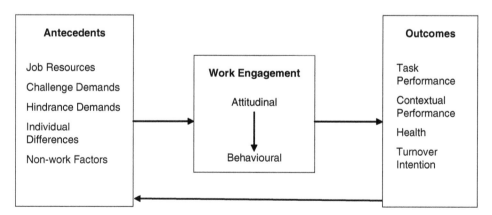

Figure 16.1 Overall framework of antecedents and outcomes of employee work engagement

Note: Only main effects are shown in the figure (i.e. potential interaction effects are excluded). Main potential correlates of work engagement (e.g. job satisfaction, organisational commitment, job involvement) are discussed in the text but are excluded from the figure.

Key Approaches to the Conceptualisation and Measurement of Work Engagement

As noted, the focus here is on employees' engagement with their job or work, including specific tasks or activities that are part of the job. Before examining the notion of work engagement in greater detail, however, it is important to highlight two points in order to clarify the focus and conceptual boundaries of the present analysis. The first point has to do with the fact that work engagement is not the only type of engagement that has been identified in the literature. The most common other type of engagement that is identified, particularly in the applied management literature, is the engagement of employees with their organisation as a whole (Vance 2006). The main problem with the notion of organisationally-focused engagement is that this construct is commonly conceptualised in terms of employees' overall commitment to and/or satisfaction with their organisation and, as such, is virtually indistinguishable from existing constructs designed to capture individuals' general attitude towards their employing organisation (Saks 2006). Here, therefore, while acknowledging the possibility of different focuses of engagement, I will not examine the notion of organisational engagement any further and will, instead, focus the discussion on the more distinctive concept of work engagement.

The second and related point has to do with the way in which work engagement is defined in the applied management literature. Over the past decade a growing number of consultancy firms have developed their own particular approach to employee engagement, leading to a proliferation of definitions and measures. With the possible exception of Gallup's Q^{12} employee engagement scale, none of these measures have been subjected to systematic scrutiny and testing (Wefald and Downey 2009). As noted by a number of researchers (Schaufeli and Bakker 2010; Macey and Schneider 2008), a key feature of these practitioner-based conceptualisations is that, by and large, they do not focus on engagement itself, but rather, tend to define engagement in terms of its correlates, antecedents or consequences. Gallup's Q^{12} scale, for instance, does not actually assess individuals' experience of engagement as such, but rather, as argued by Schaufeli and Bakker (2010: 15), it measures the '*antecedents* of engagement in terms of perceived job resources'. In a similar vein, the UK's Chartered Institute of Personnel and Development (CIPD) defines employee engagement in terms of some of its potential correlates and consequences, such as aspects of organisational commitment and citizenship behaviour, arguing that engagement 'can be seen as a combination of commitment to the organisation and its values and a willingness to help colleagues' (www.cipd.co.uk). More generally, definitions of engagement in the practitioner literature vary substantially and include issues such as personal support from one's supervisor, recognition for one's contribution, job satisfaction, commitment, intention to stay, job performance and discretionary effort (MacLeod and Clarke 2009; Wefald and Downey 2009). Here I will not focus on these various definitions.

Useful summaries and critiques of industry approaches to engagement, including critiques of some of the most popular engagement scales used by organisations, such as Gallup's Q^{12} scale, can be found in Wefald and Downey (2009) and Schaufeli and Bakker (2010). Instead, I will concentrate on the main approaches to work engagement that have been proposed in the academic literature.

There are a number of conceptualisations of work engagement in the academic literature (Macey and Schneider 2008; Schaufeli and Bakker 2010). By and large, these different conceptualisations fall into two main categories, namely, those that view work engagement as a psychological state or attitude and those that view it as a form of behaviour (Macey and Schneider 2008). The attitudinal approach to WE is best exemplified by the work of Schaufeli, Bakker and colleagues (Schaufeli *et al.* 2006; Schaufeli *et al.* 2002), while the behavioural approach is best represented by the stream of research based on the work of Kahn (1990, 1992). Each of these approaches will be considered in turn. However, when reviewing the attitudinal approach I also consider a temporal dimension and draw attention to the distinction emphasised by Sonnentag and her colleagues (Sonnentag 2003; Sonnentag *et al.* 2008) between work engagement as a relatively stable phenomenon and engagement as a more temporary or transient psychological state that may fluctuate on a weekly or even a daily basis and vary, for example, depending on the particular tasks being undertaken. I start with a critical evaluation of the attitudinal approach to work engagement.

Attitudinal approach: work engagement as a psychological state

The dominant conceptualisation of work engagement in the academic literature is that proposed by Schaufeli, Bakker and colleagues (Schaufeli *et al.* 2002; Schaufeli *et al.* 2006) in a series of articles published in the early 2000s and measured with the Utrecht Work Engagement Scale (UWES). Here, work engagement is explicitly viewed as a relatively stable, positive, affective-cognitive psychological state. Specifically, Schaufeli *et al.* (2002: 74) define work engagement as 'a positive, fulfilling, work-related state of mind that is characterised by vigour, dedication and absorption'. Vigour refers to 'high levels of energy and mental resilience while working, the willingness to invest effort in one's work, and persistence even in the face of difficulties', while dedication is characterised by feelings of significance, inspiration, pride, enthusiasm and challenge. Absorption refers to 'being fully concentrated and engrossed in one's work' (Schaufeli *et al.* 2002: 74-75).

This particular conceptualisation of WE as a relatively stable three-dimensional psychological construct, measured with either the nine or the 17-item version of the UWES (see Table 2.3 in Schaufeli and Bakker 2010: 17), is the most widely used approach to the study of work engagement in the academic literature, one that has been employed in dozens of studies covering a wide range of employees in a number of different countries (Shimazu *et al.* 2010). However, a key question that needs to be asked of any new construct in the social sciences, including the notion of attitudinal work engagement, or AWE for short, is whether it is conceptually and empirically distinct from existing, potentially related constructs in the area. As a number of scholars (Le *et al.* 2010; Schwab 1980) have argued, failure to establish the discriminant validity of new constructs relative to existing constructs is a particularly acute problem in organisational research, since it results in the unnecessary proliferation of constructs and in construct redundancy.

The problem of construct redundancy is particularly marked with respect to the attitudinal approach to work engagement for two reasons. First, as a positive affective-cognitive psychological state, AWE is likely to overlap conceptually with a number of other well-established work-related constructs including, for example, job satisfaction, organisational commitment, job involvement and burnout (Christian *et al.* 2011; Cole *et al.* 2011; Halbesleben 2010; Newman and Harrison 2008). Second, even if engagement can be argued to be theoretically and conceptually distinct from these other constructs, there remains the question of the empirical distinctiveness of AWE, in this case, as measured by the UWES. As suggested by Le *et al.* (2010: 113), although for two constructs to be considered distinct they must be both conceptually and empirically non-redundant, empirical distinctiveness is key since 'constructs can be conceptually distinct but empirically redundant'. Here, therefore, the focus is primarily on the empirical distinctiveness or otherwise of the AWE construct, as measured by the UWES. The need to explore the empirical non-redundancy of this construct is all the more important because, as Newman and Harrison (2008) have noted, the vast majority of the UWES items are virtually identical to items found in pre-existing, well-established measures of organisational commitment, job satisfaction, job involvement and positive job affect.

As noted by Le *et al.* (2010), two constructs can be said to be empirically distinct and non-redundant if, after downward bias created by measurement artifacts is corrected for, (a) they do not correlate very highly (1.00 or near to 1.00), and (b) they do not exhibit a similar pattern of correlations with other key antecedents and/or outcome variables in a coherent nomological network. Before examining the evidence in relation to these two key criteria, it is important to note that establishing the empirical distinctiveness of AWE is made more difficult by the fact that the conceptualisation of this construct has, to some extent, evolved over time. In particular, there is a growing tendency to downplay the importance of absorption in recent conceptualisations of AWE and to focus just on vigour and dedication as the 'core' of engagement (Bakker *et al.* 2011b; Schaufeli and Salanova 2011). As discussed more fully below, this redefinition of attitudinal engagement excluding the absorption component is particularly problematic when trying to establish the discriminant validity of AWE in relation to burnout.

To explore the discriminant validity of attitudinal engagement I relied primarily on data from four recent meta-analyses that have examined the relationship between AWE, measured with the UWES, and a range of cognate constructs (Christian *et al.* 2011; Cole *et al.* 2011; Halbesleben 2010; Newman *et al.*, 2010). These four quantitative reviews, based on scores of studies covering many thousands of respondents, provide the most robust, comprehensive and up-to-date evidence available about the empirical distinctiveness of AWE.

Attitudinal engagement and workaholism

Overall, the evidence concerning the distinctiveness of attitudinal engagement is quite mixed. In terms of the relationship between AWE and workaholism, the evidence, although not based on meta-analytic results, is generally supportive. Workaholism is commonly defined in terms of a strong inner drive to work hard, in combination with high effort expenditure (i.e. working excessively and compulsively) (Schaufeli *et al.* 2008). As such, it shares some of the same conceptual space as attitudinal engagement (Taris *et al.* 2010). As noted by Taris *et al.* (2010), all the empirical evidence suggests that AWE and workaholism are interrelated but separate constructs. Moreover, the pattern of relationships of engagement and workhaholism with a range of other work characteristics, work outcomes and health-related variables is sufficiently different to suggest that AWE and workaholism are indeed empirically distinct constructs (Taris *et al.* 2010).

Attitudinal engagement, job satisfaction, organisational commitment and job involvement

In contrast, the picture in relation to classical job attitudes, including job satisfaction (JS), organisational commitment (OC) and job involvement (JI), is less clear. On the positive side, although the meta-analytic corrected correlations between AWE and JS, OC and JI are all high, ranging from 0.52 to 0.59 (Christian *et al.* 2011), they fall considerably short of unity, indicating discriminant validity (Le *et al.* 2010). Based on these results, therefore, it would appear that although attitudinal engagement is clearly related to job satisfaction, organisational commitment and job involvement, and shares some of the same conceptual space as these three key job attitudes, it nevertheless is a separate construct in its own right. In other words, contrary to what is sometimes claimed in the literature (Macey and Schneider 2008; Newman and Harrison 2008), attitudinal engagement would not appear simply to be 'old wines in new bottles'. Rather, it is a separate construct that is conceptually and empirically distinct from a number of other well-established job attitudes.

In contrast, however, Newman *et al.* (2010) in their meta-analysis show that there is a very strong overlap between AWE and an overall higher-order job attitude factor comprising JS, OC and JI. The corrected meta-analytic correlation between engagement and this higher-order so-called 'A-factor' is 0.77. On this basis, Newman *et al.* (2010: 55) conclude that 'employee engagement as measured by the UWES is largely redundant with the A-factor', suggesting that the incremental explanatory value of AWE, above and beyond that of well-established job attitudes, may well be limited.

Attitudinal engagement and job burnout

The relationship between attitudinal engagement and job burnout is also quite complex and subject to continuing debate. Burnout is commonly defined as a negative psychological state characterised by mental fatigue (emotional exhaustion), a distant attitude towards one's work (cynicism) and reduced personal efficacy (Maslach *et al.* 2001), with emotional exhaustion and cynicism increasingly coming to be regarded as the 'core' of burnout (Schaufeli and Taris 2005).

There are two main views about the relationship between attitudinal engagement and burnout. The first view considers engagement as the polar opposite of burnout (Maslach *et al.* 2001; Schaufeli and Bakker 2010). In other words, engagement and burnout are thought to constitute opposite ends of a common continuum and are therefore said to represent 'two sides of the same coin' (Bakker *et al.* 2011b). Indeed, in line with the growing interest in positive psychology, when the notion of atti-tudinal engagement was first proposed, it was explicitly presented as the positive antipode of burnout (Bakker *et al.* 2008). In particular, the vigour and dedication dimensions of engagement are said to be the direct opposites of the exhaustion and cynicism dimensions of burnout (Schaufeli *et al.* 2002). To the extent, therefore, that there is a tendency to conceptualise attitudinal engagement primarily in terms of vigour and dedication, and burnout primarily in terms of exhaustion and cynicism, the conceptual and empirical overlap between the two constructs is likely to be considerable (Cole *et al.* 2011). The second view considers engagement and burnout to be independent states that, although negatively related, can, to some extent, vary independently of each other (Cole *et al.* 2011; Schaufeli and Bakker 2004). In other words, engagement and burnout are not just thought to be opposite ends of a single continuum. Rather, they are distinct concepts in their own right and can, therefore, be said to represent 'two different coins' (Schaufeli and Salanova 2011).

The relationship between engagement and burnout has been examined in a large number of individual studies and reviewed and summarised in the recent meta-analyses by Halbesleben (2010), Crawford *et al.* (2010) and Cole *et al.* (2011). Here the focus will be on the results of Cole *et al.*'s (2011) meta-analysis since these researchers provide the most detailed and comprehensive quantitative review of the engagement-burnout relationship, focusing specifically on studies that have employed the UWES.

Three points stand out. First, Cole *et al.* (2011) show that the underlying dimensions of engagement and burnout (measured with the Maslach Burnout Inventory) are relatively highly negatively interrelated, with an average corrected correlation of - 0.55. But even though the dimensions of engagement and burnout are not perfectly negatively correlated, supporting the view that the two constructs are 'two separate coins' rather than 'opposite sides of the same coin', engagement and burnout nevertheless share considerable variance. A meta-analytic confirmatory factor analysis (CFA) model 'allowing for substantial cross-loadings between burnout and engagement' significantly outperformed alternative models, including one where the dimensions of engagement and burnout loaded only on their respective constructs (Cole *et al.* 2011: 16). Second, with the exception of job demands, the various dimensions of engagement and burnout exhibit a very similar, if not nearly identical, pattern of association with a range of important antecedent and outcome variables. Finally, Cole *et al.* (2011) found that the effect sizes associated with the engagement dimensions were substantially reduced once the burnout dimensions were controlled for in meta-regressions predicting job satisfaction, organisational commitment and health complaints, thereby raising serious doubts about the incremental validity of engagement. Taken together these results not only fail to support the discriminant validity of AWE relative to burnout, but also question the added explanatory value of the attitudinal engagement construct, suggesting that it may be largely empirically redundant with burnout.

Overall, the evidence reviewed above raises serious concerns, at the very least, about both the discriminant and incremental validity of attitudinal engagement relative to a number of other well-established job attitudes, including job satisfaction, organisational commitment, job involvement and burnout. As suggested by Parker and Griffin (2011), however, it is also important to locate attitudinal engagement in a wider nomological net of motivational work constructs. As argued by Bakker et al. (2011b), a key feature of attitudinal work engagement is that it represents a proactive, positive psychological state combining both pleasure and activation. Conceptually and empirically, therefore, there may be considerable overlap between AWE and a number of other proactive psychological states and motivational work constructs, such as positive affect and mood at work (Fisher 2000; Warr 1994), a proactive work orientation (Parker 2000), intrinsic work motivation (Deci and Ryan 1985) and psychological empowerment (Spreitzer 1995). The conceptual and empirical relationship between engagement and these various proactive psychological and motivational states has not been examined systematically to date and hence, as argued by Parker and Griffin (2011), requires further attention.

State work engagement

In recent years there has been growing interest in intra-individual variations in attitudinal work engagement over time. That is, in the idea that individuals' engagement at work may be quite variable and fluctuate from week to week, day to day, or even from hour to hour depending on the particular work tasks and activities involved (Sonnentag 2003; Sonnentag 2011; Sonnentag et al. 2008; Xanthopoulou et al. 2008). Sonnentag et al. (2010b) have labelled this more momentary and transient form of work engagement that fluctuates within individuals within short periods of time, state work engagement (SWE).

Quantitative studies of SWE based on diary techniques using adapted versions of the UWES have demonstrated that there can be substantial weekly and daily within-individual fluctuations in work engagement, above and beyond any more stable and durable between-individual differences in overall levels of AWE (Bakker and Bal 2010; Sonnentag 2003). Not surprisingly, the analysis of SWE is increasingly argued to be central to gaining a better understanding of the nature and dynamics of engagement at work (Bakker and Leiter 2010b; Sonnentag 2011). As emphasised by Sonnentag et al. (2010b), however, research on SWE is still limited so there remain important, unanswered questions about the conceptualisation and measurement of state engagement. Particularly important is whether state work engagement is best conceptualised as a three-dimensional construct involving the same vigour, dedication and absorption dimensions as more enduring attitudinal engagement, and whether SWE should indeed be measured with the UWES, albeit using different time anchors for the items (Sonnentag 2011).

Behavioural work engagement

The behavioural approach to work engagement is rooted in the work of Khan (1990, 1992) and represents the main alternative to the attitudinal perspective reviewed above. The behavioural approach is particularly popular with US researchers who, by and large, have tended to ignore the attitudinal approach in favour of a conceptualisation that views work engagement in explicitly behavioural terms – as a directly observable behaviour in the job context rather than as a psychological state.

Behavioural work engagement, or BWE for short, has been conceptualised in a number of ways in the academic literature. Harrison *et al.* (2006: 316), for example, define behavioural engagement as 'a general tendency of employees to contribute desirable inputs towards their work roles rather than withholding those inputs', suggesting that engagement is a broad higher-order behavioural construct that captures the overlap among job performance, organisational citizenship behaviour and various aspects of withdrawal, such as lateness, absence and turnover (Newman and Harrison 2008; Newman *et al.* 2010). However, the best known conceptualisation of BWE is that provided by Kahn (1990, 1992) who views engagement at work as a separate motivational behavioural construct in its own right. Specifically, Kahn (1990, 1992) conceptualises engagement as the harnessing by employees of their full selves to their work roles by investing high levels of personal physical, cognitive and emotional energy into the performance of their job. Engaged individuals invest physical effort into their job, are cognitively vigilant and attentive, and are emotionally connected to their work. In other words, engagement 'involves investing the 'hands, head and heart' in active, full work performance' (Rich *et al.* 2010: 619).

Importantly, behavioural engagement, like attitudinal engagement, can vary not only between individuals, but also within individuals over time and across tasks. Employees' propensity to invest physical, cognitive and emotional energy in their work may, for instance, fluctuate from week to week, day to day, or even hour to hour. It may also vary depending on the particular tasks involved. Behavioural engagement as conceptualised by Khan (1990, 1992), therefore, represents a genuine alternative to notions of attitudinal and state work engagement currently dominant in the academic literature.

Research focusing specifically on behavioural work engagement is relatively limited, however. Consequently, little or no systematic evidence is available about the distinctiveness of BWE relative to other potentially overlapping attitudinal and behavioural constructs in the area. Rich *et al.* (2010), for example, argue that because BWE involves the simultaneous investment of physical, cognitive and emotional energy, it is broader and therefore different from narrower motivational constructs such as job involvement, job satisfaction and intrinsic motivation. Similarly, it can be argued that because behavioural engagement is a general construct that does not specify any particular action, it is conceptually different from a range of more specific or targeted proactive work behaviours, such as taking charge, personal initiative, and various forms of innovative and continuous improvement behaviour (Bindl and Parker 2010; Crant 2000; Griffin *et al.* 2007). However, the empirical relation between BWE and these various other constructs has not been examined in any detail by researchers, thereby making it difficult to judge the actual discriminant and incremental validity of behavioural engagement.

The situation is made more difficult by the fact that there is no widely accepted measure of BWE in the literature comparable to the UWES for attitudinal engagement. Recently, however, Rich *et al.* (2010) have proposed an 18–item measure of BWE designed to assess the extent to which individuals, in line with Kahn's (1990, 1992) conceptualisation, invest physical, cognitive and emotional energy in their work. Although this is a welcome contribution to the measurement of BWE, some aspects of the measure are in need of clarification. In particular, it is not clear whether the emotional engagement items in the scale provide an appropriate behavioural operationalisation of the notion of investment of emotional energy, one of the three key components of behavioural engagement. Many of the items appear to be little more than a rephrasing of items designed to measure feelings of positive affect at work, thereby raising questions about their inclusion in a behavioural engagement scale. More generally, further thought needs to be given to what the notion of investment of emotional energy at work actually means and how it might best be operationalised in behavioural terms.

In summary, there is a rich and impressive stream of work based on the attitudinal approach to work engagement. All the main contributors to this stream of research strongly argue in favour of treating work engagement as a positive motivational psychological state involving feelings of vigour, dedication and possibly also absorption (Bakker *et al.* 2011a, 2011b; Schaufeli *et al.* 2002; Schaufeli and Salanova 2010; Sonnentag 2011). However, there is substantial evidence questioning the discriminant and incremental validity of AWE, suggesting that the notion of attitudinal engagement, as currently conceptualised and operationalised, may need some rethinking. At the same time, more work also needs to be done in terms of the notion of state work engagement and its measurement. The notion of behavioural work engagement linked to Kahn's (1990, 1992) contribution, provides an interesting and potentially promising way forward for engagement research. Although intuitively appealing and, as argued by Newman and Harrison (2008: 34), more in line with practitioners' interest in 'bottom–line behavioural results', the concept of behavioural engagement still requires considerably more work, both conceptually and empirically. In particular, there is a need explicitly to compare behavioural with attitudinal notions and measures of engagement as a basis for gaining a better understanding of the nature of these constructs and their interrelation (for a similar point see Sonnentag 2011).

This is all the more important because recent meta-analyses (Christian *et al.* 2011; Crawford *et al.* 2010; Halbesleben 2010) show that the relationship between work engagement and a wide range of potential correlates, antecedents and outcomes does not vary significantly depending on the particular measure of engagement (mainly UWES vs. non-UWES) used in the analysis. The non-UWES analyses are not necessarily based only on behavioural measures of engagement. They also include meta-correlations incorporating some attitudinal measures that are not UWES-based. However, to the extent that the non-UWES measures are behaviourally based, the similarity in the pattern of meta-correlations across measures suggests a marked empirical overlap between attitudinal and behavioural notions of engagement. This overlap may, in part, be a function of strong underlying causal links between the attitudinal and behavioural manifestations of engagement. Nevertheless, the observed lack of empirical differentiation in patterns of meta-correlations raises important questions that need to be addressed about underlying differences and links between attitudinal and behavioural approaches to engagement, about overall construct redundancy in this area, and about the best way forward for engagement research.

Antecedents of Work Engagement

Much of the research on the antecedents of engagement at work has focused on attitudinal engagement using the UWES. As noted, however, recent meta-analyses (Christian *et al.* 2011; Crawford *et al.* 2010; Halbesleben 2010) show little differentiation in patterns of correlations across measures of engagement. Here, therefore, I will not distinguish between attitudinal and behavioural engagement but rather refer to work engagement in general and review its antecedents in overall terms. Later in the discussion I briefly consider antecedents that may be of specific relevance to state and behavioural work engagement respectively.

There are a large number of factors that have been proposed as potential antecedents of work engagement (see, for example, Albrecht, 2010b; Bakker and Leiter 2010b; Christian *et al.* 2011). The key predictors can be grouped under three broad categories of work-related factors, individual traits and dispositions and non-work factors.

Work-related antecedents: job demands and resources

Work-related factors have received the most research attention as potential antecedents of engagement. These factors cover a wide range of work conditions and experiences that are hypothesised to have a direct effect on individuals' level of engagement at work. Based on the job demands-resources (JD-R) model (Demerouti *et al.* 2001), these various job attributes and related work experiences can be parsimoniously classified into two broad categories, namely, demands and resources. Job demands refer to those aspects of the job that require sustained physical, mental or emotional effort and are therefore associated with certain physiological and psychological costs (Demerouti et al. 2001). They include, for example, role overload, role ambiguity, role conflict, time and work pressure, and emotional dissonance (Bakker and Demerouti 2007; Hakanen and Roodt 2010). Job resources, instead, refer to those aspects of the job that can help to reduce job demands, stimulate personal growth and development, and are functional in achieving work goals. Examples of job resources are job control, social support, performance feedback, task variety and opportunities for development (Bakker and Demerouti 2007; Hakanen and Roodt 2010).

The JD-R model is the most widely used framework for explaining the relationship between work-related factors and engagement. Central to this model is the idea that, by fostering personal growth and development, and helping the achievement of work goals, job resources satisfy basic individual needs for autonomy, relatedness and competence (Van den Broeck et al. 2008). As a result, job resources are assumed to enhance the willingness of employees to dedicate their efforts and abilities to the work task, thereby activating a motivational process that is expected to foster work engagement (Bakker and Demerouti 2007; Schaufeli and Bakker 2004). In contrast, the sustained effort and associated physiological and psychological costs involved in meeting job demands are assumed to drain individuals' energy. As a result, job demands are expected to activate an energy depletion process that is inimical to engagement (Schaufeli and Bakker 2004). Thus, job resources are expected to be positively related to engagement, while job demands are expected to be negatively related to engagement, although engagement is expected to be generally more strongly related to resources than to demands (Hakanen and Roodt 2010; Halbesleben 2010). Recently, Crawford et al. (2010) have extended and refined the JD-R model by suggesting a distinction between two kinds of job demands – challenge demands (e.g. job complexity, job responsibility, subjective workload) and hindrance demands (e.g. role ambiguity, role conflict, role overload). Drawing on the transactional theory of stress (Lazarus and Folkman 1984) they theorised that challenge demands are positively related to work engagement, while hindrance demands are negatively related to engagement.

The results of recent meta-analyses (Christian et al. 2011; Crawford et al. 2010; Halbesleben 2010) summarising the empirical evidence about the antecedents of engagement from multiple studies in various occupations and countries are summarised in Table 16. 1. Consistent with the JD-R model and its refinement by Crawford et al. (2010), the meta-analytic correlations show that a wide range of job resources are all significantly positively related to work engagement (mean correlation = 0.38), as are a range of challenge demands (mean correlation = 0.20), while hindrance demands are all significantly negatively related to engagement (mean correlation = -0.21). In line with expectations, engagement is also, on average, more strongly related to job resources than to job demands. The strongest work-related predictors of engagement are job variety, work-role fit, task significance and opportunities for development (corrected correlations = 0.53, 0.52, 0.51 and 0.47 respectively).

Table 16.1 Antecedents of employee work engagement: Summary of meta-analytic results

Antecedent	Corrected Correlations	Source
Job Resources		
Job variety	0.53	Study 2 ($k=9$, $N=9211$)
Work-role fit	0.52	Study 1 ($k=6$, $N=4559$)
Task significance	0.51	Study 2 ($k=4$, $N=5870$)
Opportunities for development	0.47	Study 1 ($k=6$, $N=4980$)
Job autonomy/control	0.39	Study 2 ($k=43$, $N=24499$)
Feedback	0.35	Study 1 ($k=19$, $N=12125$)
Social support	0.32	Study 2 ($k=38$, $N=18226$)
Leader-member exchange	0.31	Study 2 ($k=4$, $N=4695$)
Positive workplace climate	0.28	Study 1 ($k=13$, $N=10322$)
Transformational leadership	0.27	Study 2 ($k=4$, $N=777$)
Rewards and recognition	0.21	Study 1 ($k=7$, $N=6372$)
Challenge Demands		
Problem solving	0.28	Study 2 ($k=9$, $N=9578$)
Job complexity	0.24	Study 2 ($k=6$, $N=1662$)
Time urgency	0.21	Study 1 ($k=9$, $N=6561$)
Job responsibility	0.15	Study 1 ($k=7$, $N=2583$)
Work load	0.13	Study 1 ($k=16$, $N=6963$)
Hindrance Demands		
Organisational politics	-0.25	Study 1 ($k=4$, $N=3042$)
Role conflict	-0.24	Study 1 ($k=12$, $N=3698$)
Role overload	-0.20	Study 1 ($k=5$, $N=6152$)
Emotional conflict	-0.19	Study 1 ($k.=4$, $N=3220$)
Resource inadequacies	-0.18	Study 1 ($k=11$, $N=11770$)
Administrative hassles	-0.17	Study 1 ($k=7$, $N=7187$)
Individual Differences		
Self-efficacy	0.59	Study 3 ($k=17$, $N=5163$)
Proactive personality	0.44	Study 2 ($k=6$, $N=4304$)
Optimism	0.44	Study 3 ($k=5$, $N=1799$)
Trait positive affectivity	0.43	Study 2 ($k=14$, $N=6715$)
Conscientiousness	0.42	Study 2 ($k=12$, $N=5821$)
Non-work Factors		
Family-work conflict	0.25	Study 3 ($k=6$, $N=5517$)
Recovery	0.24	Study 1 ($k=3$, $N=350$)

$k=$ number of unique samples; $N=$ total sample size. For all correlations $p<0.001$.

Note: When the relationship between a particular antecedent and work engagement was examined in more than one meta-analysis, the corrected correlation from the meta-analysis that included the largest number of individual studies/samples is reported.

Source: Study 1 = Crawford *et al.* (2010); Study 2 = Christian *et al.* (2011); Study 3 = Halbesleben (2010).

Two additional aspects of the JD-R model are worth noting. First is the possible interaction between demands and resources. As noted by Bakker and Demerouti (2007), the model suggests that in addition to having a direct relationship with engagement, job demands and job resources mutually moderate each other's relationship with engagement. Indeed, a key assumption of the model is that resources have a stronger positive effect on engagement when employees are confronted with high job demands and that, conversely, resources act as buffers and diminish the negative effect of high demands on engagement (Bakker and Leiter 2010b; Bakker *et al.* 2008). Few studies have explicitly examined these moderator hypotheses. However, the available evidence from two separate large scale studies of Finnish dentists and teachers shows clear support for the proposed interaction between demands and resources in predicting work engagement (Bakker *et al.* 2007; Hakanen *et al.* 2005).

The second point concerns the temporal relationship between, in particular, job resources and engagement, including the possibility that resources and engagement may be reciprocally related and reinforce each other over time. Mauno *et al.* (2010) have provided a qualitative review of recent longitudinal research on engagement involving two-wave designs covering time lags of between three weeks and three years. The ten studies reviewed by Mauno *et al.* (2010) generally confirm the positive temporal relationship between job resources and engagement, showing that high job resources predict high work engagement over time. Beyond this temporal link from resources to engagement, Salanova *et al.* (2010) have argued for a dynamic reciprocal relationship between job resources and engagement. Specifically, drawing on Hobfoll's (1989) conservation of resources (COR) theory and the notion of 'gain spirals', they suggest that job resources, such as autonomy and supervisor support, foster engagement that, in its turn, can contribute to the further accumulation of resources by, for instance, facilitating the achievement of work goals. There are only a handful of studies that have examined the reciprocal relationship between job resources and work engagement, but the available evidence is generally consistent with the notion of 'gain spirals' and the idea that resources and engagement mutually reinforce each other over time (Salanova *et al.* 2010). Clearly, though, more research is required in this area.

Individual difference antecedents

The second major group of predictors of work engagement consists of individual differences. These include various personal traits and dispositions and aspects of psychological capital (Sweetman and Luthans 2010), such as trait positive affectivity, proactive personality, conscientiousness, self efficacy and optimism. In an extension of the JD-R model to the individual level, these personal traits and dispositions are often conceptualised as personal resources and hypothesised to facilitate work engagement (Bakker and Leiter 2010b; Sweetman and Luthans 2010). Specifically, personal resources, such as positive affectivity, conscientiousness and self-efficacy, involve positive self-evaluations, are associated with the tendency to experience work in positive and active ways, and enhance individuals' sense of their ability to control and affect their environment successfully. Hence, personal resources are expected to be positively related to engagement (Bakker and Leiter 2010b; Sweetman and Luthans 2010; Wildermuth 2010).

The results of recent meta-analyses confirm this expectation. In particular, as can be seen from the meta-analytic correlations in Table 16. 1, conscientiousness, proactive personality, self-efficacy and optimism are all strong positive predictors of engagement. What is less clear, however, is the extent to which levels of engagement are affected by the interaction between individual and work-related factors – the extent to which self-efficacy or optimism, for example, help to reduce the negative effect of hindrance demands on engagement. Future research could usefully adopt an explicit person-situation perspective and examine the extent to which individual traits and dispositions moderate the relationship between job demands, job resources and engagement.

Non-work antecedents

Non-work factors represent the third main group of predictors of engagement. Examples of non-work antecedents include family-work conflict covering home demands (e.g. quantitative and emotional home demands) and home resources (e.g. family support), and opportunities for recovery outside of work (e.g. off-job unwinding and recuperation, and mentally switching off work) (Hakanen *et al.* 2008; Sonnentag 2003; Sonnentag *et al.* 2010a). Paralleling arguments from the JD-R model, home demands are expected to create strain for individuals and deplete their overall store of energy, thereby inhibiting engagement at work, while home resources are expected to have the opposite effect and hence facilitate engagement (Bakker *et al.* 2005; for an alternative interpretation, see Rothbard 2001). Similarly, recovery and psychological detachment from work during off-job time should help to replenish individuals' overall store of energy and are therefore expected to facilitate engagement at work (Sonnentag 2003).

There are only a few studies that have examined the relationship between home demands, home resources and work engagement. The results, on the whole, are not in line with expectations. Rothbard (2001), for instance, found no support for the idea that home demands undermine engagement at work, while Bakker *et al.* (2005) found that home demands are indeed negatively associated with engagement, but only for women. In line with expectations, Bakker *et al.* (2005) also found a positive relationship between home resources and engagement. In contrast, though, Hakanen *et al.* (2008) failed to find a significant link between engagement and either home demands or home resources. Moreover, and again contrary to expectations, Halbesleben (2010), in his meta-analysis, found a significant positive rather than negative correlation between family-work conflict and engagement (see Table 16. 1).

Clearly, the relationship between engagement and both home demands and resources requires further theoretical and empirical work.

Research examining the effects of recovery on state work engagement is also limited (e.g. Sonnentag 2003, and Sonnentag *et al.* 2010a). But the results in this case are more positive in that they are generally consistent with the idea that short-term processes of off-job recovery facilitate engagement at work. The results in this area are summarised in Crawford *et al.'s* (2010) meta-analysis showing a significant and positive corrected correlation of 0.24 between off-job recovery and work engagement (see Table 16.1).

Additional antecedent issues

In terms of the antecedents of work engagement, it is important to note that, in addition to the factors reviewed above, there are a number of other potential predictors that have been identified in the literature. Two points stand out in this respect. First, in his behavioural approach to work engagement, Kahn (1990) proposed that individuals' perceptions of their work context and their own personal characteristics foster psychological conditions that directly influence their propensity to invest physical, cognitive and emotional energy in their work role. In particular, Kahn (1990) theorised that engagement is a direct function of the psychological conditions of meaningfulness, safety and availability (Rich *et al.* 2010). As noted by Crawford *et al.* (2010), these psychological conditions fall outside the scope of the JD-R model and are, in their turn, affected by factors that only partly overlap with the antecedents reviewed above. As suggested by Rich *at al.* (2010: 621), these factors include the extent to which individuals 'believe that their personal values are congruent with those of the organisation' (value congruence), perceive that the organisation is supportive and cares about their well-being (perceived organisational support), and have a positive view of their 'own worthiness, effectiveness and capability as people' (core self-evaluations). In line with theoretical expectations, each of these factors were shown by Rich *et al.* (2010) to be positively related to behavioural work engagement.

The second point concerns the role of state positive affect (i.e. positive moods and emotions) as a potential predictor of work engagement. There is considerable disagreement in the literature about the precise nature of the relationship between positive affect and engagement, with some researchers treating positive affect as an antecedent of engagement (Binneweis and Fetzer 2010), and others as a consequence of engagement (Bakker *et al.* 2008). In principle, there is no reason why engagement, especially state work engagement, should not be both an antecedent and a consequence of positive affect. This would be consistent with more dynamic models of the unfolding of engagement over time which posit a more complex reciprocal relationship between positive affect and engagement (Sonnentag *et al.* 2008). However, research using and testing more complex dynamic models of the reciprocal relationship between state affect and engagement at work is still in its infancy and undoubtedly represents an important area for further theoretical and empirical development. Particularly fruitful, in this respect, would be to extend this more dynamic analysis to a consideration also of state negative affect (George 2011), focusing specifically on engagement at the level of individual tasks (Maslach 2011; Sonnentag 2011). The overall aim would be to gain a better understanding not only of the reciprocal relationship between positive and negative affect and task engagement, but also of how positive and negative affect interact with task-specific factors to influence individuals' engagement across tasks and over time.

Consequences of Work Engagement

Underlying the current widespread interest in employee engagement is the belief that engagement pays off. As noted, particularly strong claims to this effect can be found in the practitioner literature where engagement is often presented as the key to increased profitability, 'through higher productivity, sales, customer satisfaction and employee retention' (Schaufeli and Bakker 2010: 11). Researchers have questioned the validity of many of these claims (Schaufeli and Bakker 2010). There is no doubt, however, that the consequences of engagement are a central concern also in the academic literature where work engagement is, by and large, thought to have a positive effect on a range of outcomes important to both individuals and organisations. These include, for example, various aspects of task and contextual performance, turnover, absence and employee health outcomes. A number of researchers also treat key employee attitudes, such as job satisfaction and organisational commitment, as outcomes of engagement (Albrecht 2010b; Cole *et al.* 2011). In line with our earlier discussion, however, these job attitudes are more appropriately conceptualised as correlates rather than as outcomes of engagement and will not, therefore, be examined again in this section. Here I focus primarily on key performance, turnover and health-related outcomes that have been examined in a range of individual studies and summarised in Christian *et al.'s* (2011) and Halbesleben's (2010) recent meta-analyses. Some of the potential negative effects of engagement, or what is sometimes referred to as the 'dark side' of engagement (Bakker and Leiter 2010b, Bakker *et al.* 2011a), will also be briefly considered.

Job performance outcomes

Research on the relationship between work engagement and job performance has focused on both task and contextual performance. Task or in-role performance refers to how well an individual performs the duties required by the job, while contextual or extra-role performance refers to discretionary behaviours on the part of the individual that are not formally required as part of the job, but which contribute to the effective functioning of the organisation (Borman and Motowidlo 1993). Contextual performance can take many forms, including various kinds of organisational citizenship (Organ 1988); prosocial (Brief 1998) and proactive behaviour at work (Crant 2000), such as helping co-workers with their work duties, championing the organisation to outsiders and taking personal initiative.

A number of explanations have been proposed for a positive effect of work engagement on performance. One explanation, for example, draws on Fredrickson's (2001) broaden-and-build theory of positive emotions and the idea that positive emotions, such as happiness and enthusiasm, can contribute to job performance by heightening awareness, enhancing creativity and broadening individuals' thought-action repertoire. Hence, to the extent that work engagement is associated with higher levels of positive outcomes, it can be expected to contribute to both task and contextual performance by enhancing individuals' capacity to cope with job demands, stimulating problem-solving and heightening search and creative behaviour (Demerouti and Cropanzano 2010; Salanova *et al.* 2010). A parallel explanation draws on Hobfoll's (1989) conservation of resources theory and the idea of a 'gain spiral' between work engagement and resources (Salanova *et al.* 2010). To the extent that engagement based on access to resources enables individuals to accumulate further resources, such as support from others, it can be expected to contribute to better performance by enabling individuals better to deal with their own job demands and to achieve their work goals (Bakker *et al.* 2008; Demerouti and Cropanzano 2010).

A further argument is that because engaged employees tend to experience better psychological and physical health, they are more likely to perform better on the job because they are in a better position to focus and use all their mental and physical resources at work (Bakker *et al.* 2008). Finally, as argued by Rich *et al.* (2010) in relation to behavioural engagement, the investment of high levels of physical, cognitive and emotional energy into work tasks can be expected to contribute to both in-role and extra-role performance by ensuring higher levels of sustained effort on the job, and promoting more vigilant, attentive, focused and collaborative behaviour characteristic of what Kahn (1990, 1992) termed more complete and authentic role performance.

The results of Christian *et al.*'s (2011) meta-analysis summarising the relationship between work engagement and task and contextual performance respectively, are shown in Table 16. 2. As can be seen, the corrected correlation between engagement

Table 16.2   Outcomes of employee work engagement: Summary of meta-analytic results

Outcomes	Corrected Correlations	Source
Task performance	0.43	Study 1 ($k = 14$, $N = 4562$)
Contextual performance	0.34	Study 1 ($k = 10$, $N = 3654$)
Health	0.20	Study 2 ($k = 17$, $N = 11593$)
Turnover intention	-0.26	Study 2 ($k = 4$, $N = 1893$)

k = number of unique samples; N = total sample size. For all correlations $p < 0.001$.

Note: When the relationship between work engagement and a particular outcome was examined in more than one meta-analysis, the corrected correlation from the meta-analysis that included the largest number of individual studies/samples is reported.

Source: Study 1 = Christian *et al.* (2011); Study 2 = Halbesleben (2010).

and task performance is positive, significant and moderately strong (0.43). Although slightly weaker, the corrected correlation between engagement and contextual performance is also positive and significant. Overall, therefore, the available empirical evidence clearly supports the link between work engagement and performance.

Despite the positive results, some researchers have recently questioned current understanding of the engagement-performance relationship. In particular, Bindl and Parker (2010) and Parker and Griffin (2011) have argued for a more nuanced analysis of the impact of work engagement on job performance. Drawing on the work of Griffin *et al.* (2007) they suggest the need for a more fine-grained analysis that goes beyond the standard distinction between task and contextual performance and explicitly distinguishes between different sub-dimensions of positive work role performance, while taking into account the nature of the work involved. This would involve, for example, examining the detailed motivational paths linking engagement to specific forms of proactive work behaviour, such as personal initiative and improving work methods, and exploring the conditions under which these paths become activated. This more fine-grained approach to the analysis of performance opens up important new avenues of research on the engagement-performance relationship, particularly if combined, as suggested above, with a more dynamic approach to the analysis of engagement that focuses at the level of individual tasks.

Turnover intention and health outcomes

In addition to the performance outcomes reviewed above, work engagement has been hypothesised and found to be related to a number of other desirable outcomes, including lower employee turnover intention and better employee self-reported health (e.g. lower psychosomatic health complaints, anxiety and depression) (Demerouti *et al.* 2001; Hakanen *et al.* 2006). The meta-analytic evidence on these two additional outcomes is shown in Table 16.2. Although of only moderate strength, the turnover intention corrected correlation is negative and significant, indicating that, as expected, work engagement is associated with lower employee intention to leave the organisation. In contrast, the corrected correlation for the health outcomes is positive and significant, indicating that, again as expected, engagement is related to positive health outcomes for employees. However, in this context it is important to note that, as emphasised by Bakker *et al.* (2011a), recent research has failed to find any evidence for a link between work engagement and more objective psychophysiological indicators of health, suggesting that further research is required in this area.

Dark side of engagement

Recently researchers have begun to draw attention to the fact that there may also be a dark side to work engagement, in the sense that engagement may have negative as well as positive consequences (George 2010; Halbesleben 2010; Sonnentag 2011). The potentially negative consequences of engagement include, for example, the possibility that, in order to maintain their interest, employees may craft their own job so as to focus on only the more interesting aspects of their work, ignoring potentially important but less challenging or interesting tasks. The net result is that these more mundane, nevertheless important tasks are ignored, performed less well, or delegated to others (Bakker 2010). In addition, individuals who are highly engaged at work may end up investing less of themselves in non-work domains at the expense, for example, of family or community life (Sonnenteg 2011). There is also the possibility that high levels of engagement at work may have long-term negative health consequences for individuals (Bakker and Leiter 2010b). As a number of scholars have noted, however, research on the potentially negative consequences of engagement at work is still limited (Bakker et al. 2011b). This is clearly an important area for future work.

In summary, there is considerable evidence showing that, as theorised, work engagement does indeed have a generally positive effect on a range of important individual and organisational outcomes, including core aspects of job performance. However, the precise mechanisms linking engagement to some of these outcomes need further explication. Further research is also needed on the effect of engagement on different aspects of proactive behaviour at work and on various forms of performance in different types of tasks and work situations. In addition, the potentially negative consequences of engagement need more systematic research attention, including any longer-term consequences that engagement may have for individuals' health and well-being at work.

Practical Implications: Building Engagement at Work

Because of the potential benefits involved, the question of how to enhance employee engagement at work has attracted a great deal of interest in both the academic and the practitioner literature. A detailed review of this aspect of the engagement literature is beyond the scope of the present discussion. Interested readers are directed to a number of recent research-based overviews of possible ways to promote work engagement in organisations. These more evidence-based discussions cover not only organisational-level, but also job and individual-level interventions and drivers of engagement, with particularly interesting contributions by Albrecht (2010b), Bakker et al. (2011a), Fleck and Inceoglu (2010), Leiter and Maslach (2010), and Schaufeli and Salanova (2010). Here it is sufficient to note three main points.

First, at a general level, the research evidence on the antecedents of work engagement reviewed above suggests that the development of a more positive resource-rich work environment should contribute to enhancing employee engagement. These engagement-maximising work environments are ones that are characterised, for example, by careful person-job fit, job discretion and autonomy, new learning and development opportunities, systematic communication and support for employees, opportunities for participation in decision-making at different levels of the organisation, and various forms of distributive, procedural and interactional justice. More generally, these are the kind of work environments that are commonly associated with more progressive types of human resource management (HRM) systems. These include, for instance, high commitment and high involvement HRM systems emphasising systematic recruitment and selection, extensive training and development, decentralised job design, competitive benefits and rewards, extensive information-sharing and longer-term job security for employees (Appelbaum *et al.* 2000; Pfeffer 1998). Importantly, these more progressive types of HRM systems can contribute to the development of more positive work orientations amongst employees, including aspects of their psychological capital. For example, careful processes of selection, induction, training and development, coupled with systematic information-sharing and delegation of control, can promote greater value congruence and more positive core self-evaluations by employees, while at the same time encouraging the taking of personal initiative and contributing to a stronger sense of self-efficacy (Schaufeli and Salanova 2010). In other words, the adoption by the organisation of a more progressive system of HRM can have a beneficial effect on engagement, not only by helping to generate a generally more positive and resource-rich work environment, but also by contributing to the development of employees' personal resources.

Second, the available evidence, as we have seen, also highlights the importance of two additional factors or considerations. First is the need for organisations to contain and minimise potentially deleterious hindrance demands capable of undermining work engagement, while at the same time emphasising various kinds of challenge demands that are conducive to engagement. Particularly important in this respect is the need to maintain an appropriate balance between the demands that are placed on employees and the resources that are available to them at work (Demerouti *et al.* 2001). The second consideration concerns the contribution that processes of recovery can make to engagement and the need, therefore, for organisations to take this into account more explicitly in the design of work systems and the allocation of job responsibilities. This may involve, for example, building more opportunities for respite and recovery into job roles by introducing longer rest pauses, shorter and more flexible working hours, or more balanced work duties (Albrecht 2010b; Schaufeli and Salanova 2010).

The final point concerns the need for evaluation studies of real-life engagement programmes or initiatives in organisations, including before and after quasi-experimental field evaluations of specific interventions explicitly designed to build workforce engagement. Such systematic evaluation research is central to a better understanding both of how work engagement can be enhanced in practice, and of what effect this can have on a range of individual and organisational outcomes. Yet, as noted by Leiter and Maslach (2010: 165), 'work on designing, implementing and evaluating interventions to build engagement has barely begun'. Undoubtedly, therefore, this is an important area of further research.

Future Research

Key areas of further research have been identified at various points in the present chapter and will not, therefore, be considered in detail again here. The review, however, necessarily had to be selective. As a result, it did not cover all possible topics related to engagement, including important areas of research linked, for example, to questions about the role of leadership in fostering work engagement (Bakker *et al.* 2011a), about engagement as a higher-level collective or team-level phenomenon (Schaufeli and Salanova 2011), about the contagion or crossover of engagement among members of the same work group (Bakker *et al.* 2011a), and about the notion of a climate for engagement (Bakker *et al.* 2011b). These, and a range of other important areas that deserve further research attention, are discussed in greater detail in a number of recent overviews of the state of play in the study of work engagement, with particularly useful and wide-ranging contributions by Albrecht (2010b), Bakker and Leiter (2010b), and Bakker *et al.* (2011a, 2011b).

Here, however, it is worth highlighting two key research priorities. First is to examine in greater detail the relationship between attitudinal and behavioural engagement, ideally using longitudinal designs that would allow for a fuller exploration of the distinctiveness, as well as of the dynamic link, between the two forms of engagement over time. And second is to use longitudinal designs covering different time lags to examine the dynamic relationship between work engagement and its possible consequences and antecedents both at the level of discrete job tasks and activities over potentially short periods of time (micro-task engagement), and at the level of the job as a whole over a longer time scale (macro-work engagement). An important aim of this research would be to gain a better understanding of the dynamics of engagement at each level of analysis, viewed in the context of a comprehensive, nomological network of antecedent and outcome variables at each level. A further aim would be to look across levels of analysis and explore the relationship between micro-task and macro-work engagement over time in greater detail, including possible overlaps and interactions between the nomological networks at the two levels of analysis.

Conclusions

The present chapter has sought to provide a systematic up-to-date overview of work engagement research covering an analysis of the meaning and measurement of engagement, as well as of its key antecedents and consequences for both individuals and organisations. As the review shows, the study of employee work engagement is an important research area in its own right, characterised by an impressive and rapidly growing body of theoretical and empirical work. There is no doubt, however, that considerable more work needs to be done in this area.

As part of the present review, a number of key gaps in the extant literature were identified, as well as a number of important areas of future research. Of fundamental importance is the need to clarify the meaning and definition of work engagement itself, including the extent to which engagement differs, theoretically and empirically, from other potentially overlapping work-related constructs. This means revisiting existing conceptualisations and operationalisations of work engagement, focusing on both attitudinal and behavioural approaches and covering engagement at the level both of individual tasks/activities and of the job as a whole. In particular, it means giving priority to gaining a better understanding of the relationship between attitudinal and behavioural engagement at both the micro- and the macro-level of analysis, while at the same time exploring the discriminant validity between different aspects or manifestations of engagement and other key potentially overlapping work-related attitudes and behaviours.

Improved theoretical and empirical understanding of these core issues can then provide the basis for a more systematic and cumulative programme of longitudinal research on the dynamics of employee engagement at work, covering important antecedents and consequences of the phenomenon. This programme of research should contribute to a better and more realistic evidence-based understanding of how to enhance employee engagement at work and of the consequences of doing so for both the individual and the organisation. As such, it should be of direct interest to organisational scholars and practitioners alike.

REFERENCES

Albrecht, S.L. (ed.) 2010a: *The Handbook of Employee Engagement: perspectives, issues, research and practice*, Cheltenham, UK: Edward Elgar.

Albrecht, S.L. 2010b: Employee engagement: 10 questions for research and practice, in S.L. Albrecht (ed.), *The Handbook of Employee Engagement: perspectives, issues, research and practice*, 3-19. Cheltenham, UK: Edward Elgar.

Appelbaum, E., Bailey, T., Berg, P. and Kalleberg, A. 2000: *Manufacturing advantage: Why high performance work systems pay off*, New York: Cornell University Press.

Bakker, A.B. 2010: Engagement and 'job crafting': Engaged employees create their own great place to work, in S.L. Albrecht (ed.), *The Handbook of Employee Engagement: perspectives, issues, research and practice*, 229-244. Cheltenham, UK: Edward Elgar.

Bakker, A.B., Albrecht, S.L. and Leiter, M.P. 2011a: Key questions regarding work engagement, *European Journal of Work and Organizational Psychology*, **20**, 4-28.

Bakker, A.B., Albrecht, S.L. and Leiter, M.P. 2011b: Work engagement: Further reflections on the state of play, *European Journal of Work and Organizational Psychology*, **20**, 74-88.

Bakker, A.B. and Bal, P.M. 2010: Weekly work engagement and performance: A study among starting teachers, *Journal of Occupational and Organizational Psychology*, **83**, 189-206.

Bakker, A.B. and Demerouti, E. 2007: The job demands-resources model: State of the art, *Journal of Managerial Psychology*, **22**, 309-328.

Bakker, A.B., Demerouti, E. and Schaufeli, W.B. 2005: The crossover of burnout and work engagement among working couples, *Human Relations*, **58**, 661-689.

Bakker, A.B., Hakanen, J.J., Demerouti, E. and Xanthopoulou, D. 2007: Job resources boost work engagement particularly when job demands are high, *Journal of Educational Psychology*, **99**, 274-284.

Bakker, A.B. and Leiter, M.P. (eds.) 2010a: *Work engagement: A handbook of essential theory and research*, New York: Psychology Press.

Bakker, A.B. and Leiter, M.P. 2010b: Where to go from here: Integration and future research on work engagement, in A.B. Bakker and M.P. Leiter (eds.), *Work engagement: A handbook of essential theory and research*, 181-196. New York: Psychology Press.

Bakker, A.B., Schaufeli, W.B., Leiter, M.P. and Taris, T.W. 2008: Work engagement: An emerging concept in occupational health psychology, *Work and Stress*, **22**, 187-200.

Bindl, U.K. and Parker, S.K. 2010: Feeling good and performing well? Psychological engagement and positive behaviours at work, in S.L. Albrecht (ed.), *The Handbook of Employee Engagement: perspectives, issues, research and practice*. 385-398. Cheltenham, UK: Edward Elgar.

Binneweis, C. and Fetzer, B. 2010: Affective states and affect regulation as antecedents of dynamic work engagement, in S.L. Albrecht (ed.), *The Handbook of Employee Engagement: perspectives, issues, research and practice*, 245-252. Cheltenham, UK: Edward Elgar.

Borman, W.C. and Motowidlo, S.J. 1993: Expanding the criterion domain to include elements of contextual performance, in N. Schmitt and W.C. Borman (eds.), *Personnel selection in organizations*, 79-98. San Francisco: Jossey-Bass.

Brief, A.P. 1998: *Attitudes in and around organizations*, Thousand Oaks, CA: Sage.

Christian, M.S., Garza, A.S. and Slaughter, J.E. 2011: Work engagement: A quantitative review and test of its relations with task and contextual performance, *Personnel Psychology*, **64**, 89-136.

Cole, M.S., Walter, F., Bedeian, A.G. and O'Boyle, E.H. 2011: Job burnout and employee engagement: A meta-analytic examination of construct proliferation, *Journal of Management*, August, 1-32.

Crant, J.M. 2000: Proactive behavior in organizations. *Journal of Management*, **26**, 435-462.

Crawford, E.R., LePine, J.A. and Rich, B.L. 2010: Linking job demands and resources to employee engagement and burnout: A theoretical extension and meta-analytic test, *Journal of Applied Psychology*, **95**, 834-848.

Deci, E.L. and Ryan, R.M. 1985: *Intrinsic motivation and self-determination in human behaviour*, New York, NY: Plenum Press.

Demerouti, E., Bakker, A.B., Nachreiner, F. and Schaufeli, W.B. 2001: The job demands-resources model of burnout, *Journal of Applied Psychology*, **86**, 499-512.

Demerouti, E. and Cropanzano, R. 2010: From thought to action: Employee work engagement and job performance, pp. 147-163. In Bakker A.B and Leiter M.P. (eds) *Work engagement: A handbook of essential theory and research*, New York: Psychology Press.

European Journal of Work and Organizational Psychology 2011, **20**, 3-88.

Fisher, C.D. 2000: Mood and emotions while working: Missing pieces of job satisfaction? *Journal of Organizational Behavior*, **21**, 185-202.

Fleck, S. and Inceoglu, I. 2010: A comprehensive framework for understanding and predicting engagement, in S.L. Albrecht (ed.), *The Handbook of Employee Engagement: perspectives, issues, research and practice*, 31-42. Cheltenham, UK: Edward Elgar.

Fredrickson, B.L. 2001: The role of positive emotions in positive psychology: The broaden-and-build theory of positive emotions, *American Psychologist*, **56**, 218-226.

George, J.M. 2010: More engagement is not necessarily better: The benefits of fluctuating levels of engagement pp. 253-263. In Albrecht, S.L. (ed), *The Handbook of Employee Engagement: perspectives, issues, research and practice*, Cheltenham, UK: Edward Elgar.

George, J.M. 2011: The wider context, costs, and benefits of work engagement, *European Journal of Work and Organizational Psychology*, **20**, 53-59.

Griffin, M.A., Neal, A. and Parker, S.K. 2007: A new model of work role performance: Positive behavior in uncertain and interdependent contexts, *Academy of Management Journal*, **50**, 327-347.

Hakanen, J.J., Bakker, A.B. and Demerouti, E. 2005: How dentists cope with their job demands and stay engaged: The moderating role of job resources, *European Journal of Oral Sciences*, **113**, 479-487.

Hakanen, J.J., Bakker, A.B. and Schaufeli, W.B. 2006: Burnout and work engagement among teachers, *Journal of School Psychology*, **43**, 495-513.

Hakanen, J.J. and Roodt, G. 2010: Using the job demands-resources model to predict engagement: Analysing a conceptual model, in A.B. Bakker and M.P. Leiter (eds.), *Work engagement: A handbook of essential theory and research*, 85-101. New York: Psychology Press.

Hakanen, J.L., Schaufeli, W.B. and Ahola, K. 2008: The job demands-resources model: A three-year cross-lagged study of burnout, depression, commitment, and work engagement, *Work and Stress*, **22**, 224-241.

Halbesleben, J.R.B. 2010: A meta-analysis of work engagement: Relationships with burnout, demands, resources, and consequences, in A.B. Bakker and M.P. Leiter (eds.), *Work engagement: A handbook of essential theory and research*, 102-117. New York: Psychology Press.

Harrison, D.A., Newman, D.A. and Roth, P.L. 2006: How important are job attitudes? Meta-analytic comparisons of integrative behavioral outcomes and time sequences, *Academy of Management Journal*, **49**, 305-325.

Hobfoll, S.E. 1989: Conservation of resources: A new attempt at conceptualizing stress, *American Psychologist*, **44**, 513-524.

Industrial and Organizational Psychology 2008: **1**, 3-56.

Kahn, W.A. 1990: Psychological conditions of personal engagement and disengagement at work, *Academy of Management Journal*, **33**, 692-724.

Kahn, W.A. 1992: To be fully there: Psychological presence at work, *Human Relations*, **45**, 321-349.

Lazarus, R.S. and Folkman, S. 1984: *Stress, appraisal, and coping*, New York: Springer.

Le, H., Schmidt, F.L., Harter, J.K. and Lauver, K.J. 2010: The problem of empirical redundancy of constructs in organizational research: An empirical investigation, *Organizational Behavior and Human Decision Processes*, **112**, 112-125.

Leiter, M.P. and Maslach, C. 2010: Building engagement: The design and evaluation of interventions, in A.B. Bakker and M.P. Leiter (eds.), *Work engagement: A handbook of essential theory and research*, 164-180. New York: Psychology Press.

Macey, W.H. and Schneider, B. 2008: The meaning of employee engagement. *Industrial and Organizational Psychology*, **1**, 3-30.

MacLeod, D. and Clarke, N. 2009: *Engaging for success: Enhancing performance through employee engagement*, London: Department for Business, Innovation and Skills.

Maslach, C. 2011: Engagement research: Some thoughts from a burnout perspective, *European Journal of Work and Organizational Psychology*, **20**, 47-52.

Maslach, C., Schaufeli, W.B. and Leiter, M.P. 2001: Job burnout, *Annual Review of Psychology*, **52**, 397-422.

Mauno, S., Kinnunen, U., Makikangas, A. and Feldt, T. 2010: Job demands and resources as antecedents of job engagement: A qualitative review and directions for future research, in S.L. Albrecht (ed.), *The Handbook of Employee Engagement: perspectives, issues, research and practice*, 111-128. Cheltenham, UK: Edward Elgar.

Newman, D.A. and Harrison, D.A. 2008: Been there, bottled that: Are state and behavioral work engagement new and useful construct wines? *Industrial and Organizational Psychology*, **1**, 31-35.

Newman, D.A., Joseph, D.L. and Hulin, C.L. 2010: Job attitudes and employee engagement: Considering the attitude 'A-factor', in S.L. Albrecht (ed.), *The Handbook of Employee Engagement: perspectives, issues, research and practice*, 43-61. Cheltenham, UK: Edward Elgar.

Organ, D.W. 1988: *Organizational citizenship behavior: The good soldier syndrome*, Lexington, MA: Lexington Books.

Parker, S.K. 2000: From passive to proactive motivation: The importance of flexible role orientations and role-breadth self-efficacy, *Applied Psychology: An international Review*, **3**, 447-469.

Parker, S.K. and Griffin, M.A. 2011: Understanding active psychological states: Embedding engagement in a wider nomological net and closer attention to performance, *European Journal of Work and Organizational Psychology*, **20**, 60-67.

Pfeffer. J. 1998: *The human equation: Building profit by putting people first*, Boston: Harvard Business School Press.

Rich, B.L., LePine, J.A. and Crawford, E.R. 2010: Job engagement: Antecedents and effects on job performance, *Academy of Management Journal*, **53**, 617-635.

Rothbard, N.P. 2001: Enriching or depleting? The dynamics of engagement in work and family roles, *Administrative Science Quarterly*, **46**, 655-684.

Saks, A.M. 2006: Antecedents and consequences of employee engagement, *Journal of Managerial Psychology*, **7**, 600-619.

Salanova, M., Schaufeli, W.B., Xanthopoulou, D. and Bakker, A.B. 2010: The gain spiral of resources and work engagement: Sustaining a positive worklife, in A.B. Bakker and M.P. Leiter (eds), *Work Engagement: A Handbook of Essential Theory and Research*, 118-131. New York: Psychology Press.

Schaufeli, W.B. and Bakker, A.B. 2004: Job demands, job resources and their relationship with burnout and engagement: A multi-sample study, *Journal of Organizational Behavior*, **25**, 293-315.

Schaufeli, W.B. and Bakker, A.B. 2010: Defining and measuring work engagement: Bringing clarity to the concept, pp. 10-24, in Bakker, A.B. and Leiter, M.P. (eds), *Work Engagement: A Handbook of Essential Theory and Research*, New York: Psychology Press.

Schaufeli, W.B., Bakker, A.B. and Salanova, M. 2006: The measurement of work engagement with a short questionnaire: A cross-national study, *Educational and Psychological Measurement*, **66**, 701-716.

Schaufeli, W.B. and Salanova, M. 2010: How to improve work engagement? In S.L. Albrecht (ed.), *The Handbook of Employee Engagement: perspectives, issues, research and practice*, 339-415. Cheltenham, UK: Edward Elgar.

Schaufeli, W.B. and Salanova, M. 2011: Work engagement: On how to better catch a slippery concept, *European Journal of Work and Organizational Psychology*, **20**, 39-46.

Schaufeli, W.B., Salanova, M., Gonzalez-Roma, V. and Bakker, A.B. 2002: The measurement of engagement and burnout: A two sample confirmatory factor analytic approach, *Journal of Happiness Studies*, **3**, 71-92.

Schaufeli, W.B. and Taris, T.W. 2005: The conceptualization and measurement of burnout: Common ground and worlds apart, *Work and Stress*, **19**, 356-362.

Schaufeli, W.B., Taris. T.W. and Van Rehnen, W. 2008: Workaholism, burnout, and engagement: Three of a kind or three different kinds of employee well-being? *Applied Psychology: An International Review*, **57**, 173-203.

Schwab, D.E. 1980. Construct validity in organizational behaviour, in B.M. Staw and L.L.Cummings (eds.), *Research in organizational behaviour*, 3-43. Greenwich, CT: JAI Press.

Shimazu, A., Miyanaka, D. and Schaufeli, W.B. 2010: Work engagement from a cultural perspective, in S.L. Albrecht (ed.), *The Handbook of Employee Engagement: perspectives, issues, research and practice*, 364-372. Cheltenham, UK: Edward Elgar.

Sonnentag, S. 2003: Recovery, work engagement, and proactive behavior: A new look at the interface between non-work and work, *Journal of Applied Psychology*, **88**, 518-528.

Sonnentag, S. 2011: Research on work engagement is well and alive, *European Journal of Work and Organizational Psychology*, **20**, 29-38.

Sonnentag, S., Binnewies, C. and Mojza, E. 2010a: Staying well and engaged when demands are high: The role of psychological detachment, *Journal of Applied Psychology*, **95**, 965-976.

Sonnentag, S., Dormann, C. and Demerouti, E. 2010b: Not all days are created equal: The concept of state work engagement, in A.B. Bakker and M.P. Leiter (eds.), *Work Engagement: A Handbook of Essential Theory and Research*, 25-38. New York: Psychology Press.

Sonnentag, S., Mojza, E., Binnewies, C. and Scholl, A. 2008: Being engaged at work and detached at home: A week-level study on work engagement, psychological detachment, and affect, *Work and Stress*, **22**, 257-276.

Spreitzer, G.M. 1995: Psychological empowerment in the workplace: Dimensions, example. measurement, and validation, *Academy of Management Journal*, **38**, 1442-1465.

Sweetman, D. and Luthans, F. 2010: The power of positive psychology: Psychological capital and work engagement, in A.B. Bakker and M.P. Leiter (eds.), *Work Engagement: A Handbook of Essential Theory and Research*, 54-68. New York: Psychology Press.

Taris, T.W., Schaufeli, W.B. and Shimazu, A. 2010: The push and pull of work: The differences between workaholism and work engagement, in A.B. Bakker and M.P. Leiter (eds.), *Work Engagement: A Handbook of Essential Theory and Research*, 39-53. New York: Psychology Press.

Vance, R.J. 2006: *Employee engagement and commitment: A guide to understanding, measuring and increasing engagement in your organization*, Alexandria, VA: SHRM Foundation.

Van den Broeck, A., De Witte, H., Lens, W. and Vansteenkiste, M. 2008: The role of basic need satisfaction in explaining the relationship between job demands, job resources, burnout and engagement, Work and Stress, **22**, 277-294.

Warr, P. 1994: A conceptual framework for the study of work and mental health, *Work and Stress*, **8**, 84-97.

Wefald, A.J. and Downey, R.G. 2009: Job engagement in organizations: Fad, fashion, or folderol? *Journal of Organizational Behavior*, **30**, 141-145.

Wildermuth, C. 2010: The personal side of engagement: The influence of personality factors, in S.L. Albrecht (ed.), *The Handbook of Employee Engagement: Perspectives, Issues, Research and Practice*, 197-208. Cheltenham, UK: Edward Elgar.

Work and Stress 2008: **22**, 2-54.

Xanthopoulou, D., Bakker, A.B., Heuven, E. and Demerouti, E. 2008: Working in the sky: A diary study on work engagement among flight attendants. *Journal of Occupational and Health Psychology*, **13**, 345-356.

CHAPTER SEVENTEEN

HRM and Employee Well-being

Michael Clinton and Marc van Veldhoven

Introduction

The broad aim of the chapter is to review the existing literature on the relationship between Human Resource Management (HRM) and employee well-being. The main competing perspectives on this relationship in the academic literature are discussed and the relevant empirical evidence evaluated. As both concepts are broad and potentially multi-dimensional, each requires some detailed elaboration. It is suggested that such multi-dimensionality adds complexity to the understanding of any simple relationship between HRM and employee-well being. Future research areas are subsequently presented and the issue of where the responsibility for employee well-being ultimately lies is debated in the final section.

Competing Perspectives on the Impact of HRM on Employee Well-being

History

The link between management principles and employee well-being is one with a long history in social science. One can trace the issue back in time to the work of important nineteenth century scholars such as Marx, Engels, Weber and Durkheim (Watson 1995). During that period one could also witness early attempts to improve worker well-being by building 'model worker villages', like Bournville and Port Sunlight in the UK, where industrialists offered to house their workers in a hygienic environment in contrast to slum dwellings elsewhere. Most textbooks, however, take 'scientific management' as advocated by Taylor (1911) as a starting point, perhaps because of its emphasis on detailed specification of job tasks, job simplification and its strict division of labour seeming to be at odds with employee well-being as we see it now. The Tayloristic approach soon provoked opposition and wide-spread calls for job enlargement and/or job rotation (e.g. Vernon *et al.* 1924). By switching between several simple tasks, or by combining a series of simple tasks into a more varied job, employee well-being was supposedly increased. Over time these and other initiatives developed into a countermovement oriented towards 'human relations'. Ever since, the issue of management principles and employee well-being has been at the forefront of management research, taking on different forms over the years, seeing a series of theoretical models come and go, and witnessing a substantial growth and differentiation in the factors and processes that are thought to be involved (Parker *et al.* 2001).

Debate on the HRM, well-being and performance linkage

The link between HRM and employee well-being can be considered a special case of a wider issue: how do multiple types of management (strategic management, financial management, HRM etc.) influence multiple organisational performance outcomes (productivity, quality, innovation, social legitimacy)? There appears to be general recognition that multiple, parallel outcomes are important to modern organisations (Quinn and Rohrbaugh 1983; Paauwe 2004; Boxall and Purcell 2011). Management is not a matter of simple optimisation. There is considerable debate still, however, on how HRM, employee well-being and organisational performance are related. Two main positions can be identified in this debate and below we shall describe these in more detail (Peccei 2004; Peccei *et al.* 2012).

HRM is 'good' for employees and organisation alike

The most dominant approach in the literature states that HRM is good for both employer and employees alike. By bringing training, development and additional responsibilities to workers, for instance, their jobs become more varied and more independent. Similarly, by giving feedback about performance, coupled with bonus or pay schemes linked to performance, work becomes literally more rewarding. This is supposed to increase employee well-being and, in turn, the increased well-being on-the-job is expected to pay itself back to the organisation in terms of increased organisational performance. Because of its argument being based on increased job satisfaction causing increased levels of organisational performance, this approach is called the 'happy-productive worker' thesis (Staw 1986; Wright and Staw 1999).

One might discern two variants of the happy-productive worker thesis, depending on how strongly one argues for well-being playing a role in increasing productivity. In the weaker version, positive effects for employers and employees are parallel, but not necessarily intentionally connected results of HR initiatives. HRM is simply causing two – equally important – positive effects. In its stronger version, HRM is aiming for increased organisational performance by trying to positively affect employee attitudes and behaviours. This is what is advocated in so-called 'high-commitment' or 'high-involvement' HRM (Walton 1985; Pfeffer 1998). So, in the stronger version of the happy-productive worker thesis, not only is HRM beneficial for both employees and employers, gains in positive employee attitudes and behaviours are instrumental in creating sustained competitive advantage and profits for employers.

HRM is 'good' for the organisation but 'bad' for employees

More critical views can also be found. Labour process theory (Godard 2001; Appelbaum 2002) argues that HRM initiatives targeted at increasing employee abilities, motivation and opportunities are likely to bring positive changes to job variety and autonomy for employees. However, at the same time, output expectations as to the quantity and quality of employees' work are simultaneously increased. In combination, HR practices targeted at high performance, high involvement and/ or high commitment entail work intensification. Accordingly, it is this work intensification, it is suggested, that causes negative effects for worker well-being (Delbridge and Turnbull 1992; Ramsay *et al.* 2000).

Again, we might discern weaker and stronger versions of this proposition. In the weaker version, the effect of HRM on employee well-being may be viewed as an unintended negative side-effect accompanying the broader positive impact of HRM on organisational performance. In the stronger version, management is well aware of the increasing demands placed on the workforce by HRM and is strategically planning for financial gains based on a combination of increased skills and opportunities in the workforce with increased targets (productivity, innovation, quality) at the same time (Legge 1995). In short, there may be a possible element of exploitation here (Nishii *et al.* 2008; Kroon *et al.* 2009).

Conceptualising HRM in the Context of Employee Well-being

From the preceding discussion, we can already see that the effect of HRM on employee well-being may depend, to a great deal, on what we consider HRM to be. Within the academic literature, HRM has been conceptualised in numerous ways. One conceptualisation is to consider HRM very broadly as relating to all activities linked to the management of work and people within organisations (Boxall and Purcell 2011). Other conceptualisations have suggested that HRM is a distinctive approach to management that aims to enhance organisational performance through certain sets of 'high performance' HR practices, thereby providing a competitive advantage (Storey 1995). However, how HRM may best enhance organisational performance remains a hotly contested and evolving debate (see Chapter2). Accordingly, any understanding of what HRM is, in terms of the range and form of management practices adopted by organisations to achieve competitive advantage, can also be seen as an emerging and shifting entity. In this section we will consider some key distinctions in conceptualisations of HRM to date that are relevant to our discussion of employee well-being.

Soft and hard approaches to HRM

A preliminary distinction between approaches to HRM closely linked to the consideration of employee interests is between suggested 'soft' and 'hard' approaches to HRM. Mainly discussed within the UK literature, soft HRM is associated with the human relations movement, focusing on the elicitation of positive employee responses via self-regulated mechanisms such as commitment to the organisation, rather than management controls such as employee monitoring (Truss et al. 1997). In contrast, hard HRM takes a more quantitative and calculative view of employee management, stressing the importance of tight management control over employee outputs (Storey 1995). Guest (1999: 5) suggests that 'the "hard" version (of HRM) is widely acknowledged to place little emphasis on workers' concerns. In contrast, "soft" HRM, while also having business performance as its primary concern, would be more likely to espouse a parallel concern for workers' outcomes'. One would therefore assume that hard HRM is generally ambivalent to the well-being of employees, while softer HRM approaches have the scope for benefits for employees as well as organisations. This distinction between soft and hard HRM perhaps mirrors that between the 'happy-productive worker' approach and the labour process approach to understanding the impact of HRM discussed earlier.

However, in practice, the distinction between hard and soft approaches to HRM is perhaps blurred. It does not appear that organisations strictly take one approach over the other, but can incorporate both hard and soft elements within their HRM systems. Truss et al's (1997) study of eight large UK organisations revealed that while the rhetoric of soft HRM existed in terms of what was presented to employees, the reality was often more described as hard HRM. This supports the views of Legge (1995) and Keenoy (1990), and a more insidious view of employment relations under HRM (Guest 1999), that softer forms of HRM often pretend to be concerned for workers' interests, while in practice doing the opposite.

Another option is that different approaches are adopted for different kinds of workers within the organisation. Workers that are in essential, strategic jobs for the organisation may be treated with 'soft' HRM, whereas less essential, peripheral workers are treated more along the lines of 'hard' HRM. For example, managers and key technical staff in a larger manufacturing company may have high levels of discretionary freedom and be treated from a long-term, relational and developmental perspective. On the other hand, the jobs of maintenance personnel (contractors) in the same company may be more tightly controlled and managed from a short-term, transactional perspective. Such HR differentiation, e.g. differentiation between strategic jobs and job of lesser strategic importance, is becoming increasingly common in larger organisations (Lepak and Snell 1999; Huselid and Becker 2011).

High performance work systems

Conceptualisations of HRM have most often referred to strategic HR systems; combinations of HR practices aligned towards achieving a particular goal or set of goals. One of the features of recent approaches to HRM is that it is argued that sets of practices, either in systems or in bundles, have a stronger effect on their intended outcomes than the individual practices independently (Combs *et al.* 2006). Examples of HRM systems are Walton's (1985) 'high-commitment management' which places gaining employees' commitment as its core goal (to then achieve better organisational performance), 'high-involvement work systems' that are based on ideas developed by Lawler (1986) focus upon involving employees in more work-related decisions, and 'high-performance work systems' (HPWSs) that seek to enhance organisational performance through integrating many of the practices contained within the previous two approaches (Appelbaum *et al* 2000).

HPWS is the term that has perhaps become most commonly used in recent years to describe strategic systems of HRM aimed at enhancing organisational performance. While no consensus exists about what HR practices actually formulate an HPWS, there is some agreement that at the core of each are practices relating to training and development, contingent pay and reward schemes, performance management and careful recruitment and selection (Boselie *et al.* 2005). Other practices that are often conceptualised as forming part of these strategic HRM systems include protected employment security and work-life balance initiatives, which may be more directly related to (positive) employee well-being.

But are strategic approaches to HRM examples of soft or hard HRM? Well the answer to that is, it depends. HPWSs contain elements that have the potential to have, on the one hand, a hard, controlling and intensifying effect. At the same time the identical elements may also be interpreted as soft, emancipating and rewarding. Taking contingent pay as an example, management may use this to simply reduce fixed wage costs, dictate employee behaviours and monitor employee contributions. Alternatively, contingent pay may be seen as a means to reward employees more fairly, based upon their achievements and to allow employees to take ownership of their level of output and pay.

It may be that the precise formulation and emphasis of an HPWS and its balance between harder and softer elements of the system is the key issue for employee well-being. Similarly, it may be important how an HRM system is implemented within an organisation by line-managers and their interpretation of the organisation's HR policies. Research has found that when we focus on the actual implementation of HR practices within organisations, the intensity, duration and coverage of the application of the practices can vary considerably across a workforce (Purcell *et al.* 2009).

Other HR practices

It is important to consider that a number of other HR practices exist that are used by organisations but are often not considered part of an HPWS. Firstly, there are some practices that may be viewed as more extreme examples of hard HR practices or 'low road' HRM. For example, we might consider the design of narrow and repetitive work roles, regular requirements for working over-time, low basic pay, and the widespread use of non-permanent employment contracts to represent examples of such practices. Current thinking would suggest that, on balance, the use of such 'low-road' practices is related to neither superior employee performance nor well-being (e.g. Boxall and Purcell 2011).

Secondly, there are a number of HR practices that may be assumed to have a more direct effect on employee well-being rather than organisational performance, such as those promoting generous leave provision, supportive and friendly line-management, and the prevention of workplace inequality and/or bullying. Recent research by the Chartered Institute of Personnel and Development (CIPD 2007) in the UK has acknowledged a range of organisational practices that may be seen as 'well-being initiatives'; including private healthcare insurance, access to counselling services/employee assistance programmes, and the provision of support for exercise and healthy eating. These may each be seen to have employee well-being more as their target than employee performance. Therefore, it is important to remember that HRM can relate to a broad number of different HR practices used by organisations, not only HPWSs, many of which can potentially affect employee well-being.

This brief discussion on the conceptualisation of HRM highlights the complexity of the concept and the multitude of ways in which it may be conceived. This is problematic for researchers in the area who are still struggling to develop valid and reliable measures of HRM that can be used across a range of different organisations and allow comparable data to be collected. Moreover, the preoccupation with organisational performance as the main outcome variable has led HR researchers to focus on HPWSs when trying to measure HRM. The study of the relationship between HRM and employee well-being is relatively new. In addition to the problems mentioned in relation to conceptualising HRM, we should be aware that there are other HR practices that may be highly influential on employee well-being but are not typically included within HPWSs and research inspired by HPWSs.

Conceptualising Employee Well-being in the Context of HRM

Employee well-being as a multi-dimensional construct

As Warr (1990) makes clear, employees are people who have general feelings about their lives. Such general well-being is not what is implied, however, with employee well-being. With this term we usually refer to job-specific well-being, e.g. 'people's feelings about themselves in relation to their job' (p. 393). In a recent review by Grant, Christianson and Price (2007), well-being is divided into three important sub-areas specifically for the workplace: these authors mention health, happiness and relationships as the main types of well-being in workers. For each of the three sub-areas a considerable array of concepts, theories and research has been accumulated over the years. Below we discuss some of this work in detail, specifically in relation to HRM.

Physical well-being/health and safety

Work can be dangerous and a hazard to employee safety and health. It is therefore logical that in the area of physical well-being the main focus has, for a long time, been on minimising risks and hazards. As such, HR researchers and managers have tended to neglect this area somewhat, considering it a field for dedicated specialists in occupational health and safety. By the 1990s a sub-area of research on psychosocial working conditions and job risks had evolved and large-scale epidemiologic studies were presenting clear evidence that psychosocial job risks were badly affecting employee health. This was demonstrated for a range of health indicators such as cardiovascular disease, depression, exhaustion and hypertension (Karasek and Theorell 1990). Psychosocial workload and associated fatigue are now also recognised as main causes of accidents and injury at work (Swaen et al. 2003).

Recently, researchers have begun to realise that the amount of energy or vigour that employees feel during work may also be relevant for optimal job performance (Shirom 2007). Indeed, factors such as vigour, enthusiasm and dedication form part of the increasingly popular concept of work engagement that has seen a massive growth in interest from both the academic and practitioner communities in recent years (Bakker and Leiter 2010 and see Chapter 16). In particular, work that requires initiative, creativity, complex problem solving and/or emotion regulation would seem to benefit from the employee not only being free from infirmity and disease, but also being vigorous and energetic. With this change in perspective from negative (risk prevention) to positive (health promotion, positive organisational behaviour), stimulating employee health suddenly becomes a possibly important target for HRM (Nelson and Cooper 2007).

Mental well-being/happiness

In HRM research and practice, mental well-being has hitherto been the sub-factor of the well-being factor that has been considered most often. There are thousands of studies on job satisfaction and related positive worker attitudes/psychological states, like affective commitment, job involvement and work engagement.

The importance of positive worker attitudes and psychological states, driving positive work behaviours and hence job performance is hard to overestimate. It lies at the basis of many theoretical models of HRM, including streams of HRM relating to HPWSs and high-commitment/high-involvement HRM. Given the large amount of interest in mental well-being as an antecedent for good job performance, one would expect the research evidence on the link between positive work attitudes and job performance to be particularly strong. This is not the case, however. Rather, a series of reviews on the extensive literature available on the issue has demonstrated significant, but rather modest, effects of job satisfaction on performance (Judge *et al.* 2001) and of affective commitment on performance (Meyer *et al.* 2002).

Social well-being/relationships

This well-being sub-area is frequently addressed in the HR literature. There it is emphasised how fairness, trust and open communication, vertically between managers and employees, but also horizontally between colleagues, are important factors in managing the workforce. Also, in HRM theory the classical starting point is that workers who experience negative attitudes and psychological states, whether because of an imbalance in their exchange relationship with the employer or because of a violation of the expectations they have as to their job or employer, may seek to compensate such negative attitudes and psychological states by showing negative behaviour towards the organisation, e.g. turnover, reporting absent when not ill, time theft, or other counterproductive behaviours. In other words, the imbalance in their social exchange with the employer may drive employees into withdrawal and compensatory behaviour (Blau 1964; Whitener 2001; Guest 1998).

Direct negative aspects of social relationships are not often mentioned in the HR literature, much similar to a lack of mention of physical working conditions and safety hazards. Topics like workplace bullying, sexual intimidation, discrimination, aggression and violence are considered risks to worker health and safety, and are considered to be more in the realm of occupational health and safety experts. However, it is hard to imagine how, in a workplace where employees experience negative acts from supervisors and/or colleagues, this could be compatible with the kind of trust, fairness and commitment which is the common 'high road' towards good performance in standard HR textbooks.

Well-being: integration and trade-offs

Now that we have briefly introduced the physical, mental and social dimensions of employee well-being, we can address two issues which relate to multiple well-being dimensions. The first issue concerns the conceptual integration of different well-being dimensions. One important such integrated model is the so-called circumplex model (Warr 1987; 2007). The circumplex model states that employee feelings can

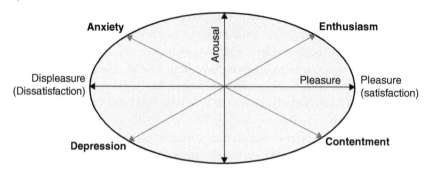

Figure 17.1 The circumplex model of subjective well-being
Source: Peter Warr (1990) *Work and Well Being* Penguin

be classified using a circular shape that is described by two main axes. Any feeling by a worker can be classified somewhere on the circle. In Figure 17.1 this is graphically represented. The first axis ranges from feeling good to feeling bad, e.g. the pleasure dimension. The second axis, the arousal dimension, ranges from fatigued to alert. The model is further elaborated by splitting the second (arousal) axis into two sub-dimensions. The first of these relates to the level of motivation or enthusiasm that the employee is feeling. On the opposite end of feelings of enthusiasm are feelings of depression at work. The second sub-dimension relates to the level of strain or anxiety that the employee is feeling during his/her job. Here, the opposite of anxiety is contentment or comfort.

It is important to note that this model integrates the health and mental dimensions of well-being. Whereas many instances of health and safety consequences exist which are not related clearly to employee subjective feelings, it has become established that sustained cognitive activation is a common cause for a series of health problems which are mediated by the accumulation of fatigue, or in other words by a mechanism of progressive exhaustion (Meijman and Mulder 1998; Ursin and Eriksen 2004; Van Veldhoven 2008).

This leads into the second issue: as a consequence of the multi-dimensional nature of employee well-being there is the possibility of trade-offs between different types of employee well-being. Management strategies and decisions as well as HRM practices and systems may benefit one type of well-being while harming another. For example, in a study of well-being in a call centre environment, Holman (2002) found that the more attentional demands required by a role, the more anxious workers reported to be, but also the more satisfied they were with their job.

Well-being trade-offs can be both deliberate on behalf of employers and employees as well as unwanted. Some examples may explain this. As a first example, consider shift work and dangerous work (like working under water, working in pressurised cabins, working with explosives). It is common to compensate workers for such 'inconveniences' with extra income. Here we see work factors which are clearly recognised as bad and/or risky for employee health and safety, which is traded off for higher income (and, by inference, for more employee happiness/satisfaction).

Mostly, such deals around 'inconveniences' are deliberate decisions on behalf of both employees and employers.

The second example illustrates unwanted effects. In many workplaces, programmes have been implemented over the last few decades to increase job autonomy, job skills and worker participation. Based on theory and research, as well as zeitgeist, HR practitioners and researchers expected to find positive effects of such programmes on employee well-being. However, this has not always been the case. In some instances, unwanted side-effects have been reported, with workers showing symptoms of more job strain; even when appreciating the better opportunities for control at work (Warr 2007).

In summary, we have noted that employee well-being, like the concept of HRM, is potentially multi-dimensional. So when considering the impact of HRM on employee well-being, it may make a difference which dimension of well-being is in question. However, the relationship between the dimensions of well-being is also likely to be complex. On the one hand, one might assume that physical, mental and social well-being dimensions are positively related to one another. However, trade-offs can also exist between dimensions, whereby well-being on one dimension is enhanced at the expense of well-being on the other.

Research on the Relationship between HRM and Employee Well-being

A growing number of research studies have examined the relationship between HRM and employee well-being. A number of comprehensive reviews already exist elsewhere (e.g. Van de Voorde *et al.* in press) so we will not be exhaustive in our coverage of the literature. Instead we will focus on some of the key pieces of research that have informed the debate and on some of the latest evidence that has emerged in recent years.

Seminal studies of HRM and well-being

Guest (1999), in one of the first UK studies of the relationship between HRM and employee well-being, presented what he termed the 'workers' verdict' of HRM. He found uniformly positive relationships between the number of strategic HR practices experienced by employees and their reports of organisational fairness, and trust, job security, job satisfaction and motivation. However, findings were more equivocal with regard to feelings of being under excessive pressure at work. While employees reporting the fewest HR practices in place also experience the greatest pressure at work, there was also a high degree of pressure reported by those experiencing the greatest number of HR practices – which is suggestive of a non-linear, U-shaped relationship between HRM and pressure at work.

Broadly similar findings have been reported by researchers who used the UK Workforce Employee Relations Survey (WERS) 1998 data. For example, Ramsay *et al.* (2000) used these data to construct an HPWS measure and measures of work intensification and job strain. Their findings indicated that HPWSs were linked to higher work intensification and more job strain. However, they also found relationships between HPWS and positive indicators of well-being, including job discretion, management relations, pay satisfaction and perceived job security. Green (2004) used the same data to consider whether HR practices designed to engender greater worker involvement and effort had caused work to have become more intensified in UK workplaces. He found some support for this notion, although the effects were patchy; being mainly observed in small rather than large organisations.

Peccei (2004) also used the WERS 1998 data but focused on 33 individual HR practices rather than any HRM system. He found that while some practices had a positive effect on well-being, others had a more negative impact. Happy workplaces were found to be those that have reasonable workloads and demands, jobs with moderate levels of control and variety, fair pay, job security and positive perceptions of managerial support. Accordingly, the HR practices associated with such workplaces included greater use of full-time permanent employment contracts, restrictions on working hours, job design focused on multi-skilling and loose specification but not work pressure, high rates of pay with additional benefits and low internal dispersion of pay, systematic management communication and a range of family-friendly and work-life balance polices. Importantly, Peccei notes that these practices do not resemble those one might find in an HPWS.

Appelbaum *et al.* (2000) conducted a large study of HPWSs within the US manufacturing sector. They generally found positive effects of HPWS elements on employee well-being. In particular they focused on opportunity to participate, finding a positive link to job satisfaction and negative relationship with stress, once a number of other control and background variables were accounted for. The strongest associate of higher job satisfaction was found to be fair pay, although family-friendly practices and promotion opportunities were also positively linked to satisfaction. Lower stress was also associated with greater levels of pay and work-family practices. However, it is important to note that the overall effect sizes for the relationships, as with most of the studies in this area, are fairly small (Vidal 2007).

More recent studies

More recent studies have sought to replicate and extend the original studies, with research being conducted in a larger range of countries. For example, Macky and Boxall (2007) found a positive link at the individual level between reports of HPWSs and job satisfaction, among other employee attitudes, amongst a representative sample of employees from New Zealand. Castanheira and Chambel (2010) conducted research in a number of Portuguese call centres, finding that HR control systems were associated with greater burnout and HR involvement systems were linked to lower burnout. The well-being effects of involvement-related HR practices were tested in a recent study using data from the WERS 2004 (Wood *et al.* 2012). In as far as the involvement practices related to job design (autonomy, skill use etc.) results mostly confirmed that employee well-being (happiness) mediated positive performance effects of HRM. When considering high-involvement practices that relate more to participation (quality circles, idea capturing schemes etc.) results were different: such high-involvement practices are associated positively with organisational performance but negatively with employee well-being (happiness as well as health) (see also Wood and De Menezes 2011).

A recent review has been conducted of the research evidence regarding the links between HRM, well-being and organisational performance by van de Voorde *et al.* (in press). The study reviewed 36 quantitative research studies that included measures of all three well-being constructs (happiness, relationships and health) published between 1995 and 2010. The authors noted that, in the majority of studies, a positive association was found between the HRM and happiness well-being (which included satisfaction, commitment or other happiness concepts). Indeed, they found that no studies reported a negative association between HRM and happiness. For the relationships aspect of well-being, similarly mostly positive findings were documented in the studies. However, in the six studies that included a measure of 'health-related well-being' (which included measures of workload, intensification and employee strain) the authors did find negative effects. Therefore, they conclude that there is a distinction between the effects of HRM on happiness and relationships-related well-being and on health-related well-being, the former having the potential to be positive and the latter having the potential to be negative.

Other recent studies have sought to better understand the mechanism behind the association between HRM and well-being. Takeuchi, Chen and Lepak (2009), in a study of 76 Japanese organisations, used a multi-level design to find support for the positive relationship between HPWSs and job satisfaction. They then found that this effect could be explained by organisational climates that scored highly on concern for employees. Here the suggestion is that HPWSs produce these supportive climates, which, in turn, affect employee well-being. Wu and Chaturvedi (2009) also examined the effect of HPWSs on job satisfaction in a number of organisations in China, Singapore and Taiwan. Again a positive relationship was found, however they found that procedural justice largely explained this effect. This suggests that the effect of HPWSs on employees' perceptions regarding the fairness of decision-making within organisations is the causal mechanism. Harley *et al.* (2010) found evidence within an Australian sample that HPWSs create an orderly and predictable work environment for employees, which partly explained their findings of a positive influence of HPWSs on employee commitment and satisfaction and negative link with emotional exhaustion. Finally, Jenson *et al.* (2012), in a study of Welsh local government authorities, found that negative associations between HPWSs and both experiences of role overload and feelings of anxiety were observed only when employees had insufficient autonomy and discretion over issues relating to their jobs.

Summary of research findings

The findings seem to be fairly conclusive that when conceptualised as a system, HRM, and most usually operationalised as HPWSs, has a positive effect on employees' happiness at work. In other words, employees report more satisfaction with their jobs and have more positive work experiences when they also experience 'more' HRM. However, findings are more mixed when physical measures of well-being are used. Early research that culminates in the reviews of van de Voorde *et al.* (at press) and Peccei (2012) suggests broadly negative effects of HRM in terms of perceptions of work intensification and stress. However, even this conclusion remains equivocal, highlighted by the more recent research by Castanheira and Chambel (2010) and Harley *et al.* (2010) that finds HPWSs sometimes help reduce aspects of employee burnout and the study by Wood *et al.* (2012) suggesting that different groups of practices can have divergent effects. Findings become considerably more complex when HRM is disaggregated into individual practices as in Peccei's (2004) study. However, this importantly shows that practices one would expect to find in an HPWS are not the practices that maximise employee well-being. So, while we may find that HPWSs are largely benign or even slightly positive for employee well-being, if people are interested in enhancing employee well-being then HPWSs may not be the most effective HR practices to achieve that. Indeed, it may be that any negative influence of HPWSs on well-being might be offset by other practices adopted by organisations more directly targeting employee well-being, which may not have been accounted for in the research conducted to date, such as the offering of Employee Assistance Programmes (see later discussion) or practices that enhance employees' job autonomy, as suggested by the recent research by Jenson and colleagues (2012). Finally, research that has tried to examine the reason why HRM is related positively to well-being has identified a number of different potential mediators. Broadly, these studies suggest that HRM promotes more favourable employee attitudes towards the organisational environment, which at least partially explains its association with well-being. Clearly, though, more work is required to better understand this mechanism.

Future Research Directions in the HRM-Well-being Debate

As mentioned previously, the study of the relationship between HRM and employee well-being is relatively new. At present there remains a lot that we do not know about this relationship. The following three areas could be particularly interesting for future knowledge generation.

Contingency variables

The notions of 'best-practice' and 'best-fit' approaches to HRM have dominated debate about the role of HRM in organisational performance for more than 20 years.

The search for contingency variables has preoccupied advocates of the 'best-fit' school, who have attempted to better understand the conditions under which certain systems of HRM are likely to be most effective in promoting organisational performance. A contingency variable is a third factor that explains why the association between two other concepts may vary.

Support for the best fit approach to HRM has been mixed (e.g. Delery and Doty 1996; Youndt *et al.* 1996), but there is an intuitive logic to the notion that organisations may need to tailor their HR practices to suit their strategic needs. Despite the interest in contingency variables in HRM research more generally, there has been very little investigation of them in the study of HRM and employee well-being to date (Jenson *et al.* 2012 being an exception).

Considering the mixed findings regarding the impact of HRM on employee well-being, examination of contingency factors that may explain this variation in effects may be very relevant. A number of potential contingency variables have been identified by Peccei *et al.* (2012), including the role of national institutions and legislation, industrial sector, trade unions, organisational turbulence and workforce characteristics. One may also propose that the other organisational characteristics, such as climate and line-manager attitudes towards HR practices, may further influence the implementation of HR practices on the shop-floor, and therefore affect the nature of their influence on employee well-being. One may also consider non-HPWS practices as potential contingency variables. For example, an HPWS that is implemented in conjunction with other practices that represent 'hard' or 'low road' HRM may tip the balance towards a negative impact overall on well-being. Alternatively, the addition of further 'soft' practices to an HPWS may off-set any negative effects so that the net effect is positive.

Alternative dimensions of employee well-being

As discussed in a previous section, employee well-being is a multi-dimensional concept. Existing research has mainly focused on work-related mental well-being and happiness. Measuring aspects of this dimension of well-being is relatively straightforward within the employee attitude surveys, which are the dominant data collection method in this research. A smaller amount of research has studied employee physical health. As previously discussed, these studies point toward different and often negative effects of HRM on measures of physical health. However, to date these studies have predominantly used self-report survey measures of employee physical health, which may not be as accurate as more objective biological (e.g. cardio-vascular) or clinical (e.g. assessment by psychotherapist) measures of employee health or measures of employee health behaviours (e.g. workplace accidents, sleeping behaviours). Further work may also consider a broader spectrum of subjective health measures to encompass desirable aspects of health, such as employee energy and proactivity, and HRM's impact on such measures (Dorenbosch 2009).

The role of employees

A final suggestion for future research concerns the role of employees within the HRM–well-being relationship. Employees are mainly portrayed (in negative depictions of HRM) as the 'victims' of management's efforts to enhance organisational performance or (in more positive representations of HRM) rather mechanistically as 'human capital'. But are employees simply passive recipients of HR practices or should we instead think of employees as more actively involved in the shaping of their experiences of HRM? Researchers studying job stress realised more than 20 years ago that employees' appraisal and evaluation of stimuli within their working environment, rather than the objective features of stimuli *per se*, was fundamental to understanding the impact of 'stressors' (see the Transactional Theory of Stress; Lazarus and Folkman 1984). However, research on HRM often assumes a more 'stimulus–response' approach to understanding employee well-being, which may not tell the whole story.

Recent work in the US by Nishii and colleagues suggests that the employees within the same organisation may perceive and interpret the same HR practices very differently (Nishii and Wright 2008). In one study, it was found that employees make different attributions about the reasons why management adopts certain HR practices (Nishii *et al.* 2008). They find that some employees perceive the HR practices within their organisation to be implemented due to management's concerns for service/production quality and employee well-being. In contrast, other people will attribute HR practices to management's attempts at cost reduction and employee exploitation. Their findings indicate that attributions based upon quality and employee enhancement are positively associated with job satisfaction. In contrast, cost reduction and employee exploitation attributions had a slight negative association with job satisfaction. While employee attribution processes may indeed play an important role in the impact of HR practices, little is known about what influences employee HR attributions and whether they are reflective of rather stable attitudes and personality characteristics or are more open to contextual influences, perhaps by line-managers and work colleagues.

In addition to the role of employee perception and attribution in influencing the impact of HRM, several recent developments within the literature suggest a more proactive role for employees in physically shaping their working conditions. Firstly, job crafting theory (Wrzesniewski and Dutton 2001) posits that, over time, employees driven by their need for control, positive self-image and human connection with others, change the cognitive, task and relational boundaries within their work roles. The ultimate goal for job crafters is the achievement of greater work meaning and identity through successful alterations to their job design and social environment. For example, a cleaning services employee may decide to enhance his/her job by adopting a friendly, sociable approach to the workers in the offices he/she is supposed to clean. Though this is not specified in the job description, this employee contributes to the work atmosphere in this way, but also importantly shapes the job in a way that makes it more pleasurable and possibly more meaningful to perform.

A second mechanism through which employees have been found to influence their working conditions is through the development of idiosyncratic deals, which represent individually negotiated work arrangements between workers and their employers (Rousseau 2005). Typically reserved for more valued employees, idiosyncratic deals offer a means through which workers can actively shape their conditions of work and potentially the HR practices they receive. For example, it may be that, over time, some employees seek out certain HR practices (e.g. flexible working) within their organisation and try to avoid experiencing others (e.g. unnecessary job training). However, there is much to learn about any 'bottom-up' influence of employees on the HR practices they receive.

Debate: Whose Responsibility is Employee Well-being?

So far we have considered the nature of HRM and employee well-being and the likely relationship between the two. But whose responsibility is it to enhance the quality of working life within organisations? And what examples are there of initiatives aimed at enhancing the health and happiness of employees? By tradition, employee well-being has been a policy issue for governments, triggering all kinds of national and international initiatives trying to prevent harm and promote well-being. Such institutional impetus towards employee well-being concerns the organisation's social legitimacy (Paauwe 2004; Boxall and Purcell 2011), much like other policy issues like environmental hazards and financial risks. Organisations vary in how they deal with such legitimacy issues. Some opt for doing no more than their institutional context allows; others opt for maximising well-being and taking it to levels well beyond basic requirements. It is also perhaps useful to question the responsibilities of employees for their well-being at work, beyond the role played by the state and employers.

National and international responsibilities

National interests in the issue of the well-being of citizens have been recently highlighted in the UK with the coalition government's plans to begin measurement of the country's psychological and environmental 'well-being' as part of a collection of indicators used to better assess quality of life. Indeed, the UK is not alone in considering such initiatives aimed at moving beyond simple economic wealth metrics as the benchmarks of national progress and prosperity, with both France and Canada engaged in similar activities. While the details of these endeavours are still in the process of being established in 2012, they represent an overt acknowledgement that well-being is increasingly being viewed as an important outcome of national interest and of the State's responsibility in looking after the health and happiness of its citizens.

Perhaps more explicitly targeted at the health of workers, there are two kinds of national and international initiatives aimed at stimulating organisational attention for employee well-being: general and specific. With general, we imply in this context those initiatives that have wider aims than only employee well-being; with specific, we imply those initiatives expressly targeted at improving employee well-being.

Some of the most important examples of general initiatives are national and international pieces of legislation that influence worker well-being. Such legislation deals with important issues like working conditions, working time arrangements and work contracts. Existing rules as to how heavy loads are allowed to be for lifting in the workplace, how many work hours are allowed without rest, and how easily contracts can be dissolved are likely to influence employee well-being. Also, legislation can create all kinds of procedural instruments that may help improve conditions, time arrangements and contracts that are conducive to worker well-being. For example, the European Union issued a framework directive on working conditions and working time, which each member state needs to translate into national laws. As the framework directive suggests that every workplace should make a list of working condition risks and health hazards, laws are accepted in member states, like the UK, to assess and monitor such risks and hazards. This also holds for risks that are related to job content and workplace aggression and violence.

It is also worthwhile to mention general initiatives at a global level. While maybe not directed at common problems for Western organisations and workers, the possible impact on employee well-being worldwide is huge. For example, there is the 'Decent Work' initiative by the International Labour Office in Geneva, which wants to have an impact globally by creating proper jobs, guaranteeing rights at work, extending social protection and promoting social dialogue, as well as stimulating gender equality at work.

Whereas many general initiatives exist that may affect worker well-being, very few specific initiatives exist. One notable exception for the UK is the Management Standards approach for stress at work (Cousins *et al.* 2004; Mackay *et al.* 2004). These constitute a government initiative to combat stress in UK workplaces. A taxonomy was made of factors causing stress in the workplace and measures were developed to operationalise these (risk assessment). Subsequently, several programmes have been directed at getting UK organisations to adopt the standards, use the measures and take initiatives at the workplace level to either prevent future problems or intervene in existing problems. Cox *et al.* (2007) have evaluated this implementation process and conclude that where such specific initiatives as the Management Standards are concerned, researchers and policy makers still need to experiment and better understand how to effectively change organisational practice. Implementation of national policy with regard to employee well-being does not appear to work in the orderly, sequential fashion that many would lead us to believe.

Organisational initiatives

The former may give the impression that organisations only do something about worker well-being because they are required to do so by law and pressures from society. But this is not true. There have always been visionary business owners and managers who have stimulated attention for worker well-being beyond what is required by law. Strangely enough this brings us back to Frederick Taylor. He inspired Henry Ford to build automobile plants in the US that were based on the principles of scientific management. Looking back now on the kinds of jobs Ford was offering his employees, we tend to perceive them as simple and maybe inhuman in terms of a lack of autonomy and skill use. However, Ford had no trouble at all finding workers: at that moment in time he was perceived as a visionary employer, taking important organisational initiatives to offer workers jobs that were relatively safe, in a relatively clean environment, and with a very reasonable amount of pay (Nelson 1992).

So, some employers have always taken initiatives aimed at attracting and retaining good personnel, and at optimising operations. More recently, it has become common practice to rank employers according to how well they practise good 'employership', albeit on a voluntary basis for the organisations involved. For instance, we have witnessed market initiatives like 'Great Place to Work' and 'Triple P (People, Planet, Profit)'. Such initiatives generate a lot of positive media attention for the participating organisations which end high in such rankings, but they also widely advertise the fact that good initiatives emerge in organisations.

There are many more good examples of organisations and HR practices documented in the field. For instance, Kompier and Cooper (1999) presented a series of European case studies under the title 'preventing stress, improving productivity'. Similarly, Leka and Cox (2010) present some international examples of good practice in psychosocial risk management. What becomes apparent from such Occupational Health and Safety initiatives is that some form of systematic data collection on employee perceptions of psychosocial job risks and stress levels is a common denominator of many of these approaches.

Some examples of organisations providing specific programmes aimed at improving and/or maintaining employee well-being are mentioned in Box 17.1. Initiatives may range from isolated activities like offering employees access to a local gym or providing counselling services, to more elaborate employee assistance and/or health promotion programmes. In these more elaborate programmes employees can choose to participate in specific courses or activities depending on their lifestyle problem/wishes (Kirk and Brown 2003; Cascio and Boudreau 2008).

Interestingly, employee survey research in relation to well-being is common in companies, but not as much on the negative side (e.g. checking risks and stress levels) as on the positive side (e.g. checking engagement/satisfaction levels and the drivers thereof). Here lies another important organisational initiative in relation to employee well-being. Employee engagement/satisfaction surveys are intensively linked with

---

Box 17.1 Some examples of organisational initiatives directed at improving and/or maintaining employee well-being

Well-being initiatives put in place by AstraZeneca, a multinational pharmaceutical company, were the focus of one case study reported by the UK's Health and Safety Executive (HSE). Introduction of a work-life balance programme, rehabilitation and treatment services such as physiotherapy, counselling and return to work programmes, and health promotion encompassing sports facilities and health screening produced a range of reported benefits, including reduced health insurance costs, absence levels 31% lower than the UK average and improvements in safety records and work-related stress cases. A further case study reported by the HSE looked at a relatively simple initiative. Barts and the London NHS Trust provided their employees with a voluntary flu vaccination and found that this led to a reduction of 25% in sickness absence amongst those who took up the vaccination.

A further case study reported by the CIPD examined a 'feeling good' initiative introduced by the Prudential, a multinational financial services company. The main aim of the initiative was to provide employees with the tools to manage their own well-being both at and away from work. This included basic benefits such as health insurance and gym membership, but went further to include advice on nutrition, stress management and sickness prevention. Over 80% of employees signed up to the health programme, and benefits of the initiative were reported to be reductions in short-term absence and turnover and increases in productivity.

Kraft Foods employs around 1,500 people in UK and Ireland and introduced a programme in 2004 based around three key areas. Firstly, Kraft sought to provide employees with more information about health and well-being issues through communication on the intranet and displayed in working environments. Secondly, Kraft held special events such as bike rides, Healthy Living weeks and nutrition and cookery demonstrations. Thirdly, Kraft provided individual initiatives such as massage and reflexology therapies and exercise, yoga and pilates classes.

---

the development of measures for organisational culture and climate. Many large companies have company surveys in place, which are facilitated by larger research institutes (like ISR, Cyrota, Valtera). Macey *et al.* (2009) describe how an engagement survey can be integrated into a larger employee engagement campaign, building on years of experience in company survey work. They also suggest integrating attention for positive (HRM) and negative (Occupational Health) aspects of well-being into one survey, which makes a lot of sense from a business process perspective.

Employee responsibility

In the previous section of the chapter we questioned whether employees are simply passive recipients of HRM or play a more active role in dictating their work experiences. But to what extent should we consider employees as being responsible for managing their own well-being at work? Are employees simply unable to protect themselves when asked by their organisations to do things that may be harmful to them? Or should we think of employees as willing accomplices; happy to make sacrifices that may harm their health in order to perform well for their companies and enhance their own careers?

It is certainly true that for many employees there are great pressures to meet what is expected of them by their organisations. Low status and power within organisations, processes of social conformity, limited or no protection through employee representation and limited alternative employment opportunities elsewhere may all contribute to the perceived inability to resist unreasonable requests from an employer. For example, the request to work unusually long hours at short notice would be difficult to turn down if a person is at a relatively low hierarchical level, has colleagues who all work extra hours, has no workplace representation and works where the local labour market provides few job alternatives. So it would be very harsh to suggest that all individuals can and should take responsibility for their work-related well-being. The concern here is firmly on the role of organisations and national institutions in promoting healthy work practices and protecting such precarious employees.

However, it is also likely that there is a further group of employees who are better able to manage their own work-related well-being. Here we are referring to employee groups with greater status and power within the labour market. This is not to say that, for these individuals, organisations don't have any responsibility in looking after them, but that such employee groups have some opportunity to choose how they respond to organisational demands and dictate the nature of the employment relationship. For such groups it might be fair to attribute a share of responsibility for their own work-related well-being.

Whether employees, if they have the opportunity, always choose to maximise their own well-being is not clear. While we might assume that individuals are interested in their health and happiness, we might not expect them to always aim to maximise their own well-being. For example, many employees may happily trade moderate workloads, low responsibility, leisure time, or sleep and recovery if this provides them with a more rewarding job in terms of remuneration, career progression or success. People's own interests in their economic well-being and broader self-concept as a 'successful person' may conflict with their psychological and physical health. As an extreme example we can mention, in this context, the issue of 'workaholism', which has recently been considered as possible collateral for being overly engaged in one's work (Schaufeli *et al.* 2008). A less extreme form of this behaviour might be 'presenteeism', which represents the decision to attend work when ill. Perhaps, contrary to much common thinking, research has discovered that, rather than being a positive behaviour often informally endorsed by organisational cultures, 'soldiering on' when ill is associated with productivity losses, which may constitute a problem for organisations; and potentially the development of more serious medical conditions, which is bad for both employee and organisation (Johns 2010).

Conclusions

The chapter has discussed the relationship between HRM and employee well-being from a number of different perspectives. The impact of work and the organisation of work on the well-being of employees has been a long-standing area of interest and contention. The recent interest in the specific relationship between HRM and well-being, and in particular between HPWSs and employee mental and physical well-being, has been the focus of a great deal of debate and research activity. While there are difficulties in defining, and therefore measuring, both HRM and employee well-being, research has begun to uncover some broadly consistent findings: HRM has the capacity to make work more stimulating and satisfying, at the same time as making it possibly more challenging and intense. On balance, findings point towards a more positive effect of HRM on employees than negative. However, there is scope for much more research work in this area and an ongoing debate about where the responsibility for employee health and well-being ultimately lies, depending on the employee groups involved.

REFERENCES

Appelbaum, E. 2002: The impact of new forms of work organisation on workers, in G. Murray, J. Belanger, A. Giles and P.A. Lapointe (eds.), *Work employment relations in the high-performance workplace*, London: Continuum.

Appelbaum, E., Bailey, T., Berg, P. and Kalleberg, A. 2000: *Manufacturing advantage: Why high performance work systems pay off*, New York, NY: Cornell University Press.

Bakker, A. B. and Leiter, M. P. 2010: *Work Engagement: A Handbook of Essential Theory and Research*, New York, NY: Psychology Press.

Blau, P. 1964: *Exchange and Power in Social Life*, New York, NY: John Wiley & Sons Inc.

Boselie, P., Dietz, G. and Boon, C. 2005: Commonalities and contradictions in HRM and performance research, *Human Resources Management Journal*, **15**, 67–94.

Boxall, P. and Purcell, P. 2011: *Strategy and human resource management* 3rd edn, Basingstoke: Palgrave Macmillan.

Cascio, W. F. and Boudreau, J. W. 2008: *Investing in People*, Upper Saddle River, NJ: Pearson.

Castanheira, F. and Chambel, M. J. 2010: Reducing burnout in call centers through HR practices, *Human Resource Management*, **49**, 1047–1065.

Chartered Institute of Personnel and Development 2007: *What's happening with well-being at work?* (Ref. 3869), London: Chartered Institute of Personnel and Development.

Combs, J., Liu, Y., Hall, A. and Ketchen, D. 2006: How much do high-performance work practices matter? A meta-analysis of their effects on organisational performance, *Personnel Psychology*, **59**, 501–528.

Cousins, R., MacKay, C., Clarke, S., Kelly, C., Kelly, P. and McCaig, R. 2004: 'Management Standards' and work-related stress in the UK: Practical development, *Work & Stress*, **18**, 113–136.

Cox, T., Karanika, M., Mellor, N., Lomas, L., Houdmont, J. and Griffiths, A. 2007: *Implementation of the Management Standards for work-related stress: Process evaluation*, Report to the Health & Safety Executive, Nottingham: Institute of Work, Health & Organisations, University of Nottingham.

Delbridge, R. and Turnbull, P. 1992: Human resource maximisation: The management of labour under Just-in-Time manufacturing systems, in P. Blyton and P. Turnbull (eds.), *Reassessing Human Resource Management*, London: Sage.

Delery, J. E. and Doty, D. H. 1996: Modes of theorizing in strategic human resource management: tests of universalistic, contingency, and configurational performance predictions, *Academy of Management Journal*, **39**, 802–835.

Dorenbosch, L. W. 2009: *Management by Vitality*, Dissertation, Tilburg University.

Godard, J. 2001: Beyond the high-performance paradigm? An analysis of variation in Canadian managerial perceptions of reform program effectiveness, *British Journal of Industrial Relations*, **39**, 25–52.

Grant, A. M., Christianson, M. K. and Price, R. H. 2007: Happiness, health, or relationships? Managerial practices and employee well-being tradeoffs, *Academy of Management Perspectives*, **21**, 51–63.

Green, F. 2004: Why has work become more intense? *Industrial Relations*, **43**, 709–741.

Guest, D. E. 1998: Is the psychological contract worth taking seriously? *Journal of Organizational Behavior*, **19**, 649–664.

Guest, D. E. 1999: Human resource management – the worker's verdict, *Human Resource Management Journal*, **9**, 5–25.

Harley, B., Allen, B. C. and Sargent, L. D. 2007: High performance work systems and employee experience of work in the service sector: The case of aged care, *British Journal of Industrial Relations*, **45**, 607–633.

Harley, B., Sargent, L., and Allen, B. 2010: Employee responses to high performance work system practices: An empirical test of the disciplined worker, *Work, Employment and Society*, **24**, 740–760.

Holman, D. 2002: Employee Well-being in Call Centres, *Human Resource Management Journal*, **12**, 35–51.

Huselid, M. A. and Becker, B. E. 2011: Bridging micro and macro domains: workforce differentiation and strategic human resource management, *Journal of Management*, **37**, 421–428.

Jenson, J. M., Patel, P. C. and Messersmith, J. G. 2012: High-Performance Work Systems and Job Control: Consequences for Anxiety, Role Overload, and Turnover Intentions, *Journal of Management*, **38**.

Johns, G. 2010: Presenteeism in the workplace: A review and research agenda, *Journal of Organizational Behavior*, **31**, 519–542.

Judge, T. A., Thoresen, C. J., Bono, J. E. and Patton, G. K. 2001: The job satisfaction-job performance relationship: A qualitative and quantitative review, *Psychological Bulletin*, **127**, 376–407.

Karasek, R. A. and Theorell, T. 1990: *Healthy work: stress, productivity, and the reconstruction of working life*, New York, NY: Basic Books.

Keenoy, T. 1990: HRM: A case of the wolf in sheep's clothing? *Personnel Review*, **2**, 3–9.

Kirk, A. K. and Brown, D. F. 2003: Employee Assistance Programmes: A review of the management of stress and wellbeing through workplace counselling and consulting, *Australian Psychologist*, **36**, 138–143.

Kompier, M. A. J. and Cooper, C. L. 1999: *Preventing stress, improving productivity: European case studies in the workplace*, London: Routledge.

Kroon, B., van de Voorde, K. and van Veldhoven, M. 2009: Cross-level effects of high performance work practices – two counteracting mediating mechanisms compared, *Personnel Review*, **38**, 509–525.

Lawler, E. E. 1986: *High Involvement Management*, San Francisco, CA: Jossey-Bass.

Lazarus, R. S. and Folkman, S. 1984: *Stress, appraisal and coping*. New York, NY: Springer.

Legge, K. 1995: *Human Resource Management: Rhetorics and Realities*, Basingstoke: Macmillan.

Leka, S. and Cox, T. 2010: Psychosocial risk management at the workplace level, in S. Leka and J. Houdmont (eds.), *Occupational Health Psychology*, Chichester: Wiley-Blackwell.

Lepak, D. P. and Snell, S. A. 1999: The human resource architecture: Toward a theory of human capital allocation and development, *Academy of Management Review*, **1**, 31–48.

Macey, W. H., Schneider, B., Barbera, K. and Young, S. A. 2009: *Employee Engagement: Tools for analysis, practice and competitive advantage*, New York, NY: Wiley-Blackwell.

MacKay, C., Cousins, R., Kelly, P., Lee, S. and McCaig, R. 2004: 'Management Standards' and work-related stress in the UK: Policy background and science, *Work and Stress*, **18**, 91–112.

Macky, K. and Boxall, P. 2007: The relationship between 'high-performance work practices' and employee attitudes: an investigation of additive and interaction effects, *International Journal of Human Resource Management*, **18**, 537–567.

Meijman, T. and Mulder, G. 1998: 'Psychological aspects of workload', in P. Drenth and H. Thierry (eds.), *Handbook of Work and Organizational Psychology*, Vol. 2: Work Psychology, pp. 5–33. Hove, UK: Psychology Press.

Meyer, J. P., Stanley, D. J., Herscovitch, L. and Topolnytsky, L. 2002: Affective, continuance, and normative commitment to the organization: A meta-analysis of antecedents, correlates and consequences, *Journal of Vocational Behavior*, **61**, 20–52.

Nelson, D. 1992: *A mental revolution: scientific management since Taylor*, Columbus: Ohio State University Press.

Nelson, D. L. and Cooper, C. L. 2007: *Positive Organizational Behavior: Accentuating the Positive at Work*, Thousand Oaks, CA: Sage.

Nishii, L. and Wright, P. 2008: Variability within organisations: Implications for strategic human resource management, in D. B. Smith (ed.), *The people make the place: Dynamic linkages between individuals and organisations*, New York, NY: Taylor & Francis.

Nishii, L. H., Lepak, D. P. and Schneider, B. 2008: Employee attributions of the "why" of HR practices: their effects on employee attitudes and behaviors, and customer satisfaction, *Personnel Psychology*, **61**, 503–545.

Paauwe, J. 2004: *HRM and performance: Achieving long term viability*, Oxford: Oxford University Press.

Parker, S. K., Wall, T. D. and Cordery, J. L. 2001: Future work design research and practice: towards an elaborate model of work design, *Journal of Occupational and Organizational Psychology*, **74**, 413–440.

Peccei, R. 2004: *Human resource management and the search for the happy workplace*, Inaugural address, Rotterdam: Erasmus Research Institute of Management (ERIM).

Peccei, R., van de Voorde, K. and van Veldhoven, M. J. P. M. 2012: HRM, performance and well-being, in D. E. Guest, J. Paauwe and P. Wright (eds.), *Managing people and performance*, Chichester: Wiley-Blackwell.

Pfeffer, J. 1998: *The human equation*, Boston, MA: Harvard Business School.

Purcell, J., Kinnie, N., Swart, J., Rayton, B. and Hutchinson, S. 2009: *People Management and Performance*, Oxford, UK: Routledge.

Quinn, R. E. and Rohrbaugh, J. 1983: A spatial model of effectiveness criteria: Toward a competing values approach to organizational analysis, *Management Science*, **29**, 363–377.

Ramsay, H., Scholarios, D. and Harley, B. 2000: Employees of high-performance work systems: Testing inside the black box, *British Journal of Industrial Relations*, **38**, 501–531.

Rousseau, D. M. 2005: *I-deals: Idiosyncratic deals workers bargain for themselves*, New York, NY: M. E. Sharpe.

Schaufeli, W. B., Taris, T. W. and van Rhenen, W. 2008: Workaholism, burnout and engagement: Three of a kind or three different kinds of employee well-being, *Applied Psychology: An International Review*, **57**, 173–203.

Shirom, A. 2007: Explaining vigor: on the antecedents and consequences of vigor as a positive affect at work, in D. L. Nelson and C. L. Cooper (eds.), *Positive Organizational Behavior: Accentuating the Positive at Work*, Thousand Oaks, CA: Sage.

Staw, B. M. 1986: Organizational psychology and the pursuit of the happy/productive worker, *California Management Review*, **27**, 40–55.

Storey, J. 1995: *Human Resource Management: A Critical Text*, London: Routledge.

Swaen, G. M. H., Van Amelsvoort, L., Bultmann, U. and Kant, I. J. 2003: Fatigue as a risk factor for being injured in an occupational accident: Results from the Maastricht cohort study, *Occupational and Environmental Medicine*, **60**, 88–92.

Takeuchi, R., Chen, G. and Lepak, D. P. 2009: Through the looking glass of a social system: Cross-level effects of high-performance work systems on employees' attitudes, *Personnel Psychology*, **62**, 1–29.

Taylor, F. W. 1911: *The Principles of Scientific Management*, New York, NY: Harper & Brothers.

Truss, C., Gratton, L., Hope-Hailey, V., McGovern, P. and Stiles, P. 1997: Soft and Hard Models of Human Resource Management: A Reappraisal, *Journal of Management Studies*, **34**, 53–74.

Ursin, H. and Eriksen, H. R. 2004: The Cognitive Activation Theory of Stress, *Psychoneuroendocrinology*, **29**, 567–592.

Van de Voorde, K., Paauwe, J. and van Veldhoven, M. In press: Employee well-being and the HRM-organizational performance relationship: a review of quantitative studies, *International Journal of Management Review*.

Van Veldhoven, M. 2008: Need for recovery after work: An overview of construct, measurement and research, in J. Houdmont and S. Leka (eds.), *Occupational health psychology:*

European perspectives on research, education and practice (Vol. 3), Nottingham: Nottingham University Press.

Vernon, A. M., Wyatt, S. and Ogden, A. D. 1924: *On the extent and effects of variety in repetitive work*, Report 26, Industrial Fatigue Research Board, London.

Vidal, M. 2007: Lean Production, Worker Empowerment, and Job Satisfaction: A Qualitative Analysis and Critique, *Critical Sociology*, **33**, 247–278.

Walton, R. E. 1985: From 'control' to 'commitment' in the workplace, *Harvard Business Review*, **63**, 77–84.

Warr, P. B. 1987: *Work, unemployment, and mental health*, Oxford: Clarendon Press.

Warr, P. B. 1990: The measurement of well-being and other aspects of mental health, *Journal of Occupational Psychology*, **63**, 193–219.

Warr, P. B. 2007: *Work, happiness, and unhappiness*, London: Lawrence Erlbaum Associates.

Watson, T. J. 1995: *Sociology, work and industry*, London: Routledge.

Whitener, E. M. 2001: Do high commitment human resource practices affect employee commitment? *Journal of Management*, **27**, 515–535.

Wood, S. and De Menezes, L. 2011: High involvement management, high-performance work systems and well-being, *International Journal of Human Resource Management*, **22**, 1586–1610.

Wood, S., van Veldhoven, M., Croon, M. and De Menezes, L. 2012: Enriched job design, high-involvement management and organizational performance: the mediating roles of job satisfaction and well-being, *Human Relations*, **65**, 419–445.

Wright, T. A. and Staw, B. M. 1999: Affect and favorable work outcomes. Two longitudinal tests of the happy-productive worker thesis, *Journal of Organizational Behavior*, **20**, 1–23.

Wrzesniewski, A. and Dutton, J. E. 2001: Crafting a job: Revisioning employees as active crafters of their work, *Academy of Management Review*, **26**, 179–201.

Wu, P. C. and Chaturvedi, S. 2009: The Role of Procedural Justice and Power Distance in the Relationship Between High-Performance Work Systems and Employee Attitudes: A Multilevel Perspective, *Journal of Management*, **35**, 1228–1247.

Youndt, M., Snell, S., Dean, J. and Lepak, D. 1996: Human resource management, manufacturing strategy, and firm performance, *Academy of Management Journal*, **39**, 836–866.

CHAPTER EIGHTEEN

Employer Branding: Developments and Challenges

Martin R. Edwards

When the earlier version of this chapter (Edwards 2005) was written, employer branding was still a phenomenon in its relatively early stages of development, having been introduced as an activity for HR less than 10 years previously (by Ambler and Barrow 1996). Since 2005, however, the interest in employer branding has continued to grow. As evidence for how seriously HR is taking the idea of employer branding, the UK HR practitioner body, the Chartered Institute of Personnel and Development (CIPD), produced no less than six reports and guides to employer branding between 2007 and 2010 (CIPD 2007ab; CIPD 2009; CIPD 2010abc) and in 2008 its Chief Executive held employer branding up as representing how the personnel department has transitioned into the management of human resources. She argued that the HR profession is going through a 'quiet revolution' and that 'it used to be Christmas parties and inductions, now we talk about employer branding' (cited by Logan 2008: 8). In addition to the practitioner literature, numerous academic papers have now been published specifically on employer branding, which indicates that it is a topic that has arrived (indicative examples include: Aggerholm *et al.* 2011; Backhaus and Tikoo 2004; Berthen *et al.* 2005; Edwards 2010; Foster *et al.* 2010; Lievens 2007; Moroko and Uncles 2009) and that many are taking it seriously.

Despite the growth in interest in employer branding, a degree of ambiguity still exists as to what employer branding actually involves, partly because as an HR initiative it has the potential to cover and involve a broad range of HR activities (e.g. communications, recruitment, training, performance management). As Edwards (2010) argued 'In its full scope, employer branding cuts across many traditional HR specialisms and becomes an umbrella programme that provides structure to previously separate policies and practices' (p. 5). What this means is that no single policy or practice can necessarily be used to define what it involves for HR. A further reason why it is not straightforward to identify what employer *branding* involves, is that some of the central ideas at the heart of employer brand notion, such as the 'employment experience', are potentially intangible, making them difficult to define. Furthermore, each organisation will vary considerably on what the employment experience may involve. This latter issue may go some way to explaining why there is yet to be any definitive research on the topic which can be identified as fundamentally contributing to our understanding of the concept, and whilst there may be numerous articles and case studies written about employer branding, as Lievens argued in 2007, 'empirical studies examining its assumptions and effects are scarce' (p. 62). This may, however, change over the next few years as a number of academic research projects currently under way begin to produce information examining some of the core assumptions made.

One of the challenges that any researcher (or for that matter any organisation/consultancy) faces when trying to identify what an organisation's employment brand consists of, is that isolating a central idea at its heart – the 'unique employment experience' offered to employees – can entail so many different things and each organisation is likely to have fundamentally different features on offer. Identifying in the first instance 'the package of functional, economic and psychological benefits provided by employment' (Ambler and Barrow 1996: 187) or 'what makes a firm different and desirable as an employer' (Lievens 2007:51) is by no means a simple task, as the possible range of things that could make up an employment 'experience' is extremely broad. Researching the area of employer branding to examine its assumptions and effects will require a sophisticated and highly sensitive set of research tools.

The chapter begins with a discussion about why there is so much interest in employer branding, it then moves on to outline definitions of employer branding followed by a discussion of what activities it entails. There have been a number of developments in the literature over recent years and these are discussed along with some of the challenges often mentioned. These developments include a growing argument being presented that the target population or customers of the branding exercise (in this case the employee workforce) needs to be segmented and the brand offering tailored, depending upon the constituent workforce segment. The developments also include a continuation of arguments presented by other authors that employee branding and internal branding should necessarily become part of any employer branding activity. The chapter reflects on this practice and discusses some of the challenges that this introduces (including challenges to diversity and inclusion). The chapter then discusses the link between employer branding and Corporate Social Responsibility (CSR) initiatives. It then goes on to make a link between employer branding, CSR and behavioural ethics and raises the ethical challenges that this focus brings to the HR function.

Why the Continuing Interest in Employer Branding?

There are a number of reasons why employer branding continues to be a focus of interest for the HR field. First, it follows the dominance of the idea of 'branding' in management as a powerful business tool. Second, developments in the field of marketing place employees at the centre of a company's marketing strategy, which means that employee branding initiatives are often a key part (and sometimes a driver) of broader employer branding programmes. Third, employer branding is seen as an opportunity for the HR function to become more strategically focused. Fourth, employer branding provides HR with a framework to deal with growing pressure for organisations to demonstrate their Corporate Social Responsibility. Finally, employer branding as an initiative nicely dovetails with now familiar models of HRM as an employment relations model, which aims to encourage employees to be organisationally committed and to share organisational values.

As mentioned, one explanation for the growing interest in employee and employer branding is that companies place so much emphasis on the importance of having a strong brand in general (to ensure that they remain competitive in the market place). As such, the introduction of branding into the HR function is simply an extension of the dominance of branding as a business idea (Edwards 2005; Edwards and Kelan 2011). As Olins (2000: 51) argues, brands are 'taking over the corporation'. According to the marketing literature, brands help distinguish a company from its competitors, they help create customer loyalty and identification, they guarantee a certain level of quality and satisfaction for customers and they help to promote the product (Hollensen 2003). It is argued that, fundamentally, branding helps improve market share and helps to increase organisational profits (Gobe 2001), which supports the idea that strong brands can have considerable financial worth. These ideas can apply equally to employer branding or any other form of branding, thus many authors argue that a strong employer brand will help increase an organisation's overall 'brand equity' (Cable and Turban 2003; King and Grace 2009; Willmot 2011).

A second reason why employer branding has become more of an HR activity is that there is growing emphasis in the marketing field that employees are fundamental to an organisation's marketing activity. Although branding as a notion has grown in emphasis over recent decades, so have calls from authors that organisations need to 'brand from the inside' (Sartain and Schumann 2006) and that employees should 'live the brand' (Ind 2003). The reason presented in favour of this employee branding is that they are considered key 'ambassadors' of an organisation's brand; that employees are important to an organisation's marketing activity as they actively help maintain a consistent, branded message when interacting with customers (de Chernatony and Drury 2006; Miles and Mangold 2004; Punjaisri and Wilson 2007). Although these calls are more specifically focused on employee branding (where employees are encouraged to align their values and/or behaviour to fit the organisation's corporate or broader brand values − see Table 18.1 below) rather than employer branding, employer branding programmes often entail and include some degree of employee branding, and numerous authors argue that the two should go hand in hand (Mosley 2007; Sartain and Schumann 2006; Foster et al. 2010). The growth in interest in employee branding is also symptomatic of wider changes in the economy. Brannan et al. (2011), for example, point out that the increasing interest in employee branding is due to knowledge economies becoming more important (Arvidson 2006) and because of an increase in the importance of service work. Brannan et al. (2011) argue that these wider shifts can help explain the interest in employee branding as 'the brand resides in the employee: employees simply are the brand' (p. 7).

A third potential reason why employer branding has become popular is that it represents an opportunity for the HR department to be more strategically focused and more involved in other key functions of organisations such as marketing (Martin and Beaumont 2003). Such an argument could be very seductive to HR departments which have often struggled with legitimacy in the more technical hard-nosed business environment. As Legge (1978), Ulrich (1997) and Caldwell (2003) have argued for some time, there is a serious issue with the HR function in terms of what its role is within the company, the extent to which it is faced with role ambiguity and the extent to which it is taken seriously as an influential and legitimate managerial force within organisations. The notion of employee or employer branding necessarily pulls the HR function into the strategic engine room of the organisation. Out of necessity, the HR function will need to cooperate and work with the marketing function to help manage and control the organisation's corporate identity and the employer brand. Some go as far as to argue that this form of collaboration with marketing is needed and important because HR lacks the competencies required (Barrow and Mosley 2005). The increasing strategic centrality that employer and employee branding actively provides for the HR department through greater involvement in the management of corporate reputation and image, is considered by some as a positive move, one which should arguably legitimise a greater strategic role for the HR function.

A fourth possible reason why employer branding continues to become more popular amongst the HR function is that it helps provide HR with a potential vehicle to respond to the consequences of an increasing emphasis on organisations acting with social responsibility. A recent survey by Edwards et al. (2008) reported that 58 per cent of 665 multinationals made explicit claims that they had CSR codes of practice; the pressure for organisations to be demonstrating their CSR credentials is apparently 'ratcheting up' (Bartels and Peloza 2008). An early CIPD (2002) paper on CSR and its role in HR emphasises the importance of branding activities in conjunction with the growing corporate social responsibility movement. They suggest that CSR will have a positive impact on an organisation's brand and corporate image. A number of other authors and reports also make the link between corporate responsibility and employee branding (Aggerholm et al. 2011) and argue that CSR and employer branding initiatives complement each other. HR's involvement in employer branding will mean carefully considering what the organisation stands for. Where organisations have CSR initiatives, the moral and ethical dimensions involved in making such commitments will provide important input into this process. It is argued that responsible business practices can be used to help enhance the employer brand and this will mean that the organisation will be more attractive to new recruits. In particular, a report by Business in the Community (2003) suggests that graduates are becoming increasingly concerned about a company's values and how socially responsible organisations are when considering where to work. The growth in interest in CSR means that what the organisation stands for, its values, and its corporate reputation image (or brand) has become of greater importance.

Whilst not necessarily an explanation for the increase in interest in employer branding by itself, the continuing use of HRM as an employment relations model, in particular the focus on the management of HR practices and policies to ensure that employees are committed to the organisation, naturally fits with the idea of employer branding. Inherent in the HRM model as a model of employment relations is a unitarist perspective that employees within an organisation share a common purpose, and the interests and goals of employees are integrated with those of the organisation's goals (Guest 1997). HRM therefore fits with ideas of employer branding as it strives to create committed workers and aims for a degree of fusion between the employees' self and organisational interests (Meyer and Allen 1997). Although employer branding exercises may well be seen as more external facing to potential recruits, a key aim with both employer and employee branding is to encourage current employees to commit to the organisation and identify with its values.

Employer versus employee branding

Employer branding involves identifying, strengthening and communicating the unique 'employment experience' offered by an employer, which describes and attempts to encapsulate the totality of tangible and intangible reward features that a particular organisation offers to its employees (Edwards 2010). It is carried out by organisations in order to clarify what it is about working for a particular organisation that is attractive (generally) to current and potential employees as a place to work. As defined by Ambler and Barrow (1996), the range of possible things contained within the brand include 'the package of financial, economic and psychological benefits provided by employment and identified with the employing company' (p. 187). Importantly, however, the benefits being referred to here go well beyond the traditional idea of employee benefits or rewards, they will involve aspects of the employment experience that include more intangible experiences that are valued by employees. Employer branding activities will, therefore, involve identifying 'subjective, abstract and intangible attributes' associated with a particular employer (Lievens *et al.* 2007: S48). Dell and Ainspan's (2001) broader definition states that 'employer branding establishes the identity of the firm as an employer. It encompasses the firm's value systems, policies and behaviours toward the objectives of attracting, motivating and retaining the firm's current and potential employees' (p. 10). Importantly, however, as Backhaus and Tikoo (2004) argue, the particular employment experiences that are set out as part of an organisation's employer brand help separate and distinguish the employer and it 'suggests differentiation of a firm's characteristics as an employer from those of its competitors, the employment brand highlights the unique aspects of the firm's employment offerings or environment' (p. 502).

There is a distinction between employer and employee branding. Many employer branding programmes will include some degree of employee branding, as a recent CIPD (2007a) survey indicates, the 'alignment to vision/value' was generally ranked by HR practitioners as the most important objective of an employer branding programme. If HR practitioners are expressing this as a main objective, then presumably they are considering employee branding as part of their employer branding initiatives. Having said this, although the two are often carried out together, they can be separated and employer branding does not have to involve specific employee branding, and vice versa.

Employee branding, often referred to as internal branding, can be seen as an extension of the management of corporate culture with a particular branding slant. Harquail (2005) advocates 'a system of socialisation and communication practices intended to deliver on a brand's promise' (p. 4) and more recently Harquail (2009) suggests that 'employee branding is the practice of "aligning" an employee's behaviour and often the employee's point of view with the image that the organisation wants to project to its customers and external stakeholders'. With employee branding, the organisation's corporate and/or recognised product brand is taken as a starting point with a view to encouraging employees to internalise central characteristics such as its values. The culture of the organisation and its branded image is being engineered and communicated internally. Importantly with employee branding, the norms, attributes, values and goals of the organisation are made explicit, and are presented as an ideal that all staff should identify with to guide their work behaviour.

Miles and Mangold (2004) define employee branding as 'the process by which employees internalise the desired brand image and are motivated to project the image to customers and other organisational constituents' (p. 68). Ultimately, employee branding attempts to achieve consistency and a degree of coordination in employee actions. Punjaisri and Wilson (2007: 59) argue that this is required because (in their view) employees are the 'company's most tenuous and vulnerable asset' and continuous efforts need to be made to ensure that the employees' actions are reinforcing the organisation's brand. Free (1999) argues that managing employee brands can be seen as a 'control strategy' used to ensure that employees act in accordance with how the organisation wants them to. With employee branding the purpose is specifically to align employees' behaviour to be 'on brand'. Principally it involves an employer trying to develop or manage staff attitudes and mould how they behave towards each other and, importantly, how they behave to customers to ensure that they become 'walking, talking brand agents'. With employee branding, the employee is part of the brand, they are exemplars of the brand, it is the employees who have been branded. To some extent, employee and employer branding can be seen as distinct practices due to the difference in what has been branded. With employer branding, the organisation is the entity being branded and current and potential employees are the targeted recipients of the branding exercise. With employee branding, however, the employee is the entity that has been branded and customers are the recipients of the branding through their experiences with branded employees. The terminology used with employee and employer branding can be confusing and terms are often used interchangeably. A branded employee is the end result of an internal (employee) branding exercise, but at the same time employer branding is partly directed internally because it involves demonstrating to current employees why the organisation is an employer of choice. In practice, employer and employee branding activities are complementary and often carried out as one initiative, but it is important to note that the two activities have a different emphasis (see Table 18.1).

Table 18.1 Features of employer and employee branding

	Employer Branding	Employee Branding
Direction of branding activities	External and internal	Internal
Branded entity	The organisation	The employee
Ultimate brand audience	Current and potential employees	Customers who interact with branded employees
Roots	Personnel/HR Management Marketing literature	The management of culture literature Organisational socialisation literature Marketing literature
HR activities	Recruitment and selection Advertising External and internal communication Benchmarking	Induction Training and development Performance management Competency based HR systems Internal communications
Aims	To ensure the company attracts new recruits of quality and retains existing employees	To ensure employees act 'on-brand' and share the values of the organisation's brand
Intended outcome	Winning the war for talent High quality, motivated and high performing workforce Having the competitive edge	Increased employee commitment and identification Increased customer satisfaction and loyalty/identification

Source: Edwards (2005)

What does employer branding entail?

It is important to indicate what branding activities might involve from an HR perspective. When reviewing the literature on employee, employer or internal branding, the practices that an HR department should be involved in can seem rather esoteric. How does an HR function translate these ideas into policy and practice? Much of what is involved is related to image presentation and communication activities. An integral activity will be to establish an image of the organisation and consistently communicate this in a number of different ways to current and potential employees.

Employer branding may involve a number of different steps and activities. The first step will be to clarify the organisation's employer brand; this step is referred to as the 'discovery' and 'analysis, interpretation and creation' phases of an employer branding initiative (CIPD 2010a). As the branding activity needs to be linked to the corporate brand, if one exists, then the attributes of the corporate brand will need to be taken into account. If the organisation does not have an existing corporate brand, then the HR department will need to develop a brand from scratch that will involve identifying recognisable core values that the staff will identify with and recognise. As well as the values of the company, the HR department will have to determine what is good about working at the organisation.

Identifying organisational values and what is good about the employment experience offered by the employing organisation tends to involve surveying staff to clarify the advantages and benefits of working for that particular company (Microsoft, for example, sent surveys to 7,300 staff to identify their 'value proposition', Universum 2005). Focus groups are often used at this stage to get staff to talk about the organisation, in particular what attributes, characteristics and values they see as being associated with the organisation. Where recruitment agencies and head-hunters are used, these can be an important source of information about what outsiders or applicants consider to be key elements: the organisation's likely employment experience. Recent joiners are often identified in this research phase to find out how the organisation came across in the recruitment phase and what messages the organisation seemed to give as to what the employment experience would be upon joining. The messages that the organisation sends out to job applicants and potential new recruits need to be thoroughly audited and a comprehensive analysis of the recruitment material needs to be carried out – including a content analysis of recruitment advertising sections of corporate websites. Recruitment advertising sections of company websites are particularly important sources of information for potential new recruits about the organisation's employer brand (particularly the 'offer' aspect to what is referred to as the 'employment offering') and the messages sent out on these pages need to be carefully assessed.

An employer branding activity will also involve rigorous HR benchmarking to identify how the organisation is different from competitors in the labour market and to establish what it offers over and above other potential employers. This is a key part of the branding activity as the brand and its employment experience need to be unique, differentiated and distinct (Backhaus and Tikoo 2004). Employer branding initiatives may also go beyond this to include introducing new benefits or terms and conditions that make it stand out even more from other employers. Importantly, employer branding does not just involve obtaining a static picture of the current 'package of financial, economic and psychological benefits'. Employer branding initiatives often involve an active construction or adjustment of the benefits provided by employment to make the organisation look more attractive than its competitors in the labour market.

The organisation will need to define what it stands for in terms of its values and vision and then communicate this systematically. This stage will fall under the 'implementation and communication' phase of an employer branding initiative

(CIPD 2010a). Employer branding activities will include attempts to market externally and internally. Once the image (especially its shared values) of the organisation and employment experience/employment offering has been identified, the organisation will then consistently use this information in communication to both current employees and in its advertising or recruitment material.

As well as being central to an employer branding programme, a key starting point for a programme involves deciding what values legitimately reflect the organisation (also usually tied to the established corporate brand if one exists), or rather what values those in the organisation should strive for. This can be a bottom-up process where the employees are asked (in focus groups for example), or it can be driven by the top of the organisation and reflect an imposition of values on employees in order to try and encourage employees to act consistently 'on brand'. Subsequent to this is the portrayal of the particular values or norms that have been decided upon as representing the organisation. The brand of the organisation should be consistently communicated to employees. This is carried out both by the communication of a recognisable logo, espoused organisational values and also via a more indirect route by presenting images and pictures that reflect characteristics of the organisation's brand. Companies such as easyJet, for example, presented pictures of young people with big smiles on their faces looking very energetic. These pictures seem to give the impression of staff having fun. EasyJet also used pictures of a clenched fist next to the word 'passionate'. These images were presented to conjure up impressions of the culture that they felt characterises the company's identity.

Persistent and consistent internal communication is integral to employee branding activities. At Southwest Airlines, for example (a company that McDonald suggested was at the 'forefront of the employee branding revolution' 2001: 57), a sophisticated programme of internal communication was introduced linked to the corporate brand notion of 'freedom'. Providing freedom to customers was a key part of the firm's corporate brand (advertised externally) and the company extended this and directed communication efforts internally with the tagline 'At Southwest freedom begins with me'. Employees were expected to take on board the principles of Southwest's brand to ensure that customers experienced the brand when interacting with staff. The firm categorised the 'employment experience' into eight freedoms: freedom to learn and grow, freedom to create financial security, freedom to make a positive difference, freedom to create and innovate, freedom to stay connected, freedom to pursue good health, freedom to travel, freedom to work hard and have fun. Southwest's 'people department' presented these freedoms to employees with a number of different media including intranet, posters and booklets.

Aside from communication, sophisticated employee branding initiatives will involve the adjustment or introduction of a number of HR-related practices, with the aim of assisting in the alignment of employee values to those of the brand. A central part of employer and employee branding will involve socialisation practices where new recruits are presented with the internal value system of the organisation. The socialisation of new recruits starts at the beginning of the recruitment process, where organisational values and norms are presented via a branded job advertisement, branded application materials (such as graduate application packs) and selection activities. Subsequently, induction courses and activities are carefully designed to ensure that a consistent message is presented to employees about what the organisation represents and what is expected of the employee. Induction courses in general can be considered a central technique to achieve a degree of organisational socialisation; a process by which an individual employee assimilates the attitudes, behaviour and knowledge needed to participate as an employee (Van Maanen and Schein 1979). Although a combination of self-selection and careful recruitment and selection practices might mean that when the employee arrives at the organisation there is likely to be some value (or brand) fit, this match will never be perfect (see Chapter 7).

According to Dose (1997), because there will be natural variation between the organisational values and those of new recruits, 'some amount of socialisation is in order' (p. 234), or using alternative terminology, some internal branding is 'in order'. Klein and Weaver (2000) found a link between attendance at an induction session/ orientation training programme and the extent to which employees shared the organisation's values and were affectively committed. Ashforth and Saks (1996) investigated factors influencing how recognisable and meaningful an organisation's identity was to new graduates; and deliberate, institutionalised socialisation practices were found to be important. They found that 'the more institutionalised the socialisation tactics, the more coherent sense will be conveyed of what the organisation purportedly represents' (p. 155). Specifically linked to employee branding, a recent research paper showed a significant positive relationship between levels of organisational socialisation and employee reports of 'brand citizenship behaviours' (King and Grace 2012).

Harquail (2005) suggested three main activities which are important ways to foster an employee brand. Firstly, suggested as the most common activity, is branding training (a form of brand socialisation) where 'all employees are taught the basics of branding and market principles' where they are 'instructed on the attributes to be associated with their [the organisation's] brand'. Brand training such as this has been carried out at LEGO, where employees were sent to 'Brand School' (Hatch and Schultz 2008) which was 'devoted to helping employees develop a shared understanding of the LEGO brand's essence' (p. 189). At such training courses employees are trained in what the organisation's brand stands for and how this is distinct from the brands of competitors. The Marketing and PR functions direct their efforts internally to employees 'as tools to influence employees and encourage on-brand behaviour' (Harquail 2005: 7). More indirectly, 'employees are branded by organisational décor that reflects the brand, such as brand consonant aesthetic schemes' (e.g. open plan spaces and décor in line with brand colours) and sophisticated employee initiatives that involve the distribution of branded 'artefacts' such as promotional materials and decorative accessories (the use of which at Domino's Pizza is discussed by Ulrich and Smallwood 2003). Examples of such materials and accessories would be corporate pens, branded stress balls, paperweights and mugs.

A policy vehicle that is used to help transmit or align organisational values to employees is competency frameworks (see Chapter 9). Competency frameworks are often used to help 'translate organisational expectations into employee action' (IRS 2003) and are likely to be used with both employer and employee branding activities. Indeed, competencies are a key tool that organisations use to instil consistency of behaviour and attitude across the organisation, particularly the use of 'core competencies' that employees are judged against. Competency frameworks are often used during the recruitment process to select new hires to ensure that employees have the appropriate person–organisation fit. Competency frameworks, however, are also used in conjunction with a much wider range of HR policies and practices. They can be used with recruitment, pay systems, appraisal schemes, training, development and succession planning programmes. Competencies are ultimately used as a form of control where employees' actions are determined indirectly rather than through over-the-shoulder management.

As mentioned above, an early stage of socialisation will involve communicating the organisation's values and norms in branded job advertisement, application materials and selection activities. For those that join, this will have been the beginning of their socialisation experiences. However, it would also serve to ensure that those who do (or don't) apply are aware of the organisation's culture and assist in the process of ensuring person–organisation fit. Much has been written about the importance of person and organisational fit (Judge and Cable 1997; Kristof-Brown et al. 2005) which suggests (separate from the employee branding literature) that person–organisation fit has numerous positive outcomes. Research in this area has reliably found a relationship between job satisfaction, organisational commitment, co-worker satisfaction, intention to stay and person–organisation fit (Kristof-Brown et al. 2005).

There is a lack of empirical work focusing on the area of employer branding, and research in the area is still developing, however, a recent project supports some of the assumptions underlying branding authors' recommendations. Chang et al. (2012) tested whether there was a relationship between HR practices that have a brand focus (including having policies that aim to align employee values with the organisation's brand through training courses and value-based fit assessments in recruitment) and the degree to which employees report 'brand psychological ownership' and 'brand citizenship behaviours'. They found a positive relationship between 'brand-centred training and reward' and 'brand sportsmanship' as well as between 'brand-centred evaluation and selection' and 'brand consideration' – both of these outcomes were positively correlated with independent ratings of customer satisfaction. This provides a degree of evidence for a key assumption from the employer and employee brand literature that brand-focused HR practices may well ultimately follow through and have a positive impact on the employee-customer profit chain.

The Rise of Segmentation

The employer brand project is still an emerging project, but it can be considered to have moved from infancy to adolescence in its development. Many organisations now have an employer brand and numerous consultancies focus on assisting organisations to manage and develop their employer brand; because the employer brand project has evolved so much, there are some key developments that have occurred over recent years. Probably the most significant of these is the idea of employer brand segmentation, which has become much more of a prominent consideration than in the past.

In the marketing field, segmentation is a well-practised activity required to take into account the fact that consumers or customers can be divided into subsets with similar needs or interests (intra-segment similarity). The assumption being that subsets of customers can be differentiated from each other (inter-segment differences) and that key messages and what is provided to them as a product should be targeted at each segment according to their specific needs.

This is, to some degree, a natural development and a number of authors have recently argued for the importance of considering segmented employment experiences and employer brands (Moroko and Uncles 2009; Tuzuner and Yuksel 2009). The reality of people management ensures that there will be sub-groups of the organisation (vertically or horizontally across function specialisms) that have very different employment experiences. Therefore, whilst an employer branding initiative involves identifying a unique employment experience offered by an organisation, the organisation is unlikely to have a single shared employment experience. As Martin (2009) notes, a number of theoretical HR models exist that lend themselves to the idea of employer brand segmentation. The resource-based view of the firm's arguments (see Chapter 2) centres around the idea that organisations should have a different level of investment in subsets of the organisation. Employees whose activities have high levels of strategic impact should, the theory argues, be invested in to a greater degree. An assumption with the resource-based view of the firm is that the organisation determines which segments get what HR practices, depending upon the strategic value of the employee segments. Central to the idea of employer brand segmentation, however, is an understanding that there will, and should, be variation in HR organisational practices partly due to the fact that different groups will desire and want different employment experiences.

One only has to explore a number of websites to see how this segmentation plays out in terms of the messages and imagery being communicated to different segments of potential employees. At the time of writing (2012) the Apple job opportunities website is divided into two main functional groups, 'retail' versus 'corporate'. These are two fundamentally different segments within the Apple employer brand. The imagery in the corporate part of the website has potential workers in casual clothes, jeans and polo shirts, whereas the retail staff all wear a coloured uniform (blue polo shirt). Fundamentally different employment experiences are being 'offered' to these two segments of the potential Apple employee population.

In some of the recent work carried out that has looked at employer branding, Moroko and Uncles (2009) provide a number of examples of how employee groups could be segmented. These include segments across age (baby boomers versus generation X versus generation Y), seniority (graduates versus managers for example), job type (technical versus client facing versus support services for example). Lawler (2011) also argues that organisations should segment the workforce to take into account that different generational groups have different needs or wants. It is clear from the number of authors who have recently argued for the consideration of segmentation in employer branding that there is a call to have an increasingly sophisticated understanding of the target population in terms of being aware of the possible heterogeneity in interests and values. A key question that remains somewhat unanswered in the employer brand segmentation literature is, when the different segments have been identified, what should actually be done about this?

Moroko and Uncles (2009) present examples of where employer branding segmentation is carried out, and graduate jobs are a good example of a segment which has tended to receive a unique set of HR practices (e.g. special training and induction) and terms and conditions (usually transferable skills and a clear career structure). Moroko and Uncles also discuss how particular conditions within financial service and pharmaceutical firms (greater retention strategies), were developed for employees who were involved in generating direct profit (e.g. sales staff). One of the challenges that such approaches might lead to for the HR function, apart from the logistical challenge of managing many different sets of HR practices, is that such differences could lead to a varied array of different sets of terms and conditions provided to different groups. This, in itself, could cause a degree of dissatisfaction amongst staff when certain groups make instrumental comparisons and feel worse off than another group that has different treatment. Such an issue is raised by Martin (2009) when discussing differential provision of terms and conditions to 'talent' versus 'non-talent' employee segments (a categorisation being increasingly referred to in the HR field): 'segmentation can lead to invidious comparisons and endemic employee relations problems because the "losers" in the war for talent resent the success of "winners"' (p. 230). The equity-based challenges are clear. As Adams's (1963) equity theory suggests, individuals make continuous comparisons about how much they receive in exchange for their efforts and weigh this up against other people's inputs and outputs. Therefore, having different terms and conditions across different groups could well lead to problems of morale across certain groups. Employees will see different employment experiences being provided to different groups and ask why. A considerable body of research exists which indicates that where organisations provide a varied distribution of rewards or resources across organisations, the decision-making that led to these differences needs to be fair and just. Employees' judgements of the fairness of both how resources have been distributed and the procedures in place when making decisions are extremely important in leading to positive or negative employee responses (Colquitt et al. 2001).

Of course, as much of employer branding is linked to the provision and communication of a focused message, when segmentation is introduced, a tension arises. This tension revolves around the fact that if employer branding activities need to account for different needs and wants of different groups, then this would require multiple sub-brands within the organisation. This would lead to difficulties when the organisation hopes to communicate (and potentially provide) a brand reflecting its shared and unique employment experience. Where segments exist in the workplace (in reality this is likely), the organisation needs to make a choice whether to direct different HR systems and terms and conditions to different groups. If an organisation does this then it will need to recognise that the employment experience isn't shared by the workforce and reflect this is in the brand communication; the alternative is, of course, that the organisation only presents a simplified brand message that fails to mention the actual differences in employment experiences across the segments. Either way, segmentation provides a challenge to the idea that an organisation can identify a shared, unique employment experience that differentiates it from other employers and use this to communicate to current and potential employees to attract and retain. A further challenge also exists with segmentation of the employment brand, as Lawler (2011) explains, 'The major problem with the segmentation approach is obvious. It assumes that the organisation can figure out what individuals want and respond correctly' (p. 306) and that there are risks if the organisation gets it wrong.

Socially responsible corporate brands and employee behavioural change

An interesting trend which can be considered to have influenced the area of employer branding is the continuing and growing focus on corporate social responsibility in corporate identity and brand management. Organisations are coming under increasing pressure to act with social responsibility and a number of authors discuss how important it is that employees are committed to an organisation's CSR principles themselves, if the corporate CSR programme is to be successful (Colliers and Esteban 2007; Powell 2011); Hollander argues that the values associated with CSR 'must live in the hearts and minds of every employee' (2004). A point worth raising in this regard is that when employer and employee branding programmes themselves involve imposing CSR and ethical principles onto employees, a conundrum exists where the imposition of values (whether ethically oriented or not) onto employees can potentially undermine the CSR principles associated with the programme, as employees themselves are stakeholders whose rights and individuality should be respected. The extent of this conundrum would obviously depend upon the degree to which employees are induced into taking on board CSR-based values. This issue was discussed by Flanders (1970) who raised the problem that where an organisation might attempt to act ethically or to undertake moral 'conversion' of employees, it may run the risk of being overly paternalistic. Where Corporate Social Responsibility principles are included in employer and employee branding programmes, some 'conversion' may be involved. The organisation, or agents of it, will have decided upon a set of values that potentially improve its reputation, either for ethical or profit reasons, and will be attempting to influence (or 'cajole' as Flanders 1970 puts it) employees to encourage an integration of beliefs and attitudes ensuring value 'synergy' or congruence within the organisation.

Where employer and employee branding programmes undertake to encourage employees to take 'on-board' the principles associated with the organisation's corporate CSR framework, the HR function (or the marketing function depending upon who is driving the initiative) is effectively getting involved in the management of behavioural ethics; defined by Trevino *et al.* (2006) as 'individual behaviour that is subject to or judged according to generally accepted norms of behaviour' (p. 952). Where organisations are attempting to prescribe a set of norms or accepted forms of potentially ethical or moral behaviours, they are involved in the management of behavioural ethics. In general, research exists to show that employees will respond positively (with organisational commitment for example) where they perceive their employer to act with social responsibility (Peterson 2004; Ellemers *et al.* 2011) and when they themselves get involved in such programmes (Jones 2010). A number of recent authors have presented arguments and evidence which suggest that the likely success of efforts to encourage employee buy-in of corporate CSR programmes will require consistency and authenticity in the organisation's activities.

Treviño and Weaver (2001) demonstrate the importance of the organisation acting in accordance with its own ethics programme. When the organisation was judged to have demonstrated ethical programme 'follow through', employees were more likely to be committed to the ethics programme themselves and less likely to observe unethical behaviour amongst colleagues (see also Brown, *et al.* 2005). Cropanzano and Stein (2009) highlight that when employees observe their employer's senior representatives acting in an ethical manner, they are more likely to behave ethically themselves. This is referred to as the 'trickle down' effect. Recent research (Edwards and Edwards 2012; Edwards and Edwards in press) shows that employees' judgements of their organisation acting in accordance with its CSR claims lead to a range of positive employee responses, including subsequent identification with their employer and, importantly, the degree to which employees take on board and commit to the ethical principles associated with this CSR programme. What this points to, from an employer branding perspective, is that where organisations make an effort to ensure that employees internalise the organisation's corporate CSR principles, a key thing that would influence success is that the organisation actually 'walks the talk' itself. What follows from this is that if organisations espouse CSR values as part of their corporate identities and this is decreed rhetoric by employees, they will be unlikely to commit to these corporate values themselves.

Continuing Challenges Faced by the Employer Branding Project

Employer and employee branding projects pose a number of interesting challenges to the HR function itself. These challenges include 1) The potential to create tension for the HR function as to what is considered acceptable 'HR Turf'; 2) In responding to profit/market driven motives HR may lose legitimacy rather than gain it; and 3) tensions may arise between management of diversity and employer branding initiatives.

Where an organisation carries out sophisticated employer and employee branding activities, it is not automatic that the HR function will necessarily be in complete charge of the process. As a survey by Universum indicates, whilst 84 per cent of employer branding projects involve the HR department, 48 per cent involve the information/communications department and 38 per cent involve the marketing department (Universum 2006). Where the marketing function has greater influence in an organisation, then it may not (automatically) be HR that drives the programme. Also, employer brand consultancy firms are often marketing or communications consultancy firms rather than HR consultancy firms (e.g. Universum). Given the nature of practices and activities that employer and employee branding initiatives can involve, turf wars may occur when marketing functions want to drive an internal marketing programme to strengthen the employee–customer profit chain. An HR function that gets the marketing function involved in their employer branding initiative may begin to find that a key part of their remit (e.g. performance management) becomes driven or influenced by other functions with different agendas.

As mentioned above, one of the possible motives for the HR function to get involved in employer branding programmes is that it may serve to increase the HR function's involvement in the organisation's 'strategic engine room'. There is a danger, however, that in attempting to become more strategic, this 'new look' HR department will look like it has 'learnt the rules of the game' (Legge 1978; Guest and King 2004) but in the process, loses a degree of credibility. As well as there being a danger that HR might end up involved in turf wars, its involvement with the marketing function could mean that the remit of the HR function may become blurred. When employer branding projects are driven by the marketing function, the main purpose of such activities should be to increase company profit. In such a scenario HR would only be considered a function that helps achieve these wider marketing aims, rather than a strategic driver of activities itself. Whilst involvement of the HR function in strengthening the organisation's corporate brand may involve the function in core strategic activities, there is a danger that in doing so, HR ends up weakening its own identity and legitimate strategic role as the function becomes subservient to helping achieve brand influence. In such a scenario, an increase in strategic involvement through managing the organisation's brand might come at a cost to the HR function.

An interesting difference exists in discourse around employees when one compares HR perspectives from those found with writers coming from a marketing slant. Some marketing authors, for example, argue that employees are 'the company's most tenuous and vulnerable asset' (Punjaisri and Wilson 2007: 59). Such statements feel very different from edicts common in the HR practitioner and academic literature where employees are considered the organisation's 'most important asset'. The danger of the HR function following marketing edicts is that it loses its legitimacy to focus on employees' welfare and well-being; these concerns come second to their role in boosting the organisation's corporate brand. The brand management literature seems to refer to employees as a tool to be used as a means to an end. In contrast to prescriptive accounts that suggest the involvement of the HR function in branding will lead to greater strategic involvement, there is a danger that employer branding may have unintended consequences that undermine the HR function rather than bolster its influence.

Recently, concerns have been raised over the potential tensions created by employer branding programmes with regard to diversity and inclusion management. Edwards and Kelan (2011) argue that employer branding initiatives (especially those that involve a degree of employee branding) can potentially undermine attempts to manage diversity within organisations. The arguments centre around the idea that the 'organisational approaches to diversity try to bring out the individual differences between and among people; this is diametrically opposed to what employer branding aims at doing' (p. 175). Edwards and Kelan draw on arguments presented by Cornelissen (2002) who suggested that managerial efforts to present a uniform set of values that everyone in the organisation does and should share, presents 'managerially induced' values 'rather than offering individuals free choice of values and identification' (p. 267). So the key point made here is that managerial activities that suggest a homogenous and shared set of beliefs or values create a tension with the essence of the management of diversity initiatives which allow for (and celebrate) differences amongst the workforce. Furthermore, the indirect effect of an organisation suggesting that it, and by implication its employees, has a single set of values is twofold. Firstly, if you do not fit, do not bother applying – this will have an effect of reinforcing a lack of diversity. Secondly, if you are an employee but your attitudes or behaviour differ from the organisation's branded message or they differ from the suggested 'on-brand' attitudes or behaviour, they are, in effect, de-legitimised. Even if these values or an organisation's 'who we are' or 'about us' statements include a commitment to diversity (as many organisational value statements do), it is unclear whether this is enough to alleviate the (deliberately) homogenising forces of an employer and employee branding programme.

Ethical concerns linked to value and behaviour steering from HR

As discussed above, employer and employee branding initiatives both include a key aim of aligning the values and interests of the workforce. Whether this attempted value and behavioural change is for reasons of person–organisation fit or in order to encourage 'on-brand' behaviour with a view to driving the 'employee–customer profit chain', the question remains whether such activities are ethical. The ethics of such activities have been discussed previously by Winstanley and Woodall (2000) who suggested that 'a desire to capture the hearts and minds in the service of corporate goals' (p. 8) 'raises ethical issues'. These concerns are particularly relevant with employee branding. As mentioned above, there is a challenge that employees are being considered as merely a means to an end, as a device or vehicle to achieve further customer loyalty; one that can be moulded and steered to help increase customer satisfaction, loyalty and, subsequently, profits. Many authors from the marketing and branding literature do not seem to even consider the idea that organisations might be doing something unethical when attempting employee branding. No consideration seems to be given to what this actually might mean to the individual who is being branded or that employees might actually resist being branded. When suggesting that employees should be 'on-brand', 'brand agents' or that they should have 'brand engagement', there is a danger that the HR function will appear to have scant regard for human dignity.

Within the employee branding literature, recommendations seem to indicate the legitimate commodification and commercialisation of employee values and attitudes. Employee values can now be seen as a commodity which the organisation can utilise for the purposes of unlocking required commitment and high performance (Bunting 2004) and to ensure greater customer satisfaction and loyalty. HR's involvement in this naturally leads to questioning the function's ethical status or role. It is very reasonable to ask where the boundaries lie of appropriate interference by the HR function and its representatives in what can be considered to be personal and private aspects of employee selves. Is the management of organisational and, more importantly, employee value systems a step into the realm of manipulation, potentially threatening employees' right to privacy and dignity? Such a point is raised by Bunting (2004) who suggests that companies (such as Microsoft and Asda) that attempt to ensure that the corporate brand is internalised by employees amounts to 'an unprecedented invasiveness as management practices reach after parts of the employee's personality which have hitherto been considered private' (p.92).

Given the arguments presented (e.g. by the CIPD) for the branding and corporate social responsibility movement to be combined, it would be valid to question whether employee or internal branding is socially responsible. Imposing corporate brand values onto employees purely to strengthen the employee-customer profit chain does not seem an ethical activity. Although some employee branding exercises may involve employees in the process of determining the organisation's values (which some authors, such as Ind and Bjerke 2007, suggest is important), the decision to carry out employee branding will invariably be made by managers at the top of the organisation and the employees will be seen as an internal target of these marketing and PR activities. It could be argued that the very nature of employee branding emasculates employees, it highlights the idea that they are a resource to be moulded and it is very unlikely that with such programmes they would be treated as legitimate stakeholders.

REFERENCES

Adams, J.S. 1963: Toward an understanding of inequity, *Journal of Abnormal and Social Psychology*, **67**(5), 422–436.

Aggerholm, H.K., Anderson, S.E. and Thomsen, C. 2011: Conceptualising employer branding in sustainable organisations, *Corporate Communications: An International Journal*, **16**(2), 105–123.

Ambler, T. and Barrow, S. 1996: The employer brand, *The Journal of Brand Management*, **4**, 185–206.

Arvidson, A. 2006: *Brands: Meaning and Value in Media Culture*, Oxon: Routlege.

Ashforth, B. and Saks, A.M. 1996: Socialisation tactics: Longitudinal effects on newcomer adjustment, *Academy of Management Journal*, **39**, 149–178.

Backhaus, K. and Tikoo, S. 2004: Conceptualizing and Researching Employer Branding. *Career Development International*, **9**(4/5), 501–517.

Barrow, S. and Mosley, R. 2005: *The Employer Brand: Bringing the best of brand management to people at work*. Chichester: John Wiley & Sons Ltd.

Bartels, S. and Peloza, J. 2008: Running Just to Stand Still? Managing CSR Reputation in an Era of Ratcheting Expectations, *Corporate Reputation Review*, **11**(1), 56–72.

Berthen, P., Ewing M. and Hah, L.L. 2005: Captivating company: Dimensions of attractiveness in employer branding, *International Journal of Advertising*, **24**(2), 151–172.

Brannan, M.J., Parsons, E.P. and Priola, V.P. 2011: Introduction, in M.J. Brannan, E. Parsons and V. Priola (eds.), *Branded Lives: The Production and Consumption of Identity at Work*, 1–16. Cheltenham: Edward Elgar.

Brown, M., Treviño, L.K. and Harrison, D. 2005: Ethical leadership: A social learning perspective for construct development and testing, *Organizational Behavior and Human Decision Processes*, **97**, 117–134.

Bunting, M. 2004: *Willing slaves: How the over work culture is ruling our lives*, London: Harper Collins.

Business in the community report 2003: Responsibility: Driving innovation, inspiring employees, *FastForward Research*, www.bitc.org.uk/document.rm?id=5253 *(downloaded March 2012)*.

Cable, D.M. and Turban, D.B. 2003: The value of organizational reputation in the recruitment context: A brand equity perspective, *Journal of Applied Social Psychology*, **33**(11), 2244–2266.

Caldwell, R. 2003: The changing roles of personnel managers: Old ambiguities, new uncertainties, *Journal of Management Studies*, **40**, 983–1004.

Chang, A., Chiang, H-H, and Han, T-S. 2012: A multilevel investigation of relationships among brand-centered HRM, brand psychological ownership, brand citizenship behaviors, and customer satisfaction, *European Journal of Marketing*, **46**(5), 626–662.

CIPD 2002: *Corporate Social Responsibility* (Guide), Autumn, London: CIPD.

CIPD 2007a: *Employer branding: a no-nonsense approach*. Guide http://www.cipd.co.uk/hr-resources/guides/employer-branding-approach.aspx, *(downloaded March 2012)*.

CIPD 2007b: *Employer branding: the latest fad or the future of HR* Research insight, http://www.cipd.co.uk/NR/rdonlyres/56C8377F-256B-4556–8650–8408B0E07576/0/empbrandlatfad.pdf, *(downloaded March 2012)*.

CIPD 2009: *Employer branding: maintaining momentum in a recession. Resource Summary*, http://www.cipd.co.uk/hr-resources/guides/employer-branding-maintaining-momentum-recession.aspx, *(downloaded March 2012)*.

CIPD 2010a: *Employer Brand Fact Sheet*, http://www.cipd.co.uk/hr-resources/factsheets/employer-brand.aspx, *(downloaded March 2012)*.

CIPD 2010b: *Your Employer brand: Keeping it real through mergers and acquisitions*. Online Practical Tool, http://www.cipd.co.uk/hr-resources/practical-tools/employer-brand-mergers-acquisitions.aspx, *(downloaded March 2012)*.

CIPD 2010c: Research Report *Employer branding and total reward*.

Colliers, J. and Esteban, R. 2007: Corporate Social Responsibility and Employee Commitment, *Business Ethics: A European Review*, **16**, 19–33.

Colquitt, J.A., Conlon, D.E., Wesson, M.J., Porter, C.O.L.H. and Ng, K.Y. 2001: Justice at the Millennium: A Meta-Analytic Review of 25 Years of Organizational Justice Research, *Journal of Applied Psychology*, **86**(3), 425–445.

Cornelissen, J.P. 2002: On the Organizational Identity Metaphor, *British Journal of Management*, **13**(3), 259–268.

Cropanzano, R. and Stein, J. H. 2009: Organizational justice and behavioral ethics: Promises and prospects, *Business Ethics Quarterly*, **19**, 193–233.

de Chernatony, L. and Drury, S.C. 2006: Internal brand factors driving successful financial services brands, *European Journal of Marketing*, **40**(5/6), 611–633.

Dell, D. and Ainspan, N. 2001: *Engaging employees through your brand*, The Conference Board: Press Inc.

Dose, J.J. 1997: Work values: An integrative framework and illustrative application to organizational socialization, *Journal of Occupational and Organizational Psychology*, **70**, 219–240.

Edwards, M.R. 2005: Employer and Employer Branding: HR or PR? In S. Bach, (ed.) *Human Resource Management: Personnel Management in Transition*, Oxford: Blackwell.

Edwards, M. R. 2010: An integrative review of employer branding and OB theory, *Personnel Review*, **39**(1–2), 5–23.

Edwards, M.R. and Edwards, T. 2012: Internalizing Corporate CSR Principles: Authenticity and the Moderating Role of Justice, *Academy of Management Congress*, Boston.

Edwards, M.R. and Edwards, T. in press: Employee responses to changing aspects of the employer brand following a multinational acquisition: A longitudinal study, *Human Resource Management*.

Edwards, M.R and Kelan, E.K. 2011: 'Employer branding and diversity: foes or friends?' In M.J. Brannan, M. Parsons and V. Priola (eds.), *Branded Lives: The Production and Consumption of Identity at Work*, 168–184. Cheltenham: Edward Elgar.

Edwards, T., Marginson, P., Edwards, P., Ferner, A. and Tregaskis, O. 2008: 'Corporate social responsibility in multinational companies: Management initiatives or negotiated agreements', *IILS Working Paper, Geneva*: ILO.

Ellemers, N., Kingma, L., van de Burgt, J. and Barreto, M. 2011: Corporate social responsibility as a source of organisational morality, employee commitment and satisfaction, *Journal of Organizational Moral Psychology*, **1**, 97–124.

Flanders, A. 1970: *Management and unions: The theory and reform of industrial relations*, London: Faber.

Foster, C., Punjaisri, K. and Cheng, R. 2010: Exploring the relationship between corporate, internal and employer branding, *Journal of Product & Brand Management*, **19**(6), 401–409.

Free, C. 1999: The Internal Brand, *The Journal of Brand Management*, **6**, 231–236.

Gobe, M. 2001: *Emotional Branding: The new paradigm for connecting brands to people*. New York: Alworth Press.

Guest, D. 1997: Human resource management and performance: a review and research agenda. *International Journal of Human Resource Management*, **8**(3), 263–276.

Guest, D. and King, Z. 2004: Power, innovation and problem solving: The personnel manager's three steps to heaven? *Journal of Management Studies*, **41**, 367–519.

Harquail, C.V. 2005: Employees as Animate Artifacts: Employee branding by "wearing the brand", in A. Rafaeli and M. Pratt (eds.), *Artifacts and Organizations*, MahWah, NJ: Lawrence Erlbaum.

Harquail, C.V. 2009: Employer Branding vs. Employee Branding available at http://authenticorganizations.com/wp-content/uploads/2008/03/employee-branding-online.pdf (accessed 15 February 2012).

Hatch, M.J. and Schultz, M. 2008: *Taking Brand Initiative: How companies can align strategy, culture, and identity through corporate branding*, San Fransisco: Jossey Bass.

Hollander, J. 2004: What matters most: Corporate Values and Social Responsibility, *California Management Review*, **46**(4), 111–119.

Hollensen, S. 2003: *Marketing management: A relationship approach*, Harlow: Prentice Hall.

Ind, N. 2003: Inside out: How employees build value, *Brand Management*, **10**, 393–402.

Ind, N. and Bjerke, R. 2007: *Branding Governance: A participatory approach to the brand building process*, Chichester: John Wiley & Sons Ltd.

IRS 2003: Employer branding: fad or fact? *IRS Employment Review*, **778**, 42–47.

Jones, D. 2010: Does serving the community also serve the company? Using organizational identification and social exchange theories to understand employee responses to a volunteerism programme, *Journal of Occupational and Organizational Psychology*, **83**, 857–878.

Judge, T.A. and Cable, D.M. 1997: Applicant personality, organizational culture, and organization attraction, *Personnel Psychology*, **50**(2), 359–394.

King, C. and Grace, D. 2009: Employee based brand equity: A third perspective, *Services Marketing Quarterly*, **30**(2), 122–147.

King, C. and Grace, D. 2012: Examining the antecedents of employee brand-related behaviour. *European Journal of Marketing*, **46**, 469–488.

Klein, H. and Weaver, N. 2000: The effectiveness of an organizational-level orientation training program in the socialization of new hires, *Personnel Psychology*, **53**, 47–66.

Kristof-Brown, A.L., Zimmerman, R.D. and Johnson, E.C. 2005: Consequences of individuals' fit at work: A meta-analysis of person–job, person–organization, person–group, and person–supervisor fit, *Personnel Psychology*, **58**, 281–342.

Lawler, E.E. III 2011: Creating a new employment deal: Total rewards and the new workforce, *Organizational Dynamics*, **40**(4), 302–309.

Legge, K. 1978: *Power, innovation and problem solving in personnel management*, London: McGraw-Hill.

Lievens, F. 2007: Employer Branding in the Belgian Army: The importance of instrumental and symbolic beliefs for potential applicants, actual applicants and military employees, *Human Resource Management*, **46**, 51–69.

Lievens, F., van Hoye, G. and Anseel, F. 2007: Organizational identify and employer image: Towards a unifying framework, *British Journal of Management*, **18**, S45–S59.

Logan, G. 2008: "Jackie Orme tells directors HR's quiet revolution not over yet", *Personnel Today*, 14 October, 8.

Martin. G. 2009: Driving corporate reputations from the inside: A strategic role and strategic dilemmas for HR? *Asia Pacific Journal of Human Resources*, **47**(2), 219–235.

Martin, G. and Beaumont, P. 2003: *Branding and People Management*, CIPD Research Report.

McDonald, D. 2001: HR earning its place at the table, *World at Work Journal*, First Quarter.

Meyer, J.P. and Allen, N. J. 1997: *Commitment in the workplace: Theory, research and application*, Thousand Oaks: Sage.

Miles, S.J. and Mangold, G. 2004: A conceptualisation of the employee branding process, *Journal of Relationship Marketing*, **3**(2/3), 65–87.

Moroko, L. and Uncles, M.D. 2009: Employer branding and market segmentation, *Journal of Brand Management*, **17**(3), 181–196.

Mosley, R. 2007: Customer experience, organizational culture and the employer brand, *Journal of Brand Management*, **15**, 123–134.

Olins, W. 2000: How brands are taking over the corporation, in M. Schultz, J. Hatch and M.H. Larsen (eds.), *The Expressive Organization*, Oxford: Oxford University Press.

Peterson, D. 2004: The relationship between perceptions of corporate citizenship and organizational commitment, *Business and Society*, **43**, 296–319.

Powell, S. 2011: The nexus between ethical corporate marketing, ethical corporate identity and corporate social responsibility: An internal organisational perspective, *European Journal of Marketing*, **45**(9/10), 1365–1379.

Punjaisri, K. and Wilson, A. 2007: The role of internal branding in the delivery of employee brand promise, *Journal of Brand Management*, **15**, 57–70.

Sartain, L. and Schumann, M. 2006: *Brand From the Inside Eight Essentials to Emotionally Connect Your Employees to Your Business*, San Fransisco: John Wiley & Sons Inc.

Treviño, L. K. and Weaver, G. R. 2001: Organizational justice and ethics program "followthrough": Influences on employees' harmful and helpful behaviour. *Business Ethics Quarterly*, **11**, 651–671.

Treviño, L. K., Weaver, G. R. and Reynolds, S. J. 2006: Behavioral Ethics in Organizations: A Review, *Journal of Management*, **32**, 951–990.

Tuzuner, V.L and Yuksel, C.A. 2009: Segmenting potential employees according to firms' employer attractiveness dimensions in the employer branding concept, *Journal of Academic Research in Economics*, **1**, 46–61.

Ulrich, D. 1997: *Human resource champions*, Boston: Harvard University Press.

Ulrich, D. and Smallwood, N. 2003: *Why the bottom line isn't*, NJ: John Wiley & Sons Inc.

Universum 2005: *Employer branding: Global best practices*, Universum Communications.

Universum 2006: *Universum Quarterly*, Issue # 2.

Van Maanen, J. and Schein, E.H. 1979: Toward a theory of organisational socialisation, in B.M. Staw (ed.), *Research in organizational behavior*, **1**, 209–264. Greenwich, CT: JAI Press.

Willmot, H. 2011: Considering the 'bigger picture': Branding in the processes of financialization and market capitalization, in M.J. Brannan, E. Parsons and V. Priola (eds.), *Branded Lives: The Production and Consumption of Identity at Work*, 17–34. Cheltenham: Edward Elgar.

Winstanley, D. and Woodall, J. 2000: The ethical dimensions of human resource management, *Human Resource Management Journal*, **10**, 5–20.

Index

Lightning Source UK Ltd.
Milton Keynes UK
UKHW03f1039070918
328457UK00004B/12/P